D0073371

THE PAPERS OF
WOODROW WILSON

VOLUME 58

APRIL 23-MAY 9, 1919

SPONSORED BY THE WOODROW WILSON
FOUNDATION
AND PRINCETON UNIVERSITY

THE PAPERS OF WOODROW WILSON

ARTHUR S. LINK, *EDITOR*

DAVID W. HIRST, *SENIOR ASSOCIATE EDITOR*

JOHN E. LITTLE, *ASSOCIATE EDITOR*

FREDRICK AANDAHL, *ASSOCIATE EDITOR*

MANFRED F. BOEMEKE, *ASSOCIATE EDITOR*

DENISE THOMPSON, *ASSISTANT EDITOR*

PHYLLIS MARCHAND AND MARGARET D. LINK,
EDITORIAL ASSISTANTS

Volume 58

April 23-May 9, 1919

PRINCETON, NEW JERSEY

PRINCETON UNIVERSITY PRESS

1988

L. C. card 66-10880
I.S.B.N. 0-691-04748-0

Note to scholars: Princeton University Press subscribes to the Resolution on Permissions of the Association of American University Presses, defining what we regard as "fair use" of copyrighted works. This Resolution, intended to encourage scholarly use of university press publications and to avoid unnecessary applications for permission, is obtainable from the Press or from the A.A.U.P. central office. Note, however, that the scholarly apparatus, transcripts of shorthand, and the texts of Wilson documents as they appear in this volume are copyrighted, and the usual rules about the use of copyrighted materials apply.

Printed in the United States of America
by Princeton University Press
Princeton, New Jersey

INTRODUCTION

THE opening of this volume finds Wilson confronting two crises which now come to a head and threaten to dash all hopes for Allied unity during the peace conference and cooperation in the postwar period.

The first crisis has been set off by Italy's intransigent demand for the Port of Fiume and the Dalmatian littoral. Wilson has already made it clear that he will not countenance what he believes to be such flagrant violence to the principle of self-determination as would be involved in handing over these Serbian regions to Italy. His appeals to Italian altruism futile, Wilson, on the very day on which this volume opens, issues an appeal to the Italian people "to exhibit to the newly liberated peoples across the Adriatic that noblest quality of greatness, magnanimity, friendly generosity, the preference of justice over interest." All of Italy explodes with bitter anti-Wilson passion; the Council of Four resounds with emotional recriminations; and Orlando goes to Rome on April 24 to receive, as it turns out, the plaudits of the Italian Parliament and people. In Paris, Clemenceau and Lloyd George say that they will have to stand by their countries' commitments under the Treaty of London of 1915, which had awarded the Dalmatian coastal areas and islands, but *not* Fiume, to Italy. Over and over, Wilson retorts that the two Prime Ministers will have to choose between him and the Italians, and that he will leave the conference before he will sign a treaty that grants the Italian demands. Even though an unyielding Orlando returns unannounced to a surprised Council of Four on May 7, the impasse between Wilson and the Italian Prime Minister remains to portend insoluble difficulties for the conference.

Orlando's departure on April 24 coincides with a second crisis occasioned by the demands of the Japanese delegates that the preliminary peace treaty include provisions which unequivocally confirm earlier secret treaties giving to Japan all of Germany's former rights and concessions in the Chinese province of Shantung. The Japanese demands put Wilson in the most agonizing dilemma that he faces during his entire stay in Paris, and he lies awake at night searching for a just solution. The Japanese make it clear that they will sign no treaty nor join the League of Nations unless the Big Three yield, at least formally, to their demands. Wilson concludes that it is better to have Japan in the League of Nations committed to the new postwar world order than to see her left free to run amuck in the Far East. Thus he acquiesces, but, with Clemenceau's and Lloyd George's support, he extracts from the Japanese a solemn promise that they will remove their armed forces from the Shantung province, restore full political sovereignty over that province to China, and retain in it only such economic privileges as Germany had enjoyed at the outbreak of the war.

In spite of these alarms and discords, the Big Three complete the preliminary treaty of peace with Germany. All the while, they keep a close eye on political developments in Germany and anticipate what they might have to do if no German government can be found that will accept the treaty's terms. What Wilson regards as the heart of that treaty—the Covenant of the League of Nations—he presents to a Plenary Session of the peace conference on April 28. That same day, the Plenary Session approves a Covenant which has been heavily amended in order to assuage its critics in the United States. Then, on May 7, Clemenceau, in a brief ceremony at the Trianon Palace at Versailles, delivers the preliminary treaty to a sullen German delegation, whose chairman, Brockdorff-Rantzau, replies in a salvo that will reverberate through the next two decades.

The pressures on Wilson during these weeks of controversy and compromise take a heavy physical toll. Already weakened by a severe gastrointestinal illness in early April, he suffers a cerebrovascular accident, most likely a small stroke, on April 28—the result, perhaps, of the strain of the past week or ten days—which affects his judgment, functioning, and behavior. He speedily enjoys what seems to be a good recovery, but in fact his great intellectual power, resolve and determination, and physical resources are and remain severely compromised.

"VERBATIM ET LITERATIM"

In earlier volumes of this series, we have said the following: "All documents are produced *verbatim et literatim*, with typographical and spelling errors corrected in square brackets only when necessary for clarity and ease of reading." The following essay explains our textual methods and review procedures.

We have never printed and do not intend to print critical, or corrected, versions of documents. We print them exactly as they are, with a few exceptions which we always note.

We never use the word *sic* except to denote the repetition of words in a document; in fact, we think that a succession of *sics* defaces a page. We usually repair words in square brackets when letters are missing. As we have said, we also repair words in square brackets for clarity and ease of reading. Our general rule is to do this when we, ourselves, cannot read the word without having to stop to puzzle out its meaning. Jumbled words and names misspelled beyond recognition of course have to be repaired. We correct the misspelling of names in documents in the footnotes identifying those persons.

However, when an old man writes to Wilson saying that he is glad to hear that Wilson is "comming" to Newark, or a semiliterate farmer from Texas writes phonetically, we see no reason to correct spellings in square brackets when the words are perfectly understandable. We do not correct Wilson's misspellings unless they are unreadable, except to supply in square brackets letters missing in words. For example, he consistently spelled "belligerent" as "belligerant." Nothing would be gained by correcting "belligerant" in square brackets.

We think that it is very important for several reasons to follow the rule of *verbatim et literatim*. Most important, a document has its own integrity and power, particularly when it is not written in perfect literary form. There is something very moving in seeing a Texas dirt farmer struggling to express his feelings in words, or a semiliterate former slave doing the same thing. Second, in Wilson's case it is essential to reproduce his errors in letters which he typed himself, since he usually typed badly when he was in an agitated state. Third, since style is the essence of the person, we would never correct grammar or make tenses consistent, as one correspondent has urged us to do. Fourth, we think it is very important that we print exact transcripts of Charles L. Swem's copies of Wilson's letters. Swem made many mistakes (we correct them in footnotes from a reading of his shorthand books), and Wilson let them pass. We thus have to assume that Wilson often did not read his letters before signing them, and this, we think, is a significant fact.

We think that our series would be worthless if we produced unreliable texts, and we go to considerable effort to make certain that the texts are authentic.

Our typists are highly skilled and proofread their transcripts carefully as soon as they have typed them. The Editor sight proofreads documents once he has assembled a volume and is setting its annotation. The Editors who write the notes read through documents several times and are careful to check any anomalies. Then, once the manuscript volume has been completed and all notes checked, the Editor and Senior Associate Editor orally proofread the documents against the copy. They read every comma, dash, and character. They note every absence of punctuation. They study every nearly illegible word in written documents.

Once this process of "establishing the text" is completed, the manuscript volume goes to our editor at Princeton University Press, who checks the volume carefully and sends it to the printing plant. The galley proofs are read against copy by the Press' proofreaders. We ourselves read the galley proofs three times. Our copyeditor gives them a sight reading against the manuscript copy to look for remaining typographical errors and to make sure that no line has been dropped. The Editor and Senior Associate Editor also sight read them against documents and copy. We then get the page proofs, which have been corrected at the Press. We check all the changes three times. In addition, we get *revised* pages and check them twice.

This is not the end. The Editor, Senior Associate Editor, and Dr. Boemeke give a final reading to headings, description-location lines, and notes. Finally, our indexer of course reads the pages word by word. Before we return the pages to the Press, she brings in a list of queries, all of which are answered by reference to the documents.

Our rule in the Wilson Papers is that our tolerance of error is zero. No system and no person can be perfect. There may be errors in our volumes. However, we believe that we have done everything humanly possible to avoid error; the chance is remote that what looks at first glance like a typographical error is indeed an error.

We call our readers' attention to the essay, "Wilson's Neurologic Illness at Paris," and to the commentaries which follow, which we print as an Appendix to this volume. We reiterate our expression of gratitude to Dr. Bert E. Park for the essay and also thank Dr. James F. Toole and Dr. Edwin A. Weinstein for their additional observations on the nature and course of Wilson's neurologic illness.

Regardless of what biographers, historians, and medical specialists might conclude about Wilson's health during an earlier period, there is now general agreement that, at least from mid-1918 onward, he suffered, increasingly, from the cerebrovascular disease that would severely handicap him during the Paris Peace Conference and the summer of 1919 and culminate in major, devastating strokes in late September and early October of that year. It is impossible to define *precisely* the degree to which this disease affected Wilson's personality, judgment, behavior, and decision during the peace confrence, but, from early June 1919 onward, the impact of his neurologic illness becomes increasingly clear and is self-evident after his massive strokes. Thus we are here confronted by some of the most important events in Wilson's life, events with monumental significance for the United States and the entire world. The essay and commentaries in the Appendix to this volume constitute the first installment of an account of Wilson's medical history during a crucial period. We plan to publish additional installments as may be appropriate.

We continue to be indebted to other persons for aid in the preparation of this volume. John Milton Cooper, Jr., William H. Harbaugh, Richard W. Leopold, and Betty Miller Unterberger all read the manuscript and were helpful critics. As in the case of earlier peace conference volumes, Philippe-Roger Mantoux reviewed very carefully our translations of his father's notes of the conversations of the Big Four. Alice Calaprice was editor of this volume for Princeton University Press.

We take this opportunity to extend our heartfelt thanks to Pendleton Herring. As President of the Board of Directors of the Woodrow Wilson Foundation since 1962, he has of course been much concerned about the proper funding and management of the Wilson Papers. But Dr. Herring has done much more: he has attended all the meetings of the Editorial Advisory Committee for many years and has been a friend of and a wise and valued counselor to the Editors. We owe him more gratitude than words can express. We also note with great pleasure the award to him, in August 1987, by the American Political Science Association of its highest honor, the James Madison Award, for his distinguished contributions to the field of political science.

We also pay our tribute of thanks and affection to William G. Bowen, now President of the Andrew W. Mellon Foundation. As President of Princeton University, 1972-1987, Dr. Bowen was a member of the Board of Directors of the Woodrow Wilson Foundation. He attended every meeting of that board during these years, took a keen and lively interest in the affairs of *The Papers*, and was one of the Editors' most valued counselors. We extend our warm wishes to him upon the beginning of his new career of service to American scholarship, learning, and public affairs.

THE EDITORS

Princeton, New Jersey
October 19, 1987

CONTENTS

The Papers, April 23-May 9, 1919

The Paris Peace Conference

General Diplomatic and Military Affairs

Domestic Affairs

ILLUSTRATIONS

Following page 330

On his way to a meeting with the American Commissioners at the Hôtel Crillon

National Archives

The German delegation just before leaving for Versailles. From left to right: Robert Leinert, Carl Melchior, Johann Giesberts, Ulrich Karl Christian, Count von Brockdorff-Rantzau, Otto Landsberg, and Walther Max Adrian Schücking

National Archives

Clemenceau addressing the Plenary Session of the Peace Conference in Trianon Palace at Versailles before the conditions of peace were presented to the German delegates. The principal delegate, Count von Brockdorff-Rantzau, can be seen sitting far to the left center with his colleagues. Wilson is sitting at Clemenceau's right, Lloyd George at his left.

National Archives

The German delegation listening to Clemenceau. From center front: Schücking, Giesberts, Brockdorff-Rantzau, Landsberg, Leinert, and Melchior (partly hidden).

National Archives

Robert Lansing, foreground, and Henry White, immediately behind, leaving Trianon Palace after the presentation of the peace terms to the German delegation.

National Archives

The Chinese delegation to the Peace Conference. Lu Cheng-hsiang is in the front row, fifth from the left, followed by Wang Cheng-t'ing and Alfred (Saoke) Sze. V. K. Wellington Koo is also in the front row, third from the right.

Princeton University Library

The Japanese delegation to the Peace Conference. Seated from the left: Baron Nobuaki Makino, Marquis Kimmochi Saionji, and Viscount Sutemi Chinda.

Princeton University Library

Enjoying a day at the races. At Longchamps Race Course with, among others, Mrs. Wilson, Admiral Grayson (in uniform), and far to the right, Bernard M. Baruch.

National Archives

ABBREVIATIONS

A.C.N.P.	American Commission to Negotiate Peace
ALS	autograph letter signed
ASB	Albert Sidney Burleson
CC	carbon copy
CCI	carbon copy initialed
CCL	carbon copy of letter
CCLS	carbon copy of letter signed
EBW	Edith Bolling Galt Wilson
EMH	Edward Mandell House
FLP	Frank Lyon Polk
FR 1919, Russia	*Papers Relating to the Foreign Relations of the United States, 1919, Russia*
GFC	Gilbert Fairchild Close
HCH	Herbert Clark Hoover
Hw, hw	handwriting, handwritten
HwI	handwritten initialed
JPT	Joseph Patrick Tumulty
MS, MSS	manuscript, manuscripts
PPC	*Papers Relating to the Foreign Relations of the United States, The Paris Peace Conference, 1919*
RG	record group
RL	Robert Lansing
T	typed
TC	typed copy
TCL	typed copy of letter
THB	Tasker Howard Bliss
TI	typed initialed
TL	typed letter
TLS	typed letter signed
TNP	Thomas Nelson Page
TS	typed signed
WCR	William Cox Redfield
WGM	William Gibbs McAdoo
WW	Woodrow Wilson
WWhw	Woodrow Wilson handwriting, handwritten
WWsh	Woodrow Wilson shorthand
WWT	Woodrow Wilson typed
WWTLI	Woodrow Wilson typed letter initialed
WWTLS	Woodrow Wilson typed letter signed

ABBREVIATIONS FOR COLLECTIONS AND REPOSITORIES

Following the National Union Catalog of the Library of Congress

CaOOA	Public Archives Library, Ottawa
CSt-H	Hoover Institution on War, Revolution and Peace
CtY	Yale University
DLC	Library of Congress
DNA	National Archives

IaWbH	Herbert Hoover Presidential Library
MH-BA	Harvard University Graduate School of Business Administration
NHpR	Franklin D. Roosevelt Library, Hyde Park
NjP	Princeton University
PRO	Public Record Office
PSC-P	Swarthmore College Peace Collection
RSB Coll., DLC	Ray Stannard Baker Collection of Wilsoniana, Library of Congress
SDR	State Department Records
WC, NjP	Woodrow Wilson Collection, Princeton University
WP, DLC	Woodrow Wilson Papers, Library of Congress

SYMBOLS

[May 7, 1919]	publication date of published writing; also date of document when date is not part of text
[*April 24, 1919*]	composition date when publication date differs
[[May 5, 1919]]	delivery date of speech when publication date differs
* * * * * * *	text deleted by author of document

THE PAPERS OF

WOODROW WILSON

VOLUME 58

APRIL 23-MAY 9, 1919

THE PAPERS OF
WOODROW WILSON

From the Diary of Dr. Grayson

Wednesday, April 23, 1919.

The President had breakfast at 8:25 o'clock, and until 11:00 o'clock he worked on official matters relating to home affairs and disposed of his correspondence. At 11:00 o'clock the President met with Lloyd-George and Clemenceau. They discussed the Italian developments, especially the defiant attitude which had been adopted by Orlando, Sonnino, and the remainder of the Italians. The President made it very plain to his colleagues that so far as he was concerned he would never consent to a surrender of principles even for the benefit of Orlando, whom he likes very much. They also discussed the Shantung proposition at further length, the Chinese having filed a supplementary brief dealing with the case.[1]

The President, Mrs. Wilson and I had lunch at one o'clock. During the lunch our conversation was carried on in a light vein. The President told us a number of stories. He wanted to know who I saw at the reception last night, which the Secretary of State had given to the new Ambassador to France.[2] I then related conversations which I had had with Vice-Admiral Gleaves, ex-Ambassador Henry White, Admiral Benson, Secretary Lansing, and others.

Immediately after lunch the President read to me the statement which he had prepared concerning the Italian situation[3] and asked me what I thought of it. I told him I could not find a point in it to criticise. He then requested me to give it out to the three press associations and to Ray Stannard Baker.

I asked the President whether he had shown it to Clemenceau and to Lloyd-George. He said that Clemenceau had said that he would not change a word in it and that it was fine. The only thing in his (Clemenceau's) mind was the question as to when the best time was to publish it, but he was in favor of publishing it. He said it would have a good effect in France. Lloyd-George approved it, the President said, and declared that he would back it up. He thought it was a remarkable statement. But the President said to me, confidentially: "He is as slippery as an eel, and I never know when to count on him." The President also read it to the other members of the American Peace Delegation, and it met with their hearty approval.

The statement is as follows:[4] . . .

The publication of the President's statement caused the utmost consternation in Italian circles. The Italians had gathered together in the King Edward Hotel, where they had their headquarters, and were preparing a statement to be issued defining their position when the word reached them that the President had forestalled them. Immediately the representatives of Orlando and Sonnino announced that the Italians were prepared to quit the conference. Their especial complaint was that the President had addressed himself directly to the people of Italy along the lines which he had used to eliminate the Hohenzollerns as the ruling class of Germany. However, the majority of the Americans, French and British, who read the statement, endorsed it in its entirety.

The President and Mrs. Wilson dined alone. I had dinner at the Ritz Hotel with Admiral Long,[5] who was entertaining in honor of Vice-Admiral Albert Gleaves.

The President spent a quiet evening with Mrs. Wilson playing Canfield. When I came in at twelve o'clock, one of the secret service men informed me that the President had asked for me three times in the past hour. I went into his room and he was just retiring. He said: "I do not feel sleepy. I have been sitting up talking with Mrs. Wilson and playing Canfield, trying to get my mind disconnected from the things that have been going on throughout the day. And before going to bed I wanted to know what reflections you have heard over my statement concerning the Italian situation." I told him that taking it all in all the statement was making a fine impression and that the Italians had stated that they were leaving at two o'clock the next afternoon, withdrawing from the Peace Conference.

I then related a conversation I had with Sir Campbell Stuart[6] during the afternoon. Sir Campbell is Lord Northcliffe's right-hand man and he is very close to him, spending a great deal of his time with Lord Northcliffe. He told me that Lord Northcliffe was a most enthusiastic admirer of President Wilson, and that if the President would show him some personal attention, Lord Northcliffe would make all of his papers turn hand-springs at the President's suggestion and advocate his policies. Northcliffe is a great believer in the President's principles and is a very fine man, Sir Campbell said, but he easily succumbs to personal attention and to personal flattery. Sir Campbell suggested to me that if I would go down to Fontainebleau and spend Sunday with Lord Northcliffe and convey to him a personal message of greeting of some sort from the President, or better still, if the President would invite him to call on him or to have lunch with him, Northcliffe would then do anything in the world for the

President. He said to me: "Northcliffe is now depressed and blue and a visit from you as suggested would be a great tonic to him and would stimulate him to support the President." I told him that this was all very fine but did he not think it would be inadvisable from the standpoint of the President for the President to mix up in any of the controversies between Northcliffe and Lloyd-George when he (the President) was working with Lloyd-George daily in this conference. I suggested that Northcliffe support the President's principles loyally, thereby doing the fine thing for the world, and when it was all over and the Peace Conference was over we would send an invitation to Northcliffe to come to America, and we would then give him a royal welcome in America. In response to my suggestion regarding the inadvisability of the President interfering between Northcliffe and Lloyd-George, Sir Campbell smiled and said: "There might be something in that." The President said: "I think you handled it just right. You are a diplomat."

T MS (in possession of James Gordon Grayson and Cary T. Grayson, Jr.) About this diary, see n. 1 to the entry from the Grayson Diary printed at Dec. 3, 1918, Vol. 53.

[1] See RL to WW, April 21, 1919, n. 1, Vol. 57.

[2] That is, Hugh Campbell Wallace.

[3] It is printed as the following document.

[4] Here follows a newspaper clipping of Wilson's statement.

[5] Rear Adm. Andrew Theodore Long, U.S.N., at this time a Naval Attaché at the American embassy in Paris.

[6] At this time managing director of both the Paris *Continental Daily Mail* and the London *Times*.

A Statement on the Adriatic Question

April 23, 1919

In view of the capital importance of the questions affected, and in order to throw all possible light upon what is involved in their settlement, I hope that the following statement will contribute to the final formation of opinion and to a satisfactory solution.

When Italy entered the war she entered upon the basis of a definite, but private, understanding with Great Britain and France, now known as the Pact of London. Since that time the whole face of circumstance has been altered. Many other powers, great and small, have entered the struggle, with no knowledge of that private understanding. The Austro-Hungarian Empire, then the enemy of Europe, and at whose expense the Pact of London was to be kept in the event of victory, has gone to pieces and no longer exists. Not only that. The several parts of that empire, it is now agreed by Italy and all her associates, are to be erected into independent states and associated in a League of Nations, not with those who were recently our enemies, but with Italy herself and the powers that stood with

Italy in the Great War for Liberty. We are to establish their liberty as well as our own. They are to be among the smaller states whose interests are henceforth to be as scrupulously safeguarded as the interests of the most powerful states.

The war was ended, moreover, by proposing to Germany an armistice and peace which should be founded on certain clearly defined principles which should set up a new order of right and justice. Upon those principles the peace with Germany has been conceived, not only, but formulated. Upon those principles it will be executed. We cannot ask the great body of powers to propose and effect peace with Austria and establish a new basis of independence and right in the states which originally constituted the Austro-Hungarian Empire and in the states of the Balkan group on principles of another kind. We must apply the same principles to the settlement of Europe in those quarters that we have applied in the peace with Germany. It was upon the explicit avowal of those principles that the initiative for peace was taken. It is upon them that the whole structure of peace must rest.

If those principles are to be adhered to, Fiume must serve as the outlet and inlet of the commerce, not of Italy, but of the lands to the north and northeast of that port: Hungary, Bohemia, Roumania, and the states of the New Jugo-Slavic group. To assign Fiume to Italy would be to create the feeling that we had deliberately put the port upon which all these countries chiefly depend for their access to the Mediterranean in the hands of a power of which it did not form an integral part and whose sovereignty, if set up there, must inevitably seem foreign, not domestic or identified with the commercial and industrial life of the regions which the power must serve. It is for that reason, no doubt, that Fiume was not included in the Pact of London but there definitely assigned to the Croatians.

And the reason why the line of the Pact of London swept about many of the islands of the eastern coast of the Adriatic and around the portion of the Dalmatian coast which lies most open to that sea was not only that here and there on those islands and here and there on that coast there are bodies of people of Italian blood and connection but also, and no doubt chiefly, because it was felt that it was necessary for Italy to have a foothold amidst the channels of the Eastern Adriatic in order that she might make her own coasts safe against the naval aggression of Austria-Hungary. But Austria-Hungary no longer exists. It is proposed that the fortifications which the Austrian Government constructed there shall be razed and permanently destroyed. It is part, also, of the new plan of European order which centres in the League of Nations that the new states erected there shall accept a limitation of armaments which puts aggression out of the question. There can be no fear of the unfair treatment of groups of Italian people there because adequate guarantees will be given, under international sanction, of the equal and equitable treatment of all racial or national minorities.

In brief, every question associated with this settlement wears a new aspect,—a new aspect given it by the very victory for right for which Italy has made the supreme sacrifice of blood and treasure. Italy, along with the four other great powers, has become one of the chief trustees of the new order which she has played so honourable a part in establishing.

And on the North and Northeast her natural frontiers are completely restored, along the whole sweep of the Alps from northwest to southeast to the very end of the Istrian peninsula, including all the great watershed within which Trieste and Pola lie and all the fair regions whose face nature has turned towards the great peninsula upon which the historic life of the Latin people has been worked out through centuries of famous story ever since Rome was first set upon her seven hills. Her ancient unity is restored. Her lines are extended to the great walls which are her natural defence. It is within her choice to be surrounded by friends; to exhibit to the newly liberated peoples across the Adriatic that noblest quality of greatness, magnanimity, friendly generosity, the preference of Justice over interest.

The nations associated with her, the nations that know nothing of the Pact of London or of any other special understanding that lies at the beginning of this great struggle, and who have made their supreme sacrifice also in the interest, not of national advantage or defence, but of the settled peace of the world, now unite with her older associates in urging her to assume a leadership which cannot be mistaken in the new order of Europe. America is Italy's friend. Her people are drawn, millions strong, from Italy's own fair countrysides. She is linked in blood as well as in affection with the Italian people. Such ties can never be broken. And America was privileged, by the generous commission of her associates in the war, to initiate the peace we are about to consummate,—to initiate it upon terms she had herself formulated, and in which I was her spokesman. The compulsion is upon her to square every decision she takes a part in with those principles. She can do nothing else. She trusts Italy, and in her trust believes that Italy will ask nothing of her that cannot be made unmistakably consistent with those sacred obligations. Interest is not now in question, but the rights of peoples, of states new and old, of liberated peoples and peoples whose rulers have never accounted them worthy of right; above all, the right of the world to peace and to such settlements of interest as shall make peace secure.

These, and these only, are the principles for which America has fought. These, and these only, are the principles upon which she can consent to make peace. Only upon these principles, she hopes and believes, will the people of Italy ask her to make peace.

Woodrow Wilson

T MS (WP, DLC).

From David Lloyd George, with Enclosure

Dear Mr. President, Paris. 23rd April 1919.

The Chancellor of the Exchequer[1] and Lord Robert Cecil, on behalf of the British representatives on the Supreme Economic Council, have forcibly urged on the notice of His Majesty's Government the necessity of some bolder solution for the rehabilitation of the credit and economic life of Europe than is now available. For the time being the United States is providing on a generous scale for the urgent food requirements of the non-enemy countries of Europe. We, on our part, are furnishing assistance on a more modest scale. But these measures which are primarily directed to the relief of immediate distress, are inadequate, as Mr. Hoover himself is the first to recognise, to the solution of the whole economic problem. On the one hand, the United States may not be able to continue indefinitely her present assistance; on the other hand, this assistance does not touch the problem of supplying raw materials to any of the countries concerned and does not apply to the enemy countries at all.

The position as it is reported by the British representatives on the Supreme Economic Council is as follows: In the case of Germany the existing financial provision is not expected to look after food supplies alone much beyond June, and for raw materials there is no provision at all, which, in view of the existing unemployment, are not less necessary if order is to be preserved in that country, peace to be signed and the obligations of the peace to be fulfilled. The other enemy countries are at a complete economic standstill and there is at present no plan whatever for dealing with them or for preserving their social and economic organisation from disruption and decay. The condition of the new States, of Serbia and of Rumania is hardly better. Mr. Hoover is meeting their immediate food requirements, but their economic and commercial fabric cannot be created or recreated unless they can be put in the possession of purchasing power with which to enter the markets of the world. France, Italy and Belgium present a different problem. But here also the external financial position has been represented to the Chancellor of the Exchequer by the Finance Ministers of these countries to be little short of desperate, and the need of outside assistance to be essential if they are to restore their countries and recommence the normal activities of peace. The United Kingdom enters upon the peace in a somewhat less unfavourable condition, with the question as to how we are to pay what we owe to the United States Treasury as the chief problem of our external finance; but we are in no position to give assistance to others on anything appraoching [approaching] the scale which they require. I may add this, however, that the difference between the position in England and the complete economic prostration of some of the other countries named above is so enormous, that our own serious difficulties in getting the wheels of industry going may be some index to the appalling magnitude of the problem in these other countries. In short, the economic mechanism of Europe is jammed. Before the war, as Mr. Hoover has said, 400,000,000 Europeans by working their hardest just managed to feed, clothe and house themselves, and perhaps six months' capital on which to live. That capital has vanished; the complicated machinery of internal and external production is more or less smashed; production has to a great extent ceased. The largely increasing population of Europe has only been maintained by the increasing development and interconnection of world industry and finance. If this is not only checked, but for the time being destroyed it is difficult to see how the population can be maintained, at any rate during the very painful period of drastic re-adjustment. If free movement were possible and other countries could absorb it, there would inevitably be a vast emigration from Europe, until an equilibrium were established between the numbers of the population and the means of livelihood. As that is not possible this equilibrium must be reached in some other way. In Russia it is being reached, it appears, by reduction of population by starvation, and by drastic changes of occupation, e.g., by the town population being forced out on the land as labourers.

To what extent the same conditions spread over the rest of Europe must depend largely on whether or not the obstacles to the resumption of production can be rapidly overcome.

What, in such circumstances, are the alternatives before us? In some quarters the hope is entertained that with the early removal of obstacles in the form of the Blockade and similar measures to free international intercourse, private enterprise may be safely entrusted with the task of finding the solution. I am in accord with the view that an early removal of such obstacles is an essential measure, and that in the long run we must mainly look for our salvation to the renewed life of private enterprise and of private initiative. Indeed so far as trading and manufacture is concerned, as distinct from finance, no other measures should be necessary from the outset. Nevertheless, in the financial sphere, the problem of restoring Europe is almost certainly too great for private enterprise alone and every delay puts this solution further out of court. There are two main obstacles; (a) the risks are too great; (b) the amounts are too big and the credit required too long. The more prostrate a country is and the nearer to Bolshevism the more presumably it requires assistance. But the less likely is private enterprise to do it. To a small extent and with a great margin some trade will be done and some barter. But not enough to meet the situation.

Apart from private enterprise His Majesty's Government see only two possible courses—direct assistance and various forms of guaranteed finance, on a very much larger scale than is at present contemplated, by the more prosperous of the Allied and Associated countries, which probably means to an extent of not less than 90%, the United States; or an attempt to re-create the credit system of Europe and by some form of world wide co-operation to enable the countries whose individual credit is temporarily destroyed to trade on their prospects of Reparation from the Enemy States or to capitalise their future prospects of production. Every consideration of policy and interest indicates the superiority of the second. The people of Europe will have to live on the fruits of their own daily labour and not on the bounty of another country.

His Majesty's Government, therefore, desire to lay before the Governments of the United States, of France and of Italy the concrete proposal contained in the paper annexed to this letter as their constructive contribution to the solution of the greatest financial problem ever set to the modern world. They are prepared to commit themselves immediately to participation in such a scheme, subject to the legislative sanction which it will presumably require in all countries; and they invite your observations and your criticisms.

I do not propose to enter upon any detailed explanation or justification of this proposal until it has been examined in outline by yourself and your advisers. There are many points in it which will require very careful discussions between our experts, and it is doubtless capable of much modification and improvement without detriment to the main ideas which underly it. But these ideas I recommend to your judgment.

I may, however, at the present stage say this much. The scheme is an attempt to deal simultaneously in as simple a way as possible with several distinct problems. The countries which have been the victims of devastation are enabled to convert the bonds of the enemy into immediate purchasing power for the purpose of early restoration. France is probably the greatest gainer from this scheme and is offered a way out from her almost overwhelming financial difficulties. The acute problem of the liquidation of inter-ally indebtedness, while not disposed of, is sensibly ameliorated. The Governments of the new States are enabled to prepare definite economic programmes which will consolidate their at present precarious positions and inspire confidence in their peoples. The Neutrals are shown that their claims against the estate of the enemy will not be overlooked, in spite of the circumstances of these claims' origin, provided they are prepared to play their part in a world wide scheme for the preservation of the credit of Europe. The enemy peoples are shown a way of discharging a part of their obligations and are given a reasonable measure of security for their economic existence in the immediate future. The good faith of the world as a whole is pledged for the carrying out of a scheme, the sole object of which is to set on its feet the new Europe. On the other hand it opens prospects of a renewal of trade to those countries primarily the United States and secondarily the British Empire, who have surplus goods to export or a favourable balance of trade to liquidate. It cannot be supposed that the two great continents, America and Europe, the one destitute and on the point of collapse and the other overflowing with goods which it wishes to dispose of, can continue to face one another for long without attempting to frame some plan of mutual advantage. And if it be admitted, as it must be, that trade can only recommence on the basis of credit of some kind, what better security can the lenders hope to secure than is herein proposed? But chief of all, perhaps, only a scheme of large and broad dimensions, which can be announced to and understood by the whole world, can inspire that sentiment of hope which is the greatest need of Europe at this moment. A proposal which unfolds future prospects and shows the peoples of Europe a road by which food and employment and orderly existence can once again come their way, will be a more powerful weapon than any other for the preservation from the dangers of Bolshevism of that order of human society which we believe to be the best starting point for future improvement and greater well being.

I suggest that the relation of this scheme to the Reparation Terms, which we are about to place before the German Government might be as follows. In these terms as at present drafted we demand an immediate payment of £1,000,000,000 from which sum is first to be deducted the cost of the Armies of Occupation and of approved supplies of food and raw material to the enemy. I suggest that if the present proposal is adopted the initial payment might be £1,000,000,000 *exclusive* of the cost of the Armies of Occupation and of approved supplies, and that the enemy might be permitted to pay £724,000,000 out of this sum in special Bonds thus to be created, providing the balance and also the cost of the Armies by the transfer of ships, gold, securities and so forth.

Ever sincerely D Lloyd George

TLS (WP, DLC).

[1] (Joseph) Austen Chamberlain.

ENCLOSURE

SECRET.

Scheme for the Rehabilitation of European Credit and for Financing Relief and Reconstruction.[1]

April, 1919.

1. (i) German Bonds to be issued to a *present* value of £1,000,000,000 and to a *face* value of £1,200,000,000, carrying interest at the rate of 4 per cent. per annum and sinking fund at the rate of 1 per cent. per annum as from January 1st, 1925, these payments to have priority over all other German obligations whatever, including additional claims for reparation not covered out of the above, the difference between the face value and the present value representing the funding of interest from January 1st, 1920, up to January 1st, 1925.

(ii) Austrian, Hungarian and Bulgarian Bonds to be issued to the present value of £125,000,000, £170,000,000 and £50,000,000 respectively on similar conditions. (N.B.—Turkey to be dealt with separately.)

(iii) Roumanian,* Polish, Czecho-Slovakian, Jugo-Slav* and Baltic States Bonds to be issued to the present value of £15,000,000, £40,000,000, £20,000,000, £15,000,000 and £10,000,000 respectively on similar conditions.

2. Interest on each of the issues of Enemy Bonds under 1 (i) and (ii) above to be guaranteed jointly and severally by the other Enemy states, in the event of any one of them failing to provide the payments due.

3. In the event of the failure of the above guarantees,[2] interest at 4 per cent. on all the above Bonds to the aggregate present value of £1,500,000,000 (or £1,800,000,000 as from January 1st, 1925), to be guaranteed by the principal Allied and Associated Governments,

* Roumania and Serbia also to receive a share of Reparation.

by the three Scandinavian Governments and by the Governments of Holland and Switzerland.

4. In the event of the guarantee under (3) becoming operative, the guaranteeing Governments to be responsible in proportions determined in advance, as set forth in the accompanying Schedule A.

5. In the event of any of the guaranteeing Governments failing to meet their guarantee, the remaining guaranteeing Governments to make good this failure in the same proportions amongst themselves as under (4).

6. A failure of any Government to meet its guarantee under the above clauses to be considered by the Financial Section of the League of Nations, and if judged by them to have been avoidable shall be punished by such penalty or forfeiture of a financial, economic or commercial character as the League of Nations may determine.

7. The Bonds to be free of all taxation in all the issuing or guaranteeing States.

8. Of the £1,000,000,000 Bonds to be issued by the German Government £724,000,000 shall be paid over to the Allied and Associated Governments on account of sums due for Reparation; £76,000,000 shall be utilised for the discharge of existing debts to the three Scandinavian countries, Holland and Switzerland; and the remaining one-fifth of the total, namely, £200,000,000, shall be left in the hands of the German Government to be made available for the purchase of food and raw materials.

9. Of the Bonds amounting to £345,000,000 in all to be issued by the Austrian, Hungarian and Bulgarian Governments, four-fifths in each case shall be paid over to the Allied and Associated Governments on account of sums due for Reparation, the remaining one-fifth being left in the hands of these Governments for the purchase of food and raw materials.

10. The Bonds amounting in all to a present value of £1,000,000,000 to be received by the Allied and Associated Governments on account of Reparation to be divided between them in the proportions determined upon by them for the division of Reparation receipts generally.

11. The Bonds to be accepted at their par value plus[3] accrued interest in payment of all indebtedness between any of the Allied and Associated Governments.

12. The Bonds to be acceptable as first-class collateral for loans at the Central Banks of all the issuing or guaranteeing States, subject to such terms and limitations as may be in force with these institutions from time to time.

SCHEDULE A.

	Per cent.
United Kingdom	20
United States	20 = 90,000,000[4]
France	20
Italy	10
Japan	10
Belgium	5
Norway, Sweden, Denmark, Holland, Switzerland	15

Printed copy (WP, DLC).

[1] The author of this memorandum was John Maynard Keynes.

[2] Wilson drew a mark on the right-hand margin opposite paragraph 3 through paragraph 6.

[3] Wilson drew a double line in the left-hand margin opposite this paragraph.

[4] WWhw.

Hankey's and Mantoux's Notes of a Meeting of the Council of Four[1]

President Wilson's House,
I.C.-175F Paris, April 23, 1919, 11 a.m.

(1) MR. LLOYD GEORGE produced a communication he had received from M. Orlando giving the latest Italian proposal (*Appendix I*). [It reads as follows: "ITALIAN PROPOSALS I. The line of the Alps (Brenner) to the sea, East of Volosoa. II. Fiume under the sovereignty of Italy. Italy will establish in the port of Fiume free zones in accordance with the terms of articles 8, 9 and 10 of the Peace clauses drawn up by the Commission of Ports, Waterways, and Railways and will extend to Fiume those facilitations which may be arranged for later on in a general convention with reference to free ports. III. Italy will have all the islands mentioned in the Pact of London except Pago. IV. Zara and Sebenico will be placed under the League of Nations with Italy as Mandatory Power."]

He felt this offered no basis for negotiation. He suggested it might be desirable to ask the Italian delegates whether they intended to meet the Germans when they came to Versailles.

[1] The complete text of Hankey's minutes is printed in *PPC*, V, 149-54.

M. CLEMENCEAU thought it was a good idea.

PRESIDENT WILSON suggested that when we came to deal with Austria, if the Italians were standing out of the Conference the boundaries should be settled as fairly as though Italy were in. Italy should be treated on absolutely fair lines and shown that their interests were taken care of.

MR. LLOYD GEORGE suggested that if Italy was not present in the negotiations with Germany it would be difficult for the Allied and Associated Powers to put forward claims on their behalf for reparation, for example.

PRESIDENT WILSON referred to a report which he had received from a M. Poupin,[2] a scientist of Yugo-Slav nationality, who was working in Columbia University. The memorandum was by no means of a menacing character, but it did convey the impression that the result of a peace unsatisfactory to the Jugo-Slavs would be to drive them into the hands of the Bolshevists. They would unite with the rest of the Slav peoples. One interesting point in M. Poupin's memorandum was a reference to an Italian Socialist meeting which had been held at Rome at which Italian claims, as recognized by the Socialists, had been outlined. No mention was made of Dalmatia, Fiume, Gorizia, or of Carinthia.

After some further discussion on this subject, which was taken up after other subjects had been discussed, PRESIDENT WILSON said that it was his intention to publish his memorandum on the Italian question this evening.

MR. LLOYD GEORGE read a memorandum which Mr. Balfour had prepared at his request and which presented the point of view of France and Great Britain.[3] In the course of the reading of Mr. Balfour's memorandum the following corrections were suggested:

(1) An alteration in certain phrases which conveyed the impression that Fiume was not mentioned in the Treaty of London. It was pointed out that Fiume was mentioned in a note to Article 5.

(2) Fiume, it was pointed out, was not on the Dalmatian but on the Croatian coast.

(3) The addition, after a sentence in which it was mentioned that Fiume was one town and not two, of the following words "and that is Slav."

(4) That it would be better to omit a passage on the last page referring to the forthcoming withdrawal of Italy from the Con-

[2] See the memorandum by M. I. Pupin printed at April 19, 1919, Vol. 57.

[3] There is a carbon copy of Balfour's memorandum, dated April 23, 1919, in the RSB Coll., DLC. The final version is printed as Appendix I to the minutes of the Council of Four printed at April 24, 1919, 4 p.m.

ference. It was pointed out that although Italy had withdrawn from these conversations they had not formally withdrawn from the Preliminary Peace Conference. It was suggested it would be better to prepare the memorandum to deter Italy from doing so rather than to suggest that it was a probable contingency.

MR. LLOYD GEORGE and M. CLEMENCEAU agreed on the following:

(1) That the letter should be revised on the above lines.

(2) That a copy should be sent to M. Clemenceau for him to have translated and examined.

No decision was taken as to when the letter should be forwarded to the Italian representatives.

There was some discussion as to the difficult position which would arise if Italy persisted in her present attitude. It was pointed out that if Italy should insist on holding on to Fiume, this would be itself a breach of the Treaty which definitely allotted Fiume to Croatia. If, on the other hand, Italy should abandon her position in Fiume, the situation would be very difficult, because then France and Great Britain would be bound by their Treaty to sign a Treaty with Austria which President Wilson did not feel himself in a position to sign, since Italy could insist on the portion of Dalmatia comprised in the Treaty being transferred to her sovereignty. It was generally agreed that anything which caused a difference between Great Britain and France on the one hand, and the United States of America on the other, would be most deplorable, since the future peace of the world depended so much on these three nations standing together. The danger of uniting the whole of the Slavs in a possible Bolshevist regime was also commented on.

Attention was also drawn to the fact that Italy had, on the 26th April 1915, adhered to the Pact of London of the 5th September 1914, thereby engaging herself mutually with Great Britain, France, and Russia, not to conclude a separate peace in the course of the War, and that when there was a question of discussing the terms of peace none of the Allied Powers should propose conditions of peace without previous agreement with each of the other Allies.

§ Mantoux's notes:

Lloyd George. If Italy is not represented when we open the negotiations with Germany, it will be impossible to inscribe her on the list of the powers which have the right to reparations.

Wilson. I believe we should treat Italy in the most equitable and even the most liberal way when we deal with Austria.

Lloyd George. Undoubtedly. I must say that I persist in believing that it is imprudent to have the Germans of the valley of the Adige included within Italy's frontiers, and I shall perhaps have to make some observations on this point. But in any case, I do not see how we could ask the Germans for reparations for Italy if she is not present.

Wilson. I received a memorial from a Yugoslav who has a position in the United States, M. Pupin, the conclusion of which is that, if the Yugoslavs have the impression that they have not been treated justly, they will throw themselves on the side of the Slavic world against the western world. What we have to fear is a coalition of which Russia would be the soul.

Lloyd George. In fact there is a danger from that side.

Wilson. Is it not better to risk exciting the temporary discontent of Italy than the permanent hostility of all the Slavs? [Discussion of other subjects, printed below.]

Clemenceau. What are we going to do about the Italians? We must respond to them. You know what M. Barzilai[4] proposes. The Italians continue to insist on the possession of Fiume.

Lloyd George. Mr. Balfour has drafted a rather satisfactory document setting forth the point of view of the signatory powers. He declares himself in the clearest way possible against the annexation of Fiume to Italy.

Wilson. I will also have to publish my declaration. [Discussion of other subjects, printed below.]

Mr. Lloyd George reads Mr. Balfour's draft of a letter to the Italian government.

Wilson. Why give arguments against the departure of the Italians before they have firmly declared their intention to leave?

Lloyd George. They indicated that their departure was imminent.

Wilson. They withdrew from these discussions, but they did not say that they were withdrawing from the conference. This letter assumes that their decision is taken. Now, if we want to divert them from a fatal decision, it is better not to treat the question as if it was settled.

Lloyd George. On the other hand, Mr. Balfour's letter gives no answer to the last message that I received from M. Orlando. I also fear that Mr. Balfour did not stress sufficiently our resolution to respect the commitments that we have taken by the Treaty of London. Rather, it is an appeal made to Italy that she herself free us from one part of these commitments.

Wilson. Undoubtedly; but there is nothing more honorable than such an effort.

[4] That is, Salvatore Barzilai.

Lloyd George. What we must avoid is having the Italians be told that we went back on our word to them by accepting the letter of the treaty but putting pressure on them to modify its clauses.

Wilson. The responsibility for the situation rests on me.

Lloyd George. Not entirely, because, in whatever concerns Fiume, we are with you; or rather, it is especially from us that the objection comes, and I am persuaded that if there is a rupture it will be over Fiume.

Wilson. What will you do if they say to you: "We demand the execution, pure and simple, of the Treaty of London," and if, in that way, they force you to separate yourselves from the United States?

Clemenceau. It must not come to that. We will say to them: "Keep these territories if you can."

Lloyd George. We can do it. But they will stay in Fiume, and that is against the treaty. As for everything outside Fiume, it is impossible for us to say that we had a crisis of conscience after the victory, whereas we did not have it when Italy's cooperation was necessary for us.

About Fiume, I am prepared to follow you completely and to cut off imports of coal to Italy if necessary.

Wilson. When we make our treaty with Austria, we will have to fix the frontiers carefully. Then it will be a question of knowing if you stay with Italy or if you range yourselves on the side of the United States. I cannot consent to give to Italy what would be the cause of a dangerous separation between the Slavic world and western Europe. We are facing an alternative: either we shall draw the southern Slavs toward western Europe and the League of Nations, or we shall throw them toward Russia and Bolshevism.

The Italians must realize that there is no comparison possible between the so-called necessities of the defense of Italy and the general peace of Europe. The Slavs have behind them the immense reservoir of the populations of Asia, whose attitude and destiny will be the great problem of the future. There are 800 million men there, against whom our 200 million would seem a small thing. Must we alienate half of Europe for a strategic boundary which, in the opinion of the American experts, is without importance?

Lloyd George. What matters is not one frontier line or another, but the sanctity of treaties. Say if you wish that the Treaty of London should never have been signed. It was done by Mr. Asquith and by M. Briand. Sir Edward Grey did not really like it, and the English cabinet was poorly impressed with it when it found out about it. But, after all, our signature is at the bottom of that treaty.

Wilson. I would be not at all scandalized if I saw France and England repudiate a treaty which was concluded in a world situation today completely modified.

Clemenceau. I am not inclined to do anything like that. But what I ask myself is if the Italians, by withdrawing from the conference, are not withdrawing from the treaty.

Lloyd George. We can say to them: "We decided with you that Fiume should go to the Croatians; if you do not accept that, the treaty no longer exists, and if you keep Fiume, you violate the treaty."

Wilson. And what will you do if they answer: "We are abandoning Fiume"?

Lloyd George. In that case, we are caught; we will have to execute the treaty.

Wilson. And you will be obliged to break with us.

Clemenceau. I tell you that they will never give up Fiume.

Wilson. The Treaty of London is an agreement that I would never have approved of, and with which I cannot associate myself.

Lloyd George. You can be satisfied with refusing your signature.

Clemenceau. My point of view is that if the Italians withdraw from the conference, they break the treaty.

Lloyd George. They can be told that to withdraw from the conference is to break the alliance. For they adhered to the Pact of London of 1914, which binds us for the war and for the conclusion of the peace. §

2. MR. LLOYD GEORGE said that he had just seen Captain Gibson,[5] an officer who had returned from Berlin and who had given us consistently very valuable information. Captain Gibson said that the best of the German Delegates was named Melchier,[6] who desired peace. Melchier was very much in with the industrialists, who desired peace. Rantzau,[7] whom he did not think very much of, was, he believed, opposed to peace.

M. CLEMENCEAU doubted if the present German Government could make peace.

3. MR. LLOYD GEORGE said that Captain Gibson had explained that the most important factor inducing the Germans to sign peace was their desire to re-start their national life. This brought him to the question of a scheme for re-starting Europe. No trade was at present moving anywhere in Europe. In Belgium there were many unemployed, and the same was true of other countries and particularly of

[5] That is, Capt. Thomas Gibson. See his report printed as Appendix II to the minutes of the Council of Four printed at April 20, 1919, Vol. 57.

[6] That is, Carl Melchior.

[7] That is, Ulrich Karl Christian, Count von Brockdorff-Rantzau.

Germany. Mr. Keynes had prepared a scheme, the broad outline of which was that the first thousand million pounds which Germany had to pay should be taken and guaranteed by all the Powers. Cash should be raised on it in order to enable all countries, including Germany, to get raw material and re-start their industries. Unless something of the kind was done, Melchier would not be able to make peace.

PRESIDENT WILSON said he had given Captain Gibson's paper to Mr. Hoover, who had some 40 agents travelling about in Europe in connection with relief work. Mr. Hoover had said that the paper was extraordinarily correct, but he thought nothing could be done unless the people could get food and start their industrial life. At present, they were in a hopeless position. The ordinary life could not grow on the present soil and Bolshevism was the only system that could. Hence, he thought that the blockade ought to be raised.

MR. LLOYD GEORGE pointed out that there was the same paralysis in countries that had no blockade.

M. CLEMENCEAU thought it would be a great mistake to raise it.

PRESIDENT WILSON pointed out that it could be reimposed.

M. CLEMENCEAU said that the moment was bad for raising the blockade. The Germans were about to arrive for the purpose of signing peace and we must not appear to be weakening.

4. M. CLEMENCEAU read information which showed that the German Delegation contemplated bringing journalists to Versailles. He asked whether the French ought to allow them to come to Versailles. His own view was strongly opposed, and he would like authority not to admit them. His information was more and more in the direction that Rantzau was coming to cause a breakdown in the negotiations.

MR. LLOYD GEORGE pointed out that Melchier was not coming with this object.

5. PRESIDENT WILSON considered that, in view of Melchier's presence, the attitude of the Germans would depend largely upon the economic terms. If the Germans found that chains were to be imposed on them, they would not sign, but if a fair basis were offered, they would. He had talked to the United States experts on the subject and the attitude they took was that the Allied and Associated Powers should only require that there should be no discrimination by Germany against any particular belligerent. That is to say, all should have the most favoured nation terms.

6. M. CLEMENCEAU read a telegram from the Chief of the Military Mission at Warsaw to Marshal Foch, reporting that by midnight of the 20th, 12 trains had passed through Warsaw conveying a portion of General Haller's Army. He reported a number of incidents where the Germans had molested the trains and broken open wagons and

taken foodstuffs, such as biscuits, preserved meat and sacks of oats and clothing. These incidents had mainly taken place at Glogau.

MR. LLOYD GEORGE said he was surprised that the troops had got through with so little trouble. He thought the attention of Marshal Foch ought to be called to the matter and that he should be directed to make representations.

PRESIDENT WILSON agreed.

(It was agreed that M. Clemenceau should instruct Marshal Foch to call the attention of the Germans to the molestation of trains conveying General Haller's Army to Poland and should insist on their carrying out their engagements.)

7. PRESIDENT WILSON said he had received an appeal from Persia,[8] who had sent a Delegation to the Peace Conference and complained that [not] only had she not been admitted or heard at the Peace Conference but that no reply had even been made to communications addressed to the Bureau of the Conference.

MR. LLOYD GEORGE said that he was informed by Sir Maurice Hankey that Mr. Balfour was opposed to the admission of Persia to the Conference, though he did not know the reasons. He asked that the matter might be postponed until he had consulted Mr. Balfour.

§Mantoux's notes:

Wilson. I am now receiving claims from all sorts of people who think they have a claim to present or a grievance to make known. I received a message of this kind from the Minister of Foreign Affairs of Persia. He recalls that Persia asked to participate in the conference; that during the war, at the demand of the Allied powers, she maintained a benevolent neutrality; that that neutrality was violated by the enemy; and that Persia suffered the horrors of the war. Not having received a response to the first message to this effect, the Minister of Foreign Affairs sends me a note about the claims that Persia would like to present to the peace conference. He insists on the right of Persia to national independence, to the restitution of territories which have been occupied, and to reparation for damages. If the Persians cannot be admitted to the peace conference, they ask at least to be heard.

Lloyd George. We must wait to settle that question until we arrive at the discussion of the peace treaty with Turkey; it has no place in our present debates.

Hankey. May I remind you that Mr. Balfour expressed an opinion against hearing the representatives of Persia.

[8] Mochaverol-Memalek, Minister for Foreign Affairs of Persia, to WW, April 8, 1919, TLS (WP, DLC), enclosing two printed pamphlets setting forth the claims of Persia (WP, DLC). Wilson summarizes these materials well in the extract from Mantoux's notes printed below.

Wilson. In any case, we must respond to them.

Lloyd George. I will see Mr. Balfour on this subject. He must have good reasons, for he is a man of very moderate judgment. Permit me to consult him on that question. §

8. PRESIDENT WILSON said the time had come for holding a Plenary Conference. Lord Robert Cecil had written to him about the desirability of discussing the League of Nations Covenant there.[9] He proposed that the Covenant should be laid before the Plenary Conference without any further speech making, although he would make a statement to the effect that the last revision which had been made to consider such criticisms as had been offered only clarified certain points. After this, anyone who wanted to discuss the question could do so. There would probably be only a few speeches. There were also several other reports which had been called for by the Plenary Conference which should be laid before them.

MR. LLOYD GEORGE agreed that there must be a meeting.

M. CLEMENCEAU also agreed.

(After some futher discussion, it was decided:

(1) That a plenary meeting of the Preliminary Peace Conference should be held on Monday, April 28th, when the following reports should be considered:
   The League of Nations Covenant
   The Labour Clauses
   Responsibility and Breaches of the laws of War.

(2) That the clauses being drafted by the Drafting Committee to give effect to the conclusion of the Supreme Council on the subject of the Responsibility and Breaches of the laws of war should be circulated for the meeting.

(3) That a second plenary meeting of the Conference should be held on the day preceding the night on which the Germans were due to arrive at Versailles. The object of this meeting would be to communicate the contents of the Peace Treaty.)

9. The question of publicity was discussed several times during this meeting.

M. CLEMENCEAU strongly urged that the Treaty should be published when it was communicated to the Germans. It would not be fair to our own people to let the Germans see the Treaty and to conceal it from them. His own position would be an impossible one if the Treaty were not published. It was absolutely certain that the Germans would publish it, particularly if they wished to make mischief for us and it would make a very bad impression in the countries of the Allied and Associated Powers if the public first learnt of the terms of the Treaty of Peace from the German wireless.

[9] See R. Cecil to WW, April 21, 1919, Vol. 57.

MR. LLOYD GEORGE suggested that the Germans might not want to publish the Treaty and that negotiations would be easier for all concerned without publicity.

Both Mr. Lloyd George and President Wilson laid the utmost stress on the preparation of a good summary for publication.

MR. LLOYD GEORGE pointed out that the reception of the Peace Treaty would depend largely on the first impression made.

M. CLEMENCEAU said he was preparing a summary for communicating to the Preliminary Meeting and he thought this might also serve for the Press. He undertook to communicate it to and to discuss it with his colleagues.

MR. LLOYD GEORGE suggested that a notice ought to be issued to the Press of the Allied and Associated Powers to the effect that the moment for publication would be after the communication of the Treaty to the Germans and that premature publicity might have very serious effects.

(M. Clemenceau undertook to draft a preface notice on the subject.)

§ Mantoux's notes:

Clemenceau. The question of the publication of the preliminaries of peace has already been raised. In any case, we will be obliged to publish them as soon as they are in the hands of the Germans; otherwise, they would come back to us through the German press.

Lloyd George. The Germans will only publish them if they want everything to fail, and, if we publish them prematurely, we shall have embarrassing and dangerous discussions in the press.

Clemenceau. I believe, however, that when our conditions of peace are known, they will not make a bad impression on the public; they can defend themselves.

Lloyd George. There are newspapers which have taken their stand and which will not trouble themselves to know if these conditions are truly good or bad.

Clemenceau. I swear to you that the opinion of those newspapers does not matter to me. What we cannot risk is having our own compatriots read the text of the treaty in the *Berliner Tageblatt*.

Lloyd George. If Bismarck had published the text of the treaty before it was signed, would the negotiation have succeeded?

Clemenceau. First, the Germans had made no mystery of their intentions, and, next, I should tell you that, although I voted against the treaty of 1871, there was absolutely nothing else to do.

Wilson. It will be impossible to read to the plenipotentiaries of the Allied and Associated Powers the complete text of the preliminaries.

Clemenceau. We are preparing a summary in view of the meeting of the powers.

[Discussion of the Italian question, printed above.]

Clemenceau. I believe that we must agree on the procedure to follow when the Germans are here. I propose that all the objections which they have to make about the terms of the treaty be presented in writing. That is the only way to stay out of trouble. If we begin to make and to listen to speeches, there will be no end of that.

Lloyd George. What have we decided about the publication of the treaty?

Clemenceau. It is not possible not to publish it.

Lloyd George. Remember that the first impression is the one that counts. We do not have to hand over this document, which will be of very considerable size, to ordinary journalists who will take elements from it at random. Moreover, they will not find there the treaty of guarantee given to France by America and England.

Clemenceau. I just said that we were preparing a summary. We will submit it to you.

Lloyd George. That summary must be very well done. I wonder if there would not have to be one for each country, because the concerns of the public are different in your country and in ours.

Wilson. The important thing is indeed the wording of that summary.

Clemenceau. I will submit it to you.

Lloyd George. We must also warn the journalists that we will be giving them this document at the time of the communication of the conditions of peace to the German delegates, and that any infraction would entail grave consequences. §

T MS (SDR, RG 256, 180.03401/115, DNA); Paul Mantoux, *Les Délibérations du Conseil des Quatre, 24 mars-28 juin 1919* (2 vols., Paris, 1955), I, 340-46; printed with the approval of Philippe-Roger Mantoux and Jacques Mantoux.

A Memorandum by the American Representatives on the Reparation Commission

April 23, 1919.

REPARATIONS

POINTS FOR DECISION BY COUNCIL OF FOUR

(1) Categories of Damage.

(a) Shall damage be defined so as to include that caused by Germany's allies? The American delegation believes that the principle of joint and several liability is just in theory and in fact and should be adopted. If so, there should be introduced a provision for crediting to Germany any payments made by Germany's allies.

(b) It should be made clear that the categories of damage apply to acts as therein defined committed against the Allied and Associated Governments even though prior to a declaration of war. (e.g., Lusitania, Sussex, etc.).[1]

(c) In prior discussion of categories of damage the American delegation pointed out that Belgium did not appear to be fully protected and it made reservation in favor of the rights of Belgium. Since then the Belgian delegation has submitted its demands to the Council of Four and it is important that the decision of the Council be known so that such changes if any in the categories as such decision may require shall be made.

(d) The French propose to submit certain new categories, the text of which has not been furnished us.

(e) There is a question relative to the computation of damage on account of pensions, etc., and interest on such damage, which, however, chiefly concerns the British and French.

(2) Constitution of the Commission.

(a) The American delegation insists that each Government represented on the Commission shall have the right to withdraw on six month's notice. The British, French and Italian delegations are unwilling to concede this right.

(b) The British, French and Italian delegations propose a clause providing that the business and proceedings of the Commission must be secret, except for communications of the delegates with their Governments. The American delegation believes that the Commission should be trusted to ensure such secrecy as is desirable, but that secrecy should not be proclaimed in a formal way in the constitution of the Commission on account of political disadvantages.

(c) The British delegation is unwilling that the issue by Germany of bonds other than issues expressly stipulated for, and the distribution of bonds, should require the unanimous vote of the Commission. The American delegation regards those questions as of such a vital nature that the action should not be taken without unanimous consent.

(d) There is a difference of opinion as to the nature of the certificates which the Commission may issue to the several interested Governments, stating their interests in assets held by the Commission. The British wish certificates in small denominations, readily negotiable, which the Americans regard as dangerous and tending to defeat the principle that the Commission should hold German bonds until it feels that German credit is sufficiently stable to permit safely of the general distribution of such bonds.

(e) The British propose an elaborate clause requiring detailed investigation of taxation in Allied countries as compared to Germany, which the American delegation regards as impracticable.
(f) If the principle is maintained that German purchases for food and raw materials out of the initial $5,000,000,000 payment are to be made only with the approval of the Allied Governments, the Commission should be designated as the agency to approve.

(3) Restoration in kind of land destruction.

(a) An agreed text has been arrived at, subject to the decision of the Council of Four, as to whether the benefits thereof shall run only in favor of France, Italy and Belgium.

(4) Restoration in kind of marine destruction.

(a) There is an important difference between the American and other delegations as to title to ships seized during the war.

(5) Payment through deliveries of raw materials.

(a) There is agreement as to giving the Allies a limited option on German coal.
(b) The delegations other than the United States desire the extension of this option principle to chemicals and certain other materials.

(6) Guarantees.

(a) The French, with British and Italian concurrence, have proposed guarantees which are in the nature of punitive acts closely allied to acts of war. The Americans propose an alternative and milder form authorizing in the event of default certain economic reprizals that each nation may see fit to take.

(7) Status of certain Allied countries.

(a) It is important that there be a decision by the Council of Four as to the status in regard to reparations of Russia in particular and also certain other countries, as Poland, Czecho-Slovakia, Jugo-Slavia, etc.

CC MS (WP, DLC).

[1] Wilson placed a large "X" on the left side of this paragraph.

From the Peace Conference Diary of Thomas William Lamont

1919 Wednesday 23 April

Worked office in a m. Noon lunch w. NHD Dulles MC C & BMB & at 3 went to Pres't. Hr's talk w. him re final reparation. He sided w. me on giving year's notice of withdrawal from High Comn. We talked about guarantees & WW. explained French idea of small army of occupation. At 4 we went upstairs for Big 3. (Orlando home, sulking) W.W. sat me at his right. We went thro' the moot questions & beat the British on almost all, Sumner & Cunliffe were wild. L-G slipped over to me & said "I like your text on German taxation much better than the British text & will adopt it." In the midst L-G was called out on 'phone for 10 minutes. When he came back he whispered to W.W. with me there that Orlando asked him some questions about the Dalmatian Coast that made him think there might be something doing in the way of a solution. Later on word came in that W.W.'s statement re Italy was all over Paris. L-G spoke of it & seemed quite pleased. L-G took a lot of falls out of the French on the Restitution clauses.

Loucheur was very decent about it all. They adopted my text on guarantees with hardly a word. Later in the afternoon we planned how we should tell the small powers about Reparation. Adjrnmt after 7.

Hw bound diary (T. W. Lamont Papers, MH-BA).

From the Diary of Vance Criswell McCormick

April 23 (Wednesday) [1919]

Meeting of Blockade at 10.00 o'clock to discuss plans relaxation, de-rationing neutrals. Reported to the Supreme Economical Council upon plan for simplifying machinery by cutting out German rations of foodstuffs.

Lunched with advisers Davis, Lamont, Baruch and Dulles at Crillon to get together on final reparation draft to be submitted to the President at 3.00 at his house.

Coached the President on points under dispute.

At 4.00 went to session with Lloyd George, Clemenceau and respective advisers in a large room upstairs in the President's house, Orlando being absent, still on a huff and threatening to go home over Fiume discussion.

During the conference Lloyd George left the room to telephone and when he came back he sat down on sofa with President Wilson and was heard to say that he thought Orlando was calming down and would not go. He walked across the room and whispered to Clemenceau, giving apparently the same information. Clemenceau seems to me to be aging rapidly.

The Chiefs are all in a good humor and much progress made, practically settling all questions of difference. We called their attention to the fact that small nations must see the Reparations clauses, which they had evidently overlooked in the excitement of settling the differences among themselves, so we were divided up into sub-committees to break the news to the lesser powers and I can already hear the kicking. Was much impressed by good nature and cordiality of the Chiefs after the trying time they are passing through. Left President's house after 7.00 o'clock.

Dined at Hoovers with Paderewski; an interesting dinner as he told us all his troubles in Poland, the importance of Danzig. Says revolution if Poland does not get satisfactory settlement. Worried over Czecho-Slovak-Poland dispute over Teschen. He seems reasonable and has more force than I imagined.

Printed copy (V. C. McCormick Papers, CtY).

From the Peace Conference Diary of Bernard Mannes Baruch

April 23, 1919.

At three o'clock we went to see the President in reference to various reparation clauses. The matter had only been presented to me at luncheon an hour and a half before. We discussed the various points, and at four o'clock went into the Council of Three, when I was handed a printed form of the Reparation matter and the clauses, many of which probably had never been seen by my associates. Some of the objectionable ones were removed. The one referring to the surplus of money in the Enemy Property Custodian Fund appeared probably for the first time.

I notified Messrs. Dulles, Davis, Lamont, and McCormick that I could not accept that reference as I had not seen it before and did not know what it meant. Davis and Lamont told me that it has not even been discussed, and that it would not be accepted. I informed Dulles that it could not be included; and furthermore that we had to include reparational claims, so far as the Lusitania, Frye, and Sussex were concerned.

The subject of options on certain machines and tools, building material and reparational matters were brought up, and the document involving them was very seriously (and very rightly) changed.

The reference to coal was discussed, and I informed Loucheur that some protective measures must be taken regarding the industrial life of Germany in order to protect reparational matters. He was very insistent, and proposed a *force major* clause which I accepted; but I told him that that did not solve the problem. Lord Sumner said that he would accept the other matters only on condition that his views on dyestuffs were granted. In other words, he did not care what happened so long as he secured the acceptance of his dyestuffs program. I informed him that this was under negotiation, and that the proposition of Sir Hubert Llewellyn Smith[1] seemed more reasonable than the others, but that my objection was upon the general principle that it would lead to difficulty. He pressed me for an answer.

I partially explained the situation to the President who said that he had no objection and that I could handle it in the best way I knew how.

In view of the previous attitude of the German dye industry and the dependency upon it of the Allies, and in view of the extreme difficulty that has developed in the home market situation of the Allied and Associated Governments, I concluded to make a compromise, which I asked MacDowell[2] to draw up. This leaves it in its least objectionable form.

T MS (B. M. Baruch Papers, NjP).

[1] Permanent Secretary of the Board of Trade and Director General of the Economic Section of the British delegation.

[2] Charles Henry MacDowell, president of the Armour Fertilizer Works, former director of the Chemicals Division of the War Industries Board, and an economic adviser to Baruch at the peace conference.

Hankey's Notes of a Meeting of the Council of Four[1]

President Wilson's House,
I.C.-176A. Paris, April 23, 1919, 4 p.m.

REPARATION.

The Council had before it a printed Memorandum on the various documents prepared by the Committees in connection with Reparation.[2]

1. MR. LLOYD GEORGE doubted the expediency of only having one representative for each nation on the Commission. He thought the number should be two as it might be desirable to have two types of men, for example, a financial and judicial expert.

MR. DAVIS pointed out that substitute members were provided for.

MR. LAMONT said the point had been carefully considered and provided for by means of coadjutor delegates. It had been considered that if there were two delegates for each of the five nations the Commission would become unwieldy and it would hamper progress. In any case delegates would require experts and sub-commissions would have to be appointed.

PRESIDENT WILSON pointed out that it was the difference between the Quai d'Orsay Council of Ten and the recent conversations of the Council of Four.

[1] The complete text of Hankey's minutes is printed in *PPC*, V, 155-201.

[2] It is printed in *ibid.*, pp. 165-87.

MR. LLOYD GEORGE agreed this was a very substantial difference.

M. CLEMENCEAU suggested that the coadjutor delegates practically provided what Mr. Lloyd George asked for.

MR. LLOYD GEORGE said he would not press the matter.

2. Attention was next drawn to a clause prepared by the American Delegation providing for the right of withdrawal upon six months notice by any nation on the Commission. (This will be found annexed to Clause 23 on page 11 of the Appendix, having been inserted here by a drafting error instead of in Clause 5 of Annex 2.)[3]

PRESIDENT WILSON explained that, in his opinion, no nation ought to withdraw from a Commission but his legal advisers had informed him that no Treaty can be withdrawn from, or even renounced, unless there was a provision to that effect. He thought that public opinion in the United States would demand that there should be such a clause, although he hoped it would never be necessary to use it.

MR. LLOYD GEORGE asked for the substitution of 12 months notice instead of 6.

PRESIDENT WILSON agreed to accept this substitution.

(It was agreed that the clause providing for the right of withdrawal should be adopted with the substitution of 12 months notice instead of 6.)

Secrecy. Appendix Annex 2. Article 8.[4]

3. MR. DAVIS said that the American Delegation considered that the secrecy provision should be withdrawn. The feeling was that to set up a secret clause in a public Treaty would make a bad public impression. If the delegates on the Commission were honest, they would not give out information; if they were dishonest, they would do so whether the clause were there or not.

MR. LLOYD GEORGE pointed out that the object of the clause was not to exclude Governments from making announcements but to prevent the officials on the Commission from doing so. He pointed out that it was vital in matters of finance that information which might affect the money markets should not be allowed to leak out.

PRESIDENT WILSON said that their objections were not to the actual secrecy but they wished to protect the Peace Conference against the attacks of those who declared that everything should be public. He agreed with Mr. Davis that if discreet people were put on the Commission they would not give information away.

MR. LAMONT suggested that every Government would give its own instructions to its own Delegates.

It was agreed that Article 8 should be deleted.

[3] It is printed in *ibid*., p. 182.

[4] It is printed in *ibid*., p. 171.

Arrangements for determining the amount and conditions of Bonds, etc.

Appendix Annex 2 Article 10 Clause (b)[5]

4. MR. DAVIS said that the French and Italian Representatives were in agreement with the American proposal.[6]

LORD SUMNER said that the Italians had agreed with the British Delegates; the United States and French Delegates were opposed to the British and Italian Delegates.

MR. LLOYD GEORGE explained that the British experts apprehended that if one Power was in a position to veto an issue of Bonds, it might be able to use this power to extort special terms. They might refuse to agree to an issue of Bonds, unless some special conditions were agreed to.

MR. LOUCHEUR said that he agreed with the United States proposal.

MR. LLOYD GEORGE said that as he was alone in this matter, he would not press the objection.

The American proposal for Clause (b) was adopted.

5. M. LOUCHEUR said that a point affecting the rate of interest had been overlooked from Article 20. He then read the following extract from an Article prepared on the subject:

> La Commission déterminera périodiquement, à la majorité, le taux de l'întérêt (au maximum 5 p.100) dont sera débitée l'Allemagne sur sa dette, telle que l'aura fixée la Commission, et aussi les dates à partir desquelles l'intérêt sera débité sur les montants respectifs de la dite dette.

This, M. Loucheur said, was an American proposal. He said that originally a different text had been proposed based on the principle that a rate of 5% should be fixed leaving the Commission the right to fix a lower rate. Mr. Norman Davis had objected to this. M. Loucheur's recollection was that Mr. Lloyd George had supported Mr. Norman Davis on the ground that he considered it better from a political point of view to determine the rate of interest on the lines now proposed. The original proposal would appear to make concessions to the Germans and would create a bad impression from a political point of view.

[5] It is printed in *ibid.*, p. 172. It reads as follows: "The Commission will from time to time issue for negotiation or sale to third parties, bonds of the hereinafter-mentioned issues delivered by Germany. In doing so, it will have regard both to the financial requirements of the Allied Powers and to the necessity of avoiding depreciation of the bonds still unissued by negotiating excessive amounts. Up to four thousand millions of marks per annum, it may decide upon such issues by a majority, but for the amounts in excess of that sum unanimity shall be required."

[6] "In all questions of determining the amount and conditions of bonds or other obligations to be executed by Germany, and of fixing the time and manner for selling, negotiating or distributing such bonds, a unanimous vote of the Commission shall be required." *Ibid.*, p. 172.

MR. LLOYD GEORGE said that if the Germans were given a lower rate than 5% when the Allied and Associated Governments had to pay 5% themselves, public opinion would ask why the Germans should be allowed to pay less. On the other hand, if the general rate of interest should fall, he thought that Germany should have the benefit thereof and that the Commission should have the right to fix a lower rate of interest. So long as we pay 5%, the Germans should pay 5%. The Commission should not have the power to give the Germans any preferential rate of interest. He thought that it was more a question of form than of substance. Did not the American delegates agree that if we paid 5% the Germans should do the same?

PRESIDENT WILSON said that they all did. The only question was as to who should have power to lower the rate.

MR. LLOYD GEORGE proposed to leave this to the Commission. He would rather regulate the payment of interest altogether than the rate.

M. CLEMENCEAU and M. LOUCHEUR said that they agreed.

(On Mr. Lloyd George's proposal, the drafting of a revised paragraph was left to the Expert Committee.)

Interest on Pensions.

6. M. LOUCHEUR read the following clause which was a continuance of the clause quoted in the preceding section and which it was proposed should be added to Article 10:

> L'intérêt sera débité: (1) sur le montant des dommages matériels (pour la fraction correspondant à la valeur d'avant guerre), à partir du 11 novembre 1918; (2) pour les pensions, à partir du jour où elles sont payées par chaque pays intéressé.

MR. LLOYD GEORGE considered a proposal as regards interest on material damage to be a mistake. If repairs were made in kind, it would mean interest was being paid on things rebuilt and it would be very difficult to assess the value. He did not, however, press the point. He did object strongly, however, to the arrangement for pensions under Clause (2). He explained that he only wanted equal treatment for damage of all kinds. He could not acknowledge that damage to houses was more important than damage to human life. The latter was irreparable. No fair interest on this could be paid unless the value of the pensions was capitalised. The same thing should be done whether it referred to a house or to a man. Supposing by May 1st, 1921, the Commission had established that the Bill for Housing was five thousand million pounds and for pensions three thousand million pounds. Both ought to be in the same category. He then called attention to Annex I, Article I, Clause (e) and suggested that a clause based on the following words should be substituted for M. Loucheur's proposal:

"The amount due to the Allied and Associated Governments to be calculated for all of them as being capitalised cost of such payments on the basis of the scales in force in France at the date of the signature of this Treaty."[7]

This, he pointed out, would provide that Germany should not be responsible to go on paying for 60 years. The sum would be capitalised as arranged by the Commission.

M. LOUCHEUR said that French delegates would agree.

(Mr. Lloyd George's proposal was accepted.)

7. M. LOUCHEUR pointed out that the original date for the calculation of pensions, namely, November 1918, did not take into account the fact that pensions had been paid by the various Governments long before that date. He suggested that some provision should be made for this.

MR. LLOYD GEORGE pointed out that this would be covered if the words "at the date of the signature of this Treaty" were added in the above clause after the words "capitalised cost."

(The addition of these words was approved.)

PARTICIPATION OF GERMANY IN THE PROCEEDINGS OF THE COMMISSION. APPENDIX: ANNEX 2, ARTICLE 13.[8]

8. MR. LLOYD GEORGE said he did not like the proposal that the Germans should not have power to challenge any proposal of the Commission. He agreed that they should not be able to prolong the discussion for years. Nevertheless, they ought to be able to make representations on any subject.

(At this moment Mr. Lloyd George withdrew to keep another appointment.)

LORD SUMNER said that Mr. Lloyd George's proposal was to leave out the following words: "in the discussion of the general rules as to the measure of damages only."

PRESIDENT WILSON pointed out that this clause contravened the original bases laid down in Clause 3 of the Reparation Provisions.[9] He proposed to cut the whole clause out.

[7] The original Clause (e), Annex I, Article 1, reads as follows: "As damage caused to the peoples of the Allied and Associated *States*, all pensions and compensations in the nature of pensions to naval and military victims of war, whether mutilated, wounded, sick or invalided, and to the dependents of such victims." Lloyd George's clause was added to the original draft. *Ibid.*, p. 168.

[8] "The Commission shall be at liberty, but shall not be bound, to allow Germany to take such part, if any, as the Commission may think right, in the discussion of the general rules as to the measure of damages only, but not in any decision of the Commission whatever." *Ibid.*, pp. 173-74.

[9] "The amount of such damage (as set forth under the specific categories attached hereto) for which compensation is to be made by *Germany* shall be determined by an Inter-Allied Commission, to be constituted in *the* form *and with the powers set forth hereunder and in the Annexes hereto.* This Commission shall examine into the claims and give to the *German Government* a just opportunity to be heard. The findings of the Com-

(After some discussion, it was agreed that the Clause should read as follows: "The Commission shall examine into the claims and give to the German Government a just opportunity to be heard but not to take part in any decision of the Commission whatever.")

BASIS FOR ESTIMATING GERMANY'S CAPACITY TO PAY. APPENDIX: ANNEX 2, ARTICLE 15 (b).[10]

9. PRESIDENT WILSON drew attention to the article the American Delegation proposed to substitute.[11]

LORD SUMNER said that the fact was that at present the burden of taxation was heavier in Allied countries than in Germany. Yet Germany might plead her poverty, and say she could not pay. It was common ground that the actual taxation was a related matter that must be taken into account. (President Wilson agreed.)

What the British Delegation submitted, and thought it was not too much to ask, was that the Commission should not have the right to relieve Germany until Germany had made an attempt to raise her taxation to the amount borne by the most heavily taxed of the Allied Powers represented on the Commission. They recognised that additional taxation would not necessarily bring in money which could be used to pay outside Germany. They recognised also that such taxation might even depreciate Germany's capacity to pay. That was

---

mission as to the amount of damage defined as above shall be concluded and notified to Germany on or before the 1st May, 1921, as representing the extent of their obligations. The Commission shall concurrently draw up a schedule of payments prescribing the time and manner for securing and discharging the entire obligation within a period of thirty years from the 1st May, 1921. In the event, however, that within the period mentioned, Germany shall have failed to discharge her obligation, then any balance remaining unpaid may, within the discretion of the Commission, be postponed for settlement in subsequent years: or may be handled otherwise in such manner as the Allied and Associated Governments, acting through the Commission, shall determine." *Ibid.*, p. 166.

[10] These clauses declared that Germany should be considered as able to pay the total amount of the proved claims against her or any annual installment thereof approved by the Reparation Commission as long as her internal taxation per capita for the service of the debt due the Allies was not at least equal to the taxation per capita of the population of the most heavily taxed of the Allied powers for the service of its public debt, unless the commission should be unanimously of the opinion that any further increase in German taxation would diminish Germany's capacity to pay. Germany was also to be considered able to pay so long as she paid any principal or interest on her own war debt or on any other debt contracted prior to the beginning of the war. The clauses further provided that the sums payable by Germany for reparation were to be a charge upon all her revenues prior to the service or discharge of any domestic loan and that the commission was to study the German system of taxation from time to time to ascertain its relation to the systems of the nations represented on the commission. *Ibid.*, pp. 175-76.

[11] "In estimating Germany's periodical capacity to pay, the Commission shall examine the German system of taxation, first to the end that the sums for reparation which Germany is required to pay shall become a charge upon all her revenues, prior to that for the service or discharge of any domestic loan, and, secondly, so as to satisfy itself that, in general, the German scheme of taxation is fully as heavy proportionately as that of any of the Powers represented on this Commission." To this the French added the following sentence: "The decision of the Commission relative to the total or partial cancellation of the capital or interest of any verified debt of Germany must be accompanied by a statement of the grounds for its action." *Ibid*, p. 175.

the reason why they said that if the taxation was too high the Commission should be permitted to accept the plea of poverty. The British Delegation felt that it was not right that the Commission should be able to remit, unless German taxation was proportionately as high as that of the most heavily taxed Allied country. He agreed it was certainly necessary to trust the Commission, but the whole of these arrangements would be subjected to very close criticism, and it would be difficult to convince public opinion if it thought that Germany could be relieved of taxation on the ground of its poverty, whilst we ourselves were more heavily taxed and had equally heavy engagements to meet. If the Commission exercised great wisdom, he agreed that the difficulty would be avoided.

PRESIDENT WILSON said that under the American scheme the Commission would not be able to admit the plea of poverty unless Germany had taxed herself to an extent at least equal to the taxation of other Powers. He agreed that the Commission must be given some standards of taxation by which to judge of Germany's ability to pay. It might be, however, that an additional burden would not give a greater yield of power to pay. He felt, however, that it was making a mistake to try to foresee situations too far in advance. If this were done, only second-rate men would be induced to serve on the Commission. He wished to get the biggest men possible, since the financial arrangements of the world would depend on its operations. Hence, he would deprecate definite and rigid instructions, and his French colleagues agreed with him. He thought that the standard of justice was as distinctly laid down in one draft as in the other.

M. LOUCHEUR said he agreed with the American draft.

MR. LLOYD GEORGE (who had meanwhile returned) said he would withdraw his objections.

(The American proposal with the French additions was adopted.)

ISSUE OF CERTIFICATES BY THE COMMISSION REGARDING BONDS HELD FOR THE BENEFIT OF DIFFERENT GOVERNMENTS APPENDIX: ANNEX 2, ARTICLE 16.[12]

10. MR. LLOYD GEORGE accepted the French proposal.

SANCTIONS: APPENDIX: ANNEX 2, ARTICLE 18.[13]

11. PRESIDENT WILSON pointed out that the United States representatives had accepted the principle of Sanctions, but were not prepared to approve the form of words proposed in the draft. He then read a simpler and shorter formula.

[12] It is printed in *ibid.*, p. 178.

[13] "In case of voluntary default by Germany in the performance of any obligation, of whatever kind, to comply with and satisfy its decisions, the Commission will forthwith give notice of such default to each of [the] interested Powers and may make such rec-

M. KLOTZ said that he would accept, with the addition of the words (underlined below) "or financial" after "economic." The following substitute for the second and third sub-paragraphs of this Article was adopted:

"The measures which the Allied and Associated Governments shall have the right to take, and which Germany hereby agrees not to consider as acts of war may include economic or financial prohibition and reprisals, and in general such other measures as the respective Government may determine to be necessary in the premise."

NOTE Just as the Meeting was breaking up, it was agreed in addition to omit the last paragraph of Article 18.

FORM OF PAYMENTS. APPENDIX ANNEX 2, ARTICLE 19.[14]

12. MR. LLOYD GEORGE thought that this Article was too stiff. It would give the Commission power practically to take any property or material to which it took a fancy.

PRESIDENT WILSON agreed with Mr. Lloyd George. He had seen this clause for the first time. What he wanted was to avoid even the appearance of a Brest-Litovsk forced Treaty.

---

ommendations as to the action to be taken in consequence of such default as it may think necessary.

"These measures, which the Allied and Associated Powers shall have the right to take, and which Germany agrees not to regard as acts of war, may be in particular the following:

"1. Prohibition against German vessels entering ports situated in the territory of the Allied and Associated States or of their possessions and dependencies and from utilising any coaling stations belonging to the said States.

"2. Seizure whether in the ports of the Allied and Associated States, whether on the high sea, of all German vessels, under reserve of the rights of neutrals, which should be safeguarded.

"3. Prohibition from entry into the territories of the Allied and Associated States or of their possessions and dependencies to all German subjects and all goods of German origin.

"4. Prohibition of the negotiation on the territories of the said States of German securities of any kind.

"5. Suspension of all postal, telegraphic, and telephonic communication with Germany.

"6. Seizure on the territories of the said States of all German goods.

"These rights shall not be exclusive of the exercise of any others.

"The engagement of the German Government in the financial protocol in the Armistice signed at Trèves on the 13th December, 1918, shall be maintained until Germany has paid the first 20,000,000,000 M. bonds referred to in Article [blank], unless the Commission should previously accept some other guarantee in lieu thereof." *Ibid.*, pp. 179-80.

14 "Payments required to be made in gold or its equivalent on account of the proved claims of the Allies may at any time be demanded or accepted by the Commission in the form of properties, chattels, commodities, businesses, rights, and concessions in German territories or in territories other than the territories of Germany, ships, bonds, shares, *or* securities of any kind, currencies or bonds of Germany or of other States, the value of such substitutes for gold being fixed at a fair and just amount by the Commission itself.

"The German Government proposes and undertakes to take any necessary measures to acquire, in cases where it is not already the owner, and to transfer to the Commission all goods, rights, and interests of German nationals which the said Commission may find acceptable." *Ibid.*, pp. 180-81.

MR. LLOYD GEORGE suggested that his objections would be surmounted by omitting in line 3 "demanded or." He had no objection to the Commission accepting payment in the forms proposed, but they should not have power to demand it.

PRESIDENT WILSON agreed.

(It was agreed to omit in line 3 the words "demanded or," and in addition, to omit the second sub-paragraph of Article 19.)

MERCHANT SHIPPING. (Appendix, Annex 3) German Ships in American Ports.[15]

13. PRESIDENT WILSON drew attention to amendments proposed by the United States Delegation (see Commission on Reparation Supplementary Interim Report of the second Sub-Committee, dated April 18th, 1919, Appendix 2).[16]

President Wilson said that the claim for the German ships seized in United States ports was almost the only reparation claim put forward by the United States of America. Other powers, with their full acquiescence, were to be reimbursed for pensions. In the course of the war, the United States of America had taken over the German ships in their ports and had secured their title to them by law. The ships had been so damaged that millions of dollars had had to be spent on their repairs and new methods that had to be devised. Throughout, these ships had been used for the indispensable transport of the American armies to France. It would not be tolerable to public opinion in the United States if their title to these ships was not recognised. This had nothing to do with the payment of owners which the United States contemplated, but only to their title. It would be intolerable if anyone questioned the title which had been legally established under full process of their rights as a belligerent.

MR. LLOYD GEORGE said that if he went into the whole case, he would show there were serious grounds which made it impossible for the British Government to accept. If he accepted it would not be merely a matter affecting the United States of America. This was an easy matter which he would not contest. It would, however, affect neutrals and other belligerents. Neutrals would benefit by this to the extent of 794,000 tons of shipping, Brazil to the extent of 216,000 tons. This meant a loss not of cash but of ships which were even more important. Brazil lost 25,000 tons and had seized 216,000 tons

[15] It is printed in *ibid.*, pp. 182-84.

[16] This report is printed in *ibid.*, pp. 187-93. The amendments proposed by the American delegation required Germany to acknowledge the validity of the seizures of ships made by each individual Allied or Associated Power and to recognize the title of that power to the ships which it had seized. The report devoted considerable space to the arguments for and against the American amendments. These arguments are well summarized below by Wilson and Lloyd George.

in her ports and would consequently profit enormously by the transaction. France lost 950,000 tons and would only be able to keep 45,000 tons; that is to say, France would only get less than 1/20th of her loss. The United States lost 389,000 tons and would get 628,000 tons. The British Empire lost 7,740,000 tons and would only get 400,000 tons. During the war Great Britain after allowing for shipbuilding had lost a balance of 4,500,000 tons. There was a great difference between the value of ships to Great Britain and the United States. It was like the value of ships to a fisherman compared with ships to a swell yachtsman. Great Britain lived on ships and it was a very serious matter to her. There was first the case of the neutrals who would walk off with 800,000 tons. In reply to President Wilson's suggestion that this could be avoided he thought it would be difficult. The German ships in American ports had been driven to take refuge there by the action of the Navies of France and Great Britain. They only escaped capture because they took refuge in United States' ports. He could not help thinking that the whole of shipping should be put in "hotchpot." The United States would then certainly get all that she had lost.

PRESIDENT WILSON said they had lost not only ships but thousands of lives. In other countries such lives were being provided for by reparation arrangements, but that America was making no such claim and it would be intolerable to public opinion if it were not agreed that the United States should retain these ships.

MR. LLOYD GEORGE said he would be glad to enter into an arrangement but objected to the participation of Brazil, who had no claim for walking off with so many ships. Brazil's whole trade was protected by our Fleet.

PRESIDENT WILSON said this argument did not apply to the United States, who had made an invaluable contribution to the war. The United States did not mean to take over the ships without payment.

MR. LLOYD GEORGE said he did not object to some arrangement whereby the United States would retain all of the Enemy ships which they had taken over, but that he did object to the proposed American clauses being put into the Peace Treaty which would permit other countries whose rights were not the same as those of the United States, to retain the enemy ships taken over by them.

Mr. Lloyd George proposed, therefore, that Annex III should stand as at present for insertion without alteration in the Peace Treaty, but that an agreement be made by the Allied Governments with the United States, providing for the retention by the United States of enemy ships now in its possession, against payment.

PRESIDENT WILSON stated this would be acceptable to him provided a satisfactory agreement in accordance with the American amendment is drawn and executed by the Allies with the United States prior to the execution of the Treaty.

(The following alterations were made during the interval when the Conference had broken up into groups.

The Secretary was unable to follow the precise reasons for the decision.)

PAYMENT IN KIND (Appendix 1, Annex 4)[17]

14. After some discussion it was agreed to omit para 2 (c) and (d) and the last para of 6.[18]

15. (It was agreed to omit the following words at the end of para. 10: "and to the decisions and orders of the above named Commission from time to time." The para. therefore reads as follows: "Germany undertakes to pass any legislation and to issue any orders and decrees that may be necessary to give complete effect to these clauses."

MR. LLOYD GEORGE asked what would be the position of Czecho-Slovakia and Poland.

PRESIDENT WILSON considered that these would not be entitled to claim reparation since they had been part of enemy countries.

MR. LLOYD GEORGE asked what would be the position of Roumania and Serbia, which had annexed very large territories in Transylvania and Jugo-Slavia respectively. These countries would not only escape the debts of the Austrian Empire to which they had formerly belonged, but would also escape the burdens imposed on the Allies. He thought the best plan was that proposed by M. Orlando, that there should be a sort of ledger account in relation to these territories. On one side of the account would be the liability that the annexed territories would have had for a share of the Austrian debt and indemnity and on the other side of the account would be their share in the claim of Roumania and Serbia respectively for indemnity. This would be set off one against the other and they would be credited with the balance.

MR. NORMAN DAVIS asked what would happen if the balance was a debit instead of a credit.

MR. LLOYD GEORGE said in that case there would be no claim.

(The above arrangement was agreed to.)

[17] Printed in *ibid.*, pp. 184-86.

[18] Paragraphs 2 (c) and (d) concerned lists which the several Allied and Associated Powers might file with the Reparation Commission dealing with the number of German workmen they might desire for reconstruction labor and with destroyed objects of artistic, historical, or literary value which they might desire to have replaced by "similar objects which are in being in Germany." The last paragraph of Section 6 declared that a maximum of 500,000 German workmen might be required at any one time by all of the Allied and Associated Powers. The Reparation Commission would determine work rules for these men, and the countries employing them would have to provide proper working and living conditions.

CLAIMS BY THE SUBJECTS OF ALLIED AND ASSOCIATED POWERS RESIDENT IN POLAND AND CZECHOSLOVAKIA.

17.[19] M. KLOTZ asked what would be the position of the subjects of Allied and Associated countries established in a country like Poland whose property had been destroyed. They would not claim compensation from Poland; ought it not to be provided that they should claim against Germany?

MR. LLOYD GEORGE pointed out that they were provided for by Annex I, Article I(a).

It was also pointed out that they were provided for by Article 3, where the words used were "wherever situated."

CONSULTATION WITH THE SMALLER POWERS.

18. After a somewhat prolonged discussion, the following arrangements were agreed to for consultation with the Powers with special interest on the subject of the reparation clauses. The Expert Committee, which had been advising the Supreme Council, should divide itself into groups and each group should see a group of nations of the Powers with special interests. M. Loucheur undertook to organise this arrangement. Those States which had observations to make should subsequently have the right of consulting the Supreme Council.

THE RETURN OF ANIMALS TAKEN FROM INVADED TERRITORIES.

19. M. LOUCHEUR proposed the following addition to Article 7 of the reparation clauses:

> "Si une moitié au moins des animaux pris par l'ennemi dans les territoires envahis ne peut être identifiée et restituée, le reste, jusqu'à concurrence de la moitié du nombre enlevé, sera livré par l'Allemagne à titre de restitution."
>
> (After considerable discussion, it was agreed that M. Loucheur's proposed addition to Article 7 should not be inserted in the Treaty of Peace; his proposal should, however, form the subject of a separate agreement between the Allies, a draft text of the agreement to be prepared and submitted by M. Loucheur.)

CATEGORIES OF DAMAGE.

20. M. KLOTZ proposed the addition of the following new category of damage:

> "(h) Dépenses engagées par l'Etat, ou pour son compte et avec son autorisation, pour ravitailler, transporter ou secourir la pop-

[19] There is no "No. 16."

ulation civile des territoires occupés et la population civile refugiée ou évacuée."

MR. LLOYD GEORGE said that if new categories were put in, the British Government would have a number of new categories which it would wish to introduce.

(It was agreed that the addition proposed by M. Klotz related to a question of the interpretation to be given to the categories already accepted and should be referred without delay for consideration to the Commission on Reparations.)

21. M. KLOTZ made a proposal for putting a valuation clause in the Treaty in regard to property for which reparation was to be given. This was necessary owing to the change of value between 1914 and the present time.

(It was agreed that the Expert Committee should meet to prepare a text.)

(The Conclusions, as revised by the Expert Drafting Committee, will be forwarded later.)

T MS (SDR, RG 256, 180.03401/116, DNA).

To Herbert Clark Hoover, with Enclosure

My dear Hoover: Paris, 23 April, 1919.

I think the enclosed is all right[1] and I hope you will feel at liberty to give it out.

In unavoidable haste,

Cordially and faithfully yours, Woodrow Wilson

TLS (Hoover Archives, CSt-H).

[1] About Hoover's two earlier drafts and what happened to them, see the extract from the Diary of Colonel House printed at April 19, 1919, and n. 2 thereto, and H. C. Hoover to EMH, April 19, 1919, and the Enclosure thereto, all in Vol. 57.

E N C L O S U R E

21 April 1919.

The favorable reply of the Associated Governments to the proposals of Doctor Nansen[1] that a neutral commission should be allowed to undertake the feeding of the people of the principal cities in Russia, is based on three conceptions:

First, that in giving permission to a Neutral commission to undertake the humanitarian work, it in no way comprises any negotiations between the Allies and the government of Russia, nor does it imply any approval of their methods of government. The situation in this particular is very much akin to the Belgian Relief Commission, through which the Allied Governments did not make a recognition of the German Government of Belgium.

Second, that there shall be complete justice in distribution to all classes, regardless of all distinctions, and the guarantees of a strong neutral commission that this will be the case.

The third conception is that the Bolsheviki are to keep themselves within a certain circumscribed area, ceasing all military action and attempts at invasions.

The primary reasons for this action are purely humanitarian. Hundreds of thousands of people are dying monthly from starvation, and beyond even this it is the wish of the world that fighting and the killing of men should cease. Other reasons have been also brought to bear. The newly born democracies of Siberia, Kuban, Finland, Esthonia, Lettlant [Lettland], Livonia, Poland, Ruthenia, Roumania, Armenia, Serbia, Bulgaria, and Austria, and other nationalities which surround Bolshevik Russia must have a breathing spell to build up some stability. There is little hope of setting any orderly government in these places, and of getting their people back to production unless they can raise food and necessities for next year, unless they can be relieved of the constant threat of Bolshevist invasion and the necessity to keep armies in being out of resources founded on misery.

Again the brunt of this famine in Russia is being thrown by the Bolshevik upon the skilled workmen who refuse to accept their doctrine, upon the merchants, the storekeepers, and professional classes, and unless food is put into Russia all these classes will be dead before next harvest.

T MS (Hoover Archives, CSt-H).

[1] See the Enclosure printed with F. Nansen to WW, April 17, 1919, Vol. 57, and F. Nansen to WW, April 3, 1919, Vol. 56.

To Tasker Howard Bliss

My dear General: Paris, 23 April, 1919.

I thank you sincerely for your letter of April 21st about the immediate publication of my statement with regard to the Italian question.[1] I find my colleagues, Mr. Lloyd George and M. Clemenceau, opposed to its immediate publication because they believe that that would end the possibility of agreement with Italy, but I am standing out for my rights and shall not hold it back too long.

Cordially and faithfully yours, Woodrow Wilson

TLS (T. H. Bliss Papers, DLC).
[1] THB to WW, April 21, 1919 (first letter of that date), Vol. 57.

To Henry Mauris Robinson

My dear Mr. Robinson: Paris, 23 April, 1919.

How do you think a clause of this sort would do as a substitute for clause number eight in the Labor Resolutions:[1]

"The standards set by law in each country with respect to the conditions of labor shall have due regard to the equitable and humane treatment of all foreign workers lawfully resident therein."

Cordially and sincerely yours, Woodrow Wilson

TLS (WP, DLC).
[1] About which, see the Enclosure printed with H. M. Robinson to WW, March 24, 1919, Vol. 56. The original version of Clause 8 included therein reads as follows: "In all matters concerning their status as workers and social insurance foreign workmen lawfully admitted to any country and their families should be ensured the same treatment as the nationals of that country." For other versions of Clause 8 up to this time, see EMH to WW, April 20, 1919, and the notes thereto, Vol. 57.

To William Shepherd Benson

My dear Admiral: Paris, 23 April, 1919.

Thank you for your note of yesterday about the GEORGE WASHINGTON.[1] I am quite satisfied with the arrangement which keeps the ARIZONA here and would feel easier if the GEORGE WASHINGTON were not retained but were to continue at the transportation work assigned her.

I would be very much obliged to you if you would, if you can, send me a list of the transports and the dates at which they are severally due at Brest. Grayson tells me that there will probably be one each week.

With warm appreciation,

Cordially yours, [Woodrow Wilson]

CCL (WP, DLC).
[1] W. S. Benson to WW, April 22, 1919, TLS (WP, DLC). Benson asked if Wilson wished the *George Washinton* held at Brest in case he should wish to make an early departure for the United States. Otherwise, the liner would be used to transport American troops home, and could not return to Brest before May 20. Benson pointed out that *U.S.S. Arizona* was presently at Brest and could be held there for Wilson should the *George Washington* be released.

A Memorandum

23 April, 1919.

MEMORANDUM for the President.

Count de Cellere, the Italian Ambassador, asks for an appointment at the earliest possible time. He wishes to see the President on behalf of Mr. Orlando.

Notify Count de Cellere at following address:

Telegraph Service,
Hotel Edouard VII,
Room 120.

T MS (WP, DLC).

From Nikola P. Pašić

Mr. President, Paris, April 23-rd 1919.

From the depth of my heart and my soul I thank you. Your righteous and divine words have saved from slavery a part of our nation. With your declaration[1] you have revived the faith of all feeble nations that there verily begins a new era of fraternity and equality in rights of all nations. Our nation with three names will eternally praise you as our saviour of a new bondage and will always be unshakeably grateful, to you and to your great Nation which has heroically shed its blood, not demanding anything else but the freedom and the develo[p]ment of all nations, great and small, and a durable world's peace.

I avail myself with the greatest pleasure of this opportunity to renew to Your Excellency the assurance of my highest consideration, with which I am,

Mr. President, yours very sincerely, Nik. P. Pashitch

TLS (WP, DLC).

[1] That is, Wilson's statement on the Adriatic question, printed earlier at this date.

From Robert Lansing, with Enclosure

My dear Mr. President: Paris, April 23, 1919.

I enclose for your information a copy of an extremely interesting and important telegram[1] which has just been received from Mr. Dresel. Faithfully yours, Robert Lansing

TLS (WP, DLC).

[1] From Ellis Loring Dresel and George Herbert Harries. Dresel, accompanied by Lithgow Osborne, a Second Secretary in the American Foreign Service, had left Paris on his second mission to Germany on April 16. His assignment was to prepare German leaders

to accept the terms of peace as well as to report on conditions in Germany and to appraise the mood of the German government and the people. Dresel remained in Berlin until early May. Brig. Gen. Harries had been chief of the United States Military Mission in Berlin since December 3, 1918. See *PPC*, XII, 82-117, and Klaus Schwabe, *Woodrow Wilson, Revolutionary Germany, and Peacemaking, 1918-1919: Missionary Diplomacy and the Realities of Power*, trans. Rita and Robert Kimber (Chapel Hill, N. C., 1985), pp. 313-18.

E N C L O S U R E

Third Army. April 20, 1919.

CONFIDENTIAL. In talk with Rantzau Saturday evening, he began by stating that formal invitation to Versailles had astonished him, and that he should only go if he were specifically directed by the government to start. As far as he could see an ultimatum was intended as it was not clear why he should have to go to Paris to receive this. Passing to discussion of terms he said that conditions apparently proposed would reduce Germans to abject slavery. An eminent financier had just assured him that full possession of the Sarre district and upper Silesia were absolutely indispensable to economic existence of nation. He would never sign any peace nor would the ministry in his opinion agree to one which deprived Germany even temporarily of these two districts and he was convinced that the German people would back this up. If another ministry chose to accept such conditions that was their look out. Questioned as to how, in case of refusal of terms, German people could continue to exist, he made no definite answer and repudiated my suggestion that possibly an arrangement with Russia might be attempted.

Throughout the interview he insinuated a peace, such as apparently will be imposed, could not be in accordance with President's fourteen points. He stated that he made no specific (#), as to Alsace Lorraine, specially Wiesbaden, or the size of the indemnity as announced, and I gather that the protests on these points will not be serious. The free port for Danzig will, as I infer, also not meet with much opposition.

His attitude was of great depression and he showed a remarkable irritation towards the French. He gave the impression of sincerity although I *not* convinced he will not ultimately recede from his position. From the papers, a proclamation just issued by Ebert, and interviews with several well informed persons, I have guarantees that the views of Rantzau meet with much support. A plebiscite on the question of acceptance of the terms is now being much discussed and appears entirely probable. As to this Rantzau would not commit himself. The independent socialists would undoubtedly favor acceptance of the terms as published but it is exceedingly doubtful whether their influence will be decisive.

I venture to suggest that whatever definite statement can be made indicating that at least a limited amount of discussion of terms will be permitted might have reassuring influence.

I emphasized throughout the talk the belief that German economic rehabilitation will be in the interests of the whole world and that on the conclusion of peace our attitude will be only cooperation to this end. I also pointed out the ruinous consequences of summary rejection of peace. I shall endeavor to impress this as strongly as possible in future conversations and shall be grateful for suggestions as to anything that can be said further along these lines. Dressel Harries.

Apparent Omission.
T telegram (WP, DLC).

From Edward Thomas Williams

Dear Mr. President: Paris, April 23, 1919.

In compliance with your request of last evening[1] I send you herewith copies of the agreements between Germany and China relating to the lease of Kiaochow and to railway and mining rights in Shantung.[2]

I beg to call attention to the provision in Section II Article 4, of the first document, for thirty li (10 miles) zone along the railways, which as you will note from section 3, Article I of the fourth document, has been cancelled in exchange for certain definite mining areas.

All these documents will be found also in the pamphlet[3] which you held in your hands last evening; pages 25-39 inclusive.

I shall reply very soon to the question which you put to me last evening. In accordance with your suggestion I shall try to confer with Mr. Macleay[4] of the British Delegation and Mr. Gout[5] of the French Foreign Office.

I am, my dear Mr. President,

Your obedient servant, E. T. Williams

TLS (WP, DLC).

[1] See the extract from the Diary of E. T. Williams printed at April 22, 1919, Vol. 57.

[2] *CONVENTION BETWEEN CHINA AND GERMANY RESPECTING THE LEASE OF KIAOCHOW TO GERMANY*, March 6, 1898; *AGREEMENT BETWEEN CHINA AND GERMANY RESPECTING THE KIAOCHOW-CHINAN RAILWAY REGULATIONS*, March 21, 1900; *CONVENTION BETWEEN CHINA AND GERMANY RESPECTING THE WITHDRAWAL OF GERMAN TROOPS FROM KIAOCHOW AND KAOMI*, November 28, 1905; and *AGREEMENT BETWEEN THE PROVINCIAL AUTHORITIES OF SHANTUNG AND THE CHINO-GERMAN MINING COMPANY FOR DELIMITING MINING AREAS OF THE COMPANY IN THE PROVINCE OF SHANTUNG*, Sept. 24, 1911; all mimeograph and CC documents (WP, DLC).

[3] *THE CLAIM of China*, about which see V. K. Wellington Koo to WW, April 17, 1919, n. 1, Vol. 57.

[4] James William Ronald Macleay, member of the British diplomatic service and a technical expert in the British delegation on political and diplomatic questions relating to the Far East.

[5] That is, Jean Étienne Paul Gout.

From Norman Hezekiah Davis

My dear Mr. President: Paris, 23rd, April, 1919.

The Secretary of the Treasury has cabled me that he desires to formulate in writing a definite agreement with the French and Italian Governments, similar to that already concluded with the British Government, to cover commitments made by them in the United States with his knowledge and approval. In obedience to your suggestion that, pending developments, the establishment of additional credits for Italy be withheld, I have cabled the Secretary that I shall advise him when your approval is given, but that in the meantime he should postpone making any further commitments to Italy until he hears from us.

As regards the French Government, however, the Secretary desires your approval for the establishment of credits up to $100,000,000 in addition to amounts previously authorized by you. His tentative estimate of France's needs exceeds by about $25,000,000 the amount of credits for France already approved by you. He therefore deems it advisable to establish an additional credit of $100,000,000 for France, for which he would like to have your consent, and I am enclosing a formal letter to this effect for your signature in case this request meets with your approval.

I judge from the cables received from the Secretary that he desires to obtain your approval now for the establishment of these credits in order to be in a position to establish the credits only when necessary to cover commitments made in the United States with his knowledge and approval.

I am, my dear Mr. President,

Cordially and respectfully yours, Norman H. Davis

TLS (WP, DLC).

To Carter Glass

Dear Mr. Secretary: [Paris] April 23rd, 1919.

Mr. Norman H. Davis has transmitted your request for my approval of the establishment of further credits in favor of the French Government, up to $100,000,000, beyond amounts previously authorized by me, and I have pleasure in advising you of my approval of the establishment of this additional credit.

Cordially yours, [Woodrow Wilson]

CCL (WP, DLC).

From the Diary of Colonel House

April 23, 1919.

The Italian situation is almost the sole topic of conversation. This morning I suggested to the President that he put out his statement, but *I advised him to confer with Clemenceau and Lloyd George before doing so.* I told him that Orlando had a statement ready and I thought it well for him to anticipate him. He agreed to this, and said he would take it up with the two Prime Ministers at this morning's meeting. . . .

Mrs. Wilson has just called over the telephone to give some messages from the President. He was too tired to come to the telephone himself, but she went back and forth from his room to the study, where our private telephone is, to carry on the conversation. He wished to know how his statement, which he gave out this afternoon, had been taken. He said Balfour was also writing a statement which the British would give out tomorrow, and which maintained our position regarding Fiume. They confine themselves to Fiume because the Pact of London made it inadvisable for them to mention Dalmatia.

T MS (E. M. House Papers, CtY).

From Samuel Gompers

Sir: Washington, D. C. April 23, 1919.

I am in receipt of a number of communications from many parts of the country, all in bitter complaint and in protest against the conduct of Postmaster General Burleson toward the employes in the Postal Telegraph and Telephone Departments. His austere and autocratic course toward the employes of the Department has caused resentment through the entire country and the sympathetic expressions of the citizenship generally with the employes' position, have been manifested in many ways. The men and women in the organized labor movement stand entirely with the protest of the employes.

It may be interesting to say that a large number of the employes in the various branches of the Department are organized in voluntary associations of workers and they have often but vainly pleaded with Postmaster General Burleson for an opportunity to be heard through their representatives in presenting grievances or just causes of complaint, and to lay before him for consideration as the head of the Department the request for consideration of their condition.

I have had several conferences with the Postmaster General. I have endeavored to prevail upon him to afford the opportunity for the employes of the Department to be heard through their representatives and spokesmen, but in vain.

Perhaps a statement as accurately as my memory affords may be interesting, as occurring between Mr. Burleson and the undersigned. In suggesting to Mr. Burleson both the wisdom and the practicability for the good of the service, in the interest of the government and the interest of the employes of the Department, that the representative of the workers should be given the opportunity of appearing before him at some stated period for the purpose of presenting the subjects [subject] matter referred to above to his consideration, his attention was called to the course pursued by the Secretaries of the various Departments, the declarations of the War Labor Board approved by you, etc., etc.

Mr. Burleson declaimed as to his high-mindedness, his generosity and his sympathy with the employes, and said that if any one of them had anything to present to him they could come to him and present it in person. Of course everyone knows that such a course would be unsatisfactory from all points of view; that further, if any would have the temerity to go to the Postmaster General to present any particular grievance, many of them would not be the grievances of the employes as such.

Closing an hour's conference with Mr. Burleson in his office, I felt constrained to say to him somewhat as follows: "General, it seems to me that you do not fully understand the cause for which our government entered this war. We went into the war, among other things, for the destruction of militarism, autocracy and dictatorship, and though you may be kindly disposed, the American people are as much opposed to an industrial despot as they are opposed to a political despot; they are opposed even to a benevolent despot." The interview closed rather abruptly even if courteously, by my leaving Mr. Burleson's office.

Your aid has been sought by the Governors of the New England States in regard to the strike of the telephone operators in New England and with justification you have cabled your reply stating that you are at too great a distance to intelligently understand the situation, and be of any practical assistance in its adjustment.[1] But the situation, condition and feeling have not been materially changed. All through the country the same feeling of unrest among the employes and their sympathizers is manifest, and the immediate future is not at all reassuring from the present outlook. Let me add that this feeling and manifestation is not confined to the rank and file alone, but also to their immediate superior officers.

Among the communications I have received is one from the manager of the Postal Telegraph Company of Detroit, Michigan, Mr. Minnis,[2] in which he says in substance that the employes are so completely disgusted with the administration of the Postmaster General and with the treatment they have had under that administration that, in his opinion, both organized and unorganized men from messengers up to superintendents will all walk out in the event that a strike is called. He says that this is his opinion though he is not an organization man. A strike vote is now being taken. Viewing the whole situation, it is the opinion of this superintendent that in the event of a strike "they (the companies) won't be able to turn a wheel." He further says "The newspapers will be paralyzed and as people are so disgusted with the Burleson administration, what injury will it do to the Democratic Party when all the newspapers in the country get after the administration." * * * "Mr. Burleson has done more injury to the party than any ten thousand men in or out of Washington. He has undone all the good work that Mr. McAdoo has done for the party."

Mr. Minnis points out that the Commercial Telegraphers' Union of America has two and one half million pamphlets ready for distribution throughout the country when the strike vote is recorded. These pamphlets he says will give an account of the treatment accorded telegraph employes by Mr. Burleson's administration.

Of course I am fully aware of the fact that you will not view this matter from the standpoint of the Democratic Party, nor do I view it from that standpoint. The case is one that no one can consider except as from the viewpoint of the good of the nation. I cite the letter merely as showing the state of mind that is far more general than I would care to believe did I not have such a volume of correspondence before me.

This morning the "Washington Post" (April 23, 1919) contains a dispatch from New York, which I quote:

HALT PRESS MESSAGES

New York Wire Chiefs Refuse Telegrams Offered

[1] For both of these telegrams, see WW to JPT, April 17, 1919 (first telegram of that date), and n. 2 thereto, Vol. 57.

[2] He cannot be further identified.

"APPEARED TO BE IMPROPER"

Queries on Article Purporting to tell about Postmaster General and Addressed to Various Newspapers Rejected by Both Postal and Western Union.

(Special to the Washington Post.)

New York, April 22.—The New York World tomorrow will publish the following:

In the issue of the World of Monday last there was printed a fairly complete and comprehensive analysis of the conduct of the Postoffice Department by the Postmaster General, the Hon. Albert Sidney Burleson.

In accordance with the terms of existing contracts, the World offered to transmit by telegraph the article dealing with the administration of the Postoffice Department under Mr. Burleson to their contract newspapers throughout the country, which included the Cincinnati Enquirer; Star, Indianapolis; the Times, Toledo Ohio; the Commercial Appeal, Memphis, and several others.

SCHEDULE SENT TO NEWSPAPERS.

A schedule paraphrasing the headlines that the World used over the article and giving a brief outline of the character and scope of it was prepared by the night manager of the World News Bureau and addressed to the newspapers named.

The schedule read as follows:

"3. Washington—Seibold.[3] Burleson pictured as snoop, trouble maker, disorganizer, autocrat and arch-politician. Postoffice employes call their chief slave driver, convict laborers having been whipped on his farm; misgovernment of mail system alleged; he is credited with having put national prohibition through; 5,000 (words)."

SUBMITTED TO THEIR CHIEFS.

The representatives of the two telegraph companies in the World Office submitted the Burleson schedule to their respective chiefs, Night Manager Coney,[4] of the Postal, and Leipmann[5] of the Western Union.

Those officials said tonight that they had passed on the matter and decided against sending it over the wires operated by their companies. The reason advanced by them was the same—that the article described by the schedule "appeared to be improper."

Under authority of Congress and through executive designa-

[3] That is. Louis Seibold.

[4] Edward A. Coney, night manager of the Postal Telegraph-Cable Co. of New York.

[5] He cannot be further identified.

tion by the President the telegraph and cable systems of the country are under the control of the Postmaster General.

SUSPENDS "POSTAL" PAPER

(By the Associated Press)

New York, April 22. Distribution of "Postal Telegraph" the house organ of the Postal Telegraph Cable Company, to employes of the company through "regular channels" has been ordered suspended by Postmaster General Burleson, according to a statement issued tonight by William J. Deegan,[6] secretary of the Mackay companies.

Mr. Deegan added that distribution to the public of literature "which in any way reflects on Burleson's control" also had been ordered suspended and that any employe who expressed any opinion against the present control "must give a promise to keep his mouth shut or face instant dismissal."

SPY SYSTEM ALLEGED.

In addition to orders against distribution of any literature attacking the Postoffice Department regime, Mr. Deegan declared that "a system of post office espionage has been instituted on our lines which would do credit to the Russian secret service."

"Employes," he declared, "Are being lectured by Burleson's representatives that they must not criticize any act of Burleson or in any way express their opinion of Burleson's control. Any one expressing such opinions is reported to the Postoffice Department by Burleson's spies. By means of these threats an organized reign of terror has been instituted on the lines of the Postal Telegraph system, and every effort is being made to shake the confidence of the staff in their belief that the company will eventually have its lines returned."

Crowded as you are with many duties before you, and being so far distant from the United States, it is impossible for you to know the feeling which has been engendered by the course pursued by Postmaster General Burleson. It is twelve days now since I returned to the United States, and I beg to assure you that though I had been keep [kept] fairly well informed of the situation in the Postoffice Department while I was in Paris, I feel constrained to say that I was much surprised at the intensity of the feeling which has been aroused by the course pursued by Mr. Burleson, and there is no telling what may arise both on account of his course towards the employes coming under his department, and by the course he has pursued in regard to the subject matter with which the above clipping deals.

[6] William Joseph Deegan, secretary of the Messenger Commercial Cable Co.

It seems to me a duty I could not escape to present this entire matter to you so that at least on your return voyage to the United States you may give this matter your consideration, and such action as you may deem proper to pursue in the premises on your return.

With every earnest hope for your entire success, and wishing you a safe return to our beloved country, I have the honor to remain,

Yours very respectfully, Saml. Gompers.

TLS (WP, DLC).

From the Diary of Dr. Grayson

Thursday, April 24, 1919.

The President got up early, had breakfast at 8:15, and immediately went to his study, where he worked until 11:00 o'clock. At that hour the Big Three resumed their conference. The Italian situation had developed materially overnight. Orlando and Sonnino had held a number of conferences which had lasted until five o'clock in the morning, and before the Big Three met Orlando sent a request to Lloyd-George to visit him at their hotel, which Lloyd-George did. Orlando requested the British Premier to arrange for another conference on the Adriatic-Fiume situation, which Lloyd-George promised he would do. The Big Three session resolved itself into a further discussion of the Fiume situation and the applicability of the Pact of London to present Italian demands. Lloyd-George told the President that Orlando wanted a meeting in the afternoon and that he (Orlando) would appreciate it very much if, in order to "save his face" the meeting was held at the home of Lloyd-George. Naturally the President had no objection whatever to going there for a meeting of this character, and it was arranged that this should be done. The question of the effect of the Italians leaving was discussed by the Big Three, and it was the consensus of opinion that it could have no real effect on the outcome of the negotiations with Germany. As a matter of fact, it developed later that the French attitude was that Italy in insisting on having Fiume ceded to her had of her own volition violated the Pact of London, thereby making impossible any insistence by Italy that Great Britain and France refrain from signing a separate peace. This was officially given out as the French attitude and did a great deal to depress the Italians who had believed that the President was acting entirely on his own initiative in issuing his now famous statement of principle.

Just before lunch Orlando sent his secretary[1] to see the President.

[1] Count Luigi Aldrovandi Marescotti.

When he arrived the President was in conference with Clemenceau and Lloyd-George. As Orlando's secretary was leaving the President's study, Lieutenant *Mantou* (?),[2] the French officer who was selected by Clemenceau on his own initiative to act as the personal interpreter of the Conference, and who is a member of the French General Staff, joined him in the hall and said to Orlando's secretary that Mr. Clemenceau did everything he could to prevent the President's statement from being published and that he (Clemenceau) regretted its publication exceedingly; that he had heard Clemenceau say this; he also said that Clemenceau thought it was a great mistake and that he would do everything in his power to correct it. As a matter of fact, this was a direct lie and simply illustrated the manner in which the lesser French officials have attempted to reflect their own views and to interpret the opinions of their chiefs without knowing what their chiefs actually believed. This is not the first time this same individual has tried to do the same thing.

Dr. J[ohn]. Chalmers DaCosta, the noted Philadelphia Surgeon, who is serving as a Lieutenant Commander in the Navy during the emergency, called today to pay his respects. He had arrived on the GEORGE WASHINGTON and was chagrined over the publication prior to his departure of a story that intimated that he had been hurriedly summoned to France in connection with the President's health. He told me that he knew nothing whatever about the story but that he had come here in accordance with routine orders. He told me that he hoped that I would see that I wrote everything regarding the personal side of the President's visit to Europe and the developments from day to day. "Write, write, write," he said to me; "everything that takes place here should be chronicled—and you are the only person in a position to chronicle the facts for the generations to come." Doctor DaCosta then related a story of a Philadelphia Republican, who had gone to hear the President when the latter was campaigning as a candidate for Governor of New Jersey. The man had listened to the speech for about five minutes when he suddenly seized his hat and started out of the hall. A friend stopped him and said: "What's the matter? Where are you going? This is a good speech. You ought to hear it." To which the Republican replied: "Yes, I know it is a good speech, but if I stay here that man will convert me and make a Democrat out of me." Doctor DaCosta said that while he had never met the President, he had followed his writings and he was convinced that the President was the greatest author, as well as the greatest statesman that the United States ever has produced.

The President, Mrs. Wilson and I had lunch at one o'clock, and

[2] That is, Paul Mantoux.

after lunch the President and I had a long talk. He showed me some of the maps which he keeps in his study and called my attention to the various points under discussion. He went into the subject of the Pact of London in detail and explained just what promises it carried in Italy's behalf. He also told me what would happen should the Pact of London be rigidly adhered to, especially in view of the conflicting claims and the necessity for Italy surrendering certain privileges which were granted her at a time when the solidarity of Austria-Hungary seemed certain. The President told me that so far as he was concerned there would be no compromise on a question of principle which was so sharply defined as the present one, and he made it very plain that he would let Lloyd-George and Clemenceau both understand before the afternoon session was concluded that they must decide whether they would break with Italy or break with the United States should Italy refuse to accept the principles of self-determination in the settlement of the Adriatic problem. He recalled that Lloyd-George and Clemenceau, as well as Orlando, had agreed when the armistice was signed that the principles underlying the fourteen points would be the principles that would be their guide in arriving at final determinations, and the President was simply insisting that they make good the promises which America had accepted whole-heartedly.

It was very clear from the information which had reached the President that Clemenceau and Lloyd-George had been taking one position while they were with the President and assuming another when they debated the Adriatic question with the Italians. It was also very clear that Colonel House had been telling the Italians that in the last analysis they would find that the President would compromise, and that he (House) would be able to persuade him to do so. As a matter of fact, what House had apparently been trying to accomplish was to have Orlando defeat the Italian claims and have the President pocket his principles and permit him (House) to arrive at a settlement based entirely on his ideas of what a compromise should be regardless of how it fitted in with the announced principles upon which the President had taken such a determined stand. It was rather singular that Colonel House, when the President read his statement to him, had approved it completely and whole-heartedly, and yet within a very few moments after the President left he was endeavoring to bring about a compromise that would entitle him to further consideration as the King of Compromisers.[3]

The afternoon session was held at Lloyd-George's house and until

[3] For a careful review of the evidence of the extent to which Clemenceau, Lloyd George, and House were willing to compromise on the Adriatic question at this time, see René Albrecht-Carrié, *Italy at the Paris Peace Conference* (New York, 1938), pp. 131-40.

6:30 in the evening the President, Clemenceau, Lloyd-George, Orlando and Sonnino debated the merits of Italy's claims. Orlando insisted that he could not himself settle the problem and said that it would be necessary for him to go back to Italy at eight o'clock in order that he might make a complete explanation to the Italian people and to the Italian Parliament. The meeting finally adjourned without any decision having been reached, and an official communique, which was issued, simply stated that the Italian question had been debated without a definite conclusion having been reached and that Orlando would proceed to Rome in the hope that the Italian Parliament would be able to assist in bringing about an amicable agreement. Orlando went to the Italian headquarters from the meeting at the Lloyd-George house and went on to Rome at 8:30 in the evening. Before leaving he said that he hoped to come back but that he would have to find out exactly how the Italian people felt before he could decide what his future course of action would be. The President's statement on Fiume and the Adriatic had not been printed in Italy before Orlando left, but he promised that he would see that it was printed in full together with his own rejoinder as soon as possible.

Tired out by the events of the day and unable to secure much-needed exercise, the President retired reasonably soon after dinner.

I dined at the Ritz with Mr. Henry Morgenthau, who had just come back from Turkey. Most of the guests were Red Cross officials.

While the meeting was in progress during the afternoon I took advantage of the opportunity to get a little fresh air for a couple of hours by visiting the thoroughbred training farm of W. K. Vanderbilt,[4] at Poissy, just outside of Paris. The Vanderbilt trainer, Mr. William Duke, received us and said that Mr. Vanderbilt regretted that he could not be there; that he had an engagement which was previously made, and was unable to be there; he requested us, however, Mr. Duke said, to come sometime when he could be there. Mr. Duke showed me his horses and his training tracks, which are very fine in every way.

After having inspected the stables we were invited by Mr. Duke to go to the house for tea. He said: "We have tea here for every one but there is a liberal supply of champagne in the house for any one who does not want tea. Whereupon Colonel Percy L. Jones[5] scratched his head and said: "To be perfectly frank with you, I am not a tea-drinking man." It developed that there were others in the party who were not tea-drinking men.

[4] William Kissam Vanderbilt (1849-1920), now largely retired from the family railroad enterprises, a noted Francophile, collector of fine art, and owner of racehorses.

[5] Commander of the United States Ambulance Service which served with the French armies during the war.

A Memorandum by Tasker Howard Bliss

April 24, 1919.

MEMORANDUM for the President.
FROM General Bliss.

One of General Pershing's Staff Officers gave General Bliss the information that Marshal Foch had called a meeting of the Commanders-in-Chief of the Allied Armies in France to be held today, for the purpose of considering the condition of the Armies for a general advance or for what might be called an offensive action. General Bliss thought the President ought to have this information.

T MS (WP, DLC).

Hankey's and Mantoux's Notes of a Meeting of the Council of Four[1]

President Wilson's House,
I.C.-176B. Paris, April 24, 1919, 11 a.m.

1. MR. LLOYD GEORGE reported a conversation that he had had with M. Orlando that morning, in which he had pointed out the whole of the difficulties in which M. Orlando was placed. M. Orlando had said that he was contemplating a reply to President Wilson's manifesto. Publication of President Wilson's manifesto had been held up [in Italy] and it would only be published together with M. Orlando's reply. This reply M. Orlando had promised would be couched in moderate language and would not close the door to further negotiations. MR. LLOYD GEORGE had especially pressed that it should not commit the Italians in regard to Fiume. M. Orlando had agreed on this point. M. Orlando had said that he was willing to leave Baron Sonnino in Paris. MR. LLOYD GEORGE's impression, however, was that M. Orlando would like to stay. He had intimated that it would help him if a communique could be issued in the Press to the effect that at the request of M. Clemenceau and Mr. Lloyd George, as representing the countries signatory to the Treaty of London, he had agreed to defer his departure.

PRESIDENT WILSON pointed out that this would place him in an invidious position. The issue was fundamental to him as to whether the United States could take part in any part of the Treaty of London referring to districts south of Istria. The impression had already been conveyed in the Press that the Signatories of the Treaty of London were divided from the United States of America. It had not been

[1] The complete text of Hankey's minutes is printed in *PPC*, V, 202-209.

possible for him to let the Italian people get their version of what had occurred from a poisoned Press; consequently, he had been bound to issue his manifesto. It was a friendly message to set out the case to the Italian people. If only some time were gained, he thought that the Italian people would realise their position and that the present ferment would settle down. Hence, he would be glad if M. Orlando could remain in Paris at least a week.

MR. LLOYD GEORGE asked M. Clemenceau whether he were satisfied with Mr. Balfour's draft letter to M. Orlando.

M. CLEMENCEAU said that with a few verbal alterations he was satisfied. He said he would bring these in the afternoon.

PRESIDENT WILSON said he had not seen the latest version of the draft.

MR. LLOYD GEORGE promised him a copy.

After some further discussion, the following conclusions were reached:

1. Mr. Lloyd George should ask M. Orlando if he would issue the following communique:

   At the request of President Wilson, Monsieur Clemenceau and Mr. Lloyd George, Signor Orlando has agreed to defer his departure to Italy with a view to seeing whether it is not still possible to accommodate the difficulties which have arisen about Fiume and the Dalmatian coast.

2. Mr. Lloyd George and M. Clemenceau should arrange for the final draft of the letter to M. Orlando and sign it jointly.
3. Mr. Lloyd George should send President Wilson a copy of the proposed letter to M. Orlando.

Mr. Philip Kerr was sent by Mr. Lloyd George with the draft communique to M. Orlando but the latter did not consider publication desirable. At the very end of the meeting, at the moment of adjournment, Count Aldrovandi arrived with a message from M. Orlando to the effect that he and his colleagues had come to the conclusion that the best plan would be for them to meet the Supreme Council that afternoon at President Wilson's house.

This was agreed to.

§ Mantoux's notes:

Lloyd George. This morning I saw M. Orlando again. I would like to prevent him from doing anything which could really separate our countries. If he goes to Rome, he will be met there by a surge of public opinion, and he will not be able to make any concession, especially concerning Fiume. I told him that. I warned him that we would not consent to cede Fiume to Italy and that, if Italy kept Fiume, that would put an end to the Treaty of London. That made a great impression on him. He has prepared a sort of manifesto in response to President Wilson's open letter. I said to him: "If you speak about Fiume in that declaration, that will close the door to negotiations." He promised me to modify the text in such a way as to avoid this danger.

I insisted before M. Orlando that he should not leave. He told me that if he left, he would leave Baron Sonnino here. I answered him that his very presence in Italy would be enough to provoke a disturbance extremely dangerous for the success of our pourparlers.

Do you see any problem if we make a statement to the press saying that the discussions are continuing and that we are seeking a way to give the question a satisfactory solution?

Wilson. It is a question whether I can lend myself to a compromise. I will ask you to observe that nothing in my manifesto separates me from you.

Lloyd George. You criticize the Treaty of London rather sharply, and you say that it should never have been signed.

Clemenceau. I have nothing much to say against that.

Wilson. My argument is that the circumstances which justified the treaty have since then completely changed.

Clemenceau. Unfortunately, it is impossible for me to look at it from that point of view.

Lloyd George. That would mean that Italy has succeeded so well that she must not come near the prize of her victory.

Wilson. That is not what I meant. But I showed that the annexation of Dalmatia no longer makes sense after the fall of Austria, which can no longer menace Italy.

Lloyd George. It is impossible for us to discuss the Treaty of London, which we signed. But I will willingly put all dignity aside if I can arrive at an acceptable arrangement. Think about what the Germans can make out of the departure of the Italians when they arrive here in a few days.

Clemenceau. I do not attach a very great importance to that.

Lloyd George. I am not of your opinion.

Wilson. All that I wanted was to inform the Italian people of my true attitude in view of all that has been said by a venal press. But I surely believe that it is desirable to give the representatives of Italy time to reflect. I truly hope that M. Orlando can stay here at least a week and that some arrangement would thereby become possible.

Lloyd George. I will ask you to treat him with respect and circumspection. We have nothing to lose by giving him the opportunity to think again about the risks of the situation and the means by which to disentangle himself from it.

Wilson. Yes, but he must understand your position and mine.

Lloyd George. I left him in no doubt about our attitude concerning Fiume.

Clemenceau. In this case, I would do best not to respond to the letter addressed to me by M. Orlando;[2] that would only make things worse.

Lloyd George. You can write him a personal letter; but you must try at the same time to treat him with discretion and to make some accommodation possible. Unfortunately I fear that the harm already done prevents peace from being concluded.

Clemenceau. I expect the Germans to refuse. But it is a difficulty which will not last longer than a few weeks.

Lloyd George. I am not sure of that. I would fear this refusal very much.

Wilson. If we omit from the treaty secondary details which, while without real importance for us, are of a kind to alarm the Germans, that will render the signing easier.

Lloyd George. I propose anew to send a communiqué to the press indicating that we made an effort to persuade M. Orlando not to leave before a new conversation.

Clemenceau. I see no objection to that.

Wilson. As for myself, I was going to write to him to beg him to stay.

Lloyd George. For his part, he has consented to publish his declaration in a form which will not close the door to an acceptable solution.

I was categorical on the question of Fiume.

Mr. Lloyd George's proposal is adopted.* §

2. M. CLEMENCEAU said that since the discussion of the previous day the Germans had announced officially that seven journalists would accompany their Delegation. He asked what attitude he was to take.

PRESIDENT WILSON pointed out that although he did not much care to have the journalists present, nevertheless, they would be confined by the same restrictions as the Plenipotentiaries.

M. CLEMENCEAU said that he could not have them free to move about in Paris.

MR. LLOYD GEORGE thought that, so long as they were restricted in

* After the session, the communiqué to the press was postponed at M. Orlando's request.

[2] From a report from Paris, datelined April 23, 1919, in the *New York Times*, April 24, 1919: "Premier Orlando this evening addressed an official communication to Premier Clemenceau as President of the Peace Conference, saying that as a result of the declaration by President Wilson the Italian delegation had decided to leave Paris at 2 o'clock tomorrow afternoon."

the same manner as the Plenipotentiaries, the German papers were entitled to receive such information as they could obtain from them.

It was agreed that:

Journalists should be allowed to accompany the German Delegation but should be confined by the same restrictions as the Delegation itself.

3. MR. LLOYD GEORGE again reverted to the question of publicity on which he said he felt very strongly, so strongly, indeed, that he would almost have to make a protest. Since the previous discussion, he had seen Captain Gibson, an Officer just returned from Berlin, who had expressed the view that if the terms were published it might be impossible for the Germans to sign, as publication would strengthen the hand of the extremists. He himself felt that it would make it difficult, if not impossible, for the Allied and Associated Powers to give way on points that really were not of very great importance. There was a long discussion on this subject, which followed much the same lines of the discussion on the previous day, and it is only very briefly summarised below.

M. CLEMENCEAU's point of view was that publication was quite unavoidable. If the Allied and Associated Powers did not publish the Germans would. He had had to grant them free telegraphic and telephonic facilities; the German Delegation would be accompanied by 40 telegraphists; and it was certain that within three days the whole Peace Treaty would be published by the enemy. The Allied peoples ought not to learn the contents of the Peace Treaty first from enemy sources. Public opinion would, in a few days, compel publication of the Peace Treaty. In any case there would be leakages.

MR. LLOYD GEORGE's view was that leakages were not of very material consequence. In Great Britain the public did not attach much importance to leakages. Once everything was announced officially they knew it to be true and it would be extremely difficult to recede from any position taken up.

PRESIDENT WILSON's point of view was that although publication was undesirable it was, he believed, also unavoidable. He quoted some information that he had received from an Officer in the United States 3rd Army, who had had a talk with Brockdorff-Rantzau.[3] The latter expressed surprise at receiving an invitation to Versailles and assumed that it meant that Germany would be asked to sign practically an imposed Peace. He had considered the terms, as published, to amount to slavery for Germany and had referred particularly to the Saar Valley and Silesia. He said that he should never consent to a Peace giving up these districts, even temporarily, and that the Ger-

[3] See the Enclosure printed with RL to WW, April 23, 1919.

man Ministry could not agree to such terms. He had believed that the German people would support them in not signing such terms. When asked as to how Germany could continue to exist without outside relief, in the event of her not signing, he had given no reply, though he had thrown out the suggestion that they might turn towards Russia. The American Officer had gathered that there would be no strong protest against the provisions as regards Alsace-Lorraine and Indemnity, although some difficulty would be made over Danzig. The serious points of the Treaty, however, would be the Saar Valley and Silesia. Brockdorff-Rantzau had appeared very depressed. The same informant had stated that the idea of a plebiscite was being discussed a good deal in Germany and might be carried out. The independent socialists would accept it. PRESIDENT WILSON interpreted this telegram to mean that Brockdorff-Rantzau typified the extreme point of view. In the background he believed there was a more submissive body of opinion. His informant had suggested that the German people ought to know that a certain amount of discussion would be permitted. He himself was inclined to agree in the proposal that the discussion should take place in writing. As regards publicity, he inclined towards Mr. Balfour's view that a summary rather than the actual text should be published in the first instance. The preparation of the summary was a matter of the very first importance.

M. CLEMENCEAU said he would consult M. Tardieu in regard to this. He asked how long the summary should be.

MR. LLOYD GEORGE thought it should be as short as possible.

§ Mantoux's notes:

Wilson. The question is to know who will lead the German delegation, Brockdorff-Rantzau or Melchior.

Clemenceau. Then we limit ourselves to the publication of a summary.

Lloyd George. The summary will be enough to create the danger I dread. The certainty that Germany will have to lose Silesia and Danzig will be enough to provoke a serious resistance. I do not want to act in such a way as to make it impossible for any German government to sign the peace. Could we not try to find out what the German government itself thinks of that question of the publication of the treaty? If it itself said that this publication would make the conclusion of the peace impossible, we would be assuming a serious responsibility in deciding it.

Wilson. Cannot the difficulty be avoided by publishing a summary written in very general terms? For example, it could be said that the frontiers of Germany had been traced according to ethnographic lines, without any other specifics.

Clemenceau. We can try.

Wilson. Everything depends upon the nature of the summary. It can be written now; for if it is only a matter of a general declaration, we do not need to wait for the final drafting of all the articles.

Clemenceau. What will be the length of a document of this kind?

Lloyd George. As for myself, I do not see any disadvantage in publishing in full our agreement with France to guarantee her against the danger of an invasion. That publication will make a useful impression in Germany; it will show that we are sticking together.

Wilson. General Pershing tells me that Marshal Foch's orders prescribe preparations for a military advance.[4]

Lloyd George. It is only the result of our recommendations; we must make provision in case the Germans should refuse to sign.

Clemenceau. What will we do with M. Orlando? I think it is preferable not to send an answer to the letter which I received from him; but I will put my signature at the bottom of Mr. Balfour's letter.

Wilson. Will M. Orlando make new proposals?

Lloyd George. He must meet with his colleagues today, and they will inform us what they have decided. I believe that they will accept the suggestion to make Fiume a free city. When I spoke to him about it, he restricted himself to asking me what Fiume's diplomatic representation should be. He would have desired, naturally, that it were assumed by Italy. I believe that it is an easy problem to settle; the city of Fiume can have itself represented as it wishes. §

4. PRESIDENT WILSON read a report from the Ports and Waterways Commission, which had been asked to consider the question of the Kiel Canal. (Appendix I.)[5] The only controversial point was Article 7. in regard to which two versions had been submitted, one by the United States of America, British, Italian and Japanese Delegations, and one by the French.

M. CLEMENCEAU said he was particularly anxious that Admiral de Bon[6] should be heard on the subject of the fortifications of the Canal.

PRESIDENT WILSON said that his feeling on this matter was that if Germany had no fortifications, she might be unable to carry out her obligation to keep the canal open if she ever became involved in war with any power. The provision for no fortification was not consistent with the provision for keeping the Canal open.

(It was agreed that Admiral Hope,[7] Admiral Benson, and Admiral de Bon should be seen that afternoon.)

[4] He meant General Bliss. See the preceding document.
[5] There is a TC of this document in WP, DLC.
[6] That is, Vice Adm. Ferdinand Jean Jacques de Bon.
[7] That is, Rear Adm. George Price Webley Hope.

NOTE: This was subsequently cancelled, in consequence of the receipt of a communication from M. Orlando. (Minute 1.)[8]

5. MR. LLOYD GEORGE read a memorandum which had been presented to him by Mr. Headlam-Morley on the subject of the Saar Valley. (Appendix 2.)[9]

(After a short discussion, it was agreed that the United States, British, and French experts should be authorised to visit the Saar Valley, in order to advise on the question.)

6. SIR MAURICE HANKEY stated that the report of the Economic Commission had been circulated. He learned by telephone from Sir Hubert Llewellyn Smith that some of the principal delegates on the Commission, namely, M. Clementel, M. Crespi, Mr. Baruch, and himself, had met on the previous evening, and after a very long discussion, had agreed to four out of the five outstanding points.

(Sir Maurice Hankey was instructed to summon the Economic experts for 4.30 p.m. in the afternoon.

NOTE: This was subsequently cancelled, owing to the receipt of a communication from M. Orlando, (see Minute 1).

§ Mantoux's notes:

Lloyd George. I have in hand the report of Professor Haskins. According to the observations made by the French delegates, the northern limit of the Saar region, such as it has previously been provided for, does not coincide with the natural limit of this district, which is rather well marked by hills and by a narrowing of the river. The difference between the two lines represents thirty-two square kilometers and 4,000 inhabitants who are, moreover, attached to the Saar region by their occupations. The American representative wishes that this question be submitted to our judgment, and the experts propose first of all to go to the site next Sunday.

The British delegate agrees with Mr. Haskins, and he is of opinion to accept the French proposal.

Wilson. The experts agree; but they prefer to go first to the site; I believe they must be encouraged to do so.

Concerning the Saar, there is a question which always troubles me. The production of this basin is only seventeen million tons; the production of which France was deprived in the Nord was twenty-one million tons. Now the coal from the Saar is consumed in the neighboring region; consequently, it is not in that way that the losses suffered by France in another region can be repaired.

M. Loucheur insists strongly that Germany be obligated to sell the quantity of coal necessary for French industries at the current price.

[8] It is missing.

[9] There is a TC of this memorandum, signed by Haskins and Headlam-Morley, enclosed in C. H. Haskins to WW, April 24, 1919, TLS (WP, DLC).

The difficulty is this: we have already taken from Germany several of her coal basins; we must avoid placing her industries in a situation which would not permit her to recover and to pay us what is due us.

Clemenceau. It is a question of figures.

Wilson. M. Loucheur must be heard on this subject, and at the same time our experts must be summoned.

Lloyd George. I would also like you to hear Mr. Gibson who is returning from Berlin.

Count Aldrovandi, introduced, makes it known that the Italian ministers will return to a meeting in the afternoon to study anew the question of the Adriatic. §

APPENDIX I

DRAFT ARTICLES CONCERNING THE KIEL CANAL FOR INSERTION IN THE PRELIMINARY TREATY OF PEACE WITH GERMANY.

ARTICLE I.

The Kiel Canal and its approaches shall be maintained free and open to the vessels of commerce and of war of all nations at peace with Germany on terms of entire equality.

ARTICLE II.

The nationals, property and vessels of all States shall, in respect of charges, facilities, and in all other respects, be treated on a footing of perfect equality in the use of the Canal, no distinction being made to the detriment of nationals, property and vessels of any State, between the latter and the nationals, property and vessels of Germany or of the most favored nation.

No impediment shall be placed on the movement of persons or vessels other than those arising out of the police customs, sanitary, emigration or immigration regulations, and those relating to the import or export of prohibited goods.

Such regulations must be reasonable and uniform, and must not unnecessarily impede traffic.

ARTICLE III.

Only such charges may be levied on vessels using the canal or its approaches as are intended to cover in an equitable manner the cost of maintaining in a navigable condition, or of improving, the canal or its approaches, or to meet expenditures incurred in the interests of navigation. The schedule of such charges shall be calculated on the basis of such expenses and shall be posted up in the ports. These charges shall be levied in such a manner as to render any detailed examination of cargoes unnecessary, except in the case of suspected fraud or contravention.

ARTICLE IV.

Goods in transit may be placed under seal or in the custody of customs agents; the loading and unloading of goods, and the embarkation and disembarkation of passengers, shall only take place in the ports specified by Germany.

ARTICLE V.

No charges of any kind other than those provided for in the present regulations shall be levied along the course or at the approaches of the Kiel Canal.

ARTICLE VI.

Germany shall be bound to take suitable measures to remove any obstacle or danger to navigation and to ensure the maintenance of good conditions of navigation. Germany shall not undertake any works of a nature to impede navigation on the canal or its approaches.

ARTICLE VII.

(English, American, Japanese and Italian Proposal)

In the event of violation of any of these conditions, or of disputes as to the interpretation of the present Convention, any interested State can appeal to the jurisdiction instituted for the purpose by the League of Nations and can demand the formation of an International Commission.

In order to avoid reference of small questions to the League of Nations, Germany will establish a local authority at Kiel qualified to deal with disputes in the first case and to give satisfaction so far as possible to complaints which may be presented through the Consular representatives of the Interested Powers.

(French Proposal)

The Kiel Canal and its approaches shall be under the control of an International Commission which shall include:

2 representatives of Germany.
1 representative of Great Britain.
1 representative of France.
1 representative of Poland.
1 representative of Denmark.

This International Commission shall meet within three months from the signature of the Preliminary Peace Treaty and shall proceed immediately to prepare a project for the revision of the existing regulations; this project shall be drawn up in conformity with the General Convention on International Navigable Waterways should such Convention have been previously concluded. In the absence of such Convention, the project for revision shall be in conformity with the provisions of the preceding Articles.

ARTICLE VIII. (French and Italian Proposal).

The following shall be demobilised or suppressed under the direction of the Allied and Associated Powers and within the period fixed by such powers:

All fortified works situated within fifty kilometres of either bank of the Canal or of the mouth of the Elbe, and of all means of obstruction the object or effect of which might be to interfere with the liberty and the entire security of navigation.

Germany shall be prohibited from erecting any new fortifications, from installing any battery within the zone specified above and from placing any obstruction in the approaches or in the canal.

APPENDIX II.

Memorandum by the American and British Representatives in the matter of the Saar Basin.

Our attention was yesterday called to new information which had reached our French colleague bearing on the proposed frontier of the Saar Basin. It appears that the proposed north-west frontier in the Valley of the Saar itself does not extend quite to the natural geographical and economic boundary which is formed by the narrows of the river and the hilly district extending to the north and west. In order to rectify this, it would be necessary to add a district comprising about 32 square kilometres (12 square miles) with a population of slightly over 5,000. The district has its natural centre in the adjoining towns of Mettlach and Keuchingen with a joint population of 2,500. The population of these towns is industrial and they are connected by daily workmans' trains with the Saar Basin; on the other side they are partially cut off from any easy connection with the German territory lying towards Trèves.

The American and British Representatives are agreed that it is beyond their power to accept proposals for an extension of the frontier which has been definitely accepted by the Council of Four; they consider it however their duty to call attention to this new information.

The members of the Committee are prepared to pay a visit to the spot on Sunday next. Meanwhile, an alternative description of the frontier has been prepared for insertion in the text of the Treaty if the proposed modification were approved either before or after an inspection on the spot. (Intd.) (C.H.H.
(J.W.H.M.

23.4.19.

T MS (SDR, RG 256, 180.03401/117, DNA); Mantoux, I, 347-49, 352-53, 353-54.

From Lu Cheng-hsiang, with Enclosure

My dear Mr. President: Paris, April 24, 1919.

With reference to the Kiaochow-Shantung question, I beg leave to enclose a brief memorandum giving a summary of the views of the Chinese Delegates and submitting on behalf of the Chinese Government certain propositions as a settlement of the question.

I am, my dear Mr. President,

Yours sincerely, Y. R Loutsengtsiang

TLS (WP, DLC).

E N C L O S U R E

Paris April 23, 1919

In regard to the Kiaochow-Shantung settlement, the Chinese Delegates have carefully considered the question which the Council of Four put to them at its meeting of April 22nd, namely, Which China would prefer—the treaty with Japan, or the transfer to Japan of the German rights? If they find neither alternative acceptable, it is only because they see difficulties in both. To hold China to the treaty and notes of 1915 would be to give countenance to serious encroachments on Chinese sovereignty committed without provocation and consummated only after the delivery of an ultimatum on China; while to substitute Japan for Germany in Shantung would be to create a graver situation because of Japan's propinquity to China, and because of her domination of Manchuria, which lies closely to the north of Shantung.

As regards the notes of 1918, they grew out of the treaty and notes of 1915. They were made by China out of a desire to relieve the tense situation in Shantung Province. The presence of the Japanese troops along the railway and the establishment of Japanese civil administration offices in the interior of Shantung evoked such opposition from the people thereof that the Chinese Government were obliged to take some step to induce Japan to withdraw her troops and remove her civil administration establishments, pending a settlement of the whole question by the Peace Conference.

The Chinese Delegates regret that there exist certain secret agreements between France and Japan, and between Great Britain and Japan, pledging to support Japan's claims to the German rights in Shantung. China was not consulted when they were made; nor was she informed of their contents when she was invited to join the War. But she, on her part, has been a loyal co-belligerent on the side of the Allies. Is it just that her rights and her future welfare should be thus sacrificed to the policy of aggrandizement of Japan?

The Chinese Delegates desire to point out that since the said agreements were made, France, Great Britain and Japan as well as China and other Allied and Associated Powers have all accepted, as the basis of the peace now being made, certain principles with which the said agreements appear to be in conflict. As it is an established principle that a subsequent act supersedes a previous one in case of their incompatibility, the agreements in question would appear to be no longer applicable to the claims of Japan.

The Chinese Delegates are in full accord with the desire of the Council to uphold, as a principle, the sanctity of accepted obligations, but they question themselves whether there is not a higher obligation resting on the Council now to remove serious obstacles to the maintenance of a durable peace in the Far East as elsewhere. The Council now has the solution of the Kiaochow-Shantung question in its hands: if it makes a settlement compatible with justice, it means peace in the Far East at least for half a century; and if it declines to make a just settlement merely because of the existence of certain obligations either imposed on China by threat of force or contracted by France and Great Britain in circumstances since entirely changed, it may be sowing seeds of a grave discord in the years soon to come.

Besides, China is now at the parting of the ways. She has come to the West to ask for justice. If she should fail to get it, her people would, perhaps, attribute the failure not so much to Japan's insistence on her own claims as to the attitude of the West, which declined to lend a helping hand to China merely because some of its leading Powers had privately pledged to support Japan.

Appreciative, however, of the sympathetic interest of the Council of Four in this question and desirous to aid it in every way possible in its earnest effort to find a solution at once compatible with China's welfare and conducive to peace in the Far East, the Chinese Delegates beg leave to submit the following four propositions as a settlement thereof:

I. Germany renounces to the five Allied and Associated Powers her holdings, rights and privileges in Shantung for restoration to China.

II. Japan, being in possession of the said holdings, rights and privileges, engages to effect the said restoration to China within one year after the signature of the treaty of peace with Germany.

III. China agrees to make a pecuniary compensation to Japan for the military expenses incurred in the capture of Tsingtao, the amount of the said compensation to be determined by the Council of Four.

IV. China agrees to open the whole of Kiaochow Bay as a commercial port, and to provide a special quarter, if desired, for the residence of the citizens and subjects of the treaty powers. Y.R.L.

TI MS (WP, DLC).

From Edward Thomas Williams, with Enclosure

Dear Mr. President: Paris, April 24, 1919.

Mr. Macleay of the British Delegation, M. Gout of the French Foreign Office and myself have agreed upon a reply to the question, which was referred to us last Tuesday evening, concerning the cession of German rights in the province of Shantung, China. A copy of the reply is enclosed.

I reserved the privilege, however, of making, with your permission, an additional statement setting forth the reasons which convince me that neither alternative should be adopted by the Conference.

1. The proposal to grant Japan the rights enjoyed by Germany before 1914, although less objectionable than the alternative is open to very serious objection. To claim that because Japan took Kiaochow from Germany she has any right to it is as though we were to claim from France St. Mihiel because we took it from Germany. Japan in Shantung is far more dangerous to China and to the peace of the Far East than Germany ever was. For four years and more this has been proved by the gross violation of Chinese rights by the connivance at smuggling and the promotion of vice. To give her a fortified naval base for 78 years at Tsingtao and *permanent* control of the railways and mines of Shantung is to make a thrust at the very heart of China.

2. The alternative would be still more injurious. The Conventions of 1915,[1] as it seems to me, ought not to be recognized at all in the settlement. Rather they ought to be declared not binding, for they are even more objectionable than the Treaty of Brest-Litovsk. The latter grew out of war: the former were extorted from a peaceful and defenceless people, without provocation and by the pressure of troops landed in China and an ultimatum issued. In one of these Conventions Japan promises to restore the leased territory of Kiaochow to China upon certain conditions, one of which was the establishment of an exclusive Japanese settlement at Tsingtau, so that instead of a lease yet to run 78 years she would obtain a concession that would be *permanent*. She does not offer to return the railway or the mines. Moreover she proposes to control the policing of the railway which Germany never attempted and she will station troops at

the capital of the province, a thing Germany never did. Her offer to return Kiaochow therefore is merely an offer of the shell. She would keep the kernel.

3. Is it not possible to find a third course? I beg to suggest a formula something like the following:

All treaties between China and Germany having been abrogated, Germany relinquishes (in favor of the Five Powers) all rights and privileges derived therefrom

But with respect to former German holdings and property in Shantung province, since they were taken in military operations by Great Britain and Japan before China declared war, and since they are now in possession of Japan, it is agreed that Japan shall transfer them to China within one year after the signature of the Treaty of Peace upon the following conditions;

1. That an *international settlement* shall be established at Tsingtau in which Chinese citizens shall enjoy the same political rights as those of foreign nations.
2. China agrees to reimburse Japan for her expenses in connection with the taking of Kiaochow.

If this should not be satisfactory to the Japanese, it might be intimated to them that the mines (which are their chief concern) could be made over to a Sino-Japanese company.

It is most important that Japan shall not be left in possession of the railway.

Such a settlement would seem to save Japan's face while preventing the making by her of any excessive demands upon China.

The terms of peace accepted by Germany were those laid down by you in your address to the Congress on January 8, 1918 and "the principles of settlement" set forth in your "subsequent addresses."

One of the latter was delivered at Mt. Vernon on July 4, 1918 and contained the following statement:

"The settlement of every question, whether of territory, of sovereignty, of economic arrangement, or of political relationship upon the basis of the free acceptance of that settlement by the people immediately concerned, and not upon the basis of the material interest or advantage of any other nation or people which may desire a different settlement for the sake of its own exterior influence or mastery."

Were not these terms of peace agreed to by all the powers?

The reservations made by certain powers did not apply to this principle.

The Provincial Assembly of Shantung, the Provincial Educational Association and the Provincial Chamber of Commerce have telegraphed you begging your good offices.[2] These we are pledged by treaty to give.

Nowhere have the people of a district spoken more plainly.

Faithfully yours, E. T. Williams

TLS (WP, DLC).

[1] About which, see the documents on Shantung and the notes thereto in Vol. 57.

[2] Provincial Assembly of Shantung, Shantung Chamber of Commerce and Agriculture, Shantung Educational Association, and Shantung Industrial Association to Ammission, Paris, April 3, 1919, T telegram (WP, DLC).

ENCLOSURE

We are directed to express an opinion as to whether it would be more advantageous for China if Japan were merely to inherit the rights possessed by Germany in Shantung and Kiaochow or if she were to accept the position created by the Sino-Japanese Treaties and Agreements of 1915 and 1918.

We find that either course presents serious disadvantages for China.

In the first case China would not recover her rights of sovereignty over Kiaochow Bay and the leased territory until the termination of the lease in 1997, i.e., for another 78 years.

Under the terms of the lease the Japanese would have the right to erect fortifications, to use the port as a naval base and to exercise rights of administration in the ceded territory. The rights in the railways, mines and presumably the other ex-German concessions in the Province of Shantung would persist after the termination of the lease of Kiaochow.

In the second case China would recover from Japan possession of the leased territory of Kiaochow, but not of the railway and mining rights in the Province of Shantung. It is presumed that the restoration of the leased territory to China would take place immediately after the ratification of the Treaty of Peace, provided that that Treaty gives Japan the free disposal of the German rights. The retrocession of the leased territory to China by Japan is, however, made dependent upon certain conditions and especially upon the establishment of an exclusive Japanese residential Concession in the town and port of Tsingtao. This Concession presumably would be permanent and if, as is understood to be the case, it is intended that this exclusive Japanese area shall include the greater part of the business portion of the town of Tsingtao, the docks, quays and the railway terminus, its effect, in our opinion, will be to diminish to a great extent the value of the immediate restoration to China of the leased territory. Moreover the Sino-Japanese Agreement of the 24th September, 1918, gives Japan the right to maintain a contingent of Japanese troops at Tsinanfu, which is in the centre of the Province of

Shantung and is a place of strategic importance as the junction of the Kiaochow-Tsinan and Tientsin-Pukow Railways. The Agreement further provides for the employment of Japanese at the headquarters of the Chinese police force charged with the policing of the Kiaochow-Tsinanfu railway. Japanese are also to be employed at the principal railway stations and at the police training school. We venture to call attention to the fact that these rights, which would appear to constitute an infringement of China's sovereignty and independence, were not enjoyed or exercised by Germany under the 1898 Convention or any subsequent Agreement with China.

In these circumstances we are of opinion that it would be more advantageous for China to accept the first alternative and to agree to Japan succeeding to the rights and the position which Germany possessed in Kiaochow and in the Province of Shantung in 1914 on the outbreak of the war, provided that Japan's rights, both in the leased territory and in the Province, are confined strictly to those secured to Germany by the Treaty of March 6th, 1898, and by the subsequent Sino-German Agreements in regard to mines and railways.

We desire to call special attention to the fact that these Sino-German Treaties and Agreements did not confer upon Germany the right to establish outside the leased territory any form of civil administration in the Province of Shantung, or to maintain troops in any district or town of the Province, or to employ German troops or police to guard the Kiaochow-Tsinanfu railway. It is further to be noted that, in accordance with the terms of the Agreement concluded between Germany and China on the 31st December, 1913, the two railways in the Province of Shantung, which Germany obtained the concession to build in place of the lines originally contemplated in the 1898 Convention, were to be constructed as Chinese Government railways, i.e., they would become the property of the Chinese State and not of the Concessionaires.

Signed: Jean Gout
E. T. Williams
Ronald Macleay.

T MS (WP, DLC).

Hankey's Notes of a Meeting of the Council of Four[1]

Mr. Lloyd George's Residence,
I.C.-176C. Paris, April 24, 1919, 4 p.m.

1. MR. LLOYD GEORGE asked M. Orlando to put his view.

M. ORLANDO said that he must declare that he had most carefully reviewed the situation, which was undoubtedly very serious. Already he had had two conversations with his colleagues at Rome and he must declare the situation to be a very painful one. There was one very difficult aspect of the situation which came before the territorial difficulty, namely, the effect produced by President Wilson's declaration. He must state at once that his esteem and admiration and personal friendship towards President Wilson, to which he had always given testimony, had not been in the least altered by the declaration. Before he heard what President Wilson had to say he wished to assure him that he realised his intentions towards M. Orlando, himself, and his country to be only that of a friend. In politics, however, the public impression of circumstances often had an importance surpassing their actual substance. Thus the impression of this document, which he himself declared had nothing in it that was not friendly and courteous, nevertheless was that of an appeal to the people of Italy and to the people generally. The consequence of this was that it put in doubt M. Orlando's own authority, as representative of the Italian people. That was the impression that he had received and, consequently, it was necessary for him to return to consult the source of his authority, that is to say, the Italian Parliament. The situation, therefore, was a very delicate one and it was only after much reflection that he had decided to return to Rome; his doing so had no connection with the territorial arrangements. There was no rupture of negotiations but his conscience compelled him to return to his people, and to call Parliament together within 48 hours so as to consult as to his position and establish his authority. For the moment the territorial situation was, for him, in the background. If his colleagues were to repeat to him the proposals that had been suggested yesterday, even so, it would be necessary for him to reply "I must return to Italy." His difficulty was as to the plenitude of his powers.

PRESIDENT WILSON said that M. Orlando had made a very frank and, if he might say so, an admirable statement of the position. The feelings expressed towards himself were most heartily reciprocated. He felt nothing but respect and consideration for him and his motives. Nothing should mar their relations and he felt it a very gra-

[1] The complete text of these minutes is printed in *PPC*, V, 210-28.

cious act of M. Orlando to express himself as he did. There was one aspect of the question that had not been in his mind. He had never thought of his statement as going behind the back of M. Orlando and appealing to the Italian people. If that were the effect, he, personally, regretted it. He welcomed this opportunity to say why he had published the statement. He would remind M. Orlando that his attitude in this matter had been the same from the first. Through all these months there had been a misunderstanding in the public mind as to the nature of the controversy and its basis. Things had been said, not once only, but often, in the Press both of France and Italy that put the attitude of himself and his Government in so false a light that it had become necessary to let his own people know, not only the position that the Government took up, but the basis of its attitude. It was necessary to state the grounds of the principles on which all the attitude of the United States Government was based. It was necessary to clear the mists which had arisen concerning the conditions of the Conference. The state of mind of other nations also was affected (as he had had evidence of this very day) in regard to the position of the Government of the United States of America. He was reassured by M. Orlando's statement that he was going back to Italy to seek instructions from his people and that there would be no rupture from the Conference. It would not only be serious, but perhaps fatal, if Italy were to withdraw and he was very happy to have M. Orlando's assurance on this point. He hoped that M. Orlando would make it evident to the world that his errand was to seek the instructions of Parliament, and not what the public believed a withdrawal from the Peace Settlement.

M. ORLANDO said he owed his thanks to President Wilson for his noble declaration for what he had spontaneously said that he recognised that M. Orlando excluded every intention and thought that was not kindly towards him. He felt that President Wilson would appreciate the reasons why he had to go to Rome. In the circumstances, it was absolutely essential for him to seek contact with his people and he recalled the moment when President Wilson himself had suggested that he (M. Orlando) ought to return and explain the situation to the Italian people. It was the more necessary since it had appeared not only in these conversations but was realised by the masses of the people that there had been some differences. It was necessary, therefore, to explain this situation to his people. He would explain to Parliament the result of these conversations, namely, the choice that Italy had to make. Speaking among friends, the fact was that Italy had made Fiume a national question. On that point not only the United States of America but also Italy's allies had declared quite specifically that they could not consent. In these circumstances to continue the conversations was useless. The people must decide when he explained the situation to them.

PRESIDENT WILSON said he would ask M. Orlando to be kind enough in explaining the situation to call attention to the fact that, in the view of the United States of America, the Treaty of London was not in the interest of the relations that ought to prevail between Italy and the Yugo-Slavs, nor to the peace of the world.

M. ORLANDO said that, in making his declaration to Parliament, he would explain openly the reasons put forward by President Wilson not only in his published statement but also in the memorandum he had sent him[2] and which President Wilson had authorised him to read to the Italian Parliament and which accordingly he intended to read.

M. CLEMENCEAU asked M. Orlando to explain his point of view which he thought was also Mr. Lloyd George's point of view about Fiume. This was that the same treaty which bound the Allies to Italy also granted Fiume to the Slavs. If they could not fail in their word to Italy, neither could they fail in their word to the Slavs.

MR. LLOYD GEORGE agreed, but said that beyond this there was no use in pretending that a new element had not been introduced since the signature of the Treaty of London. There was the advent of the United States of America into the war unbound and free not only from treaties but from the necessity that had compelled us to sign treaties and covenants all the world over. He would not say that this modified his views in regard to the Treaty of London, but, in certain circumstances, it would necessitate a reconsideration in regard to Fiume as well. In the circumstances, he felt justified in modifying the Treaty in regard to Fiume. The treaty gave Fiume to the Croatians. If it was modified in part with the assent of Italy in regard to Dalmatia, we should be free to make a modification also in regard to Fiume. This modification would be to make Fiume a free port controlled by its own population, Italians, Hungarians and Slavs, with free and equal access to all parts served by the port. To that extent he felt free to assent to a modification of the treaty if his Allies agreed. He did not feel free to challenge the decision of M. Orlando to go to Rome. He, himself, had felt it necessary to go to London in much less serious circumstances, so he could understand M. Orlando's position. Meanwhile, he asked what was the position of Italy? If this were an ordinary week, the absence of M. Orlando would not be so very serious. But on Tuesday next, the Germans would most likely be coming to Versailles. Would Italy be represented there? M. Orlando could hardly reach Rome before Saturday. When could he meet the Italian Parliament?

[2] See Wilson's memorandum printed at April 14, 1919, Vol. 57.

M. ORLANDO said on the 28th.

MR. LLOYD GEORGE asked when the Germans would be at Versailles? He presumed it would be on Tuesday. Between today and Tuesday was Italy not to be consulted? Only yesterday very important questions had been discussed on which the British and Italian experts had taken the same view, but the Italian experts had not attended. He referred to the question of indemnities. This afternoon, the economic question ought to have been under consideration. He thought that the people as a whole were more interested in economic than in territorial questions, which mainly concerned the newspapers and special persons who interested themselves in foreign politics. Then there was the question of coal. Would M. Crespi be here? Was Italy to be unrepresented altogether? There were great questions regarding the export of German coal. Had the Allies the right to put forward demands on behalf of a country that was not represented? Or was Italy ready to put herself in the hands of the Allies? Would she agree to what they accepted for her or would she say that they had no right to accept? Was Italy to be present when questions affecting her own economic life were under consideration? There was also the question of a joint credit for re-establishing life in Europe. Would Italy be in or out of this scheme? Who was to discuss it on Italy's behalf? Were we to put forward Italy's demands? Because Italy was not satisfied about the prospective peace with Austria, was she to have no peace with Germany? These were practical questions on which he wanted to have an answer.

M. CLEMENCEAU said he wished to add that after the events of the last days, the Germans would say that there was a schism among the Allies and, if the Italians were not represented at Versailles, the situation would be very serious. This would make peace much less probable.

PRESIDENT WILSON said he hoped that the Italian Delegation would remain and he understood that to be the object of what Mr. Lloyd George had said.

MR. LLOYD GEORGE said that was the object.

M. ORLANDO said he took note of the declarations of M. Clemenceau and Mr. Lloyd George in regard to the Treaty of London. This was, however, not a moment to enter into a detailed discussion of it. He would expose to the Italian Parliament the different points of view. In regard to Mr. Lloyd George's observation on the practical side, there seemed to him two questions. The first question related to the days between now and the discussions with Germany. During the last few weeks the Treaty had been discussed, and Italy was satisfied at the decisions taken, and had no objection to accepting. Without doubt many questions remained to be settled, including some of grave importance. Nevertheless, he felt confidence in his

Allies that Italy's interests would be considered all the more fairly because she was not represented. He trusted them as a judge, who is on his guard to be just in the case of a prisoner who has no advocate. He would discuss this matter with his colleagues, and find some practical way of settling it. He would leave M. Crespi, who could be consulted by the Allied experts on technical questions. The second question, which was a graver one, was that of the presence of Italy when the Germans came. He had read in the papers that the Germans were endeavouring to secure delay.

M. CLEMENCEAU said he had no official news of this. They said they could not leave Berlin before April 28th at the earliest.

M. ORLANDO said he hoped he would be back before then. While accepting Mr. Lloyd George's and M. Clemenceau's remarks that we must not give the Germans the impression that the Allies were less solid than before, the fundamental questions at stake were so vital to Italy that he considered it preferable to encounter the difficulties that Mr. Lloyd George mentioned rather than to stay away.

M. CLEMENCEAU asked whether Italy would be represented at the meeting with the Germans or not.

M. ORLANDO said it would depend on the decision taken in Italy.

PRESIDENT WILSON said that, strictly speaking, the decisions in regard to the Italian frontiers did not affect the peace with Germany, but only with the Austro-Hungarian Empire. Hence, personally, he could see no inconsistency between Italy's taking part in the Treaty with Germany and reserving the Treaty with Austria.

MR. LLOYD GEORGE said he still maintained that if Italian representatives were not present, however much they might trust their Allies, their claims could not be put forward. If they were not present at the meeting on May 1st, and M. Orlando had not obtained the consent of his Parliament to participate, how could their claims be put forward?

M. CLEMENCEAU said that we could hardly meet the Germans, for it would involve a change in the whole drafting of the Treaty.

MR. LLOYD GEORGE said that the Germans would ask who were the representatives of Italy. We could not put forward claims for Italy unless they were present or unless M. Orlando wrote and asked the Allies to put in a claim on Italy's behalf.

M. ORLANDO said that in his view if Mr. Lloyd George's objection was considered by itself, he was right. He agreed that it was impossible to propose conditions on behalf of a Power that was not present. This question would have to be carefully examined and a decision would have to be taken according to the circumstances. He agreed with Mr. Lloyd George that if Italy was not present, she would not be entitled to make any claims on Germany. He did not agree with

M. Clemenceau that the drafting of the articles would be much affected, because Italy was only concerned in a few questions in the Germany Treaty, mainly in regard to Reparation. Mr. Lloyd George's objection, however, must be considered in relation to the suggestion that President Wilson had made,—that Italy could make peace with Germany and postpone the Treaty with Austria. To this he had two answers. The first was that the general interpretation of the Pact of London of April, 1915, and the Treaty of September, 1914,—in fact, that the spirit of these two Pacts—was that there ought to be a general Peace. It would not be general, however, if the rest of the world were at peace and Italy still remained at war. Although President Wilson was not bound by these Pacts, he would put it to him that the question was one that must be regarded from the point of view of general equity, not only between the Allies, but also between the Associated Powers, that the peace ought to be a general Peace. On the other hand, he would remark to President Wilson that in signing the Treaty of Peace with Germany, the League of Nations Statute would also be signed. One clause of the League of Nations Covenant provided for mutual and reciprocal guarantees of territory among the signatories. The effect of this would be that Italy would engage herself to guarantee the territories of other countries without being guaranteed herself. Another difficulty was that the League of Nations Covenant included an arrangement for avoiding future wars, and for resolving difficulties between nations. If Italy adhered to the League of Nations, that would mean that the question of frontiers between Italy and the Yugo-Slavs would have to be resolved through the League of Nations instead of as the direct result of the war which had been won. This was a reason of grave difficulty in signing the peace with Germany, if questions affecting the peace with Austria-Hungary—that is to say, the question of the frontiers—was not also settled.

MR. LLOYD GEORGE said that if M. Orlando left, a very carefully drawn communique would have to be sent to the press.

BARON SONNINO, starting from the basis of M. Orlando's statement, said that it was proposed that M. Orlando should present to the Italian Parliament a statement of the question in general terms. It was difficult, however, to state the question if he had no clear idea of the intention of the other parties. He had thought that when they were invited to come here this afternoon, they would receive some suggestion of the latest point of view of the Allied and Associated Powers. Up to now this had not been given. President Wilson had made a statement as though the position was where it was a few days ago before certain additional proposals had been made. Mr. Lloyd George, in regard to Fiume for example, had said that he would not refuse to change in some degree the elements of the Treaty of London provided that concessions were made by Italy. M. Clemenceau did not take the same point of view, and said that Fiume had been promised to Croatia.

MR. LLOYD GEORGE said he never went beyond what his colleagues had agreed to. The Treaty of London gave Fiume to Croatia. He now proposed that it should be a free port, or rather he should say a free city. He would take it from the Croatians and give it to its own inhabitants of all races. This was a serious modification of the Treaty from his point of view, but he would agree to it if Italy would modify the Treaty of London.

BARON SONNINO asked if M. Clemenceau agreed.

M. CLEMENCEAU said he did. Mr. Lloyd George's point of view was his own.

BARON SONNINO asked if that was President Wilson's view also.

PRESIDENT WILSON said that in his memorandum he had expressed his readiness to the erection of Fiume into a free city, and he had accompanied his memorandum with a map.

BARON SONNINO said that in President Wilson's memorandum other frontiers, for example in Istria, were not the same as in the Treaty of London. Did President Wilson consent to leave these frontiers as in the Treaty? He only asked the question to clear the situation.

PRESIDENT WILSON said that in his memorandum he had stated what he felt to be the position of the United States of America. From that he did not care to depart. He hoped that in any statement to the Italian Parliament, M. Orlando would limit himself to that memorandum.

BARON SONNINO said that that raised a new difficulty.

M. ORLANDO said he would like to resume briefly Baron Sonnino's idea. He himself was under the necessity of explaining the position to the Italian Parliament. His explanation must be a very clear one. He had the memorandum of President Wilson and the declaration of the Governments which adhered to the Treaty of London. Then, he thought, Baron Sonnino asks: Can we tell Parliament what is the middle situation in which all parties are agreed? He would like to be able to state that. If his colleagues could not tell him this tonight, perhaps they could tell him tomorrow. He could say at present that his Allies adhered to the Pact of London. Then he would be asked: Have you the signature of President Wilson?

PRESIDENT WILSON said that if he agreed to any middle course, it would be contrary to what his people expected and had given him authority for.

MR. LLOYD GEORGE said that his impression was not that President Wilson had proposed a middle course, but the exact contrary. He himself and M. Clemenceau had suggested a middle course, which did not commend itself to President Wilson, but which, as he understood the matter, President Wilson was prepared to accept if his Italian colleagues would agree. He himself had taken the liberty to tell the Italians that this was the position. If he had been wrong in this, he regretted it. He put it to the Italian representatives that if they would be prepared to abandon their rights in Dalmatia, leaving Zara and Sebenico as free cities, and would content themselves with the islands other than those which form practically part of the mainland, he thought an agreed basis might be arranged.

PRESIDENT WILSON said he had never committed himself in this arrangement. All he had done was to ask Mr. Lloyd George to ascertain if the Italians would be ready to discuss on this basis, and the reply he had received was that they were not. He had reserved his judgment in every case. He regretted if there had been any failure on his part to make his position clear.

MR. LLOYD GEORGE said he had understood that if the Italians saw their way to assent, President Wilson would not have stood in his way.

PRESIDENT WILSON said this point of view was that he did not want his Italian friends to think that he would not discuss any aspect of the question. He was willing to go over the ground a hundred times if necessary.

MR. LLOYD GEORGE said he thought from the way that President Wilson had pressed for Spalato and the inner island to be left out, that he would have been willing to agree.

BARON SONNINO recalled the course of events.* On the previous afternoon, the Italians had sent proposals which would have given the line of the Alps to the Sea east of Volosca to Italy, and would have put Fiume under the sovereignty of Italy, and provided for the establishment by Italy in the port of Fiume of free zones. Italy would also have received all the islands mentioned in the Pact of London except Pago; and Zara and Sebenico would have been placed under the League of Nations with Italy as Mandatory Power. If that had been accepted, Italy would have had some assurance. An answer was received in regard to the sovereignty of Fiume, namely: that this could not be a basis of discussion, but, as regards the rest, it had been understood that if Italy gave up Fiume, it would form a basis of acceptance in a general way. This had been the impression received.

PRESIDENT WILSON asked if it was an impression of a joint agreement.

MR. LLOYD GEORGE said that he had understood this to be the case,

* The Secretary was out of the room during a portion of this statement.

except as regards the question of Mandates, which was a point that he had overlooked. He understood, however, that the remainder was generally agreed.

BARON SONNINO said the reply had been that Fiume was not acceptable, but that the rest might be acceptable. The Italian Delegation had sent word to say that if Italian sovereignty over Fiume could not be accepted, no explanation was available as to what would be substituted for it. He then asked Count Aldrovandi if any answer had been received.

COUNT ALDROVANDI said that the Marquis Imperiali[3] had seen Mr. Lloyd George, who had informed him that the League of Nations would take the place of Italy.

PRESIDENT WILSON said that Mr. Lloyd George had returned to the room where they were discussing with the experts the question of Reparation, and had told him what the message meant. He had, however, not consulted him as to any reply to be given to the message.

BARON SONNINO said that the impression that he had formed was that Fiume was to be a free city with a wide contour.

MR. LLOYD GEORGE said that that was the proposal contained in President Wilson's document.

PRESIDENT WILSON said that Baron Sonnino's contention was that a message had been sent to them during the afternoon when they were consulting with the experts on Reparation. All that he could remember was that Mr. Lloyd George had left the room to see the Marquis Imperiali, and had returned and merely told M. Clemenceau and himself what the Marquis had said. Baron Sonnino, however, said that he had received a message.

M. CLEMENCEAU said that he had never agreed to any message.

MR. LLOYD GEORGE said that in the morning the question had been discussed at great length, and he himself had said nothing that was not in accordance with what had then been agreed to. The only point of difference was in regard to Mandates, and on this there had been a misunderstanding. It had not been Count Aldrovandi's fault, but he himself had overlooked the mention of Mandates in connection with Zara and Sebenico. Everything else that he had said resulted from the conversation of the morning. All that had happened with the Marquis Imperiali was that he had asked where the sovereignty of Fiume would lie if it was not vested in Italy. He himself had replied: In the League of Nations. The other question raised had been one of the diplomatic responsibility in regard to Fiume.

BARON SONNINO said that on the Marquis Imperiali's return he

[3] That is, Marquis Guglielmo Imperiali.

and his colleagues had just begun to discuss the question, when they had received a copy of President Wilson's statement. They had then felt that the whole position was changed, and it was no use discussing details any more. He expressed his thanks for Mr. Lloyd George's intervention. He had narrowed the gulf between them to some extent, and he had hoped that they might learn to what extent their three colleagues could agree on a basis for discussion. If they had such a basis, things could be stated in a clear way. It was no use telling Parliament that two of the Allies would do one thing, and the third another.

MR. LLOYD GEORGE said that he was in his usual disagreeable role of trying to effect a conciliation when both sides were inclined to refute him. Nevertheless, he would again endeavour to make a suggestion. He understood, however, that whatever was suggested the Italian Delegates were not in a position to accept it.

BARON SONNINO said that they were in a very difficult position. If they only knew the gulf that separated them it would be better.

MR. LLOYD GEORGE said that he fully understood the difficulty President Wilson was in to say that he agreed when he could not reconcile agreement with his principles. The Italian representatives might return to Italy with a proposal agreed to by their three colleagues, but they might then find themselves in an entirely different atmosphere where only one point of view was understood. He therefore fully understood President Wilson's difficulty in telling the Italian representatives beforehand what he could agree to. He, himself, had a good deal of experience of industrial disputes. He always said "Will you, the workmen, take the responsibility of recommending this proposal if the other party will do the same?" He now said the same to the Italian representatives. Would they take the responsibility of recommending an arrangement?

BARON SONNINO said if it were acceptable they would.

M. ORLANDO said he would not have the power to accept any proposition whatever it was. To do so would be contrary to his original declaration at the beginning of the meeting. He had to put his position before Parliament. He had asked the three Powers, two of whom were allied and the other associated, whether they were agreed. The reply was in the negative. This was all he wanted to know. In their latest proposal, as he understood it, they had spoken of making Zara and Sebenico free cities and of handing over the islands to Italy and making Fiume a free city, but they had overlooked one point, namely Istria. It was essential to Italy that the frontiers should go right down to Volosca.

BARON SONNINO recalled that Mr. Lloyd George had asked whether the Italian Delegation would be prepared to accept a proposal if the three were in accord. He had asked if they were in a position to recommend acceptance. He had replied that if the proposals were acceptable they would recommend them to Parliament. Mr. Lloyd George had explained President Wilson's difficulties in making a precise proposal. The chance, however, was not great if the whole case had to be presented to the Italian Parliament without receiving a detailed proposal.

MR. LLOYD GEORGE said that unless the Italian Ministers were prepared to take the responsibility of recommending the proposal to Parliament, it was idle to discuss the matter further.

BARON SONNINO said that if proposals could be made to them that were acceptable they would undertake to recommend them with all their weight. Up to the present, however, he had not received an offer.

PRESIDENT WILSON said that M. Orlando would explain the difficult position of the several nations. Great Britain and France were bound by the pact and the United States by principles. He would put this position to the Italian Parliament and say to them "Have I authority to go back and settle as best I can?" He did not think it would be right to make a proposal for M. Orlando to present to Parliament.

BARON SONNINO asked what would happen if they asked Parliament for authority to find a settlement between the two positions, and should obtain the necessary authority and then go back and fail? Our position would be quite hopeless. They would then come back with a mandate and would have no chance of success. Their position would be much better if they had some idea of an acceptable middle course now.

M. ORLANDO said that he agreed with President Wilson that the best course was to go back and explain the situation to Parliament and ask for a general authority. Why, he asked, should we exercise this pressure on President Wilson to make a proposal that he was not prepared to make? He, himself, remained in the same position as he had been at the beginning. He would go back to Parliament and ask them to take their decision. He realised, however, that he must give Parliament his own opinion. If Parliament would not accept it, the Government would be confided to other hands. He hoped, however, that the generous feelings of the Italian people would enable him to find a solution. At any rate the result would be a clear cut situation.

PRESIDENT WILSON said he thought this was an admirable position to take up. Supposing M. Orlando were to say that President Wilson, having published his statement, was now ready to abate it, what would be the opinion in Italy?

BARON SONNINO asked what was the danger of attempting some application of principles? He could not go as President Wilson suggested and simply say "Give us confidence for any plans we like to adopt." It would be much harder to make a compromise after going before Parliament. If only a compromise could be agreed to now, Parliament could be asked to accept it.

MR. LLOYD GEORGE said that unfortunately there was a conflict of principles in this case. There were President Wilson's principles, in which he agreed to and which he had defended in spite of a certain amount of opposition. There was also the principle of International engagements and standing by the signature of treaties. He could not see the danger of compromise. In such a case it was best to make the best arrangement and the best compromise possible. The proposal he had made did not give way on any of the principles. If the Dalmatian coast were free, President Wilson's principles were not impugned. He did not know the best way of getting things through the Italian Parliament, but he knew the British Parliament, having been 30 years a member, and there he would want to know where he stood and what to make for in dealing with such a question.

M. CLEMENCEAU agreed.

MR. LLOYD GEORGE said that in the question of reparation for example, he could not have gone to Parliament and asked for a free hand.

BARON SONNINO said that was exactly what he had maintained.

PRESIDENT WILSON said that as a matter of fact this was what Mr. Lloyd George had done.

MR. LLOYD GEORGE said this was not the case. He had been able to reassure Parliament exactly as to where he stood. If it had been otherwise Parliament would not have given him its confidence. They would not have done so unless he had confidence in himself.

PRESIDENT WILSON said that the Italian representative could go to the Italian Parliament and tell them that neither the Allied nor Associated Powers could consent to give them Fiume. The British and French felt bound to stand by their agreement as allies. In regard to the agreement they could state that he, himself, understood the difficulty of his colleagues and was ready to agree with anything consistent with his principles, although he had no proposal to make.

M. ORLANDO re-stated what President Wilson had said in almost identical terms.

MR. LLOYD GEORGE said that President Wilson's position seemed to be that he was unwilling to propose any arrangement but that he insisted that it must be made clear that Fiume was not to go to Italy.

PRESIDENT WILSON said he must remind his colleagues that the Italian Parliament has never known the position of the United States Government which had been set forth in his Memorandum. His proposals in that Memorandum had been not merely negative, they had also been positive. It included measures necessary for providing the security of the eastern coasts of Italy in the Adriatic. It called attention to the necessity of providing for this and included the limitation of armaments, the destruction of fortifications, etc. to meet these difficulties. Hence it was constructive as well as negative. He wanted the Italian Parliament to know what he did say in this respect.

At this moment M. Orlando said it was time for him to go as he had to catch his train.

Before leaving Sir Maurice Hankey, on behalf of Mr. Lloyd George, handed M. Orlando a letter signed by M. Clemenceau and Mr. Lloyd George. (Appendix I.)

2. A press communique was agreed to in regard to the afternoon's meeting.

3. PRESIDENT WILSON read the report of the Committee that had been set up to consider the Chinese position in regard to Shantung. (Appendix II.)[4]

SIR MAURICE HANKEY was instructed to ascertain from the Chinese Delegation whether any written note was being sent in regard to the question that had been put to them by the Supreme Council.

The Meeting adjourned until 4 p.m. on the following day when the Economic and Financial Clauses were to be considered.

APPENDIX I.

PARIS. 23.4.19.

FIUME AND THE PEACE SETTLEMENT.

We learn with a regret which it is difficult to measure that, at the very moment when Peace seems almost attained, Italy threatens to sever herself from the company of the Allied Nations, through whose common efforts victory has been achieved. We do not presume to offer any opinion as to the effects which so momentous a step would have upon the future of Italy herself. Of these it is for the Italian people and its leaders to judge, and for them alone. But we, who have been Italy's Allies through four anxious years, and would gladly be her Allies still, are bound to express our fears as to the disastrous effects it will surely have upon us, and upon the policy for which we have striven.

When in 1915 Italy threw in her lot with France, Russia and the British Empire in their struggle against the Central powers, Turkey and Bulgaria, she did so on conditions. She required her Allies to promise that in case of victory they would help her to obtain in Eu-

[4] It is printed as an Enclosure with the preceding document.

rope the frontier of the Alps, the great ports of Trieste and Pola, and a large portion of the Dalmatian coast with many of its adjacent islands. Such accessions of territory would enormously strengthen Italy's power of defence, both on land and sea, against her hereditary enemy, and would incidentally result in the transfer of over 200,000 German-speaking Tyrolese and over 750,000 Southern Slavs from Austrian to Italian rule. Under this arrangement Fiume was retained by Great Britain, France and Italy herself for Croatia.

Such was the situation in April, 1915. In November, 1918, it had profoundly changed. Germany was beaten; the Dual Monarchy had ceased to exist: and side by side with this Military revolution, the ideals of the Western Powers had grown and strengthened. In 1915 the immediate needs of self-defence, the task of creating and equipping vast Armies, the contrivance of new methods for meeting new perils, strained to the utmost the energies of the Allies. But by 1918 we had reached the double conviction that if the repetition of such calamities was to be avoided, the Nations must organise themselves to maintain Peace, as Germany, Austria, Bulgaria and Turkey had organised themselves to make war; and that little could be expected, even from the best contrived organisation, unless the boundaries of the States to be created by the Conference were framed, on the whole, in accordance with the wishes and lasting interests of the populations concerned.

This task of re-drawing European frontiers has fallen upon the Great Powers; and admittedly its difficulty is immense. Not always, nor indeed often, do race, religion, language, history, economic interests, geographical contiguity and convenience, the influence of national prejudice, and the needs of national defence, conspire to indicate without doubt of ambiguity the best frontier for any State:—be it new or old. And unless they do, some element in a perfect settlement must be neglected, compromise becomes inevitable, and there may often be honest doubts as to the form the compromise should take.

Now as regards most of the new frontier between Italy and what was once the Austrian Empire, we have nothing to say. We are bound by the Pact of London, and any demand for a change in that Pact which is adverse to Italy must come from Italy herself. But this same Pact gives Fiume to Croatia, and we would very earnestly and respectfully ask whether any valid reason exists for adding, in the teeth of the Treaty, this little city on the Croatian coast to the Kingdom of Italy? It is said indeed, and with truth, that its Italian population desire the change. But the population which clusters round the port is not predominantly Italian. It is true that the urban area wherein they dwell is not called Fiume; for it is divided by a narrow canal, as Paris is divided by the Seine, or London by the tidal estuary of the Thames, and locally the name, Fiume, is applied in strictness only to the streets on one side of it. But surely we are concerned with things, not names; and however you name it, the town which serves the port, and lives by it, is physically one town, not two; and taken as a whole is Slav, not Italian.

But if the argument drawn from the wishes of the present population does not really point to an Italian solution, what remains? Not the argument from history; for up to quite recent times the inhabitants of Fiume, in its narrowest meaning, were predominantly Slav. Not the arguments from contiguity; for the country population, up to the very gates of the city, are not merely predominantly Slav, but Slav without perceptible admixture. Not the economic argument; for the territories which obtain through Fiume their easiest access to the sea, whatever else they be, at least are not Italian. Most of them are Slav, and if it be said that Fiume is also necessary to Hungarian and Transylvanian commerce, this is a valid argument for making it a free port, but surely not for putting it under Italian sovereignty.

There is one other line of argument on this subject about which we would ask leave to say a word. It is urged by some, and thought by many, that the task of the Great Powers is not merely to sit down and coldly re-arrange the pieces on the European board in strict, even pedantic, conformity with certain admirable but very abstract principles. They must consider these great matters in more human fashion. After all (so runs the argument), the problems to be dealt with arise out of a Great War. The conquerers in that War were not the aggressors: their sacrifices have been enormous; the burdens they have to bear seem well-nigh intolerable. Are they to get nothing out of victory, except the consciousness that State frontiers in Europe will be arranged in a better pattern after 1918 than they were before: and that nations who fought on the wrong side, or who did not fight at all, will have gained their freedom through other peoples' losses? Surely the victors, if they want it, are entitled to some more valid reward than theoretical map-makers, working in the void, may on abstract principles feel disposed to give them.

There is something in this way of thinking which at first sight appeals to us all; and where no interests are concerned but those of the criminal aggressors, it deserves respectful consideration. But in most cases of territorial redistribution it is at least as important to enquire what effects the transfer will have on the nations to whom territory is given, as upon those from whom it is taken: and when, as in the case of Jugo-Slavia, the nation from whom it is taken happens to be a friendly State, the difficulty of the problem is doubled.

We do not presume to speak with authority on the value of the strategical gains which Italy anticipates from the acquisition of the islands and coastline of Dalmatia. They seem to us to be small; though, small as they are, they must greatly exceed the economic advantages which will accrue to Italian trade from new opportunities, or to the Italian Treasury from new sources of revenue. We cannot believe that the owners of Trieste have anything to fear from Fiume as a commercial rival, or the owners of Pola from Fiume as a Naval base.

But if Italy has little to gain from the proposed acquisition, has she not much to lose? The War found her protected from an hereditary enemy of nearly twice her size by a frontier which previous Treaties had deliberately left insecure. Her Eastern sea-board was almost bare of harbours, while Austria-Hungary possessed on the opposite side of the Adriatic some of the finest harbours in the world. This was her condition in 1914. In 1919 her Northern and Eastern frontiers are as secure as mountains and rivers can make them. She is adding two great ports to her Adriatic possessions; and her hereditary oppressor has ceased to exist. To us it seems that, as a State thus situated has nothing to fear from its neighbours' enmity, so its only interest must be to gain their friendship. And though memories belonging to an evil past make friendship difficult between Italians and Slavs, yet the bitterest memories soften with time, unless fresh irritants are frequently applied; and among such irritants none are more powerful than the constant contemplation of a disputed and ill-drawn frontier.

It is for Italy, and not for the other signatories of the Pact of London, to say whether she will gain more in power, wealth and honour by strictly adhering to that part of the Pact of London which is in her favour, than by accepting modifications in it which would bring it into closer harmony with the principles which are governing the territorial decisions of the Allies in other parts of Europe. But so far as Fiume is concerned the position is different. Here, as we have already pointed out, the Pact of 1915 is against the Italian contention; and so also, it seems to us, are justice and policy. After the most prolonged and anxious reflexion, we cannot bring ourselves to believe that it is either in the interests of Jugo-Slavia, in the interests of Italy herself, or in the interests of future peace—which is the concern of all the world—that this port should be severed from the territories to which economically, geographically and ethnologically it naturally belongs.

Can it be that Italy on this account is prepared to separate herself from her Allies? The hope that sustained us through the perilous years of War was that victory, when it came, would bring with it, not merely the defeat of Germany, but the final discredit of the ideals in which Germany had placed her trust. On the other hand, Germany, even when she began to entertain misgivings about the issues of the campaign, felt sure that the union of her enemies would never survive their triumph. She based her schemes no longer on the conquest of Europe, but on its political, and perhaps also on its social disintegration. The Armistice might doubtless produce a brief cessation of hostilities: but it would bring no repose to a perturbed and over-wrought world. Militant nationalism would lead to a struggle between peoples; militant internationalism to a struggle between classes. In either event, or in both, the Conference summoned to give us peace would leave us at war, and Germany alone would be the gainer.

This, or something like this, is the present calculation of a certain section of German politicians. Could anything more effectually contribute to its success than that Italy should quarrel with her Allies, and that the cause of quarrel should be the manner in which our common victory may best be used? We are calling into being a League of Nations; we are daily adding to the responsibilities which, under the approaching Treaty, it will be called upon to assume; yet before the scheme has had time to clothe itself in practical form, we hasten to destroy its credit. To the world we supply dramatic proof that the association of the Great Powers, which won the War, cannot survive Peace: and all the world will ask how, if this be so, the maintenance of Peace can safely be left in their hands.

For these reasons, if for no other, we beg our Italian colleagues to reconsider their policy. That it has been inspired by a high sense of Patriotism we do not doubt. But we cannot believe either that it is in Italy's true interests, or that it is worthy of the great part which Italy is called upon to play in the Councils of the Nations.

G. CLEMENCEAU.
D. LLOYD GEORGE.

T MS (SDR, RG 256, 180.03401/118, DNA).

To Nikola P. Pašić

My dear Mr. Pashitch: Paris, 24 April, 1919.

Thank you very warmly for your letter of yesterday. I do not think that I deserve your generous words of appreciation. I merely did my obvious duty.

Cordially and sincerely yours, [Woodrow Wilson]

CCL (WP, DLC).

Three Telegrams from Thomas Nelson Page to the American Mission

Rome April 24, 1919

259. IMPORTANT.

French Chargé d'Affaires[1] called ostensibly to ask news. Informed me that his government has instructed him to approach the Italian press in a form much more conciliatory than that in the President's statement and to say that they and the British were actually in conference with Italian representatives over the Eastern Adriatic question and believed a settlement was being reached when the President's statement appeared in the press. He, I think, reflects French governmental opinion over situation. Evidently they mean to dissociate themselves wholly from America's action in matter. He says France must keep on good terms with Italy. He appears considerably disturbed over danger, *First*: starting up, if they must again, to new military efforts; *Secondly*, of internal commotions and peril to public order.

I judge France will avail herself of situation, then have all credit for herself. He rather intimated that France would consider herself unable to (apparent omission) peace treaty without Italy.

Nelson Page.

[1] François Jules Charles-Roux, Counselor of the French embassy in Rome.

Rome, April 24, 1919.

260. The tone of the press of last night and this morning is one of intense anger. The tenseness of the situation created can hardly be exaggerated. The attitude of the press and people daily becomes more threatening and the newspapers are full of violent attacks on the President but also on the Allied Representatives denouncing latter for disloyalty and lack of good faith.

Yesterday evening a solemn demonstration in Piazza Colonna was called to reaffirm Italy's rights in demanding an immediate adjustment of her frontiers and a settlement of her claims in the Adriatic. In spite of Ragout [holiday?], many thousands, with the flag of the country, the municipality, and those of the cities of the Adriatic, collected at the appointed hour and amid great enthusiasm marched towards the Capitol where they were addressed by Dona Prospero Colonna, Mayor of Rome. "Against every formation," said Mayor, "which offends justice and which denies our rights, the people of Italy will rise, rise against all and every one. The word of Rome tells the world that Italy will not support reductions in her national rights. It is a duty which our dead from their glorious tombs impose upon us that we shall not profane them with pusillanimous weakness." Roars of applause met these words. Prior to reaching the Capitol the procession marched to the Japanese Embassy where it was halted amid loud cheering.

Deputy Federzoni[1] has telegraphed d'Annunzio[2] requesting that he come to Rome to reaffirm the will of the nation. Several members of this Embassy joined the meeting to gain some idea of feeling of the people. It was very antagonistic especially to America. While marching the crowd chanted "Down with America," "Down with England," "Down with the Violators of Treaties," "Down with Jugo-Slavs."

This morning's MESSAGGERO contained a telegram from Paris stating that the position is much graver and in a few hours it will be known how and why.

The POPOLO ROMANO says Italy cannot abandon Fiume and the other Adriatic cities to the Balkan assassins.

"The knees of Germany, says the VALA, pressed heavily upon the breast of the Allies and alone they would never have been able to breathe again when we arrived to their aid and they weeping at the mere sight of our flag (the color of which they barely now know) swore on their dead that they would never forget the services rendered by Italy to civilization, which they today barter on the Jugo-Slav market. It is well to recall that Mr. Wilson has given nothing to us Italians; has given nothing of that which he has given to the other Allies which can be considered an obligation on our part towards him. To the other Allies he has given two and a half million men for their war against Germany. To us beyond loans which are business matters and beyond the aid of Red Cross which can eventually be liquidated, nothing has been given us to win the war. We must be placed in a position of suspicion before the world; accused before the people of Europe of delaying and obstructing Peace—Wilsonian peace—because we do nothing to lay at the feet of Jugo-Slav, the late servants of Austria, our shores and our peoples of Dalmatia."

According to information press, the English troops were to have left Fiume on April 23rd.

According to the Press the Government is receiving telegrams from Senators and Deputies from all over Italy affirming their intention to stand with the Government even in the gravest measures for the revindication of Italy's rights. #260. Nelson Page

[1] Luigi Federzoni, cofounder and leader of the Italian Nationalist Association, a conservative and imperialist political organization.

[2] Gabriele D'Annunzio, poet, novelist, playwright, and war hero, who was already making inflammatory speeches looking toward Italian annexation of Fiume and who was being considered by various ultranationalist groups as a potential leader of an expedition to that city. See Michael A. Ledeen, *The First Duce: D'Annunzio at Fiume* (Baltimore and London, 1977), pp. 1-57.

Rome, April 24th, 1919.

Important. 261. Paris press telegrams announcing that the Italian, French and British Delegations were actually in session discussing Lloyd George's counter-proposals when President's statement appeared in the Paris papers, and that he declared Italy's claims outside of Alpine Line to be sheer imperialism have aroused tremendous feeling.

Under Secretary of State Borsarelli[1] called to suggest for the present I take steps to keep our people out of crowds and other places where excitement may exist. Troops, including cavalry, are out and quite a lot of soldiers are posted in the courtyard of the Embassy.

Press will I hope this evening publish full text of President's message, but in state of public feeling it will probably be accompanied by bitter editorial comments which will prevent any immediate effect.

The Secretary of State Borsarelli, who has always been very friendly, showed great feeling speaking of President's decision, declaring himself unable to comprehend why Italy should be restrained from having what she has won at such immense sacrifices and Fiume, which is Italian, be given up to her most bitter enemies, while on the other hand France is given everything and more than she expected. I cite this as showing present Italian feeling.

Consuls have been warned to instruct Americans and especially soldiers in uniform, for the present to keep out of crowds.

Placards are up calling on the people to assemble in mass meeting at 7:30, about an hour from now, in the Piazza Colonna to denounce the treachery of the Allies. Sent Secstate 2814.

Nelson Page.

T telegrams (WP, DLC).

[1] That is, Marquis Luigi Borsarelli di Refreddo.

From George Lansbury

Dear President Wilson: London E.C. 4 April 24th 1919.

Your manifesto has given us all great hope; we have been watching the proceedings at Paris with a good deal of anxiety this last three months. Rumours and reports of every sort and kind are floating here—one day France is to occupy the whole of the Rhine Valley, another day, Britain, France and America are to form a new kind of Triple Alliance. But your manifesto seems to all of us to blow these things sky-high into thin air and we are all trusting that at long last all the Allied statesmen will come into line and join with you in creating the only sort of peace which can be lasting.

There is not much outward sign of interest about anything just now as far as our people are concerned, but underneath this calm there is I am sure, a great force working which will overthrow any Government that comes back with a peace based on militarism, or that continues to carry on war in Russia or elsewhere. There is a sort of unspoken longing for peace and for the commencement of that new social order of which we have all heard so much. But it is to you that everyone is looking who is taking part in affairs at all. They are pinning their faith to your personal honour and to your determination that come what will, America under your leadership shall stand for a peace of understanding, of good-will and of righteousness.

I hope you are very well and that you will continue in good health until the work you have in hand is successfully accomplished.

Yours very truly, George Lansbury

P.S. I got together a few labour men yesterday & sent you the wire[1] also Clemenceau & L. George

TLS (WP, DLC).

[1] It is missing. However, a dispatch from London, datelined April 24, 1919, printed in the *New York Times* on the following day, reported that Arthur Henderson and other British labor leaders had sent a telegram to Wilson congratulating him on his "magnificent declaration for peace based on the fourteen points." The dispatch added that the same persons had sent a telegram to Lloyd George, commending him for the support that he was giving to Wilson, and another telegram to Filippo Turati, leader of "the Intransigeant Socialists" at Rome, appealing to Italian workers to support the President of the United States.

From Bernard Mannes Baruch

My dear Mr President, Paris Thursday [April 24, 1919]

Your note on the Italian situation was fine and timely.

It took the kind of courage which you have always shown and which makes us all so proud of you.

The new world dawning for all needs this fearless frank leadership and while you are with us it will never be wanting.

I shall always follow when and where you point the way so will millions of others. The result will be as you have wished.

Sincerely Bernard M Baruch

ALS (WP, DLC).

From Emma Alice Margaret Tennant Asquith

Dear President [London] April 24th, 1919

It is impossible to say how fine, how wise, & how *brave* I think yr. appeal to these *wretched* misguided Italians is!

Margot Asquith

ALS (WP, DLC).

From Tasker Howard Bliss

My dear Mr. President: Paris April 24th, 1919

Before the preliminary terms of peace, which the Allied and Associated Powers desire to impose upon Germany, are handed to the representatives of that government, I beg to again draw your attention to the matter of control in Germany by Inter-Allied Commissions. I feel that the question is one of such great importance that I cannot emphasize too strongly the views your military and naval advisers have so often expressed.

In all the discussions during the preparation of the military, naval and air clauses of the treaty to be imposed upon Germany, from the time of the first meeting of the committee presided over by Marshal Foch to the time of the meeting of the Supreme Council on March 17th, when the clauses were discussed, the American military and naval representatives on all committees dealing with the subject strongly opposed any wording involving the United States in perpetual control, or even control for an extended period of time, by Allied Commissions in Germany. When these terms were presented to the Supreme Council on March 17th there appeared, as a foot-note, in the draft of the terms, a statement to the effect that the American Representatives had made complete reservation concerning the articles calling for perpetual control in Germany.

From the beginning, I have held to the view that the treaty stipulations should contain a definite statement that the control commissions would function only until the conditions for which a definite and reasonable time-limit was fixed had been complied with and that if these conditions were not complied with in the time fixed then the delegates should report to their respective governments for new instructions.

It should be noted that the treaty stipulations in their present form provide that the Inter-Allied Commissions of Control establish their organizations at the seat of the Central German Government and entitle them to proceed to any point whatsoever in German territory, or to send sub-commissions to any point they desire in German territory. These commissions are to supervise matters which may require the representatives to be functioning simultaneously over a large part of German territory. They are to be charged with supervising not only the disarmament of Germany and the required reduction of her army and destruction of material but also with supervising the limitation of the number of gendarmes and police officials, her coast guards, forest guards, custom house officials, the supervision of instruction in schools as well as abolishment of certain schools, and perhaps the supervision of certain of her manufacturing plants, etc. All this will require an extremely large commission, the personnel certainly numbering in the hundreds and probably in the thousands, its representatives operating all over Germany.

Although the opening article of Section V, on the subject of control commissions, as it appears in the present draft of the military, naval and air terms, provides that—

> "All military, naval and air clauses contained in the present stipulations, for the execution of which a time-limit is prescribed, shall be executed by Germany under the control of INTERALLIED COMMISSIONS,"

the article is silent as to the withdrawal of the commissions.

Having in mind the dangerous situation which it is believed would be created by having Inter-Allied Commissions functioning for an indefinite time in Germany, and because there seems to be some vagueness in the wording of the control section of the present draft stipulations, I strongly urge that it be made clear to the governments with which the United States is associated that American representation on any Control Commission in Germany will cease when Germany has complied with the terms for which a definite time-limit for their execution has been fixed, unless, because of Germany's failure to comply within the time-limit, the United States issues new instructions to its delegates, in which case the United States reserves the right to determine for itself the extra period of time, if any, that it will continue its representation on the control commissions. Sincerely yours, Tasker H. Bliss.

TLS (WP, DLC).

Hugh Campbell Wallace to Frank Lyon Polk

[Paris] April 24, 1919

107, URGENT.

With the exception of the Socialist papers and the Paris edition of the DAILY MAIL, which express hearty approval of President Wilson's action and his declarations about Fiume, the French press, including the Paris edition of the NEW YORK HERALD, are solid in their opposition to the attitude taken by the President. Most of the papers which have distinguished themselves of late for their anti-American tone are immoderate in their denunciations. LE MATIN, L'ECHO DE PARIS and LE GAULOIS are particularly violent, declaring that France will stand by her signature to the treaty of London, and accusing President Wilson of substituting himself for the Conference as well as placing the Allies in an embarrassing position with regard to Germany. Other papers like LE JOURNAL, LE FIGARO, LE PETIT PARISIEN, LE PETIT JOURNAL express regrets at the President's action and represent that it will do harm instead of good. The Socialist Press however may be said to be united in its support of President Wilson. LE POPULAIRE, LA LANTERNE L'OEUVRE condemn Italy's pretentions and L'HUMANITE, the official organ of the Socialist Party, goes so far as to remark that it would have been well if President Wilson had taken the same stand with the French in the matter of their "shameful annexationism" and the Sarre Basin. Most of the papers, regardless of opinions, publish a statement from Signor Orlando, which is given in fullest detail by LE MATIN.[1] The Italian Premier freely criticises the President's action and declares that he is himself supported by the Italian Parliament and public opinion.

Wallace.

T telegram (WP, DLC).

[1] Printed in *Le Matin*, April 25, 1919, late night edition. The news report printed as the next document is a good summary of the full text and quotes all its essential portions.

A News Report

[*April 24, 1919*]

ORLANDO MAKES PROTEST

Accuses the President of a Breach of Diplomatic Usage.

SEES OFFENSE TO AN ALLY

PARIS. April 24.—Vittorio Orlando, the Italian Premier, issued a long statement today replying to President Wilson in which he says in so many words that he is compelled to withdraw from the Peace Conference after President Wilson's action, which is regarded as a departure from diplomatic customs, and leaves the Italians no other course.

"Yesterday," says the Premier's statement, "while the Italian delegation was discussing counter-propositions which had been received from the British Prime Minister and which had for their aim the conciliation of contradictory tendencies which were manifested concerning Italian territorial aspirations, the Paris newspapers published a message from the President of the United States, in which he expressed his own thought on one of the gravest problems which has been submitted to the judgment of the Conference.

"The practice of addressing nations directly constitutes surely an innovation in international relations. I do not wish to complain, but I wish to record it as a precedent, so that at my own time I may follow it, inasmuch as this new custom doubtless constitutes the granting to nations of larger participation in international questions, and, personally, I have always been of the opinion that such participation was the harbinger of a new order of things.

"Nevertheless, if these appeals are to be considered as addressed to nations outside of the Governments which represent them, (I might say even against the Governments) I should feel deep regret in recalling that this process, heretofore applied to enemy Governments, is today applied for the first time to a Government which has been and intends to remain a loyal ally of the great American Republic, namely, to the Italian Government."

Premier Orlando says that he might complain that such a message addressed to the Italian nation had been published at the very moment when the allied and associated powers were negotiating with the Italian Government, the help of which had been sought and appreciated in numerous serious questions, heretofore discussed in intimate and complete solidarity.

"Above all," he continues, "I should have the right to complain if the declarations of the Presidential message have the purpose to oppose the Italian people to the Italian Government, because it would misconstrue and deny the high degree of civilization which the Italian people have attained and its democratic and liberal régime.

"To oppose (place in opposition?) the Italian people and Government would be to admit that this great free nation would submit to the yoke of a will other than its own, and I should be forced to protest strongly against suppositions unjustly offensive to my country."

Premier Orlando declares that President Wilson "is treating the Italians as if they were a barbarous people without a democratic Government."

Signor Orlando says that he has never denied that the Treaty of London did not apply to Fiume, but says that the Italian claim is based on the principles of President Wilson's Fourteen Points.

Referring to President Wilson's statement, Premier Orlando says it purports to demonstrate that the Italian claims beyond certain limits laid down in his message violate the principles upon which must be founded the new régime of right, justice, and liberty among peoples, and adds that he never denied these principles, and that even President Wilson would do him the justice to say that in the long conversations they had had together, he (Orlando) had never relied upon the formal authority of a treaty by which he knew President Wilson was not bound, but merely relied upon reason and justice, upon which Italy's claims were based.

Signor Orlando deplores his failure to convince Mr. Wilson, although he says the President admitted that justice and truth were the monopoly of no man, and that all men erred. The Conference, he points out, has had to change its mind many times, and he does not think himself disrespectful by asking it to change it again.

"I consider as unjustified the application that, in his statement, President Wilson makes of his principles toward the Italian claims," Premier Orlando continues. "It is impossible for me in a document of this nature to repeat the detailed arguments which have been produced in Italy's behalf. I may simply say that no one will receive without reserve the affirmation that the collapse of the Austro-Hungarian Empire should imply the reduction of Italian aspirations."

Citing the President's argument that the concessions granted bring Italy to its natural defenses, the Alps, Signor Orlando says:

"This recognition is of great importance, provided that the eastern flank of this wall does not remain open and that the right of Italy should be interpreted to include the line of Monte Nevoso, (north and west of Fiume) which separates the waters running toward the Black Sea and the Mediterranean." He recalls that the Latins from the earliest dawn of Italian history designated this mountain as "the Italian limit."

"Without this protection," says the Premier, "a dangerous breach is left in this admirable barrier of the Alps, rupturing the unquestionable political, economic, and historical unity of the Istrian Peninsula. I contend, furthermore, that he who is entitled to the honor of proclaiming to the world the right of the free determination of peoples should recognize this right for Fiume, an ancient Italian city which proclaimed its Italian nature before the Italian ships arrived—an admirable example of national conscience perpetuated throughout centuries.

"To deny this right only because of the small number concerned would mean the admission that the criterion of justice toward peoples varies according to their territorial extent."

Premier Orlando then points out that Antwerp, Genoa, and Rotterdam are international ports serving as an outlet to divers peoples and territories without having to pay for the privilege by sacrificing national conscience, and continues:

"It is impossible to qualify as excessive the Italian aspirations toward the Dalmatian coast, Italy's boulevard throughout centuries, which Roman genius and Venetian activity made noble and grand,

and whose Italian character, defying for centuries implacable persecutions, still shares the same thrill of patriotism with the Italian people."

The principle proclaimed with reference to Poland, that denationalization based on violence does not create rights, the Premier contends, should be applied to Dalmatia.

Passing to the argument of "cold statistical statements," the Premier affirms that among the national reconstructions occupying the Peace Conference none of the reconstructed nations will count within its frontiers a relatively slighter number of persons of alien race than would be attributed to Italy, and asks why only Italians should be suspected of imperialistic cupidity. The history of the negotiations, he declares, will show that the Italian delegation acted not only with firmness, but with a grand spirit of conciliation.

He concludes his statement as follows:

"The Presidential message ends with a warm declaration of America's friendship for Italy. I reply in the name of the Italian people, and proudly claim the right and honor to do this as one who in the most tragic hour of this war proclaimed the cry of resistance at all costs. This cry was heard and replied to with courage and abnegation of which there are few more striking examples in the world's history.

"Italy, thanks to the most heroic sacrifices and purest blood of her children, was able to ascend from the abyss of misfortune to the radiant crest of most glorious victory. In the name, therefore, of Italy I express with all my power the sentiment of admiration and profound sympathy which the Italian people professes toward the American people."

Premier Orlando and the other members of the Italian delegation apparently are much angrier over President Wilson's worldwide publication of his position on the Adriatic questions than over his opposition to their claims, and they resent what they term his violation of diplomatic procedure and the insult which they feel has been offered to the Italian Government in that the President made his position known to the Italian people over the heads of their peace delegation.

Discussing this contention today, a member of the American peace delegation said:

" 'Fiume or nothing' has been the Italian delegation's unalterable formula for nearly eight weeks, and their insistence upon the settlement of the Adriatic questions before an agreement upon the peace terms forced President Wilson to tell the world where he stood. The atmosphere of the conference simply had to be cleared, and there was no other way for the President to clear it.

"This statement was more for the American public than for the Italian public, and it was of such an unmistakable character that it should not leave any one in the dark as to the American position on secret agreements."

The effort of the Europeans to invoke the rules of diplomatic procedure and the conflicting statements, clouded in obscurity, have been noted by the American delegates and the American correspondents who are endeavoring to obtain the actual facts. The professions of surprise by the Italians at President Wilson's statement are amazing to the correspondents, who have positive knowledge that the statement was submitted to Premier Orlando several days before its publication, and that he sought advice about drafting a reply.

Printed in the *New York Times*, April 25, 1919.

Tasker Howard Bliss to Ignace Jan Paderewski

Your Excellency: Paris, April 24th, 1919.

I beg to state that on the evening of April 18th, immediately after the interview with which you had honored me in my apartments, I communicated to President Wilson the fact that you desired me to say to him that you and your Government accept in principle the suggested armistice and express their cordial desire to meet in every way possible the wishes of the President and of the Council. I also informed him that in execution of this idea you had sent a radio message that morning to the Government in Warsaw requesting it to send a general officer of the Polish Army to Paris as soon as possible in order that with his knowledge of the exact situation as between the Polish and the Ukrainian forces he may arrange the technical details in a way that will be satisfactory to the Polish people.

The President asks me to express to you, in his name and in that of Mr. Lloyd George and Mr. Clemenceau, their united appreciation of the cordial sentiments conveyed by you to them. In this connection he asks, also in his name and that of his colleagues, that I should communicate to you the following.

He and his colleagues express the hope and desire that, the principles of an armistice having been accepted by the Polish Government, a temporary truce preliminary to the permanent armistice be now arranged. If the two contending parties, the Poles and the Ukrainians, are to arrange an armistice here in Paris under the good auspices of the Supreme Council, there seems no reason why the generals in the field should not suspend hostilities and avoid further effusion of blood. With this same object in view, they express the earnest hope that General Haller's divisions which are now en route to Poland be not sent to Lemberg. If you can notify them that this truce has been promptly arranged, they will at once take up the questions relating to the settlement of the disputed frontier and thus make further fighting unnecessary.

I trust that Your Excellency will enable me to communicate your views to the President at an early moment.

With sentiments of the highest respect, I remain

Very sincerely yours, [T. H. Bliss]

CCL (T. H. Bliss Papers, DLC).

A Memorandum by Robert Lansing

THE EXPLOSION OVER FIUME.

April 24, 1919.

The President gave to the press last night his statement on the Italian claims, which he read to the Commissioners on Monday, the 21st, and which we all heartily approved.

The Italians at once "blew up." Orlando leaves for Italy tonight and Sonnino follows him tomorrow. Unless Italy is given Fiume her representatives say they will not sign a treaty with Germany. They are in a fine rage and all Italy will be in a turmoil. What I anticipated at the end of March has come to pass.

The President's statement is excellent. It is well balanced and temperate. The only trouble is that it should have been issued a month ago, and then we would have avoided the embarrassment of having summoned the Germans to Versailles before the Allies were of one mind.

It is hard to preduct [predict] the outcome if the President remains firm as I hope he will.

T MS (R. Lansing Papers, DLC).

From the Diary of Edith Benham

April 24, 1919

I wonder if I have made clear the stages of our negotiations as I have gathered them in from what the P. and Mrs. W. have said. Orlando has wanted to withdraw for some time, in fact, has practically withdrawn since he delivered his ultimatum when he went to the window and sobbed. Saturday Mr. W. went down to the Crillon and consulted with the other members of our Peace Commission to see if they could suggest anything else, and none of them could suggest anything else. Then Mr. W. withdrew so that Clemenceau and L. George should confer with Orlando and Sonnino and see if they could arrive at any solution. Mr. W. prepared a statement for Orlando to read before parliament if he wanted to make a frank statement before the Italian people, but he decided—Orlando did—not to do this. The situation, of course, is very tense. The Echo de Paris has the nastiest article in it about Americans and the P. so I suppose that is one of the papers the French have bought up.

After luncheon: The house is just as tense today as it was the day before war was declared at home. At luncheon Hoover came in to say Mr. Kerr, Mr. Balfour's Secretary, was there and he wanted to know if the P. would come to Mr. L. George's apartment, as they looked on that as neutral territory and would prefer going there to coming here. The P. said "What children!"

He went out, saw Mr. Kerr and came back with a statement Mr. Balfour had written for the press. Of that he read a few extracts, but it will all probably be out in the papers. L.G. and Clemenceau are both saying they thought the P.'s statement all right, but premature, yet privately they had said that now was the time for it to be published. The P. remarked today he wished he had a less slippery customer to deal with than L.G. for he is always for temporizing and making concessions. He said he was praying the Italians would not invoke the pact of London, made after Italy came into the war that they could not make peace separately, for in that event Italy had them absolutely, that she could prevent everything, League of Nations, all they had worked for, as the British and French felt they must stand by the pact. He said it was for the British to decide if they would stand with Italy or the United States.

Later: After luncheon he saw Paderewski, and then at four had his appointment across the street. About 3:30 Col. House came up and saw Mrs. W. and told her to be sure to have a stenographer to go along with the P. as the others had such persons, and he should have every word he took down there put on paper. The P. was busy with some delegations so she sent word to Close (his stenographer). My bedroom windows look across the street on L.G.'s apartment, and there are the Italian cars and their secret service men, Clemenceau's car and his secret service, and our S.S. men with the P. It is absorbingly interesting with the fate of nations and the destiny of the world going on so close at hand. Just now at seven I have watched Orlando come out, and a few newspaper men with cameras waiting; no crowds are allowed, and I have just gone to the window in time to see our P. come out. If he had yielded one thing about Fiume the world would never believe in us or our idealism. On the boulevards and on the streets it is the one thing people are talking about. Sir William Wiseman asked to bring a poet friend, Ian Malcolm,[1] who writes amusing verses, particularly one on the Peace Congress[2] and he, Sir Wm., says it was the one thing to do. I invited Mrs. W. to come to tea and we had a very nice time. It was good to have the strain of the afternoon relieved a little.

T MS (Edith Benham Helm Papers, DLC).

[1] Ian Zachary Malcolm, M.P., former diplomat and Red Cross officer, at this time secretary to A. J. Balfour.

[2] "The 'Peace' Congress," printed in Ian Zachary Malcolm, . . . *Stuff—and Nonsense: A Book of War Verses* (London, New York, Toronto, 1919), pp. 89-91.

From the Diary of Colonel House

April 24, 1919.

Mrs. Wilson called up last night and said the President would like to know whether I had heard anything further about the Italians. I had not, but a little later I did hear that they were getting ready to leave Paris at two o'clock today. I did not tell the President because he was so tired and so worried and I wanted him to be undisturbed for the night.

I have been at the Italian matter all day. Wiseman and others have been the go-betweens. I myself went to see the President, but he was closeted with Clemenceau and I had a talk with Mrs. Wilson instead and gave her some messages for the President. I am constantly afraid the President will isolate himself when there is no need of his doing so. The situation is so delicate and frought with so much peril that it is needful to watch each step. This is not a time to do things in a casual way. Every move should be carefully throught [thought] out and nothing done without a good reason.

To Joseph Patrick Tumulty

Paris, 24 April, 1919.

Thank you for your cable about the Industrial Board.[1] On the whole I think they have got into a blind alley but I am glad you are going to obtain Mr. Hines' opinion. Do not give yourself any concern about secret treaties. You may be sure I will enter into none.[2]

Please give McAdoo and Mrs. McAdoo my love and thank them for the message just received from them by cable.[3]

Woodrow Wilson.

T telegram (WP, DLC).

[1] See JPT to WW, April 22, 1919 (first telegram of that date), Vol. 57.

[2] Tumulty, on April 24, issued the following statement to the press: "In view of the fact that certain newspapers of wide circulation throughout the country have intimated that the President had entered into a secret alliance or treaty with some of the Great Powers, I conveyed this information to the President and am today in receipt of a cablegram from him giving positive and unqualified denial to this story." CC MS (J. P. Tumulty Papers, DLC).

[3] WGM to WW, April 21, 1919, CC telegram (WP, DLC). The significant portion of the telegram reads as follows: "Have just returned from Pacific Coast. Made twenty speeches from rear platform of car along railroad between coast and Mississippi discussing League of Nations in each speech. Found the people overwhelmingly for a League especially if amended as reported in recent publications here. Am sure country is with you and hope you will make speeches throughout West on your return."

Two Telegrams from Joseph Patrick Tumulty

[The White House] April 24; 10 A.M.

No. 73. At seven o'clock this morning I read your statement. I have not been able to gather the comments of the country with reference to the attitude you have taken, but am sure the country and the world will respond in the most enthusiastic manner. The position you have taken is unassailable and I hope you will not yield in the slightest way. You have put the nations of the world to a great test of their character and integrity. Let the nations who believe in secret treaties follow Italy. The people of the world will back you up.

This is your supreme hour and I have never been so proud of you.

Temporarily, in our country, your attitude, with the consequences that may ensue, will shock, but when they realize that you are fighting for open covenants and against secret treaties, they will rally to your standard. Tumulty.

[The White House] April 24; 2 P.M.

No. 74 As we see it from this distance, the selfish designs of Japan are as indefensible as are those of Italy. The two situations appear to parallel each other in their bearing upon the fate of weak and helpless nations. Would it not be an opportune time to cast another die, this one in the direction of Japan that the whole world may know once and for all where America stands upon this the greatest issue of the peace we are trying to make? Now is the time to use your heavy artillery and emphasize the danger of secret treaties and selfish designs of certain big nations. Tumulty.

T telegrams (WP, DLC).

From Albert Sidney Burleson

[The White House] April 24, 1919.

No. 76 Following from the Postmaster General:

"Information involving no reflection on any person connected with the Wire Administration or the conduct of the service has reached me that convinces me that it is imperative in the public interest that cable lines be returned to their respective owners at a date not later than May tenth. I recommend that you authorize me as Postmaster General to announce at once that necessity for further control having passed, the cable lines will be returned as soon as steps to accomplish this can be taken. It will be necessary to prepare a proclamation for your signature which I will take steps to have done through the Attorney General and cable same to you as soon as I have a reply to this cablegram. This recommendation is made after conference with former Attorney General Gregory who concurs in same and urges that prompt action be taken. Full details of reasons will be given you upon your return and I know they will have your approval. Please reply at once." Tumulty.

T telegram (WP, DLC).

From Walker Downer Hines

Dear Mr. President: San Francisco, April 24, 1919.

In the course of your voyage from France to the United States last February you read a draft of the statement I had prepared for the Senate Committee on Interstate Commerce.[1]

In that statement I made the following points with reference to the problem of a permanent solution of the railroad question:

1. That the public and labor suspect that there is serious over-capitalization of the railroad companies and that to perpetuate existing capitalization will amount to perpetuating suspicion and unrest and will defeat any plan despite the other good qualities the plan may have.

2. That no plan can be permanently successful that leaves railroad operations with a large number of railroad corporations, some strong and some weak. There are about 180 railroad companies having gross earnings of $1,000,000 or more per year and there are several hundred railroad companies having smaller earnings. They present every degree of prosperity and adversity.

[1] This draft statement was sent as an enclosure with W. D. Hines to WW, Jan. 31, 1919, TLS (WP, DLC), cited in n. 1 to W. D. Hines to WW, Feb. 24, 1919, Vol. 55 (first letter of that date). The Enclosure printed with the latter document covers much of the same ground.

3. That if any plan of private management is to be successful it ought to provide for the participation of the Government and perhaps of labor in the profits in excess of some comparatively moderate return, so as to prevent the public and labor from fearing that the public interests are being exploited for the benefit of private capital.

4. That definiteness ought to be given to the doctrine that the railroads shall have a fair return and no more through the giving of a direct Government guaranty, with a provision for participation in the excess profits, to the end that with much less aggregate burden in the way of freight and passenger charges, there may be adequate certainty so as to attract the capital needed in order to accomplish the necessary railroad development.

When you were in Washington you discussed this matter briefly with me. You indicated that any successful solution must be really constructive through making adequate provision for the attraction of the great volume of additional capital which would be needed to develop the railroads so as to care for the vast additional development of the country's business, and I promised to write you further such suggestions as I could make as to the solution which would best accomplish this purpose.

I enclose memorandum which I have prepared and which presents the suggestions which I believe will best meet the necessities of the case, including the fulfillment of the requirement you emphasized as to the attraction of the necessary capital.[2]

[2] W. D. Hines, memorandum, April 23, 1919, TS MS (WP, DLC). Hines first set forth the arguments against permanent governmental ownership and operation of the American railway system. It would be too expensive, would drive the best railroad officials into other occupations, would lead to political interference in the running of the railroads, especially by Congress, and would create problems with the powerful and well-organized railway labor unions. Above all, the American public not only wanted to see competition restored in railroad service but had "the most violent hostility . . . to Government ownership of railroads or anything else."

Hines then listed the objections to continuing the prewar system of public regulation but private management of the railroads. "The all-embracing objection," he declared, "is that the old system did not afford sufficient certainty and assurance to attract the sorely needed large volume of new capital into investment in the railroads." The old system left both shippers and labor continually dissatisfied with established rates and wages. The strong railroads benefited too much from any rate and wage structure, while the weak ones benefited too little. Moreover, there was "no adequate provision for appropriating to the benefit of the public or to the benefit of public and labor any due proportion of the excess profits which may be realized in the case of fortunately situated railroads and in the case of nearly all railroads in good years."

"The practical solution," Hines decided, "appears to be private management combined with a Government guarantee of a moderate return and a division of the profits in excess of that return." Under this plan, the railroads would be returned to the management of private corporations, subject to "strict regulation both as to rates and service and including regulation of security issues." The profits in excess of the governmental guarantee (the amount of which was not specified in the plan) would be divided either between the government and stockholders or among the government, stockholders, and labor. Hines also suggested that the railroads of the country be consolidated into "a comparatively few systems, say for example from twelve to twenty." In this way, rates could be made uniform for all systems. The consolidated systems should be competitive throughout the var-

So far there has been no crystallization of view on the part of the public. There has been a strong tendency to assume that mere non-essential changes in the old form of regulation would suffice. A Special Committee of the Chamber of Commerce of the United States has been giving careful study to the subject and is continuing its deliberations. I have taken several occasions to impress upon this Committee the view that nothing short of radical changes which will deal with the fundamentals I have indicated can solve the problem. I am to address the Annual Convention of the Chamber of Commerce on this subject at St. Louis a week from today.

Feeling that it was highly important to stimulate thought on the subject I have availed myself of such opportunities as presented to emphasize the thoughts set forth in those portions of the attached memorandum dealing with the objections to the return to the old regulation and the necessity for having a radically improved form of regulation. I have suggested as illustrative of what this form ought to be the plan outlined in the memorandum of private management through a form of consolidated competitive corporations with a moderate Government guaranty and a division of the excess profits, with Government representation on the Boards of Directors, such Government representatives to be a portion of the governmental regulating body. I have stated in these various talks that personally I believe it is advisable to retain the advantages of private management and private initiative under the strict form of regulation I have proposed, but I have not dwelt upon any arguments against Government ownership. I have felt this would serve no useful purpose because for the time being the feeling is so nearly unanimous against Government ownership and I did not wish to elaborate any argument which might be inconsistent with the views you may form on the subject. In all of these talks I have made it clear that I was not authorized to speak for you but that I was putting forward my own views simply in order to illustrate the difficulties and to serve as a basis for discussion. In all my talks I have made it plain both at the beginning and at the conclusion that my sole function as Director

---

ious regions of the country, and no one system should have a monopoly within a particular region. Another desirable, although not essential, feature of Hines' plan was to have "government Directors" on the boards of the various railroads and for some of these governmental directors to be members of the federal regulating body. The best mechanism Hines could see for solving labor problems was the creation of a bipartisan board, or boards, made up equally of representatives of labor and management. He believed that in most cases such a board would be able to reach agreement. If both sides were equally represented, then "there would be little that could be done except to have the bi-partisan Board submit all the facts to the public." Another difficult problem would be the jurisdiction of the states in railroad matters. Hines suggested that the states should have jurisdiction in intrastate matters, but that the federal regulating body should have the final decision in such matters if, in its opinion, the national interest was not served if such federal control was not exercised.

General was to do all in my power during the temporary period of Federal control to provide an adequate and satisfactory public service just as far as it was reasonably practicable under the difficult conditions of the readjustment period. I have put forward these ideas at Pittsburgh, Chicago (on three different occasions), Atlanta, St. Paul, Spokane, Seattle, Tacoma and Portland, Ore., and in the present week expect to develop the same thoughts at San Francisco, Los Angeles, Denver, Topeka and Kansas City, prior to my talk to the Chamber of Commerce of the United States at St. Louis on the 30th instant.

In my judgment these talks are aiding in stimulating public thought on the subject, but the whole question is still in a highly nebulous state.

Senator Cummins[3] will, I understand, be the Chairman of the Senate Committee on Interstate Commerce. For many years he has given more attention to railroad problems than any other man in the Senate. He has pronounced views in support of the general principles indicated in the attached memorandum, although I am not advised as to the character of legislation he has in mind for effectuating these principles. By reason of his expert knowledge and his position in the Senate I believe he will be a highly important factor in accomplishing a solution. He indicates he is most anxious to press the matter to the earliest possible conclusion along these lines.

As far as I can learn the dissatisfaction with the service rendered by the railroads under Federal control is gradually diminishing as we are able, by reason of the disappearance of war conditions, to eliminate some of the war inconveniences. The momentum which the dissatisfaction obtained, however, during the war still carries the criticism forward to a considerable extent. At present there is more of a disposition to stress the heavy costs which have developed under Federal operation, but I believe by degrees I will succeed in impressing upon the public the view that these costs were not due to Federal control but were due to the war and relatively are less heavy than increased costs in other industrial enterprises which remained under private control. For the time being our operations are exceedingly unsatisfactory and we are falling far short of earning the guaranteed rental, but this is unavoidable during the period of readjustment through which we are going at present. I hope on your return to be able to give you a clear statement of the conditions as they then existed and as they appear in prospect. The relations of the Railroad Administration with labor appear to be fairly satisfactory and I believe the representatives of labor, generally speaking, have confi-

[3] Albert Baird Cummins, Republican of Iowa.

dence in the purpose of the Administration to accord just treatment.

It seems to me that from all angles it would be extremely helpful if the Congress would settle upon a permanent policy for the railroads, during the extra session, which I understand you contemplate calling. Otherwise a great cause of doubt and hesitation will be prolonged into, and perhaps throughout, 1920. For example, railroad improvements are not likely to be resumed upon a proper scale until a solution can be decided upon. Hence I think that whatever tends to assist in crystallizing the thought of the people and of the Congress in favor of an early solution is clearly in the public interest.

I need not add that anything which you may deem it wise to say upon the subject would have more effect toward crystallizing this sentiment than anything else that could be done, and I therefore take the liberty of suggesting that in my opinion it would prove very beneficial for you to discuss the subject in a message to the Congress as soon as possible after the extra session convenes, laying particular stress on the urgency of prompt consideration of the entire question, and of the great importance (if you agree with this view) of dealing with the problem in a drastic and radical way rather than by statutory amendments which are not fundamental. In my opinion a statement of this kind from you would immediately center the attention of the entire country on the problem and bring about a discussion both in and out of the Congress which would prove highly beneficial. I think this is particularly important, if you decide to adopt the recommendation which I have already made to you, that you announce that the railroads will be relinquished from the present Federal control on December 31, 1919. If following such announcement of relinquishment you thus urge the importance of a prompt and thorough solution, and if Congress then fails to act during the extra session, the country could hardly hold you and your Administration responsible for any embarrassments arising from the non-passage of remedial legislation.

Faithfully yours, Walker D. Hines.

TLS (WP, DLC).

From the Diary of Dr. Grayson

Friday, April 25, 1919.

The President had breakfast at eight o'clock, and immediately after went to his study. There was no meeting of the Big Three in the morning but the President had a number of engagements, a list of which follows:

A delegation of Slovenes, composed of Bogumil Vosnjak, Dr. Gustave Gregorin and Dr. Ivan Shvegal.[1]

General Cherif Pasha, President of the Kurdish Delegation.[2]

Committee from the Workmen's Organization, "La Wilsonienne"—[3] to present a valuable frame to the President.

Mr. F. W. Taussig, Chairman of the U. S. Tariff Commission.

Mr. H. Wilson Harris,[4] of the London Daily News, to pay respects.

General Bliss.

Mr. B. M. Baruch.

Before the President started with his appointments I went in to see him and he read a telegram which he had received from Secretary Tumulty complimenting the President on the stand he had taken in the Italian situation, and assuring him that the American people would endorse that stand solidly. He also said to me: "I am constantly finding that England and France are bound by numerous secret treaties. Yesterday I found that England had a secret treaty with Japan against China. It seems they bind themselves up without any principle, thinking that they are strengthening themselves all the time. Every few days a new secret treaty seems to turn up. When I question them closely as to why a certain matter cannot be submitted, I am told that it is in conflict with a secret treaty of which nothing was known to the nations not involved. We are now in the midst of being enmeshed in a network of secret treaties. It is quite a proposition to unravel them."

When the committee from the Workmen's Organization, "La Wilsonienne," presented the picture they told the President that they had placed his picture in their society hall because they looked upon him as the great man for justice and for peace and for guidance of all people, including the poor man; they looked upon him as the great man of the world who will do the right thing for all people. Their knowledge of English was quite limited. The President replied and thanked them for the picture and for the honor which they had paid him, and he expressed the hope that he might be instrumental in bringing about a better understanding between employer and employee. In many instances, he said, things go the wrong way between the employer and the employee, and he hoped that in the future they could be gotten closer together and come to a better understanding and cooperate with each other. Both the President and the men seemed touched. As they were leaving they said to the President in English: "*Good night*; you are very dear to the hearts of the working people of France." Before leaving they apologized for appearing in their working clothes, stating that they did not have time to change.

Colonel Tom Birch,[5] the American Minister to Portugal, and a long-time admirer of the President, called after lunch to bid farewell before returning to his post at Lisbon. The Colonel presented a picturesque appearance looking very much like a red rose in full bloom. His extremely florid face was flanked by grey side-burns and was set off by a veritable halo of grey hair. The Colonel wore a sky-blue suit, ox-blood spats, and a tie that matched, and carried a walking stick of unusual size. Altogether, he typified the rich man in American diplomatic life.

The President, Mrs. Wilson and I lunched informally. This afternoon at four o'clock there was a meeting of the Big Three, which took up with the economic experts the economic sections of the Peace Treaty, to be submitted to the German delegates next week. At five o'clock the naval experts headed by Admiral Benson were called in to present their report on the future of the Kiel Canal and on certain sections of Heligoland.

The President, Mrs. Wilson and I had dinner together. After dinner we sat around the fire. I read to the President extracts from editorials and newspaper comments on various international subjects, including the Italian situation. The President remarked that he feared the Italian situation would be only a tempest in a tea-pot compared with the coming controversy with Japan covering the Shantung Province in China. He said: "It worries me a great deal because I discovered today in conversation with Lloyd-George another secret treaty between England and Japan giving Japan another stronghold on China." He discussed the question at length with me, saying that he felt his duty to stand by his principles as laid down in the Fourteen Points, but that he was confronted with a proposition which went against the "grain" of playing worldly wise. He said: "England's secret treaty with Japan would mean that when it came to a show down England would side with Japan. And don't you see what that would mean? If Japan refused to stand by the Fourteen Points it would mean that she would withdraw from the Conference; England might follow, and with Italy already out, it would leave only America and France, which would defeat all the purposes of the Peace Conference, including the League of Nations. Japan has the strategic advantage of now occupying Kiao Chow, which was formerly occupied by the Germans, and if we demanded that she withdraw and she refused, it would mean that we would have to resort to arms. If I only had men of principle to stand by me. For instance, Lloyd-George and Clemenceau absolutely approved of my Italian statement and the stand which I took and today they are straddling the issue. And now when the question arises of England standing with Japan or the United States, owing to these secret treaties, Lloyd-George, I feel sure, would side with Japan. That would leave only America and France—two against three—in the Peace Conference. It is a question of judgment as to what is the best course to pursue. If I follow out the principles of what is just and right it will mean that Japan, Italy and England will not sign the Peace Treaty, and I will have to shoulder the blame for obstructing the peace of the world. It is not that I care personally so much, but the question is what is the best course to pursue for the world in a crisis like this. My only hope is that I can find some outlet to permit the Japanese to save their face and let the League of Nations decide the matter later. It is a matter to which I will have to give profound study and attention between now and the middle of next week. The experts whom I have had study the matter seem only to give me one answer and that is to stand by the principles; but they do not seem to realize what the results might be at this crucial time in the world's history."

The President retired at about 11:00 o'clock.

[1] Vošnjak was Secretary General of the Yugoslav delegation to the peace conference; Ivan Švegelj was a member of the press section of that delegation; and Gustav Gregorin was a member of the Yugoslav Committee, a nationalist organization of exiles with branches in Paris and London.

[2] Cherif (or Sherif) Pasha, formerly an associate of Sultan Abdul Hamid II of Turkey, who had remained in Europe during the war as a sympathizer of the Allies and in early 1919 had founded a "League of Ottoman Liberals" in Geneva to defend Turkish interests. It was widely suspected, both at this time and later, that he had become a self-appointed spokesman for the cause of Kurdish autonomy only in order to limit the boundaries of the new Armenian state and thus preserve more of the old Ottoman dominions under at least nominal Turkish sovereignty. See Richard G. Hovannisian, *The Republic of Armenia* (2 vols. to date, Berkeley and Los Angeles, Calif., 1971-82), II, 443-47.

[3] About which, see GFC to A. H. Frazier, March 22, 1919, Vol. 56.

[4] That is, Henry Wilson Harris.

[5] That is, Thomas Howard Birch.

Hankey's Notes of a Meeting of the Council of Four[1]

President Wilson's Residence,

I.C.-176D. Paris, April 25, 1919, 4 p.m.

1. M. LOUCHEUR said that he and Lord Cunliffe and Mr. Lamont, in accordance with the decision taken the previous day, had interviewed the representatives of Belgium, Serbia, Portugal and Brazil, and had explained to them the reparation clauses. The results of the interview had been set forth in a memorandum which M. Loucheur had prepared, but might be summarised as follows:

Belgium had demanded the costs of the war, provisions as regards certain works of art and certain new categories of damage.

Serbia had demanded to be represented on the Commission and had made some small demand in regard to categories.

[1] The full text of these minutes is printed in *PPC*, V, 229-34.

Brazil had claimed the same treatment as the United States of America in regard to captured enemy ships.

Portugal claimed the costs of the war and reparation for shipping.

All had asked to be heard by the Supreme Council.

M. LOUCHEUR suggested that, as Belgium was the most important, her representatives should be heard separately.

PRESIDENT WILSON thought this was quite right.

MR. LLOYD GEORGE said he had received a letter from Lord Sumner describing the interview which he and some of his colleagues had had with the representatives of Roumania, Greece and Japan. Roumania had said nothing, but had given the impression of being not very contented. Greece had been satisfied. The Japanese representative had been enigmatic and they had not been able to judge of his attitude.

No complaints nor demands had been made. This was a matter that would have to be dealt with by the Supreme Council. In regard to the ships, he had always felt that Brazil would take this attitude.

PRESIDENT WILSON remarked that the difference between the case of Brazil and that of the United States was very great.

2. The Supreme Council had before them the articles prepared by the Economic Commission.

PRESIDENT WILSON said that the differences between the experts were now very few and he proposed that they should only discuss those articles to which his colleagues wished to draw attention.

PRESIDENT WILSON said that one of the points in which the United States of America were especially interested was raised in Part 1, Chapter D, Article 1. Although it was a matter of policy, it did not directly affect the United States of America. The point he wished to raise referred to the limitation to be imposed on the duration of these clauses. What the United States were particularly interested in was a uniform provision as to the length of time for which these articles were to be applicable. They desired an automatic application of a term of 5 years, at the end of which the articles should cease to be operative except under some action by the League of Nations. The alternative proposal was that they should remain operative until they were terminated by some affirmative action by the League of Nations. The United States' view was that they ought to terminate automatically unless renewed.

SIR ROBERT BORDEN said that the discussion at the British Empire Delegation had centered on this point. The general view had been that the articles should be terminated unless renewed by the League of Nations.

PRESIDENT WILSON said this was precisely his view.

MR LLOYD GEORGE asked how the matter stood in the report.

MR. BARUCH said that the articles would continue until terminated by the League of Nations.

M. CLEMENTEL said that there were two classes of articles to be considered. The first class dealt with customs and the second class dealt with the treatment of nationals of Allied and Associated Powers in ex-enemy countries, etc. and shipping. In regard to customs, it had been generally accepted that the provisions should terminate automatically at the end of 5 years, unless renewed by a decision of the League of Nations, which, he remarked, was rather difficult and uncertain, because a unanimous decision was necessary and any one party was at liberty to refuse assent. He asked that it should be remembered what Germany had done not only during the war but before the war. Countries like France, for example, had suffered very much from Germany's action before the war, in her attempts to capture the iron trade; to obtain control of such articles as bauxite in order to get the aluminium trade under control; and in regard to dyestuffs, where she had checked competition. To this must be added what had happened during the war, when prodigious damage had been inflicted by Germany, both of a material and personal character. When this was borne in mind, the difficulty would be realised for peoples who had so suffered to forget within so short a term as 5 years. If the provisions came to an end at the end of 5 years, those countries would be obliged to receive the Germans in the same position as before the war. If they refused, they would, of course, be exposed to reciprocal treatment by Germany. It had been suggested that the invaded countries should receive separate treatment, and that the provisions should continue automatically unless stopped.

PRESIDENT WILSON said that M. Clementel's argument proved too much. If the League of Nations could not extend the period because it would not be able to reach a unanimous decision, it would equally be unable for the same reason to terminate the operation of the provisions. He, himself, thought that it was a mistake to suppose that the League of Nations would not be able to reach unanimity.

M. CLEMENTEL said that it was realised that the system could not be permanent. What was proposed was a maximum period within which the provisions should operate. The first proposal was for 20 years. Now, however, this had been reduced to 10 years. Five years was, in his opinion, too short a period. The result of fixing only 5 years would be that France would have to shut the Germans out, in which case they would receive reciprocal treatment in Germany.

M. CLEMENCEAU said that he would accept the demand for 10 years as a maximum for countries that had been ravaged.

M. BARUCH said that the United States Delegates on the Commission had thought five years too long. He hoped, therefore, that five years would be accepted as the maximum unless the League of Nations decided to prolong it. His personal view was that five years was too long.

M. CLEMENCEAU said that it should be taken into account that the different nations had not been affected during the War in the same manner. In France damage had been done which would be perceptible for more than a century. Nations which had taken part in the War and had not been exposed to the same terrible suffering as France naturally had not the same mentality as a country which could not be completely repaired for more than a century. In his view, five years might be adopted for all countries but a special provision should be made for countries like France which were in a different position.

SIR ROBERT BORDEN suggested that the five years which had already been fixed should be adopted as a minimum and ten years should be taken as the maximum period. The League of Nations should have power to appoint a Commission which should, by majority, fix a period for which in particular cases an extension should be granted, such extension not to go beyond a maximum of ten years from the original date.

M. CLEMENCEAU said France would accept that proposal.

MR. LLOYD GEORGE also agreed in the proposal.

PRESIDENT WILSON said that one aspect was constantly in his mind in regard to the whole of the Treaty with Germany. When the German plenipotentiaries came to Versailles they would be representatives of a very unstable Government. Consequently, they would have to scrutinize every item, not merely to say that it was equitable, but also as to whether it could be agreed to without their being unseated. If the present Government were unseated, a weaker Government would take its place. Hence the question had to be studied like a problem of dynamics concerning the action of forces in a body in unstable equilibrium. Any special restrictions on their nationals which they would not meet by corresponding restrictions would place them in difficulties. The Treaty would hit them very hard since it would deprive them of their Mercantile Marine; would affect their international machinery for commerce; would deprive them of their property in other countries; would open their country by compulsion to enterprising citizens of other countries without enabling their enterprising citizens to try and recover their position in foreign countries. He did not think that the fact had been sufficiently faced that Germany could not pay in gold unless she had a balance of trade in her favour. This meant that Germany must establish a greater foreign commerce than she had had before the war if she was to be able to pay. Before the war the balance of trade in Germany's favour had never equalled the amounts which she would now have to pay. If too great a handicap was imposed on Germany's resources we should not be able to get what Germany owed for reparation. Moreover, if the business world realised that this was the case the securities on which the payment of reparation would depend would have no value. If this reasoning was sound it provided a formidable argument. He only looked towards reaching a peace and in doing so putting Germany in the position to build up a commerce which would enable her to pay what she ought to pay in order to make good the robbery and destruction she had perpetrated. But if the robber was to be in such a position that he could not pay, the penalties would be inoperative. These penalties ought to be operative and real. We ought to see that Germany could put herself in a position where she could be punished. At the present time we were sending food to Germany but she would not be able to pay for that for more than about two months.

M. CLEMENTEL said he thought there was some misunderstanding. There was perfect agreement as far as customs clauses were concerned, namely, that they should terminate at the end of five years or that at the end of four years the League of Nations should consider whether there was to be any extension. As regards persons it was not desirable from Germany's point of view that it should be automatically terminated too soon, as if it were, Germans in countries like France would be exposed to violence. He would be quite satisfied if Sir Robert Borden's proposal were adopted. The countries concerned would then have a right to state before the Commission set up by the League of Nations whether public opinion would enable them to terminate the provisions at the end of five years or would render it desirable to extend the term of their operation. Nothing would be gained by Germany by unduly shortening the period. In accepting Sir Robert Borden's proposal France was making a considerable concession when it was remembered that 20 years had been the period originally proposed.

PRESIDENT WILSON said he did not much like Sir Robert Borden's proposal and he thought it was a mistake. He thought it would be quite safe to decide that the provisions should terminate in five years unless continued by the League of Nations. He would point out that the term used should either be "Council of the League" or "Body of Delegates."

MR. LLOYD GEORGE said that this was the case.

PRESIDENT WILSON said that he wanted in every possible case to yield to the desire of his French colleagues. He realised to the full the position of the French Government and people and the suffering which France had undergone. Although it was a serious matter for the treaty as a whole, therefore, he would accept Sir Robert Borden's suggestion but he urged that the clauses should be very precisely drawn.

SIR ROBERT BORDEN said he would be glad to cooperate with the Drafting Committee.

Sir Robert Borden's proposal was accepted, namely that the period during which the provisions should apply should be fixed at five years unless extended by the League of Nations. The maximum period to which the extension could be made should be ten years from the original date. The League of Nations should by majority vote set up a Commission which by majority vote should decide the length of any extension within the total period of ten years.

The Drafting Committee of the Commission should formulate the necessary amendments to be forwarded to the Drafting Committee of the Peace Conference.

PRESIDENT WILSON asked Dr. Taussig to explain points which arose on these clauses.

DR. TAUSSIG illustrated the point raised by this Article in the following manner: Supposing a German subject possessed property in Italy, the Article provided that such property could be utilised towards the payment of amounts due to subjects of the Allied or Associated Powers in regard to property which they had in German territory. The question was whether, in the event of there being a surplus on the German property, it could be used to make good debts owed to Allied and Associated subjects in Austria or other enemy territory. The Italian Delegation had taken the view that it could be so used, but the United States Delegation had reserved their adhesion.

MR. LLOYD GEORGE said he agreed with the Italian view. The principle of joint liability by enemy powers had been accepted in regard to reparation, and he thought it would be difficult to avoid applying the principle here also.

SIR HUBERT LLEWELYN SMITH pointed out that compensation to the enemy subjects in such case was provided for, but would have to be paid by the enemy Government concerned.

PRESIDENT WILSON said he did not much like the Article, but he would not press his objections.

(The Article was accepted.)

(It was agreed that the foot-note should be deleted.)

Sir Maurice Hankey was instructed to forward the Report of the Economic Commission to the Secretary General for communication to the Drafting Committee of the Preliminary Peace Conference as soon as the expert Drafting Committee had completed the necessary alterations in the Articles.

T MS (SDR, RG 256, 180.03401/119, DNA).

From the Peace Conference Diary of Bernard Mannes Baruch

April 25th, 1919.

The work of the Economic Commission was brought up at the President's house first at 2:15 P.M. Accompanying me were Messrs. Lamont, Taussig, and Bradley Palmer.[1] The whole subject was briefly brought to the attention of the President, the various points of difference being referred to. I explained to him those questions which would appear to be unnecessary, such as the strictures placed upon Germany, which were not reciprocal until after five years, particularly those which remain operative unless the League of Nations acts. A compromise regarding the last question was reached by making them operative unless the League of Nations acts, but with the proviso that a majority of the League could act, and that they should continue no longer than ten years. Also the matter of regional appel[l]ation which was objectionable but on which the French were very insistent & which it appeared was agreed to in principle between Portugal & Germany.

An agreement was reached that all monies now in the hands of the Alien Enemy Custodian should remain in the hands of Congress in order that Congress might do whatever it was decided was wise and proper to do with these monies. My understanding was that no strictures would be placed upon Congress.

This was all agreed to in the meeting which took place at 4:00 o'clock in the President's house, at which were present besides the President Messrs. Lamont, Taussig, Bradley Palmer, Chandler Anderson[2] and myself; Mr. Lloyd George, Sir Hubert Llewellyn Smith, Sir Robert Borden, Monsieur Clemenceau, Monsieur Loucheur, and Monsieur Clementel.

It was further agreed that the financial clause should be the one adopted by the Financial Commission, and Mr. Lamont was requested to see that it was put in.

I drew Mr. Lamont's attention to the extreme care with which he should look into the work of the Reparations Commission, in order that nothing there should conflict with our action in regard to leaving free the hands of Congress to dispose of the funds of the Alien Property Custodian and other monies that might be placed at its disposition. The President asked Mr. Lamont what he thought of Mr.

Keynes' proposal. Mr. Lamont did not think it was a good one, but he himself suggested that he would prepare a statement in conjunction with Messrs. McCormick, Davis and Baruch to bring to the attention of the President.

I informed the President that he had already approved of a committee composed of two representatives of France, Great Britain and the United States to look into general economic conditions. Mr. Lamont suggested that that was not necessary, and that it should not be undertaken. I was surprised to find Mr. Lamont taking the position which he did, because both he and Mr. Davis had previously told me that the United States should take no part in the financial discussions at this time; that they were sure the Treasury would be opposed to it, and that the United States should be kept entirely free from such discussions.

On further discussing the matter with Mr. Lamont, he said that I had not understood it, as what he wanted to do was something quite different from what he had talked about; but I felt sure that such was not the case, and I stated to him the embarrassment that had been caused by getting the President to take the position that he had taken.

Later on I called up Mr. Davis and told him of my astonishment at the action of his associate, and he told me that I had not understood it, and that he himself was surprised, because he had not consulted with Mr. Lamont concerning it.

It looks to me as if the keen disappointment they both felt in the matter having been discussed by others than themselves had led them to undertake the very thing which they had said should not be undertaken.

I am fearful in having the United States Government tied up even in any indirect way in the reparation that is to be paid by Germany, because of the disappointment that some day may come to the people of the world in not receiving as much money as had been indicated by the Reparations Commission's report.

Before taking this subject—Economic Com. report—up with the President, I had received the full approval of Messrs. Taussig, Young, Anderson, Nielsen, Pennie, Brown, Summers and Legge[3] of all the clauses, with certain exceptions which were finally adopted and approved by them.

[1] Bradley Webster Palmer, at this time a technical adviser on economic and commercial questions in the American delegation.

[2] Chandler Parsons Anderson, at this time in France as counsel for the Red Cross in organizing the League of Red Cross Societies. Baruch and others were consulting him informally about proposed economic clauses of the peace treaty. See C. P. Anderson to the Editor, the *New York Times*, Nov. 29, 1921.

[3] Those not previously identified in this series were Fred Kenelm Nielsen, Assistant Solicitor for the Department of State and a technical adviser for economic and commercial

questions in the A.C.N.P.; John C. Pennie, lawyer of New York and a technical adviser on patent law; and Jo Baily Brown, lawyer of Pittsburgh and a technical adviser on industrial property, patents, trade marks, and copyrights.

From the Diary of Vance Criswell McCormick

April 25 (Friday) [1919]

Papers still full of the Italian fracas. The President has called their bluff in good style. They can gain nothing by holding out. Looks to me as though their game is to save their Ministry by grandstand play and throw the responsibility on the Allies if they fail, which they will do. . . .

We are at a great disadvantage here in regard to publicity. French papers under strictest censorship and Government control and are antagonistic to the President whenever their Government wants to pass the buck. Paris-New York Herald, a rotten anti-Wilson sheet, evidently carrying on a distinct propaganda to embarrass the President. Chief is holding his own in great shape, has himself well in hand. Knows what he wants and is going to get it, in my opinion.

All advisers busy today discussing new financial scheme of British to consolidate debt and have all Allies guarantee interest and principal. That means the United States would guarantee all the bankrupt nations. The more the plan is studied the less enthusiastic our people become. It is the same old game they have been working on all through the conference, to get the United States to underwrite their debts. We will have to help but I don't believe in quite that way.

From the Peace Conference Diary of Thomas William Lamont

Friday 25th [April]

Lunch w. Monet[1] at Crillon re Keynes' bond proposal. At 2.15 Prest's w. BMB Taussig & Palmer re Econ. Comn. Report. Re the 5 yr clauses etc. At 4 to Big 3 with same crowd. I sat at left of Pres't & he pd me more attention than BMB. He decided to yield on 5 yr question of reciprocal treatment of nationals & also on question of taking, say Austrian money for German private debts. On Question #1 it was 5-10 yr compromise offered by Sir Rob't Borden. Then W.W. made quite a long declaration in wh. he explained again that he tho't it unwise to carry out these provisions wh. meant impairment of Germany's ability to pay reparation, but he "could not bear to turn down his French colleagues who had suffered so much."

Loucheur presented briefly report of our little subcomn on smaller nations on reparation.

At first interview earlier in day W.W. asked me if I had read Keynes' memo. re bonds. I said yes, it was impracticable. He wished I would prepare some constructive suggestion along American lines. I asked him if he was convinced that U.S.A. *must* help the small nations—must help the European situation & he said *yes*. To me this is very significant. We must get him to make a statement. L-G may be able to help in this.

[1] That is, Jean Omer Marie Gabriel Monnet.

Hankey's Notes of a Meeting of the Council of Four[1]

President Wilson's Residence,
I.C.-176E. Paris, April 25, 1919, 5:30 p.m.

The Supreme Council had before it the draft of articles concerning the Kiel Canal for insertion in the Preliminary Treaty of Peace with Germany. (Appendix.)[2]

MR. LLOYD GEORGE pointed out that the French and Italian Delegates had put forward a proposal for the destruction of the fortifications of the Kiel Canal. He understood that the subject of fortifications was dealt with in the Naval Terms, which only permitted Germany to retain works of a defensive nature. The result of the application of this principle was that no works of defence would be allowed at the Kiel end of the Canal, because these would have an offensive character since they would threaten the entrances to the Baltic.

ADMIRAL BENSON said that the object in prohibiting these defensive works at the Kiel end was not connected with the Kiel Canal at all, but was to prevent interference with the natural waterway into the Baltic.

MR. LLOYD GEORGE pointed out that against the proposal to destroy the defensive measures at the Elbe end of the Canal was the argument that in 15 minutes the Canal could be rendered unnavigable by dropping mines in it.

ADMIRAL DE BON said the reason for which the French and Italian Admirals had proposed the destruction of the defences at the Elbe end of the Canal was because, if the navigation of the Kiel Canal was to be free at all, it must be absolutely free. As regards the argument that the Canal could be rendered unnavigable by laying mines, he

[1] The complete text of these minutes is printed in *PPC*, V, 235-43.

[2] An identic copy of this Appendix is printed as Appendix I to the minutes of the Council of Four, April 24, 1919, 11 a.m.

pointed out that by doing so the Germans would deprive themselves of the use of the Canal. Nothing could suit us better than that. The Kiel Canal doubled the efficiency of the German Fleet, and if they deprived themselves of it, nothing could be better. From a commercial point of view, the traffic through the Kiel Canal might become very important. It was capable of carrying 11,000,000 tons a year, and might become as important a waterway as the Belts.[3] As regards the argument which had been used in informal conversation while the Council was assembling, that fortifications could be rapidly improvised, this was equally true as regards the Belts. Fortifications could be improvised here also. Hence, there was no argument in regard to the Belts that could not be equally applied to the Elbe.

MR. LLOYD GEORGE said that in the Naval Terms it had been decided that Germany should be in a position to defend her ports against the enemy. We could not deprive the Kiel Canal of its fortifications without leaving the Elbe unfortified.

ADMIRAL BENSON raised the question of the removal of the fortifications at the Kiel end. He was inclined to question whether we were not going too far. This would leave a large part of the Baltic coast totally undefended. The British representative had suggested that Germany might be allowed some fortification at the Kiel end of the Canal. The general principle to which we were working was that natural waterways should not be fortified. There should be free communication through them both in Peace and in War. It had been decided to remove the defences at the Kiel end because the range of modern guns placed to command the approaches to the Belts happened to take in the Kiel Canal and Baltic Coast of Germany.

MR. LLOYD GEORGE said he hoped the French Delegation would not press for the inclusion of this Article.

PRESIDENT WILSON said that as a matter of fact the provisions it was proposed to impose for the Kiel Canal were practically identical with the United States arrangements for the Panama Canal, which had been arranged between the United States of America and Great Britain. These provisions were based on the principle of the Canal being available for use on the same terms by ships of all countries, except in time of war. The Panama Canal, however, was very vulnerable to attack, and provision had had to be made for its defence. Consequently, it had been very heavily fortified.

M. CLEMENCEAU pointed out that the Suez Canal had no fortifications, and these were prohibited.

ADMIRAL HOPE pointed out that we could not use the Canal if we were at war with Germany.

[3] That is, the Great Belt and the Little Belt, straits in Denmark connecting the Kattegat and the Baltic Sea.

ADMIRAL BENSON said that nothing could suit the enemy better than to get ships into the Canal in the event of war, and then to block them in there.

M. CLEMENCEAU said that Admiral de Bon's point was that such arrangements ought to be made that if we could not use the Kiel Canal in time of war, neither should Germany be able to.

PRESIDENT WILSON pointed out that the Kiel Canal was entirely within German territory and sovereignty. This was not true of the Suez Canal, which was not in the body of any single country.

ADMIRAL BENSON said that his feeling was very strong that it was a mistake to touch the Kiel Canal at all. It established a precedent of a very dubious character. If it was regarded as a purely punitive measure, then he would have nothing to say. But to go into a country and make special provision for a Canal was very similar to going in and taking its railways. The Kiel Canal had been a German national enterprise, and was no concern of the outside world.

ADMIRAL HOPE pointed out that we had Bismarck's declaration that the Kiel Canal had been built solely for strategic purposes. It was for this reason that Admiral de Bon went so far as to say it ought to be destroyed. In these provisions, however, Germany had been treated more leniently.

PRESIDENT WILSON said the Canal had some commercial importance.

ADMIRAL HOPE said that this was not great. The greatest distance saved between the nearest Dutch port and the nearest Baltic port was only 200 miles as compared with the route through the Belts.

ADMIRAL DE BON pointed out a certain inconsistency between our attitude with regard to the Kiel Canal and the other provisions that had been made for internationalising the course of the Elbe and many other waterways. If these waterways were to be internationalised, why not the Kiel Canal also? Surely it ought to be on the same basis?

(It was decided to omit Article 8.)

Article 7.

MR. LLOYD GEORGE asked whether it was worth while setting up an International Commission to control a purely German Canal. This Canal had no very great value from a commercial point of view. Most ships would still prefer to use the Belts, and only a few ships trafficking between Dutch and Baltic ports were likely to use the Canal. The reason for this was that there were no dues in the Belts, and there must be dues in the Canal. He asked if it was worth while to hurt German pride and add to our own difficulties for so small a matter.

M. CLEMENCEAU agreed that it was not, and withdrew the French draft of Article 7.

(The British, American, Japanese and Italian proposal for Article 7 (Appendix), was adopted.[4])

Naval, Military and Air Terms. Reserve Clauses. Article 25.[5]
Sinking of Surface Ships.

2. ADMIRAL HOPE said that the first question raised was as to whether surface ships enumerated in the Article were to be sunk.

PRESIDENT WILSON asked whether after these ships had been handed over, Germany would retain any surface ships.

ADMIRAL HOPE replied that they would.

ADMIRAL BENSON considered that too much was at stake to settle this Article in a hurry. He pointed out that the ships now lying in the British Port of Scapa Flow had not been surrendered but were merely interned.

ADMIRAL HOPE pointed out that by Article 24, the ships interned in compliance with the Armistice were to be definitely surrendered. This Article had already been accepted.

ADMIRAL BENSON pressed that the disposal of the surface ships should be definitely dealt with in the Peace Terms. What, he asked, would happen if it had not been decided before the Peace Terms were signed, what should be done with these ships now in German ports. Were the British or French Navies prepared to take them into British and French ports, and look after them? To decide this question now would ease the situation as far as Germany was concerned. To leave it unsettled was to risk misunderstandings.

MR. LLOYD GEORGE suggested that no prolonged discussion on this should be embarked on, as there were still many questions to be settled before the Germans arrive at Versailles. A discussion on this point might last a day or two. In the meanwhile, he proposed that the terms should simply state that the ships were to be surrendered to the Allied and Associated Powers. He was desirous of reaching some arrangement; for example, it might be agreed to sink some of the German ships.

PRESIDENT WILSON suggested that a promise might be given to Germany that a decision would be reached on the subject before the Treaty of Peace was actually signed. The question could be discussed while the Peace Treaty was being examined by the Germans.

[4] These drafts are printed in Appendix I, Article 7, to the minutes of the Council of Four, April 24, 1919, 11 a.m.

[5] The proposed naval terms of the treaty are included in the minutes of the Supreme War Council printed at March 17, 1919, Vol. 56.

ADMIRAL BENSON asked what would happen if a decision had not been reached.

PRESIDENT WILSON said his proposal was to say definitely that a decision would be reached, and then it would have to be reached.

ADMIRAL BENSON pointed out that any decision, except to sink the ships, meant an increase of armaments.

MR. LLOYD GEORGE said he could give Admiral Benson his proposal for stopping the increase of armaments, and even bring about a decrease, but he doubted if the Admiral would accept it. The British Government did not want these ships and were ready to discuss even the decrease of Navies, provided all would agree. This, however, was a very big question.

PRESIDENT WILSON said he understood the French had made a reservation in regard to this Article. He asked for the reason.

ADMIRAL DE BON said the reason was, first, that by sinking the ships, valuable property would be destroyed, and there would be an increase in the general losses of the war. French public opinion was strongly against this. A more especial reason was, however, that if the ships were divided among the Allied and Associated Powers, it would make a considerable addition, perhaps not of great fighting value, but nevertheless, a useful addition to the peace strength of the French Navy. During five years, owing to the immense efforts of French industries in supplying the armies, it had not been possible to complete any capital ships. These ships would be very useful to show the French flag and spread the national influence in the world. France's naval strength was greatly reduced, especially as compared with other nations. For no aggressive desires of any kind, France did not want to lose this opportunity for repairing her losses.

MR. LLOYD GEORGE said that Admiral de Bon was also well aware that the French taxpayer would not be content to pay for more ships. He fully agreed that the French position in this matter ought to be considered. His idea was that France should have some of these ships, and sink a corresponding number of old ships, or if unwilling to sink them, she might break them up, which Admiral Hope told him would be a business proposition.

PRESIDENT WILSON proposed that if the German Peace delegates should raise the question, a promise should be given them that the question would be settled for the signing of the Peace Treaty.

MR. LLOYD GEORGE and M. CLEMENCEAU agreed in this.

(Article 25 as finally revised is as follows:

> Within a period of two months from the coming into force of the present stipulations, the German surface warships enumerated below will be surrendered to Allied and Associated Governments.
>
> These warships will have been disarmed as provided in Article

23 of the Armistice dated the 11th November, 1918. Nevertheless they must have all their guns on board.

Battleships.

Oldenburg.	Posen.
Thüringen.	Westfalen.
Ostfriesland.	Rheinland.
Helgoland.	Nassau.

Light Cruisers.

Stettin.	Strassburg.
Danzig.	Augsburg.
München.	Kolberg.
Lübeck.	Stuttgart.

and, in addition, forty-two modern destroyers and fifty modern torpedo boats, as chosen by the five Allied and Associated Governments.)

Article 28. Destruction of Submarines.

3. ADMIRAL HOPE said that the reserved portion of this Article related to the question of whether surrendered submarines were to be destroyed and broken up.

MR. LLOYD GEORGE asked what objection there was.

ADMIRAL DE BON said it was the same objection as before, namely, the destruction of material.

MR. LLOYD GEORGE demurred to the idea that any nation should add to its submarines.

PRESIDENT WILSON said that he himself was opposed to submarines altogether, and hoped the time would come when they would be contrary to International Law. In his view, they should be regarded as outlaws.

MR. LLOYD GEORGE pointed out that many of the submarines that had been handed over by the Germans had been broken up altogether. A decision to this effect had been taken earlier.

M. CLEMENCEAU said that this had been agreed to, but when he had discovered it, he had intervened.

PRESIDENT WILSON pointed out that M. Clemenceau's objection was to the destruction of material. If the submarines were broken up, the material would not be wasted.

M. CLEMENCEAU asked Admiral de Bon what was his policy towards submarines.

ADMIRAL DE BON said that his policy was to keep the German submarines, of which France had received some 50. France had very few of her own.

MR. LLOYD GEORGE said that he did not think that Navies ought to be strengthened by submarines.

M. CLEMENCEAU said that if ever France had another war with Germany they might be useful, although he hoped long before that they would be obsolete.

MR. LLOYD GEORGE said he would like to destroy all the German submarines.

M. CLEMENCEAU said that France had very few, whereas Great Britain had very many.

ADMIRAL DE BON said the question had never been discussed by experts.

(It was agreed:

1. That the words in the second clause of Article 28 "there to be destroyed or broken up" should be struck out.
2. That the Admirals of the Allied and Associated Powers should further consider the question of the disposal of the German submarines.)

ADMIRAL HOPE suggested that the following words in Article 32, which had been reserved, "such arms, munitions, and war material will be destroyed or rendered useless" should be omitted, as a corresponding article had been inserted in the Military clauses.

(This was agreed to.)

T MS (SDR, RG 256, 180.03401/120, DNA).

A Translation of a Letter from Marquis Kimmochi Saionji to Georges Clemenceau

Mr. President, Paris, April 25, 1919.

The Heads of the Governments of the Great Powers, having already listened to the Delegates of China on the subject of the question of the Province of Chantong [Shantung], I take the liberty of expressing to you, in the name of the Japanese Delegation, the desire that there be called, in the nearest possible future, a new meeting in order to hasten the definite settlement of this question.

On the other hand, in view of the particular gravity for Japan of the question concerned, I would be very grateful, Mr. President, if, as far as possible, you would be kind enough to keep us informed of all the phases of its development.

I beg you to accept, Mr. President, with all my thanks for the action which you will be kind enough to take on this request, the assurances of my highest consideration. (Sgd) Saionji

T MS (WP, DLC).

Hankey's and Mantoux's Notes of a Meeting of the Council of Four[1]

President Wilson's Residence,
I.C.-176-F. Paris, April 25, 1919, 6:30 p.m.

1. M. CLEMENCEAU handed to Mr. Lloyd George a new set of articles concerning the guarantees for the execution of the Peace Treaty with Germany. (Appendix I.) President Wilson, he said, had agreed to these.

MR. LLOYD GEORGE said he considered Clause 2(c) to be a very dangerous one, although he realised M. Clemenceau's difficulties. He undertook to examine the question.

2. SIR MAURICE HANKEY said that Mr. Hurst, the British Representative on the Drafting Committee, had told him that the Drafting Committee was now waiting for more material on which to work. Mr. Hurst had represented to him that a decision in regard to the language of the Peace Treaty was urgently required. In reply to President Wilson, he said that the Italian representative had throughout pressed strongly that Italian, as well as French and English, should be the official languages in the Peace Treaty. On the previous day, however, M. Orlando had stated that he could not say definitely whether Italy would be present at Versailles to meet the Germans. Moreover, Mr. Hurst informed him that the Italian representative had withdrawn from the Drafting Committee and there was no one on that Committee who could put the clauses into Italian. In view of the uncertainty as to whether the Italians would be at Versailles at all; in view of the withdrawal of the Italian representative from the Drafting Committee; and in view of the very short time available for printing and setting up the Peace Treaty, he said the Drafting Committee urgently required a decision.

(It was agreed that the Peace Treaty should be printed in the French and English languages, which should be the official languages of the Treaty.)

3. The Supreme Council had before them the following documents:

A letter from the Marquis Saionji to M. Clemenceau, asking him to press on the settlement of this question. (Appendix II.)[2]

A Report by the Expert Committee appointed by the Supreme Council. (Appendix III.)[3]

A Statement by the Chinese Delegation, (Appendix IV.)[4]

[1] The complete text of Hankey's notes is printed in *PPC*, V, 244-50.
[2] The French version of the preceding document.
[3] It is printed as an Enclosure with E. T. Williams to WW, April 24, 1919.
[4] It is printed as an Enclosure with Lu Cheng-hsiang to WW, April 24, 1919.

PRESIDENT WILSON said that this question was almost as difficult as the Italian question. After calling attention to the reports mentioned above, he asked if the British and French were bound to transfer Kiauchau and Shantung to Japan.

MR. LLOYD GEORGE said that sooner or later they were.

M. CLEMENCEAU agreed.

PRESIDENT WILSON said that, on a previous occasion, Mr. Lloyd George had said that he was in a position to insist in common that, [like] the islands south of the Equator, Kiauchau and Shantung should be transferred in trust to the Allied and Associated Powers.

MR. LLOYD GEORGE said he had discussed the question with Mr. Balfour, who had made a useful suggestion. His suggestion had been that we were bound to transfer the German rights in Shantung and Kiauchau to Japan, but we should like to talk over the terms on which Japan would hand them back to China. That proposal would meet the Japanese sentiments of pride, which compelled them to insist on the transfer of Kiauchau and Shantung to them and not to the Allied and Associated Powers. There was something to be said for Japan in this respect, since the Far East was the only sphere in which Japan was greatly concerned. She was not much concerned in the Western settlement. Then there was a suggestion which had been made by the Chinese and, excepting for their first proposal, Mr. Balfour thought the Japanese might accept it and he thought there was something to be said for starting on that basis.

PRESIDENT WILSON pointed out that the treaty between China and Japan gave to Japan more and not less than Germany had had. In fact, Japan would practically hand back nothing to China. In the meantime, if his information was correct, Japan had gained possession of the foreshore of Kiauchau bay.

MR. LLOYD GEORGE said that we ought to discuss with Japan the conditions on which she would cede the territory to China. Undoubtedly, we should get the conditions which were best for China. He felt that he must point out that, if it had not been for Japanese intervention, the Germans would still have been in Shantung. The Chinese did nothing to help get rid of them. We must not forget that Japan had rendered considerable assistance in the war.

SIR MAURICE HANKEY, at Mr. Lloyd George's request, explained the naval assistance that Japan had given. By capturing Kiauchau, she had deprived Germany of her naval base in the Far East and her ships had had to leave the Pacific and had eventually been brought to action and sunk off the Falkland Islands. Japan, after helping to clear the seas and to escort the troops from Australia and New Zealand, had continued to police the Far East, thus setting free cruisers for operations elsewhere and particularly in the North Sea. She had also sent 12 or more destroyers to the Mediterranean.

MR. LLOYD GEORGE pointed out that, but for the assistance of Japan, it would have been difficult to transport the Australian and New Zealand troops.

PRESIDENT WILSON doubted if the Germans would have remained in possession of Kiauchau even if Japan had not captured it. The representatives of Japan had said they were willing to discuss with the other Powers the renunciation of the unusual rights which the Powers possessed in China. This would be a great relief to China, although these rights possessed no practical importance to the Powers. If China would agree to discuss with us the terms on which these rights could be ceded to China, then we could agree as an inducement to liberal terms to allow Kiauchau and Shantung to be ceded direct to Japan.

MR. LLOYD GEORGE said that the British Government could not agree to Japan having a special position in Shantung as well as a general position in the Yangtse Kiang. The Japanese, however, wanted special powers for exploitation in the territories they occupied.

PRESIDENT WILSON said his object was to take the chains off China.

MR. LLOYD GEORGE said that the difficulty was that we could not allow other nations to co-operate in the Yangtse Kiang, although we should like to, since we had not sufficient capital ourselves for development. The reason we could not do so was because we should have to allow the Japanese in.

PRESIDENT WILSON said that he understood this and that the Japanese were apt to make special arrangements, which excluded other people.

MR. LLOYD GEORGE said that when the British built railways they handed them over to China. The Japanese, however, were apt to keep the railways and exploit them.

PRESIDENT WILSON pointed out that the larger part of Japanese territory was barren and consequently they required room for their population. They had found some space in Korea and Manchuria but they were now seeking more in China.

MR. LLOYD GEORGE suggested the best plan to be for someone to sound the Japanese before they saw the Supreme Council.

PRESIDENT WILSON suggested that they should be told that the Allied and Associated Powers could not consent to the return of Kiauchau and Shantung to the Japanese on the terms on which they had agreed with China. He suggested that Mr. Lloyd George and Mr. Balfour should see Baron Makino and Viscount Chinda.

(Mr. Lloyd George undertook that Mr. Balfour should see the Japanese Representatives, and instructed Sir Maurice Hankey to inform Mr. Balfour accordingly.)

§ Mantoux's notes:

Wilson. I would like us to exchange a few words about the Japanese question; it is nearly as difficult as the Italian question.

Lloyd George. Yes, but the Japanese are much more determined; with them there is no bluffing.

Wilson. What are we going to do? We have the report of our experts on the question that we asked. They say that the transfer to the Japanese of the rights previously accorded to the Germans would be preferable to the execution of the treaty concluded between Japan and China. Do your treaties with Japan obligate France and England to grant the transfer of the German rights to Japan?

Lloyd George and Clemenceau. Yes.

Wilson. So you cannot ask that the German rights be handed over to the five Powers?

Lloyd George. Mr. Balfour proposes to say to the Japanese: "We will assure you the transfer of the German rights; but we are asking you to discuss with us the conditions under which you propose to restore Kiaochow to China." The Chinese propose a compromise; but I do not believe that the Japanese will accept.

Wilson. Suppose they refuse; we really cannot sanction the treaty between Japan and China. It was obtained by violence and under threat; it gives the Japanese more than the Germans ever possessed, and, moreover, they acquired not only the control but also the ownership of a large part of the bay. I will discuss with them before Thursday the conditions under which they will have to restore Kiaochow to China. But we must take into account the fact that, without the intervention of Japan—and I can add our own—Kiaochow would still be German.

What do you think of the Japanese assistance on the sea?

Hankey. The Japanese cleaned up the Pacific and made possible the transport of Australian and New Zealand troops.

Lloyd George. We cannot forget that; we had great need of these troops.

Wilson. The Japanese declared themselves, on the other hand, ready to abandon, if we ourselves did it, the special rights of foreigners in China. If they accept the transfer pure and simple of German rights to Japan and really want to discuss with us the modification of the conditions which they imposed on China, we can find a solution to the problem.

Lloyd George. We could not agree to abandon our special rights in the Yangtze Valley if Japan retained a privileged position in Shantung. What we can propose is a perfect equality of treatment.

Wilson. The question is to know if that equality, which would open the Yangtze Valley to the Japanese, would be advantageous for

China or not. What I seek is to liberate China from the chains which weigh on her.

Lloyd George. Make no mistake, the Japanese are working on a plan of conquest. When it's a question of constructing railways in China, while we limit ourselves to construction, they retain the administration of them, they install themselves in the stations and in the countryside. There are in China 400 million men who, if they were organized militarily by Japan, would constitute a formidable mass.

I was struck the other day to see Baron Makino handle with perfect dexterity and a certain disdain the phraseology of the West about the rights of humanity and the League of Nations. The Japanese are truly the Prussians of the Far East.

Wilson. We must remember that their country is too small and much too infertile for their growing population. They found room in Korea and in Manchuria; but that is not sufficient for them.

Lloyd George. I will see with Mr. Balfour what can be done.

Clemenceau. I believe that the Japanese will hold fast to what they call their rights.

Wilson. They will have satisfaction by the transfer of the German rights. But we will tell them that we want to discuss with them the conditions under which they will restore Kiaochow to China, and that in no case will we agree that the rights which will be conceded to them shall exceed those which the Germans possessed.

It is agreed that Mr. Balfour will be charged with studying that question. §

4. MR. LLOYD GEORGE informed President Wilson that he had now ascertained the numbers of British troops sent to Archangel, which reached a total of 5,000.

5. There was some discussion on the question as to whether the Syrian Commission should start.

The following decisions were reached:

(1) The French Government should immediately nominate their representatives.
(2) The Commission should start as soon as possible.
(3) No announcement should be made until the Germans had come to Versailles.

§ Mantoux's notes:

Lloyd George. On the subject of Syria, should I send my two commissioners there and what instructions should I give them?

Wilson. It seems to me that we go through a change of attitude on that question every day. I have already sent and called back my people.

Clemenceau (to Lloyd George). You informed me of the dangers of the commission and you told me: "First let us agree between ourselves."

Wilson. If you settle the question between yourselves, to send a commission to the site would be a mockery.

Clemenceau. I only saw one man who insisted on the commission: it is Faisal; he told me that he was certain that Syria would ask the commission to place him at its head.

Wilson. I do not believe it wise to proceed as you want to, and, on the other hand, we agreed that the population would be consulted.

Clemenceau. I said that, and I will not go back on my word.

Lloyd George. There are three parties in Syria; Faisal is not the favorite of everyone.

Wilson. That is not the question. If it is a question of establishing a mandate of the League of Nations in Syria, can you decide between yourselves to whom that mandate should go?

Lloyd George. All I have to say is that, as far as the British government is concerned, its absolute decision is not to accept a mandate in Syria. For us, the friendship of France is worth ten Syrias.

Wilson. Nor do I wish a mandate for the United States; but the question of the mandate cannot be resolved simply by an arrangement between you two. In my opinion, a question other than the one you are concerned with arises: I think that it would be necessary that there be a single mandate for all the Arab countries.

Lloyd George. To tell the truth, these countries have never been united among themselves, except in the great empires of antiquity. As for the Bedouins, no one has ever succeeded in governing them. In any case, the members of that commission must be told if they must leave or not. First I told them to go, then to stay.

Clemenceau. I would prefer that that commission leave only after the arrival of the Germans here. That would make the thing much easier for me. §

APPENDIX I TO I.C. 176.F.

24 AVRIL 1919

ARTICLES CONCERNING THE GUARANTEES OF EXECUTION OF THE TREATY

1. As a guarantee of the execution by Germany of the present treaty, German territories west of the Rhine, including the bridgeheads, are to be occupied by allied and associated forces during fifteen years.

2. If the conditions of the treaty are executed by Germany, occupation to be successively reduced according to following schedule:

a) to be evacuated after 5 years: the bridgehead of Köln and the territories north of a line running along the Roer, then along the railroad: Julich, Duren, Euskirchen, Rheinbach, then the road Rheinbach to Sinzig, and reaching the Rhine at the confluence with the Ahr river (the roads, railroads and localities above mentioned included in the occupied territory).

b) to be evacuated after 10 years: the bridgehead of Coblentz and the territories north of line to be drawn from the intersection between the frontiers of Belgium, Germany and Holland, running about 4 kilometres south of Aix-la-Chapelle, then to and following the crest of Forts Gemünd, then east of the railroad of the Urft Valley, then along Blankorheim, Valdorf, Dreis, Ulmen to and following the Mosel from Bremm to Nehrin, then passing along Kappel, Simmern, then following the ridge of the heights between Simmern and the Rhine and reaches the river at Bacharach (all localities, valleys, roads and railroads above mentioned included in the occupied territory).

c) to be evacuated after fifteen years the bridgehead of Mainz, the bridgehead of Kehl and the remainder of German territories still occupied. If at that time the guarantees against unprovoked aggression by Germany are not considered satisfactory by the present allied and associated Governments, Germany consents to accept such similar guarantees as they may require.

3. In case, either during or after this fifteen years delay, the Interallied Commission of Reparations recognise that Germany refuse to execute the whole or part of the conditions agreed upon by her according to the present treaty, the reoccupation by Allied and Associated forces of part or the whole of the areas defined by articles 2 will take place immediately.

4. If, before fifteen years, Germany meets all the engagements taken by her according to the terms of the present treaty, the withdrawal of the Allied and Associated troops would immediately follow.

T MS (SDR, RG 256, 180.03401/121, DNA); Mantoux, I, 376-78, 378-79.

To Tasker Howard Bliss

My dear General Bliss: Paris, 25 April, 1919.

Thank you for your reminder about the commissions which are to function in Germany. As you know, my judgment is entirely with you in these matters, and I thought we had eliminated the commissions which are to work without limit of time. I would be very much indebted to you if you would have a memorandum made for me of those whose duration is not limited.

Cordially and faithfully yours, Woodrow Wilson

TLS (T. H. Bliss Papers, DLC).

To Herbert Clark Hoover

My dear Hoover: Paris, 25 April, 1919.

I think the case you make out for the wives of your associates is an unanswerable one.[1] Your associates are after all not in any proper sense part of the staff of the Peace Mission. Their job is all but permanent, if one looks both backward and forward, and they may be said to be feeding Europe. I am perfectly willing that you should say to the Secretary of State that I shall make no objection.

Cordially and faithfully yours, Woodrow Wilson

TLS (Hoover Archives, CSt-H).

[1] Wilson was replying to HCH to WW, April 22, 1919, TLS (WP, DLC), in which Hoover requested that "the very proper ruling prohibiting wives of members of the Peace Mission from coming to Europe" should be relaxed for members of his staff engaged in relief work. He gave several arguments in favor of his case but the basic one was simply that he would soon lose some of his best men unless their wives were allowed to join them.

From Robert Lansing, with Enclosure

My dear Mr. President: Paris, April 25 1919.

I enclose herewith a copy of a note of April 22d, from the French Ministry of Foreign Affairs to the American Ambassador at Paris, with regard to the apportionment between the Allied and Associated Governments of their respective obligations to extend credits to Roumania for the purpose of enabling that country to provide itself with provisions, supplies and armament. The Council of Four has evidently decided on a policy to offer facilities to the Roumanian Government in this matter.

May I inquire of you whether, in the Council of Four, it has been agreed that the United States Government shall take part in the apportionment of credits to Roumania for the purpose set forth in the note from the Foreign Office? If so, I shall, upon receipt of your advice, communicate with the Treasury Department with a view to having someone designated to represent the United States Government.

I am, my dear Mr. President,

Faithfully yours, Robert Lansing

TLS (WP, DLC).

E N C L O S U R E

Paris, 22 April 1919.

His Excellency Mr. Sharp is not unaware of the fact that after deliberation the Council of the Four decided to facilitate on a large scale, provisioning, supplying and armament of Roumania, for the purpose of barring the road into Europe for Bolshevism.

This decision involves important financial effects and the French Government is obliged to reiterate that nothing has been done up to the present to determine the extent of the respective obligations of each of the Allied and Associated Governments in this matter.

M. Pichon therefore requests His Excellency Mr. Sharp to communicate the preceding statement to his Government and to ask it to appoint for this purpose representatives qualified to fix the rules of financial distribution and the opening of credit necessary for the accomplishment of the decisions of the Council of Four.

The delegates could advantageously meet at the Ministry of Finances as soon as their names are known.

T MS (WP, DLC).

Joseph Clark Grew to Gilbert Fairchild Close

My dear Mr. Close: Paris, April 25, 1919.

I am enclosing, for the information of the President, a copy of, "The Claim of China."[1]

This pamphlet purports to submit for abrogation by the Peace Conference the treaties and notes made and exchanged by and between China and Japan on May 25, 1915, as a transaction arising out of and connected with the war between the Allied and Associated States and the Central Powers.

Very sincerely yours, J. C. Grew

TLS (WP, DLC).

[1] Chinese Delegation, Peace Conference, *THE CLAIM OF CHINA, SUBMITTING FOR ABROGATION BY THE PEACE CONFERENCE THE TREATIES AND NOTES MADE AND EXCHANGED BY AND BETWEEN CHINA AND JAPAN ON MAY 25, 1915, AS A TRANSACTION ARISING OUT OF AND CONNECTED WITH THE WAR BETWEEN THE ALLIED AND ASSOCIATED STATES AND THE CENTRAL POWERS, PARIS: APRIL 1919,* printed copy (SDR, RG 256, 185.1158/75, DNA); reprinted in David Hunter Miller, *My Diary at the Conference of Paris, With Documents* (21 vols., New York, 1924), VI, 213-51. This document presented an extensive analysis of the background and content of the Twenty-One Demands and the treaties resulting therefrom and set forth extensive arguments in favor of their abrogation.

Two Letters from Edward Mandell House

Dear Governor: Paris, April 25, 1919.

I have been told that there was some effort being made in Poland to discredit Paderewski because he has accepted without protest the decisions of the Council of Four. It is insisted by his enemies that he should have taken the same attitude towards Dantzig as the Italians have taken towards Fiume.

Wiseman tells me that Lloyd George is in favor of your writing such a letter as the one I enclose[1] and is willing to have his name used in the way in which it appears in this draft or in any other way that you see fit. Affectionately yours, E. M. House

[1] Wilson sent House's draft as WW to I. J. Paderewski, April 26, 1919.

Dear Governor: Paris, April 25, 1919.

I notice you have given the D.S.M. to Commander Gaunt.[1] May I suggest that you also give one to Lt. Col. Sir William Wiseman.[2]

Wiseman is leaving Paris next week to resume his personal affairs. If any Englishman deserves one, surely, he does.

Affectionately yours, E. M. House

TLS (WP, DLC).

[1] That is, Commodore Sir Guy (Reginald Archer) Gaunt.

[2] Wilson apparently never awarded the D.S.M. to Wiseman.

From Henry White, with Enclosure

Dear Mr. President: Paris 25 April 1919

I enclose, for your information, the copy of a letter which I have received from our mutual friend, Bryce, and which speaks for itself. The document referred to therein has not yet reached me, and, in any case, I imagine you have too much to read at the present time to be able to give attention to anything on the subject beyond the enclosed letter. I am afraid the matter has been settled and therefore probably Bryce's letter is too late.

You are probably aware that, if the Brenner boundary be given to the Italians, 239,000 Germans (than whom none more patriotic or more devoted to their country, which is that of Andreas Hofer, exist anywhere) would be handed over to the former.

Pray do not take a moment of your time to answer this note, as no reply is required. I am only sending Bryce's letter to you because he asks me to do so. Of course, if you should wish to see Douglas Freshfield's paper, I shall gladly send it to you as soon as it reaches me.

Yours very sincerely, Henry White

TLS (WP, DLC).

E N C L O S U R E

James Viscount Bryce to Henry White

CONFIDENTIAL

Forest Row, Sussex, England.
My dear White: April 20, 1919.

An old friend of mine, Douglas Freshfield, a famous traveler, ex-president of the Alpine Club and also ex-president of our Royal Geographical Society, who is, like myself, interested in saving the worthy German-speaking Tyrolese, who dwell in Germanic Tyrol south of the main chain of the Rhaetian Alps from being annexed by and subjected to Italy, asks me to send to you for the purpose of the American Commission to Negotiate Peace, a copy of a paper he wrote recently showing the boundaries between the Italian-speaking and the German-speaking population in Middle Tyrol. Thinking it may be of service to you and your colleagues, I am asking your Embassy to forward it to you. You will know when to show it to the President. I hope that the determination of the boundaries between the Italian-speakers and the German-speakers will be entrusted to an impartial commission, as a similar determination of boundaries between the Greek, Serb, Albanian, and Bulgarian populations in the Balkans ought to be, for this will be the only satisfactory way of dealing with the discordant and always extreme claims made by each of these peoples. The Italian Government, I understand, claims to extend its territory up to the Rhaeti watershed on strategic grounds, but this is no justification for a flagrant disregard of the principles of nationality and self-determination. There is a good strategic line of defense which would correspond nearly with the line demarcating the two languages.

Ever sincerely yours, James Bryce

P.S. I congratulate you all most heartily on the practical certainty now attained that the American people will accept the League of Nations Covenant as amended. This is a real victory, for the Senate will obey the wish of the people.

TCL (WP, DLC).

From Thomas William Lamont

The Case of Belgium.

Dear Mr. President: Paris, April 25, 1919.

Referring to our brief conversation over the telephone yesterday morning:

The various sub-committees, as designated on Wednesday, explained to the smaller powers yesterday the general scheme and terms of reparation. As I anticipated, the first questions that the Belgians asked us privately, when the session was over, were (a) as to their priority of $500,000,000 and (b) as to what their share is to be in the total of reparation payments.

As to question (a), you will recall that America has consistently urged the wisdom of this $500,000,000 priority for Belgium, and we have thought that the other Chief Powers had acquiesced; but of late Mr. Lloyd George has seemed somewhat doubtful about the matter.

As to the question (b), McCormick tells me that he has explained to you the importance of having all these proportions promptly determined; for while America is not directly concerned in the proportions, America is likely to be called in as an arbitrator, and if she is to occupy such position, we should complete the work in the immediate future.

Mr. Davis and all of us are in accord on these points, and also upon the advisability of permitting Belgium to meet the Big Four in a brief session apart from the one where the other smaller powers will be present. Politically, we think the same remarks apply to Japan.

With great respect, I am,

Sincerely yours, Thomas W. Lamont

TLS (WP, DLC).

From Jane Addams and Others

Dear Mr. President Paris, April 25, 1919

As a group of American women profoundly interested in the establishment of a League of Nations and of a just settlement which would be its worthy prelude and basis, we wish to express to you our appreciation of your disinterested and convincing statement with which you yesterday appealed to the public opinion of the world, in support of the principles which you have so consistently advocated.

May we take advantage of this opportunity to express our great admiration for the courage and steadfastness with which, in the face of extraordinary difficulties, you have upheld those principles of international righteousness so essential to the establishment of permanent peace?

Sincerely yours, Jane Addams.
Emily G. Balch
Alice Thacher Post
Lucia Ames Mead

Rose M. Nichols
Mary Church Terrell
Grace H. White
Alice Hamilton
Jeannette Rankin
Lucy Biddle Lewis
Lillian D. Wald[1]

TLS (WP, DLC).

[1] Those persons not heretofore identified in this series were Mary Eliza Church (Mrs. Robert Heberton) Terrell of Washington, a long-time advocate of the rights of blacks and women; Grace Hoffman (Mrs. John Jay) White, a leader of the National Women's party; Alice Hamilton, M.D., a social worker at Hull-House, Chicago, and the leading American scientific expert on industrial diseases and industrial poisons; and Lucy Biddle (Mrs. J. Reece) Lewis of Philadelphia, a leader in the peace movement. Rose M. Nichols cannot be further identified. All of the signers of this letter were in Europe to attend the International Congress of Women held in Zurich, May 12-19, 1919. This congress, which included delegates from both the Allied nations and the former Central Powers, concerned itself primarily with the problems of the peace settlement and the proposed League of Nations and, at its conclusion, transformed itself into a permanent organization, the Women's International League for Peace and Freedom. See Gertrude Bussey and Margaret Tims, *Women's International League for Peace and Freedom, 1915-1965: A Record of Fifty Years' Work* (London, 1965), pp. 17-33.

Two Letters from William Shepherd Benson

My dear Mr. President: [Paris] 25 April, 1919.

Replying to the inquiry contained in your letter of the 23rd instant, relative to the dates of sailings of transports from Brest, I beg to quote the following despatch which has been received from Brest:

"Predicted sailing dates as follows: LEVIATHAN and GREAT NORTHERN May 8; VON STEUBEN May 9; MOUNT VERNON and AMERICA May 11; AGAMEMNON May 14; PRESIDENT GRANT May 30. The sailings are predicted from past performances; no date has been received for sailings of these vessels from the United States."

These dates are only tentative, but it indicates generally the vessels which may be considered available. As you will notice, the list includes the largest and most comfortable of the transports. As more definite information becomes available, I shall keep you informed, or will see that the information is transmitted direct to Grayson, who will have it available for your information.

I have issued instructions for the GEORGE WASHINGTON to sail on the 27th instant. Reservations have been made for the Secretary of War and his party and the vessel will await them before departing. The GEORGE WASHINGTON should be in Brest again before May 25th.

Very sincerely yours, W. S. Benson.

My dear Mr. President: Paris, France. 25 April, 1919.

I have just received the following despatch from Rear Admiral Andrews,[1] Commanding our Naval Forces in the Adriatic, which I deem of sufficient importance to send to you without delay:

"Following information from USS SCHLEY at Pola: SCHLEY requested to land no liberty parties at Pola. Italian Commander-in-Chief[2] states situation very delicate. Heavy troop movement toward Fiume, Austria. SAN GIORGIO sailed for Fiume today. 123635 Andrews." Sincerely yours, W. S. Benson.

TLS (WP, DLC).

[1] That is, Philip Andrews.

[2] Vice Adm. Umberto Cagni, commander of the Italian occupation force at Pola.

From the Diary of Ray Stannard Baker

Friday April 25th [1919]

The more critical & important the days the less my opportunity for writing here, for I am occupied early & late as never before. We are in the midst of the Italian crisis which was precipitated on Wednesday when the President sent down his statement by Admiral Grayson for me to give out. It caused a terrific sensation & precipitated upon us all the newspaper men in Paris, of all nationalities. We got it at once on the wireless & cables, had it translated into French & Le Temps succeeded in publishing it in a second edition. It marked, in many ways, the greatest moment of the Conference, for it brought the two forces which have so long been struggling in secret to the surface & outlined the issue. The President had been talking with me for several days about the message which he had read aloud to both Lloyd-George & Clemenceau, who approved it, or said they did. But it took tremendous courage to put it out & risk breaking up the Conference. The Italians have steadily threatened to go home. It will clear the air & reestablish the prestige of the Conference. . . .

I had a long talk with the President. The Japanese & Chinese question is up & the President admits its great difficulty. I asked him if he had this problem in mind when he issued the Italian message, for many people see its application also to the claims of Japan "No," he said, "not specifically: but when you lay down a general truth it may cut any where."

He told me he could not see clearly just where his principles applied & remarked, with a smile, that he had been reading over the 14 points to refresh his memory! . . .

I talked with him again tonight, told him about press opinion, brought up a fine letter from Jane Addams, Lilian Wald & others commending him. But he is rather low, I think, in his spirits. The Japanese question worries him. "They are not bluffers," he said, "& they will go home unless we give them what they should not have."

"The opinion of the world," I said, "supports the Chinese claims."

"I know that," he said.

"Especially American public opinion," I added.

"I know that, too," he replied "but if Italian [Italy] remains away & Japan goes home, what becomes of the League of Nations?"

He is at Gethsemane

Hw MS (R. S. Baker Papers, DLC).

Thomas Nelson Page to the American Commissioners

Rome April 25, 1919.

262. Intense excitement prevailed Rome yesterday. President Wilson's newspaper statement to the American people appeared in the press. Manifestoes printed and distributed calling upon all citizens of capital to demonstrate against decision of President and to reaffirm invincible will of Italy that her claims should be recognized in accordance with demands of country. In view of possible hostile demonstrations against the Embassy La Piazza San Bernardo heavily guarded and closed by heavy cordons infantry and carabiniers. Likewise at the Embassy cavalry also in readiness in case of emergency. It is possible that the excitement may be kept up until after May 1st as it will tide over period of danger, in fact all American places were guarded, Red Cross, Y.M.C.A., etc. It looked as though the Government considered situation more serious than it appears to us. In fact so far Americans treated with every civility.

Papers this morning contain full accounts of the demonstrations of yesterday evening which for most part were carried on in an orderly manner although MESSAGERO in its account thereof is considerably censored. It was undoubtedly strengthened by expression of national feeling. One incident only reported; flags, one American, one British over a shop, two British soldiers rescued their flag, ours rescued by group of young Italians and taken to Questor[1] who returned it this morning with due apologies after finding. Young men who rescued it called at the Embassy to explain that incident was accident few young ruffians and did not represent the feeling of sober people. I informed them I also hold this view. Further demonstrations are ordered for today and the troops and cavalry are out, residence of Ambassador again guarded by many soldiers, also arrangements are being made on large scale to receive Orlando. Press states that immediately upon his return to Rome Parliament will be opened and interrogated as to future attitude of the country in regard to settlement of the matter; also hear resolution will be presented declaring all the Adriatic eastern coast now in controversy an integral part of Italy. All the press is full of violent attacks on the President, whose action in addressing a statement to the American people which is taken as an appeal to the Italian people over heads of king and government, while efforts were apparently being still made to provide for settlement of Italy's claims, is much criticised and resented. Prime Minister Orlando's reply to telegram of President[2] appears in the morning papers. The Italian spirit has been unquestionably tremendously excited. Press declares that huge demonstrations held Naples and other cities resenting President's appeal to the Italian people. Have learned that Cabinet received yesterday, press representatives and gave keynote to campaign which is to try to dissociate President from the American people and appeal to friendship of American people while concentrating attack on President also that the parliament will send appeal to American Congress directly in line with this understanding. A paper published last night a squib saying I had resigned because I was in dis-accord with the President. Nelson Page.

T telegram (WP, DLC).

[1] Actually, *questore*, the chief of police.

[2] See the news report printed at April 24, 1919. The "telegram" was a reference to Wilson's statement on the Adriatic question.

Gilbert Fairchild Close to Edward Thomas Williams

My dear Mr. Williams: Paris, 25 April, 1919.

The President asks me to thank you for your letter to him about the Chino-Japanese question and to say that it will be of the greatest service to him. Sincerely yours, [Gilbert F. Close]

CCL (WP, DLC).

Two Telegrams to Joseph Patrick Tumulty

Paris, 25 April, 1919.

Am very grateful for your message of approval about the Italian business. It has warmed my heart mightily. The difficulties here would have been incredible to me before I got here. Your support keeps me in heart. Woodrow Wilson.

Paris, 25 April, 1919.

Please convey this message to Mr. George P. Hampton of the Farmer's National Council: QUOTE

Your message on behalf of the farmers about secret treaties[1] is warmly appreciated. The fight is hard but worth while. UNQUOTE.

Woodrow Wilson.

TC telegrams (WP, DLC).

[1] G. P. Hampton (via JPT) to WW, April 24, 1919, T telegram (WP, DLC). Hampton, the managing director of the Farmers' National Council, stated that the members of his organization strongly supported Wilson's stand against secret treaties.

Two Telegrams from Joseph Patrick Tumulty

[The White House, April 25, 1919]

No. 78 Please do not reply to message from Burleson re cables[1] until I can cable you further. Tumulty.

[1] ASB to WW, April 24, 1919.

[The White House, April 25, 1919]

No. 79 In connection with the suggestion of the early return of the cables, I owe it in frankness to say to you that there is no present source of irritation and popular discontent affecting all classes of the people comparable with that growing out of the continuance of control of cables, telegraph and telephone lines by the Postmaster General. There is no reason apparent to the public why this control should be continued. I understand, however, that the Postmaster General believes that the financial position of the telegraph companies, and possibly of the telephone companies, might be very grave if they were returned at this time.

I am inclined to think that it would be very desirable to return the cables at an early date but that a failure to return the telegraph and telephone lines or to take steps by public announcement looking towards their return at the same time would be construed as an evidence of an intention on the part of the Administration to retain the telegraph and telephone lines indefinitely. The Republican leaders openly announce that one of the first things they intend to do when they take hold is to pass a resolution providing for the immediate return of these instrumentalities. This would be very good politics from their standpoint and give our opponents a tremendous advantage over us. I am on the job here and every friend of yours who is acquainted with the serious conditions throughout the country and has weighed the same would concur with me.

I am satisfied that public opinion is not ready for government control of railroads, telegraph or telephone lines or cables, and that the wise, constructive thing for you to do is to announce immediately after the close of the Victory Loan, May tenth, that you have definitely determined to return all of these instrumentalities to private control but that you will insist on the immediate enactment by the Congress of appropriate legislation to protect the rights of the security-holders in that connection. It is evident that this is the practical politics of the situation. Frankly, the people are sick of all kinds of control and war restrictions. They submitted only during the period of the war. The war is over and they want to go about their business in their own way. Even the successful conduct of these great undertakings will not be popular; success is not possible in the absence of the kind of legislation which is necessary. The American people are going through a period of reaction following the enormous moral and physical effort which they put forth during the period of the war, and they are irritable and impatient of every interference, however laudable its purpose, with the result that the tremendous achievements of the war are being forgotten. The release under proper conditions by the Government of the control of these agencies will do more to hearten American business and clarify the air than anything you can do. Our failure to do so will give our enemies their great opportunity. I would suggest that in reply to the Postmaster General you diplomatically inquire if the time is not opportune to release government control over the telegraph and telephone lines.

Tumulty.

T telegrams (WP, DLC).

Cary Travers Grayson to Joseph Patrick Tumulty

Paris, 25 April 1919.

Situation clearing rapidly. The President's Italian action endorsed unanimously everywhere. You are secretary to the greatest statesman in the world. All well. Ask Doctor Dennis,[1] Naval Dispensary, to rush me 500 Urotropin[2] five grain capsules by next courier.

Grayson.

T telegram (WP, DLC).

[1] Edward Guy Dennis, pharmacist.

[2] Urotropine, or hexamethylentetramine, a compound used as an antiseptic for infections of the urinary tract.

From the Diary of Dr. Grayson

Saturday, April 26, 1919.

The President had breakfast at 8:30 o'clock; and at 11:00 he attended a meeting of the Big Three. At 2:00 o'clock the President went to the Crillon Hotel to confer with the various members of the American Commission. At 3:00 o'clock the Big Three met with the financial experts. They considered the amended report of the American and British financiers, who had revised the questions of reparations to be dealt with in the Peace Treaty.[1] At the meeting at the Crillon Hotel the questions at issue ranged from responsibilities to a cursory discussion of the Italian situation. No important decision was reached.

We had dinner at 7:00 o'clock, and after dinner the President said to me in our evening conversation: "I made a pun today that amused Lloyd-George. Lloyd-George was standing at the window and said: 'I notice that the foliage in Paris is much further advanced than it is out in the country, and I wonder what is the cause of this.' " The President replied, "I would suggest that it is because our soldiers come to Paris for their leaves."

The President loves to tease and it is a characteristic which he himself says often threatens to get him into trouble. He said: "I suppose I came by it honestly, because my father was the greatest tease I ever knew." He then told the following story about his father: In Augusta, Georgia, where his father was a Minister of the Presbyterian Church, one day while driving he stopped at a watering place on the street to water his horse, and a member of his congregation, who knew him very well, said to him: "Doctor Wilson, your horse is looking exceedingly well; in fact, he looks better cared for than you." Whereupon his father replied: "Yes, I agree with you, and there is a good reason for it; I myself take care of my horse, and my congregation takes care of me." He told me that his father always advised him that he should not indulge in extemporaneous speaking without writing something every week—not particularly regarding his speech, but to see his own thoughts in writing. He told the President that he should do this at least once a week. He would then have an opportunity to see the defects in his expressions, which he might not be able to detect from an extemporaneous speech. His father would not let him write a speech at length and then re-write it by cutting it down. He would tell him to go on the principle of building a house—lay the foundation and erect the frame-work, and then build up around it.

Today I had my first horse-back ride in France. I joined Mr. Henry

Morgenthau, ex-Ambassador to Turkey, for a ride through the Bois. We were accompanied by his niece, Miss Edith Strauss.

[1] Hankey's brief minutes of this meeting, which began at 3:15 p.m., April 26, 1919, are printed in *PPC*, V, 302-307.

Hankey's and Mantoux's Notes of a Meeting of the Council of Four[1]

President Wilson's Residence,
I.C.-176H. Paris, April 26, 1919, 12:15 p.m.

REPARATION, DYE STUFFS AND CHEMICALS, DRUGS
COAL AND COAL DERIVATIVES

1. (Sir Hubert Llewellyn Smith who had remained on from the previous Meeting[2] and Commandant Aron[3] were present during the short discussion of this subject.)

The Articles having been agreed by the British and United States Experts and Commandant Aron having assured M. Clemenceau that M. Loucheur had accepted them, the Articles in Appendix I[4] were approved and Sir Maurice Hankey was instructed to forward them to the Secretary General for a Drafting Committee.

Sir Hubert Llewellyn Smith and Commandant Aron then withdrew.

2. Attention was drawn to reports of the movements of Italian troops towards Fiume apparently from Austria and of Italian naval movements towards Fiume.

§ Mantoux's notes:

Wilson. I have telegrams about the state of opinion in Rome.[5] The crowd marched tumultuously to the Capitol, and on the way stopped to cheer in front of the Japanese embassy: it is rather significant.

Moreover, I have received telegrams informing me of the movement of Italian troops toward Fiume, and warning me that the battleship *San Giorgio* is leaving for Fiume today.[6] That promises no good.

Lloyd George. I fear that M. Orlando will be carried away by the movement which he has allowed to develop. Today he is in the po-

[1] The complete text of Hankey's minutes is printed in *PPC*, V, 291-98.

[2] A meeting of the Council of Four at 11 a.m. on April 26, 1919, when the report of the Commission on the International Regime of Ports, Waterways and Railways was presented and approved with modifications. The minutes of this meeting and the report are printed in *ibid.*, pp. 251-90.

[3] Head of technical and economic services of the French Ministry of Industrial Reconstruction. The Editors have been unable to learn his given name or names.

[4] It is printed in *PPC*, V, 294-97.

[5] That is, T. N. Page to the American Mission, April 24, 1919 (second telegram of that date).

[6] See W. S. Benson to WW, April 25, 1919 (second letter of that date).

sition of a secretary of a labor union who has allowed a strike to run wild. §

3. PRESIDENT WILSON suggested that Roumania should be asked to cease their aggressive action towards Hungary. Roumania had had considerable assistance from the Allies and was pressing her advantage of numbers and equipment. Her action was distinctly aggressive and might constitute a danger to the Peace. He recalled General Smuts' suggestion that the Austrians should be invited to come to Paris. He suggested that an invitation might be sent giving a date a short time in advance to quiet things in Austria. This might arrest the danger to the Hungarian ferment extending to Austria. If Austria were put on a footing of respect this danger might be checked. This suggestion,[7] President Wilson said, came from Mr. Hoover who had very good sources of information through his Relief Agencies. Mr. Hoover was afraid of a collapse in Austria. He asked if General Franchet d'Esperey commanded the armies in that region.

M. CLEMENCEAU said that General Graziani[8] was now in command there.

MR. LLOYD GEORGE suggested that M. Bratiano might be invited to attend and asked to stop the Roumanian aggressive movement.

PRESIDENT WILSON suggested that in view of the pressure of time it might be better to send him a joint letter.

M. CLEMENCEAU thought it would be best to hear M. Bratiano for ten minutes after which a letter might be sent.

PRESIDENT WILSON suggested that the Austrians might be invited for the 15th May.

MR. LLOYD GEORGE said there was not a great deal to be settled now with the Austrian Treaty.

PRESIDENT WILSON said it was particularly confined to questions of boundaries, which were in process of settlement and the proportion of Austria's debt to be borne by the States formerly constituting the Austro-Hungary Empire.

MR. LLOYD GEORGE said that he was not sure if the proportions could not be fixed. His view was that general principles should be stated first, and then a Commission should be set up to work out details. The calculation was a very difficult one involving not only the population but also the wealth of the country.

PRESIDENT WILSON agreed that the best plan would be to get a Commission set up.

This question was then dropped without any actual decision being taken.

[7] Undoubtedly made orally. There is no letter from Hoover to Wilson about this subject at this time.

[8] Gen. Jean César Graziani.

4. The Council had before them a document prepared by the Secretary General assisted by the United States, British and Japanese Secretaries (Appendix II).[9]

5. The first proposal for an examination of credentials by an Examining Commission presided by M. Jules Cambon was approved.

The proposal that the President of the Conference should determine the date and hour of the examination as soon as the German Delegates arrived was also agreed to.

6. It was pointed out that the question of the recognition of the Jugo-Slavs was raised by the suggestion that the Germans might ask for an examination of the Allies' credentials.

PRESIDENT WILSON said that the United States had already recognised Jugo-Slavia.

MR. LLOYD GEORGE and M. CLEMENCEAU said that Great Britain and France had not.

(It was agreed that a provisional decision should be taken for the British and French Governments to recognise the Jugo-Slavia Government before the Germans arrived at Versailles but that action should be suspended pending M. Orlando's return. Unless some reason was shown to the contrary however, the Jugo-Slavs would be recognised before the arrival of the Germans.)

§ Mantoux's notes:

Wilson. For our approaching meeting with the Germans, the first question which arises is that of the verification of credentials. The Germans will present their credentials and will ask for ours. What will we say on the subject of the Kingdom of the Serbs, Croats, and Slovenes?

Clemenceau. It is true that we have not recognized it until now, in order to please the Italians.

Lloyd George. Why not simply present the Serbian letters of credence?

Wilson. That is what M. Trumbić will not accept.

Clemenceau. Obviously, the recognition at this time of the Kingdom of the Serbs, Croats, and Slovenes will increase the danger from the Italian side. But I do not see how we can avoid it.

Has America not recognized the Yugoslavs?

Wilson. Yes.

Lloyd George. I propose to decide that, if the Italians are not present at the time when the negotiations with Germany open, we recognize the Kingdom of the Serbs, Croats, and Slovenes.

Adopted. §

[9] It is printed in *PPC*, V, 297-98. It was about the communication of the preliminary peace terms to the German delegates.

7. It was agreed that the Germans should submit their observations on the Treaty of Peace in French and English.

8. (1) It was agreed that the maximum time limit to the Germans to make their observations on the Peace Treaty should be fifteen days.

(2) That they should be required to make their observations on particular subjects within such shorter period as might be determined.

(3) That M. Clemenceau should instruct the Secretary General to place himself in communication with the groups which had considered the different subjects and invite their suggestions as to how long a time should be permitted to the Germans for the consideration of each of the subjects mentioned in his list.

It was pointed out that the League of Nations was not included in the Secretary General's list.

9. The Secretary General's proposal that the President should hand over the Treaty to the German Delegation in the presence of the Plenipotentiaries of the Five Great Powers and of the Belgian Delegation only was not approved.

It was agreed:

1. That the full number of the Plenipotentiaries of all Belligerents should be present when the Treaty was handed over.

The question of the inclusion of the Polish and Czecho-Slovak Delegation as belligerents was discussed but not decided.

§ Mantoux's notes:

Wilson. Should we not agree about the time which we will allow the Germans to study the treaty and to present us with their written observations?

Lloyd George. I propose two weeks.

Wilson. That is not much; the document will be very voluminous.

Clemenceau. They will not be much more satisfied with this document at the end of fifty days. I propose two weeks. It goes without saying that, if the Germans ask for more time and seem to be preoccupied about arriving at a solution, we cannot refuse them an extension. It is understood that the communications and the replies will take place in writing.

Shall we invite all the belligerents to the opening session? I do not believe that it would be possible to do otherwise.

Lloyd George. That will mean a lot of people. I do not know if we must include among the belligerents the newly formed powers which did not fight against the Germans, such as Poland and Czechoslovakia.

Wilson. Before taking a decision about the amount of time we will allow the Germans to examine the text of the treaty, I propose to ask each of the commissions which knows the parts of the treaty on which they have worked, how much time it seems to them reasonable to grant.

Adopted.

Lloyd George. In the list of questions asked the Germans, which correspond to the different chapters of the treaty, I see neither the fundamental act of the League of Nations, nor the international agreement relating to conditions of work.

Wilson. They only have to be added.

Clemenceau. How will we divide the time which will be granted to the Germans to examine the document? We do not intend to allow them to work for two weeks without our receiving any response from them.

Lloyd George. I believe it would be necessary to fix time limits for each of the principal questions, with two weeks as the absolute limit. We cannot remain idle for two weeks.

Clemenceau. I will have the text revised in this sense. §

10. MR. HEADLAM-MORLEY stated that in a conversation on Thursday the 24th with M. Paderewski he had explained to him the proposed arrangement for Danzig. M. Paderewski had obviously been seriously disturbed, but had recognised that the matter had been decided in principle. He had asked, however, that two points should be provided for to which he attached the greatest importance:

(1) That there should be secured to Poland not only the use and service of the docks, etc., but the actual ownership, especially of those situated at the mouth of the Vistula and outside the walls of the city.

(2) He suggested that the Polish control over Danzig would be secured by the disarmament of Germany, and that in order to help the general principle of disarmament it would not be desirable that Poland should make any display of military force in Danzig. While acquiescing in this idea he still wanted the power of protection against unorganised attacks by German "free-booters."

Mr. Headlam-Morley had then said he would try and secure something giving to Poland the right if required for the protection of Danzig against external attack.

Mr. Headlam-Morley said he had not been able to ascertain who were the present owners of the docks.

PRESIDENT WILSON did not consider that either of these requests by M. Paderewski could be acceded to.

MR. LLOYD GEORGE suggested that M. Paderewski would be satisfied with power of development of the Port of Danzig.

(This proposal was agreed to, and Mr. Headlam-Morley was instructed to draft the final clauses on this assumption.

It was also agreed that the protection of Danzig against external attack would be vested in the League of Nations.)

T MS (SDR, RG 256, 180.03401/123, DNA); Mantoux, I, 384, 385, 386.

From the Diary of Colonel House

April 26, 1919.

The President came to the Crillon at two o'clock for a meeting of the Commissioners. He wanted our opinion as to what action had best be taken in the differences between Japan and China. Both he and Lansing lean toward China, while in this instance, my sympathies are about evenly divided with a feeling that it would be a mistake to take such action against Japan as might lead to her withdrawal from the Conference. I argued the matter at some length with the President, and I think there will not be much difficulty in reaching an agreement with Japan.

I am greatly disturbed at the President's almost childish action in going into conferences with Lloyd George and Clemenceau without having any of our secretaries to make a proces verbal. He relies entirely upon Mantoux and Hankey. Lloyd George is now telling the British correspondents that he, George, did not agree to the President's publication of his Italian statement, and that it was read to him hastily. He also intimates that he did not approve the statement, and that he disapproved of its being given out. This is just the reverse of what the President tells me and the President is taking great chances in dealing with him as he does without taking better means to protect himself.

Hankey's and Mantoux's Notes of a Meeting of the Council of Four[1]

President Wilson's House,

I.C.-176I. Paris, April 26, 1919, 3 p.m.

The Drafting Committee of the Preliminary Peace Conference, consisting of Mr. Brown Scott,[2] Mr. Hurst, and M. Fromageot were present.

1. The question was raised as to whether the Treaty of Peace with Germany should be "agreed" or "imposed."

(After a short discussion it was decided that it should be an "agreed" peace and should be prepared in this form.)

The question was raised as to whether the preamble of the Peace Treaty should state the principles on which peace was being made.

MR. BROWN SCOTT said it was extremely difficult when attempted in detail, and it was also pointed out that the Covenant of the League of Nations contained a preamble stating principles.

(It was decided not to state the principles on which peace is being made in the preamble.)

(The project for the Treaty of Peace attached in the Appendix was approved, subject to the addition of a reference to the effect that Germany had declared war on France.)

2. PRESIDENT WILSON suggested that it would make the Naval, Military, and Air terms more acceptable to the enemy if they were presented as preparing the way for a general limitation of armaments for all nations.

M. CLEMENCEAU said he would like to see the formula before [he] agreed.

(The following formula was accepted:

With the object of rendering possible the preparation of the general limitation of armaments of all nations, Germany undertakes to observe strictly the Naval, Military, and Aerial Clauses laid down below.)

3. M. CLEMENCEAU said that the Germans were due to arrive on next Wednesday evening, April 30, and that the first meeting would be held on May 1st at Versailles.

(At this point the Financial Experts were introduced.)

§ Mantoux's notes:

Clemenceau. The Germans will be here Wednesday evening; the work can begin on Thursday. What shall we do if the Italians are not there?

Lloyd George. The Drafting Committee must be told to put everywhere, instead of "the five Powers," "the principal Allied and Associated Powers," a formula which neither mentions nor excludes the Italians.

The financial delegates are introduced. §

T MS (SDR, RG 256, 180.03401/124, DNA); Mantoux, I, 387.

[1] The complete text of Hankey's minutes is printed in *PPC*, V, 299-301.

[2] That is, James Brown Scott.

To Ignace Jan Paderewski

My dear Mr. Paderewski: Paris, 26 April, 1919.

Before you leave Paris I would like to express our appreciation for the help you have given in aiding us to reach decisions in the difficult and delicate questions which have arisen regarding Poland and her neighbors.

Your grasp of the various problems, your keen insight into the historic and ethnic relations governing that part of Europe, and your willingness to accept a broad rather than a narrow basis of settlement has impressed us all. I speak for my colleagues as well as myself when I say that your attitude has given us confidence that Poland will soon again take her place among the potential powers, and become an influence towards the political liberty and advancement of mankind.

I am, my dear Mr. Paderewski,

Sincerely yours, Woodrow Wilson

TLS (Paderewski Collection, CSt-H).

To Emma Alice Margaret Tennant Asquith

My dear Mrs. Asquith: Paris, 26 April, 1919.

I warmly appreciated your little note about my declaration about the Italian claims, and I know that you will be generous enough to excuse a man who has no time that he can call his own, for sending you this typewritten note. It is very delightful to know that you are looking on and approving.

Cordially and sincerely yours, [Woodrow Wilson]

CCL (WP, DLC).

To Bernard Mannes Baruch

My dear Baruch: Paris, 26 April, 1919.

Thank you with all my heart for your note about the Italian statement. You always cheer me with your generous support.

Cordially and faithfully yours, [Woodrow Wilson]

CCL (WP, DLC).

To Jane Addams

My dear Miss Addams: Paris, 26 April, 1919.

I deeply appreciate the letter which you, Mrs. Balch, Mrs. Post, and other generous friends were kind enough to write me under date of yesterday about my attitude with regard to the Italian claims. It not only strengthens me, but cheers me, in a way much needed to receive such assurances from those whom I highly respect and whose support I know to mean so much.

Sincerely yours, Woodrow Wilson

TLS (Jane Addams Coll., PSC-P).

From Robert Joseph Kerner,[1] with Enclosure

My dear Mr. President: [Paris] April 26, 1919.

Should you so desire, I shall be delighted to send you the weekly interpretations of the political situation in Central Europe which I prepare for the Inquiry. I am enclosing a copy of the same for this week.

Most respectfully yours, Robert J Kerner

TLS (WP, DLC).

[1] Associate Professor of Modern European History at the University of Missouri, a member of The Inquiry specializing in eastern Europe.

E N C L O S U R E

THE POLITICAL SITUATION IN CENTRAL EUROPE.

by R. J. Kerner, April 26, 1919.

The General Situation.

The attempted revolution in German Austria and the Rumanian advance into Hungary have been the two main events of the week. By contrast the general situation in Czecho-Slovakia has continued to improve.

Full reports of the situation in German Austria and of the intended extent of the Rumanian advance into Hungary are not yet at hand. It is clear, however, that the developments in both states have led to the renewal of appeals on the part of Entente (including American) officials at Vienna for armed intervention—an intervention which the Smuts fiasco[1] and the recent events demonstrate should have taken place *a month ago.*

[1] About the Smuts mission, see the Memorandum by J. C. Smuts, and the notes thereto, printed at April 9, 1919, Vol. 57. For additional details and a more critical view of the mission, see Arno J. Mayer, *Politics and Diplomacy of Peacemaking: Containment and Counterrevolution at Versailles, 1918-1919* (New York, 1967), pp. 724-31.

In Hungary, as was to be expected, Kun has embarked upon a campaign for the virtual extermination of the bourgeoisie, and it sufficed for the Rumanians to advance in order to point out how feeble was the Bolshevik grip upon Hungary. In order to be carried out at the least cost, the intervention should be initiated before the Magyars and the Russians can effect a junction.

In German Austria, the grievances of the war invalids and of the unemployed, fostered by foreign agitators, led to an attempt to overthrow the government. The police proved loyal, and fortunately the People's Guard did not go over to the side of the disturbing elements. Had the Renner-Bauer government[2] taken a firmer stand from the beginning against the foreign agitators and their own radical elements, instead of conniving with them, the attempt would not have occurred.

It is too early as yet to estimate, except in general terms, the reaction of Jugo-Slavia to President Wilson's statement on Fiume and the Italian "withdrawal" from the Peace Conference.

CZECHO-SLOVAKIA.

As pointed out in the last two reports, conditions in Czecho-Slovakia have continued to improve materially. The disorders in Germany and Hungary have caused even the Bolshevists themselves to declare that they do not want to repeat the example of Russia. Muna,[3] one of the leading Bolshevist agitators in the new republic, complains that Czecho-Slovak nationalism is too strong and too solidly entrenched. Putting his hopes in his comrades of Kladno,[4] he "hopes" nevertheless for better days. The Teschen affair and the Bolshevik disorders in Munich and Budapest may therefore be regarded as having had a beneficial effect on national solidarity in the Czecho-Slovak State. For the time being it has silenced the non-Czecho-Slovak elements in the new state.

The recent announcement that the boundary between Germany

[2] Karl Renner and Otto Bauer, both leaders of the Austrian Social Democratic party, had played dominant roles in the revolutionary government of Austria since the first meeting of the provisional National Assembly on October 21, 1918. Renner had drawn up the first constitution of the new state, adopted by the assembly on October 30, and he was appointed Chancellor of the new government on that date. Bauer became Foreign Minister on November 21, following the death of Viktor Adler, the first holder of that position under the republic.

The attempted left-wing coup mentioned above took place on April 17, 1919, when huge crowds of the unemployed and invalids assembled before the Vienna city hall, heard speeches calling for relief of harsh living conditions and the establishment of a soviet government, and then marched to the Parliament building, where they tried to force an entrance. The crowds were dispersed by police and loyal units of the *Volkswehr* (Peoples' Army). See *ibid.*, pp. 731-34, and Charles A. Gulick, *Austria From Habsburg to Hitler* (2 vols., Berkeley and Los Angeles, Calif., 1948), I, 51-78.

[3] Alois Muna, a founder of the Czech Communist party while a prisoner in Russia.

[4] A coal-mining town, located fifteen miles west of Prague, which had long been a center of radical socialist agitation.

and Czecho-Slovakia would be the old historic limits has led to a discussion of what terms the Germans will be able to get within the new state. For the time being the proposals discussed are those of "*individuals*" only. President Masaryk recently expressed himself as having "in mind the example of Switzerland." The Germans will bargain for full "*territorial autonomy*." The Czechs will perhaps offer full political, economic and cultural rights—i.e. rights of "*personal nationality*" as distinguished from "*territorial nationality*." It is a salutary sign that the discussion has begun and that the Germans will take part in the communal elections next month.

The situation in Slovakia continues likewise to improve largely owing to the increased efficiency of the administration and to the scare produced by the Bolshevik regime in Hungary. The Slovak administrators are beginning to tackle the problem of the liquor monopoly which is at the root of a great deal of evil. This is in the hands of the Jews who form a strong pro-Magyar element in all of Hungary.

The Land Expropriation Law lays down the principle that estates will be expropriated and sets the lowest limit at 350 hectares (200 ha. arable, 150 ha. forest) and the highest limit at 500 ha.

It is only a skeleton law and will require a host of minor laws and considerable legislative machinery to carry it into effect. This law is on the whole a great achievement in spite of the haste in which it was passed. It delays detailed action until more information may be gathered, and it appears to leave a fairly high limit for the size of landed estates. At the same time it is calculated to allow some 1,300,000 ha. arable land and 3,000,000 ha. of forest land for expropriation.

HUNGARY.

Two tendencies are to be noted here. As pointed out in the last report, Bela Kun has proceeded with ever more radical measures to overcome the Magyar bourgeoisie, until during the last week he was reported to have said that he "would wipe them out." This is the natural evolution in all such turnovers as have taken place in Russia and Hungary. It was also pointed out *a month ago* that it needed only a blow from without to topple over this Bolshevist house of cards. Since then the Smuts fiasco has exposed how little the question of Magyar Bolshevism has been understood in dominant Allied circles. It required the advance of the Rumanian army to convince the American representatives at Vienna after weeks of indecision to urge intervention. It will take more troops now than it would have a month ago, and it may take many more later if the Russians make a direct connection with the Magyars. It should also be noted that our position as regards the Magyars is a different one in contrast to the

Russians. The Russians were our allies, and we might excuse ourselves from intervening in internal affairs on this basis. But the Magyars were conquered by the Allies, and the question at issue is the fulfilment of terms laid down by the Peace Conference. In other words, the two questions should be judged separately and be treated by different methods. The Magyar problem in itself is not half so dangerous as the possibilities it opens up in regard to making Central Europe Bolshevik. For the solution of this question men are needed who have a *thorough understanding* of the problems of Central Europe and who are resolute.

The intervention should take place under Entente orders and under Entente military control and should be accompanied with a definite announcement that within the territorial limits laid down by the Peace Conference the Entente will insist on the establishment of a democratic government representing all classes of society and will furnish immediately and effectively the necessary supplies of food, coal, and capital and guarantee the resumption of normal relations with the outside world. The time for letting the "peoples of Hungary" to "determine themselves" is past. The Czecho-Slovaks, Rumanians and Jugo-Slavs may well answer: "Certainly, we shall accept self-determination for branches of our peoples within the borders of old Hungary, but *after a certain time*, so as to give us an equal chance with the forty years of Magyar oppression." Or they may insist that all the Czecho-Slovaks, Rumanians, and Jugo-Slavs within the limits of the states they now form be allowed to determine themselves.

GERMAN AUSTRIA.

During the last week Vienna witnessed an attempt, fostered largely by foreign agitators, to overturn the government. The war invalids, whose grievances are many, the hungry and unemployed proletariat, but most of all the weak and vacillating policy of the Renner-Bauer government contributed to make the attempt look more serious than it really was. It is too early to judge the movement because of the lack of decisive details. Serious or not, the events of the week have definitely convinced our representatives in Vienna that the Entente must intervene in Hungary and occupy German Austria. It is certain likewise that with the increasing influence of Bolshevism at Vienna the provinces of German Austria tend more and more toward separatist tendencies and toward an open Bolshevist movement at Graz and among the soldiers along the Jugo-Slav-German frontier.

In the meanwhile, it appears that Renner has urged the quickening of the socialization legislation before the National Assembly and the continuation of the negotiations for union with Germany.

How the Italian "withdrawal" from the Peace Conference will affect German Austria cannot now be foretold. But should the "withdrawal" be consummated and Orlando receive the backing of the Italian nation, it may lead to a stiffening of the Italian position in Tyrol and more open dickerings for an understanding between Italy and Germany at the cost of German Austria.

JUGO-SLAVIA.

The important event this week for Jugo-Slavia has been the statement of President Wilson on Fiume and the "withdrawal" of the Italians from the Peace Conference. For the Jugo-Slavs, the situation has brought *renewed hope*. The Croats will be encouraged to range themselves with increasing solidarity behind Jugo-Slavia. The Slovenes, who stand the chance of losing one-third of their number by the decisions at the Peace Conference, naturally have been disquieted. They hold that not only should the Italo-Slovene boundary be drawn so as to include the least number of Slovenes in Italy, but the Slovenes in Italy should be told that they will get a guarantee of political and cultural freedom from the League of Nations. As regards the Germano-Slovene boundaries in the valley of the Drau, the internationalization under the League of Nations for a decade of such cities as Klagenfurt and Villach would tend to allay the fears of the Slovenes. The main railroads from the Adriatic will undoubtedly be internationalized and the inclusion of these two cities under that regime with guarantees of complete political liberty to both Germans and Slovenes would lead to a juster settlement and to better relations between the Slovenes and the Germans.

The increasing activity of the Bolsheviks along the Germano-Slovene and Magyaro-Croat border has caused alarm in certain circles. For the present this appears as yet unfounded. It is interesting to note that the Slovene Social Democrats whose center is at *Laibach recently voted down* Bolshevik methods, while both Slovene and Italian Social Democrats in the regions occupied by Italy centering at *Trieste* voted "*for the proletariat dictatorship*" In other words, while Jugo-Slavia *still remains Bolshevik-proof*, the western, northern, and north-eastern borders are being more and more exposed to the movement. This has led to protective measures on the part of the government.

The strong anti-Italian and pro-Jugo-Slav feeling of the vast mass of the people in the territory occupied by Italy can no longer be doubted. The policy of the Italian military and administrative officers is partly to blame. The reports which are coming in bear witness to that fact.

T MS (WP, DLC).

From Vance Criswell McCormick

My dear Mr. President: [Paris] April 26, 1919.

I enclose herewith an extract from the Minutes of the Conference on Reparations, held at your house on Wednesday, April 23, at 4 P.M.[1] It occurs to me that there is the possibility of a misunderstanding as to the meaning of your statement at the beginning of the second paragraph, page 2: "President Wilson said that the claim for German ships seized in United States ports was the only reparation claim put forth by the United States of America." The balance of your remarks seem to me to make clear what I think was in your mind, namely, that we were waiving a claim for pensions and separation allowances to an amount far in excess of the value of the German ships, and it was a waiver of this particular claim, and not of every other claim whatsoever, that you had in mind.

I enclose a brief analysis of estimates made of damage suffered by the United States, from which you will see that we have claims approximating $280,000,000, exclusive of (a) claims for pensions and separation allowances; (b) claims on account of any failure to restore intact to their owners United States property in enemy and occupied territory; and (c) expense of army of occupation which, under the armistice, constitutes a special claim against Germany.

If, as I believe, you did not intend by your remark of last Wednesday to waive our claims for damage resulting from acts of aggression before entry into war (e.g., Lusitania, etc.) and shipping losses suffered during the war, and similar direct damage as indicated in the enclosed statement, you may perhaps think it desirable to call the attention of Mr. Lloyd George and of Mr. Clemenceau to this fact.

I am, my dear Mr. President,

Very sincerely yours, Vance C McCormick

CCLS (V. C. McCormick Papers, CtY).

[1] "Memorandum of conversation between President Wilson and Mr. Lloyd George, at the President's house, on Wednesday, April 23, at 4 o'clock P.M.," T MS (V. C. McCormick Papers, CtY). A different version of this conversation appears in the minutes of the Council of Four printed at April 23, 1919, 4 p.m. It should be noted that the sentence quoted by McCormick below, while accurate in substance, does not appear verbatim in either version of the conversation.

From Milenko R. Vesnić

My dear Mr President, Paris, le 26 Avril 1919

I have the honour to acknowledge the receipt of your exceedingly kind letter of the 21st inst.,[1] for w[h]ich I beg to express my most sincere thanks. My gratitude is all the greater, as your opening gives me the long wished-for opportunity of explaninig [explaining] to you the Montenegrin chapter in the Yougoslave problem.

Permit me however to begin by thanking you for the truly friendly solicitude you are displaynig [displaying] towoords [towards] the progress of our national question. I am sure that I am hereby only giving expression to the inmost feelings of my entire people.

At the same time I would add at once, that I have not failed to bring to the notice of my Government the interest which you in your generous friendship are taking in the Montenegrin affair, and I am convinced in advance that the Royal Government will give your views every possible consideration.

May I furthermore add, that His Excellency Mr. Sharp had already on the 4 inst. inst [*sic*] drawn my attention to the advisability of proce[e]ding deliberately in regard to the Montenegrins implicated in the recent political disturbances, and especially to put off the carrying out of the sentences until the final conclusion of peace.

I begged my Government to pay every deference to this suggestion, and I am happy to say that it has declared itself prepared to act upon it. May I say that I was sure in advance of the reply?

The present Government of my country is largely composed of men who have themselves been the victims of political prosecution [persecution], and have experienced in their own persons the inconvenience of summary proceedings. Indeed, our present Prime Minister, Mr Protitch,[2] has spent holf [half] his life in prison on account of his fight for political liberty; Mr Pashitch has suffered in the same way and was at one time condemned to death, and I myself have passed through similar vicissitudes.

The Montenegrins are as much Serbian as the people of New Jersey are American. The population of those highlands is as patriotic as the most loyal citizen of Serbia, and it has always aspired to reunion in one State with the other Serbs.

Since your proclamation in your glorious messages, promising the peoples the right to dispose of their own destinies, and especially since the moment when the whole Yougoslav race believed that it was on the threshold of union in one free and democratic State; since our Croat and Slovene kinsmen have succeeded in grasping our hands, our Montenegrin brothers have considered that they, too, and perhaps more than anyone else, had the right to realize their dream of centuries, and that no one would contest them this right.

But apart from their national sentiments, they were forced into this pathe by the autocratic and tyrannous rule of King Nicholas, and that more particularly since they perceived that he did not look upon them as citizens, but rather as cattle to traffick in.

It is very painful to me to speak in these terms of a Serbe Sovereign, but I have the habit of always telling the truth and your cordiality prompts me to be perfectly frank, and especielly [especially] because I am afraid that unscrupulous persons may mislead you in regard to this question.

The people of Montenegro has resolutely made up its mind to unite for good and all with its brothers. This union has in former times been frustrated by the Government of Vienna. For the last three years the Rome Government has replaced that of Vienna in this action, and I have good reason to believe, that King Nicholas would have already resigned himself to the will of the people, if Baron Sonnino had not decided to use him as an instrument of his policy in the Balkans.

The way in which you have met me from the first moment, when I had the honour to approach you, and the gratitude with which this reception inspires me towards yourself, could not but impose the obligation upon me to lay the whole truth before you, even if it were not the future of my nation which is at stake.

Pray believe me therefore, that King Nicholas and his present associates are men totally undeserving of the interest you extend to them in the greatness of your heart, and that on the contrary this interest could only reflect a shadow upon your personality, which I would fervently wish to keep guarded from all misinterprestation [misinterpretation].

If the world is to be made safe for democracy, I beg you to believe me that King Nickolas is not the man to assure it, as he was always been an autocrat, a tyrant, and that at his time of life—sevently [seventy] six years of age—he is in the nature of things not likely to change. Unfortunabily his son is, if possible, worse than himself; and even if either of them were to change, the people would never believe it. I tremble at the thought, that under your protection he might return to Montenegro. His return would be the signal for fresh bloodshed, which would be a veritable calamity for our people.

I am sorry to say, I have grounds to fear that the Italians will endeavour to reinstate him, as I know that they [have been] organizing an expedition for that purpose.

I beg you, my dear Mr President, to consider the foregoing more in the light of a confession, and to ascribe it to a wish to give you the most exact information possible; than to take it as special pleading in defence of the policy of my Government.

But for this wish I should not have taken the liberty of encroaching so long upon your precious time.

Needless to say, we shall always be ready to fall in with your suggestions and extremely gratiful to you for them.

I trust that you will take all I have said in the spirit in which I have written it, and I have the honour

to remain

yours very sincerely Milenko R. Vesnitch

TLS (WP, DLC).

[1] WW to M. R. Vesnić, April 21, 1919, Vol. 57.

[2] Stojan Protić.

A Summary of a Letter from Marcel Laurent

[Paris, April 26, 1919]

Ass't Secretary of General Confederation of Labor begs Pres. to adhere to his 14 points, and promises support of the members. Imperialistic ambitions of all nations should be curbed.[1]

T MS (WP, DLC).

[1] This summary scarcely does justice to this eloquent and important letter, which Wilson almost certainly did not read. Laurent began by saying that the "grave incident" which had divided the United States and Italy at the peace conference gave "striking evidence of the dangers of annexationism which continue to tempt the spirit of the supporters of secret diplomacy." "Your strong and public protest," he continued, "against the Italian pretentions has found, we wish to assure you of it, an approbation without reserve in the conscience of the French working masses, in whose name we thank you for that new mark of courage and fidelity to the principles of peace of which you have been made the champion, and which must be imposed on all the belligerents in the sacred interest of the peoples and of the peace." Wilson had voiced on the subject of Fiume and Dalmatia "the profound sentiment of all right consciences, of all those who only participated in the war in a sentiment of legitimate defense, of resistance to imperialism and annexationism." The French working people had suffered too much in the war against imperialistic and militaristic Germany to tolerate seeing similar ambitions develop in the Allied governments. Even if imperialism and annexationism had changed sides after the victory, they remained nonetheless "strictly condemnable." Wilson had called on the peoples themselves for a discussion in broad daylight to enable them to form their own judgments. "We respond to you, Mr. President," Laurent wrote, "by applauding your gesture and by ranging ourselves on your side." Wilson had given the working people "the necessary encouragement to continue to defend against all the crooked dealers of diplomacy the Fourteen Points which you have set forth, which we have made our own, and which must serve as the basis of the humane peoples' peace." M. Laurent to WW, April 26, 1919, TLS (WP, DLC).

Norman Hezekiah Davis to Gilbert Fairchild Close

Dear Mr. Close: Paris, 26th April, 1919.

I wish to acknowledge and thank you for your letter of April 25th enclosing the President's letter to the Secretary of the Treasury approving the establishment of credits to the amount of $100,000,000, in favor of the French Government, beyond amounts already established by him. Sincerely yours, Norman H. Davis

TLS (WP, DLC).

A Memorandum by Edward Thomas Williams

[April 26, 1919]

Conversation between Secretary Lansing and Viscount Chinda

At 9:15 p.m. April 26, 1919, in accordance with the request of Secretary Lansing I went to his office where I found him in conversation with Viscount Chinda.

They were discussing the disposition to be made of the Shantung Railway. Viscount Chinda said: "It is to be made a joint undertaking." "What do you mean by that" asked Mr. Lansing. The Viscount turned to me and said: "What is the proper term for "*ho-pan*." I said it was a "joint undertaking" and explained that I understood that the railway was to be managed by a Sino-Japanese corporation. The Viscount said that was the meaning.

Mr. Lansing asked what it was that Japan wanted done. The Viscount said they simply wanted their agreements with China executed. That China had entered into an agreement with Japan in regard to the disposition of the German rights and property. He referred to the treaty containing the 21-Demands. Mr. Lansing asked why Japan had made these 21-Demands upon China. The Viscount replied that they were necessary in order to the settlement of the Shantung question. The Secretary pointed out that the 21-Demands covered a great deal more than the Shantung question.

Viscount Chinda acknowledged that this was so, but said there were many other unsettled questions pending at that time in relation to Manchuria and other places and that it seemed desirable to settle them all at once.

Mr. Lansing pointed out that the convention was extorted from China and was therefore of doubtful validity; of no more validity than the Treaty of Bucharest. Viscount Chinda said the Chinese delegates were making much of this point and he then proceeded to say that at the close of the Chino-Japanese war Japan had entered into a treaty with China by which South Manchuria was ceded to Japan. Thereupon Russia, France and Germany advised Japan to retrocede it to China. Japan was too weak to resist these three powers and acquiesced, but Japan did not go about complaining of it. It was ridiculous for a nation of 400,000,000 of people to go around complaining that they had made a treaty under duress.

The Viscount added that they had promised to return the place to China only if Germany should hand it over unconditionally and without compensation. This Germany had not done and Japan had had to go to war to obtain it. Japan therefore was under no obligation to return it to China. They had taken it by conquest and had a right to retain it, if they so desired.

Secretary Lansing again reminded him that it was nevertheless a treaty made after an ultimatum issued and that there was a difference between exaction made of a belligerent and one made in time of peace. Mr. Lansing asked what were the provisions for the return of these rights to China. The Viscount replied that they were stated in the Convention. "Yes but there is much besides in the Conventions" said the Secretary, turning to me. I remarked that the conditions for the restoration of the lease were four, enumerating them:

1. The opening of the whole of Kiaochow Bay to foreign trade.
2. The establishment of an exclusive Japanese settlement.
3. The establishment of an international settlement, if so desired.
4. The disposition of the public buildings and property by arrangement between China and Japan.

Mr. Lansing asked what the conditions of such transfer of public property would be. The Viscount said: "How do I know? It will depend upon the negotiations between China and Japan." He evidently did not catch Mr. Lansing's meaning, who was thinking of a return of these buildings to China. Viscount Chinda probably had in mind the taking of them over by Japan for the "exclusive Japanese Settlement." Mr. Lansing endeavored to explain and asked if he meant that the transfer was to be made for a money consideration, say for a stated sum like $5,000,000. "No," said the Viscount, they had never thought of receiving money for the return of Kiaochow to China. Mr. Lansing asked how soon Japan would return the place to China. The Viscount didn't know. "Would it be so long as two years," asked the Secretary. The Viscount thought it would not possibly be so long as that. He then explained that he had himself attended to the opening of Hangchow, Changsha and Shashih where foreign settlements were established and that it had taken some months, because they had to agree with the Chinese authorities as to the locality and boundaries of the settlements; and in the case of Tsingtao it would be necessary first to know whether an international settlement was to be established or not and what the boundaries would be.

Mr. Lansing asked then if China would at once thereafter come into control of Kiachow.* "Certainly" said Viscount Chinda. (He did not, however, state that while the lease would be returned to China, the possession of an exclusive Japanese settlement covering the best part of Kiaochow would replace a lease of 78 years with a permanent Japanese city, as will indeed be the case, if the terms of the convention are carried out.) Mr. Lansing asked what about the other

* Mr. Lansing also asked him, if Japan were not taking the place over as trustee for China, to which the Viscount assented. Secretary Lansing said that trustees could not profit by such transaction. The Viscount did not appear to get the implication.

German rights in Shantung. "What do you mean?," said the Japanese Ambassador. "Well the railway, for instance." "Why it will be a joint undertaking" he replied. "Will it belong to the Japanese Government?" He said he did not know but he added there were very few rights in Shantung. There was this railway and options on two other lines. (He did not mention the mines nor the option on all supplies of engineers, money and materials for public works in the province.) Mr. Lansing said that the American desire was to see the matter amicably settled between China and Japan. The German rights in Shantung were founded upon a gross wrong—founded in blood. They had bargained with the blood of their people and this was an indemnity for murder. We could not bear to see such a situation perpetuated. We looked upon the people of Shantung as a people wronged and oppressed and now that the enemy was removed we could not bear to see the evil continue through replacing one foreign nation by another.

Viscount Chinda admitted the charge against Germany, but said Japan did not intend to treat the people as the Germans had done. Mr. Lansing pointed to the attitude of the United States as regards the principles upon which peace was to be made; the rights of nationalities, the right of self-determination of peoples.

"O but the situation is quite different," Viscount Chinda said. "We have express conventions with China dealing with this question and we mean to insist upon their *exact fulfillment.*" Mr. Lansing asked why the conditions of return to China could not be stated in the Peace Treaty. Viscount Chinda replied that the treaty of peace was with Germany and not with China and Germany was to renounce her rights unconditionally and cede them to Japan. They could not tell the Japanese what they should do with it. Mr. Lansing said that did not prevent a statement by Japan of her generous intentions. The Viscount said Japan had already proclaimed her generous intentions. They were stated in the Convention which had been published to the world. He charged that we were always suspecting them, doubting their good faith.** Mr. Lansing denied this, and said our only desire was to find some way of reconciling the claims of Japan and China: That we wanted to save the face of Japan, but also the face of China. The Viscount then launched into a confidential attack upon the conduct of the Chinese delegates. He repeated the story of the alleged instructions issued by the Peking Government to the delegates to work in harmony with Japan and to the alleged agreement made by Minister Lou as he came through Tokyo to co-

** He also asked if we came here to sit in judgment on them, saying that Japan could not submit to that; that we all came as representing sovereign states, compeers, and no one could call in question the actions of another.

operate with the Japanese delegation and said their own delegation had instructions to support China as far as possible in such matters as the abolition of spheres of influence, the abolition of extraterritoriality and the obtaining of tariff autonomy, etc. They were, he said, taken by surprise by the action of the Chinese Delegation in presenting a claim to the direct return of Kiaochow. The Japanese delegates had kept quiet, however, and had asked for further instructions from their government. He said the propaganda of the Chinese delegates had grossly misrepresented Japan and that such misrepresentation was still going on. He pulled a telegram from his pocket from Viscount Ishii saying that a Mr. Selden,[1] correspondent of the New York Tribune (?) had telegraphed to his paper that a member of the Chinese delegation had charged Japan with having a secret treaty with Germany.

Mr. Lansing said that he had heard that rumor too; turning to me to ask as to the origin, I said it had been published in a Moscow paper.†

He mentioned another little incident showing a disposition on the part of the Chinese to misrepresent them.

All this he said had stirred up a great deal of feeling in Japan and it was a point of honor with them now to insist upon the exact fulfillment of the treaty with China.

They had had instructions from home that if the German rights were not renounced in favor of Japan the Japanese delegates were not to sign the Treaty. They, therefore, had no option in the matter.

E.T.W

† We have received a great deal of evidence showing conclusively that the Japanese consular officials in Sweden have had frequent interviews with German agents.

TI MS (WP, DLC).

[1] Charles Albert Selden, at this time a Paris correspondent of the *New York Times*, not the *New York Tribune*. His telegram, dated Paris, April 18, was printed in the *New York Times*, April 19, 1919. It consisted largely of quotations from a dispatch from the Chinese Foreign Office in Peking to the Chinese legation in Paris. The dispatch reported that the Bolsheviks were circulating an "alleged treaty of alliance between Germany and Japan," said to have been drawn up, but never ratified, while Prince Max of Baden was Chancellor of Germany (that is, between October 4 and November 9, 1918). The dispatch gave details of what it referred to as the "bogus" treaty. Selden noted, however, that the Chinese diplomats in Paris believed that there was some truth behind the report, even if the treaty was a forgery.

From the Diary of Edith Benham

April 26, 1919

These are eventful days, but the P. is so tired when he comes home he seldom speaks of what has gone on. In speaking of Clemenceau he said he seems to have the conception of what is right and wrong, but he seems afraid of the French people, and afraid to publish what he considers right. He has always been considered such a lion of courage that such timidity seems curious. L. George seems to be the slippery customer, and it seems impossible to tell which way he is going to jump from day to day. Secret advice today is to the effect that the Italian fleet is ordered to Fiume, and the Army is told to advance toward it. Our Navy there is advised to hold their men all aboard ship. This is the first time the Italian Navy has been known to come out, for during the war they said proudly they had never lost a ship, because they had never risked going to sea and meeting the Austrians.

From the Diary of Ray Stannard Baker

Saturday the 26 [April 1919]

Colonel House agreed with me on my arguments for better press arrangements at Versailles, but thought I ought to take it up with the President: that no one else had authority enough. I did so this evening when I met the President. I had quite an argument with him: & finally he thought there was justice in our demand for admission to see the treaty presented to the Germans but he was decidedly against the second proposal—to meet the spokesman of the Germans. He said that he agreed here with the French. He said there were two factions in the delegation—the unbending & arrogant Brockdorff-Rantzau group & the more amenable Melchior group & while they were to be given free communication with Germany he felt that the feeling was too intense here to make it advisable for our men to talk with any of the Germans.

The President seemed proud of the accomplishment of the day by the Big Three—they finished with ports & waterways this morning & with the financial clauses this afternoon.

From James Grover McDonald

New York Apl 26 1919

League of free nations association[1] heartily congratulate you on your courageous appeal to the public opinion of the world on behalf of a peace settlement based upon the principles agreed to by the Allied and Associated powers and accepted by the enemy states at the time of the signing of the armistice.

James G McDonald, Chairman of Executive Committee.

T telegram (WP, DLC).

[1] About which, see N. Hapgood to WW, Feb. 26, 1919, n. 1, Vol. 55.

From Joseph Patrick Tumulty

[The White House, April 26, 1919]

No. 80 It appears to me from this end that the Japanese demands will soon produce another crisis. If such a crisis arises, I hope you will in any statement you make emphasize again America's purpose and her unwillingness to consent to any imperialistic peace. The whole country will be with you in this matter as never before.

I think that your Italian statement was the beginning of a real peace and a real League of Nations.

In the Italian situation you took the offensive in the matter of secret treaties, plots, etc. You cannot yield it for anything no matter what the consequences. Tumulty.

T telegram (WP, DLC).

From the Diary of Dr. Grayson

Sunday, April 27, 1919.

Owing to the strenuous week that the President had passed, and in view of the fact that he had a conference all day last Sunday over the Italian situation, I begged him to cancel the conferences which he had previously arranged for including church. I told him that I had arranged a Sunday outing for him and Mrs. Wilson. He agreed to follow my prescription. He arose at about 10:30; had a light breakfast; and at 12:00 o'clock the President, Mrs. Wilson, Miss Benham and I went for a motor ride, arriving at 1:00 o'clock at a country place near Versailles, which is occupied by Mr. Bernard M. Baruch. It was a delightful change for the President to come unannounced to this little cottage for an informal lunch with no one to disturb him or even to notice that he was President of the United States. We all walked around the grounds and through the flower gardens, and it was a most restful relaxation for him. Mr. Baruch was in Germany on business but returned in time for lunch, and much to his surpise and pleasure, found us there. He joined us at lunch. No one else was present. At the luncheon Mr. Baruch discussed with the President some of the men prominent in French official life. No business of any kind was taken up.

I had arranged for Mr. Baruch's French chauffeur to accompany us from the temporary White House to the country place as a guide. He was told to be at the President's house promptly at 12:00 o'clock. When 12:00 o'clock arrived, the chauffeur failed to put in his appearance. The President, always punctual, was ready. We waited five minutes, and then the President said to me: "We will not wait any longer." So I had to act as pilot through this net-work of roads, over which I had traveled only once. I succeeded, however, in getting to Mr. Baruch's place without difficulty. The President and Mrs. Wilson were amazed at my being able to accomplish this.

After lunch at Mr. Baruch's place we motored to Fontainebleau. We drove around the Palace, and went to the spot where Napoleon said farewell to the grenadiers of his Old Guard on April 20, 1814, just as he was leaving for Elba. We visited the gardens and the pond in the rear of the Palace, and afterwards took an extended drive through the forest. On the main road between Paris and Fontainebleau is a monument. We were told that at this place Napoleon met Pope Pius VII. It appears that the Pope was to reach Fontainebleau at a certain hour. Failing to put in his appearance at the hour fixed, Napoleon became very impatient and started on the road to Paris to meet him. He met him at the cross roads, in the center of which stands a monument.

I took the liberty of saying to the President that in respect to his appointments he resembles Napoleon; that is, he becomes very impatient when his callers are late. The President simply smiled. I recalled to the President the remark which he made on one occasion when William Jennings Bryan, who was Secretary of State, had an appointment with the President at two o'clock at the White House. After waiting about five minutes, and Mr. Bryan failing to put in his appearance, I noticed the President walking up and down the floor impatiently. The President at the time turned to me and said: "Doctor, I hate for any one not to be punctual with their engagements. I feel inclined now to make a few 'cursory' remarks."

While returning to Paris the President slept for about a half hour. I also dozed off for a few minutes. The President, however, woke up first and said to me: "This is wonderful scenery we have just passed, isn't it?" The remark seemed to amuse Mrs. Wilson.

We reached the temporary White House at six o'clock. The President, Mrs. Wilson and I had dinner at seven o'clock. He showed that the outing had refreshed him very much. It produced a healthy fatigue. At 8:30 the President saw General Pershing, the two remaining together for a half hour. General Pershing discussed with him the French military report which had been completed by Marshal Foch and presented to the French Cabinet on Thursday. Marshal Foch had told the French Cabinet that he could not be responsible for guarding the frontiers of France unless a real army was kept on the Rhine, and the President asked General Pershing to discuss with him exactly what was necessary.

From the Diary of Edith Benham

April 27, 1919

Today we went off on rather a spree. Mr. Baruch has taken a little house at St. Cloud, about twenty minutes ride. He told Dr. G. he could lease it for the day any time he wanted, so the Dr. heard he had gone to Strasburg and invited the P., Mrs. W. and me to go out there to luncheon. The host turned up early this morning and wanted to go off to town so as not to be around when the P. was there, but Dr. G. persuaded him to stay and it was much nicer having him. He really lives at the Ritz most of the time and comes to this place for the weekends. It is a cunning little house with a charming garden and very quiet and retired. We had a very nice luncheon. As usual, conversation turned on the slipperiness of the various delegates. The P. spoke of Allenby for whom they had sent and whom he characterized as a man in every sense of the word, height and breadth and a splendid face. He advised strongly against giving the French a hand in Syria, said their measures would surely provoke an insurrection and massacres, so it was decided by L.G. and the others to follow Allenby's advice and they were proceeding along that line when L.G. produced a Col. Wilson[1] (British) who is very pro-French and he advised giving the French full sway in Syria which, of course, pleased old Clemenceau. Then it was agreed to let a Commission go to Syria to study the subject and the P. appointed Mr. Charles Crane and another man, the head of Oberlin College,[2] to go with the French and British Commissioners to study the matter, and one day Clemenceau and L.G. decide to let them go and change their minds the next. The P. said that if he had had three honest men who were strong enough to live up to their convictions peace would have been settled six months ago.

He says he hated the idea of meeting the Germans. He would not have minded so much meeting the old blood and iron people of the old regime, but he hates the thought of seeing these nondescript creatures of the new, and he had searched diligently in his mind for some method to avoid meeting them. The question came up of Herbert Hoover as a Presidential candidate—Democratic—and Baruch seems to think he rather wants to run. The P. does not think him a man sufficiently able to carry the many questions to a practical conclusion as a President should.

[1] That is, Capt. Arnold Talbot Wilson, about whom, see n. 4 to the minutes of the Council of Four printed at April 11, 1919, Vol. 57.

[2] That is, Henry Churchill King.

From Henry Mauris Robinson, with Enclosure

Dear Mr. President: Paris 27 April 1919

In agreement with Sir Robert Borden, Mr. Barnes, the Japanese Delegation and the Belgian Delegation, the Labour Clauses are as set out in the draft attached.

Sir Robert Borden stated that he must take the matter up with the British Delegation, that he did not believe there would be any general objection but suspected there might be one objection (Hughes's).

It is our belief that the French Delegation will agree, and we are hopeful that the entire British Delegation also will agree.

Very respectfully yours, Henry M. Robinson

TLS (WP, DLC).

ENCLOSURE

INTERNATIONAL LABOUR LEGISLATION

CLAUSES PROPOSED FOR INSERTION IN THE TREATY OF PEACE

The High Contracting Parties, recognising that the well being, physical, moral and intellectual of industrial wage earners is of supreme international importance, have framed a permanent machinery associated with that of the League of Nations to further this great end.

They recognize that differences of climate, habits and customs, of economic opportunity and industrial tradition, make strict uniformity in the conditions of labour difficult of immediate attainment. But, holding as they do, that labour should not be regarded merely as an article of commerce, they think that there are methods and principles for regulating labour conditions which all industrial communities should endeavour to apply so far as their special circumstances will permit.

Among these methods and principles, the following seem to the High Contracting Parties to be of special and urgent importance:

First. The guiding principle above ennunciated that labour should not be regarded merely as a commodity or article of commerce.

Second. The right of association for all lawful purposes by the employed as well as by the employers.

Third. The payment to the employed of a wage adequate to maintain a reasonable standard of life as this is understood in their time and country.

Fourth. The adoption of an eight hours day or a forty-eight

hours week as the standard to be aimed at where it has not already been attained.

Fifth. The adoption of a weekly rest of at least twenty-four hours which should include Sunday wherever practicable.

Sixth. The abolition of child labour and the imposition of such limitations on the labour of young persons as shall permit the continuation of their education and assure their proper physical development.

Seventh. The principle that men and women should receive equal remuneration for work of equal value.

Eighth. The standards set by law in each country with respect to the conditions of labour should have due regard to the equitable economic treatment of all workers lawfully resident therein.[1]

Ninth. Each State should make provision for a system of inspection in which women should take part, in order to insure the enforcement of the laws and regulations for the protection of the employed.

Without claiming that these methods and principles are either complete or final, the High Contracting Parties are of opinion that they are well fitted to guide the policy of the League of Nations; and that, if adopted by the industrial communities who are members of the League, and safeguarded in practice by an adequate system of inspection, they will confer lasting benefits upon the wage earners of the world.

T MS (WP, DLC).

[1] About the final wording of this clause by Wilson, see WW to H. M. Robinson, April 23, 1919. Robinson later explained the provenance of this clause, as follows:

"In respect of the eighth principle, which had to do with 'aliens lawfully resident in a country,' against our opposition it was carried through in a form which the Peace Conference felt it could not adopt. For that reason, the draft convention, including the Principle 8, was returned to the conference for further discussion and action. The only important objection was the one named to Principle No. 8.

"We obtained the assistance of stylists in English of all degrees, including David Hunter Miller and other prominent men in words, and last but not least Sir Alfred Balfour [*sic*].

"They worked for two weeks and were unable to find a phraseology which was satisfactory to the Conference. It looked as though we might be forced to eliminate the eighth principle, thus reducing the total to eight.

"I was naturally disturbed by this and I felt that President Wilson would be also. One afternoon I wrote him that I feared this was going to happen. I told him of our difficulty and the following morning at ten o'clock, I received from him the suggested form of clause contained in his letter. Fearing that it would be unwise to inform the group that he had written it and that it might be turned down, I took on the authorship as my own and it was promptly accepted unanimously by the Conference.

"This long story is written as one of the many proofs of President Wilson's ability as a stylist. My admiration for him, however, went way beyond the question of style and the limited contacts I had with him were always very satisfactory." H. M. Robinson to EBW, Nov. 13, 1936, TLS (WP, DLC).

A Memorandum by Arthur James Balfour

April 27, 1919.

The result of my conversations with the Japanese may, I think, be summarized somewhat as follows:

In the first place, the Japanese strenuously deny either that they intended to modify in their own favor the conditions which the Germans had imposed upon the Chinese in connection with the Shantung Peninsula, or that, in fact, their treaties with China would have had that effect.

They say, on the contrary, that they propose surrendering all military control over the Peninsula, including the 50-kilometre zone round KAIAOCHOW within which German troops were allowed but not Chinese, and all interference with the civil administration of the territory. Their intention is fully to restore Chinese sovereignty within the leased territory.

The provisions that appear in the Treaty of 1918, with regard to maintaining a garrison at TSINAN and guarding the railway with Japanese troops, are purely provisional, and refer only to the period of transition immediately following peace, and this period it is their intention to make as short as possible. No date was named, however, for the determination of this transitory arrangement.

In these circumstances, the German rights which the Japanese propose still to retain are economic in their character. They consist in:

1. A right to claim a concession at Tsingtau, which, however, does not exclude, and was not intended to exclude, the right also for other countries to organize an international concession, if that is desired.

2. The German rights in the railways already built, and the mines associated with them. The railways are built on land which is in full Chinese sovereignty, and subject to Chinese law.

3. Concessions granted to the Germans for building two other railways. These railways are to be built with Japanese capital, and the Japanese capitalists are at this moment negotiating with the Chinese Government as to the terms on which the necessary money will be provided. The Chinese Government will be able to secure the same position in regard to these railways as it has over other railways constructed by foreign capital.

The Japanese Plenipotentiaries, for reasons of national dignity which are easy to understand, are unwilling to modify the letter of the treaties which they have made with China, but they are ready (if I understand them rightly) to give explicit and binding assurances:

(a) That any concession which China gives them at Tsingtau will not exclude other foreign enterprise from the Port.

(b) That the economic control of the railway, which the possession of the majority of the shares gives them will not be used in any way to discriminate between the trade facilities of different nations.

T MS (WP, DLC).

From Albert Sidney Burleson

[The White House, April 27, 1919]

No. 81 Following sent at the request of the Postmaster General: "If you do not object I desire to give out the following statement: 'The cable congestion resulting from war conditions having largely passed and the resumption of the sending of commercial code messages having materially lessened, the cable [loads and the diminished use of the cables following][1] as the result of the agreement on the terms to be embodied in the treaty of peace with Germany, make it possible to return the cable lines to their respective owners, and the Postmaster General has so recommended to the President. He hopes that the return may be effected by May second.' "

Tumulty.

T telegram (WP, DLC).

[1] Addition from the "telegram sent" in the J. P. Tumulty Papers, DLC.

From the Diary of Dr. Grayson

Monday, April 28, 1919.

The President had breakfast at 8:15 o'clock. He then went to his study to dispose of his correspondence. At 11:00 o'clock he met with the Big Three. The Japanese situation was discussed. Immediately after lunch he conferred with Mr. Balfour. The Plenary Session then followed at three o'clock, adjourning at 5:45 o'clock.[1] The League of Nations Constitution, as originally agreed upon by the special committee, was debated and adopted unanimously, the Japanese delegates reserving the right to bring up the question of "the equality of nations" after the League actually has been constituted. The President made a speech in moving the adoption of the League Constitution.

The President, Mrs. Wilson and I went for a motor ride in the Bois.

In referring to Mr. Bourgeois, one of the French Delegates, who is a long-winded and tiresome speaker, and who gives the impression of a man of mediocre ability, I said to the President: "I wonder how that man ever became Prime Minister of France."[2] He replied: "I asked that question of Mr. Clemenceau, and Mr. Clemenceau laughingly replied: 'Those were the days when I was out tearing down French Cabinets. Bourgeois did not amount to much—I put him off towards the last—but before I got to him, he was about the only available one left, so they elected him Prime Minister.' " Mr. Clemenceau is not very complimentary about a number of his French colleagues. In referring to Mr. Klotz, the Minister of Finance, Mr. Clemenceau repeated a statement previously made by him that he (Klotz) was the only Jew that he had ever known who did not know anything about finance.

After dinner the President signed some mail and read some important papers he had on his desk concerning the Japanese claims.

[1] The complete minutes of this session are printed in *PPC*, III, 285-332.
[2] Bourgeois served as Prime Minister from November 1, 1895, to April 22, 1896.

Hankey's and Mantoux's Notes of a Meeting of the Council of Four[1]

President Wilson's Residence,
I.C.-177-A. Paris, April 28, 1919, 11 a.m.

. . . 13. PRESIDENT WILSON read a letter he had received from Mr. Hoover pleading for the recognition of the Finnish Government.[2] This letter gave very powerful reasons in support of the proposal, pointing out that Finland at the present time had ships which could not sail the seas because they had no flag to sail under; that they had need of credit but no banker would give it to a Government that was unrecognised; that they were subjected to severe censorship and had no means of issuing recognisable passports. (The remainder of the Letter was not heard as the Secretary was called out of the room.)

MR. LLOYD GEORGE pointed out that the attitude of the Finnish Government up to very recently had been very dubious. One of the reasons for the Murmansk expedition had been to prevent the Finns with the help of the Germans from getting possession of the Murman coast. Until the collapse of Germany Finland had, on the whole, been hostile. After that he had for a time been very doubtful whether Finland would be Bolshevist or Anti-Bolshevist. Now she had put on white gloves and was demanding recognition.

PRESIDENT WILSON admitted that it would be agreed [wise to agree?] to recognise Finland as this was the equitable course.

[1] The complete text of Hankey's minutes is printed in *PPC*, V, 308-26.
[2] HCH to WW, April 26, 1919, CCL (IaWbH). It is printed as Appendix I to the minutes of the Council of Four, April 30, 1919, 11 a.m., *PPC*, V, 357-59.

MR. LLOYD GEORGE said that personally he had no objection, but he would wish to consult the Foreign Secretary.

M. CLEMENCEAU said he would have to consult M. Pichon.

14. MR. LLOYD GEORGE handed round a memorandum which Mr. Balfour had prepared as a result of his conversation with the Japanese undertaken at the request of the Supreme Council on Saturday last. (Appendix VI.)[3]

PRESIDENT WILSON said that this was not sufficiently explicit but showed a decided approach in the Japanese attitude.

MR. LLOYD GEORGE said that Baron Makino had, on behalf of the Japanese Delegation, accepted Mr. Balfour's memorandum.

PRESIDENT WILSON asked what the effect would be of saying to the Japanese—"We transfer to you the German rights but we do not confirm any arrangement you made with the Chinese earlier in the war and we do this provided that you give a definite assurance that you will not exercise your provisional rights for employing military forces in Shantung." There was nothing on which the public opinion of the United States of America was firmer than on this question that China should be not oppressed by Japan. Public opinion expected him to take the same line for Japan as he had taken for Italy. There was certainly some difference between the two cases inasmuch as there was a definite undertaking by China to transfer territory to Japan.

§ Mantoux's notes:

Lloyd George. I have to inform you about an interview which took place Saturday between the representatives of Japan and Mr. Balfour.

The Japanese denied that the arrangement claimed by them was more advantageous than that which the Germans profited from. They called to our attention that they proposed to evacuate militarily all of Shantung, including the zone of fifty kilometers occupied by the Germans around Kiaochow. They repeat that their intention is to restore Chinese sovereignty in that province; the occupation of the railway line by Japanese troops is, they say, a temporary measure.

Their demands are essentially economic. What they want is a Japanese concession in the bay of Kiaochow, and the transfer of the German rights over the railway and the mines, which belong to the same company. The other lines that they propose to construct with Japanese capital will be established under the same conditions as the other railways constructed in China by foreign capital.

National pride stands in the way of the Japanese accepting a mod-

[3] See the memorandum by A. J. Balfour printed at April 27, 1919.

ification of their treaties with China. But they do really want an agreement with us not to oppose the establishment of an international concession in the bay of Kiaochow and to restore in all its plenitude Chinese sovereignty in Shantung.

What is your impression of that conversation?

Wilson. It is certainly better.

Hankey. Mr. Balfour also informs you that the Japanese have approved the summary which you just heard read.

Wilson. Can we say to the Japanese that we will leave them in possession of all the rights previously conceded to the Germans on the condition that they do not exercise their temporary right of military occupation? Notice that nothing would so easily inflame American opinion as the idea of an injustice done to China in favor of Japan. The news that I receive from America shows not only that public opinion supports me strongly in the position which I took concerning the Italian question, but that it expects to see me take the same position on the Japanese question.

Lloyd George. We must speak to the Japanese about it; Japan is a great power which must be treated as such.

Clemenceau. We must speak to them frankly and show them on what bases we believe we can agree with them.

Wilson. In that case, I would propose that we should see them tomorrow.§

(After an interval during which other subjects were discussed, Mr. Balfour was introduced and the discussion was continued.)

MR. BALFOUR said that by the instructions of the Supreme Council he had seen Baron Makino and Viscount Chinda on Saturday. The Supreme Council had his memorandum in their hands. Baron Makino had come again to see him on Sunday evening. With great delicacy but perfect clearness he had indicated that Japan wanted a decision on the Japanese claims as a whole. He had pointed out that Japan was asked to agree to the League of Nations although she could not obtain recognition of her claims for equality of treatment. He did not want to make trouble, but public opinion in Japan was very much concerned on this question. If Japan was to receive one check in Shantung and another check as regards the League of Nations the position would be very serious. Consequently, it was very important to obtain a decision on the question of Shantung before the Plenary Meeting to be held the same afternoon on the subject of the League of Nations. He understood that if Japan received what she claimed in regard to Shantung, her representatives at the Plenary Meeting would content themselves with a survey of the inequality of races and move some abstract resolution which would probably be rejected. Japan would then merely make a protest. If, however, she regarded herself as ill treated over Shantung, he was unable to say what line the Japanese delegates might take.

PRESIDENT WILSON asked if they would go to the length of refusing to adhere to the League of Nations. His difficulty was that he could not possibly abandon China. He had told the United States' delegation that his line was this: "If Japan will return Kiaochow and Shantung to China and relinquish all sovereign rights and will reduce her claims to mere economic concessions, foregoing all military rights, I would regard it as returning these possessions to China on better terms than Germany had held them."

MR. BALFOUR said that there was no doubt whatsoever that Japan was returning these territories to China on incomparably better terms than Germany had held them.

PRESIDENT WILSON said his experts did not agree.

MR. BALFOUR said that the United States' experts had not heard the Japanese case. The same had applied to his expert, Mr. Macleay, who had signed the expert Report furnished at the request of the Supreme Council.[4] After hearing the Japanese representatives and cross-examining them for an hour he had been entirely satisfied.

MR. BALFOUR continued that the Japanese Government now in power was not the same Government as had made the Treaty of 1915 with China. He honestly believed that this Government intended adopting a more liberal policy and had been influenced by what the Japanese representatives had learned in Paris. He said that Baron Makino had arrived on Sunday evening just after he had dictated his memorandum. His shorthand-writer had read it out to Baron Makino who had accepted it.

MR. LLOYD GEORGE said it showed a very considerable improvement in the position.

PRESIDENT WILSON drew attention to the fact that Japan retained the right to keep troops in Shantung and Germany had had no such rights, even temporarily.

MR. BALFOUR said that the Japanese representatives had made it clear that this right would only be exercised temporarily during the period of transfer, from Japan to China.

PRESIDENT WILSON said that if the Japanese would concede all military rights and make their agreement a purely economic one, he would agree to what they desired. He referred to a subject he had mentioned at previous meetings, namely, that when the League of Nations was set up he would make a proposal for the cession by all the Powers concerned, including Japan, of their rights of extra territoriality.

[4] See the Enclosure printed with E. T. Williams to WW, April 24, 1919.

MR. BALFOUR thought that Japan would be willing to limit herself to purely economic claims. He suggested that he should be authorised to write a letter to Baron Makino.

(After a short discussion as to the line to be taken in the letter, it was agreed that Mr. Balfour should do as he had proposed and he accordingly sent the letter attached in Appendix VII.[5]

It was also agreed that the Japanese representatives should be asked to meet the Supreme Council on the following day at 11 a.m.)

§ Mantoux's notes:

Lloyd George. Mr. Balfour is here; he says that the Japanese are expecting to be received today.

Mr. Balfour is introduced.

Balfour. I saw the Japanese on Saturday. Baron Makino came back to see me yesterday evening at seven o'clock and, in a very delicate way, made me understand that Japan needed a decision. He told me: "We cannot adhere to the League of Nations, in spite of the great interest that we take in its founding, without having protested against the refusal to adopt the principle of the equality of the races. But we cannot accept at the same time the refusal of this principle and the rejection of our claims to Kiaochow. Before the meeting on Monday, we ask you to let us know where we stand on that latter question." I replied to him that the explanations given by the Japanese delegation were not of the kind to displease the heads of governments. But the Japanese expect to be heard this afternoon.

Lloyd George. If not, what will they do?

Balfour. I think they will make a protest against the refusal to accept the principle of the equality of the races. But if they were not satisfied about Shantung, they could go much further.

Wilson. Would they go as far as to withdraw from the League of Nations?

Balfour. No, if they expect a solution acceptable to them on the problem of Kiaochow.

Wilson. I cannot return to America saying that I abandoned China. If the Japanese give up Kiaochow and content themselves with economic rights without any military advantage, we then would have the feeling that they are giving China better conditions than the Germans.

Balfour. That is what the Japanese promise.

Wilson. That is not at all the opinion of our experts.

Balfour. Whatever the policy of Japan may have been in 1915, do not forget that it is not the same today. The government has

[5] It is printed as the next document.

changed; the military party is no longer in power. The men we are dealing with are ready to agree with the western powers to grant China reasonable treatment.

Wilson. That's all very well, but I would like to see it in black and white.

Balfour. They will give you the same assurances which are expressed in the memorandum which I sent to you and which summarizes our conversation.

Wilson. They want to maintain their troops on the railway line.

Balfour. Temporarily.

Wilson. What I will ask them is to be content with economic rights. Later we can propose a general renunciation of special rights for foreigners in China.

Balfour. I believe that one can get a promise from the Japanese that they are content with purely economic advantages. They are prepared to give you the most explicit assurances. Authorize me to write to them that the declaration of their intention to renounce all sovereignty has satisfied you, and that you object only to the military occupation of the railway and the organization of the police by the Japanese. Lastly, I propose that you have a short conversation with them on this subject before the Plenary Session which takes place at three o'clock.

Wilson. So be it; it is possible to come to an understanding if there is accord on the last point. But I do not want this question to be settled hastily, and I would prefer to see them tomorrow at leisure. §

15. M. CLEMENCEAU drew attention to the military engagements to be imposed upon Germany, which had been approved at a meeting held on April 22nd. (I.C.175.B. Minute 5, and Appendix 3.)[6] The last paragraph of this he pointed out was as follows:

> "As long as the present Treaty remains in force the pledge by Germany to respond to any enquiry that the Council of the League of Nations may deem necessary."

He pointed out that according to Article 5 of the League of Nations Covenant decisions, except as provided in the Covenant, would require the agreement of all the members of the League represented at the meeting. It might, however, he pointed out, be difficult to obtain a unanimous decision, and he suggested that in these matters the Council of the League ought to be able to decide by majority.

PRESIDENT WILSON reminded his colleagues that a decision had been taken within the last few days with the Council of the League of Nations, and decided certain economic questions by majority

[6] See the minutes of the Council of Four printed at April 22, 1919, 11 a.m., and Appendix III thereto, Vol. 57.

vote, not by unanimity. Mr. Miller, his legal adviser on the League of Nations Covenant, pointed out that this was not consistent with the Covenant, and had proposed to insert in Article 5, line 1, after the word "Covenant" the following words "or except as otherwise provided in this Treaty." If this was decided upon action ought to be taken in the matter in the afternoon.

M. CLEMENCEAU considered it very necessary in this case.

PRESIDENT WILSON said that it might be supposed that there would be unreasonable persons on the Council.

MR. LLOYD GEORGE pointed out that sooner or later Germany or Austria might enter the League of Nations and be represented on the Council, and in this case it would be impossible to get a unanimous vote on this subject.

(The following alterations were agreed to:

(1) In the League of Nations Covenant, Article 5, the first clause should run as follows:
"Except where otherwise expressly provided in this Covenant *or* in the terms of this Treaty decisions at any meeting of the Assembly or the Council shall require the agreement of all the members of the League represented at the meeting."

(2) In the document entitled military engagements imposed upon Germany, Clause 3 should be as follows:
"As long as the present Treaty remains in force, a pledge to be taken by Germany to respond to any enquiry that will be deemed necessary by the Council of the League of Nations, which, in this matter, will act by a majority vote."

N.B. The new passages are underlined.)

(Sir Maurice Hankey was instructed to notify these decisions to the Secretary-General for the information of the Drafting Committee.)

T MS (SDR, RG 256, 180.03401/126, DNA); Mantoux, I, 396-97, 399-400.

Arthur James Balfour to Baron Nobuaki Makino

Dear Baron Machino, [Paris] April 28th, 1919.

Through no fault of mine there has, I fear, been some misunderstanding with regard to to-day's Meeting, and the business of Shantung in which you are particularly interested.

I was not myself present at the Meeting until I accidentally heard that the question of Shantung was deferred till to-morrow, when they propose asking you to give them the honour of your presence. As soon as I heard of this decision I went over to President Wilson's house, and again explained that you thought it due to you to have the Shantung question settled one way or the other before the discussion on the League of Nations came on this afternoon at the Plenary Conference. It was unfortunately then much too late to ask you to discuss the matter with your colleagues from America, France and England. But after hearing what I had to say in supplement on the paper which I read to you yesterday, I was authorised to tell you that if—which they did not doubt—the view which I represented to them as being yours was held by you, they were quite satisfied as regards the permanent arrangements come to between Japan and China on the question of Shantung. The essence of these arrangements, as I repeated to them, is that after German rights have been ceded to Japan, Japan will hand back to China the whole of the leased territory in complete sovereignty; that the only rights which Japan will retain are the economic rights enumerated in my Memorandum; and that Japan proposes to take every precaution to prevent undue discrimination in matters of railways rates, or port and harbour dues, or other cognate matters between nation and nation; in fact, that the policy of the open door should be fully carried out in the spirit as in the letter.

The only points on which your colleagues expressed anxiety were the temporary arrangements with regard to guarding the line and garrisoning Tsinan. These, as they pointed out, were not merely interferences with Chinese sovereignty, but interferences in excess of anything which the Germans could claim under their Shantung arrangements. They hoped you would consent to discuss this relatively unimportant aspect of the Shantung problem to-morrow at 11 o'clock. They quite recognise, and greatly regret, the inconvenience to which you may have been put owing to the fact that the Plenary Conference will, under this arrangement, precede the Shantung discussion; but they hoped that, inasmuch as the main doubts and difficulties connected with the surrender of the German lease appear to be already satisfactorily disposed of, you will forgive the inevitable postponement of conversations upon the purely temporary arrangements which still in their view seem to raise questions of difficulty. [Sincerely yours, A. J. Balfour]

CCL (WP, DLC).

A Memorandum by Robert Lansing

JAPANESE CLAIMS AND THE LEAGUE OF NATIONS.

April 28, 1919.

At the Plenary Session of the Peace Conference this afternoon Baron Makino spoke of his proposed amendment to the Covenant declaring "racial equality" but said he would not press it.

I concluded from what the President said to me that he was disposed to accede to Japan's claims in regard to Kiau Chau and Shantung. He also showed me the copy of a letter approved by the Heads of State from Balfour to Makino saying that he was sorry their claims had not been finally settled before the Session.

From all this I am forced to the conclusion that a bargain has been struck by which the Japanese agree to sign the Covenant in exchange for admission of their claims. If so, it is an iniquitous agreement.

Apparently the President is going to do this to avoid Japan's declining to enter the League of Nations. It is a surrender of the principle of self-determination, a transfer of millions of Chinese from one foreign master to another. This is another of those secret arrangements which have riddled the "fourteen points" and are wrecking a just peace. I believe House is at the bottom of it. I said to him today that to give Kiau Chau to Japan was to barter away a great principle. He replied, "we have had to do it before." I answered with some heat: "Yes, it has been done and it is the curse of this Conference that that method has been adopted." He made no reply, but that may have been because we were talking across a corner of the peace table in whispers.

In my opinion, it would be better to let Japan stay out of the League than to abandon China and surrender our prestige in the Far East for a "mess of pottage"—and a mess it is. I fear that it is too late to do anything to save the situation.

T MS (R. Lansing Papers, DLC).

From the Diary of Colonel House

April 28, 1919.

Today has been eventful to me. The Plenary Session unanimously adopted the draft of the Covenant for the League of Nations which our Committee wrote. It also passed the Resolution which I instigated and had David Miller write, and which the President offered. This Resolution as adopted is a part of the record. It not only names the nations which are to compose the Council of Nine, but also names the nations which are to compose the Committee on Organization. In other words, the Organization Committee is now practically in my hands as I had hoped it would be. Clemenceau put the "steam roller" promptly to work as soon as those who wanted to make speeches to go in the *proces verbal* had finished. Every thing was passed almost before the Conference could catch its breath.

Hughes of Australia never got an opportunity to make the speech which he has been threatening to make all winter against the Covenant. I do not believe he realized that the Covenant had been adopted until after the Conference adjourned.

And this reminds me of some of the biting sayings of Clemenceau. Someone remarked to him not long ago "Stephen Pichon said so." Clemenceau quickly asked "Pichon, Pichon, who is Pichon?" The reply came, "Why, Pichon is your Minister for Foreign Affairs." "So he is," said Clemenceau, "I had forgotten it."

Another time he spoke to [of] Klotz, his Minister of Finance as being "the only Jew I ever knew who knew nothing of finance."

Again he told someone, "Colonel House is practical, I can understand him, but when I talk with President Wilson, I feel as if I were talking to Jesus Christ." Again he said, "The Almighty gave us Ten Commandments, but Wilson has given us Fourteen."

When Bourgeois was rambling along this afternoon about his amendments it was worth while being bored to watch Clemenceau's expression of contempt as he looked at his worthy confrere. Lloyd George remarked to Clemenceau, "how did Bourgeois ever become Prime Minister of France?" to which he replied, "During a period when I was unmaking Cabinets, the material ran out, and they took Bourgeois." When Bourgeois began his argument, which the President and I had heard innumerable times in our League of Nations meetings, I wrote on a slip to the President, "Lest old acquaintance be forgot." He replied, "I wish I could forget both the speech and the man."[1] . . .

Before going into the Conference this afternoon, Balfour took me aside and we went into Pichon's room for a conference. He told me how unsatisfactory and impossible the Council of Four were as a working body. His grievance related to the Japanese-Chinese misunderstanding over the Shangtung Peni[n]sula. He asked if I would not help him straighten it out.

Lloyd George afterward took me aside and asked if I would not get the President in a more amenable frame of mind. He thought the President was unfair to Japan and so does Balfour, and indeed, so do I. The concessions the Germans obtained from China in the first instance, and which the Japanese have taken over as a part of their spoils of war, is bad enough, but it is no worse than the doubtful transactions that have gone on among the Allies themselves and, indeed, that are going on now. They are dividing up the Turkish Empire in the same way as the Japanese are using to secure a sphere of influence in China, but with this difference: The Allies intend to hold what they take in Asia Minor, while the Japanese have promised to return the concessions to China, provided the Allies permit Japan to save her fast [face] by first taking them over.

[1] This handwritten exchange is in the E. M. House Papers, CtY. Wilson actually wrote "I'd rather forget speech and man."

From the Diary of Edith Benham

April 28, 1919

Today I went with Mrs. W. to the Plenary session of the Peace Conference. As a spectacle it was very interesting to see how the delegates sit, the room in which they sit, but the session itself was singularly dull. Everyone had expected it to be full of sensation, for the P. said in going over he had almost forgotten the Italian question in the trouble the Japanese are giving, and he feared the session might be stormy, but his opening speech was the only new thing. The Japanese delegate was very mild, only serving notice that the race question would come up again. The delegate from Uruguay[1] made an excellent and very short speech. The P. in commenting on it tonight said that Uruguay in its legislation and laws is the most advanced country in the world, and he said he wrote a little note to the delegate complimenting him on what he said which bore out the reputation his country enjoyed. The bore of the conference spoke, Leon Bourgeois. The P. said he had heard the same matter discussed at all the meetings of the committee to draft the League of Nations, and Col. House, who came over to speak to us, said he had calculated that Bourgeois had consumed 10 hours of the time of the conference in repeating the same thing. Clemenceau (the P. said) said of him when questioned how Bourgeois had ever happened to be Prime Minister, that the time he (Clemenceau) was making Ministries fall so fast that the supply had run out.

[1] Juan Antonio Buero, Minister of Foreign Affairs.

From the Diary of Vance Criswell McCormick

April 28 (Monday) [1919]

At 3.00 o'clock went to Quai d'Orsay to attend a meeting of the Plenary Peace Conference to see the final passage of the League of Nations Covenant which was an historic event. The President presented the amendments to the original draft which had been approved by the Commission and then the Japanese delegates stated their objection with a good argument about the equal treatment of all races, etc., but stated they would not press the issue at this time. Bourgeois spoke for France; Hymans for Belgium, as did several others, and then Clemenceau declared the thing passed unanimously. Sir Robert Borden, Canada, proposed amendment to labor clause of treaty which was adopted. Meeting adjourned.

The conference room was packed as more and more spectators are slipping in under the guise of advisers and newspaper men. I saw Mrs. Wilson and Miss Benham and Admiral Grayson present.

Some of the speeches were pretty long and as we sat close behind Clemenceau, Lloyd George and the President we could hear Lloyd George chaffing Clemenceau about permitting such long speeches and he asked him why he had not read over the speeches first, etc., much to the old gentleman's delight. They all seemed in good humor today and did not seem to miss the Italians, who, I think, will be back soon after they have blown off a little steam.

The Covenant of the League of Nations

[April 28, 1919]

In order to promote international co-operation and to achieve international peace and security by the acceptance of obligations not to resort to war, by the prescription of open, just and honorable relations between nations, by the firm establishment of the understandings of international law as the actual rule of conduct among governments, and by the maintenance of justice and a scrupulous respect for all treaty obligations in the dealings of organized peoples with one another, the High Contracting Parties agree to this Covenant of the League of Nations.

Article I.

The original Members of the League of Nations shall be those of the Signatories which are named in the Annex to this Covenant and also such of those other States named in the Annex as shall accede without reservation to this Covenant. Such accession shall be effected by a Declaration deposited with the Secretariat within two months of the coming into force of the Covenant. Notice thereof shall be sent to all other Members of the League.

Any fully self-governing State, Dominion or Colony not named in the Annex, may become a Member of the League if its admission is agreed to by two-thirds of the Assembly, provided that it shall give effective guarantees of its sincere intention to observe its international obligations, and shall accept such regulations as may be prescribed by the League in regard to its military and naval forces and armaments.

Any Member of the League may, after two years' notice of its intention to do so, withdraw from the League, provided that all its international obligations and all its obligations under this Covenant shall have been fulfilled at the time of its withdrawal.

Article II.

The action of the League under this Covenant shall be effected through the instrumentality of an Assembly and of a Council, with a permanent Secretariat.

Article III.

The Assembly shall consist of Representatives of the Members of the League.

The Assembly shall meet at stated intervals and from time to time as occasion may require at the Seat of the League, or at such other place as may be decided upon.

The Assembly may deal at its meetings with any matter within the sphere of action of the League or affecting the peace of the world.

At meetings of the Assembly each Member of the League shall have one vote, and may have not more than three Representatives.

Article IV.

The Council shall consist of Representatives of the United States of America, of the British Empire, of France, of Italy, and of Japan, together with Representatives of four other Members of the League. These four Members of the League shall be selected by the Assembly from time to time in its discretion. Until the appointment of the Representatives of the four Members of the League first selected by the Assembly, Representatives of [blank] shall be members of the Council.

With the approval of the majority of the Assembly, the Council may name additional Members of the League whose Representatives shall always be members of the Council; the Council with like approval may increase the number of Members of the League to be selected by the Assembly for representation on the Council.

The Council shall meet from time to time as occasion may require, and at least once a year, at the Seat of the League, or at such other place as may be decided upon.

The Council may deal at its meetings with any matter within the sphere of action of the League or affecting the peace of the world.

Any Member of the League not represented on the Council shall be invited to send a Representative to sit as a member at any meeting of the council during the consideration of matters specially affecting the interests of that Member of the League.

At meetings of the Council each Member of the League represented on the Council shall have one vote, and may have not more than one Representative.

Article V.

Except where otherwise expressly provided in this Covenant, decisions at any meeting of the Assembly or of the Council shall require the agreement of all the Members of the League represented at the meeting.

All matters of procedure at meetings of the Assembly or of the Council, including the appointment of Committees to investigate particular matters, shall be regulated by the Assembly or by the Council and may be decided by a majority of the Members of the League represented at the meeting.

The first meeting of the Assembly and the first meeting of the Council shall be summoned by the President of the United States of America.

Article VI.

The permanent Secretariat shall be established at the Seat of the League. The Secretariat shall comprise a Secretary General and such secretaries and staff as may be required.

The first Secretary General shall be the person named in the Annex; thereafter the Secretary General shall be appointed by the Council with the approval of the majority of the Assembly.

The secretaries and the staff of the Secretariat shall be appointed by the Secretary General with the approval of the Council.

The Secretary General shall act in that capacity at all meetings of the Assembly and of the Council.

The expenses of the Secretariat shall be borne by the Members of the League in accordance with the apportionment of the expenses of the International Bureau of the Universal Postal Union.

Article VII.

The Seat of the League is established at Geneva.

The Council may at any time decide that the Seat of the League shall be established elsewhere.

All positions under or in connection with the League, including the Secretariat, shall be open equally to men and women.

Representatives of the Members of the League and officials of the League when engaged on the business of the League shall enjoy diplomatic privileges and immunities.

The buildings and other property occupied by the League or its officials or by Representatives attending its meetings shall be inviolable.

Article VIII.

The Members of the League recognize that the maintenance of peace requires the reduction of national armaments to the lowest point consistent with national safety and the enforcement by common action of international obligations.

The Council, taking account of the geographical situation and circumstances of each State, shall formulate plans for such reduction for the consideration and action of the several Governments.

Such plans shall be subject to reconsideration and revision at least every ten years.

After these plans shall have been adopted by the several Governments, the limits of armaments therein fixed shall not be exceeded without the concurrence of the Council.

The Members of the League agree that the manufacture by private enterprise of munitions and implements of war is open to grave objections. The Council shall advise how the evil effects attendant upon such manufacture can be prevented, due regard being had to the necessities of those Members of the League which are not able to manufacture the munitions and implements of war necessary for their safety.

The Members of the League undertake to interchange full and frank information as to the scale of their armaments, their military and naval programmes and the condition of such of their industries as are adaptable to war-like purposes.

Article IX.

A permanent Commission shall be constituted to advise the Council on the execution of the provisions of Articles I and VIII and on military and naval questions generally.

Article X.

The Members of the League undertake to respect and preserve as against external aggression the territorial integrity and existing political independence of all Members of the League. In case of any such aggression or in case of any threat or danger of such aggression the Council shall advise upon the means by which this obligation shall be fulfilled.

Article XI.

Any war or threat of war, whether immediately affecting any of the Members of the League or not, is hereby declared a matter of concern to the whole League, and the League shall take any action that may be deemed wise and effectual to safeguard the peace of nations. In case any such emergency should arise the Secretary General shall on the request of any Member of the League forthwith summon a meeting of the Council.

It is also declared to be the friendly right of each Member of the League to bring to the attention of the Assembly or of the Council any circumstance whatever affecting international relations which threatens to disturb international peace or the good understanding between nations upon which peace depends.

Article XII.

The Members of the League agree that if there should arise between them any dispute likely to lead to a rupture, they will submit the matter either to arbitration or to inquiry by the Council, and they agree in no case to resort to war until three months after the award by the arbitrators or the report by the Council.

In any case under this Article the award of the arbitrators shall be made within a reasonable time, and the report of the Council shall be made within six months after the submission of the dispute.

Article XIII.

The Members of the League agree that whenever any dispute shall arise between them which they recognize to be suitable for submission to arbitration and which cannot be satisfactorily settled by diplomacy, they will submit the whole subject matter to arbitration.

Disputes as to the interpretation of a treaty, as to any question of international law, as to the existence of any fact which if established would constitute a breach of any international obligation, or as to the extent and nature of the reparation to be made for any such breach, are declared to be among those which are generally suitable for submission to arbitration.

For the consideration of any such dispute the court of arbitration to which the case is referred shall be the court agreed on by the parties to the dispute or stipulated in any convention existing between them.

The Members of the League agree that they will carry out in full good faith any award that may be rendered and that they will not resort to war against a Member of the League which complies therewith. In the event of any failure to carry out such an award, the Council shall propose what steps should be taken to give effect thereto.

Article XIV.

The Council shall formulate and submit to the Members of the League for adoption plans for the establishment of a Permanent Court of International Justice. The Court shall be competent to hear and determine any dispute of an international character which the parties thereto submit to it. The Court may also give an advisory opinion upon any dispute or question referred to it by the Council or by the Assembly.

Article XV.

If there should arise between Members of the League any dispute likely to lead to a rupture, which is not submitted to arbitration as above, the Members of the League agree that they will submit the matter to the Council. Any party to the dispute may effect such submission by giving notice of the existence of the dispute to the Secretary General, who will make all necessary arrangements for a full investigation and consideration thereof.

For this purpose the parties to the dispute will communicate to the Secretary General, as promptly as possible, statements of their case with all the relevant facts and papers, and the Council may forthwith direct the publication thereof.

The Council shall endeavor to effect a settlement of the dispute, and if such efforts are successful, a statement shall be made public giving such facts and explanations regarding the dispute and the terms of settlement thereof as the Council may deem appropriate.

If the dispute is not thus settled, the Council either unanimously or by a majority vote shall make and publish a report containing a statement of the facts of the dispute and the recommendations which are deemed just and proper in regard thereto.

Any Member of the League represented on the Council may make public a statement of the facts of the dispute and of its conclusions regarding the same.

If a report by the Council is unanimously agreed to by the members thereof other than the Representatives of one or more of the parties to the dispute, the Members of the League agree that they will not go to war with any party to the dispute which complies with the recommendations of the report.

If the Council fails to reach a report which is unanimously agreed to by the members thereof, other than the representatives of one or more of the parties to the dispute, the Members of the League reserve to themselves the right to take such action as they shall consider necessary for the maintenance of right and justice.

If the dispute between the parties is claimed by one of them, and is found by the Council, to arise out of a matter which by international law is solely within the domestic jurisdiction of that party, the Council shall so report, and shall make no recommendation as to its settlement.

The Council may in any case under this Article refer the dispute to the Assembly. The dispute shall be so referred at the request of either party to the dispute, provided that such request be made within fourteen days after the submission of the dispute to the Council.

In any case referred to the Assembly all the provisions of this Article and of Article XII relating to the action and powers of the Council shall apply to the action and powers of the Assembly, provided that a report made by the Assembly if concurred in by the Representatives of those Members of the League represented on the Council and of a majority of the other Members of the League, exclusive in each case of the Representatives of the parties to the dispute, shall have the same force as a report by the Council concurred in by all the members thereof other than the Representatives of one or more of the parties to the dispute.

Article XVI.

Should any Member of the League resort to war in disregard of its covenants under Articles XII, XIII or XV, it shall *ipso facto* be deemed to have committed an act of war against all other Members of the League, which hereby undertake immediately to subject it to the severance of all trade or financial relations, the prohibition of all intercourse between their nationals and the nationals of the covenant-breaking State, and the prevention of all financial, commercial, or personal intercourse between the nationals of the covenant-breaking State and the nationals of any other State, whether a Member of the League or not.

It shall be the duty of the Council in such case to recommend to the several Governments concerned what effective military or naval force the Members of the League shall severally contribute to the armed forces to be used to protect the covenants of the League.

The Members of the League agree, further, that they will mutually support one another in the financial and economic measures which are taken under this Article, in order to minimize the loss and inconvenience resulting from the above measures, and that they will mutually support one another in resisting any special measures aimed at one of their number by the covenant-breaking State, and that they will take the necessary steps to afford passage through their territory to the forces of any of the Members of the League which are co-operating to protect the covenants of the League.

Any Member of the League which has violated any covenant of the League may be declared to be no longer a Member of the League by a vote of the Council concurred in by the Representatives of all the other Members of the League represented thereon.

Article XVII.

In the event of a dispute between a member of the League and a State which is not a Member of the League, or between States not Members of the League, the State or States not Members of the

League shall be invited to accept the obligations of membership in the League for the purposes of such dispute, upon such conditions as the Council may deem just. If such invitation is accepted, the provisions of Articles XII to XVI inclusive shall be applied with such modifications as may be deemed necessary by the Council.

Upon such invitation being given the Council shall immediately institute an inquiry into the circumstances of the dispute and recommend such action as may seem best and most effectual in the circumstances.

If a State so invited shall refuse to accept the obligations of membership in the League for the purposes of such dispute, and shall resort to war against a Member of the League, the provisions of Article XVI shall be applicable as against the State taking such action.

If both parties to the dispute when so invited refuse to accept the obligations of membership in the League for the purposes of such dispute, the Council may take such measures and make such recommendations as will prevent hostilities and will result in the settlement of the dispute.

Article XVIII.

Every treaty or international engagement entered into hereafter by any Member of the League, shall be forthwith registered with the Secretariat and shall as soon as possible be published by it. No such treaty or international engagement shall be binding until so registered.

Article XIX.

The Assembly may from time to time advise the reconsideration by Members of the League of treaties which have become inapplicable and the consideration of international conditions whose continuance might endanger the peace of the world.

Article XX.

The Members of the League severally agree that this Covenant is accepted as abrogating all obligations or understandings *inter se* which are inconsistent with the terms thereof, and solemnly undertake that they will not hereafter enter into any engagements inconsistent with the terms thereof.

In case any Member of the League shall, before becoming a Member of the League, have undertaken any obligations inconsistent with the terms of this Covenant, it shall be the duty of such Member to take immediate steps to procure its release from such obligations.

Aricle XXI.

Nothing in this Covenant shall be deemed to affect the validity of international engagements such as treaties of arbitration or regional understandings like the Monroe Doctrine for securing the maintenance of peace.

Article XXII.

To those colonies and territories which as a consequence of the late war have ceased to be under the sovereignty of the States which formerly governed them and which are inhabited by peoples not yet able to stand by themselves under the strenuous conditions of the modern world, there should be applied the principle that the well-being and development of such peoples form a sacred trust of civilization and that securities for the performance of this trust should be embodied in this Covenant.

The best method of giving practical effect to this principle is that the tutelage of such peoples should be entrusted to advanced nations who by reason of their resources, their experience or their geographical position, can best undertake this responsibility, and who are willing to accept it, and that this tutelage should be exercised by them as Mandataries on behalf of the League.

The character of the mandate must differ according to the stage of the development of the people, the geographical situation of the territory, its economic conditions and other similar circumstances.

Certain communities formerly belonging to the Turkish Empire have reached a stage of development where their existence as independent nations can be provisionally recognized subject to the rendering of administrative advice and assistance by a Mandatary until such time as they are able to stand alone. The wishes of these communities must be a principal consideration in the selection of a Mandatary.

Other peoples, especially those of Central Africa, are at such a stage that the Mandatary must be responsible for the administration of the territory under conditions which will guarantee freedom of conscience or religion, subject only to the maintenance of public order and morals, the prohibition of abuses such as the slave trade, the arms traffic and the liquor traffic, and the prevention of the establishment of fortifications or military and naval bases and of military training of the natives for other than police purposes and the defence of territory, and will also secure equal opportunities for the trade and commerce of other Members of the League.

There are territories, such as South-west Africa and certain of the South Pacific Islands, which, owing to the sparseness of their population, or their small size, or their remoteness from the centers of civilization, or their geographical contiguity to the territory of the Mandatary, and other circumstances, can be best administered under the laws of the Mandatary as integral portions of its territory, subject to the safeguards above-mentioned in the interests of the indigenous population.

In every case of mandate, the Mandatary shall render to the

Council an annual report in reference to the territory committed to its charge.

The degree of authority, control, or administration to be exercised by the Mandatary shall if not previously agreed upon by the Members of the League be explicitly defined in each case by the Council.

A permanent Commission shall be constituted to receive and examine the annual reports of the Mandataries and to advise the Council on all matters relating to the observance of the mandates.

Article XXIII.

Subject to and in accordance with the provisions of international conventions existing or hereafter to be agreed upon, the Members of the League

(a) will endeavor to secure and maintain fair and humane conditions of labor for men, women and children both in their own countries and in all countries to which their commercial and industrial relations extend, and for that purpose will establish and maintain the necessary international organizations;

(b) undertake to secure just treatment of the native inhabitants of territories under their control;

(c) will entrust the League with the general supervision over the execution of agreements with regard to the traffic in women and children, and the traffic in opium and other dangerous drugs;

(c) will entrust the League with the general supervision of the trade in arms and ammunition with the countries in which the control of this traffic is necessary in the common interest;

(e) will make provision to secure and maintain freedom of communications and of transit and equitable treatment for the commerce of all Members of the League. In this connection, the special necessities of the regions devastated during the war of 1914-1918 shall be borne in mind;

(f) will endeavor to take steps in matters of international concern for the prevention and control of disease.

Article XXIV.

There shall be placed under the direction of the League all international bureaux already established by general treaties if the parties to such treaties consent. All such international bureaux and all commissions for the regulation of matters of international interest hereafter constituted shall be placed under the direction of the League.

In all matters of international interest which are regulated by general conventions but which are not placed under the control of international bureaux or commissions, the Secretariat of the League shall, subject to the consent of the Council and if desired by the parties, collect and distribute all relevant information and shall render any other assistance which may be necessary or desirable.

The Council may include as part of the expenses of the Secretariat the expenses of any bureau or commission which is placed under the direction of the League.

Article XXV.

The Members of the League agree to encourage and promote the establishment and co-operation of duly authorized voluntary national Red Cross organizations having as purposes the improvement of health, the prevention of disease and the mitigation of suffering throughout the world.

Article XXVI.

Amendments to this Covenant will take effect when ratified by the Members of the League whose Representatives compose the Council and by a majority of the Members of the League whose Representatives compose the Assembly.

No such amendment shall bind any Member of the League which signifies its dissent therefrom, but in that case it shall cease to be a Member of the League.

ANNEX TO THE COVENANT.

1. Original Members of the League of Nations Signatories of the Treaty of Peace.

United States of America.
Belgium.
Bolivia.
Brazil.
British Empire.
  Canada.
  Australia.
  South Africa.
  New Zealand.
  India.
China.
Cuba.
Czecho-Slovakia.
Ecuador.
France.
Greece.
Guatemala.
Haiti.
Hedjaz.
Honduras.
Italy.
Japan.
Liberia.
Nicaragua.
Panama.
Peru.
Poland.
Portugal.
Roumania.
Serbia.
Siam.
Uruguay.

States Invited to Accede to the Covenant.

Argentine Republic.
Chili.
Colombia.
Denmark.
Netherlands.
Norway.
Paraguay.
Persia.
Salvador.
Spain.
Sweden.
Switzerland.
Venezuela.

2. First Secretary General of the League of Nations.

ADDENDA

At the Plenary Session of the 28th April, 1919, the following additions were made to the text of this Covenant.

In Article IV, first paragraph, last line, after the words "representatives of" add, "Belgium, Brazil, Greece and Spain."

In Article V, first paragraph, at the end of the first line, strike out the comma and add: "or by the terms of this Treaty."

In the Annex, under the caption "First Secretary General of the League of Nations," add: "The Honorable Sir James Eric Drummond, K.C.M.G., C.B."

Printed copy (C. L. Swem Coll., NjP).

Remarks to a Plenary Session of the Paris Peace Conference[1]

28 April, 1919.

Mr. President: When the text of the Covenant of the League of Nations was last laid before you, I had the honor of reading the Covenant in extenso. I will not detain you today to reread the Covenant as it has now been altered, but will merely take the liberty of explaining to you some of the alterations that have been made. The report of the commission has been circulated. You yourselves have in hand the text of the Covenant and will no doubt have noticed that most of the changes that have been made are mere changes of phraseology, not changes of substance, and that, besides that, most of the changes are intended to clarify the document, or, rather, to make explicit what we had all assumed was implicit in the document as it was originally presented to you. But I shall take the liberty of calling your attention, for fear you may not have had the time to examine the document carefully, to the new features, such as they are, some of them considerable, the rest trivial.

The first paragraph of Article I is new. In view of the insertion of the Covenant in the peace treaty, specific provision as to the signatories of the treaty who would become members of the League, and also as to the neutral states to be invited to accede to the Covenant, was obviously necessary. The paragaraph also provides for the method by which a neutral state may accede to the Covenant.

The third paragraph of Article I is new, providing for the withdrawal of any member of the League on a notice given of two years.

The second paragraph of Article IV is new, providing for a possible increase in the Council should other powers be added to the League of Nations whose present accession is not anticipated.

The last paragraph of Article IV is new, providing specifically for one vote for each member of the League in the Council, which was understood before; and providing also for one representative of each member of the League.

The first paragraph of Article V is new, expressly incorporating the provision as to unanimity of voting, which was at first taken for granted.

The second paragraph of Article VI has had added to it that a majority of the Assembly must approve the appointment of the Secretary General.

The first paragraph of Article VII names Geneva as the seat of the League, and is followed by a second paragraph which gives the Council power to establish the seat of the League elsewhere should it subsequently deem it necessary.

The third paragraph of Article VII is new, establishing equality of employment of men and women, that is to say, by the League.

The second paragraph of Article XIII is new, inasmuch as it undertakes to give instances of disputes which are generally suitable for submission to arbitration, instances of what have laterally been called justiciable questions.

The eighth paragraph of Article XV is new. This is the amendment regarding domestic jurisdiction, that where the Council finds that a question arising out of an international dispute affects matters which are clearly under the domestic jurisdiction of one or other of the parties, it is to report to that effect and make no recommendation.

The last paragraph of Article XVI is new, providing for an expulsion from the League in certain extraordinary circumstances.

Article XXI is new.

The second paragraph of Article XXII inserts the words with regard to mandatories, "and who are willing to accept it," thus explicitly introducing the principle that a mandate cannot be forced upon a nation unwilling to accept it.

Article XXIII is a combination of several former articles, and also contains the following: a clause providing for the just treatment of aborigines, a clause looking towards the prevention of the white slave traffic and the traffic in opium, and a clause looking towards progress in international prevention and control of disease.

Article XXV specifically mentions the Red Cross as one of the international organizations which is to connect its work with the work of the League.

Article XXVI permits amendment of the Covenant by a majority of the states composing the Assembly instead of three fourths of the states, though it does not change the requirement in that matter with regard to the vote in the Council.

The second paragraph of Article XXVI is also new and was added at the request of the Brazilian delegation, in order to avoid certain constitutional difficulties. It permits any member of the League to dissent from an amendment, the effect of such dissent, however, being withdrawal from the League.

And then an annex is added giving the names of the signatories of the treaty who will become members and the names of the states invited to accede to the Covenant.

These are all the changes, I believe, which are of moment.

Mr. President, I take opportunity to move the following resolutions, in order to carry out the provisions of the Covenant. You will notice that the Covenant provides that the first Secretary General shall be chosen by this conference. It also provides that the first choice of the four member states which are to be added to the five great powers on the Council is left to this conference. I move, therefore, first, that the first Secretary General of the League shall be the Honorable Sir James Eric Drummond, K.C.M.G., C.B.; second, that until such time as the Assembly shall have selected the first four members of the League to be represented on the Council in accordance with Article IV of the Covenant, representatives of Belgium, Brazil, Greece, and Spain shall be members; and, third, that the powers to be represented on the Council of the League of Nations are requested to name representatives who shall form a committee of nine to prepare plans for the organization of the League and for the establishment of the seat of the League, and to make arrangements and to prepare the agenda for the first meeting of the Assembly, this committee to report both to the Council and to the Assembly of the League.

I think it is not necessary to call your attention to other matters we have previously discussed—the capital significance of this Covenant, the hopes which are entertained as to the effect it will have upon steadying the affairs of the world, and the obvious necessity that there should be a concert of the free nations of the world to maintain justice in international relations and peace between the nations of the world.

(The President was calling on Baron Makino to speak when the President of the United States begged leave to add the few following remarks:)

If Baron Makino will pardon me for introducing a matter which I absentmindedly overlooked, it is necessary for me to propose the alteration of several words in the first line of Article V. Let me say that in several parts of the treaty, of which the Covenant will form a part, certain duties are assigned to the Council of the League of Nations. In some instances, it is provided that the action they shall take shall be by a majority vote. It is, therefore, necessary to make the Covenant conform with the other portions of the treaty by adding these words. I will read the first line, and add the words:

"Except where otherwise expressly provided in this Covenant, or by the terms of this Treaty, decisions at any meeting of the Assembly or of the Council shall require the agreement of all the Members of the League represented at the meeting."

"Except where otherwise expressly provided in this Covenant," is the present reading, and I move the addition of "or by the terms of this Treaty." With that addition, I move the adoption of the Covenant.

T MS (WP, DLC), with corrections and additions from printed copy (SDR, RG 256, 180.0201/5, DNA).

[1] Wilson read from a manuscript which he had dictated to Swem. It is a T MS in WP, DLC. Wilson repeated or paraphrased D. H. Miller, "MEMORANDUM OF IMPORTANT CHANGES MADE IN THE COVENANT . . . ," a T MS (WP, DLC), dated April 28, 1919.

It strikes the Editors that this speech by Wilson was delivered in an uncharacteristic way—mechanically, without typical flourish, and with obvious physical difficulty.

For one thing, Wilson adhered very closely to Miller's memorandum in explaining the changes that the League of Nations Commission had made in the Covenant. On the other hand, he omitted five changes, one of which, concerning advisory opinions by the Permanent Court of International Justice, was important.

Second, Wilson's interruption of Baron Makino to explain the significance of changes in Article V was obviously necessary because of a transient loss of memory.

Most important, Wilson ended his remarks abruptly without (as one might assume he would have ordinarily done) closing with an expression of thanks to the other members of the League of Nations Commission and a grand peroration on the character and future indispensability of the League of Nations, such as he had done in presenting the draft of the Covenant to the third Plenary Session on February 14, 1919. His speech upon this occasion is printed at that date in Vol. 55.

For a discussion of what seems to have been a crisis in Wilson's health, which apparently began on April 28, 1919, see the essays and commentaries printed in the Appendix to this volume.

To Henry Mauris Robinson, with Enclosure

My dear Mr. Robinson: Paris, 28 April, 1919.

Will you not be kind enough to read the enclosed letter? I think that Mr. Hoover has a real case here and I hope that you will in my name make the strongest representations to the Shipping Board at home in this matter. It is evidently, I think, a case of the unwillingness of the Franklin Committee[1] to divert ships from commercial routes which may promise large profits, but in a matter of world exigency like this the Franklin Committee should be made to yield and cooperate.

With regard to the arrangements for shipping coal to Italy, I have the greatest sympathy with that but obviously this is not the time to further Italian industrial interests at the expense of feeding a distracted world. I am sure that you will agree with me in these matters.

Cordially and faithfully yours, Woodrow Wilson

TLS (photographic copy, WP, DLC).

[1] That is, the Shipping Control Committee, of which Philip Albright Small Franklin was chairman. The other members were Harry Howard Raymond, president of the Mallory and Clyde steamship companies, and Capt. Sir Connop Guthrie, a representative in the United States of the British Ministry of Shipping, who represented Great Britain, France, and Italy. The committee had been appointed by Edward N. Hurley in January 1918 to coordinate and allocate shipping in the North Atlantic. See the *New York Times*, Jan. 31, 1918, and Edward N. Hurley, *The Bridge to France* (Philadelphia and London, 1927), pp. 101-108.

E N C L O S U R E

From Herbert Clark Hoover

My dear Mr. President: Paris, April 25, 1919.

I am extremely sorry to trouble you with any matter of lesser import than those with which you are faced.

You will recollect having sent a direction to Mr. Hurley to furnish the Relief Administration with 500,000 tons of shipping for loading in the month of April, this being a minimum on which I believed we could hold the tide of starvation during the month of May, when these cargoes would arrive. I regret to inform you that up to the present moment we have been furnished shipping for actual loading and dispatch from the United States of less than 220,000 tons since April 1st. This comes on top of the failure of the Shipping Board to keep its promises to give us 350,000 tons of loading in March, in which month we received only 200,000 tons. We are at present in the midst of a positive famine of supplies, and I am only able to eke out during the present month by borrowing from other governments as against future replacements on an extremely expensive basis.

I feel that I have at least the right to inform you of my total inability to carry out the obligation that has been placed upon me in this situation. I have no desire to desert the post, but it does not seem to me fair that I should be given this responsibility and given assurances that would enable its execution, and then to be faced with this constant failure. When you consider that the American mercantile fleet delivered into Europe duing the last days of the war nearly one million tons of commodities per month and that the Army is now delivering only 100,000 tons per month of supplies, and when you consider the very considerable increase in our fleet, I think you will appreciate that I am not asking for the impossible. We have in effect asked that in the month of April,—our most trying month,—that we should have one-third of our fleet withdrawn from commercial trades in order to save Europe.

Incidentally, I hear that Mr. Hurley is about to assign ships for loading of coal to Italy, in order to enlarge employment of our coal miners. I would like to point out that if the same rates are charged on coal to Italy that are charged on food to starving populations, it will cost from $35 to $40 a ton to deliver this coal in Italy, out of which some $4 or $5 will be the purchase price of the coal on the Atlantic seaboard and from this amount the American miner will receive less than $2.00 a ton. The Italian credits are absolutely worthless and therefore in order to give $2.00 worth of employment in the United States, our Government is about to expend $35. The British have taken the obligation, and are performing their obligation, to furnish Italy with coal. It would occur to me that it is better to stem the tide of starvation in Europe and [than] to devote the waste of $33 on sending a ton of coal to Italy to the employment of workmen at shoveling sand on the beach.

Yours faithfully, Herbert Hoover

TLS (photographic copy, WP, DLC).

To Henry Mauris Robinson

My dear Mr. Robinson: Paris, 28 April, 1919.

Pardon me for having left in doubt the appointment of Mr. Gompers as a member of the Organization Committee of the Labor Conference.[1] I heartily approve of the suggestion and wish you would take the proper steps to inform Mr. Gompers of the appointment.

I also approve of the appointment of Mr. Nathan A. Smythe[2] as Mr. Gompers' substitute if Mr. Gompers approves. There would be some awkwardness in appointing a substitute whom Mr. Gompers did not regard as a real substitute.

Cordially and sincerely yours, Woodrow Wilson

TLS (photographic copy, WP, DLC).

[1] Wilson was replying to H. M. Robinson to EMH, April 26, 1919, TLS, enclosed in H. M. Robinson to WW, April 26, 1919, TCL, both in WP, DLC.

[2] Nathan Ayer Smyth, not Smythe, lawyer of New York, formerly Assistant Director General of the United States Employment Service in the Department of Labor.

To George Davis Herron

My dear Dr. Herron: [Paris] 28 April, 1919.

Thank you for your considerate letter of the 21st.[1] I know that you will pardon the brevity of my reply, because you know how I am called upon every minute for this, that or the other conference.

I am sorry that you are so deeply discouraged about the work of the conference. It is undoubtedly true that many of the results arrived at are far from ideal, but I think that on the whole we have been able to keep tolerably close to the lines laid down at the outset, and I am confirmed in this opinion by the judgment of many conscientious men about me, by whose conscience as well as by my own I try to be guided. The treaty which ends so terrible a war must unavoidably seem harsh towards the outlaw who started the war, but when the details are read and understood I believe that the impression will be largely removed. Perhaps my judgment is affected by the consciousness that results are so much better than at one time I feared, that they now seem to me better than they are.

In haste, Sincerely yours, [Woodrow Wilson]

CCL (WP, DLC).

[1] G. D. Herron to WW, April 21, 1919, Vol. 57.

From the American Commissioners

My dear Mr. President: Paris, April 28, 1919.

Recent telegrams from Austria and Hungary and reports of observers suggest urgent action in order to strengthen the elements working for law and order in these countries.

The situation in Vienna has long been critical; the poor, who are unable to buy American flour because of depreciation in currency, are slowly starving. The present Socialist Government, threatened by famine conditions and Communist propaganda, has lost hope at receiving no intimation from the Conference that there is an immediate prospect of peace as far as Austria is concerned. Even Germany, whose representatives have now been summoned to Paris, is in a better position in this respect than German Austria, which has no reason to believe that their case has yet been considered. The situation in Hungary is more complex in view of the character of the present government, but need not be considered hopeless provided it is not left under the influence of French militaristic policy, or the cupidity of Hungary's neighbors, the Czechs, Roumanians and Serbs.

We therefore recommend as a means of removing this feeling of isolation and abandonment that Austrian representatives be allowed to proceed to Paris immediately to present their case, not necessarily before you and the Premiers but before those whom you and they might designate. In our opinion such contact will go far towards encouraging the Austrians to resist the ever-increasing propaganda of the Communists.

Similar measures could be taken in the case of Hungary as soon as a representative government exists there.

Faithfully yours, Robert Lansing.
Henry White
Tasker H. Bliss.
E. M. House

TLS (WP, DLC).

From William Shepherd Benson

My dear Mr. President: Paris, France. 28 April, 1919.

Realizing the heavy burden that you are carrying, it is with the greatest possible reluctance that I trespass upon your time or attention; nothing but a strong sense of duty compels me to do so.

It is evident that commercial interest is underlying every factor under consideration by the various nations, except ourselves. This is particularly true in the case of Great Britain; she has ever maintained her commercial supremacy by superior naval strength. In turn she has crushed Spain, Holland and Germany because they threatened her supremacy on the sea. Her objection to our building program, both Commercial and Naval, is because of a belief that we are now probably threatening that supremacy.

I feel sure that if the final disposition of the surrendered German and Austrian war vessels is not stated in the Peace Terms, they will not be destroyed, but in time will be employed against our interests in some way. It is for this reason that I beg to urge you to safeguard this point before it is too late.

Sincerely yours, W. S. Benson.

TLS (WP, DLC).

From Robert Lansing, with Enclosure

My dear Mr. President: Paris, 28 April, 1919.

Professor W. L. Westermann, one of our specialists under Dr. Mezes, has drafted certain general clauses to be embodied in mandates over parts of the present Ottoman Empire. The mandates, when finally formulated, will be specific for each case and will differ, but Professor Westermann thinks it wise to establish certain general provisions which will be more easily accepted when stated as general principles than if they should be brought forward after the mandataries have been named and the desire for strong control has begun to operate.

It is the opinion of your Colleagues of the Commission that the whole question of mandataries requires extremely careful consideration. Your Colleagues therefore would be very glad to have an expression of your opinion as to whether an American Commission should not immediately be formed to consider the matter, and also whether this commission should not be broadened as soon as possible into an Interallied Commission for the same purpose.

I am, my dear Mr. President,

Faithfully yours, Robert Lansing

TLS (WP, DLC).

ENCLOSURE

The general form to be adopted for, and certain general clauses to be included in, the specific mandates over states that may be formed through the breaking up of the Ottoman Empire.

Preamble.

Whereas His Majesty the Emperor of the Ottomans has ceded to [blank] (hereinafter referred to as the Signatory Powers) all his dominion and sovereignty in the territory of [blank] within the boundaries described in the annexed schedule:

Now therefore, the Signatory Powers hereby constitute the said territory of [blank] into a separate state under the League of Nations and appoint [blank] to be the mandatary of the League of Nations for the government and administration of the said state subject to the following limitations and obligations.

I.

Authority subject to the League of Nations.

All powers hereby conferred shall be exercised subject to the control which now is or hereafter may be vested in the League of Nations.

II.

Duration of the Mandate.

The term for the duration of this mandate shall be 25 years. At the end of this period, unless the League of Nations specifically extends it, the mandate shall cease and the autonomy of the state shall be complete. The mandate may be revoked by the League of Nations at any time and given to another power if the League shall consider that the Mandatary Power is not fulfilling its functions faithfully.

III.

Development toward complete independence.

It shall be the duty of the Mandatary Power to prepare the people of the state for complete self-government which shall be essentially popular in form. With this end in view a civil government where there is not already one in existence, shall be organized as soon as practicable, including both a higher Council which shall contain nationals of the state as well as nationals of the Mandatary Power and a House of Delegates chosen from the nationals of the state by popular vote.

Provision shall be made to promote the largest measure of regional autonomy and in the delimitation of these regions the primary consideration shall be racial distribution.

Within five years from the date of the mandate a Constitutional Convention shall be called to formulate a Constitution which shall go into immediate effect upon approval by the League of Nations.

IV.

Citizenship.

All residents born in the state and those resident therein five years prior to the date of this mandate, shall be nationals of the state, except those who, being citizens of some other state, shall within a period of one year opt for their own citizenship. No person shall be barred from the rights of nationals in this state on the ground of race, faith, or sex, or on any ground other than that of moral or mental disability.

V.

Abolition of Capitulations.

All those special rights, commonly known as Capitulations, which have been granted by the Ottoman Empire to certain nations are hereby abolished.

VI.

Preservation of existing Commercial Treaties.

Existing Commercial Treaties, concluded between the Ottoman Empire and any other Power, shall be regarded as binding upon the State except in-so-far as they shall conflict with the provisions of this mandate or be replaced by new treaties.

VII.

Rights of Foreigners.

Foreigners who shall establish themselves as residents of the state shall enjoy the same rights to hold land and to engage in commerce as the citizens of the state, and no discrimination in taxation shall be made against them.

VIII.

Toleration in Religious Belief.

Civil, political, and economic rights shall be assured to all citizens or subjects without discrimination on account of religious belief or creed. Freedom of conscience and religion shall be guaranteed and the following rights shall be assured to all:

(a) To choose freely any form of religious belief and to make a change of religion without let or hindrance.
(b) To exercise any form of divine worship publically or privately.
(c) To give religious instruction to any who desire to receive it.

IX.

Head of Religious Group.

In each state the head of any religious group shall be a citizen of that state.

X.

Religious, educational and philanthropic Organizations.

Religious, educational, or philanthropic organizations shall be allowed to exist as at present constituted and in full possession of present rights, including property rights, and with a guarantee of opportunity for future development, and full permission shall be accorded in the future for the foundation and development of similar institutions with similar rights, without discrimination in favor of or against any institution or sect, or the nationals of any foreign power who wish to develop such institutions.

XI.

Share of Ottoman Public Debt.

The State shall bear its share of the Public Debt of the Ottoman Empire, this share to be determined by the League of Nations.

XII.

Agreements with regard to Railways and Concessions.

The State shall take the place of the Ottoman Empire in all agreements made prior to the war with regard to Railways and Concessions which lie within the boundaries of the State. Subjects of the allied and associated Powers to whom concessions have been granted by the Ottoman Empire shall have the right to carry on business under the terms of concessions as granted without diminution of their existing rights.

XIII.

Transfers of Land.

In case question as to real estate titles, acquired since the beginning of the war, shall be raised within six months from the date of the mandate, the burden of proof, as between the holder before the war and the present holder, shall rest with the present holder of the title to show that the transfer was bona fide.

XIV.

Prohibition of Troops and Fortifications.

Except under emergency and on special authorization from the League of Nations, no troops other than for the maintenance of order shall be kept in the state by the Mandatary Power. Nor shall fortifications be maintained or constructed.

XV.

Prohibition to incorporate nationals of the State in the Army of the Mandatory Power.

No Mandatary Power shall incorporate in its own army nationals of the State, except in-so-far as they may freely volunteer.

XVI.

Prohibition of Transit Duties.

No transit duties shall be levied on goods passing through the State.

XVII.

Reports to be made by the Mandatory Power.

The Mandatary Power shall present to the League of Nations, at such intervals as the League shall specify, reports dealing with its trusteeship and with political and economic conditions in the State.

T MS (WP, DLC).

Thomas Nelson Page to the American Mission

Rome. April 28th, 1919.

270. CONFIDENTIAL Senator Lanciani[1] came yesterday to say a number of Senators were considering coming to express to me their great regret at present situation and friendship for America. They wished, however, first to see Orlando. I said I had thought of seeing Orlando myself to express the necessity of calming the people and of stopping vituperative attacks on the President by the press. He appeared most anxious I should see Orlando and arrange therefor, and I have just seen latter. He appears to appreciate gravity of present situation. I pointed out the importance of calming the people and curbing the continuance of the press campaign against the President which excites them by giving false information, including that regarding England, France, and the people of United States, who are, in fact, with the President. I said the President is, I know, a great friend of Italy's. He is the same who vetoed the immigration bill[2] which Italy thought against her interests, who established the system of just apportionment of world food and the world's tonnage, which saved Italy. Yet the press for some reason is allowed to pursue campaign attacking him outrageously which can only injure Italy. He said that he had given orders to try and stop the attacks; that he had also opposed the holding of a great demonstration at the Capitol, but the people did not heed him. I learned, however, that the dem-

onstration has been called off though many soldiers are out picketing the streets.

I met Barzilai as I came out with whom I had a little talk impressing on him the necessity of calming the people.

I gathered from Orlando that they did not mean to return to Paris to sign peace. He referred to the shortness of time before the German delegates arrive as a misfortune in view of the present state of mind of the Italian people. He said[3] that the situation is full of dangers whichever way he acts; but he prefers trouble from the outside to trouble in his own house and in the present state of agitation for him to sign treaty, including League of Nations, which will prevent any further acquisition of Italian territories settled by Italians, would be more dangerous than not to do it. Nelson Page

T telegram (WP, DLC).

[1] Rodolfo Amadeo Lanciani, a noted archeologist of Rome.

[2] Wilson's vetoes of the so-called Burnett bill are printed at Jan. 28, 1915, Vol. 32, and Jan. 29, 1917, Vol. 41.

[3] Wilson drew a double line on the left-hand margin of this telegram from "He said" to the end of the message.

A Translation of a Letter from Raymond Poincaré to Georges Clemenceau

My dear President: Paris, April 28, 1919.

Before definite decisions are taken, I do not believe it amiss to summarize the observations which are suggested to me by the plans prepared and which I have transmitted to you on several occasions. You will thus be in a position to communicate, if you deem it possible, my opinion to the Allied and associated Governments.

The debt which the Allied and associated Powers are to impose on Germany cannot be definitely calculated until after the estimates shall have been made by the commission created by virtue of the peace preliminaries. But at present it seems evident from the findings of the delegations that the payment will apparently be made in at least thirty annual instalments. It would seem just and logical that the military occupation of the left bank of the Rhine and of the bridgeheads should last during the same period.

One can, in the first place, invoke in favor of this occupation the grave considerations exposed by Marshal Foch in the two memoranda[1] of which the Allied and associated Governments have been apprised. The Marshal believes, in agreement with the military authorities, that the Rhine is the only barrier which really assures, in case of a new German attack, the common defense of England, Belgium and France. It is therefore advisable not to abandon this barrier until Germany has executed all the conditions of the treaty of peace.

There is, besides, something quite abnormal in renouncing a pledge before the debt involved has been completely paid.

Since the occupation must cease in case payment be made before the time set, the logical opposite of this clause is that the occupation will extend, in any case, until the payment of the balance of the debt.

After the War of 1870 the Germans occupied several French provinces until they received payment of the last centime of indemnity imposed on France, and Monsieur Thiers did not succeed in liberating the territory except by paying in advance the billions exacted by the conqueror.

The occupation as a guarantee of a debt representing the reparation for damages of war has nothing [in] contravention of the principles proclaimed by Mr. President Wilson and recognized by the Allies. It is well understood that it has no relation to annexation. It does not affect the national sovereignty of the vanquished nation; it is by its very definition temporary and subordinate to the duration of the debt which it guarantees; it constitutes only a surety, a means for the creditor to receive payment without resorting to force. It is impossible to understand how this occupation could be of shorter duration than the aggregate time of the annual payments. The period of fifteen years is entirely arbitrary and it is no less arbitrary to anticipate during the fifteen years three successive stages of evacuation, since at the end of the fifteen years, France and her Allies will still be creditors of Germany.

It is answered that once the occupation is terminated it could be resumed in case of non-payment. This option of re-occupation may seem alluring today on paper. It is fraught with difficulties and dangers.

Let us imagine the conditions sixteen or seventeen years hence. Germany has paid regularly during fifteen years. We have evacuated the entire left bank of the Rhine. We have retired on this side of the political frontiers which offer no military security. Let us suppose Germany to be again a prey to imperialism; let us suppose it to be merely dishonest. She suspends her payments. We are compelled to re-occupy. We give orders to that effect. Who can assure us that we shall be able to execute them without difficulty?

In the first place, Germany will not fail with her ordinary means of propaganda to falsify the facts and to pretend that we are the aggressors; and since, in reality, it is our troops which will re-enter German territory, we will be easily considered, in fact, as invaders.

And then will we be sure to find the left bank without German troops? One may say that Germany will bind herself to have neither troops nor fortresses on the left bank and within a zone of fifty kilometers to the east of the Rhine. But the treaty provides for no permanent control over troops and armaments, any more over the left bank than over the rest of Germany. The clause which stipulates that the Society of Nations may order investigations runs the risk, in default of this permanent control, of being entirely illusory. Nothing can therefore guarantee that after the expiration of the fifteen years and evacuation of the left bank, the Germans will not introduce little by little, troops into that region. Supposing that they may not do it in advance, how can we prevent them from doing it the day we should desire to re-occupy for default of payment?

It will be easy for them in that case to rush to the Rhine in a single night and to take possession well in advance of us, of this natural and military frontier.

The option of re-occupation, therefore, from no point of view could be substituted for occupation.

It is objected that the prolonged occupation will be a heavy military burden. Marshal Foch believes, on the contrary, that the defense of the Rhine will require a smaller number of troops than the defense of our political frontier, and no one surely is more competent in this question than he. Besides, it is not a matter, for the moment, of forcing ourselves to occupy; it is a matter of forcing Germany to accept this occupation. The Allies will always be free to renounce it if they deem it advisable.

It is also objected that by its prolongation, the occupation may embitter the relations between the troops and the population and thus provoke conflict. If the objection were well-founded, it would be just as valid against an occupation of fifteen years as against an occupation guaranteeing a debt. It would be even more valid against the first than against the second because the first, having an arbitrary duration, does not seem to have a clearly defined object; whereas the second, being a guarantee of payment, can be easily understood by the entire world and especially by the inhabitants of the occupied country. But it must be added, on one hand, that these inhabitants are among the most sociable of Germany and that they have never borne against the Allies the sentiments of hostility which animate the inhabitants of Prussia; on the other hand, (it must be added), that the French troops, once peace has been signed, will have sufficient tact not to treat these inhabitants as enemies. Were there any misunderstandings to be feared it would be rather during the first year because of the memories of the war; but as time passes the relations between the armies of occupation and the inhabitants will not fail to become better.

In a word, everything militates in favor of an occupation which is the result and the pledge of the debt. The former should cease when the latter has been paid. No sooner, no later.

No one appreciates more highly than I the offers of alliance which Mr. President of the United States and Mr. Prime Minister of Great Britain have generously made to France. The durable association of our three nations for the defense of right and liberty will be a great and magnificent thing. But the precious assistance which our friends will give us in the case of German aggression, unfortunately can never reach us at a moment's notice. Moreover, it will have no direct bearing on the guarantee of the debt. It can therefore not be a substitute for the occupation.

I have full confidence that the Allied and associated Governments will understand the situation and that they will consent to give to France, which has suffered so much, the only security which, in my opinion, will fully guarantee the payment of our debt.

Believe, my dear President, in my very devoted sentiments.

Poincaré.

T MS (WP, DLC).

[1] See the Enclosure printed with F. Foch to WW, March 14, 1919, Vol. 55, and the memorandum by Foch printed at March 31, 1919, Vol. 56.

From the Diary of Ray Stannard Baker

Monday the 28th [April 1919]

I saw the President just after the morning meeting of the Council of Three & he told me that he was much concerned over the settlement between Japan & China over Kiao Chau, regarded it as about the most difficult problem yet. The Japanese would not "bluff" but would make their demands & go home if they were not met! I had been talking with Williams & Hornbeck[1] about the whole subject, as well as with some of the Chinese, & was able to help him with some facts. . . .

When I got home to the hotel about midnight I found that the President's house had been repeatedly calling me. Though the hour was late I immediately called Admiral Grayson & he said the President wanted me to get certain information on the Chinese situation. I immediately got Hornbeck out of bed & we talked the situation until 2. a.m. I then came back here & worked on memoranda until an early hour. . . .

The Covenant is adopted! Bourgeois made an endless speech & Baron Makino withdrew, temporarily, his objection to the Covenant because it has no clause providing for racial equality.

Will the League come into being on this basis? Who knows? It now has a seat—and a Secretary General (Sir Eric Drummond)

[1] That is, Stanley Kuhl Hornbeck.

To Albert Sidney Burleson

Paris, 28 April, 1919.

For Postmaster General: I approve of your decision to return the cable lines to their respective owners at a date not later than May 10th, but suggest that you should not do so without at the same time announcing that the telegraph and telephone lines will be returned to their owners just so soon as legislation can be secured from Congress which will properly safeguard the interests of the owners in every way that it is possible to safeguard them. Only in this way I believe can the proper tone of confidence be restored in these matters. I will be obliged to you if you will send me by cable a form for my recommendation of this matter to Congress.

Woodrow Wilson.

T telegram (WP, DLC).

From Joseph Patrick Tumulty

[The White House, April 28, 1919]

No. 82. The issue which you raised in the Italian matter was inevitable. All issues of greed and grab now on trial. You took your stand on the side of justice. Whatever Orlando and Sonnino may do, the issue will have to be met. You are committed irrevocably to democratic peace and cannot yield. Sooner or later, the Sonninos in every country will have to yield.

As Springfield Republican says, "If imperialism does not capture the Peace Conference and put the peace settlements into imperialistic chains, Woodrow Wilson will have been the single force causing its defeat. Imperialists know their enemy; they can recognize him in all languages."

Tumulty.

T telegram (WP, DLC).

From the Diary of Dr. Grayson

Tuesday, April 29, 1919.

The President arose early, and after breakfast went to his study, where he received the Japanese delegates at ten o'clock. They pressed their claims for the Shantung Peninsula, again repeating that they were entitled to hold Kiao Chow and the railroads leading to the north, inasmuch as they had personally conquered Germany in the East and had simply wrested from Germany territory that China voluntarily had transferred to the Kaiser's government. Japan claimed that it kept China from becoming the prey of the Germans, as the Germans had their eye on China for a long time. The conference lasted until 1:20, when the President had lunch with Mrs. Wilson, Miss Benham and myself. After lunch the President and I went for a motor ride through the woods of St. Cloud and through the Bois. During the ride he talked freely about the difficulties of the Japanese situation. He said that the Japanese had made a number of notable concessions at the morning conference, agreeing to evacuate Kiao Chow and to destroy the modern fortifications which controlled the entrance to the harbor.

Upon his return the President conferred with the financial experts of the American Peace Commission, who presented him the result of the deliberations which they had had dealing with the German indemnities.

Dr. Axson was a dinner guest. He told the President of the plans that have now been completed for the internationalization of the Red Cross. They have just concluded a conference at Lyons, at which plans were perfected whereby the Red Cross movement would be continued effectively in relieving distress with the coming of peace.

The President retired at his usual hour.

Hankey's and Mantoux's Notes of a Meeting of the Council of Four[1]

President Wilson's Residence,
I.C.-177B. (*Revise*) Paris, April 29, 1919, 11 a.m.

(1) PRESIDENT WILSON said that he had taken the liberty of inviting the Japanese representatives to an hour's conversation before the Meeting. At the moment at which M. Clemenceau and Mr. Lloyd George had joined them, the discussion had reached this point: he himself had said that he understood that the Japanese were willing to re-cede to China the lease and rights in the leased territory, retaining their rights only in the leased district of Kiaochow, and outside of that only economic rights. They were willing, he understood, to forego their right to place troops along the railway and compel the Chinese to accept police instructors. That right has exceeded Germany's rights outside the leased territory, and went beyond economic rights. He understood that it was contemplated that there should be a joint Chino-Japanese control of the railway, which would be controlled by a corporation. The latter he proposed should have some control in the police also. But to give this right of

[1] The complete text of Hankey's notes is printed in *PPC*, V, 327-36.

police control to the Government would convey the same impression to the world as the German control of the Turkish army.

VISCOUNT CHINDA said that Japan's claims regarding police did not in his opinion exceed the rights actually exercised by Germany. The railway was really German-owned property. As German property the railway and its German personnel had the right to extra-territoriality, and this included the rights of policing, as it was the case with the foreign settlements in China.

MR. BALFOUR said he had thought that Viscount Chinda had on Saturday told him that the railway ran on Chinese territory and outside of German jurisdiction.[2]

VISCOUNT CHINDA said that the territory was Chinese, but the railway had in fact been German-owned, and consequently the railway and its personnel enjoyed extra-territoriality.

PRESIDENT WILSON asked why, because the railway was German-owned, it should enjoy extra-territorial rights? If, for example, the United States of America conceded the property in a railway in its own country to Germany, it would not have the right of extra-territoriality.

VISCOUNT CHINDA said that it was because in China foreigners have the right of extra-territoriality. As a matter of fact the Germans had employed Chinese as police, but had had an official of great importance not merely as instructor but as an adviser, and the whole police force had in fact been in his hands, consequently Japan, in asking for instructors, claimed less rights than Germany had exercised.

PRESIDENT WILSON said he did not mind Japan asking for these rights, but what he objected to was their imposing them. He was not arguing as to what rights Germany actually obtained by one act or another, but he was only concerned in what Germany's rights had been to which Japan succeeded.

MR BALFOUR asked if he was not right in saying that on Saturday Viscount Chinda had made the point that Japan became the heir of the German rights—that as Germany had owned the majority of the shares in the railway, Japan would inherit the same. That, however, surely did not give Japan the right of extra-territoriality. The remainder of the shares, he understood, were owned by the Chinese. It was certainly news to him that a commercial property of this kind covered extra-territorial rights, including control of police.

BARON MAKINO said he did not think it was contended that the majority of shares gave the right to extra-territoriality.

PRESIDENT WILSON asked if it was contended that the fact that the Government was the owner gave this right.

[2] See Balfour's memorandum printed at April 27, 1919.

BARON MAKINO said that it was a fact that Germany actually established the state of things which had been criticised.

VISCOUNT CHINDA said that territorial sovereignty belonged to China. Extra-territoriality applied not to the territory but to the people.

PRESIDENT WILSON said he could not admit this. He did not understand the first part of the settlement, namely, that referring to the control of life. He did not admit by inference that extra-territoriality applied to the personnel administering the railway. He was not contesting the facts of the situation that Germany had brought about, but he did contest what Germany had had the right to bring about if China had opposed it.

VISCOUNT CHINDA said that Germany had in fact enjoyed these rights. The police, however, had no right to interfere with the regions outside the railway.

MR. LLOYD GEORGE said that in the United Kingdom the police of railways and docks was very often in the hands of the Company concerned. The Company would arrange with the Home Office to hand over to it a section of the police, but it would remain under the control of the Directors of the Company. It seemed to him that some use might be made of this analogy. Control through the Directors would not be derogatory to the sovereignty of China any more than control of the London & North Western Railway police was derogatory to the sovereignty of Great Britain.

PRESIDENT WILSON pointed out the difference that the London & North Western Railway was not owned by a foreign Government. The police arrangements in the United States of America were somewhat similar, and State or City Commissioners often gave the control of railways to the Companies who paid the wages and were permitted to deal direct with these police. In law, however, the police were the employees of the municipalities, counties, etc. of the Central Government. What he contended was that if the majority of the shares was held by the Japanese, which would give a Japanese majority on the Board of Directors, they could in fact control the persons by whom the police were chosen. Why, he asked, should we compel a foreign Government to control what a majority of Directors could control in an administrative manner? If the Japanese Government insisted on Government control, and on Japanese instructors, they would offend the sovereignty of China, and get no more in fact than they could obtain through a majority of Japanese Directors. He remarked that there was no stipulation in the German lease concerning the right of police.

VISCOUNT CHINDA said that the matter might not be founded on an express understanding between Germany and China. It might be inferred from the fact of the ownership of the railway by Germany. The Japanese claim in this respect was a matter of precaution to obtain the necessary rights in China for safeguarding the railway. Practically it might work out all right if Mr. Lloyd George's proposal were adopted.

PRESIDENT WILSON objected to the form of this claim, which he regarded as an unwise one. It would give the impression of offending Chinese sovereignty. He himself was trying to get away from anything that would do this.

VISCOUNT CHINDA pointed out that China had accepted the arrangements voluntarily. In that case there would be no infringement of China's rights.

PRESIDENT WILSON said that the Chinese maintained that it was not voluntary.

VISCOUNT CHINDA said it was necessary to draw a distinction between the so called twenty-one points, and the September agreement of last year.

PRESIDENT WILSON said that circumstances and the temper of the parties had altered by 1918, but nevertheless the 1918 agreement had grown out of the 1915 agreement. One had been the supplement of the other.

VISCOUNT CHINDA said that the 1918 agreement was far from having been made under pressure. It had in fact been initiated by the Chinese Government. There had been no question of pressure.

BARON MAKINO said that the question of police instructors was related to the policy adopted in regard to these instructors. If the instructors were entered on a political basis and took part in the administrative part of their police duties, this would be going too far. The term instructors was rather a vague one. It might be abused as the Germans had done. In their case it had been a matter of a policy of vindication. If such intrusion was carried out it was a misuse. But if the arrangement was voluntarily entered into it would be regarded simply as a police arrangement.

PRESIDENT WILSON said it was extremely difficult for him in the face of public opinion in the United States of America to assent to any part of the arrangement.

He was seeking a way to make it possible for him to agree, and it was not a simple matter. Public opinion in the United States did not agree to the transfer of the concession. He was bound to tell the Japanese representatives that. He was trying to see all views and to find a way out. In these circumstances it greatly increased his difficulty if there were even an appearance of unusual control insisted on, particularly if the transfer of rights to Japan was greater than those exercised by Germany. He could not possibly justify in the United

States his assent to a transfer on such terms. Public opinion would say it did not believe in the transfer of the claims at all and that he had actually given Japan more than Germany had had. He must say frankly that he could not do this. He asked the Japanese representatives to cooperate with him in finding a way out. He wanted to support the dignity of Japan, but he thought that Japan gained nothing by insisting on these leased rights being vested in the Government.

MR. BALFOUR referred to his conversations with the Japanese representatives on the previous Saturday and Sunday. In view of these he was rather surprised at the tone of the present conversation. He understood and had stated in his memorandum that the intention of Japan was fully to restore Chinese sovereignty within the leased territory, and only to retain rights which were economic in their character. He had shown this memorandum to Baron Makino, who had expressed himself satisfied with it. Hence he was surprised this morning to find the question being discussed as to whether Japan did intend to exercise some rights of sovereignty. He had thought that that was not in dispute. He had thought that there was only a question of temporary and transitional arrangements, which did indeed transgress sovereignty, but only for a short time.

BARON MAKINO said he thought that the question of police instructors had been mentioned in their conversation. The conditions of the transfer arranged in 1918 had surely been discussed.

MR. BALFOUR said he did not deny this, but the broad issue was as to whether Chinese sovereignty was to be restored in its entirety. If this was to be done Japan would be within her rights in regard to her position in connection with the railway and the concession to negotiate was reasonable. Her position would be analogous with that of other powers which had concessions in China, although no doubt the whole system deserved to be reconsidered and was in need of revision. These concessions, however, would then only be of an economic character. He thought it was agreed that Japan should retain economic rights, and the only outstanding question related to the transitional period. Hence he had felt a good deal of surprise at the line of conversation this morning.

BARON MAKINO said he was sorry if there had been any misunderstanding. All this, however, was part of the arrangement of 1918.

PRESIDENT WILSON said that if Baron Makino relied on the agreement with China in regard to the police, he must also remind him that this agreement also provided for the maintenance of a military force by Japan in China. Japan did not insist upon that. Why should she insist upon the police?

BARON MAKINO said that in the conversation that he and Viscount Chinda had had with Mr. Balfour, they had felt considerable surprise at the interpretation that Mr. Balfour placed on the proposed concentration of troops at Chinan and Tsingtau, which he had apparently regarded as indefinite. The reason for his surprise was that the idea had never entered into his head, nor he believed into the heads of the Japanese military experts. The troops hitherto had been lined out along the railway at a number of points, and this concentration had been regarded as a mere step towards the final withdrawal of the troops. That being their standpoint he had been surprised when Mr. Balfour had assumed that it was intended to be for an indefinite period. In regard to the police, the question was of a somewhat different nature to the disposition of the troops. He was not entering into the wisdom of the arrangement, but according to his interpretation one of the stipulations was for the employment of instructors.

PRESIDENT WILSON said that no limit was imposed in regard to troops there.

BARON MAKINO agreed that on re-reading the article he had found that it might be construed in that sense. This had surprised him and he believed it to be merely a matter of wrong drafting. He admitted the phrase had been ambiguous, but the correct interpretation was the one he had given.

PRESIDENT WILSON said that one of the worst features in the whole of these transactions had been the unfortunate 21 demands and this had included a demand for police instructors, although, of course, on a much wider basis. This had caused the greatest irritation, as it was an invasion of Chinese political and administrative independence. It was impossible to divorce transactions of this kind from the public impression they made. The present arrangement was, in public estimation, tied up with the impression made by the 21 demands. He admitted that the police point in itself was a minor one, but in its implications, both in China and the United States, it was very unfortunate.

VISCOUNT CHINDA pointed out the difference that in the case of the 21 demands the idea had been to employ Japanese officers in entire regions. Here, however, it was only proposed to confine the police to the railway itself.

MR. LLOYD GEORGE said that this was a very important point. As the representative of one of the countries bound to support the transfer he was nevertheless very anxious that Japan should reach an agreement with the United States which was not signatory. Was it not possible, he asked, to reach an agreement on the basis of the practice in the United States of America and Great Britain, to which he had already referred? He could quite see that the Japanese did not wish to leave the railway entirely to Chinese administration.

They wished to ensure the security of their property and they had not their direct or indirect control. The same applied in the United Kingdom where, as elsewhere, some police administrations were better than others. He asked if this could not be done as President Wilson had proposed earlier in the discussion by putting the police under the directors? His suggestion would be to insert a clause in the agreement putting the police in the hands of the railway company, and providing that China would also do what was necessary to establish that police force. This would even give the right to the directors to employ Japanese instructors and no doubt instruction was a very important element. By these means, Japan would obtain all she wanted. She would substantially obtain the administration of the police of the railway, but the Chinese status would not be damaged.

VISCOUNT CHINDA said that the practical result of this arrangement might perhaps be adequate and satisfactory. The difficulty, however, was that it would involve a revision of the treaty or else a statement which would be regarded in Japan as of the same effect.

MR. LLOYD GEORGE asked why Japan should not merely give an interpretation of the treaty in this sense.

VISCOUNT CHINDA asked if this would be mere transitory measure.

MR. LLOYD GEORGE said it would be as a permanent measure, namely, that the arrangement was to be interpreted by Japan as one that would be worked through the directors. He quoted Article 2 of the exchange of notes of September 24th, 1918:

> "The Chinese Government may organise a police force to undertake the policing of the Kiauchao-Chinan Railway."

He asked if it could not be stated that the police force would be chosen by the directors.

VISCOUNT CHINDA said that as a practical arrangement this would perhaps do very well, as long as it did not alter the agreement or involve a public statement tantamount to a reversal of the agreement.

PRESIDENT WILSON said that he and the Government of the United States could not admit that the agreements were consistent with the terms of the German concession. What he was asked to do was contrary to the great volume of opinion in his own country, namely, to extend the German rights.

VISCOUNT CHINDA said he could not agree to this interpretation. That was the difference between them. The Japanese contended that the policing of the railway had nothing to do with the sovereignty.

PRESIDENT WILSON said he had examined it on the basis of the text of the transfer to Germany and the notes exchanged between

China and Japan. These notes certainly contained more than the German concession.

VISCOUNT CHINDA said that the German concession carried with it the right of policing.

PRESIDENT WILSON said he was willing to admit the policing being in the hands of a number of directors, the majority of which might be Japanese and he was willing to admit administrative control by them, but he was not willing to admit the right of the Japanese Government to exercise supervision over the police force.

MR. LLOYD GEORGE read the note of September 24th, 1918, and said he could not find those rights. It did not say that the Japanese would have supervision of the police force. It merely said that they were to be employed at the headquarters of the police, on the principal railway stations and at the police training school. It did not even mention instructors.

VISCOUNT CHINDA said that the right of having instructors employed was the Japanese interpretation of the clause.

MR. LLOYD GEORGE said that there was nothing in these clauses which could bear the interpretation of putting the Japanese in the position of repudiating the treaty. It merely said that Japanese were to be employed. He again suggested that there would be no departure from the terms of the treaty if the Japanese said that the Japanese chosen would be selected by the directors of the railway. He had no doubt that in fact the directors would have to apply to the Japanese Government. There would not be many suitable people in China and the Japanese Government would be the only source from which they could be obtained.

PRESIDENT WILSON said that the point was that in the treaty with Germany, we should impose the transfer of the German rights to Japan. His interpretation of the Chino-Japanese agreement was that in handing it back to China Japan would, in fact, extend her rights beyond those exercised by the Germans. The Japanese demanded that these rights should be transferred with this extension.

MR. LLOYD GEORGE said that the only extension was in respect of police. He asked if the instructors of the police had not, in fact, been Germans?

VISCOUNT CHINDA said that they had been termed advisers, but had undertaken the whole of the management. He considered that Japan was asking for less than this.

PRESIDENT WILSON said that Germany had not had any such right, although she had exercised it.

MR. LLOYD GEORGE asked Viscount Chinda to consider his proposition for leaving it to the directors to control the police.

(There was a considerable adjournment, during which Viscount Chinda conferred with his colleagues.)

After some further discussion, Mr. Balfour made certain proposals, which, in the course of the discussion were slightly amended, and eventually reached the following form:

1. The declared policy of Japan is to hand back to China in full sovereignty the Shantung Peninsula and to retain only the economic privileges possessed by Germany.

2. (The intention of the clauses relating to the*) police on the railway is merely to give the owners of the railway security for traffic and will be used for no other purpose.

3. Such Japanese instructors as may be required to assist in policing the railway may be selected by the Company.

PRESIDENT WILSON made the following proposal:

"Surrender to China of all rights of sovereignty and retention with regard to the railway and the mines only of the economic rights of a concessionaire, retaining, however, the privilege of establishing a non-exclusive settlement area at Singtau."

BARON MAKINO AND VISCOUNT CHINDA undertook carefully to consider the above two formulae and to let the Supreme Council know as soon as possible whether they could accept them or not. If they were unable to accept them or to make any public announcement in regard to them, they undertook to continue the discussion on the following day.

§ Mantoux's notes:

Mr. Balfour presents a draft statement: Japan respects the sovereignty of China in Shantung; her only desire is to succeed the Germans in the enjoyment of their economic rights. The clauses referring to the police have only the goal of assuring the security of the railway.

Lloyd George. I would add a sentence about the intention to confer on the railway company the task of organizing the police force, as certain companies in America and in England do.

Wilson. There remains this difference, that our companies cannot enroll foreigners in their police force. You would find no precedent in the West.

Lloyd George. Yes, but in many cases China employs foreigners, notably in the customs.

Wilson. Undoubtedly, but she chooses them herself, and voluntarily. I recognize with you that China is not in normal circumstances.

Lloyd George. China's stagnation justifies a great part of what for-

* To meet a criticism by President Wilson, Mr. Balfour suggested substituting the following words: "Any employment of special."

eigners have done there. The Chinese are like the Arabs, a very talented race, but arrived at a state which does not permit it to progress further. China would have been destroyed by the Taiping insurrection if Gordon had not been there to organize her army.[3] It must be acknowledged that China is not in the same situation as the great powers represented in this Conference.

Wilson. What I am saying is that I could not make the United States accept the sanction of the Sino-Japanese convention if it continued to give the Japanese, on certain points, more than the Germans possessed by virtue of their lease.

I believe what Baron Makino said about the military occupation.

Makino. I said that the troops would be withdrawn.

Lloyd George. Can we not limit ourselves to stipulating, in the treaty with Germany, that the German rights are transferred to Japan, and reserve for later the details relating to the means of this transfer?

Wilson. It is impossible to do that without knowing in advance what arrangement will follow the treaty.

Balfour. I will re-read the draft of the statement which we would ask the Japanese delegates to sign. It provides in the first place the reestablishment of China's sovereignty over the entire Shantung Province; (2) the institution of a police force along the railway line, in the interest of the railway line; (3) the appointment of the personnel of that police force by the railway company.

The Japanese delegates examine the text of the statement.

Wilson (after a moment of conversation with the Japanese delegates). Our Japanese colleagues tell me about the difficulty there is for them in appearing to abandon the treaty that Japan signed with China. Can they not declare that, to aid the success of the League of Nations, and to contribute to the peace of the world, they will willingly be content with the purely economic rights that will be granted them? Such a declaration before their Parliament would

[3] An exaggeration in several respects. The Taiping Rebellion, which had begun in 1850, had largely run its course before Maj. Charles George Gordon (often referred to as "Chinese" Gordon) first came into prominence in March 1863. He then took command of the so-called "Ever Victorious Army," a force of Chinese mercenaries, captured rebels, and volunteers, whose peak strength has been variously estimated at between 4,000 and 6,000 men, led by European and American officers. By that time the Taiping armies were already in retreat before much larger and superior forces led by Chinese generals loyal to the Manchu dynasty. Gordon did lead his army in several important battles in 1863 and 1864, but he had disbanded it before the fall of Nanking, the Taiping capital, to imperial forces on July 19, 1864, an action which marked the effective end of the rebellion. It was only after this date that Gordon spent some five months training officers for a new imperial army before returning to England in November 1864. At no time did he "organize" any Chinese military force. For the most detailed modern study of the rebellion and its suppression, see Teng Ssu-yü (S. Y. Teng), *The Taiping Rebellion and the Western Powers: A Comprehensive Survey* (Oxford, 1971). For Gordon's role therein, see *ibid.*, pp. 320-22, and Anthony Nutting, *Gordon: Martyr and Misfit* (London, 1966), pp. 32-80.

only enhance their dignity, Japan only bowing before the common ideal of civilized nations.

Makino. For my part, I do not believe that the arrangements that we have requested for the railway police implies a derogation of China's sovereignty. It is a matter of assuring the protection of the railway in the interest of the company which will use it. I do not see where the offense lies against the national integrity of China, which herself employs so many foreigners in her public services.

Wilson. According to the stipulation suggested by Mr. Balfour, the railway company would have the *option* of enrolling Japanese to serve in the police: that formula would remove my objection. If the Japanese delegation wishes to have the time to study this draft statement, it could give us its response this afternoon.

Makino. Your wish would be that the interpretation given by us to the treaty would be published?

Wilson. That is necessary for America public opinion.

Chinda. Yes, but that would have the opposite effect on Japanese opinion.

Wilson. Even with the considerations which I propose?

Chinda. I fear a real danger from that direction.

Balfour. May I suggest that possibility of making such a declaration in the form of an interview? In that way it would have the look of spontaneity which might prevent the impression which you fear. §

(2) The attached report from Mr. Headlam-Morley and Dr. Haskins was approved. (Appendix I.)

(Sir Maurice Hankey was instructed to communicate it to the Secretary-General for the information of the Drafting Committee.)

(3) MR. LLOYD GEORGE mentioned a speech by the Burgomaster of Cologne[4] which had been brought to his attention intimating the possibility of the establishment of a separate Republic for the Rhenish Provinces and Westphalia. He undertook to communicate a copy to his colleagues.

(4) SIR MAURICE HANKEY said that the British Admiralty had sent a telegram, asking that the Treaty of Peace should provide for the surrendered German ships to be handed over at such Allied ports as might be designated. The reason for this was that otherwise the Allies would have to go and fetch the ships.

PRESIDENT WILSON said he believed the ships were already dismantled.

MR. LLOYD GEORGE thought that the ships would be able to steam.

(It was agreed that the first clause of Article 25 should read as follows:

[4] Konrad Adenauer.

"Within a period of two months from the coming into force of the Present Treaty, the German surface warships enumerated below will be surrendered to the Allied and Associated Governments at such Allied ports as those Governments may direct."

Sir Maurice Hankey was instructed to communicate this decision to the Secretary-General for the information of the Drafting Committee.)

(5) M. CLEMENCEAU said that he had been advised by M. Jules Cambon that the German plenipotentiaries for Saxony and Bavaria and other States of the German Empire ought to possess credentials not only from the German Central Government but also from their State Governments. The opinion of the French jurisconsultes was that we could not proceed otherwise.

MR. LLOYD GEORGE pointed out that otherwise the Treaty might be signed by the representatives of the Central Government and yet be repudiated by the State Governments.

PRESIDENT WILSON felt some doubt as to the necessity of this.

M. CLEMENCEAU suggested the question should be remitted to an expert Committee to advise.

(It was agreed that the questions should be examined by a Committee composed of Mr. Lansing for the United States of America, Lord Hardinge for the British Empire, and M. Jules Cambon for France.)

APPENDIX I.

Memorandum by the American and British Representatives in the matter of the Saar Basin.

April 29th, 1919.

In accordance with the request of the Council of Four, we have examined on the spot the question of a slight modification in the northwestern boundary of the Saar Basin. We are clearly of the opinion that the economic and other interests of the southern portion of the canton of Mettlach require its incorporation in the territory of the Saar Basin, and that the proposed boundary should be modified accordingly. This would involve the addition of about ten square miles with a population of about five thousand which is in daily contact with the Basin.

We also recommend, in conjunction with M. Tardieu, that a clause be added to the final article concerning the Saar Basin so as to give the League of Nations power fifteen years hence to make an equitable apportionment of any obligations of the Government of the Basin of the Saar arising from loans raised by the Commission or otherwise.

(Sd) J. W. HEADLAM-MORLEY
CHARLES H. HASKINS.

T MS (SDR, RG 256, 180.03401/127, DNA); Mantoux, I, 406-408.

From Arthur James Balfour, with Enclosure

My dear Mr. President Paris. Apr. 29. 1919

Baron Makino and Viscount Chinda have just brought me a formula which embodies the result of their conversations with the Japanese Delegation on the subject of this morning's deliberations.

This formula they are quite prepared to accept: and as it differs but little from one of those discussed at your house I hope it may prove satisfactory. The two modifications they have introduced are underlined. The second of them, which is the most important of the two, and the only one which embodies any novelty, is, as you will observe, entirely in favour of Chinese sovereignty.

Y. v. srly Arthur James Balfour

ALS (WP, DLC).

ENCLOSURE

I. The declared policy of Japan is to hand back to China in full sovereignty the Shantung peninsula and to retain only the economic privileges possessed by Germany as well as that of establishing a Japanese settlement at Tsingtao.

II. The intention of the clauses relating to the police on the railways is merely to give the owner of the railway security for traffic and will be used for no other purpose.

III. Such Japanese instructors as may be required to assist in policing the railway may be selected by the Company, but shall be appointed by the Chinese Government.

T MS (Balfour Papers, Add. MSS 49751, British Library).

From Edward Mandell House

Dear Governor: Paris, April 29, 1919.

Both George and Balfour spoke to me yesterday about the Japanese settlement. They hoped you would accept the assurance which Makino gave Balfour and of which he has made a record.

My feeling is that while it is all bad, it is no worse than the things we are doing in many of the settlements in which the Western Powers are interested. I feel, too, that we had best clean up a lot of old rubbish with the least friction, and let the League of Nations and the new era do the rest.

England, France and Japan ought to get out of China and perhaps they will later if enough pressure is brought through public opinion as expressed in the League of Nations.

Affectionately yours, E. M. House

TLS (WP, DLC).

From the Diary of Ray Stannard Baker

Tuesday, April 29, 1919.

After working until about two o'clock this morning on the Chinese-Japanese problems I lay down for an hour or so, but could not sleep and soon got up and went at it again—in order to have the material ready for the President before his meeting with the Japanese. The Admiral[1] called me about 8:30 on the telephone & at nine I was at the President's house where I laid before him the Notes[2] I had made, together with various memoranda furnished me by Williams and Hornbeck *and* by Koo and Wei and others of the Chinese.[3] There is no possible doubt as to where the President's sympathies lie: he is for the Chinese. I told him that the sympathy of the world was with the Chinese "I know that," he said. Probably the most popular thing he could do would be to decide for the Chinese & go home! But it might be temporary popularity—before the storm broke. I made as strong a case as I could for the Chinese position, urging some postponement at least. The President pointed out how inextricably the whole matter was tied up with old treaties, how Britain felt herself bound to Japan—and how, with Italy already out, Belgium bitterly discontented—the defection of Japan, not an unreasonable possibility, might not only break up the peace Conference, but destroy the League of Nations.

I went up again at 2 o'clock with another load of ammunition for the President,[4] mostly provided by Hornbeck. The Council of 3 had the really critical Belgian situation up this afternoon & all the company of financial pundits was there. The Belgians feel that they have been neglected & are now hotly demanding their share of the reparations. It is curious how some crises of this conference are public property from the start—like the Italian situation, while others, almost equally serious, are scarcely heard of outside the innermost councils. Not a word has been said as to the extreme seriousness of this Belgian difficulty. They are threatening to go home!

At 6:30 I went up again & the President told me about the doings of the day, very little of which I am allowed to report to the press. The Japanese-Chinese question is still acute—and unsettled. It worries the President more than any other at any time. . . . The President is tired & looks worn.

[1] That is, Dr. Grayson.
[2] They are printed as the next document.
[3] For examples, see V. K. W. Koo to WW, April 17, 1919, n. 1, Vol. 57; the Enclosure printed with Lu Cheng-hsiang to WW, April 24, 1919; E. T. Williams to WW, April 24, 1919, and its Enclosure; and the memorandum by E. T. Williams printed at April 26, 1919.
[4] This "load" may have included, for example, S. K. Hornbeck to E. T. Williams, April 24, 1919, TS MS, enclosing "Practical Considerations with regard to *The Question of Shantung*," April 24, 1919, TS MS (SDR, RG 256, 185.1158/76, DNA).

A Memorandum by Ray Stannard Baker

[April 29, 1919]

Notes on the Japanese-Chinese Question.

The public opinion of the world, especially in America and in the British colonies sympathises with China.

Germany entered Shantung, and Japan is now there, by virtue of pursuing the "mailed fist" policy.

The Japanese-Chinese agreements of 1915 were extorted under pressure and with attempt at concealment and deceit. China, at the moment of signing, issued an official protest.

The United States is not only not committed to the support of Japan but, on the contrary, the American government specifically declared in May, 1915, that it would not recognise agreements impairing the principles of the open door, the integrity of China, and the rights of other nations. The Lansing-Ishii Notes can in no way correctly be cited as bearing on the question now in controversy.

The United States is under special moral obligation to stand for the utmost measure of justice for China, as it was at the invitation of the American government, and through the persuasion of Americans that China entered the war.

The Allied and Associated powers are all under moral obligation to refuse to sanction the doing of a wrong to China, inasmuch as they are bound by the professions which they made as to war aims and by the principles which they adopted as the basis for making peace, the Fourteen points proposed by President Wilson.

For the Conference to accept the contention that the question can be disposed of between Japan and China alone would be to evade responsibility.

To approve the Japanese contention that the settlement must conform to the terms of the agreements of 1915 and 1917 [1918] would be to set the seal of legality upon agreements decured [secured] by duress.

If the Conference renders a decision adverse to the Japanese claims it will, of course, occasion great annoyance in Japan. The effect, however, would be not that of an injury to the Japanese people;

it would constitute a rebuke to a bureaucratic group which, pursuing a policy of militaristic imperialism, has created an almost intolerable international political situation, has forced an unjust issue, and is apprehensive for its own political future.

As contrasted with this, a decision adverse to China, leaving Japan in an established political and strategic position in Shantung province, would cause a nation of 400,000,000 people to despair of obtaining justice or security except by embracing the very militarism which they fear and hate; it would destroy their confidence in the combined idealism and strength of the United States; it would embitter them against the Occident; it would make for war rather than for peace in the Far East. Left to the mercies of Japan at this critical moment, China would be forced to accept either subjugation to or an alliance with Japan, with the probability in either case that the Orient would soon be arrayed in arms against the Occident.

A decision in favor of Japan's claims would sanction the principle of conquest for profit.

A decision against Japan's Shantung claims will do Japan no injury, and will constitute a reaffirmation of the principle that the world must be made safe for those who wish to govern themselves within their own territories.

Japan, like Italy, cites her treaties, urges her particular interests, pleads consideration of domestic politics and international prestige. Here too, an individulal [individual] state places its own ambitions and self-adjudged interests above the principles according to which it has agreed that the peace shall be made. And Japan, like Italy, has alrwady [already] gained or been conceded great advantages. Has she not been relieved of the "menace" of the presence of Germany in the Pacific—in the words of her own statesman. Has she not profited enormously in material ways through the elimination of this rival from the markets in which she competes? Has she not won great political prestige? With a contribution infinaitely [infinitely] small in comparison with that made by the others, has she not been accorded recognition before the world as the equal in diplomatic authority of the greatest occidental powers? Surely Japan has been richly repaid for all that she has contributed toward the defeat of Germany.

The Japanese profession of willingness to restore the "lease of Kiaochow" and certain other things to China must be carefully considered for its exact import. The lease itself is a thing of comparative unimportance. The Japanese plan contemplates the retention by Japan of the railroads (or joint Japanese-Chinese control, which would speedily become Japanese control), the retention of the right to build additional railroads, retention of mines, the establishment of an exclusive port on Kiaochow bay, and continuation of the German right of first refusal in connection with assisting in economic enterprises throughout Shantung.

As in Manchuria, control of the railways and of a port as a terminus would enable Japan to control Shantung, and added to the control of Manchuria, would make Japan strategetically [strategically] the master of North China.

The Japanese proposals amount to "offering China the shell and securing for Japan the oyster.["] Ray Stannard Baker

TS MS (WP, DLC).

From Tasker Howard Bliss

My dear Mr. President: Paris, April 29th, 1919.

Last Saturday morning you told the American Delegation that you desired suggestions, although not at that moment, in regard to the pending matter of certain conflicting claims between Japan and China centering about the alleged German rights. My principal interest in the matter is with sole reference to the question of the moral right or wrong involved. From this point of view I discussed the matter this morning with Mr. Lansing and Mr. White. They concurred with me and requested me to draft a hasty note to you on the subject.

Since your conference with us last Saturday, I have asked myself three or four Socratic questions the answers to which make me, personally, quite sure on which side the moral right lies.

First. Japan bases certain of her claims on the right acquired by conquest. I asked myself the following question: Suppose Japan had not succeeded in her efforts to force the capitulation of the Germans at Tsing-Tau; suppose that the armistice of November 11th had found her still fighting the Germans at that place, just as the armistice found the English still fighting the Germans in South-East Africa. We would then oblige Germany to dispose of her claims in China by a clause in the Treaty of Peace. Would it occur to anyone that, as a matter of right, we should force Germany to cede her claims to Japan rather than to China? It seems to me that it would occur to every American that we would then have the opportunity that we have long desired to force Germany to correct, in favor of China, the great wrong which she began to do to the latter in 1898. What moral right has Japan acquired by her conquest of Shantung assisted by the British? If Great Britain and Japan secured no moral right to sovereignty over various savages inhabiting islands in the Pacific Ocean but, on the other hand, we hold that these people shall be governed by mandates under the League of Nations, what moral right has Japan acquired to the suzerainty (which she would undoubtedly eventually have) over 30,000,000 Chinese in the sacred province of Shantung?

Second. Japan must base her claims either on the Convention with China or on the right of conquest, or on both. Let us consider her moral right under either of these points.

a) If the United States has not before this recognized the validity of the rights claimed by Japan under her Convention with China, what has happened since the Armistice that would justify us in recognizing their validity now?

b) If Germany had possessed territory, in full sovereignty, on the east coast of Asia, a right to this territory, under international law, could have been obtained by conquest. But Germany possessed no such territory. What then was left for Japan to acquire by conquest? Apparently, nothing but a lease extorted under compulsion from China by Germany. I understand that international lawyers hold that such a lease or the rights acquired, justly or unjustly, under it cannot be acquired by conquest.

Third. Suppose Germany says to us, "We will cede our lease and all rights under it, but we will cede them back to China." Will we recognize the justice of Japan's claims to such an extent that we will threaten Germany with further war unless she cedes these rights to Japan rather than to China?

Again, suppose that Germany in her hopelessness of resistance to our demands, should sign without question a clause cedeing [ceding] these rights to Japan, even though we know that this is so wrong that we would not fight in order to compel Germany to do it, what moral justification would we have in making Germany do this?

Fourth. Stripped of all words that befog the issue, would we not, under the guise of making a treaty with Germany, really be making a treaty with Japan by which we compel one of our Allies (China) to cede against her will these things to Japan? Would not this action be really more unjustifiable than the one which you have refused to be a party to on the Dalmatian Coast? Because, in the latter case, the territory in dispute did not belong to one of the Allies but to one of the Central Powers; the question in Dalmatia is as to which of two friendly powers we shall give territory taken from an enemy power; in China the question is, shall we take certain claimed rights from one friendly power in order to give them to another friendly power.

It would seem to be advisable to call particular attention to what the Japanese mean when they say that they will return Kiachow to China. They *do not* offer to return the railway, the mines or the port, i.e., Tsingtau. The leased territory included a portion of land on the north-east side of the entra[n]ce of the Bay and another on the south-west and some islands. It is a small territory. The 50 Kilometer Zone was not included. That was a *limitation* put upon the movement of German troops. They could not go beyond the boundary of the Zone. Within this zone China enjoyed all rights of sovereignty and administration.

Japan's proposal to abandon the zone is somewhat of an impertinence since she has violated it ever since she took possession. She kept troops all along the railway line until recently and insists on maintaining in the future a guard at Tsinan, 254 miles away. The zone would restrict her military movements, consequently she gives it up.

The proposals she makes are (1) to open the whole bay. It is from 15 to 20 miles from the entrance to the northern shore of the bay. (2) To have a Japanese exclusive concession *at a* place to be designated by her, i.e., she can take just as much as she likes of the territory around the bay. It may be as large as the present leased territory, but more likely it will include only the best part of Tsingtau. What then does she give up? Nothing but such parts of the leased territory as are of no value.

The operation then would amount chiefly to an exchange of two pieces of paper—one cancelling the lease for 78 years, the other granting a more valuable concession which would amount to a permanent title to the port. Why take two years to go through this operation?

If it be right for a policeman, who recovers your purse, to keep the contents and claim that he has fulfilled his duty in returning the empty purse, then Japan's conduct may be tolerated.

If it be right for Japan to annex the territory of an Ally, then it cannot be wrong for Italy to retain Fiume taken from the enemy.

If we support Japan's claim, we abandon the democracy of China to the domination of the Prussianized militarism of Japan.

We shall be sowing dragons teeth.

It can't be right to do wrong even to make peace. Peace is desirable, but there are things dearer than peace, justice and freedom.

Sincerely yours, Tasker H. Bliss

TLS (WP, DLC).

Hankey's Notes of a Meeting of the Council of Four[1]

President Wilson's Residence,
I.C.-177C. Paris, April 29, 1919, 4 p.m.

1. M. M. G. CAHEN[2] was present for this discussion.

The Supreme Council had before them a Note by Sir Maurice Hankey setting forth the questions referred by the Council of Foreign Ministers. (Appendix I.)[3]

2. M. CAHEN said that what the French members of the Commission had had in mind was that, in case the Germans were asked, as part of the Clauses on Reparation, to supply labour for the purpose of restoring the devastated regions, a combined system of railway trains should be worked out. The same trains that brought the workmen might return with prisoners. The French representatives had felt it necessary to postpone the decision, in order that the two questions might be considered together.

M. CLEMENCEAU said that the prisoners of war ought to be returned immediately after the conclusion of Peace. Why should we mix up the question of trains with the question of prisoners?

M. CAHEN said that the only reason was that the two questions were intimately connected.

M. CLEMENCEAU said that to keep the prisoners would amount to slavery. The question of the supply of labour was another question that might be arranged at Versailles.

M. CAHEN asked if it was not proposed to enforce the supply of labour on the Germans.

M. CLEMENCEAU replied that it was not. It would be arranged.

PRESIDENT WILSON said he entirely agreed with M. Clemenceau. Forced labour would be unprecedented, unless one went back thousands of years.

MR. LLOYD GEORGE also agreed with M. Clemenceau.

(It was agreed:

> That the new Article referred to in Article 1 on the subject of Prisoners of War, should provide for the repatriation of Prisoners of War as soon as possible after the signature of the Treaty of Peace, and should be carried out with the utmost rapidity.)

3. PRESIDENT WILSON said that the proposal in Article 6 was practically to take hostages for the surrender of persons believed to have been guilty of breaches of the laws of war. It would be necessary to go back some hundreds of years to find a precedent for this also.

MR. LLOYD GEORGE said it was not as though we were dealing with the former German Government. He doubted whether it would be any use to take hostages in dealing with the present Government.

PRESIDENT WILSON asked what it was proposed to do with the hostages. In the end you would have to return them, and they would constitute no effective threat.

M. CLEMENCEAU said that all these should be kept against whom there was a presumption of personal guilt.

PRESIDENT WILSON said that this was provided for. (Article 5.)

M. CAHEN said that this had been a British proposal. The argument in favour of it was that we had evidence of crimes against the laws of war by persons in Germany. If our sanctions proved insufficient, there would be great popular discontent. We had many officer prisoners of the military caste, which was collectively guilty. We proposed that some of these officers should be kept if the accused persons were not delivered to justice. Mr. Lansing said that there must be no hostages. This was not in our minds. It was merely proposed to give Germany an inducement to hand over the accused persons. If this proposal was rejected offenders against discipline who otherwise would be released as an act of grace, might be kept.

MR. LLOYD GEORGE said that he did not agree in this.

M. CLEMENCEAU and PRESIDENT WILSON were of the same view.

(It was agreed: That Article 6 should be entirely suppressed.)

Sir Maurice Hankey was instructed to communicate this decision to the Secretary-General for the information of the Drafting Committee.

4. M. CLEMENCEAU said that the question of the recognition of the Jugo-Slavs had been cleared up. It had been ascertained that the mere acknowledgment of their credentials was equivalent to recognition, and would give occasion to no special declaration by the Allied and Associated Governments.

5. The attached Articles, prepared by Dr. Mezes, Sir Eyre Crowe, Baron de Guiffier[4] and M. Tardieu, in regard to Luxembourg, were approved, subject to the agreement of Belgium. (Appendix II.)[5]

(NOTE. M. Hymans, who was present a few minutes later at the meeting on reparation, was shown the Articles by Sir Maurice Hankey, and expressed his concurrence.)

Sir Maurice Hankey was instructed to forward the Articles to the Secretary-General, for communication to the Drafting Committee of the Preliminary Peace Conference.

6. SIR MAURICE HANKEY, at the conclusion of the meeting, consulted President Wilson as to his recollection of the decision taken in regard to Heligoland on April 15th, 1919 (I.C.171.A.),[6] when no Secretary had been present. The Drafting Committee, he pointed out, had received conflicting accounts.

PRESIDENT WILSON supported Mr. Balfour's recollection of the decision, namely that the naval harbour, as well as the fortifications, was to be destroyed, and that the island was not to be re-fortified.

Sir Maurice Hankey undertook to report this to the Drafting Committee.

(The meeting then adjourned upstairs to the meeting with the Belgian representatives on Reparation.)[7]

T MS (SDR, RG 256, 180.03401/128, DNA).

[1] The complete text of these minutes is printed in *PPC*, V, 337-43.

[2] Georges Joseph Ernest Cahen-Salvador, director of the General Service of Prisoners of War in the French War Ministry.

[3] Printed in *PPC*, V, 339-42.

[4] Edmund Ferdinand Félix Euchariste Marie Guillain, Baron de Gaiffier d'Hestroy, Belgian Minister to France.

[5] Printed in *PPC*, V, 342-43.

[6] However, see Mantoux's minutes of the Council of Four printed at April 15, 1919, 4 p.m., Vol. 57.

[7] The minutes of this meeting are printed in *PPC*, V, 344-51. Wilson made only one comment during this session. He warned the Belgians that they might not be represented in the peace negotiations if they refused to accept the terms of reparation worked out by the Big Four.

From the Diary of Vance Criswell McCormick

April 29 (Tuesday) [1919]

While working at office was sent for by the President to attend conference at his house with the Big Three and Belgians to discuss the latter's claim for reparations. Hymans, Foreign Minister Van der Heuval and Van der——[Vandervelde] representing Belgium.[1] After some discussion and counter offers of minor changes in the categories, Hymans stated that as Belgium's proposals were not acceptable for war costs, etc., the Belgium delegates would have to return to Brussels and get instructions. This struck the Big Three like a bomb shell as the Germans have arrived and with the Italian mess it would be serious. I have felt all along Belgium would play a strong hand. She has a good case and a popular one and at a prior meeting of the Big Four at Lloyd George's house, where categories were discussed, I made, during the President's absence in America, a reservation for United States until Belgium was satisfied.[2] After some discussion, we having warned President Wilson to let Lloyd George and Clemenceau bear the burden of discussion, as this trouble is of their own making, the French and British suggested a proposal to have Belgium get from Germany payments sufficient to pay her war debt to the Allies. This was not made to Belgium but discussed among ourselves and was amusing to me because I can see Great Britain and France coming to what I said all along they would be compelled to do.

During the discussion one of Lloyd George's secretaries brought in the speech of Orlando in Italian, made in Rome today.[3] It was a dramatic sight, seeing the President, Lloyd George and Clemenceau and others grouped about the interpreter in the middle of the room listening to the reading of Orlando's speech which might mean so much to the entire settlement of peace. It did not bring out anything new and there was not much comment.

While the Big Three seemed in good spirits, yet I could see underneath it all a great strain.

During the discussion the President mentioned to Davis on the side that both Lloyd George and Clemenceau had promised him to make a public statement on the Italian question but so far they had failed him. It has been unfair the way they have pushed him out into the light to bear the brunt of all the unpopular moves. Loucheur, French Minister of Reclamation, told me today that the propaganda of the Italians in French papers cost the Italians eight million francs. The French press is certainly rotten.

We did not get away from President's house until 7.30.

[1] Jules Norbert Marie Van den Heuvel, former Minister of Justice and Minister to the Vatican, at this time a plenipotentiary delegate to the peace conference; Émile Vandervelde, Minister of Justice and a plenipotentiary delegate.

[2] Actually, this meeting took place during Wilson's illness in Paris. See the minutes of the Council of Four printed at April 7, 1919, 4 p.m., Vol. 57.

[3] Orlando had delivered the same speech to separate sessions of the Italian Chamber of Deputies and the Senate in the afternoon and evening, respectively, of April 29. Wilson's public statement of April 23 on the Italian territorial claims, he declared, had made it necessary for him to renew his mandate from Parliament and the nation before continuing negotiations in Paris. After appealing for "calm and serenity" on the part of all concerned, he proceeded to a detailed exposition of his negotiations on Italy's territorial claims with Wilson and with Lloyd George and Clemenceau since mid-March. He asserted that it was only after meeting with Wilson on April 14 and reading Wilson's memorandum of that date that he had realized that their positions were irreconcilable. He said that Clemenceau and Lloyd George remained prepared to honor their commitments to Italy made in the Treaty of London but could not accept Italy's claim to Fiume. He was somewhat vague as to the course he proposed to follow in the future: he declared on the one hand that Italy must and would remain loyal to its wartime allies but made it clear on the other hand that Italy would not accept a peace settlement which did not essentially meet all of her just claims. Following his speech to the Chamber of Deputies, that body passed a resolution of confidence in the government by a vote of 382 to forty. The Socialists cast the negative votes. The Senate passed a similar resolution unanimously. Full texts of Orlando's speech and other related proceedings of the two sessions are printed in *Atti del Parlamento Italiano: Camera dei Deputati*, XXIV Legislatura, Sessione 1913-1919, Discussioni, XVII, 18849-63, and *Atti Parlamenti della Camera dei Senatori*, Legislatura XXIV, Sessione 1913-1919, Discussioni, V, 4885-96. Summaries with quotations appear in the London *Times*, May 1, 1919, and in the Associated Press reports in the *New York Times*, April 30-May 1, 1919. For other brief summaries of the events of these sessions, see Albrecht-Carrié, *Italy at the Paris Peace Conference*, pp. 147-48, and Mayer, *Politics and Diplomacy of Peacemaking*, pp. 709-11.

Thomas Nelson Page to the American Mission

Rome April 29, 1919

273. In response to a manifesto issued by the Mayor of Rome[1] and posted throughout city many thousand people gathered at the Capitol yesterday afternoon in a demonstration which had for its object

the carrying to the King at the Quirinal the vote of the country insisting on the annexation of Fiume and the settlement of the Adriatic question in accord with Italy's wishes. Great enthusiasm greeted the speech of the Mayor. A resolution read by the Mayor was voted to the effect that the people of Rome being aware of the legitimate and concrete will of Fiume to be united to Italy, invoke the immediate annexation of the territory included in the Pact of London reminding the government of its duty to liberate the other Italian cities not yet redeemed especially Spalato and Trau. Speaking to the crowd the Mayor said among other things "We will never market our national honor nor insult the tombs and blood of our heroes. The act of energetic firmness of our delegates at the Conference at Paris has been confirmed by the plebiscite of the entire people of Italy." The gathering after confirming the resolution proceeded to the Quirinal, led by the municipal band, where the Mayor and his colleagues were received by the King and Queen, and presented to the King the resolution. Everything passed over in an orderly manner amid great enthusiasm.

Today the walls of the city are covered with various colored posters calling for the annexation of Fiume and Dalmatia, some contain the single word Annexation.

Today's POPOLO ROMANO exhorting the people of Rome to calm during the sitting of Parliament says "The duty of the nation in the grave moment through which we are passing is to wait in silence but ready for any event."

MESSAGGERO deprecates further demonstrations in order that vote of Chamber may not seem due to popular pressure.

Press issues today under the heading "Wilson's message was unknown to Clemenceau," an official statement from the French Embassy as follows, "It having been asserted that well known publication made by President Wilson was inspired by Signor Clemenceau the French Embassy is authorized to make a formal denial to the above assertions." The POPULO ROMANO version of the French Embassy's denial includes the words "Neither previously known or inspired."[2]

The above is followed by official Stephani telegram[3] sent from Paris which states that French official circles flatly deny the statement issued in Sec. of Interior Lane's message that Clemenceau and Lloyd George have approved the President's declaration.[4] The same communiqué goes on to report that the French Press and public feeling is "More than ever in favor Italy as a consequence of the unexpected initiative of President Wilson, as already the French Government official and semi-official agencies are manifestly making every effort to profit by this incident. It seems strange that what the head lines announce, is not in accord with the text of the correspondence, but it is the bold words of the headlines that are remembered. According to the press the order of the day, to be presented to the Chamber by the Hon. Joachim Zatti and to the Senate by the Hon. Tittoni[5] reads as follows: "The Chamber, guardian of the dignity and interpreter of the will of the Italian people, declares itself solid with the Italian Government and reaffirms full faith in it to defend the supreme rights of the nation to obtain just and durable peace."

The Press announces that Socialist Party after lengthy meetings held the night before last and yesterday have decided to vote against the government on motion of confidence. Deputy Turati,[6] as spokesman of party, has announced that while Socialists would vote in favor of Italian rights to Fiume it will not vote in favor of motion of confidence in Orlando cabinet, which Socialist Party is unable to give.

The AVANTI has a first of May proclamation censored, about a third of it being excluded, calling upon the laboring proletariat to the Socialist party and saying to them that the Peace of the peoples is a Socialist peace, calls upon laborers who gather on May 1st to vote upon following resolution: (First) Complete freedom on land and sea, (Second) Full liberty in use of civil and political rights, (Third) General amnesty for all crimes political and military, (Fourth) Immediate withdrawal Italian soldiers from Servia. A note at foot of this article says this manifesto of May 1st is published so late because some days passed, the censor excluded it from them to the last. A criticism of the Government inspired by today's meeting of Parliament is heavily censored.

Press now working up idea of Japanese and French hostility toward American program. Under headlines, "American Imperialism Against French Interests" is a news item, to effect that our Government deported a Spanish Bolshevic from Cuba, a representative of French interests enroute to Mexico. Nelson Page.

T telegram (WP, DLC).

[1] That is, Prince Prospero Colonna.

[2] Underlining added, perhaps by Wilson.

[3] The Agenzia Stefani, not Stephani, founded by Guglielmo Stefani in 1853, was the quasiofficial news agency of the Italian government.

[4] Franklin K. Lane had, on April 26, issued a brief statement to explain "one or two matters connected with the Fiume situation that should not be overlooked." "Fiume," he said, "was not to be given to Italy by the secret treaty made on Italy's entrance into the war, called the London treaty. Under this treaty Fiume was to go to Croatia, which is now a part of Jugoslavia. And this is where President Wilson wishes it to go now. The question of giving Fiume to Italy thus becomes a question of good judgment, and President Wilson and Premiers Lloyd George and Clemenceau unitedly concluded that to give Fiume to Italy would be unjust to the new republics east of the Adriatic, as Fiume is the only port on the eastern side of the Adriatic which can be serviceable as a sea entrance to Jugoslavia and adjoining countries." *New York Times*, April 27, 1919.

[5] "Joachim Zatti" is a garbled version of Luigi Luzzatti, former Prime Minister and former Minister of the Treasury, who presented the resolution of support for the Orlando

ministry in the Chamber of Deputies on April 29. Tommaso Tittoni, former Foreign Minister, presented the resolution in the Senate on the same date.

[6] Filippo Turati, founder and principal leader of the Italian Socialist party.

From Eleutherios Vénisélos

Dear Mr. President: Paris, April 29, 1919.

The resolution adopted yesterday by the Peace Conference, on the proposition of the Great Allied and Associated Powers, to include Greece among the States of which the delegates will compose the first Council of the League of Nations, will be welcomed by the Greek people with a feeling of deep gratitude.

Allow me to thank you in their stead, Mr. President, and to assure you that they will take it to their heart to prove worthy of the honour and of the confidence of which they have been the object.

Greece will be happy and proud to contribute with all the means at her disposal, towards the success of the great work, which, owing to your initiative, will be undertaken for the purpose of safeguarding the reign of Peace and of leading Humanity towards a happier and better destiny.

Believe me, dear Mr. President,

Yours faithfully, E. K. Vénisélos

TLS (WP, DLC).

From William Allen White

Sir: [Paris] April 29, 1919.

The Conference is almost over. I believe I have known something of the inside of almost every great movement—something of what you have done. And as one American belonging to the cynical profession of the press, it may hearten you to know that every great move you have made has seemed to me wise and just and strong. I shall go home to support your course here with enthusiasm and with what force I can command.

I realize the termendous [tremendous] inertia of the French in resisting publicity. Yet I genuinely believe the world response which has come from your Italian stand, which after all was strong chiefly because it let publicity into the Conference, will well be duplicated if you insist that when the Allies meet the Germans to give the enemy his terms, the press of the world shall have some representation at the meeting. Such representation when the Covenant which has been made in the open is finally arrived at in the open would absolutely vindicate point number one.[1] And the humble people of the world who have looked so eagerly to you for championship would feel that in this final crisis you have stood by them. I hope you can feel that even an extraordinary effort to overcome the French inertia will be worth while in this final struggle for the open consum[m]ation of a just Covenant. But in any case I have the honor to subscribe myself in this splendid adventure of yours into world politics, Sincerely yours, W. A. White

TLS (WP, DLC).

[1] That is, of the Fourteen Points.

From Felix Frankfurter

My dear Mr. President, Paris April 29th, 1919.

Great gifts should not be accepted in silence. You will therefore forgive me if one more voice expresses its gratitude for the heartening message you addressed, not only to Italy, but to the liberal faith of the world. Surely no one familiar with the hopes and the feelings of the masses in England and France, as well as in the United States, can doubt that they will respond to all the calls you may make upon them in the enforcement of your principles.

Faithfully Yours, Felix Frankfurter.

TLS (WP, DLC).

From Norman Hezekiah Davis

My dear Mr. President: Paris, 29th April, 1919.

The United States Treasury, at the request of the British, French, and Italian Governments, has already established credits in favor of these Governments to the extent of $10,000,000 each, to be used for the payment of food purchased in the United States and sent to Austria for relief purposes, in order to prevent the further spread of anarchy. Mr. Hoover has estimated that it will require $15,000,000 additional to provide food for Austrian relief until the next crop is harvested, and I therefore recommended to the Secretary of the Treasury that an additional credit of five million dollars each to England, France, and Italy, a total of $15,000,000, be established on the same conditions as the previous $10,000,000 credit to each of them for food purchased in the United States and used for Austrian relief.

The Secretary of the Treasury has advised me that, before establishing these additional credits he would like to have your approval of them, inasmuch as they do not represent present commitments of the Treasury, as recently set forth by the Secretary in formal letters to each of these three Governments.

The Secretary has asked me to advise you that the estimated needs of the various countries to which the Treasury has been lending amount to a total of $9,754,747,716, leaving a balance of $245,252,284 of the original appropriation of $10,000,000,000. He wishes you to be informed, in addition, that the additional credits of $5,000,000 for each of these Governments would be in addition to the credit of $50,000,000 for Italy which he has already recommended and which is being withheld for the moment, and the additional credit of $100,000,000 for France which you have just approved.

I think it important that the $15,000,000 which Mr. Hoover considers necessary to complete his relief programme in Austria should be available, and I am enclosing a formal letter of approval to the Secretary of the Treasury for your signature in case the granting of these credits meets with your approval.

Faithfully yours, Norman H. Davis

TLS (WP, DLC).

To Joseph Patrick Tumulty

[Paris, April 29, 1919]

Please convey following message to Mr. Gompers, quote. Deeply grieved to hear of your accident.[1] Hope everything goes well with you. Warmest sympathy and regards,[2] unquote.

Woodrow Wilson.

T telegram (WP, DLC).

[1] Samuel Gompers, then age sixty-nine, had suffered two broken ribs in New York on April 27 when the taxicab in which he was riding was struck by a trolley car. *New York Times*, April 28 and 29, 1919.

[2] There is a WWhw draft of this message in WP, DLC.

Gilbert Fairchild Close to Joseph Patrick Tumulty

[Paris] April 29, 1919.

President approves statement contained your cable number eighty-one from Postmaster General.[1] Close.

T telegram (WP, DLC).

[1] ASB to WW, April 27, 1919.

From Joseph Patrick Tumulty

[The White House, April 29, 1919]

No. 84 Comment upon new draft of League most favorable and in many cases enthusiastic. Taft suppor[t]ing you vigorously especially in Fiume matter. Criticism from same old crowd led by Borah and Reed. Republican leaders conferring today at Capitol. Business situation improving every day. Wish our political situation might improve as fast, but this will improve with your return. Hope you will consider making tour of country on League of Nations. It would be a great stimulant and mean the utter rout of your political enemies.

Tumulty.

T telegram (WP, DLC).

From the Diary of Dr. Grayson

Wednesday, April 30, 1919.

The President had breakfast at 8:15 o'clock, and then went to his study where he remained until his meeting with the Big Three at 11:00 o'clock. Among other things the question was taken up of the verification of the credentials of the German delegates who have arrived at Versailles. The important proposition was to what extent those delegates could represent Bavaria in the negotiations. Bavaria occupies a peculiar position in the German Empire in that she never surrendered her own territorial rights and in all treaties that heretofore have been made Bavaria has been integrally a distinct part. The question of what should be done in case it was determined that the delegates could not act for Bavaria was gone into in detail, and it was finally decided that the Credentials Committee of the Allies, which is headed by M. Jules Cambon, should put the question direct to the Germans when they met to exchange credentials. Should it be discovered that Bavaria must be separately represented it was decided that an invitation would be sent to the government in control at Munich to be represented at the Treaty Conference.

After lunch the President went to his study. Noticing that he was very much fatigued I went to him and asked him if I could not order the car for him so that he could go for a ride with Mrs. Wilson through the Bois before the four o'clock meeting—to which he consented. He said: "I am sure to fall asleep as soon as I get into the motor, for last night I could not sleep—my mind was so full of the Japanese-Chinese controversy. But it was settled this morning, and while it is not to me a satisfactory settlement, I suppose it could be called an 'even break.' It is the best that could be accomplished out of a 'dirty past.' You know, England, and now I find out also France, had a secret treaty with Japan. I succeeded with much difficulty in getting the Japanese to agree to material concessions." The President gave me a statement to deliver to Ray Stannard Baker, the publicity representative of the Peace Commission, to take from the essential facts for the guidance of the newspapers. This was not to be used as an official statement. It was as follows: . . .[1]

The President then went for a motor ride, accompanied by Mrs. Wilson, through the Bois, returning in time for the four o'clock meeting with the Big Three.

The President made a strong plea to Lloyd-George and Clemenceau this afternoon to permit the newspapermen to be present at the conference at Versailles when the treaty is laid before the German delegates. Clemenceau objected strenuously to it. He said: "It would be undignified to have a large body of people looking on." He would not stand for it—and Lloyd-George sided with him. The President said that he was very much surprised at their attitude; that he thought it was unjust and unfair not to allow at least a limited number of representatives of the press to be present.

The Big Three also discussed Alsace-Lorraine.

Referring to the Labor Holiday tomorrow, the President said to Clemenceau: "I propose that we have a meeting here tomorrow—or do you prefer to stay indoors? I want enlightenment as to the procedure on your holidays. I have heard different versions." Clemenceau said: "Oh, no, the Socialists like you. You are very popular with them." "He said it in a vein as if he didn't like it," the President said, "and as if he were piqued at my popularity with the working people."

The President and Mrs. Wilson and I had dinner. After dinner I showed him a lot of cartoons of himself, which I had gotten in a book store this afternoon. Some of them were very amusing. He laughed at them heartily.

[1] Here follows the statement included in WW to JPT, April 30, 1919, printed below.

To Arthur James Balfour, with Enclosure

My dear Mr. Balfour, [Paris] 30 April, 1919.

I am sending enclosed (with the Japanese proposal, which I return) a form which I hope you will be kind enough to urge upon the Japanese. I hoped that I had made it clear to them that I could not accept a settlement based on the agreements with China, which all go back for the foundation to an ultimatum connected with the wrongful Twenty-one Demands. The whole settlement must, in my view, be based upon the German rights and our *present* understandings. What I have written is exactly equivalent in substance to their form.

Pardon typewriting: this is done by myself on my own "pen."

Faithfully Yours, Woodrow Wilson

WWTLS (A. J. Balfour Papers, Add. MSS 49751, British Library).

E N C L O S U R E

The declared policy of Japan is to hand back the Shantung peninsula in full sovereignty to China, retaining only the economic privileges granted to Germany and the right to establish a settlement under the usual conditions at Tsingtao.

The owners of the railway will use special police only to insure security for traffic. They will be used for no other purpose.

The police force will be composed of Chinese and such Japanese instructors as the directors of the railway may select will be appointed by the Chinese Government.

WWT MS (A. J. Balfour Papers, Add. MSS 49751, British Library).

From Arthur James Balfour, with Enclosure

My dear Mr. President, Paris. April 30th, 1919.

On receipt of your note I at once wrote to Baron Makino the enclosed letter. I sincerely hope it will lead to a successful termination of this troublesome question.

Yours Arthur James Balfour

TLS (WP, DLC).

E N C L O S U R E

Arthur James Balfour to Baron Nobuaki Makino

Dear Baron Makino, Paris. April 30th, 1919.

I have just received from the President a statement of his views upon the suggestion of yesterday. I send you a copy of the proposal which he is prepared to accept. You will observe that it differs from that which we discussed yesterday only in three particulars. The first is in Paragraph 1., in which there is a slight change in the wording which describes the settlement of Tsingtao. The second suggested alteration is in Paragraph 2. Here, as far as I can see, there is absolutely no difference in substance; but no reference is made to any Treaty arrangements, and the clause becomes merely a declaration of policy on which all parties are agreed. The third Paragraph specifically mentions the fact that the Police Force will be essentially Chinese, but, so far as I am aware, does not suggest any modification of the Japanese policy, or any other alteration in the Japanese wording.

If, as I hope and believe, these suggested modifications carry with them no alteration in Japanese policy, and no infringement of the rights and dignity of the Japanese people, I hope you may see your way to accept them. If so, I gather that the whole negotiation may be regarded as happily concluded.

Believe me, etc. etc. Arthur James Balfour.

TCL (WP, DLC).

From Vi Kyuin Wellington Koo

My dear Mr. President: Paris, April 30, 1919.

For reasons of urgency I am writing you personally in order to invite your attention to the following two points in connexion with the Kiaochow-Shantung question:

(a) The compromise offered and outlined in the Memorandum communicated by the Chinese Delegation to you on the 24th inst.[1] involves no violation of the undertakings given to Japan by the British Government on February 16, 1917 and by the French Government on March 1, 1917. These undertakings were only promises to support Japan's claim to German rights in Shantung on the occasion of the Peace Conference. While there were such rights in existence at the time of the undertaking, to-day there are none, because all German rights were abrogated by China's declaration of war as notified to, and taken cognizance of by, the Allied and Associated Governments on August 14, 1917.

(2) The indirect restitution of Kiaochow, desired by Japan, would be construed by Japan as a confirmation by the Peace Conference of the Treaties and Notes of 1915 which Japan compelled China to sign under coercion of an ultimatum, edged with a threat of war. These Treaties and Notes are now before the Peace Conference for abrogation in a separate Memorandum submitted by the Chinese Delegation.[2]

I attach a copy of the terms of the compromise referred to.[3]

I am, my dear Mr. President,

Yours sincerely, V. K. Wellington Koo

TLS (WP, DLC).

[1] See Lu Cheng-hsiang to WW, April 24, 1919.
[2] See n. 1 to J. C. Grew to GFC, April 25, 1919.
[3] They are printed in the Enclosure with Lu Cheng-hsiang to WW, April 24, 1919.

Cary Travers Grayson to Joseph Patrick Tumulty

[Paris, April 30, 1919]

Japanese situation is hanging by a thread. They are in conference now. These are terrible days for the President physically and otherwise. Grayson.

T telegram (WP, DLC).

Hankey's and Mantoux's Notes of a Meeting of the Council of Four[1]

President Wilson's House,
I.C.-177E. Paris, April 30, 1919, 11 a.m.

1. PRESIDENT WILSON said that Mr. Lansing had drawn his attention to Article 46 of the Military Terms which provided that "the Armistice of November 11th, 1918 and the subsequent Conventions thereto remain in force so far as they are not inconsistent with the above stipulations." He doubted the expediency of this.

MR. LLOYD GEORGE agreed.

(President Wilson undertook to send word to General Bliss and ask him to give a statement as to the precise signification of this Article.)

2. (It was agreed that Mr. Hoover's letter on the subject of the recognition of Finland[2] should be sent for examination and report by the Council of Foreign Ministers, Appendix I.)

3. M. CLEMENCEAU said that M. Jules Cambon was sending word to Herr Brockdorff-Rantzau, asking him to meet him on Thursday afternoon at the Hotel Trianon, with the credentials of the German Plenipotentiaries.

MR. LLOYD GEORGE urged that the meeting should be held in the morning and not in the afternoon, and that M. Jules Cambon should be accompanied by other Members of the Credentials Committee.

M. CLEMENCEAU suggested that M. Cambon should be telephoned for.

(The discussion of this subject was adjourned, pending the arrival of M. Jules Cambon.)

[1] The complete text of Hankey's minutes is printed in *PPC*, V, 352-62.
[2] Printed in *ibid.*, pp. 357-59.

4. M. CLEMENCEAU said that Article 41 had been reserved.

SIR MAURICE HANKEY read the Article, which relates to the establishment by Germany of landing places and dirigible sheds, prohibiting their establishment within 150 kilometres of any frontier.

MR. LLOYD GEORGE said he had protested against this clause and considered 50 kilometres sufficient.

PRESIDENT WILSON suggested that the whole Article was ridiculous.

(It was agreed that Article 41 should be struck out of the Air Terms.)

M. CLEMENCEAU said he was informed that Article 51 was reserved. This Article states that "the upkeep and cost of the Commissions of Control and the expenses involved by their work shall be borne by Germany."

(It was agreed that this Article should be retained.)

5. The Council had before them a letter from the Japanese Delegation, asking:

1. That Japan should be represented on the Commission for Reparations, since Reparations is a question of general interest, and
2. To see inserted in Article 16 of the Financial Clauses a particular disposition concerning Japan, which has 4,000 German prisoners while Germany has only a few civil Japanese prisoners. (Appendix II.)[3]

The discussion of this letter at once gave rise to a discussion on the letter addressed by M. Loucheur to President Wilson on the question of the application by Serbia for a seat on the Reparations Commission. (Appendix III.)[4]

(6) After some discussion, the following proposal submitted by M. Loucheur, Mr. Norman Davis, Mr. Baruch, Mr. Lamont, and Mr. Keynes, was approved:

> "Belgium shall sit, as originally proposed, as one of the five members of the Commission for all general discussions and for all other questions except those relating to damage by sea, for which Japan shall take her place, and those relating to Austria-Hungary, for which Serbia shall take Belgium's place. The Commission will thus always be limited in number to five, and the Japanese and Serbian representatives on the occasions on which they are entitled to sit will have the same power of voting as the delegates of the other four Powers."

(7) The discussions on M. Loucheur's letter gave rise to a discus-

[3] Printed in *ibid.*, p. 359.
[4] Printed in *ibid.*, pp. 359-60.

sion on the attitude to be taken if the Italian Delegation did not return to meet the Germans.

MR. LLOYD GEORGE asked if the Allied and Associated Powers were to put in a claim on Italy's behalf.

PRESIDENT WILSON replied that we could not do so.

M. CLEMENCEAU asked whether it would not be advisable to let M. Orlando know that the Germans had arrived, and that the Allied and Associated Powers would meet them in a day or two.

MR. LLOYD GEORGE advocated taking no action. They had been offered a definite proposal.

PRESIDENT WILSON said that as far as he was concerned, Italy could have any district in Austria, provided she could secure it by a majority of votes in the plebiscite. This of course, would only apply to a clearly defined district, and not to a small spot on the map. If the Italians alleged that a particular island was Italian in character, they could have a plebiscite.

MR. LLOYD GEORGE pointed out that their claim to the islands was based on security.

PRESIDENT WILSON said that argument was not a valid one. If Italy insisted on her claims to Dalmatia under the Treaty of London, it would upset the whole peace of the world and especially of the Slavonic world.

M. CLEMENCEAU said there was news this morning that an Italian dreadnought had been sent to Smyrna.

SIR MAURICE HANKEY reminded the Council that M. Clemenceau at the last meeting with MM. Orlando and Sonnino had asked a direct question, whether the Italians would be present to meet the Germans at Versailles, and M. Orlando had replied that this depended on what happened at Rome.

(There was then some short discussion as to the inferences to be drawn from MM. Orlando's and Sonnino's speeches,[5] and as to the awkward situation which would arise if the Italians returned and insisted on France and Great Britain carrying out the Treaty of London, which President Wilson was unable to support.)

MR. LLOYD GEORGE reminded his colleagues that he had asked M. Orlando if they would be justified in putting forward claims on Italy's behalf, if Italy was not present at Versailles to meet the Germans. M. Orlando had recognized that this was impossible.

PRESIDENT WILSON recalled a conversation he had had with M.

[5] Sonnino, always a very reluctant public speaker, did speak briefly to assembled crowds in Genoa and Rome on his return to Italy from Paris on April 27. The only hint as to the content of his remarks, made on April 28, was in the New York *Evening Post*, April 28, 1919, which reported that he said in Genoa "that the government is determined to obtain what is due to Italy." See also the *New York Times*, April 29, 1919.

Orlando in which the latter had shown quite clearly that he realized that if the Italian Delegates did not return, they could not sign the Treaty with Germany; they would be outside the League of Nations; and he had said some words which indicated that he considered they would be, in a sense, outcasts.

PRESIDENT WILSON had then pointed out that they were quarrelling with their best friends and M. Orlando had replied in some phrase to the effect that Italy would rather die with honour than compromise.

(No action was decided on as to making any communication.)

§ Mantoux's notes:

Lloyd George. What shall we do about Italy? The question is pressing.

Clemenceau. Must the Italians be notified that we are entering into contact with the Germans tomorrow?

Lloyd George. I would tell them nothing. They made no response to the proposal of compromise which I made to them, but I am persuaded that they will end by accepting it. In his speech in Montecitorio,[6] M. Orlando said that we had proposed to establish Fiume as a free city in exchange for concessions in Dalmatia; this opens the way to the compromise which I desire.

Wilson. As far as I am concerned, I declare that Italy can have all that she can obtain by a plebiscite. I do not see any harm, on that condition, in her occupying all the territories she wants.

Lloyd George. The Italians are invoking an argument other than that of the will of the people; they are speaking of Italy's security.

Wilson. That is an argument which does not hold. It would obviously be very dangerous for them to refuse the plebiscite, because it would be to avow, themselves, the weakness of their claims.

Clemenceau. A dispatch which we received indicates that the Italians are sending a battleship to Smyrna.

Lloyd George. This is dangerous, and it would seem that the Italians wish to cause a crisis. It is better that we attend to them.

Wilson. They are supported by their Parliament.

Lloyd George. Remember that Baron Sonnino was against the trip to Rome and in favor of a compromise. If he should return here and if we did not manage to agree, that would be worse than anything, and we, bound by our treaty, we would be in a very difficult situation. If they do not wish to come, for the love of God let us leave them where they are. If they come to ask us to execute purely and

[6] That is, Orlando's speech of April 29, 1919, about which see n. 3 to the extract from the Diary of V. C. McCormick printed at that date. The Palace of Montecitorio was the meeting place of the Italian Chamber of Deputies.

simply the Treaty of London, we are obliged to do it. I am not anxious for that to happen. The present situation is bad but not irreparable.

For the moment, it seems to me impossible to present Italy's claims to Germany.

Wilson. In the conversation which I had with M. Orlando before the debate was extended to us all, he stated to me that if Italy could receive only what I was inclined to grant her, she would be obliged to dissociate herself from us, and in this case, she would find herself, he said, as outside the law. I said to him: "Nothing would be more tragic, when we are dealing among friends." He replied to me that that seemed inevitable to him, if he only had the choice between dying honorably or living by a shameful compromise. §

8. Attention was then drawn to the last paragraph of M. Loucheur's letter (Appendix III) in which was raised the question of the joint and several liability of the enemy States.

PRESIDENT WILSON asked if that had been decided.

MR. LLOYD GEORGE said he thought it had been, subject to a bookkeeping arrangement proposed by M. Orlando.

SIR MAURICE HANKEY said that this had been discussed before he was introduced as Secretary. The only intimation on the subject that he had had was that M. Orlando had undertaken that the Italian financial expert (M. Crespi) should discuss the question with the experts of the other Allied and Associated Powers. He had heard from Lord Sumner that a preliminary discussion had taken place, but after that, the Italian Delegates had left, and he thought, no more had been done.

MR. LLOYD GEORGE considered that the question was very important. Roumania and Serbia were absorbing great slices of former Austrian territory which was entirely free from war debt, and it would seem desirable that this asset should be balanced against other liabilities.

PRESIDENT WILSON said that the question was too complicated for an off-hand decision. He saw Mr. Lloyd George's point, but it would work both ways. Germany would have to take her share of the Austrian, Bulgarian and Turkish liabilities, and to that extent, the direct indemnity obtained from Germany would be lessened.

MR. LLOYD GEORGE suggested that the matter should be settled at once.

PRESIDENT WILSON suggested that a decision should be taken that Germany should be jointly liable with her Allies.

MR. LLOYD GEORGE agreed in this, but suggested that in addition the following questions should be referred to expert examination:

1. To work out the Austrian bill of reparations on the same principle as had been adopted in the case of Germany.
2. To work out the proportion of the Austrian War debt to be borne by Jugo Slavia, Transylvania and other parts of the former Austrian Empire transferred to other nationalities.

M. CLEMENCEAU said that he would first like to consult his experts, but would inform them of his views on the following morning.

(9) The Council next took up the question raised in paragraph (a) of M. Loucheur's letter.

MR. LLOYD GEORGE said he was prepared to accept the principle that the proportions in which the successive instalments paid over by Germany in satisfaction of the claims against her should be divided by the Allied and Associated Governments, should be determined by the Permanent Commission set up under the Reparations Articles, in proportion to the claims allowed by the Commission. It was true that these would not be known before May 21st, 1919, but he was prepared to accept this principle.

PRESIDENT WILSON said that this seemed obviously fair.

M. CLEMENCEAU agreed.

(10) The Council had before them the draft Articles in Appendix IV, relating to China. These had been prepared by a Committee composed of:

Mr. E. T. Williams for the United States of America.

Mr. Ronald Macleay for the British Empire.

M. Jean Gout for France.

The Articles were agreed to, subject to a reservation by Mr. Lloyd George in Article VI, as he wished to enquire as to why the German renunciation was in one case in favour of the British concessions, and in the other, in favour of the French and Chinese Governments jointly. (NOTE: After inquiry, Mr. Lloyd George accepted the Articles.)

(11) PRESIDENT WILSON said that he was informed that the Allied and Associated journalists were very anxious to see the Treaty of Peace handed to the Germans. He understood that under present arrangements they were only to be permitted to view the approach of the Germans from behind a hedge. He was informed that there was a room separated from the Conference room by a glass screen, and that a number of journalists could be accommodated in this room, and view the proceedings.

(M. Jules Cambon entered during this discussion.)

This room was entered by a side door so that the Conference would in no way be inconvenienced.

M. CLEMENCEAU said that this description was correct. He

thought that the journalists might be admitted to this room for this particular meeting.

MR. LLOYD GEORGE suggested that it was very undignified and improper to admit the journalists and to treat the meeting almost as though it were a menagerie. He did not mind so much the presence of two or three. But it had to be borne in mind that the Germans were in a very delicate and disagreeable position and might have just cause to complain at descriptions being given of the precise manner in which they received the Treaty. He had no bowels of compassion for the Germans, but he thought that the admission of journalists on such an occasion would be unprecedented.

M. CLEMENCEAU suggested that at any rate, they might be admitted to be present at the end of the corridor in order to witness the arrival and departure of the Delegates.

PRESIDENT WILSON said he did not agree in this decision as he considered on principle that the journalists should be present, but he did not press his objection.

(It was agreed that the journalists should be permitted to witness the arrival of the Delegates from the end of the corridor in the Trianon Hotel.)

(12) It was agreed:

1. That the credentials of the German Delegates should be examined on the following morning at 11 a.m.
2. That M. Jules Cambon should be accompanied by the Members of the Committee appointed at the Peace Conference for the examination of credentials.
3. That the Committee for the examination of credentials should report the result of their interview to M. Clemenceau, President Wilson, and Mr. Lloyd George the same afternoon at President Wilson's house at 4 p.m.

(13) MR. LLOYD GEORGE asked how this matter stood.

PRESIDENT WILSON said he understood it had been decided provisionally to publish a summary when it was handed to the Germans, although that depended on the nature of the summary.

MR. LLOYD GEORGE suggested it would be desirable to ascertain from the Germans how they regarded the matter. He suggested that M. Cambon should be asked to ascertain this on the morrow.

M. CLEMENCEAU undertook to consult M. Cambon on the point.

(14) The Secretary and Interpreter were asked to withdraw from the room during this discussion. After their return, M. Clemenceau handed to Sir Maurice Hankey the following sentence to be added to Article 2(c) of the clauses approved on April 22nd (I.C.175B).[7]

[7] See Appendix IV to the minutes of the Council of Four, April 22, 1919, 11 a.m., Vol. 57. In the T MS, this incorrectly reads "(I.C. 1751)."

"Si, à ce moment, les garanties contre une agression non provoquée de l'Allemagne n'etaient pas considérées comme suffisantes par les Gouvernements Alliés et Associés, l'evacuation des troupes d'occupation pourrant être retardée dans la mesure jugée nécessaire à l'obtention des dites garanties."

§ Mantoux's notes:

M. Jules Cambon is introduced.

Clemenceau. We are asking you to see Brockdorff-Rantzau tomorrow for the presentation of credentials, with your colleagues on the Committee for the Verification of Powers. How many are you?

Cambon. Four: the Marquis Salvago Raggi,[8] Mr. Balfour, who is represented by Mr. Barnes, Mr. Henry White, and myself.

Hankey. According to the rule of the conference, it must be plenipotentiaries who present the credentials.

Clemenceau. Then the best thing is to say that M. Cambon will be accompanied by Messrs. White and Balfour. There cannot be a question of an Italian representative, since Italy, for the moment, is not present. Do that tomorrow morning and come in the afternoon to make a report to us about what took place.

Lloyd George. Must we not also try to know what the intentions of the Germans are concerning the publication of the treaty, in order to regulate our own conduct according to what we are able to learn of their frame of mind?

Clemenceau. I will ask M. Cambon to try to inform us about that.

M. Jules Cambon withdraws. §

APPENDIX IV TO I.C.177.E.

DRAFT ARTICLES IN REGARD TO CHINA TO BE INSERTED IN THE PRELIMINARY PEACE TREATY WITH GERMANY.

ARTICLE I.

Germany renounces in favour of China all claims to all benefits and privileges under the provisions of the final protocol signed at Peking on the 7th September, 1901, as well as under all Annexes, Notes and Documents supplementary thereto, and she likewise renounces in favour of China all claims to all indemnities accruing under the said protocol and supplementary annexes, notes and documents subsequent to the 14th March, 1917.

ARTICLE II.

Germany cedes to China all the buildings, wharves, barracks, forts, arms and munitions of war, vessels of all kinds, wireless in-

[8] Marquis Giuseppe Salvago-Raggi, former Italian Ambassador to France, a plenipotentiary delegate to the peace conference.

stallations and other public property belonging to the German Government, which are situated or may be found in the German Concessions in Tientsin and Hankow and in other parts of Chinese territory except in the leased territory of Kiaochow.

It is understood, however, that buildings and establishments used as diplomatic or consular residences or offices are not included in the above act of cession and, furthermore, that no steps shall be taken by the Chinese Government to dispose of the German public and private property situated within the so-called Legation Quarter at Peking without the consent of the Diplomatic Representatives of the Powers which on the signature of this Treaty remain Parties to the Final Protocol of the 7th September, 1901.

ARTICLE III.

Germany engages to restore to China within twelve calendar months, from the date of the ratification of the present Treaty, all the astronomical instruments which her troops removed in 1900-1901 from China without the latter's consent; and to defray all expenses which may be incurred in effecting such restoration, including the expenses for dismounting, packing, transporting, insurance and installation in Peking.

ARTICLE IV.

Germany agrees to the abrogation of the leases from the Chinese Government under which the German residential Concessions at Hankow and Tientsin are now held.

China, restored to the full exercise of her sovereign rights in the above areas, declares her intention to open them to international residence and trade. She further declares that the abrogation of the leases under which the concessions are now held shall not affect the property rights of citizens of allied and associated countries who are individual holders of lots in the concessions.

ARTICLE V.

Germany waives all claims against the Chinese Government or against any allied or associated Government arising out of the internment of German citizens in China and their repatriation. She equally renounces all claims arising out of the liquidation, sequestration or control of German properties, rights and interests in that country, since the 14th August, 1917. This provision, however, shall not affect the rights of the parties interested in the proceeds of any such liquidation, which shall be governed by the other provisions of this treaty.

ARTICLE VI.

Germany renounces in favour of the Government of His Britannic Majesty German state property in the British Concession at Shamun. She renounces in favour of the French and Chinese Governments conjointly the property of the German school situated in the French Concession at Shanghai.

T MS (SDR, RG 256, 180.03401/130, DNA); Mantoux, I, 422-23, 425.

Hankey's Notes of a Meeting of the Council of Four[1]

President Wilson's House,
I.C.-177F. (*Revise.*) Paris, April 30, 1919, 12:30 p.m.

1. In reply to questions by President Wilson, the Japanese Delegates declared that:

"The policy of Japan is to hand back the Shantung Peninsula in full sovereignty to China retaining only the economic privileges granted to Germany and the right to establish a settlement under the usual conditions at Tsingtao.

The owners of the Railway will use special Police only to ensure security for traffic. They will be used for no other purpose.

The Police Force will be composed of Chinese, and such Japanese instructors as the Directors of the Railway may select will be appointed by the Chinese Government."

(At this point there was a more or less prolonged conversation between President Wilson and the Japanese Delegates which at a certain point developed into a general discussion. It is only possible to record the salient features of the general discussion.)

VISCOUNT CHINDA made it clear that in the last resort, if China failed to carry out the agreements—if for example, she would not assist in the formation of the Police Force or the employment of Japanese Instructors, the Japanese Government reserved the right to fall back on the Agreements of 1918.

PRESIDENT WILSON pointed out that by that time Japan and China would be operating under the system of the League of Nations and Japan would be represented on the Council of the League. In such an event, he asked why should not the Japanese voluntarily apply for the mediation of the Council of the League of Nations.

VISCOUNT CHINDA said that even if the case was sent to the League of Nations, nevertheless Japan must reserve her right in the last analysis to base her rights on her special Agreements with China. If the Chinese Government acted loyally, such case would not arise, but if the Chinese Government refused to do so, the only course left to Japan would be to invoke the agreement.

PRESIDENT WILSON said that what he wanted to urge was this: he did not want a situation to arise which would prove embarrassing.

[1] The complete text of these minutes is printed in *PPC*, V, 363-67.

As the Japanese representatives knew, the United States Government had been much distressed by the twenty-one demands. These negotiations were based on the Notes of May 1915, and this exchange of Notes had its root in the negotiations connected with the twenty-one demands. In the view of his Government, the less the present transactions were related to this incident, the better. He would like, as a friend of Japan, to see no reference to the Notes of the last few years. If an occasion such as Viscount Chinda had postulated should arise, he hoped that the Japanese Government would not bring it before the Council of the League of Nations with a threat of war, but merely for friendly counsel, so that the Council of the League might make the necessary representations to China.

BARON MAKINO said that this was a possible eventuality but that so far as Japan was concerned, if the Chinese people co-operated with goodwill, he thought no such eventuality would arise. So far as Japan was concerned, she looked to the engagement with China, but hoped that no difficulty would arise.

VISCOUNT CHINDA said that the difficulty was that President Wilson on his side did not admit the validity of these Agreements but Japan did. He only mentioned the fact so as not to be morally bound not to invoke these Agreements. In the meanwhile he hoped that there would be no occasion for the refusal of the Chinese to carry out the Agreements.

PRESIDENT WILSON said that frankly he must insist that nothing he said should be construed as any admission of the recognition of the Notes exchanged between Japan and China.

VISCOUNT CHINDA said he had mentioned the point in order to remove any moral engagement on behalf of Japan not to invoke the Agreements in question.

PRESIDENT WILSON said that the Japanese representatives proposed to make public the policy declared at the outset of this discussion by means of an interview. He supposed he was at liberty to use the part of the declaration that most concerned him as he understood it.

BARON MAKINO said that the Japanese representatives attached the greatest importance to no impression being given that this decision was forced. They wished it to be clear that this was a voluntary expression of the Japanese Delegates' interpretation of the policy of their Government in regard to the restitution of the Province of Shantung. He hoped that this would be made quite clear.

PRESIDENT WILSON said that the following point had occurred to him. He had not appreciated from the map which had been shown him whether the Forts which Germany had built were taken over in the area of the settlement.

VISCOUNT CHINDA drew a sketch to illustrate the exact position and showed that the settlement would be part of the Town of Tsingtao and would not include the fortifications.

In reply to President Wilson, Baron Makino and Viscount Chinda gave an assurance that the Japanese troops would be withdrawn as soon as practicable.

SIR MAURICE HANKEY asked what he was to send to the Drafting Committee.

VISCOUNT CHINDA produced a revised draft of the clause to be inserted in the Treaty of Peace which included the alterations agreed to on the previous day. (Appendix I.) He gave the following explanation as to the reasons for the various alterations that had been made:

"The instructions of the Japanese Government state expressly that the surrender of the German public property should be unconditional and without compensation. Compliance with the above instruction makes it absolutely necessary to modify the Articles I and II of our claims by adding at their ends the phrase: 'free of all charges and encumbrances,' in order to exempt them from the general application of Article IX Financial Clauses.

As regards our claim upon the Tsingtao-Tsinan Railway, the Japanese Government regard the railway as German public property, but contention may possibly be advanced claiming it to be private property. In case the contention should be well established, the Japanese Government would be willing to pay for the same. In the meantime, the question is left open. This explains why the addition of the same phrase as above is not proposed in respect to the second paragraph, Article I of our claim."

(The Articles in the Appendix relative to Shantung Province were approved. Sir Maurice Hankey was directed to forward them to the Secretary-General for the information of the Drafting Committee.)

2. MR. LLOYD GEORGE handed to the Japanese representatives the following proposal which had been made by an Expert Committee, to which the question had been referred:

"Belgium shall sit, as originally proposed, as one of the five members of the Commission for all general discussions and for all other questions except those relating to damage by sea, for which Japan shall take her place, and those relating to Austria-Hungary, for which Serbia shall take Belgium's place. This Commission will thus always be limited in number to five, and the Japanese and Serbian representatives, on the occasions on which they are entitled to sit, will have the same power of voting as the delegates of the other four Powers."

M. MAKINO said that the arrangement should be altered to provide that the Japanese should be represented on the Commission (wherever their interests were concerned). There were a certain number of Japanese interned in Germany.

MR. LLOYD GEORGE said that this was not a matter for the Reparation Commission.

VISCOUNT CHINDA pointed out that the necessity for such provision arose in connection with Article 13 in the Financial Clauses.

(After some discussion, it was agreed that Japan should be represented on the Permanent Reparation Commission whenever questions relating to damage by sea were under consideration (as already provided) and in addition whenever Japanese interests under Article 13 of the Financial Clauses were under consideration.)

3. VISCOUNT CHINDA drew attention to Article 16 of the Financial Clauses which is as follows:

"The High Contracting Parties waive reciprocally all claims on account of the expenses of all kinds incurred by them in connection with enemy prisoners of war."

He pointed out that there were between 4,000 and 5,000 German prisoners in Japan. These have not been used for any sort of work as had been possible in European countries, but had been maintained at the expense of Japan under the provisions of the Hague Convention. It had been entirely a one-sided expense. In view of the fact that in the case of most other countries, the numbers of prisoners had been fairly well balanced, Japan stood in an unique position and was therefore entitled to an exceptional treatment in this respect.

MR. LLOYD GEORGE said that this was not the case in regard to civilian persons interned. The British had had four or five Germans to maintain for one British maintained in Germany.

VISCOUNT CHINDA said that German prisoners in Japan had been military. They had constituted the garrison of Kiaochow and had been in Japanese hands ever since the early stage of the war.

MR. LLOYD GEORGE pointed out that Japan had inherited the German rights in Kiaochow which might be set off against the cost of maintaining these Germans.

M. MAKINO said that that had not been taken into the calculation.

MR. LLOYD GEORGE pointed out that every time one country or another brought up some new point difficulties arose. The sums mounted up and up and Germany would not be able to pay for reparation. Hence it had been decided hitherto to stick rigidly to the principles. Japan would, of course, receive a share of reparation for pensions.

M. MAKINO said that Japan had lost less than 2,000 lives and would not receive much on this account.

MR. LLOYD GEORGE said it was very awkward to put in a special claim for one country as then all other countries would wish to put in their claims.

M. MAKINO said that if great difficulties would be created, Japan would not press her demand.

MR. LLOYD GEORGE, PRESIDENT WILSON and M. CLEMENCEAU thanked M. Makino for this declaration.

APPENDIX I TO I.C.177.F.

Corrected for Drafting Committee.

Special Conditions
relative to Shantung Province.

Article 1.

Germany renounces, in favour of Japan, all her rights, titles, or privileges—particularly those concerning the territory of Kiaochow, railways, mines and sub-marine cables—which she acquired, in virtue of the treaties concluded by her with China on the 6th March, 1898, and of all other arrangements relative to Shantung Province.

All German rights in the Tsingtao-Tsinan Railway, including its branch lines, together with its accessories of all kinds, stations, shops, fixed materials and rolling stocks, mines, establishments and materials for exploitation of the mines, are, and shall remain, acquired by Japan, together with the rights and privileges appertaining thereto.

The sub-marine cables of the State of Germany, from Tsingtao to Shanghai and from Tsingtao to Chefoo, with all the rights, privileges and properties appertaining thereto, shall equally remain acquired by Japan, free of all charges and encumbrances.

Article 2.

The rights of movable and immovable properties possessed by the State of Germany in the territory of Kiaochow, as well as all the rights which she is entitled to claim in consequence of the works or equipments set up, or of the expenses disbursed by her, either directly or indirectly, and concerning the territory, are, and shall remain, acquired by Japan, free of all charges and encumbrances.

T MS (SDR, RG 256, 180.03401/131, DNA).

From the Diary of Vance Criswell McCormick

April 30 (Wednesday) [1919]

Minister Cartier[1] of Belgium called to try to have me arrange an appointment with the President for the Belgium delegation tomorrow. Hymans, Foreign Minister, telephoned he had heard from Brussels and the Belgium government could not accept British and French proposal and two members of the cabinet were leaving for Paris tonight. I talked to President over telephone about appointment. He feels he should not meet them alone as it might make matters worse for them as Lloyd George and Clemenceau are quite excited over situation and very firm in their position. I am not sure the President has sized the situation up. I think it most important to give the fullest opportunity for Belgium to present its case.

Some of the advisers went to the President's house with Dulles to discuss joint and several liability of enemy states. I stayed behind to talk to Baruch.

[1] That is, Émile Ernest, Baron de Cartier de Marchienne, the Belgian Minister to the United States.

From Tasker Howard Bliss

[Paris, April 30, 1919]

Memorandum for the President from General Bliss.

An intelligent consideration of the question would require us to have the exact terms of the treaty, in order that we may see ourselves whether there is anything inconsistent between the terms of the armistice and the terms of the treaty.

Unless there is something in the terms of the treaty which specifically and by terms lifts the blockade at a fixed date, there will be nothing inconsistent between the treaty and the armistice term which provides for maintaining the blockade, and that armistice term being made a part of the treaty, the Allies can hold that the blockade can be kept up just as long as they please and to any extent that they please.

Unless the terms of the treaty prescribe that at a fixed date the Allied troops shall withdraw from the bridgeheads on the Rhine or from any other part of Germany now occupied by them, there will be nothing inconsistent between the treaty and that provision of the armistice which puts the Allies not only on the Rhine but across the Rhine, and that term being now embodied in the treaty by the inclusion of all armistice terms which are not inconsistent with the treaty, the Allies could remain forever in occupation of those bridgeheads.

We do not know how many more things would be discovered perfectly consistent between the armistice terms and the treaty terms, and in the absence of that knowledge we do not know what terms of the armistice would be perpetuated in the treaty very much against the wish of the United States.

There is the general objection to this proposed insertion in the treaty, continuing in force the armistice of November 11th, in that the armistice terms are terms relating to a status of war and have no place in a treaty of peace, except where a particular clause of the armistice happens to be consistent with a state of peace, and therefore the wise thing to do is to request those who proposed the insertion of this clause 48 to state what particular clauses of the armistice they desire to have retained in the Peace Treaty and then let the council decide whether they should or should not go in the treaty. Any other course is fraught with the greatest danger by reason of the vagueness and uncertainty involved.

T MS (WP, DLC).

Hankey's and Mantoux's Notes of a Meeting of the Council of Four[1]

President Wilson's House,
I.C.-178A. Paris, April 30, 1919, 4 p.m.

§ Mantoux's notes:

Mr. Lloyd George reads aloud a memorandum from Mr. Lamont: M. Hymans received a telegram from his government, which states that it cannot accept our proposals without reimbursement for the marks within a period of two years. Two Belgian ministers are leaving for Paris. Mr. Lamont told M. Hymans that it would be impossible to grant Belgium compensation for the mark at 1.25 francs. Moreover, M. Hymans understands this.

Clemenceau. We have news from Italy. It seems that there is some prospect of working out something. M. Crespi and Count Bonin Longare[2] are in contact with M. Tardieu. I believe that their present idea would be to accept Fiume as a free city while asking that Zara and Sebenico be placed under an Italian mandate.

Wilson. Such a mandate would only be a camouflage for sovereignty. What they want above all is to save face. §

(1) MR. LLOYD GEORGE said that he had learnt that at the Meeting of Foreign Ministers, Mr. Lansing had made a very powerful state-

[1] The complete text of Hankey's minutes is printed in *PPC*, V, 368-72.
[2] Count Lelio Bonin Longare, the Italian Ambassador to France.

ment, in which he had said that the German Constitution provided that the Central Government had full powers to make peace and war.[3]

M. CLEMENCEAU said that had not been the case in 1871.

PRESIDENT WILSON said it was a long time since he had studied Constitutional history, but he felt fairly sure that the Constitution of the German Empire had been drawn up since 1871, and that in it had been included the powers of making peace and war.

M. CLEMENCEAU said that great care ought to be exercised lest we should make a peace, and find a few minutes after that the German States had not accepted it.

(2) MR. LLOYD GEORGE proposed that during the following week, while the German Delegates were studying the peace treaty, the Supreme Council should study the question and get a general idea of the line they were going to take in regard to the re-arrangement of the old Austrian-Hungarian Empire. He proposed that in the following week the Delegates of Austria and Hungary should be invited to Paris.

PRESIDENT WILSON agreed.

M. CLEMENCEAU agreed.

SIR MAURICE HANKEY asked who would be responsible for sending the invitation.

MR. LLOYD GEORGE said that in case of the Germans, Marshal Foch had sent the invitation. Consequently, if the Italians had still been in the Conference, it would have been General Diaz's duty.

SIR MAURICE HANKEY said, as he was the only official present, he thought he ought to put the point of view of the officials. The Drafting Committee was so overworked in bringing out the German Treaty that he felt confident they could not possibly prepare the Austrian Treaty in so short a time.

PRESIDENT WILSON said that it was only proposed to discuss the lines of the Treaty with the Austrians. It would not be necessary to present them with a complete Treaty. He pointed out that the Hungarian de facto Government was hardly more than a local Government. By inviting them we should run the risk of our publics regarding them as a people in close intercourse with the Russian Soviets.

MR. LLOYD GEORGE said they had committed no atrocities. He was reminded, however, by Sir Maurice Hankey of a recent telegram to the effect that 200 Bourgeois had been killed in Buda Pest, though he could not vouch for its truth.

[3] The Editors have been unable to find any such statement by Lansing in the records of the Council of Foreign Ministers. Indeed, the printed minutes of the meetings do not indicate that the subject of the powers of the German central government to make peace and war ever came up. See *PPC*, IV, 515-658.

PRESIDENT WILSON said that many people had been rather alarmed at General Smuts' visit. He thought that the boundaries could be determined without consulting the Hungarians. They would not be on quite the same footing as the Austrians.

M. CLEMENCEAU asked what was to be done with the Austrians and Hungarians after their views had been heard? Were they to be let free to move about in Paris? Meanwhile, the Germans might give a good deal of work.

PRESIDENT WILSON suggested that the Austrians and Hungarians should be sent somewhere outside Paris. For example, Fontainebleau.

M. CLEMENCEAU said Chantilly would be the best place.

PRESIDENT WILSON agreed that this would be more prudent than Paris. He said that the immediate object of this proposal was the moral effect that would be produced on the Austrian people by inviting their representatives for consultation. He read a letter from his four colleagues on the American Delegation urging this course.[4]

MR. LLOYD GEORGE urged that there should be no differentiation between Austrians and Hungarians. He did not see why because the Hungarians were called the Soviet they should not be met. A workmen's Government had just as much right to be dealt with as any other.

M. CLEMENCEAU suggested that as the Hungarians and Austrians were somewhat hostile to one another, it would be necessary to house them separately.

(It was agreed that M. Clemenceau, as President of the Preliminary Peace Conference, should invite the representatives of the Austrian and Hungarian Governments to come to Chantilly on May 12th.)

(3) There was a short discussion in regard to the position in North Russia, in the course of which Mr. Lloyd George suggested that he and his colleagues should see Mr. Tchaikowski,[5] the head of the Archangel Government, who was very hopeful that the Russians at Archangel might, by their own efforts, establish contact with General Kolchak. His information in regard to the Bolsheviks did not correspond with that in the possession of the French Government. He undertook to distribute a memorandum prepared by the British Intelligence Department in regard to the situation in Russia. He suggested that a similar document should be prepared by the French and the United States Military Departments.

PRESIDENT WILSON said he thought little good would be served by

[4] See the American Commissioners to WW, April 28, 1919.
[5] That is, Nikolai Vasil'evich Chaikovskii.

seeing Mr. Tchaikowski. His views had been received by telegram. The United States only had one regiment at Archangel, and United States public opinion would not tolerate sending any more troops.

MR. LLOYD GEORGE said that the British Government had called for volunteers, and had received more offers than they could accept. The lists had had to be closed because they were full.

PRESIDENT WILSON thought perhaps experts might hear Mr. Tchaikowski's views.

(It was agreed that as the basis for discussion, the United States, British and French Military Departments should prepare memoranda for circulation.)

(4) SIR MAURICE HANKEY said that in consultation with Mr. Dutasta, he had prepared a scheme for dealing with questions raised by the Germans in connection with the Treaty of Peace. (Appendix [blank])

(The scheme was approved.)

(5) SIR MAURICE HANKEY recalled the decision that had been taken in the morning that the proportions in which the successive instalments paid over by Germany in satisfaction of claims against her should be divided by the Allied and Associated Powers should be determined by the Reparation Commission set up in the Reparation Articles, in proportion to the claims allowed by the Commission. He asked for instructions as to what action should be taken to give effect to this decision. It was not a matter which would affect any clause in the Treaty of Peace, and as these Minutes were not circulated, he felt some doubt as to the best method of placing it on record so that it should not be overlooked. He had contemplated writing a letter to M. Loucheur, Mr. Norman Davis and Mr. Keynes, so that the experts of France, the United States of America, and Great Britain, might be apprised of the decision.

MR. LLOYD GEORGE said that the matter was one of so great importance that he thought it should take the form of a letter or a formal minute signed by M. Clemenceau, President Wilson and himself.

(This was agreed to and Sir Maurice Hankey was instructed to draft the letter.)

(6) (It was decided provisionally and subject to possible revision in the event of good reason being shown to the contrary that Article 46 of the Military terms of Peace should be suppressed.)

NOTE: Article 46 is as follows:

"The Armistice of November 11th 1918 and the Convention subsequent thereto, remain in force so far as they are not inconsistent with the above stipulations."

Sir Maurice Hankey was instructed to communicate this decision to the Secretary General for the information of the Drafting Committee.

§ Mantoux's notes:

Wilson. You remember that General Bliss had to study the article of the peace treaty providing for the prolongation of certain stipulations of the Armistice. He judges that article dangerous, especially given the very general terms of the draft.

Clemenceau. I am rather of that opinion.

Wilson. So the article disappears, unless its drafters give us new reasons to keep it. §

(7) SIR MAURICE HANKEY pointed out that Article 45 was reserved.

PRESIDENT WILSON asked how the Allied and Associated Powers could change the German Laws.

MR. LLOYD GEORGE pointed out that if the German Military Service Law was not abolished, military recruits would automatically be called up for service.

(It was agreed that the form of the Article should be altered so as to provide that the German Government should undertake within a period not exceeding three months from the ratification of the Treaty to modify their law.)

(8) MR. LLOYD GEORGE read a telegram from the British Admiralty urging that an alteration should be made in Article 32 of the Naval Clauses, specially providing for the surrender of Floating Docks, and calling attention to the sale of a large Floating Dock now at Hamburg to an Engineering and Slipway Company at Rotterdam which was not prevented by the Armistice terms.

(It was agreed that no alteration should be made in the Treaty in this respect.)

T MS (SDR, RG 256, 180.03401/132, DNA); Mantoux, I, 428, 430.

From Robert Lansing

My dear Mr. President: Paris, April 30, 1919.

With reference to your letter of April 26th,[1] enclosing a number of communications regarding Montenegro, you may be interested to know that the Commission has been deluged with communications from the so-called Minister of Foreign Affairs and representative of King Nicholas.[2]

While I feel that with such a disturbed situation as at present prevails in Montenegro it is wise to reserve our judgment as to a final settlement, from the reports which have reached me I am inclined to believe that King Nicholas and his protests, such as you forwarded to me, do not represent the sentiment of the bulk of the Montenegrin people. The Montenegrins appear to be divided chiefly on the question of the manner in which they shall join the new Yugo-Slav Kingdom, some desiring wide local autonomy and others close political union with Yugo-Slavia. Those who desire complete independence or a return of King Nicholas would probably not represent more than a relatively small minority.

At the suggestion of Mr. Balfour an Anglo-American Commission of investigation is on its way to Montenegro, on which, by your appointment, the United States is to be represented by Lieutenant-Colonel Sherman Miles. I shall not fail to bring to your attention the substance of any report bearing on the desires of the people of Montenegro which this Commission may submit.

I am, my dear Mr. President,

Faithfully yours, Robert Lansing

TLS (WP, DLC).

[1] WW to RL, April 26, 1919, CCL (WP, DLC).

[2] That is, Jovan S. Plamenatz (Plamenac).

From Charles Prestwich Scott

Dear Mr. Wilson, [Manchester] April 30/19.

Will you allow me to express the admiration & the gratitude with which I, in common I am certain with all that is Liberal (not confined to the Liberal party) in England have watched your course in Paris—desperately difficult I am certain & demanding every kind of fortitude & tolerance. If good comes out of the whole business in the end, as it will, it will be due first & last to you. I am happy to think that you have had good support on the whole from our own Prime Minister, who lacks neither heart nor courage, but uncommonly little I fear elsewhere. Those whom your restraint embitters & enrages today will have reason to thank you hereafter when the moral safeguards you are building up have had time to prove their power.

It is one of the turning points of history & it will stand to the eternal credit of America that she, with you to guide and interpret her, has intervened decisively to keep us in the right course. I only wanted just to say this, remembering the great pleasure I had in meeting you in Manchester & counting on your not being at the trouble in any way to acknowledge it.

Yours sincerely C. P. Scott.

ALS (WP, DLC).

From Henry Mauris Robinson

Dear Mr. President: [Paris] 30 April 1919

Mr. Hoover had told me something of the contents of his letter to you setting forth the discrepancy between the Food Administration's tonnage needs and the amount loaded and dispatched by the United States Shipping Board during the months of March and April,[1] and I had cabled several days since asking for an explanation.

Our information is that Mr. Hurley, acting under his doctor's instructions, because of the condition of his health was compelled to go to Florida about April 1st and, we understand, has not yet returned to Washington.

From the cables received I am satisfied that no arrangements have been made for shipping coal to Italy, a course I have repeatedly advised against. However, I have cabled to Messrs. Hurley, Stevens and Rosseter[2] today, explaining in unmistakable terms your interest in and your views in respect to the furnishing of ships for Food Relief.

I feel that I should add that the Franklin Committee[3] was dissolved as of January 1st, and that since that time the allocation of the Government ships is directly under the Department of Operations of the Shipping Board.

As you know, the pressure by the producers and by the miners for the shipment of coal to Italy has been great. To this has been added Italy's insistent demands. And to this I think has been added the impression that there was not alone lack of English ships but lack of English coal, which is not the fact. All of this resulted in a meeting in Washington at which various Departments were represented, such as the Fuel Administration, Department of Commerce, and Shipping Board, at which meeting Mr. Hurley was not present.

As a result of the meeting, a cable was sent to Mr. McCormick asking the Supreme Economic Council to decide whether Italy should be furnished with coal from the United States. At the Economic Group meeting on Saturday this proposal was decided upon adversely.

This probably is the basis of Mr. Hoover's apprehensions and of his letter to you.

I have gone into this detail in order that you may have the available information.

The cable sent today will, I trust, bring a prompt reply which I will transmit to you immediately.

Very respectfully yours, Henry M. Robinson

TLS (WP, DLC).

[1] See H. C. Hoover to WW, April 25, 1919, printed as an Enclosure with WW to H. M. Robinson, April 28, 1919.
[2] That is, Raymond Bartlett Stevens and John Henry Rosseter.
[3] About this committee, see n. 1 to WW to H. M. Robinson, April 28, 1919.

From the Diary of Ray Stannard Baker

Wednesday the 30th [April 1919]

Another whirling day! At noon I was able to announce that the Shantung question had been settled by the Big Three, though Colonel House told the correspondents at 6 o'clock that it had not been!

I saw the President at 6:30 as usual & he went over the whole ground with me at length. Said he had been unable to sleep the night before for considering the question. Anything he might do was wrong! He gave me a copy of a cablegram he had just sent to Tumulty giving the gist of the decision. He said it was "the best that could be gotten out of a dirty past." He had considered every possible contingency. His sympathies were all with the Chinese. (And I found afterwards that he had been fairly bombarded by pro-Chinese arguments by our own people, including a powerful letter by General Bliss) But if he made such a decision that the Japanese went home, he felt that the whole Peace Conference would break up. With Italy & Japan out, and Belgium threatening, would Germany sign the treaty? It might mean that everyone would return home & begin to arm—wars everywhere. And this would not force Japan out of Shantung: it would only encourage deeper penetration. The only hope was, somehow, to keep the world together, get the League of Nations with Japan in it & then try to secure justice for the Chinese not only as regards Japan but as regarding England, Russia, France & America, all of whom had concessions in China. If Japan went home there was a danger of a Japanese-Russian-German alliance—and a return to the old "balance of power" system in the world—on a greater scale than ever. He knew that his decision would be unpopular in America, that the Chinese would be bitterly disappointed, that the avaricious Japanese would feel triumphant, that he would be accused of violating his own principles—but never-the-less he *must* work for world order & organization against anarchy & a return to the old unilitarism [unilateralism] (The League of Nations is a matter of *faith*: and the President is first of all a *man of faith*. He believes in the L. of N. as an organization that will save the world. All the others believe only in the old sanctions of force. On the Commission House is the only one who supports this view & House only *feels* it, where the President *sees it*, *grasps* it, *feels* it, with the mighty tenacity of a great faith. He is willing even to compromise desperately for it, suffer the charge of inconsistency for it—He is the only Man here.)

In all these dealings Lloyd-George has been as slippery as an eel: standing by the Japanese: giving promises of support inside but outside blowing cold on all the President's plans.

I urged strongly that I be allowed to announce the main lines of the settlement to-night, lest it come out garbled through Japanese sources. To this the President finally consented and I went back to No. 4 to the 40 or 50 correspondents who were awaiting me with about the biggest "story" of the conference. I had to choose my words carefully in reporting it![1] What a clacking of typewriters followed!

[1] R. S. Baker, "STATEMENT AS TO THE FACTS AS TO KIAO-CHOW AND SHANTUNG," April 30, 1919, T MS (WP, DLC). The statement reads as follows: "All rights in Kiao-Chow and Shantung province formerly belonging to Germany are to be transferred without reservation to Japan. Japan voluntarily engages to hand back the Shantung peninsula in full sovereignty to China, retaining only the economic privileges granted to Germany and the right to establish a settlement at Tsing-Tao. Owners of railroads will use special police only to insure security for traffic, the police force will be composed of Chinese, and such Japanese instructors as the Directors of the Railways may select, will be appointed by the Chinese Government. The Japanese military forces are to be withdrawn at the earliest possible moment.

"Japan thus gets only such rights as an economic concessionaire as are possessed by one or two other Great Powers and the whole future relationship between the two countries fall[s] at once under the guarantee of the League of Nations of territorial integrity and political independence."

Thomas Nelson Page to Baron Sidney Sonnino

My dear Baron Sonnino: Rome, April 30, 1919.

I have telephoned hoping to be able to see you personally to talk over informally a matter which has caused me some anxiety by reason of certain possible unhappy consequences which may result from what I wished to speak of. Inasmuch as, owing to the great pressure of the work on you, you have not been able to see me, and as the matter seems to me somewhat immediate, I am writing this personal note.

As one who has labored most ardently to cement and render deeper the friendship which has ever existed between the United States and Italy, I feel that I should request that the attention of the proper authorities be drawn to the persistent violence of the attacks made on the President of the United States by some elements of the Italian press, and to the unhappy consequences which have at times followed similar attacks in periods of great danger and excitement.

The close of a great war is always a time of deep feeling, and passions, at least of those individuals susceptible of being excited beyond control, are sometimes stirred beyond all bounds.

I have only kindness to remember personally from the Italians, and I have profound friendship for them. I know that President Wilson and the whole American people also bear a deep friendship for Italy, even though his sense of obligation to the principles enunciated by him may have placed him in opposition to the stand taken by Italy on things which have become very dear to her heart, and which are affected by the application of those principles.

Whatever may be felt here at this moment in regard to Mr. Wilson, I can not but believe that any man of temperate mind must recognize his sincerity and share, at least in part, my profound regret to see the inflammatory campaign against the Chief of a nation not second to any in the world in friendship towards Italy, continued under conditions so unhappy and which might, under such attacks, possibly become, through some untoward act, even more unhappy.

It is with a sense of the possibilities which may result from what tends to increase passions already deeply stirred that I declare this protest thus addressed to you inspired, not only by my sense of duty towards my country, but by my unalterable friendship for this great people, whom I have come to hold in real affection.

Believe me, always with great respect,

Yours very sincerely, Thos. Nelson Page.

CCL (WP, DLC).

To Joseph Patrick Tumulty

Paris, 30 April, 1919.

The Japanese-Chinese matter has been settled in a way which seems to me as sastifactory as could be got out of the tangle of treaties in which China herself was involved, and it is important that the exact facts should be known. I therefore send you the following for public use at such time as the matter may come under public discussion. In the treaty all the rights at Kiao-Chau and in Shantung Province belonging to Germany are to be transferred without reservation to Japan, but Japan voluntarily engages, in answer to questions put in conference, that it will be her immediate policy "to hand back the Shantung Peninsula in full sovereignty to China, retaining only the economic privileges granted to Germany and the right to establish a settlement under the usual conditions at Tsingtao. Owners of the railway will use special police only to insure security for traffic. They will be used for no other purpose. The police force will be composed of Chinese, and such Japanese instructors as the directors of the railway may select will be appointed by the Chinese Government." It was understood in addition that inasmuch as the sovereign rights receded to China were to be unqualified, all Japanese troops remaining on the peninsula should be withdrawn at the earliest possible time. Japan thus gets only such rights as an economic concessionaire as are possessed by one or two other great powers and are only too common in China, and the whole future relationship between the two countries falls at once under the guarantee of the League of Nations of territorial integrity and political independence. I find a general disposition to look with favor upon the proposal that at an early date through the mediation of the League of Nations all extraordinary foreign rights in China and all spheres of influence should be abrogated by the common consent of all the nations concerned. I regard the assurances given by Japan as very satisfactory in view of the complicated circumstances. Please do not give out any of the above as a quotation from me, but use it in some other form for public information at the right time. Woodrow Wilson

T telegram (WP, DLC).

Joseph Patrick Tumulty to Cary Travers Grayson

The White House, April 30, 1919.

Am sorry about the Japanese settlement. Am afraid of the impression it will make. Everybody all right. Tumulty

T telegram (WP, DLC).

Two Telegrams from Joseph Patrick Tumulty

[The White House, April 30, 1919]

No. 84 Woman suffrage organizations publicly declare suffrage amendment still lacks one vote. Urgently suggest that you send for Senator Harris of Georgia,[1] now in Paris, and ask him, upon leaving you, to announce to American newspaper correspondents substantially as follows:

"I learned recently that the suffrage amendment, in spite of Republican claims to the contrary made following the election last November, still lacks one vote. It has just been my pleasure to assure President Wilson that I am glad of the opportunity to deliver that necessary vote, in addition to my support and vote for the League of Nations, and thereby assure the success of the measure which all true workers for the suffrage cause, especially those who enjoy his confidence, know has long been so near to his heart."

Extremely important to Democratic party that Harris make such announcement in next forty-eight hours, as Republicans are desperate over failure of Keyes[2] of New Hampshire, on whom they were relying to advocate the amendment, and are working hard to recoup. Walsh, Montana, Woolley and Hale join in suggestion.[3]

Tumulty.

[1] That is, William Julius Harris.

[2] Henry Wilder Keyes, Republican senator from New Hampshire.

[3] That is, Thomas James Walsh, Democratic senator from Montana; Robert Wickliffe Woolley, member of the Interstate Commerce Commission; and Matthew Hale, formerly a lawyer of Boston and a leader of the Progressive party.

[The White House, April 30, 1919]

No. 85. Beg to call your attention to following editorial from Springfield Republican:

"The critical period in the peace making has been reached when progress can win over reaction the very least of victories only by a resolute stand of the most commanding figure in Paris. France and England cannot desert the President without branding themselves as hypocrites and ingrates. Worse things could happen than for the President to come home without a peace treaty, leaving Europe to wallow in the mire of national rivalries and hates, to which reaction would sentence it for all time. There is no compelling reason why America should sign a treaty that would merely perpetuate ancient feuds and make new wars a certainty. Our chief interest in the conference at Paris, as the President declared at Manchester, is the peace of the world. Unless this is made reasonably sure, with Europe's sincere cooperation, the time is near when 'pack up and come home' will be America's only policy." Tumulty.

T telegrams (WP, DLC).

From the Diary of Dr. Grayson

Thursday, May 1, 1919.

This was a typical French May Day—every avenue of commerce being completely closed, and the city presenting a deserted appearance in the early hours. The President had breakfast at 8:30. By his orders no effort was made to operate the automobiles assigned directly to him. It was pouring rain outside, and this had the effect of keeping the workers, and especially the Socialists, indoors up until noon. The French Government, following its policy of caring nothing for the rights of the people, had concentrated thousands of soldiers in the city, and, in addition, had drawn in gendarmes. All of the main thoroughfares were lined with troops, cavalry being used in great profusion. In the vicinity of the Crillon Hotel, where the American Peace Commission was quartered, the Republic guard and picked cavalry from the south of France were concentrated, while along the grand boulevard and through the Place de l'Opéra mounted Colonials were gathered. Despite the rain the workers began to put in an appearance shortly before noon, and by two o'clock the streets were filled. The union leaders had planned to hold a meeting outside of the Crillon Hotel in the Place de la Concorde at three o'clock in the afternoon, and their processions began to head that way shortly before that hour. The crowd was an extremely good tempered one in the early stages, although the leaders chanted "A-bas Clemenceau, A-bas Clemenceau," and when they tired of this would stop and cheer loudly, shouting "Vive Wilson." This manner of the crowd was very displeasing to the military and the police authorities, who did not like the cry of "Down Clemenceau" and the cheering for the President. The result was that the cavalry charged the crowd as it tried to pass through the Rue Royale to the Place de la Concorde, and from this time, three o'clock, on until dark serious clashes took place all over the city. Newspapermen who have had much experience with crowds and mobs were severe in their criticism of the action of the authorities, saying that if the people had been allowed to carry on their demonstration it would have simply been one of rejoicing and instead as it turned out to be one of bloodshed, in which one man was killed outright and more than 2,000 taken to the hospitals.

One soldier appeared at the window of our press representative and said: "I have been at the front for four years fighting in the trenches, and this is the thanks that my government gives me for it. This is a holiday and we are not permitted to enjoy ourselves. I am against the French government and Clemenceau."

During the evening in discussing this subject the President was very much pained to hear that the men had been treated so harshly at the hands of the government. He said: "At the meeting at the Quai d'Orsay this afternoon a note was handed Mr. Clemenceau saying that about 200 soldiers had been injured in the fighting this afternoon. I asked Mr. Clemenceau how many civilians had been injured. Clemenceau shrugged his shoulders and said: 'We do not know anything about them. They go home and we have no record of them.' Clemenceau treated the whole question as if it were only a mere matter of routine business. He showed no concern or sympathy whatever."

The President, Mrs. Wilson and I had lunch, and immediately after lunch the President and I went into the big parlor adjoining the dining-room. The President remarked: "I don't like the way the colors of this furniture fight each other. The greens and the reds are all mixed up here and there is no harmony. Here is a big purple, high-backed covered chair, which is like the Purple Cow, strayed off to itself, and it is placed where the light shines on it too brightly. If you will give me a lift, we will move this next to the wall where the light from the window will give it a subdued effect. And here are two chairs, one green and the other red. This will never do. Let's put the greens all together and the reds together." The President then pointed out and said: "Over in the right-hand corner at our meetings the British gather; in the left-hand corner the Americans; in the middle the French are seated. When we meet every day it would amuse you to see us walk to our respective corners just as if we were school children occupying our regular seats. Now, we will put all the reds over here in the American corner, next to to the red sofa; the greens we will put over here for the Britishers; the odds and ends we will put here in the center for the French, and we will harmonize them as much as possible. The other chairs that do not harmonize we will put out on the edge where the experts can occupy them when they are called in before the Big Three."[1]

The President had had a very busy morning with the Big Three discussing complicated questions, and after lunch he took a great deal of interest in arranging this furniture, seemingly to forget his exalted position. He was just like an ordinary human being. After we completed the job of re-arranging the furniture I could see such a marked improvement in the appearance of the room that I said to the President: "Mr. President, I think if you ever want a job after leaving the Presidency you would make a great success as an interior decorator." The President smilingly replied: "I don't mean to throw bouquets at myself but I do think that I have made a success of the arrangement of this furniture."

I then said: "How about going out for a ride?" The President said: "This is Labor Day here in France and every one is refraining from using their cars as much as possible. I want to fall in with the spirit of the day as much as possible and not use the cars except in case of absolute necessity. I have suggested to Mrs. Wilson that she do likewise." The President continued: "I asked Mr. Clemenceau this morning if he thought it was safe to go around the city today. I had heard so many rumors that there was going to be a great deal of disturbances among the French population. Whereupon Mr. Clemen-

[1] For one explanation of the significance of this strange episode, see Edwin A. Weinstein, M.D., *Woodrow Wilson: A Medical and Psychological Biography* (Princeton, N. J., 1981), p. 342. Wilson rearranged the furniture in the sitting room again on May 17. See the extract from the Baker Diary printed at May 17, 1919.

ceau shrugged his shoulders, threw out his hands, and said: 'It is perfectly safe for you to go because you are a great favorite among the working people of France.' He did not say this in a sarcastic way but he showed that he had a little feeling on the subject. It was plain that it did not please Clemenceau because the rank and file of the people did approve of me."

At four o'clock the President went to the Quai d'Orsay for a meeting of the Big Three. They discussed the German cable question. Japan and England were anxious to gobble them up themselves and eventually have a monopoly over them. No final decision was reached.

The President returned home after the meeting, and at seven o'clock had dinner with Mrs. Wilson, Miss Benham and myself. Just as we were finishing dinner Miss Margaret arrived from one of her singing tours. The President spent most of his time after dinner asking her what she had been doing and how she had been getting along. Miss Margaret did most of the talking.

During the day I sent the following cablegram to Secretary Tumulty: . . .[2]

[2] It is printed below.

Hankey's and Mantoux's Notes of a Meeting of the Council of Four[1]

President Wilson's House,
I.C.-178D. Paris, May 1, 1919, 11 a.m.

Kiaochau and Shantung.

1. It was agreed that:

Mr. Balfour should communicate the decision taken on this subject to the Chinese Delegation.

(An immediate message was sent to Mr. Balfour, communicating this decision.)

Responsibility of the Authors of the War & Enforcement of Penalties.

2. MR. LLOYD GEORGE brought to note certain criticisms that had been made by the British Solicitor-General and Attorney-General[2] against the articles on this subject, (Appx IV) drafted by the Drafting Committee on the basis of the instructions given to them. In re-

[1] The complete text of Hankey's minutes is printed in *PPC*, V, 389-402.

[2] Sir Ernest Murray Pollock and Sir Gordon Hewart. Actually, their criticisms were based upon a memorandum for Balfour by C. J. B. Hurst, dated April 14, 1919, TS MS (D. Lloyd George Papers, F/147/8/9, House of Lords Record Office).

gard to Article 1, attention had been drawn to the words in line: "not for an offence against criminal law but." It has been pointed out that the draft as it stands might possibly be construed as an admission on the part of the Allied and Associated Powers that the German Emperor had not committed any offences against criminal law. He proposed the omission of these words.

PRESIDENT WILSON agreed.[3]

(It was agreed that:

The first clause, Article 1, should read as follows:

"The Allied and Associated Powers publicly arraign William II of Hohenzollern, formerly German Emperor, for a supreme offence against international morality and the sanctity of treaties."

In regard to Article 2, Mr. Lloyd George said that criticisms had been made against this Article on the ground that it might be construed to enable the German Government to secure immunity to persons who are accused of having committed acts in violation of the laws and customs of war by trying them in a German Court and passing a nominal sentence.

(It was agreed that:

The Drafting Committee should be instructed to devise some means of avoiding this interpretation and the following draft of the first clause of Article 2 was suggested:

"The German Government engages that the persons accused of having committed acts in violation of the laws and customs of war shall be brought before military tribunals by the Allied and Associated Powers and if found guilty sentenced to the punishment laid down by military law.")

(Sir Maurice Hankey was instructed to communicate these alterations to the Secretary-General for the information of the Drafting Committee.)

Belgium and Reparation.

3. M. CLEMENCEAU asked if there was any news from the Belgians about Reparation.

PRESIDENT WILSON said he had received none.

MR. LLOYD GEORGE said that the Belgian financial experts had asked to see Mr. Keynes, but he did not know on what subject.

[3] It might be pointed out that Wilson here, by agreeing to this omission, which opened the possibility of the trial of William for criminal offenses, violated all the principles for which he had earlier fought so long and hard and that he gave away the victory that he had won in the protocol on responsibilities that the Council of Four had approved on April 9, 1919. See the minutes of the Council of Four printed at April 9, 1919, 11 a.m., Vol. 57. It is of course possible that Wilson was in a daze and did not know what was going on at this meeting. On the general subject, see James F. Willis, *Prologue to Nuremberg: The Politics and Diplomacy of Punishing War Criminals of the First World War* (Westport, Conn., 1982).

PRESIDENT WILSON said that Mr. McCormick had told him that the Belgian Delegation wished M. Cartier, who was the Belgian Minister at Washington, to see President Wilson, in order to place before him certain aspects of the question with which he was not familiar. He, himself, had refused to see them, as he did not think it was right to conduct, as it were, a separate negotiation. Mr. McCormick had also conveyed the impression that the Belgians were alleging that the French and British Governments had in some special way granted them the value of the German marks in Belgium. He emphasised that this was only a general impression and not an exact statement.

Credentials of the German Delegates.

4. M. CLEMENCEAU reported that the Credentials Committee would see the German Delegates at 3 p.m. The German Delegates had asked for the credentials of the Allied and Associated Powers. There had been some delay in regard to those of the Czecho-Slovaks and Poland.

Italian Credentials.

5. M. PICHON said that there would certainly be an incident when the Germans asked for the Italian Credentials and M. Jules Cambon was unable to produce them. It should be made clear, in his opinion, to the world and to the Italians that Italy was responsible for this state of affairs. Re-calling the Pact of London, to which Italy adhered, whereby France, Great Britain, Italy and Russia had agreed not to make a separate peace, M. Pichon said that we must show clearly that it was Italy who had separated. He proposed, therefore, that the incident should be notified by telegram to Italy through the President of the Conference and that Italy should be allowed to hear of it only through the press. The message should not contain any invitation to the Italians to return. The responsibility for this should be left to the Italians themselves. The message should merely show that the absence of the Italian Credentials was their fault and not ours. In reply to President Wilson he said he contemplated that the message should consist merely of a simple relation of the incident. For example, that credentials had been exchanged with the German Delegates; that Germany had asked for the Italian credentials. And that M. Jules Cambon had replied that we had not got them. If the Germans did not ask for the Italian credentials, then no incident would arise.

M. LLOYD GEORGE doubted if the Germans would ask for the Italian credentials.

M. CLEMENCEAU said that in their case he would certainly ask for them. M. Jules Cambon would certainly make no answer today about the Italian credentials, beyond merely stating that he had not got them. The Germans might raise this when they met the representatives of the Allied and Associated Powers. But M. Jules Cambon would simply say he had no power to discuss.

MR. LLOYD GEORGE asked what attitude should be taken if the Germans pressed the question when they met our plenipotentiaries.

M. CLEMENCEAU said that we should simply reply that we were ready to make peace and leave on Italy the responsibility for breaking the Treaty.

PRESIDENT WILSON pointed out that Italy had broken the Treaty or was contemplating breaking the Treaty in a most peculiar way. They said they would not agree to sign the Treaty with Germany because the Treaty with Austria was not settled, which was an irrelevant matter.

MR. LLOYD GEORGE pointed out that they represented that the League of Nations was their difficulty in the circumstances.

M. CLEMENCEAU said that Italians had promised to him, in front of his colleagues, to telegraph from Rome if they were coming back. They had not done so.

PRESIDENT WILSON said he thought it inadvisable to send any message, even of the most formal character. By implication, it would constitute an invitation to the Italians to return. His interpretation of the news from Rome was that in reality they were anxious to come back and he thought if they were left alone they might come back in 10 days' time.

In the course of the discussion, Mr. Lloyd George read the following message from M. Poincaré to Italy (published in the "Temps"):[4]

> "L'Italie et la France, étroitement unies dans la guerre, resteront unies dans la paix. Rien ne les séparers. Le refroidissement de leur amitié serait une catastrophe pour la civilisation latino et pour l'humanité. La France, fidèle a ses engagements, à ses sympathies et à ses traditions, gardera les mains jointes aux mains de l'Italie."

There was some discussion on this subject, in the course of which it was pointed out that this message might be construed as a declaration on behalf of the French Government. Under ordinary circumstances the message was perfectly beyond criticism, but at the present juncture it was susceptible of misinterpretation,

M. PICHON said he attached no importance to it.

MR. LLOYD GEORGE pointed out that to some extent it might be taken as confirming the impression conveyed in the Italian newspapers to the effect that French public opinion was rather rallying to the side of Italy.

[4] Actually, in the Paris *France-Italie*, May 1, 1919. For the background, publication, and discussion of this message, see Raymond Poincaré, *Au Service de la France* (11 vols., Paris, 1926-74), XI, 387-88, 414-16.

(After some further discussion, it was agreed that:

No message in regard to what might occur at Versailles on the subject of the Italian credentials should be sent to Italy.)

§ Mantoux's notes:

M. Stéphen Pichon is introduced.

Clemenceau. M. Pichon has come to speak to you about Italy.

Pichon. There will probably be an incident this afternoon, when M. Cambon will present the letters of credence of the Allied and Associated plenipotentiaries to the Germans. The Germans will ask where are the full powers of Italy; we will not be able to present them. It is Italy that is responsible for this situation; but this responsibility must appear clearly to the Italian public itself. It is essential to have good reason on our side. By mutual consent, we have decided that we would not make a separate peace. It must be obvious that it is Italy which separates herself from us, and not we from Italy. If there is an incident today, the Italian government would have to be notified of it by telegram, without any commentary. The Italian government will respond as it pleases. The important thing is to establish clearly that, if Italy does not return to take her place at the conference, it is her fault and not ours.

Wilson. What sort of telegram does M. Pichon propose to write?

Pichon. The telegram will only report the incident; we will say that the exchange of full powers has taken place, that the Germans asked for those of Italy, and that we had to answer that they were not in our hands.

Lloyd George. And if the Germans do not ask for anything?

Pichon. In that case, there will be nothing to do.

Lloyd George. I strongly doubt that they will ask anything whatsoever. They will say: "Who are you?" When M. Cambon will have answered them, they will not ask why such and such is not present.

Clemenceau. If there is no incident, obviously there will be no reason to telegraph the Italian government.

Lloyd George. If the Germans say: "Are you prepared to make peace in the absence of Italy? what will M. Cambon answer?

Clemenceau. M. Cambon will reply that it is the business of the heads of governments.

Lloyd George. But what will the heads of governments do?

Clemenceau. They will answer the Germans that we are prepared to negotiate with them. M. Orlando promised me to telegraph from Rome if he was ready to return; I have received nothing from him.

Lloyd George. Italy signed the Pact of London and, by withdrawing from the conference, it is she who will have broken it.

Wilson. And in a very singular way, by demanding that she be given assurances on treaties other than the one we are presently concerned with, the treaties with Austria and Hungary.

I believe that the Italians, at heart, want to return. If we don't blow things up by budging, I am persuaded that we shall see them in ten days.

Lloyd George. The news which I receive from Italy says: Italian opinion is supported by the French press and by the statement that M. Poincaré made in favor of Italy.

Clemenceau. M. Poincaré has written to Italy?

Pichon. It was three lines which appeared in the newspaper *France-Italie*, on the occasion of the anniversary of the death of Leonardo da Vinci.

Clemenceau. The President of the Republic is not to intervene without referring the matter to me.

Lloyd George. All that I can say is that, if the King had sent a message of this kind, even if the message had been perfect, that would create a serious incident in a situation like this one.

Clemenceau. In the circumstances we are in, the President of the Republic does not have the right to do that without consulting the government.

Wilson. It is an affront to the United States.

Pichon. The letter of the President of the Republic was submitted to me before its publication. I was asked if I saw a problem in its being published; I said no.

Reading of the text: "Italy and France, closely united in the war, will remain united in the peace. The cooling of their friendship would be a catastrophe for Latin civilization and for humanity. France, faithful to her commitments, to her sympathies and to her traditions, will keep her hands joined to those of Italy. Nothing will separate them.—Raymond Poincaré."

Wilson. This text can be understood as a commitment on the part of the French government.

Clemenceau. Under these conditions, my view is to send no telegram to the Italian government.

Pichon. It seemed to me that this letter from the President of the Republic was only a message of pure courtesy.

Lloyd George. The Italian press has the impression that French opinion is on her side.

Clemenceau. The French press was paid. Several months ago, Count Bonin Longare came constantly to complain about attacks by the Parisian press; if, all of a sudden, it has been seized with enthusiasm for Italy, we know what that means.

Lloyd George. So we shall send no communication to the Italian government?

Wilson. That is my opinion. §

Submarine Cables.

6. After a short discussion, it was agreed that:

The question of submarine cables should be discussed with the Foreign Ministers at the Quai d'Orsay at 4 p.m. in the afternoon.

§ Mantoux's notes:

Wilson. The question of the submarine cables is not settled. The difficulty came from us, and here is our point of view.

The article relating to the cables was first inserted into the military clauses. A discussion took place and, after a conversation with me, Mr. Balfour drafted a memorandum[5] in the following sense: When the cables were cut and diverted by the Allies, the Germans had the right to recover the abandoned section and to reestablish their former communications. Mr. Lansing and I do not find that, in the text as it has been drafted, that right left to the Germans to be sufficiently stipulated. Moreover, Germany would have to obtain new permission in order to lay her cables at certain points, for example in the Azores.

This would give Great Britain absolute control over telegraphic communications in the Atlantic, and it would be the same for Japan in the Pacific. We have a serious objection to make against a regime which would give the absolute monopoly of the cables to two of the great naval powers.

Lloyd George. You have no cables of your own?

Wilson. The American government does not have control of any, although America participates financially in some of these enterprises. Our concern is that the possession and administration of the world's cables not be in the hands of one or two powers.

Lloyd George. Until now, our representatives have not been able to agree; you are on one side, the representatives of France, Great Britain, and Japan are on the other. I believe that we cannot take a decision without again hearing our specialists.

Pichon. It was already agreed that I would come this afternoon with Admiral de Bon and Mr. Balfour with his expert.

Wilson. Let us confirm this appointment for this afternoon, at the Quai d'Orsay.

Clemenceau. Then, a meeting this afternoon at the Quai d'Orsay, at four o'clock. §

The Peace with Austria & Hungary.

7. M. PICHON asked for a re-consideration of the decision taken on the previous day to invite the representatives of Austria and of Hun-

[5] Wilson meant the resolution by Balfour embodied in the minutes of the Council of Ten printed at March 24, 1919, Vol. 56.

gary to Paris on the 12th May. (I.C.178A. Minute 2.)[6] He observed that, at Vienna, there was a Government with which the Allied and Associated Powers could negotiate. In regard to Hungary, however, the news was to the effect that the Government was tottering and that the country was not behind it. This made it desirable to wait some days before sending an invitation. This would also have the advantage of giving a few more days to see what happened on the side of Italy and it must be remembered that the great question in the Austrian settlement was the frontier of Italy. Hence, it would be better not to act too soon. If something was to be done immediately, it would be a good plan to bring the Hungarians to Paris by the middle of May. The Treaty could be ready for them, but it was not desirable to have the Austrians and Hungarians before we were ready.

PRESIDENT WILSON said that the principal reason for inviting the Austrians was to steady the Government at Vienna by showing to Austrian public opinion that we were ready to deal with it. According to his information, no delay in this matter was possible. The case of Hungary was different, and, as Mr. Lloyd George had said, perhaps stronger. Even there, we might help to prevent constant changes of Government. Our expectation of [blank] was less strong. He hoped, however, that the invitation would not be delayed and he, himself, would like to have it sent in 6 hours.[7]

M. CLEMENCEAU agreed and said he would discuss the details with M. Pichon later.

MR. LLOYD GEORGE agreed with President Wilson.

(M. Pichon withdrew.)

New States. Conditions to be accepted by them.
Protection of Jews and religious minorities.

(8) PRESIDENT WILSON said it had been brought to his attention that the Jews were somewhat inhospitably regarded in Poland.[8] In Roumania also they depended only on statutory rights. While we could not deal with Roumania, we could deal with their position in Poland and Czecho-Slovakia. Certain safeguards had been suggested to him.

(He then read the following two clauses, one of which he had drafted himself, while the other had been prepared by a United States legal draftsman:

(1) The State of ______ covenants and agrees that it will accord

[6] See the minutes of the Council of Four printed at April 30, 1919, 4 p.m.

[7] Mantoux, I, 440: "Wilson. M. Pichon does not know the reasons why we proposed to summon the Austrians at an early date. Our idea is to support the government of Vienna, by showing that we are disposed to treat with it; that admits of no delay. The same for Hungary. If the government weakens, we can have the advantage of avoiding a series of upheavals by sending our summons now. I insist on the immediate summons."

[8] See Enclosure I printed with S. S. Wise to WW, March 2, 1919, Vol. 55.

to all racial or national minorities within its jurisdiction exactly the same treatment and security, alike in law and in fact, that is accorded the racial or national majority of its people.

(2) The State of ______ covenants and agrees that it will not prohibit or interfere with the free exercise of any creed, religion or belief whose practices are not inconsistent with public order or public morals, and that no person within its jurisdiction shall be molested in life, liberty or the pursuit of happiness by reason of his adherence to any such creed, religion or belief.)

MR. LLOYD GEORGE said he was going to propose that some similar provisions should be introduced in the Mandates.

PRESIDENT WILSON then read a draft of clauses for the Treaty of Peace which had been prepared by Dr Miller concerning the protection of minorities in Poland, (Appendix I). He said that the draftsman had consulted the representatives of smaller nations and of the Jews in preparing this draft.

MR. LLOYD GEORGE said that this really formed part of a bigger subject. He himself had received a note on the subject from Sir Hubert Llewellyn Smith,[9] which opened up some wider aspects of the conditions which should be accepted by the new nations. He asked why some such provisions should not be laid down as a condition for admission to the League of Nations.

PRESIDENT WILSON said these States were already admitted to the League.

MR. LLOYD GEORGE said that M. Paderewski had made to him a very able defence of the attitude of Poland towards the Jews, and had pointed out that the Jews had themselves to blame to a considerable extent.

PRESIDENT WILSON said that the reason the Jews had caused trouble was because in those countries they were not really welcome citizens. They did not care for any country where they were badly treated. In the United States of America, Great Britain or France, those questions did not arise. They were only disloyal in countries where they were not treated properly.

MR. LLOYD GEORGE and M. CLEMENCEAU said that the Jews were very good citizens in their countries.

MR. LLOYD GEORGE said that in Poland he understood the Jews were really more efficient men of business than the Poles.

M. CLEMENCEAU said that in Poland a Pole who wanted to carry out any transaction—for example, to buy a horse—would send for a Jew.

[9] Printed as Appendix II.

PRESIDENT WILSON pointed out that in England the Jews had been bad citizens before they were properly treated.

MR. LLOYD GEORGE remarked that Cromwell was the first person to recognise the importance of treating the Jews properly.

PRESIDENT WILSON proposed that a body of experts should be got together to draw up clauses, if not for the present Treaty, at any rate for subsequent Treaties.

MR. LLOYD GEORGE thought the matter should be put in hand at once.

PRESIDENT WILSON suggested that his documents should be sent to this Committee as a basis for their enquiry. His draft about the protection of religious minorities would probably be sufficient.

M. CLEMENCEAU agreed.

MR. LLOYD GEORGE said that there were other more mundane matters referred to in Sir Hubert Llewellyn Smith's memorandum. He pointed out that the new States ought to assume the same obligations as other States in regard to matters adhering to general Conventions such as the Postal & Telegraph Convention; Industrial, Property and Copyright Conventions; and International Transit Conventions. He suggested that Sir Hubert Llewellyn Smith's memorandum should also be sent to the Committee.

PRESIDENT WILSON agreed. President Wilson suggested that the Committee should examine how these questions were to be fitted into the Treaty.

MR. LLOYD GEORGE said the difficulty was that the new States had already been recognised, but they had not been created.

PRESIDENT WILSON asked what was the act of creating a new State?

MR. LLOYD GEORGE said that the Treaty would be the act of creation, since, until the Treaties were signed, they would be part of Germany or Austria.

(It was agreed that a Committee composed as follows:

> Dr Miller for the United States of America; Mr. Headlam-Morley for the British Empire; A French Representative to be nominated by M. Clemenceau;

should meet immediately to consider the International obligations to be accepted by Poland and other new States created by the Treaties of Peace, including the protection of racial and religious minorities and other matters raised in the following documents:

- (a) The two drafts produced by President Wilson and quoted above;
- (b) The clauses forwarded by Dr Miller (Appendix I);
- (c) Memorandum by Sir Hubert Llewellyn Smith (Appendix II)

all of which should be regarded as an indication to the Committee of the subjects they were to consider.)

§ Mantoux's notes:

Protection of National and Religious Minorities

Wilson. One of the elements which troubles the peace of the world is the persecution of the Jews. They have been or are held in poor esteem in many countries. You know that they are particularly badly treated in Poland, and that they are deprived of the rights of citizenship in Rumania. In the treaty with Germany, we make stipulations as to Poland. It is necessary to demand two guarantees for national minorities and for religious minorities.

I would propose to insert in the treaty, along these lines, two articles which would be applied not only to Poland but to Bohemia and to the other new states. It is a matter of saying that (1) "the state of ______ pledges itself to grant to all racial and national minorities the same treatment in law and in fact as to the majority; (2) the State of ______ pledges itself to place no obstacle to the practice of any religion, if that practice is not contrary to public order or morals."

Lloyd George. I would propose the extension of this principle to the countries subject to the regime of mandate.

Wilson. A detailed text was prepared on the status of the citizens of Poland, which indicates that in a more explicit fashion. This plan was drafted after consultation with the representatives of the minorities. What I do not like is that they demand a sort of autonomy for the national minorities.

Lloyd George. This is a claim of the Jews, who wish to form a sort of state within the state. Nothing would be more dangerous.

Wilson. The reason why I ask that the general stipulations which I just indicated be included in the treaty with Germany is that Poland is incorporating several million German subjects into her territory.

Lloyd George. In any case, these stipulations must be imposed upon the Poles. There is obviously something to say to justify the hostile feeling of the Poles against the Jews. M. Paderewski told me that, during the war, the Jews of Poland were by turns for the Germans, for the Russians, for the Austrians, and very little for Poland herself.

Wilson. It is the result of a long persecution. The Jews of the United States are good citizens.

Lloyd George. It is the same in England.

Clemenceau. And in France.

Wilson. Remember that, when the Jews were outside the law in England, they acted as people outside the law. Our wish is to bring them back everywhere under the terms of the law of the land.

Lloyd George. I will recall the benevolence of Cromwell toward them.

Wilson. I propose to bring together a small committee of experts to draft the articles which will settle that question in Poland. If this text does not find its place in the treaty with Germany, it will be necessary in any case to insert it in the treaty which will determine the organic law of the Polish State.

Lloyd George. The best thing is to put it in the German treaty.

Wilson. We will tell the committee to prepare as short a text as possible.

Lloyd George. It will be necessary to provide many other clauses for these new states and first to impose upon them the same international obligations as those of other civilized countries.

Wilson. I do not see how all that could be inserted in the treaty with Germany.

Lloyd George. However, we cannot recognize these new states without such guarantees.

Wilson. We have already recognized them; but in reality it remains to create them. How do we do it?

Lloyd George. The best thing is to do it by the peace treaties which we are going to sign. §

Provision for the Post-bellum occupation of German territory.

(9) MR LLOYD GEORGE pointed out that no arrangements had been made to regulate the post-bellum occupation of German territory. It was important that provision should be made for the relations between the Army and the civil authorities, etc. He was informed that General Weygand was discussing this with General Thwaites and General Bliss, but, in the meantime, some provision had to be made in the Treaty of Peace. He suggested the following clause:

> "All matters regarding occupation not provided for by the present Treaty shall be regulated by a subsequent Convention or Conventions which shall have the same force and effect as if embodied in the present Treaty."

(This was agreed as a basis for the preparation of an Article by the Drafting Committee.)

Mandates.

(10) MR LLOYD GEORGE urged that the conditions of the Mandates should be fixed. He asked if they ought not to be inserted in the Treaty with Germany.

M. CLEMENCEAU said this was unnecessary.

PRESIDENT WILSON agreed.

MR LLOYD GEORGE said that at any rate there ought to be a clear understanding on the matter. The British Dominions laid great stress on this.

PRESIDENT WILSON said that there was a tacit agreement as to the assignment of the Mandates.

MR LLOYD GEORGE said it was rather the conditions of the Mandates he was referring to.

PRESIDENT WILSON said that the Supreme Council was too much pressed to take up that matter.

(11) M. CLEMENCEAU said he did not think that the Treaty of Peace would be ready before Monday. He suggested that the Plenary Conference at which he would read the summary to the States with special interests should be held on Sunday.

PRESIDENT WILSON and MR LLOYD GEORGE both demurred to a Sunday meeting.

M. CLEMENCEAU said it would have to be held on Saturday.

Enemy Ships in United States Ports.

(12) There was a short discussion on this subject, which was postponed for further consideration.

§ Mantoux's notes:

Lloyd George. We cannot meet the Germans in Versailles before Monday. My idea is to hold a meeting next Sunday in which we will transmit the text of the preliminaries to the representatives of the Allied and Associated Powers.

Wilson. That can create difficulties for me with American opinion.

Lloyd George. I go along with your opinion.

Clemenceau. Then it will be necessary to hold it on Saturday.

Lloyd George. Are there many articles which are not ready?

Clemenceau. I will bring them to you this afternoon.

Wilson. The question of the disposition of German merchant ships is not settled.

Lloyd George. The treaty will say only that the Germans surrender the ships. The division that we shall make pertains only to us. What I have proposed is that the United States keep those which they took, paying over the surplus value in relation to their losses in tonnage into a fund to be decided upon. Mr. Keynes proposes a different wording: the surplus to be deposited in a common fund would be calculated in relation to what the United States would receive if the ships which she seized were deposited in the aggregate. Mr. Keynes also proposes an amendment according to which, instead of serving as compensation to American subjects, the German properties seized in America would go into the total of the reparations.

Wilson. The difficulty arises from American legislation. The enemy properties were seized by a decision of the Congress, and it is the Congress, in principle, which must dispose of them.

The general principle is that each government compensates its nationals, and that the surplus goes into the aggregate; that general rule must obviously be applied to the ships. §

Blockade.

(13) There was a short discussion in regard to the opinions expressed by the United States, British and Italian Delegations on the Supreme Economic Council in favour of relaxation of the blockade.

PRESIDENT WILSON said that if the blockade was not removed until the Peace had been ratified, Germany would go to pieces.

MR LLOYD GEORGE pointed out that the real difficulty in victualling Germany was not so much the blockade as the fact that Germany had no financial resources wherewith to pay for goods or raw materials, hence it was necessary to provide some means for supplying credit. He had put forward a scheme which he understood was not acceptable to the United States experts.[10] He did not attach any special importance to any particular scheme, but he felt sure it was necessary to have some scheme, and the subject ought to be discussed. All his information tended to show that Germany's signature to Peace would depend mainly on her prospects of getting food and raw materials.

PRESIDENT WILSON suggested that it would not be necessary to propound any particular scheme. It would be sufficient to say that effective co-operation would be given.

MR LLOYD GEORGE said he did not think this would suffice. The Germans would say that promises of the kind were held out to them in the Armistice discussions, but that nothing had resulted. It was necessary to propound a definite scheme which would be acceptable to the Germans.

(The Subject was adjourned.)

Reparation.

(14) The formal Minute in Appendix III was signed in triplicate by M. Clemenceau, President Wilson and Mr Lloyd George as giving effect to the decision taken on the previous day as to the proportions in which the receipts paid by Germany for reparation were to be divided between the Allied and Associated Governments.

One copy was kept by President Wilson, one by M. Clemenceau and one by Mr Lloyd George.

APPENDIX I. TO I.C.178.D.

Draft clauses for the protection of Minorities in Poland.

No. 1

My dear Colonel House: 29th April, 1919.

Herewith are the proposals of draft clauses for the protection of

[10] See the Enclosure printed with D. Lloyd George to WW, April 23, 1919.

minorities in Poland, in which some very slight changes have been made since they were previously submitted to you.

In the enclosed draft it will be observed that Article VI is in two forms; that in the left-hand column is the one preferred by the Jewish representatives, and that in the right-hand column is the one which I think is preferable as I believe it allows more liberty to minorities in the future even if it would make no practical difference at present.

These clauses to be effective would have to be inserted in the Treaty of Peace if the cession of German territory to Poland is to be contained in that Treaty. If, however, the territory which Germany relinquishes is ceded temporarily to the Allied and Associated Powers the insertion of these clauses could perhaps be made in the paper subsequently granting the territory to Poland. My own view, however, is that their insertion in the Treaty of Peace is preferable.

It is my opinion that these clauses or their substance should be inserted in the Treaty if minorities in Poland are to receive proper protection.

Doubtless, if these clauses are accepted for Poland, similar clauses will be adopted for the protection of minorities in other countries, such as Czecho-Slovakia and Roumania, varying somewhat according to the circumstances therein.

If these clauses are to be inserted in the Treaty of Peace it seems to me essential that they should have the immediate approval of the Council of Four.

Yours faithfully, (Signed) DAVID HUNTER MILLER.

CLAUSES FOR THE TREATY OF PEACE

CONCERNING PROTECTION OF MINORITIES IN POLAND.

Poland undertakes the following obligations to each of the other Allied and Associated Powers, and recognizes them to be obligations of international concern of which the League of Nations has jurisdiction.

1. Without any requirement of qualifying or other proceedings, Poland admits and declares to be Polish citizens (a) all persons born in the territory recognised to be Polish in this Treaty, who have not heretofore been naturalized in some other country, and who were resident or domiciled in such territory at any time since August 1st, 1909, or who have maintained their relation to such territory within such period by passport issued by the present or the former sovereignty; (b) all persons who were inhabitants of such territory on August 1st, 1914; (c) all persons hereafter born in Poland and subject to the jurisdiction thereof. Any person belonging to classes (a) or (b) may however within two years after the coming into force of this treaty opt his former citizenship.

2. Poland agrees that all citizens of Poland shall enjoy equal civil,

religious, and political rights without distinction as to birth, race, nationality, language, or religion.

3. Poland assumes and will perform the following obligations:

(a) To protect the life, liberty and property of all inhabitants of Poland;

(b) To assure to all inhabitants of Poland freedom of religion and of the outward exercise thereof;

(c) To allow to all inhabitants of Poland the free use of any language, particularly in business transactions, in schools and other educational instruction, in the press, and at public meetings and assemblies; and,

(d) To make no discrimination against any inhabitant of Poland on account of birth, race, nationality, language, or religion.

4. Poland recognises the several national minorities in its population as constituting distinct public corporations, and as such having equally the right to establish, manage, and control their schools and their religions, educational, charitable or social institutions.

Any person may declare his withdrawal from such a national minority.

Within the meaning of these articles the Jewish population of Poland shall constitute a national minority.

5. Poland agrees that to the extent that the establishment and the maintenance of schools or religious, educational, charitable or social institutions may be provided for by any state, department, municipal or other budget, to be paid for out of public funds, each national minority shall be allotted a proportion of such funds based upon the ratio between its numbers in the respective areas and the entire population therein.

6. Poland agrees that each national minority shall have the right to elect a proportion of the entire number of representatives in all state, departmental, municipal and other public elective bodies based upon the ratio of its numbers in the respective electoral areas to the entire population therein.	6. Poland agrees to adopt and enforce the principle of proportional minority representation by means of cumulative voting in all states, departmental, municipal or other public elective bodies, conducted on a basis of justice and equality, the several electoral areas being subdivided into electoral districts which shall consist of compact, contiguous territory, and the population of the several electoral districts being equal as nearly as practicable.

7. Poland agrees that the foregoing obligations are hereby embodied in her fundamental law as a bill of rights, with which no law, reg-

ulation or official action shall conflict or interfere and as against which no law, regulation or official action shall have validity or effect, and which shall not be amendable except with the consent of the League of Nations.

APPENDIX II TO I.C.178.D.

NOTE BY SIR HUBERT LLEWELLYN SMITH.

The Chapters in the Treaty of Peace dealing with Territorial changes are supposed to provide for all the obligations which it is necessary to impose on Germany, Austria, etc. in relation to the new States or the ceded territories.

In some cases (e.g. Poland) they provide to *some extent* for obligations of the new States towards Germany, etc. But they are necessarily silent as to the obligations of the new States towards the Allies, and before the Treaties are signed compelling the Enemy States to recognise the new States and to accept obligations toward them, it seems only prudent to impose by separate instruments on the new States and ceded Territories such obligations inter se, towards the Allies and also towards the Enemy States as may be thought essential. If we miss this opportunity, we may never succeed in getting some of these obligations accepted.

Naturally nothing oppressive or one-sided ought to be imposed, but the Allies whose efforts and sacrifices have created the new States and compelled the cession of territory have an undoubted right and duty to see that the general interests and their own special interests are not prejudiced thereby, and they have also a moral obligation to secure to the transferred populations the rights which they formerly enjoyed (e.g. under such laws as the German Insurance Laws).

As an example, it would be desirable to require the new States to adhere to such general Conventions as the Postal and Telegraphic Conventions, the Industrial Property and Copyright Conventions. It would also be desirable to require them to accept some such clauses as the following:

> "The provisions of any general Conventions relating to the international regime of Transit, Waterways, Ports and Railways, which may be concluded before the expiration of five years from the coming into force of the Treaty of Peace and which may be accepted as applicable to all the European States represented on the Council of the League of Nations shall apply to ______."

It would also be very desirable if practicable, to insist on the following stipulation:

> "Pending the conclusion of a general Convention regulating the commercial relations among the States members of the League of Nations, the ______ undertake to treat the commerce of

the Allied and Associated States on a footing of absolute equality both among themselves and as compared with any other foreign country. Provided that no Allied or Associated State can claim the benefit of this provision on behalf of any part of its territories in which reciprocal treatment is not accorded."

If this is agreed to in principle, it would seem desirable for a Drafting Committee to prepare a model draft of instrument which should begin by setting out the boundaries of the new State and recognising the State within these boundaries. It would go on to impose the above obligations and any others which may be thought necessary.

There might, if preferred, be only one instrument with several Annexes setting out the various boundaries, the whole being signed by all the Allies including the new States.

It may be added that the clauses relating to free Transit and the maintenance of Insurance privileges should probably go also into the instruments relating to ceded territories (e.g. Schleswig, Alsace-Lorraine, etc.) but the commercial and treaty provisions would only be applicable to new States.

27th April, 1919.

APPENDIX III TO I.C.178.D.

At a Meeting held between M. Clemenceau, President Wilson and Mr. Lloyd George on the morning of the 30th April, 1919, it was agreed that:

The proportions, in which receipts from Germany are to be divided between the Allied and Associated Governments in accordance with Article 7 of the Reparation chapter of the Draft Treaty with Germany, shall be those which the aggregates of the claims of each against Germany which are established to the satisfaction of the Reparation Commission, in accordance with Annexes 1 and 2 of the Reparation chapter, bear to the aggregate of the claims of all against Germany which are established to the satisfaction of the Commission.

(Signed) G. CLEMENCEAU.
" D. LLOYD GEORGE.
" WOODROW WILSON.

Paris, May 1, 1919.

Signed in triplicate. Copies to United States,[11] British and French Treasuries.

[11] Wilson's copy of this document is a TS MS, dated May 1, 1919, and is in WP, DLC.

APPENDIX IV TO I.C.178.D.

DRAFT CLAUSES PREPARED BY THE DRAFTING COMMITTEE OF THE PEACE CONFERENCE,

on instructions received from

THE COUNCIL OF THE FIRST DELEGATES OF THE POWERS WITH GENERAL INTERESTS AFTER CONSIDERATION OF THE REPORT OF THE COMMISSION.

PENALTIES.

Article 1.

The Allied and Associated Powers publicly arraign William II of Hohenzollern, formerly German Emperor, not for an offence against criminal law, but for a supreme offence against international morality and the sanctity of treaties.

A special tribunal will be constituted to try the accused, thereby assuring him the guarantees essential to the right of defence. It will be composed of five judges, one appointed by each of the following five Powers: namely, the United States of America, Great Britain, France, Italy and Japan.

In its decision the tribunal will be guided by the highest principles of international policy, with a view to vindicating the solemn obligations of international undertakings and the validity of international morality. It will be its duty to fix the punishment which it considers should be imposed.

The Allied and Associated Powers will address a request to the Government of the Netherlands for the surrender to them of the ex-Emperor in order that he may be put on trial.

Article 2.

The German Government not having ensured the punishment of the persons accused of having committed acts in violation of the laws and customs of war, such persons will be brought before military tribunals by the Allied and Associated Powers, and if found guilty, sentenced to the punishments laid down by military law.

The German Government shall hand over to the Allied and Associated Powers, or to such one of them as shall so request, all persons accused of having committed an act in violation of the laws and customs of war, who are specified either by name or by the rank, office or employment which they held under the German authorities.

Article 3.

Persons guilty of criminal acts against the nationals of one of the Allied and Associated Powers will be brought before the military tribunals of that Power.

Persons guilty of criminal acts against the nationals of more than one of the Allied and Associated Powers will be brought before military tribunals composed of members of the military tribunals of the Powers concerned.

In every case the accused will be entitled to name his own counsel.

Article 4.

The German Government undertakes to furnish all documents and information of every kind, the production of which may be considered necessary to ensure the full knowledge of the incriminating acts, the discovery of the offenders, and the just appreciation of the responsibility.

T MS (SDR, RG 256, 180.03401/135, DNA); Mantoux, I, 436-39, 440-41, 442.

Two Letters from Robert Lansing

Dear Mr. President: Paris, May 1, 1919.

The question of submarine cables was placed on the Agenda for the meeting of the Ministers for Foreign Affairs yesterday afternoon at my request. I thought it desirable to have the matter brought up, inasmuch as the Drafting Committee, in my opinion, had entirely misinterpreted the intent of the resolution proposed by Mr. Balfour at the meeting of the Council of Ten held on March 24th last.

I beg to attach copies of extracts of the Secretary's notes of the meeting of yesterday afternoon, the important portions of which have been marked with blue pencil.[1]

I regret to say that after considerable discussion we came to a complete impasse, and finding no solution it was decided to refer the matter to the Supreme Council.

Briefly stated my position which was based upon our recent conversation was as follows: The Allies should not be required to return to Germany those sections of the German Cable System which they had destroyed, but that Germany should be permitted to restore such sections. In other words, the portions of the German cables which had not been destroyed, removed or diverted should revert to Germany together with the landing rights which she might have, although it would of course be within the power of any of the Allied Powers to refuse to renew German landing rights within their territories, as these rights had automatically been abrogated by the declaration of war. It was our intention that all other cables including those which have been used by the Allies should revert to Germany.

The British, French and Japanese took the position that while they were prepared to permit Germany to restore the portions of her cable system which they had removed or diverted, they were not willing to return sections which had become incorporated in their own cable system. They also refused to return to Germany any cables which had been merely used by them.

In a word, they were ready to permit Germany to rebuild a new cable system, but were not prepared to let her have her former cables or any portions of them as a nucleus on which to build up a new system.

While there is every reason in law and equity that the German cables seized during the war should be returned to Germany, nevertheless many of these cables have been removed and diverted, so that these cables now form parts of other communication systems.

As an example of a diverted cable, the cable which ran from Emden to New York via the Azores now runs from England to Canada via the Azores. Derelict ends of the former German cable lie in the sea off New York and off Emden. The cable as it now runs forms part of the British cable system.

Special considerations apply to certain of the cables:

The French claim to have expended a great deal of money on the German cable from Monrovia to Pernambuco and insist that they should be reimbursed for this expenditure should the cable be returned to Germany.

It is apparent that the Japanese expect to receive the island of Yap and as incident thereto obtain the German cable system radiating from that island.

I recommend that we stand by the basic principle which has been insisted upon by us heretofore.

I am, my dear Mr. President,

Very sincerely yours, Robert Lansing.

[1] "EXTRACT from Secretary's Notes . . . ," T MS (WP, DLC); printed in *PPC*, IV, 645-53. Lansing summarizes the issues involved very well.

My dear Mr. President: Paris, May 1, 1919.

In accordance with your directions, I beg to enclose herewith six copies of a draft resolution relating to Submarine Cables[1] which you undertook to present at the next meeting of the Council of Ten.

I am, my dear Mr. President,

Very sincerely yours, Robert Lansing.

TLS (WP, DLC).

[1] "DRAFT RESOLUTION," T MS (WP, DLC). This resolution is reproduced in the minutes of the Council of Ten printed at May 2, 1919, 5 p.m.

Hankey's Notes of a Meeting of the Council of Ten[1]

BC-59 Quai d'Orsay, May 1, 1919, 4 p.m.

M. CLEMENCEAU called on M. Pichon to explain how the question of submarine cables now stood.

M. PICHON said that on the 24th March, 1919,[2] the following Resolution proposed by Mr. Balfour had been passed by the Council of Ten, namely:

> "The Treaty of Peace should not debar Germany from repairing at her own expense submarine cables cut by the Allied and Associated Powers during the war, nor from replacing at her expense any parts which had been cut out from such cables or which, without having been cut, are now in use by any of those Powers."

It had been agreed that this text should be referred to the Drafting Committee for the submission of a draft clause for inclusion in the Treaty of Peace. The Drafting Committee had prepared a text (see I.C.178)[3] which, however, was only accepted by the American representative subject to the approval of his Government. At a meeting of the Foreign Ministers held at the Quai d'Orsay on the 30th April, 1919, the text in question had again come under discussion. Mr. Lansing had been unable to accept the draft text proposed by the Drafting Committee and had proposed certain amendments (see I.C.178), which both Mr. Balfour and Admiral de Bon had been unable to accept. Consequently, it had been decided to refer the whole question to the Heads of Government for final decision.

PRESIDENT WILSON enquired whether Mr. Balfour held the view that the Article, as drafted by the Drafting Committee, carried out the intention of the Resolution passed on the 24th March, 1919.

MR. BALFOUR, in reply, said he would like to give his version of what had occurred. On the 24th March, 1919, at the Conference of the Ten, which Mr. Lloyd George had not attended, a prolonged discussion of the cable question had taken place. A Resolution had been unanimously accepted, which was to be referred to the Drafting Committee for insertion in the Articles of the Peace Treaty. Both Mr. Lansing and he (Mr. Balfour) had adhered to that Resolution, which was to govern the action of the Drafting Committee. The question had now arisen as to the correct interpretation to be given to the original Resolution. Mr. Lansing would no doubt explain his point of view. He, himself, interpreted the clause to mean that all acts taken by the Allies in connection with enemy submarine cables during the war should stand, and that Germany should have no

[1] The complete text of these minutes is printed in *PPC*, IV, 483–92.

[2] The minutes of the meeting of the Council of Ten of March 24, 1919, are printed in Vol. 56.

[3] Actually, FM-10, printed in *PPC*, IV, 645–54. There is no I.C.178.

claim to compensation. Thus, for instance, should a cable line have been cut and diverted, the new system so established should stand. On the other hand, Germany would have a perfect right to reconstruct her former cable system as it stood before the war. To illustrate his argument, he would ask the Council to imagine a German cable line going from A to C through B. During the war the cable was cut at B and connected up with a new line from B, to D, so that the line went from A to B to D, as follows:

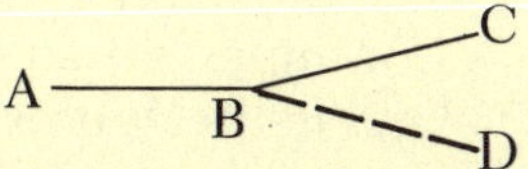

Under these conditions, Mr. Lansing held that the piece A-B should now be restored to Germany, whereas the British, French and Japanese representatives contended that as A-B was an essential part of the new line A-B-D, it could not be restored to Germany, though she should have a right to join up the piece B-C with a new line to be laid by her from B to A.

MR. LLOYD GEORGE enquired whether the Germans would have the right to the use in common of the line A-B.

MR. BALFOUR explained that it would not be practical for two separate systems to use the same cable line. Consequently, the part A-B would have to be owned by the country that had laid down the line B-D. In his opinion, unless the British interpretation were accepted, the Allies and not the Germans would have to spend an enormous sum of money in making their new cable lines effective. He fully agreed that the number of cables should not be diminished and that the more cables there were, the better it would be; but he thought that it was Germany who should be required to make the expenditure to reconstruct her lost cables. Great Britain had already spent over £400,000 on the changes necessary for adapting the lines taken over from Germany to the new cable systems.

PRESIDENT WILSON said that when he took part in the discussion, it had been with an unfortunate ignorance of technical details. He had not known that the main trunk line could not be used by two parties. He had supposed that the Germans could, at their own expense, connect up their end and operate through the common trunk line. As the trunk line lay at the bottom of the sea, in what might be called no-man's-land, it was not subject to capture, but was subject to use. He realised that there was no International law on this question. He had assented to the resolution, therefore, under an erroneous impression, which was entirely his own fault. He would take an example. There had been a cable line from Emden by the Azores to New York. The European end had been diverted to Brest, and the

American end to Halifax. This had caused great inconvenience to the United States, and he had supposed that a new branch line to New York could be attached to the main trunk line without disturbing the communication with Halifax and similarly that a new German end could be installed without disturbing the line to Brest. But, under the interpretation now given to the resolution, Germany would not have the use of the main trunk line and only the abandoned short ends of the original cable lines would be restored to her, and she would have to replace the main lengths of the line extending to a length of some 3,000 miles. In addition, Germany would have to obtain the right to land in the Azores. This was not what he had assented to, but the error was due to his ignorance. He thought that in a war in which many nations had participated and expended their share of blood and treasure, these indispensable instruments of international communication should not pass into the hands of only three of the parties in the war. He had no desire to re-establish the German cable system, but he had a very decided interest in ensuring the means of obtaining quick cable communication. Wireless, as now developed, had not the same value as cables, since anyone could pick up wireless messages. On the other hand, cables possessed a certain degree of privacy, depending on the good faith of the employees. Again the cable lines across the Pacific passed through the Island of Yap, which thus became a general distributing centre for the lines of communication of the North Pacific. Yap should not, therefore, fall into the hands of one Power.

In his opinion, the case had assumed a new aspect, since he had heard the interpretation now given to the resolution. It was proposed that the German cables were to be turned over entirely to those who had cut them during the war, even though one particular line, Pernambuco to Monrovia, actually terminated at both ends in neutral countries. If any method could be devised to put the cable systems under International control he would be quite satisfied; but it seemed to him a very serious matter that all Powers should not have a common interest in them. He thought a satisfactory solution would be reached, if the enemy cables could be turned over to the Allied and Associated Governments as trustees, and managed under the terms of an International Convention. He asked to correct a slight mistake made in his statement. He found there had actually been two cables from Emden to New York. One of these lines had been diverted so as to operate between Brest and New York, thus constituting a Franco-American line. The second line had been connected to run from Land's End to Halifax.

MR. BALFOUR said that he wished to repeat the statement made by him at a previous meeting, when discussing the same question, to the effect that he was entirely against monopolies. But the existing cable systems could not be described as monopolies in the bad sense of the word. The Cable Companies in question though registered in Great Britain were actually owned by a majority of American shareholders, which rather disposed of the idea that any undue monopoly existed.

PRESIDENT WILSON pointed out that in accordance with the laws of the United States of America a majority of directors would have to belong to the country in which the Company was registered.

MR. LLOYD GEORGE did not think that the same law applied to Great Britain in the case of international companies. He understood that, although these cable companies were owned by British companies, they were actually operated by American companies.

MR. LANSING thought that the whole question was merely one of investments. The control of the cable lines was wholey in the hands of the British.

ADMIRAL DE BON said that two definite questions called for decision by the Council, namely: Firstly, the use to which the captured German cables should be put, and, secondly, the regulations which the Allies, and especially the United States of America, wished to apply to the use of cables crossing the high seas. In regard to the first question, the cables which had previously consituted the German system could be considered under three different heads. Firstly, the lines which had been taken over by the Allied Governments and organised into new systems which were now in use. He thought no one would suggest the return of these cable lines to Germany, with the resulting disturbance of the existing lines of communication. He felt certain that complete agreement existed on this point. Secondly, bits of cables existed which had been disconnected from the main trunk line and still lay, unused, at the bottom of the sea. President Wilson maintained that these bits of cables belonged to no one and, therefore, Germany should have the right to utilise them in reconstructing her new cable lines. He saw no difficulty in accepting President Wilson's views even though these bits of cables constituted materials of war, captured during operations of war. Thirdly, there remained the question of the cable from Pernambuco-Monrovia which had been cut by the French, diverted, and made ready for use. The Government of the United States had for political reasons requested that this cable line should not be used, and to this the French Government had assented.

To sum up, complete agreement existed in regard to the first point. The second point was debatable but President Wilson's point of view could be adopted. The third point constituted a special case, since the cable in question had been diverted to Monrovia and was ready to function. Had America objected before the completion of the work, the line could have been diverted to Conakry and in that case no discussion would have arisen. In any case, he was strongly opposed to the return of that cable to Germany.

In regard to the question of cable communications in general, which the American Government wished to have assured by constituting an international system of control, the question did not appertain to the Treaty of Peace. It could, therefore, well be put aside for further study on the lines laid down by President Wilson. The present task of the Conference would, therefore, be confined to informing Germany that the cables, which, during the period of the war had been cut and utilized by the Allied and Associated Governments would not be restored to her and that they would remain the property of the Allied and Associated Governments. On the other hand, Germany would have the right to regain possession of the cables or parts of cables which had been cut and remained unutilised.

The resolution passed on March 24th stated that Germany would not be debarred from repairing at her own expense the submarine cables cut by Allied and Associated Powers during the war, nor from replacing at her own expense any parts of submarine cables which had been cut out from such cables or which, without having been cut, were now in use by any of these Powers. In his opinion, the Allied and Associated Governments should not permit Germany to lay down new cables without first obtaining the necessary licences. In his opinion, no clause should be introduced in the Peace Treaty which might appear to give Germany the right to avoid such formalities. The Governments concerned must retain the right to decide whether a new licence should be granted or not.

To sum up, as far as the Treaty of Peace was concerned, he thought it would only be necessary to lay down that the Allied and Associated Governments would retain the cables now being used by them, including the Monrovia-Pernambuco cable, which had been made ready for use; and that Germany would be allowed to pick up and re-connect the bits of unused cables. It would be unnecessary to make any statement in the Peace Treaty in regard to the future policy of the Allied and Associated Governments on the subject of the control of cables.

SIR ROBERT BORDEN said that he had not been able to study the cable situation under discussion very carefully; but Canada was deeply interested in the cables crossing the Atlantic. Though many of the cable lines landed at Halifax, the Canadian Government had no control over that line; the control being American.

MR LANSING, intervening, pointed out that only the control was American, the property itself being vested in the United Kingdom.

MR LLOYD GEORGE thought that the Americans, at all events, controlled the rate to be charged for cables.

MR LANSING doubted the correctness of that statement. The Western Union Cable Company of America merely controlled the working of the cables; but the cables themselves were owned by British Companies.

SIR ROBERT BORDEN, continuing, said that he was certain of one thing, namely, that the Canadians did not control these cable lines. The Canadian Government had been requested by the British Government to allow the cable line in question to land at Halifax. The permission asked for had been granted and he would now strongly object to its removal. In his opinion, the whole question of cable control required careful consideration by the Governments concerned.

PRESIDENT WILSON pointed out that he did not wish Sir Robert Borden to imagine that anyone held the idea of diverting the cable from Halifax.

MR LLOYD GEORGE held that if the line in question were handed back to Germany, it would as a natural consequence be diverted to New York.

PRESIDENT WILSON expressed the view that the meeting had to decide only the two following definite questions, namely:

"(i) Are submarine cables proper objects of appropriation and can they be retained without reckoning them in the total bill of reparations?

"(ii) Can any means be devised to place the cable lines under international control?"

He thought if these principles could be accepted, a satisfactory agreement would easily be reached.

SIR ROBERT BORDEN invited attention to the fact that six or seven years ago the Canadian Government had endeavoured to exercise some control over the rates charged for cables. The Government eventually only succeeded in obtaining a reduction by threatening to lay cables of their own.

MR LLOYD GEORGE maintained that whatever President Wilson's intention might be in connection with the cable line in question, the effect would obviously be to divert the cable from Halifax. The right to take cables was just as strong as the right to capture ships. He agreed that cables had not heretofore formed the subject of capture; but there had never been a war of the same kind before, and serious risks and heavy expenditure had had to be incurred in order to obtain possession of these cables. He, himself, would be quite prepared to consider the question of the payment of some sort of compensation to Germany for the surrender of the cables, but this was a new proposition and would require careful examination. A direct line of communication to Canada having now been established, the people of Canada who had suffered much in money and life during the war would feel deeply deserted if the suggestion were accepted to return these lines to Germany. In conclusion, he wished to support very cordially what Admiral de Bon had said, namely, that after peace had been established the Governments should meet together and endeavour to arrive at some agreement on the question of the international control of cable lines. The only point, however, now to be decided was whether these particular cables should be restored to Germany or not. He held the view that if such a step were now taken very bitter feeling would be raised.

PRESIDENT WILSON pointed out that there was a side of the question to which Mr. Lloyd George had not referred. If it were merely a question of returning the cables to Germany or not, the solution would be comparatively easy, as this could only be answered in the negative. But the Council was asked to decide whether these cables should remain exclusively in the hands of those who had taken them over, though all parties had taken part in the war. Should a decision to that effect be taken, that might prejudge any ulterior arrangements, whereas, in his opinion, the Treaty of Peace ought to leave the question open.

MR. LLOYD GEORGE enquired whether President Wilson could make some definite proposal.

PRESIDENT WILSON suggested that the Peace Terms should require the cables in question to be transferred to the Allied and Associated Powers as Trustees; who would be authorised to determine the future working of the cables in the interests of the Powers concerned.

MR. LLOYD GEORGE enquired whether the Trustees would have the power of diverting the cables to other places.

PRESIDENT WILSON expressed the view that the Trustees would only be empowered to do this as a result of a unanimous decision, on the grounds that such a diversion would be in the interest of the whole of the Powers concerned.

SIR ROBERT BORDEN explained that the Canadian Government had intended to make the cable in question State property to be linked up with the land telegraphic system, which already belonged to the Government. In this way, it was thought measures could be taken to reduce rates.

PRESIDENT WILSON thought that the question raised by Sir Robert Borden was not in contradiction with his own proposals, and should be considered when the question of drafting the international convention relating to cables was undertaken.

MR. LLOYD GEORGE pointed out that President Wilson's proposal would apply to all cables, and consequently would also affect the French and Japanese Governments.

BARON MAKINO said he wished to state Japan's position in the matter. At the last meeting on this subject, Mr. Balfour had proposed a resolution which had been accepted after long discussion. He had not then had time to catch the real purport of the resolution. Accordingly, he had wished to obtain some explanation, but he was told that after the text came back from the Drafting Committee, he would have an opportunity of discussing the question further. At the present moment, he was prepared to accept the policy contained in the resolution proposed by Mr. Balfour on 24th March last.

In regard to the appropriation of the cables in question, he would invite attention to the policy that had been pursued, vis-à-vis Germany, as expressed in the Peace Treaty. It would be found that a certain number of questions had been settled not strictly in accordance with the recognised usages of international law. For instance, in regard to the taking over of private property. Again, Article 13 of the Financial Clauses authorised the taking over of undertakings of public utility. That is to say, the Allied and Associated Governments had, in his opinion, gone very far in taking over German rights and much further than had ever been done heretofore. In his opinion, the same procedure could therefore well be followed in regard to cables. The Cable Company taken over by the Japanese Government had a capital of 15 million marks at its disposal and in addition received from the German Government an annual subsidy of 1½ million marks. Those facts clearly proved that the undertaking had not been a commercial one, but part and parcel of the German political system. For this reason, taking into consideration also the general policy introduced elsewhere in the Treaty to which he had just alluded, it was not unreasonable that this cable should be taken over by Japan. That clearly was the Japanese point of view, and after very careful consideration he had been led to the conclusion that the best policy would be to adopt Mr. Balfour's original resolution.

Next, in regard to the International Convention relating to the future management of cables, his personal opinion was that such an arrangement would be desirable. Such a Convention could be drawn up on the same lines as the International Postal Convention, subject to International agreement. But for the moment he was only willing to accept the proposals contained in Mr. Balfour's resolution adopted on March 24th last.

MR. LLOYD GEORGE said that President Wilson had put forward a new proposal. So far, he had only been able to have a short consultation with Mr. Balfour, who agreed with him that their experts should be consulted before reaching a definite conclusion. He would therefore ask the Council to adjourn the further discussion of the question, in order to give time for proper consideration of the new proposal. He felt very hopeful that an agreement would be reached; but he would like to consult his experts. In his opinion, it would be a mistake to discuss the proposal until it had received further consideration.

PRESIDENT WILSON explained that he had put forward his proposal for two reasons. Firstly, because he thought it was right and, secondly, because he thought it afforded a solution in the general interest, which would have the effect of creating a solidarity amongst the Allied Powers.

MR. LLOYD GEORGE agreed provided financial solidarity alone was not intended.

SIR ROBERT BORDEN was particularly anxious to avoid private companies acquiring too large a monopoly. For instance, he was anxious to approach the American Government with a view to reducing cable rates and ship rates.

PRESIDENT WILSON expressed his complete agreement with Sir Robert Borden's purpose. The common trusteeship he had proposed was intended to bring about these very objects. He thought one reason why the German cable referred to by Baron Makino had not paid was because it constituted merely an independent piece, which did not enter into the general system. With the permission of the Council, he would formulate a definite draft resolution for discussion at the next meeting of the Council.

MR. LANSING thought that the draft resolution might very well be drawn up on the lines of the Article dealing with the surrender of German Colonies.

(It was agreed that President Wilson should formulate a draft resolution for discussion at the next meeting of the Council of Ten to the effect that all German Cables seized during the war should be transferred to the Allied and Associated Powers as trustees, who would determine the future working of the cables in the interests of the Powers concerned.)

The meeting then adjourned.

T MS (SDR, RG 256, 180.03101/66, DNA).

From Tasker Howard Bliss, with Enclosures

My dear Mr. President: Paris, May 1, 1919.

I enclose, herewith, papers this moment received from Colonel Conger, one of the General Pershing's assistant chiefs of staff, and who is in charge of confidential work in Germany.

Sincerely yours, Tasker H. Bliss.

TLS (WP, DLC).

E N C L O S U R E I

Arthur Latham Conger to Tasker Howard Bliss

Dear General Bliss: Treves, April 30, 1919.

I enclose a statement of an interview with Count Brockdorff-Rantzau just before he went to Paris which I think should go to the President alone, but which you will know how best to handle. It has added interest in connection with the interviews with members of the German Cabinet being sent you through Major Tyler.[1]

Sincerely yours, A. L. Conger.

TCL (WP, DLC).

[1] That is, Maj. Royall Tyler.

E N C L O S U R E I I

Interview with Count Brockdorff-Rantzau
(April 28)

I went to see Count B.R. to arrange with him in person about communicating with him (through Berlin) while he is in Paris. After this had been done he asked my views in regard to the course the negociations were likely to take. I replied that I thought the U. S. would be very liberal in allowing Germany a free hand to speak her mind, but that a time would come when the U. S. would indicate that Germany had better sign and sign quick. He replied: "How shall we be told that: through you, or someone else?"

His manner in saying that indicated entire acceptance of the advice and my opinion is that he will sign when told that the time has arrived.

I said I did not know how we would be told. He then said: "I wish very much that I could see the President alone. If that be possible many difficulties would be cleared away."

E N C L O S U R E I I I

Treves, Germany, April 30, 1919.

INTERVIEWS OF A CONFIDENTIAL AGENT WITH MEMBERS OF THE GERMAN GOVERNMENT.

Berlin, April 26 and 27, 1919.

President Ebert: The President seemed very pessimistic as to the future and does not think that Germany can sign the peace if the conditions are on the basis indicated in the French Press. The President gave it as his opinion that world-wide chaos will result if the peace is not signed. The German Government's view of the peace question, as it has been adopted, (and the President is in entire accord with it), is to sign the peace if it be in any way possible. The President does not see any great difficulty in the Italian matter, and the German Government has no intention to exploit the situation in order to get into close relations with Italy or any other of the Allied Governments separately. The food question is still the main question in Germany and no man can say what will happen in Germany if the blockade is kept up. The President mentioned that while some members of the Cabinet were of the opinion that Germany should refuse to sign the Peace Terms if territorial cessions outside the 14 points are insisted upon, he himself has confidence that the Peace Conference will be a real conference and clear up all matters of difficulty.

Mr. Erzberger: Mr. Erzberger stated that the decision of March 30th (by this he probably refers to the statement of the peace terms which Germany could accept, previously sent in),[1] still stands. Erzberger is of the opinion that Germany will make peace in any possible way so long as the 14 points are not overstepped.

Mr. Erzberger is anxious to know whether the United States will hold back the German capital now in the hands of the public Trustee, and also whether the United States Government will forbid the extending of private credits to Germany after peace is signed.

Mr. Erzberger's opinion of the Italian affair is that President Wilson meant Clemenceau when speaking to Orlando.

The outside political work of Mr. Erzberger will close with the opening of the Peace Conference, but he will continue to be one of the most active members of the Cabinet.

Count Bernstorff: Count Bernstorff is to be acting Minister of Foreign Affairs during the absence of Count Rantzau. He is very pessimistic about signing the peace, but he is one of the party in favor of accepting peace even if the terms are more severe than are believed by others to be possible of acceptance. Bernstorff still stands on the platform of March 30th, (referring to the same document).

He wants a very close friendship to the United States and believes that only American capital can enable Germany to regain a bare economic existence. He considers the Italian situation to be good and has foreseen that President Wilson will keep his word.

Count Bernstorff also stated that he hoped that the Americans would not allow the Peace Congress to be broken up on account of difficulties which might arise, until Mr. Wilson received practical information on the question through this connection. Personally Bernstorff will forward the signing of peace in every way possible.

Mr. Scheidermann [Scheidemann]: Mr. Scheidermann wants peace signed if in any way possible. Both he and the leaders of his party have said so to Brockdorf[f]-Rantzau. He emphasized the internal difficulties of Germany and the necessity for having a big army so long as these internal difficulties keep up. As an example, he stated that he had notified the Minister of Finance[2] to put up 300,000,000 marks for the War Cripples which measure had been forced on the Government by the Independent and Communist Socialists.

Speaking of the War Indemnities, Mr. Scheidermann said that he had held a conference with the big bankers who had informed him that they could not see at present any way in which to pay Germany's debts. Various sources from which the Government formerly drew a big income are cut off at present, and worse than that, draw on the Government for immense amounts to be given their employees. Take for example, he said, the Post-office, which formerly was one of the large sources of income to the Government. Minister Giesberts was forced today to sign an agreement with the telegraph and telephone workers (not clerks), which gives them an income of from 6,000 to 8,000 marks a year. Had this not been signed all telegraph and telephone lines of Germany would have been tied up. Interference with the Railroad traffic owing to the strikes and to lack of coal, also weakened the Government financially. Mr. Scheidermann said "we are absolutely willing to sign the peace, but it must be a peace which gives Germany a living." He hopes for an economic union between [the] United States and Germany and is sure that alone can put Germany to work again. In the matter of shipping, he asked to be informed whether the German ships would be given back or not. If the German ships are not given back it will mean a destruction of Germany's entire foreign commerce. He says that the German Cabinet is a unit in hoping that the American Army of Occupation will be sent back home by way of Hamburg and Bremen. He also hopes that the United States will give private credits to the Germans and help them to build up.

He ended the interview by saying that if the present Government cannot make peace, no other government can; that the government will have to resign if it cannot make peace is certain. A government further to the left is impossible: a government by the right cannot exist as it has no basis. We know what will happen if we cannot sign the peace for no Government will then be present that can maintain order in Germany. The only way to protect Germany against disorder and by that means also to protect the other European countries, is to make the German Government able to sign the peace.

Count Brockdorf[f]-Rantzau—Says that he is prepared to sign the peace if in any way possible.

T MSS (WP, DLC).

[1] See the memorandum printed as Enclosure I with T. H. Bliss to WW, April 1, 1919, Vol. 56. The memorandum had apparently been written by Walter Loeb, a young German officer in contact with Col. Arthur Latham Conger at Trier, at the behest of Matthias Erzberger. Conger, after deleting a reference to possible joint German-American action in Russia, forwarded the memorandum to Paris for the attention of the American peace commissioners. For careful analyses of what is known of the origins of the memorandum, see Schwabe, *Woodrow Wilson, Revolutionary Germany, and Peacemaking*, pp. 309-12, and Fritz T. Epstein, "Zwischen Compiègne und Versailles: Geheime amerikanische Militärdiplomatie in der Periode des Waffenstillstandes 1918/19: Die Rolle des Obersten Arthur L. Conger," *Vierteljahrshefte für Zeitgeschichte*, III (Oct. 1955), 412-24.

[2] Bernhard Jakob Ludwig Dernburg, former German Colonial Secretary and head of the German Information Service in New York, 1914-1915.

From Tasker Howard Bliss:

Dear Mr. President: Paris, May 1, 1919.

I gave Marshal Foch a statement in writing of the information that is needed in order to understand the exact application of the proposed Article[1] which carries over into the Peace Terms all of the clauses of the Armistice which are not inconsistent with the Peace Terms. He replied in substance as follows, saying that he would follow it by a letter which I am still waiting for.

He said that the proposed Article was a blanket clause which had originally been put in by the English as a safeguard. He said that he did not know the text of the Peace Terms; that no one had ever shown him a text of the Peace Terms and that he had no information on the subject. Lacking this information he was unable to tell what clauses of the Armistice were inconsistent with the Peace Treaty as drawn up and what terms of the Armistice not being inconsistent with the terms of the Peace Treaty would remain in force.

The Marshal said that he could not even tell the relation of the Armistice Terms to the *Military* Peace Terms, not to speak of financial and economic matters which are treated of in both the Peace Treaty and the Armistice. He said that he did not know even which of the military terms drafted by his Committee had been retained and which had been thrown out, nor how those retained had been altered.

When I receive the Marshal's written statement I shall forward it to you, but I am sure that it will simply confirm the above.

The Marshal's statement is what was to have been expected and would have to be made by anyone of whom the same question was asked. It shows the danger of the introduction of Clause 46 in the Peace Terms because neither the Marshal nor anyone else can tell what it means; nor can anyone know what it means until after the Treaty is formally presented and we have an opportunity to make the necessary comparison.

Very sincerely, Tasker H. Bliss.

TLS (WP, DLC).

[1] That is, Article 46.

Hankey's and Mantoux's Notes of a Meeting of the Council of Four[1]

I.C.-179A. Quai d'Orsay, May 1, 1919, 5:45 p.m.

1. M. JULES CAMBON gave an account of his interview with the German Delegates. Having been charged with the verification of their credentials, and having invited them to meet him at Versailles, he received a telegram stating that the German representatives would be presided over by Herr Landsberg, the German Minister of Justice, and would include Herr Simons, the Commissary-General for Judicial Questions and Director of the Department of Justice, Foreign Office, [and] the Advocate Counsel, Councillor of Legation Gauss,[2] who would be at the Trianon Palace to bring the German credentials and would ask to receive in exchange the credentials of the Allied and Associated Powers. He had then sent a message to suggest that Herr Brockdorff-Rantzau as Head of the German Commission, should accompany the delegates. He had addressed a few words to the German delegates, and had asked for their credentials, which had been handed over. They had then asked for the Allied and Associated credentials and he had handed them over. He had told them that if they had any observations to make on the credentials of the Allied and Associated Powers, they would meet again. After that they separated. He had received the impression that Herr Brockdorff-Rantzau and his colleagues were profoundly moved and that their attitude towards the Allied and Associated Powers was what it

[1] The complete text of Hankey's minutes is printed in *PPC*, V, 403-406.

[2] That is, Otto Landsberg, Walter Simons, and Friedrich Wilhelm Otto Gaus.

should be. Herr Brockdorff-Rantzau, who knows and speaks French fluently, as well as his officials, had said what they had to say in German, and had brought an interpreter. He felt it his duty to submit to the representatives of the Allied and Associated Powers that it was within the right of those Governments to decide whether the Germans should be permitted to speak German or should have to speak French or English.

M. CLEMENCEAU said you could not forbid them speaking in their own language. He said that in the negotiations of 1871, Bismarck had spoken French when he was pleased, and German when he was not.

MR. BALFOUR pointed out the inconvenience of having the interpreter for speech into two languages.

PRESIDENT WILSON said that the exchange of views would be in writing and that there would be very little speechmaking.

MR. LLOYD GEORGE asked if M. Cambon had ascertained anything as to the German views of publicity of the Peace Treaty.

M. CAMBON said the question had not been raised. In reply to Mr. Lansing, he said that the credentials of the Allied and Associated Powers were in the hands of the Germans for determination and vice versa.

In reply to M. Clemenceau, he said he had not fixed the date of the next meeting. Knowing the Germans as he did, he felt sure it would take them some time to examine all the credentials of the Allied and Associated Powers. The same applied to his own Commission, which he proposed should meet the following afternoon. He asked for 48 hours for examination of the German credentials, and would not be prepared to make any report before Saturday.

PRESIDENT WILSON said it had just been learnt that the Drafting Committee would probably require until Tuesday, as the date for handing the Treaty to the Germans. He suggested, therefore, that M. Jules Cambon's Committee should make a careful scrutiny of the German credentials.

(This M. Cambon undertook to do.)

(Mr. White, M. Cambon, Lord Hardinge and M. Kimura[3] withdrew.)

2. MR. LLOYD GEORGE raised the question of whether some communication should not be made to the Italians. He suggested that a message should be sent to the Ambassador to the effect that for drafting reasons the handing over of the Treaty had been put off until Tuesday.

[3] Kimura was a secretary in the Japanese Ministry of Foreign Affairs as well as in the Japanese delegation to the peace conference. The Editors have been unable to learn his given name.

MR. BALFOUR suggested the communication should be made to the Marquis Imperiali. When the Italian Delegation left, Baron Sonnino had written him a civil note to say that the Marquis Imperiali was left in charge.

PRESIDENT WILSON thought that the Marquis Imperiali was the person to address with any communication or approach we might have to make. This, however, in his view, should not be a communication from the Conference, but merely a communication from M. Pichon to the Italian Ambassador in Paris.

M. CLEMENCEAU asked what exactly M. Pichon should say.

PRESIDENT WILSON suggested he should say that as a mere matter of opinion, the Drafting Committee did not expect to be ready with the Treaty until Tuesday.

MR. LLOYD GEORGE suggested he should add that we expected to meet the Germans on Tuesday.

(It was agreed that:

(1) M. Pichon should inform the Italian Ambassador in Paris that the Drafting Committee did not expect to have the Treaty ready for the Germans until Tuesday, and that the Allied and Associated Powers expected to meet the Germans on Tuesday.

(2) That this should merely be a message from M. Pichon to the Italian Ambassador and not a formal message from the Conference to the Italian Government.

3. M. PICHON said he had some information to the effect that there was a certain movement against the Italian Government, from the Socialist side on the part of the M. Lussati[4] and from the opposite side on the part of M. Tittoni.

(At this point M. Pichon and Mr. Lansing withdrew.)

4. PRESIDENT WILSON communicating a number of reports he had received about the attitude towards the Peace Treaty of the various members of the German Government including Herren Brockdorff-Rantzau, Ebert, Scheidemann, Bernsdorff, and others.

5. PRESIDENT WILSON read a letter he had had from General Bliss describing the conversation with Marshal Foch on the subject of the elimination of Article 46 from the Military Terms.

(This is the Article keeping the Armistice in force so far as not inconsistent with the Treaty.)

The tenour of Marshal Foch's replies had rather been that he did not know enough of the stipulation of the Peace Treaty to judge of the matter.

President Wilson recalled the previous provisional decision to

[4] Luigi Luzzatti, not Lussati, was not a member of the Socialist party. Pichon undoubtedly said "Turati," that is, Filippo Turati, a Socialist, who spoke after Orlando and said that he and his comrades would not "drink of" Orlando's "cup." London *Times*, May 1, 1919.

eliminate this Article and proposed that it should now be regarded as settled.

M. CLEMENCEAU said he had no objection.

MR. LLOYD GEORGE agreed, unless his experts should raise any objection.

§ Mantoux's notes:

Wilson. I received from Trier a letter from Colonel Conger informing me about an interview he had had with Brockdorff-Rantzau, en route to Paris, on April 28. Brockdorff asked his impression about the way in which the negotiations would take place. The Colonel told him that the United States would demonstrate much liberalism in permitting the Germans to explain themselves, but that the time would come when they would be invited to sign, and to sign without delay. Brockdorff asked if it would be known in advance when that moment would be. The Colonel responded that he would be informed about it.

Some American agents in Germany have had interviews with several of the most important people in the German state, and it could be interesting to summarize them. Ebert appears to be very pessimistic; he believes it is impossible to sign the peace on the basis which the French press seems to indicate. On the other hand, he believes that, if Germany does not sign, the consequence will be chaos for Germany and for the world. He hopes he can sign. He has shown no desire to turn the Italian incident to his advantage. He hopes that the conference will be a true conference and that Germany will not be asked to make territorial cessions in contradiction to the Fourteen Points.

Erzberger says that the decision of March 30—I think that is a declaration made by the German Assembly—is still valid. Germany will sign the treaty if the Fourteen Points are respected. He appears to be very anxious to obtain commercial credit for Germany in America. About Italy, he seems to believe that the warning given by President Wilson to Orlando is addressed indirectly to Clemenceau. Our old friend Count Bernstorff also adheres to the declaration of March 30. He wants Germany to have good relations with the United States. If he has this desire, he will do well not to return to America. He states that he will assist the signing of the peace with all his power.

Scheidemann declares himself favorable to the signature if it is not absolutely impossible. He laments over Germany's internal difficulties, speaks of the necessity of having an army in order to deal with them. About the war indemnities, he had a conference with some German bankers, who do not see how the country can ever pay its debts. The revenues of the state have considerably diminished, at the same time as the salaries of the civil servants increased in a very great proportion. The postal administration has just been obliged to accord to its subordinate personnel appointments which vary from 6,000 to 8,000 marks per years. Scheidemann says that he is prepared to sign any peace which will permit Germany to live. He asks if the German commercial ships will be returned: without them, all Germany's commerce is lost. If the present government—he says—cannot make the peace, no other government can do it. The only means of saving order in Germany and in Europe is the signature of an acceptable peace.

Clemenceau. Altogether, this information is not too bad.

Wilson. General Bliss saw Marshal Foch, as he had agreed, about maintaining in the peace treaty certain arrangements of the Armistice. The Marshal says that, not knowing the text of the treaty, he does not know whether there is a contradiction between this text and the one of the Armistice and where it would be necessary to complete the one by the other.

Balfour. I hope that what is necessary was done to prevent what General Wilson fears: he says that if certain arrangements of the Armistice are not maintained in the treaty, the army of occupation will find itself one day deprived of the right of requisition, of lodging, etc.

Wilson. I would not willingly run the risk of allowing this article to stand as it is without a precise justification. §

M. CLEMENCEAU said he had been seeking the formula for his communication to the Austrian and Hungarian Delegates.

The following is a rough translation of the Note as agreed to:

"The Supreme Council of the Allied and Associated Powers has decided to invite the Austrian/Hungarian Delegates furnished with full powers, to come to St. Germain on the 12th/15th May in the evening, in order to examine the conditions of Peace. The Austrian/Hungarian Government is therefore invited to communicate forthwith the number and quality [qualifications] of the Delegates they propose to send to St. Germain, as well as the number and quality of the persons who will accompany them. The Mission will have to remain strictly confined to its role, and should include only persons qualified for their special tasks."

NOTE. The reason for inviting the Austrians and Hungarians on different dates is that the two Governments are not friendly.

(It was agreed

1. That M. Clemenceau should, on behalf of the Preliminary Peace Conference, despatch a Note on the above lines to the Austrian and Hungarian Governments.

2. That M. Pichon should be authorised to notify this to the Italian Ambassador at the same time as the information referred to in Minute 2 above.)

Sir Maurice Hankey was instructed to ask the Secretary-General to speed up various Commissions dealing with subjects affecting Peace with Austria, and to inform them that their reports should all be complete not later than May 12th.

(M. Dutasta entered the room.)

M. DUTASTA read a communication from the Belgian Delegation, asking for—

1. The text of the Articles in the Treaty of Peace, which they would have to submit to the King of the Belgians.
2. A wording of the Articles in regard to the surrender of the German Colonies.
3. That the summary of the Peace Treaty might be communicated in advance to the Belgian Delegation, in order that it might be published in Brussels at the same time as in Paris.

(It was agreed to discuss this question on the following morning.)

T MS (SDR, RG 256, 180.03401/136, DNA); Mantoux, I, 446-47.

Two Letters to Robert Lansing

My dear Mr. Secretary: Paris, 1 May, 1919.

I would be very much obliged if you would act on the enclosed information[1] by obtaining an interview with Mr. Paderewski and expressing to him our great anxiety about this whole situation and our hope that no part of Haller's Army will be used at the Ukrainian front. The whole temper of the conference concerning the settlement of the boundary question there will undoubtedly depend upon the moderation and prudence with which the Poles as well as the Ukrainians act at this critical time. I tried myself to point that out to Mr. Paderewski the other day.[2]

Cordially and faithfully yours, [Woodrow Wilson]

[1] See THB to WW, April 18, 1919 (second letter of that date); the minutes of the Council of Four printed at April 21, 1919, 4 p.m.; WW to THB, April 22, 1919, all in Vol. 57; and THB to I. J. Paderewski, April 24, 1919.

[2] The Editors have found no record of this encounter. Perhaps it took place before or after the Plenary Session of April 28, at which Paderewski was present.

My dear Mr. Secretary: Paris, 1 May, 1919.

The fact is that while a definite decision was arrived at by the Council of Four to extend all possible assistance to Roumania in the matters mentioned,[1] I merely said that I would see what participation in that assistance was possible on the part of the United States. So far as I can see, the only possible participation is in the extension of credits to Roumania which will enable her to purchase supplies of different kinds.

If you would be kind enough to have a conversation with General Bliss about this his memory will be much more exact than mine of the conversations which I had with him immediately after the decision referred to and of the general impression that was left upon his mind and mine as to what was to be done.

Sincerely yours, [Woodrow Wilson]

CCL (WP, DLC).

[1] Wilson was replying to RL to WW, April 25, 1919.

To Felix Frankfurter

My dear Mr. Frankfurter: Paris, 1 May, 1919.

Just a line to express my very deep appreciation of your note of the 29th. In these times of perplexity and anxiety such messages are particularly refreshing and heartening.

Cordially and sincerely yours, [Woodrow Wilson]

CCL (WP, DLC).

To George Lansbury

My dear Mr. Lansbury: Paris, 1 May, 1919.

Thank you for your generous letter of the 24th of April. It did me a lot of good to get it and to recall my stimulating conversation with you.

In unavoidable haste,

Cordially and sincerely yours, [Woodrow Wilson]

CCL (WP, DLC).

To Eleutherios Vénisélos

My dear Mr. Veneselos: Paris, 1 May, 1919.

Thank you very warmly for your letter of the 29th. You may be sure that I was glad to play any part in recognizing the claim of Greece to be included in the first council of the League of Nations, and I want to take this occasion to express my warm appreciation of the very generous and effective support and very illuminating counsel you gave regarding the whole plan, while the Commission of which we were members was at work. I think the outcome is a matter for general congratulations.

Cordially and sincerely yours, [Woodrow Wilson]

CCL (WP, DLC).

From Robert Lansing, with Enclosure

My dear Mr. President: Paris, May 1, 1919.

I am sending you herewith a copy of a cablegram received by the Commission yesterday from the American Diplomatic Agent at Cairo,[1] transmitting a message from the King of the Hedjaz to the Arab Diplomatic Agent at Cairo. As this message is somewhat garbled, I am having it repeated.

May I request an expression of your views as to whether it would be advisable to show this message to General Allenby?

I am, my dear Mr. President,

Faithfully yours, Robert Lansing

TSL (WP, DLC).

[1] That is, Hampson Gary.

E N C L O S U R E

Cairo. April 22, 1919.
Rec'd. 8:25 a.m. 30th.

Urgent. April 22—9 p.m. Please forward following telegram to Department and American Peace Commission. No. 455 April 22, 9 p.m. The Arab Diplomatic Agent has called at the agency and asked that I transmit to the President the following message he has received from King of the Hedjaz. "You are directed to call at once on the American Agent at Cairo and ask him officially that he, on my behalf, inform President Wilson that I do not agree by any way or form, of splitting a span ? of the Arabic countries from their combination; otherwise I withdraw myself at once from the matter. But I do not object if Elhedjaz is annexed to Syria, Mesopotamia or Nageid[1] in a manner of uprightness and power. Inform us as soon as possible. Hussein."

I respectfully request that I be permitted to show this message to General Allenby and I ask for any special instructions in this connection that the Department may judge advisable to transmit to me.

Gary.

TC telegram (WP, DLC).

[1] A garbled form of Nejd (or Najd, Nedjed), a semiautonomous region of the Arabian Peninsula to the east of the Hedjaz, which was united with the latter in 1932 to form the Kingdom of Saudi Arabia.

From Robert Lansing

My dear Mr. President: Paris, May 1, 1919.

I have just received notice that the British have requested that the question of Finnish independence and recognition of that Government be placed on the Agenda for a meeting of the Council of Foreign Ministers. It brings us face to face with a general policy as to whether we should recognize as separate and distinct sovereignties any portion of the former Russian Empire other than the portion which is included within the boundaries of Finland and to which we have previously given our adhesion.

I do not wish to raise the merits in the case of Finland which, as you know, are exceptionally strong, but I would like your advice as to the general policy to be adopted in the case of the recognition of states carved out of Russia.

Faithfully yours, [Robert Lansing]

CCL (R. Lansing Papers, DLC).

From William Shepherd Benson

My dear Mr. President: [Paris] 1 May, 1919

With a view to assuring the safe withdrawal of our Army forces now in Northern Russia, as well as providing guns of sufficient power to cover their embarkation, we have recently increased our own Naval forces in those waters. Other vessels now enroute will give us for this duty a total of one cruiser, two gunboats, and three torpedo craft of the Eagle class. In addition to these I am holding on the Scottish coast twelve submarine chasers, which had been requested earlier. These vessels, of course, will cooperate closely with the Allied forces which are in, or will be sent to these waters. The British force is of considerable strength and the French are represented.

With a view to determining the advisability of sending the submarine chasers, I have made an inquiry through our Naval representative in London to determine the views of the British Admiralty as to the desirability and advisability of sending these small vessels to augment the Naval force of the Allies and ourselves. In reply, I have been informed that the British favor sending our submarine chasers; that Rear Admiral McCully,[1] our Naval Representative, believes that they will be of value in operations in the Dwina River, should these be decided upon; but that if intended only to assist in the evacuation of troops, they would probably not be needed.

Before taking any action, I request to be informed of what policy has been adopted and whether or not the Naval force which we send should be prepared to assist in active operations or whether it should merely be of a character such as to insure the safe withdrawal of our land forces. Very respectfully, W. S. Benson.

TLS (WP, DLC).

[1] That is, Newton Alexander McCully.

Tasker Howard Bliss to Eleanora Anderson Bliss

My dear Nellie: Hotel Crillon, Paris May 1, 1919.

. . . I also enclose some copies of letters which I wish you could carefully preserve for me. Please note the one dated April 29. This morning we were all mortified and angry at learning that the President had yielded the Japanese claims. Last Saturday he talked to us about it, being evidently disposed to yield then. He is influenced solely by Mr. H. who is a trimmer. He said he would ask our advice but didn't, evidently seeing from the attitude of Mr. L., Mr. W. and myself that we were not disposed to yield. On the morning of the 29th I expressed my views quite strongly to my colleagues (L. and W.) and they fully concurred with me. They asked me to write a letter to the President and convey to him these views. The enclosed of the 29th is a copy of it. How he can reconcile his attitude to the one he took on the Italian claims on the east coast of the Adriatic we do not see. Now this must go.

TCL (T. H. Bliss Papers, DLC).

From Norman Hezekiah Davis

My dear Mr. President: Paris, 1st May, 1919.

The Secretary of the Treasury has cabled me to request that you withdraw your approval of the establishment of $22,250,000 of the $40,000,000 credit which was authorized by you for Belgian relief but which has not yet been established by the Secretary. The Commission for Relief in Belgium will complete its operations in the early part of May, turning over its functions to the Belgian Government, and the estimated requirements for completing its relief program will necessitate establishing only $17,750,000 of the above credit of $40,000,000 originally approved by you.

I am enclosing for your signature a formal letter of authorization[1] in case such action meets with your approval.

Cordially and sincerely yours, Norman H. Davis

TLS (WP, DLC).

[1] WW to C. Glass, May 1, 1919, TLS (WP, DLC). However, see WW to N. H. Davis, May 3, 1919.

Two Telegrams from Thomas Nelson Page to the American Mission

Rome May 1st. 1919.

280. IMPORTANT. URGENT.

Learned late last night that at full meeting of Italian delegation to Peace Conference, it was decided that the delegation could not return Paris unless some step be taken there opening way for them to do so with hope of some adjustment of the Adriatic problem which they can accept, and further, until the other powers are agreed among themselves what this adjustment shall be.

Also, that Ambassador Barrère[1] was arriving Rome last night and it is hoped he may prove link between the Italian delegation and other powers at Paris opening way to adjustment. Also that my visit to Premier Orlando of previous day was discussed and Orlando said that I had nothing to offer, only expressed regret at the situation, spoke kindly and urged necessity of tranquilizing people instead of exciting them. Also learned that on a report that the Jugo-Slavs were threatening to attack Italians at Fiume, General Diaz was sent there to look over situation and take due measures to prevent surprises and he left last night for Trieste.

I believe delegation desires to return to Paris, but afraid to do so unless conditions above met. Serious Italians believe that a revolution may result if government does not get Fiume in some form so that it may be said that Italy has Fiume. Some of Orlando's friends have advised him to resign.

In order to save friendship between two peoples, might not at some opportune moment some modifications be suggested by the President with Fiume conceded as Italian under such conditions as may meet fully principle of Auto decision. This, however, will require extreme care not to permit impression that Italy first was unjustly denied everything and at last received, under compulsion, only a part of her real due. Nelson Page

[1] That is, Camille Barrère.

Rome. May 1st, 1919.

281. IMPORTANT. CONFIDENTIAL.

Monday I called on Premier Orlando to call attention to violence of persistent press attacks on the President and impress upon him the importance of tranquilizing people instead of permitting them to be continually excited. He declared his great desire to calm them and his speech was in fact more moderate in tone than when delivered on his arrival Rome.

On yesterday having failed to get an appointment with Baron Sonnino with same object I wrote him a personal note to the same effect protesting against permitting the attacks to continue.[1] I send translation of his reply just received. A more tranquil condition than formerly evident today not much affected.

"Dear Ambassador:

In reply to Your Excellency's letter of today, I do not need to assure you how well known to me is the work accomplished by Your Excellency for the purpose of improving more and more the relations between the U. S. and Italy; how much I appreciate it and how much my own conduct is inspired by similar sentiments.

The violence assumed by a part of the press is certainly deplorable even if it finds an explanation in the events of these days and I have no such facts to bring this matter to the attention of the Ministry of the Interior in order that it may in the interests of the good relations between the two countries restrain any excesses and especially any attack whatever upon the Pres. of the U. S.

Pray accept dear Ambassador the expression of my highest consideration. Signed. Sonnino." Nelson Page.

T telegrams (WP, DLC).

[1] See T. N. Page to S. Sonnino, April 30, 1919.

A Memorandum by Henry Churchill King and Charles Richard Crane

[c. May 1, 1919]

I.

THE DANGERS TO THE ALLIES FROM A SELFISH EXPLOITATION OF THE TURKISH EMPIRE.

In approaching a practicable plan for the division of the Turkish Empire, the Allies should bear clearly in mind, that their fidelity to their announced aims in the war is here peculiarly to be tested; and that, in the proportion in which the division of the Turkish Empire by the Allies approaches a division primarily determined by the selfish national and corporate interests of the Allies, in just that proportion it will be subjected to the following dangers:

1. Such a division would have to be forced upon the peoples concerned—not chosen by them.

2. A large number of troops would thus be required to establish and to maintain such a division. This might prove a very serious consideration.

3. Men like President Gates[1] of Robert College believe that the mere announcement of such a division would be likely to provoke further massacres of Christians in Turkey—a consideration of great moment.

4. Such selfish exploitation of Turkey would not only certainly call out the resentment of the most solid portion of the American people, as emphatically not illustrating the ends for which America came into the war; but would also tend to alienate the best sentiment among all the Allies. To eliminate from the cause of the Allies this weight of moral judgment would involve a loss of power not lightly to be faced.

5. Such exploitation would mean, too, the deliberate sowing of dissension of the gravest kind among the Allies themselves—threatening the moral unity of their cause and entailing serious world consequences.

6. Coupled with similar decisions already reached, it would also go far to convince men of independent moral judgment all over the world—including many previously ardent upholders of the cause of the Allies—that the aims of the Allies had become as selfish and ruthless as those of the Germans had been. That would carry with it its own consequences.

7. For one thing, when such moral condemnation became clear—as it certainly would in time—it would in itself tend to encourage rebellious uprusings [uprisings] on the part of the national groups, and to increase general sympathy with such uprisings.

8. For another thing, America cannot be expected to furnish financial backing for schemes of selfish exploitation—even sometimes directed precisely against herself.

II.

MEMORANDUM OF CONSIDERATIONS LOOKING TO THE DIVISION OF TURKEY.

1. It is desirable that the Turkish Empire as such should definitely cease to exist. The repeated massacres—Armenian and Syrian, and the demonstrated age-long incapacity for good government demand this.

2. The strategic position of Constantinople and the Straits—com-

[1] Caleb Frank Gates.

mercial, political, military and symbolic—demand that they should be clearly taken out of the hands of the Turks, and that the Sultan[2]—if he is to continue in any form—be removed to some other capital like Brusa. The moral judgment of the world calls for not less than this. The Indian protest at this point should not prevail; for there is good evidence that the Caliphate has no such present vitality for the Moslem World as is often assumed.[3]

3. There would be real danger, even under a mandate, in keeping intact the Empire as a whole, or perhaps even the Asia Minor portion of the Empire,—danger of a later revival of the Turkish Empire and repetition of its past history, on account of jealousies of the Powers, etc.

4. The age-long and hideous misrule of the Turks, coupled with their occupation of territory of critical significance to the world, make unusual restrictions necessary in their case, for the greater good of the world.

5. The Empire, too, as it has existed, is not truly a unit from any point of view—certainly not the Arabic and the non-Arabic speaking portions. Its interests—except those of good government—are not one. There would probably be real gain, consequently, in dividing its problems and seeking separate solutions of them. Syria, Mesopotamia, and Arabia, for example, each has a kind of unity of its own.

6. Moreover, the Mohammedan races of Asia Minor do not constitute a truly unified national group. (See Ramsay "Impressions of Turkey"[4] pp. 94 ff. and 99 ff. upon this point) and cannot urge the full claims of such a group.

7. If, then, the Allies are now ready, under the stimulus of the war, boldly to break with the whole previous Turkish situation, that may be better for the world than the more timid policy supported by the missionaries which suggests fear of the Turks and compromise with them, in spite of massacres and of their hideous misrule.

8. It is right that the more able, industrious and enterprising groups, like the Greeks and Armenians, should be recognized in the settlement.

9. It is right that the long relations of Greece, France, Italy and Great Britain with various parts of the Turkish Empire should be given due weight also.

[2] Mehmed VI.

[3] A reference to the protest by representatives of the Muslim inhabitants of India against the proposed separation of Constantinople and the Straits from Turkey. They argued against such a separation essentially on the ground that Constantinople was the seat of the Sultan of Turkey who, in his capacity as Caliph, was the spiritual leader of all Muslims. For a detailed review of their arguments, see the minutes of the Council of Four, May 17, 1919, 4:30 p.m., printed in *PPC*, V, 690-701.

[4] Sir William Mitchell Ramsay, *Impressions of Turkey During Twelve Years' Wanderings* (New York and London, 1897).

10. If the proposed divisions can be made genuine mandataries under the League of Nations, with real regard for the peoples under the mandates, with annual reports to the League, and with limited terms, something like a generous rivalry for good government and in service of the peoples involved might result, especially if America took a significant mandate.

All this may be said in recognition of the variety of interests involved in the problem of the breaking up of the Turkish Empire, and in favor of some division, on large lines, of that Empire.

11. But if the principles of national unity and of self-determination are to be applied at all to the Turkish people, at least a large central portion of Asia Minor, sufficient to provide for the bulk of the Turks under a single mandate, and with adequate outlets to the sea, should be left to them. For the present, such a province should be under a mandatory power, in order to secure to the Turks themselves that good government which they have so notoriously lacked. "The wishes of these communities," moreover, as the Covenant of the League of Nations says, "must be a principle consideration in the selection of the Mandatary."

12. The immemorial trade routes suggest the undesirability of breaking up the economic unity of Turkey, and so producing artificial barriers and wasteful arrangements. There should be a customs union, and other economic agreements, covering at least all of Asia Minor, and perhaps the whole of the old Empire.

13. In the light of all these considerations—local, racial, national and international—the following mandates for the old Turkish Empire might be justified.

A—For the Arabic-speaking portions of the Empire:

(1) A British Mandate for Mesopotamia, based on British fitness and the general desires of the peoples involved.

(2) The British acting as Agent for an International Mandate in Palestine, to guard the holy places and the entire territory for the benefit of all the peoples interested, and not simply for the Jews.

(3) For Arabia:

(a) The recognition of the independence of the Kingdom of the Hedjaz and of the title of King Husein.

(b) The establishment of the right of all national and racial groups among the Moslems in all countries to representation upon a Commission, acting under the League of Nations, for the Holy Places of Islam in Arabia.

(c) The recognition of Great Britain's general supervision of Arabia, with the proviso that she be held strictly responsible for the maintenance of the "open door" for all the members of the League of Nations. This would go far to remove the natural French and Italian jealousy of Britain's large territorial gains in this war.

(4) A French Mandate for Syria liberally interpreted, and frankly based, not on the primary desires of the people, but on the international need of preserving friendly relations between France and Great Britain.

B—For the non-Arabic-speaking portions of the Empire:

There seems to be good evidence that the first choice of the peoples of Asia Minor themselves would be for *a general American mandate*, perhaps with subsidiary mandates under the general mandate: recognizing the Greek and Armenian interests, the desirability of some provision for Turkish national unity, and the necessity of an international Constantinopolitan State.

This would have the double advantage of giving due deference to the wishes of the peoples concerned, and of administrative and economic unity.

But, on the other hand, so large a mandate for America would have its own peculiar difficulties, and America might be unwilling to assume so large a task; while it would also probably arouse the jealousy of the other Powers. Keeping Asia Minor intact would also involve some danger, especially with a mandate taken for a limited term of years, of a later revival of the Turkish Empire.

A composite mandate might remove some of the objections to a single and undifferentiated mandate.

If a single mandate for Asia Minor be set aside, a four-fold division is perhaps most naturally suggested:

(1) An American Mandate for an International Constantinopolitan State,—an essential world interest.

(2) A Mandate for Anatolia, under a supervision still to be determined, providing for the bulk of the Turkish people under a single mandate.

(3) An autonomous Greek region within Anatolia, covering Smyrna and contiguous territory, but not so large as to shut off the Turkish portion of Anatolia from good access to the Aegean Sea.

(4) An American Mandate for Armenia and the rest of the northern portion of Turkey, including Adana in order to give access to the Mediterranean Sea.

Henry Churchill King
Charles R. Crane
Commissioners.

Albert H. Lybyer
George R Montgomery
William Yale.[5]
Advisers.

TS MS (WP, DLC).

[5] Albert Howe Lybyer, Professor of History at the University of Illinois and a member of The Inquiry; the Rev. George Redington Montgomery, a Presbyterian minister born in Marash, Turkey, who had lived for some years in the Middle East; and Capt. William Yale, U.S.A., formerly an employee of the Standard Oil Co. in the Ottoman Empire, more recently a military observer in Palestine and Syria. All three were technical advisers to the King-Crane Commission.

From the Diary of Ray Stannard Baker

May 1st [1919]

The Chinese decision has caused a regular furor. Our whole delegation, except Col. House, who is for smoothing everything over, is for the Chinese case, & declare Wilson has made a terrible mistake. Williams, Hornbeck & others of our experts are openly sympathising with & helping the Chinese. I had a long talk with Secy Lansing, while he drew his interminable grotesque pictures on his pad of paper, & found him quite inconsolable. He said he would not, under any circumstances, defend the decision. He would not attack it. He would remain silent. He was for the right of the matter, he said, regardless of consequences. "And break up the Peace Conference?" I asked. "Even that, if necessary." Both Bliss & Henry White side with him. House is with the President: he favors all compromises, while the President knows when to compromise & when not to.

I had to tell the Commissioners what the decision of the Big Three had been: the President had not informed any of them. Lansing's secretary telephoned to me, asking about it.

I saw the President this evening & told him of the effect on the Chinese & on the correspondents. Wm Allen White is writing a strong article defending the President's position: & Frederick Moore & Smith[1] of the Associated Press, both of whom have been long in the far east, say that this, after all, however hard for the Chinese, was the only practical solution. On the whole I think we are getting over the *whole* of the problem. I do not try to make propaganda for the President's position: but I have been trying to have our correspondents see the whole thing in proportion—the problem in the broadest aspects, just as the President has had to face it. This broad view, of course, is not possible to the narrow partisans of the Chinese, like Williams—& Lansing, for that matter. *The truth is best.*

[1] Frederick Moore, correspondent for the *New York Tribune*, and Charles Stephenson Smith, correspondent for the Associated Press.

From the Diary of Edith Benham

May 1, 1919

The P. is getting so much tried by Poincaré. Constitutionally he has no right to interfere in any affairs of Government, and yet he is always meddling to the great disgust of Clemenceau. At the conference today the P. said L. George spoke of a message which he had sent to the Italian people via one of the newspapers. At this time it was most unfortunate for it stated that the Latin races should hold together now, and speaking of the close ties binding the French and Italians. Pichon, Minister of Foreign Affairs, was there and Clemenceau who heard this evidently for the first time, fairly stiffened in his chair and turned and glared at Pichon and asked if it was true, and then said it was odd that he had to hear it for the first time from the English! The P. feels that it is a grave discourtesy to him and to America. It would have been a perfectly proper message at any other time but this, but now it is a direct challenge to America. I don't hear quite so much now of what is going on because conversation has to be guarded at the table. I know what will probably appear in a few days that the Japanese question had to be compromised. I am sure he feels very uneasy and fears the situation will be misunderstood and badly viewed. There is no doubt of his dislike for Mr. Lansing, for he said bitterly, "The Secretary of State had the goodness to tell me that he, Bliss and White felt very bitterly about my arrangement in regard to China,"[1] so I imagine he has gone contrary to the views of the American delegates on that point.

[1] See the memorandum by RL printed at April 28, 1919.

Cary Travers Grayson to Joseph Patrick Tumulty

[Paris, May 1, 1919]

The solution of the Kiaochau question is regarded here both generally and by special friends of China, like Charles R. Crane, as remarkably favorable and fortunate, considering its rotten and complicated past, and the tangle of secret treaties in which she was enmeshed and from which she had to be extricated. It is regarded as a wonderful victory for the President. The Japanese themselves admit that they have made far greater concessions than they had even dreamed would be required of them. The Chinese agree that they have had their interests safeguarded in every way and they appreciate that the League of Nations eventually will look after them.

Grayson.

T telegram (WP, DLC).

Two Telegrams from Joseph Patrick Tumulty

[The White House, May 1, 1919]

No. 87 I have not made use of the Japanese statement,[1] but am keeping my ear to the ground and waiting. My feeling is that an attempt to explain the compromise, why it was made, would weaken our position instead of strengthening it. I will, therefore, do nothing about the Japanese matter unless you insist. It would help if I could unofficially say: first, the date of your probable return to this country; second, whether tour of the country to discuss the League of Nations is possible. The adoption of the labor programme as part of the peace treaty is most important, but not enough emphasis is being placed upon it. Could you not make a statement of some kind that we could use here, showing the importance of this programme as helping toward the stabilization of labor conditions throughout the world? Tumulty.

[1] That is, WW to JPT, April 30, 1919.

[The White House, May 1, 1919]

No. 88 There has been no apparent progress made between the Railroad Administration and Secretary Redfield's board in the matter of price fixing and the whole thing, [by reason of][1] the statements made by both sides, bids fair to become very disagreeably[2] ridiculous. I hope you will direct me to say to Mr. Hines that unless there is a [some] positive settlement by Saturday night, that you wish all negotiations to be at an end. Tumulty.

T telegrams (WP, DLC).

[1] Additions from the copy in the J. P. Tumulty Papers, DLC.

[2] "Disagreeably" not in Tumulty's copy.

From Samuel Gompers

Washington. May 1, 1919.

1806. For the President from Gompers:

"Redraft of preamble and nine points composing labors bill of rights[1] as presented at plenary session Monday by Sir Robert Borden not only weakens but practically nullifies whole program as outlined in bill of rights as approved by commission on international legislation. Clause one as redrafted repudiates the American principle enunciated in the Clayton Act stipulating that labor is not a commodity or article of commerce. With my associates of American Federation of Labor Mission to Paris I most earnestly urge that original draft be inserted in treaty of peace." Phillips, Acting.

T telegram (WP, DLC).
[1] Printed as an Enclosure with H. M. Robinson to WW, April 27, 1919.

From Carter Glass

Washington. May 1, 1919.

1803. VERY URGENT. For President from Glass.

As forecast in my cablegram March 15th[1] War Risk appropriation for family allowances to dependents of soldiers and sailors is exhausted. Director of Bureau[2] reports no funds available to pay April family allowances due May 1st. Amount required for April allowances is approximately $14,000,000. As allotments from soldiers' pay are included in same check with allowances it is administratively impossible for the Bureau to mail even allotments from pay without allowances although allotment fund of War Department is not exhausted. This therefore means that because of insufficiency of funds for allowances the money allotted by soldiers from their pay will also be withheld from their families. If allotment and allowance checks are delayed hardship and inconvenience will undoubtedly be visited upon families of soldiers with the result that protests will be heard in all sections of the country and find renewed expression upon the assembling of Congress. Regret necessity of burdening you with this situation but its seriousness is such to bear directly upon your decision respecting the date for the extra session of Congress. May I take the liberty of asking if it is possible for you to give me any light on this matter at this time. Meanwhile I shall have the Bureau prepare the checks with the purpose of mailing them as soon as Congress makes necessary appropriation. Bureau has sufficient funds for salaries and administrative expenses only to and including May 15th. Phillips, Acting.

T telegram (WP, DLC).
[1] See C. Glass to WW, March 15, 1919, Vol. 55.
[2] Col. Henry Dickinson Lindsley.

From the Diary of Dr. Grayson

Friday, May 2, 1919.

The President arose early and had breakfast at 8:15. He then disposed of a good deal of correspondence, and at 10:30 he saw a delegation of Congressmen—mostly members of the House of Representatives Military Affairs Committee.[1] He frankly explained to them some of the complications of the Italian and Chinese situations. They left the President fully satisfied that he was handling a

On his way to a meeting with the American Commissioners
at the Hôtel Crillon

The German delegation just before leaving for Versailles. From left to right: Robert Leinert, Carl Melchior, Johann Giesberts, Ulrich Karl Christian, Count von Brockdorff-Rantzau, Otto Landsberg, and Walther Max Adrian Schücking

Clemenceau addressing the Plenary Session of the Peace Conference in Trianon Palace at Versailles before the conditions of peace were presented to the German delegates. The principal delegate, Count von Brockdorff-Rantzau, can be seen sitting far to the left center with his colleagues. Wilson is sitting at Clemenceau's right, Lloyd George at his left.

The German delegation listening to Clemenceau. From center front: Schücking, Giesberts, Brockdorff-Rantzau, Landsberg, Leinert, and Melchior (partly hidden).

Robert Lansing, foreground, and Henry White, immediately behind, leaving Trianon Palace after the presentation of the peace terms to the German delegation.

The Chinese delegation to the Peace Conference. Lu Cheng-hsiang is in the front row, fifth from the left, followed by Wang Cheng-t'ing and Alfred (Saoke) Sze. V. K. Wellington Koo is also in the front row, third from the right.

The Japanese delegation to the Peace Conference. Seated from the left: Baron Nobuaki Makino, Marquis Kimmochi Saionji, and Viscount Sutemi Chinda.

Enjoying a day at the races. At Longchamps Race Course with, among others, Mrs. Wilson, Admiral Grayson (in uniform), and, far to the right, Bernard M. Baruch.

very delicate situation in an able manner and they so declared when seen by the newspapermen later.

At 11:00 o'clock the Big Three met here. They continued their discussion of the cable question.

The President had lunch at 1:00 o'clock, Sir William Wiseman, the British Government's personal publicity representative, being the guest. I had lunch with Ambassador Wallace, who was entertaining the Congressmen who had just called on the President. The Ambassador was anxious for me to help him out, as it was a stag lunch.

The President and Mrs. Wilson went for a ride after lunch, and the President then went to the Crillon Hotel. At four o'clock he went to the Quai d'Orsay to attend a meeting of the Big Three. This meeting was devoted to the consideration of the form that the treaty shall take when submitted to the Germans should Italy fail to announce her desire to resume her part in the negotiations. It was necessary to arrange a double form—one which would be in effect should Italy remain away from Paris and unrepresented, and another should she finally decide that the exigencies of the situation should make it necessary for her representatives to return here and resume their place in the negotiations. The question naturally was whether there should be four powers, the United States, France, Great Britain and Japan, or five, with Italy added. Arrangements were made to handle the situation no matter how it may develop.

At seven o'clock, the President, as usual, saw Ray Stannard Baker, and told him some of the things that transpired during the day, with a view to having the information conveyed to the press. . . .

The President, Mrs. Wilson, Miss Margaret, Dr. Axson and myself had dinner at seven o'clock. After dinner I asked the usual question: "What progress did you make today, Mr. President?" He said: "Most of the forenoon was consumed by Lloyd-George making erratic flights over Italy. Every day he seems to have a different view on the Italian situation, notwithstanding the fact that he approved of my statement when we discussed it. He is the most unsteady individual you can imagine. He takes one view today and settles on it. Then tomorrow he goes off on another tack. He is unstable. He is constantly turning somersaults. He is an impossible, incalculable person to do business with. Some days he is nothing more than a sentimental Tommy."

The President continued: "Today when Lloyd-George was in the midst of giving expression to his rambling ideas and uttering his fear concerning the outcome of a certain decision, I told him the following story: A young man was going along the road and he saw a young lassie milking a cow when he stopped and engaged in conversation with her. Suddenly the young man noticed a bull coming across the field with his head down, his tail up in the air, bellowing furiously, every now and then stopping and pawing the ground, and all the time approaching closer and closer to the young girl. Whereupon the young fellow said: 'Please run, my lassie, the bull is coming.' She seemed to be perfectly unconcerned and kept on in her conversation with him. He implored her again and again to leave as the angry bull was approaching. But she would not move. Finally, he said: 'My dear lassie, aren't you afraid of the bull?' She calmly said: 'Why should I be afraid of him? I am milking his mother-in-law.' " The President's object in relating this story was to calm the fears of Lloyd-George.

Tonight he discussed the characteristics of the French people—how simple they were in their thoughts. They often acted like little children. He said: "I have been frequently told that there is such a marked difference in the people of France since the armistice. Shortly after the armistice the people were most grateful and expressed their appreciation of what America had done in helping to win the war and of the warm feeling that the American people had for France. But now they show a reversal of this feeling. There seems to be a lack of appreciation and they assume the attitude that France did it all. It is really distressing when you know the French people to see how greedy they are for the material things of life. Their only feeling towards America now is one not alone ungrateful but they also appear to want money and aid of some kind from them. This applies to the rich and influential rather than to the poorer class. It is more noticeable in Paris than in rural France."

I told the President that certain American officers had told me that the feeling in Germany for the President was extremely fine; that they expressed the belief that he was the one man who would see that Germany was not looted and destroyed; that she would get justice at his hands. The President predicted that there will be intense feeling in Germany against him when the contents of the Peace Treaty are revealed. He said: "The terms of the treaty are particularly severe, but I have striven my level best to make them fair, and at the same time compel Germany to pay a just penalty. However, I fully realize that I will be the one on whom the blame will be placed. In their hearts the Germans dislike me because if I had kept America from entering the war Germany would have defeated the Allies. So I know that they blame me for their defeat. While they may be flattering me now, a reaction will set in when they read the treaty."

A day or two ago I sent to Mr. Venizelos, the Prime Minister of Greece, a photograph with the request that he autograph it for me. I had a very pleasant acquaintance with him and a great admiration for him. The President said that he considered Mr. Venizelos the greatest statesman in Europe. In response to my request, I received the following letter from Mr. Venizelos:

"I have duly received your card and the photograph—supposed to be a photo of mine—which you were asking me to autograph.

"In spite of the gloomy weather and of the weight of the duties which I am supposed to carry, I decline to be identified with the expression of the photograph.

"I have therefore taken the liberty to autograph another one which may be said to be a better likeness of me. May I hope that you will agree with me?"

[1] The Associated Press report of this meeting read as follows: "PARIS. May 2. . . . Before the Council of Three went into session today President Wilson received the members of the Military Affairs Committee of the House of Representatives, who reached Paris last evening. The meeting was a brief and purely formal one." *New York Times*, May 3, 1919. For a similar account, see the London *Times*, May 3, 1919.

Hankey's Notes of a Meeting of the Council of Four[1]

President Wilson's House,

I.C.-179B. Paris, May 2, 1919, 11 a.m.

1. PRESIDENT WILSON said that the representatives of Azerbaijan[2] were anxious to come to Paris. They had had a deputation at Constantinople for a long time, waiting for permission to come to Paris. He understood that the French Government had not given the necessary authorisation. The Georgians and other representatives of the Caucasus republics were all in Paris, and there seemed to be no reason for this exception.

M. CLEMENCEAU and MR. LLOYD GEORGE undertook to look into the matter.

2. M. CLEMENCEAU urged that the letter signed by Mr. Lloyd George and himself, and handed to M. Orlando on April 24th (I.C.176.C.)[3] should be published. He suggested that it should be published with a preamble somewhat as follows:

> "In order that there may be no misunderstanding abut the attitude of Great Britain and France in regard to Fiume, M. Clemenceau and Mr. Lloyd George have authorised the publication of the following letter to M. Orlando in regard to these matters:"

[1] The complete text of Hankey's notes is printed in *PPC*, V, 407-17.

[2] The delegates included Ali Marden Bek Topchibashev, Mohammad Hasan Hajinskii, Akbar Shaykh'ul'-Islamov, Mir Yaqub Mehdiev, Mohammad Moharramov, and Jeihun Bay Hajibekov. They arrived in Paris later in the spring. See Firuz Kazemzadeh, *The Struggle for Transcaucasia (1917-1921)* (New York and Oxford, 1951), pp. 265-66.

[3] See Appendix I to the minutes of the Council of Four printed at April 24, 1919, 4 p.m.

MR. LLOYD GEORGE said he had received a letter from the Marquis Imperiali, which he proceeded to read. The gist of it was that M. Orlando thought it better that the memorandum presented by M. Clemenceau and Mr. Lloyd George should not be published, as it would not help public opinion in Italy in its attitude towards Great Britain and France. M. Orlando had been begged by a very able French diplomatist in Rome not to read the memorandum. He felt sure that this was right, as it had made a very painful impression on the Parliamentary Commission to whom he had read it. The Marquis Imperiali urged, in these circumstances, that the memorandum should not be published.

PRESIDENT WILSON urged that it should be published.

M. CLEMENCEAU said that the Drafting Committee did not know whether to insert Italy or not.

MR. LLOYD GEORGE said he understood that the Drafting Committee had been instructed on this subject.

SIR MAURICE HANKEY said that he had not been authorised to make any formal communication to the Drafting Committee on the subject. Under Mr. Lloyd George's instructions, however, he had asked Mr. Hurst, the British member of the Drafting Committee, to try and arrange throughout the Treaty to avoid mentioning either the word "Italy," or the words "The five Allied and Associated Powers." At an interview he had had with the Drafting Committee yesterday, however, he had gathered that they had not been able to do this.

He had one other item of information he ought to mention, namely, that it had come to his knowledge that one of the Commissions, either the Economic Commission or the Commission on Ports, Waterways and Railways had sent a telegram warning the Italian representative that Austrian questions would be considered on Monday.

(The view was generally expressed that this ought not to have been done in the present situation with Italy, without authority.)

M. CLEMENCEAU said that M. Pichon had carried out his instructions the previous evening to see the Italian Ambassador, and had told him that the Germans were to be met next Tuesday, and that the Austrians and Hungarians were being asked to Paris. M. Bonin[4] did not like it at all.

Reverting to Sir Maurice Hankey's information about the communication by a Commission to Italy, he said that M. Klotz had reported the receipt of a letter from M. Crespi, dated April 30th (which M. Clemenceau proceeded to read), in which he had made a number of criticisms about the reparation decisions, and had made un-

[4] That is, Count Lelio Bonin Longare.

qualified reservations in the name of the Italian Government. Was this sort of thing to continue? M. Clemenceau asked.

MR. LLOYD GEORGE asked how M. Crespi had received word of those decisions. He wondered whether he had yet learnt of the decision that in reckoning claims for reparation against Germany, account should be taken of the proportion of the German effort on the particular front.

M. CLEMENCEAU asked what was to be done regarding M. Crespi's letter.

PRESIDENT WILSON said it would be sufficient if M. Klotz's secretary were to acknowledge receipt. He would not do more than this.

MR. LLOYD GEORGE said he would ask him the straight question as to whether he was a member of the Conference or not. He should say he wished to know because other decisions affecting Italy were being taken.

SIR MAURICE HANKEY mentioned that whenever he had known that reparation, economic, or ports, railways and waterways, or financial questions were to be considered he had sent a telephonic communication to M. Crespi, just as he had done to the other experts. M. Crespi had usually replied that he was unable to be present. This did not apply, however, to the meeting at which the decision referred to by Mr. Lloyd George had been taken, because that had not been a meeting specially organised for the subject. The experts had been present in connection with another question, namely, that of Alsace-Lorraine, and advantage had been taken of their presence to settle this question.

MR. LLOYD GEORGE said it was necessary to be very careful over this matter; if a break—and by break he did not mean hostilities—occurred with Italy it would be a very serious matter. In these moments small matters and the methods in which things were done were apt to tell. We must avoid even the appearance of incivility. He would give an air of over-courtesy. He thought that M. Klotz was entitled to write and say that other amendments were being made to the reparation clauses which affected Italy, and that he thought he ought to afford an opportunity to M. Crespi to be present.

PRESIDENT WILSON fully agreed as to the importance of courtesy. He thought, however, under all the circumstances, the only proper course was for M. Klotz's secretary to send a courteous acknowledgment of the receipt of the letter. At the present time M. Klotz's relations with the Italian representative were undefined. It would be as irregular for M. Klotz to make an official communication as undoubtedly it had been for M. Crespi to do so.

MR. LLOYD GEORGE thought that nevertheless M. Klotz was entitled to ask if M. Crespi was a member or not.

PRESIDENT WILSON said he would not answer.

M. CLEMENCEAU said he would at once telegraph to the Italian Government.

MR. LLOYD GEORGE said he had not been feeling comfortable about the decision on the subject of joint and several responsibility which had been taken in the absence of Italy, though it was to the detriment of Italian interests. He thought undoubtedly that both France and Great Britain would make a good deal out of this decision at Italian expense; France twice as much as Great Britain, and the decision had been taken the moment the Italians left.

PRESIDENT WILSON said we ought not to be too soft-hearted about the Italians, who had withdrawn from the negotiations with Germany because they could not get what they wanted about the negotiations with Austria, which were a separate matter.

MR. LLOYD GEORGE thought the decision looked rather like sharp practice.

PRESIDENT WILSON suggested that a letter should be drafted for M. Klotz to send.

(Mr. Philip Kerr was then invited into the room, and was given an outline of the question, and asked to draft a reply. Mr. Kerr retired.)

MR. LLOYD GEORGE thought that before a decision was taken as to the publication of his and M. Clemenceau's memorandum to M. Orlando, it should be carefully studied.

(Sir Maurice Hankey handed him the memorandum, which he proceeded to read.) (I.C.176.C., Appendix I.)

M. CLEMENCEAU said he thought we could not abstain from publishing the letter.

PRESIDENT WILSON reminded that the original understanding was that some document was to be published by Mr. Lloyd George and M. Clemenceau on the morning following the publication of his own statement. The impression had been created that the United States of America stood alone, in their attitude and M. Poincaré's declaration had rather heightened the impression that Great Britain and France were not with him. In these circumstances he felt that the memorandum ought to be published.

MR. LLOYD GEORGE said the effect must be very carefully considered. If the Italians did not want to come back, they would be glad of some excuse which would throw the blame on to their Allies.

PRESIDENT WILSON felt sure they wanted to come back.

MR. LLOYD GEORGE said that might be the case, but you did not want to put them in a position of saying President Wilson drove them away from the Conference, and M. Clemenceau and Mr. Lloyd George prevented them from coming back.

PRESIDENT WILSON said it was not fair to the world to abstain from publishing. The idea had been put about that Italy was expecting some arrangement to be offered them about Fiume, such as some form of independence under the League of Nations. The world needed some assurance that the Allied and Associated Powers collectively intended to do the right thing.

MR. LLOYD GEORGE said that the first thing was to patch up an arrangement with Italy if it could be patched up honourably. He would like Italy to be represented at the Council if this could be arranged without any sacrifice of principle. (President Wilson agreed.) The second point was that if they did not come back the responsibility must not be with the Allied and Associated Powers. He was afraid that publication would prejudice the position. He was not sure that publication would not make it impossible for the Italians to return. It was well known that a letter had been written, and he and his colleagues, with whom he had discussed it, took the view that the longer the declaration was withheld, the greater would be the effect. British public opinion was not with the Italians in this matter, but it really had no great interest in it. It wanted it patched up. It was not indifferent to principle, but it really did not know the question or understand it.

PRESIDENT WILSON said that public opinion in the United States was intensely interested. It could not understand why the United States was apparently left in isolation. United States public opinion was much more important than Italian. If the United States again became isolated it would break up the whole scheme on which the Peace Conference was working. He himself had less contact than Mr. Lloyd George and M. Clemenceau with Italian opinion, but his experts, with whom he had discussed the matter, assured him that the only way was to show Italy that she was in an impossible position. Once Italy realised that, a result was much more likely. If Italy was kept in a state of hope as regards Fiume, she would go on scheming, and putting her views in the Press, and would get no further. M. Clemenceau's and Mr. Lloyd George's memorandum was unanswerable. It would show clearly to Italian public opinion that Italy was in an impossible situation and must get out of it if she wanted to be in the great world movement. In the meanwhile, if nothing were done, work would have to be continued on the same difficult basis, that is to say, one of constant embarrassment in taking decisions adverse to Italy in the absence of its representatives, and not knowing whether Italy was in or out of the Peace Conference.

MR. LLOYD GEORGE said he would put some considerations on the other side. He thought President Wilson was wrong in assuming that the United States was regarded as standing alone. His opinion was that Italian public opinion regarded Great Britain as more hostile than she really was. They really thought that the British representatives had acted against them. This was undoubtedly a good deal due to the attitude of "The Times," which was still regarded as an official or semi-official organ in Italy. Only the previous evening a British soldier had told him that British officers were insulted in the streets in Italian cities, and the feeling was running strong against us. It was assumed that Great Britain had stood with the United States of America. He thought that the contrary opinion had been disseminated in the United States mainly by Mr. Hearst's papers, which were always trying to make trouble between Great Britain and the United States. It was assumed that Great Britain was pro-Jugo-Slav, but as a matter of fact British opinion knew and cared very little about the Jugo-Slavs. If he thought that public opinion would bring matters to a head and force Italy to take a decision, he would agree to it. But he feared it might only prolong the crisis by making it difficult for Italy to come in. Sooner or later, Italy must come in, and must do so voluntarily. Publication might cause a ministerial crisis in Italy, and bring back M. Giolitti and M. Tittoni, which would not be at all desirable. Moreover, to publish in the face of the Marquis Imperiali's letter, which was based on information from M. Orlando, would, he thought, be a very serious matter.

PRESIDENT WILSON said he thought he was the best judge of opinion in the United States of America, and the impression there he had no doubt from daily communications was that the United States were getting no support.

MR. LLOYD GEORGE suggested the publication of some semi-official communiqué that was obviously inspired.

PRESIDENT WILSON thought that we should prolong the present situation longer by the present method of leaving matters alone than by a drop in the test tube which was to produce precipitation. (Mr. Lloyd George interjected that he was afraid it might produce an explosion.) He believed that the only way to get the Italians back would be to make a declaration. We had now sent for the Austrians, and we should show them that if they did not come back they would be out of it altogether. He understood that they had sent a ship to Fiume and that they were increasing the number of troops in Fiume.[5] He had learnt that very morning from Mr. Lloyd George that they had sent a battleship, two cruisers and a destroyer to Smyrna. This confirmed what M. Orlando had told the United States ambassador in Rome that they would not go into the League of Nations unless they got what they wanted.[6] At Brest there was

[5] See W. S. Benson to WW, April 25, 1919 (second letter of that date).

[6] See T. N. Page to American Mission, April 28, 1919.

one of the latest United States battleships[7] waiting to take him home, but this could be sent to Smyrna or Fiume.

M. CLEMENCEAU and MR. LLOYD GEORGE said they would send it to Fiume.

PRESIDENT WILSON said that of course the danger was if a force was sent, some incident might happen. The Italians seemed to be sending forces to several places.

MR. LLOYD GEORGE said that he had sent Lieut. Harmsworth[8] to M. Venizelos with a telegram that he had received from the Central Committee of unredeemed Hellenes at Athens, to the effect that recent events, especially in the Smyrna district, indicated that the Turks, stimulated by some outside power (this, no doubt, was Italy) were continuing their policy of oppression and massacre; the telegram concluded by asking for forces to be sent. M. Venizelos had replied that the Italians were undoubtedly stirring up the Turks, and no doubt there was an understanding between them. This strengthened the view that an Inter-Allied force should be sent to Smyrna.

PRESIDENT WILSON said that the Italians would probably say they were sending battleships to Smyrna to protect their compatriots in Turkey.

MR LLOYD GEORGE suggested that the three nations should all send forces. Great Britain had a battleship in the Black Sea.

M. CLEMENCEAU said that France had battleships in the Black Sea also.

PRESIDENT WILSON said he would see Admiral Benson about it at once.

M. CLEMENCEAU said that this was the application of the principle of the League of Nations. What he asked were [was what] we [were] going to do about the Italians at Versailles.

MR. LLOYD GEORGE said that the Germans knew the position.

M. CLEMENCEAU said his information was that the Germans did not take much interest in the Italian position.

PRESIDENT WILSON said that this confirmed the information he had read yesterday.

MR LLOYD GEORGE said that the peace of the world really depended upon the United States of America, France and Great Britain hanging together.

M. CLEMENCEAU said that the Italian policy was clearly to lead the Allied and Associated Powers to the point where they could not make peace in common because Great Britain and France were bound by the Treaty of London which President Wilson could not recognise. We ought to let them know beforehand that by not com-

[7] *U.S.S. Arizona.*

[8] Esmond Cecil Harmsworth, aide-de-camp to Lloyd George.

ing to Versailles they had broken the Pact of London to which they had adhered, and by which it was agreed not to make peace separately. We should show that if they broke the Pact of London we were not bound.

PRESIDENT WILSON pointed out that it depended upon how the promise not to make a separate peace was interpreted. The Italians had been a party to the Armistice, they had been a party to the preliminary peace, a party (as Mr. Lloyd George pointed out) to the basis of the peace, and a party to the discussions on the peace. On the very eve of the negotiations with the Germans, they had withdrawn on a matter that had nothing to do with those negotiations.

M. CLEMENCEAU said that we should let them know that if they withdraw they are breaking the Pact of London, and we are not bound by the Treaty. We must let them know that if Italy breaks it, she must take the consequences.

PRESIDENT WILSON said it must be made clear that it was Italy and not France and Great Britain that were breaking the Treaty.

M. CLEMENCEAU said the day was coming when this must be made known.

PRESIDENT WILSON doubted if it was necessary to let it be known before next Tuesday when the Germans came.

M. CLEMENCEAU thought it should be made known before.

PRESIDENT WILSON thought it would be sufficient to say that we had signed the Treaty of Peace whereby Italy not signing had broken the Pact of London.

M. CLEMENCEAU recalled that when the decision had been taken to invite the Germans to Versailles, President Wilson and Mr. Lloyd George had agreed, but M. Orlando had written to him making all reservations. He had that correspondence. The communication had not been sent to the Germans with M. Orlando's consent.

PRESIDENT WILSON said that except as regards certain matters of detail, the main elements of the Treaty with the Germans had been urged with the co-operation of the Italians. They now refused to sign this Treaty unless another Treaty was settled first.

MR. LLOYD GEORGE suggested that the Italians ought to be informed if the Drafting Committee were instructed to leave Italy out of the Treaty.

PRESIDENT WILSON said that if some communication was sent every day to Italy in this sort of way, she would only be encouraged in her attitude. Surely M. Klotz's reply to M. Crespi was enough.

At this point Sir Maurice Hankey, under instruction, read extracts from the previous Minutes showing that Mr. Lloyd George had asked M. Orlando whether, in the event of Italy's absence from the meeting with the Germans, the Allied and Associated Powers were entitled to put forward demands on Italy's behalf, and that M. Orlando had made it clear that they were not. (176C.)

MR. LLOYD GEORGE said he had told the Marquis Imperiali that if Italy abstained from being present it would be an end to the Pact of London. Unfortunately there was no note of this conversation.

PRESIDENT WILSON recalled that Mr. Lloyd George had told him.

1. (It was agreed that the question should be studied by M. Clemenceau and his advisers, and by Mr. Lloyd George and Mr. Balfour, and that a form of communication to Italy should be prepared for consideration)
2. (The draft of a letter from M. Klotz to M. Crespi prepared by Mr. Philip Kerr was read and approved (Appendix I)
   M. Clemenceau took the letter to communicate to M. Klotz)

. . .

APPENDIX I TO I.C.179B.

COPY OF LETTER TO BE SENT BY M. KLOTZ TO M. CRESPI.

Dear Signor Crespi, 2nd May 1919.

I have much pleasure in acknowledging receipt of your letter of April 30th in which you suggest certain amendments in the draft of the clauses of the Treaty with Germany relating to reparation. I feel somewhat at a loss as to how to deal with your request, because, as you remind me, the Italian representatives withdrew from our deliberations on April 22nd and have taken no part in them since. I am, however, very glad to note your criticisms and suggestions and have communicated them to the American and British representatives.

I should like further to take this opportunity to inform you that the representatives of America, the British Empire and of France have been obliged to take very important decisions in regard to the draft Treaty with Germany since they have been deprived of the advice and assistance of the Italian delegation. In particular I wish to bring to your notice the following important decision regarding the question of reparation:

> "Les dommages de guerre, consequences des hostilités sur l'un des front de combat, sont réparés par l'Allemagne et ses Alliés au *pro rata* de l'effort militaire et navale fourni par chacun d'eux sur ce front. Les proportions seront déterminés par la Commission des Réparations."

I am anxious to communicate this decision to you because it specially affects Italian interests.

T MS (SDR, RG 256, 180.03401/137, DNA).

Hankey's and Mantoux's Notes of a Meeting of the Council of Four[1]

I.C.-179C. Quai d'Orsay, Paris, May 2, 1919, 4 p.m.

. . .[2] (12) After some discussion, the attached revised Article [in regard to Austria], based on a draft submitted by M. Clemenceau, was approved for incorporation in the Treaty of Peace (Appendix IV).[3]

§ Mantoux's notes:

Clemenceau. I would propose to deal finally with the question of the cables. While awaiting the arrival of the experts, we can finish with two other questions: the relations of Germany with Austria and the relations of Germany with Russia. For Austria, according to the text that I propose, Germany recognizes "the inalienable independence" of this country.

Wilson. What does "inalienable" signify? That Austria can never be united to Germany?

Clemenceau. I know very well that we cannot prevent that union indefinitely, if the populations want it. But that formula will greatly assist the Austrian party which wishes Austria to remain an independent state.

Wilson. Like you, I think that it is desirable to prevent the immediate union of Austria to Germany; but I would omit the word "inalienable."

Clemenceau. If we omit it, the use that Austria can make of her independence tomorrow is to proclaim her union with Germany.

The goal of the article about Russia is principally to prevent the Germans from colonizing Russia. I will then ask them to recognize the "inalienable" independence of all the countries which were part of the former Russian Empire, to recognize definitively the abrogation of the Treaty of Brest-Litovsk, and to accept that the rights of Russia to restitution and reparation which are due her be reserved.

Wilson. I can immediately accept the middle paragraph, that which relates to the abolition of the Treaty of Brest-Litovsk.

Lloyd George. I accept the first two; but I do not really understand the meaning of the last.

Wilson. Do we have the right to stipulate thus for Russia?

Clemenceau. We cannot allow the Germans to make themselves the masters of Russia and thereby to become again the most redoubtable power in Europe.

Lloyd George. After having examined the last clause more attentively, I understand its meaning; it can be very useful when Russia, as we hope, will be again in the hands of a government animated by friendly intentions.

Clemenceau. So we will be able to turn to the Russians and say to them: "Here is what we have done for you."

Lloyd George. That can only have good effects.

Wilson. I accept your draft for Russia. Concerning Austria, I fear committing an offense against the right of peoples to decide for themselves. It is not Germany which concerns me in that matter, but Austria. We can forbid an annexation; but we cannot refuse a country the right to unite to another if it wants to. We cannot forbid Luxembourg to unite herself to Belgium or to France.

Lloyd George. Suppose that there was an independent Rhineland and that we judged its permanent separation from Germany indispensable to the security of Europe; why not impose it?

Wilson. I cannot accept this principle. I insist on maintaining the right of peoples to decide for themselves.

Clemenceau. Even if it is not a matter of joining ourselves with our allies and associates of the League of Nations?

Wilson. I am eager to take a favorable attitude toward the Austrians.

Clemenceau. So am I.

Lloyd George. What would most risk throwing Austria into the arms of the Germans would be, rather, the annexation of part of the German Tyrol to Italy.

Wilson. It is a question to re-examine, if Italy parts company with us.

I do not want to impose a permanent obligation on Austria; but, on the other hand, to fix a time limit would be the equivalent of inviting Austria to join with Germany at the end of the determined period of time.

Lloyd George. A text presented by our experts obliges the government of Germany to refrain from maneuvers whose goal is the union of Austria to the German state.

Clemenceau. Germany will sign an article of this kind, will do the opposite the next day, and will deny the fact.

Lloyd George. I acknowledge that this text is not worth much.

Wilson. Can we not write that Germany recognizes and will respect the independence of Austria, which will remain inalienable, except by a decision approved by the League of Nations?

Clemenceau. Very good.

Lloyd George. I gladly accept this text.

Clemenceau. I am going to read the entire text relating to Russia:

"Germany recognizes and will entirely respect the inalienable independence of all the territories which were part of the former Empire of Russia.

"Germany formally accepts the annulment of the Treaty of Brest-

Litovsk and of all treaties and agreements of any kind concluded by Germany since the Maximalist[4] revolution of November 1917 with all governments or political groups formed on the territory of the former Empire of Russia.

"The Allied and Associated governments formally reserve all rights for Russia to obtain from Germany restitution and satisfaction based on the principles of the present treaty."

This text is adopted.

Mr. Balfour is introduced.

Lloyd George. Here is a question asked by the drafting committee: will Italy's name continue to figure in the Covenant of the League of Nations? Notice that Italy is inscribed in the list of the members, although she is still not a signatory of the Covenant.

Wilson. That embarrasses me. But if Italy does not finally sign the Covenant, she cannot be a member of the League.

Lloyd George. M. Orlando said that she could not sign because her signature would prejudice the solution of territorial questions.

Wilson. Precisely.

Lloyd George. Is there not a formula which permits us to get out of this?

Wilson. We can use the same expression everywhere in the treaty with Germany: "the principal powers" instead of "the five powers." The difficulty is that in the Council of the League of Nations, if there remain only four great powers, they will be equal with the small powers, whose number we cannot reduce, since those which are to sit on the Council are already designated.

Lloyd George. It would be rather serious if the mandates are distributed by a Council on which we would only have half the votes.

Wilson. The influence of the great powers could not fail to operate.

Lloyd George. That seems rather dangerous to me. I can just see Mr. Hughes' objections.

Wilson. I do not see any other way to proceed: I think that we must leave Italy off the list; we still have a lot of time to make the necessary changes until the signing of the treaty.

The proposed modification is adopted.

Lloyd George. There remains the danger of being four against four in the Council.

Wilson. It is a question that we can raise in the Plenary Session.

Lloyd George. I fear that Belgium will make difficulties and will try to blackmail us, and that Spain, whose role was doubtful during the war, will be a dangerous element. Then we would be rather badly off.

Wilson. Concerning the mandates, we will make the distribution by an agreement among ourselves, before the signing of the treaty. All that we need say for the moment to the drafting committee is to substitute everywhere the expression "the principal powers" for the words "the five powers."§

(13) PRESIDENT WILSON said that he had arranged for an American battleship of the latest type to proceed from Brest to Smyrna.

MR. LLOYD GEORGE said that he had also ordered a ship there. M. Venizelos had wanted to do the same, but he had advised him to wait until the ships of the Allied and Associated Powers had arrived there.

M. CLEMENCEAU said that France had already a battleship at Smyrna.

MR LLOYD GEORGE asked if any announcement should be made that these naval movements were taking place in consequence of the massacres of Greeks by Turks.

M. CLEMENCEAU deprecated any announcement, and the proposal was dropped.

(The experts on the subject of Cables were then introduced, and the subsequent discussion is reported as a separate Meeting.)

T MS (SDR, RG 256, 180.03401/138, DNA); Mantoux, I, 460-64.

[1] The complete text of Hankey's minutes is printed in *PPC*, V, 418-25.

[2] To this point, the Big Three discussed a variety of matters, none at any length.

[3] It read: "Germany acknowledges and will fully respect the independence of Austria within the frontiers established by the present treaty as inalienable, except by consent of the Council of the League of Nations." *PPC*, V, 425.

[4] That is, Bolshevik.

Hankey's Notes of a Meeting of the Council of Ten[1]

BC-60 Quai d'Orsay, May 2, 1919, 5 p.m.

1. M. CLEMENCEAU said that the Japanese Representatives had not yet been able to reach the Meeting. He thought, however, that a preliminary discussion might be held in regard to the draft resolution, which had been prepared by President Wilson, and which read as follows:

"It is agreed:

(1) That an article shall be inserted in the Treaty of Peace whereby Germany shall on her own behalf and on the behalf of German nationals renounce in favour of the Allied and Associated Powers jointly all rights, titles and privileges of whatsoever nature possessed by her or her nationals in the submarine cables or portion thereof mentioned below:

Emden-Vigo: from the Straits of Dover to off Vigo.

[1] The complete text of these minutes is printed in *PPC*, IV, 493-500.

Emden-Brest: from off Cherbourg to Brest.
Emden-Teneriffe: from off Dunkerque to off Teneriffe.
Emden-Azores (1) from the Straits of Dover to Fayal.
Emden-Azores (2) from the Straits of Dover to Fayal.
Azores-New York (1) from Fayal to New York.
Azores-New York (2) from Fayal to the longitude of Halifax.
Teneriffe-Monrovia: from off Teneriffe to off Monrovia.
Monrovia-Lomé:

from about	lat. 2 deg. 30′ N. long. 7 deg. 40′ W. of Greenwich
to about	lat. 2 deg. 20′ N. long. 5.30′ deg. W. of Greenwich
and from about	lat. 3 deg. 48′ N. long. 0.00

to Lomé.

Lomé-Duala: from Lomé to Duala.
Monrovia-Pernambuco: from off Monrovia to off Pernambuco.
Constantinople-Constanza[2]: from Constantinople to Constanza.
Chefoo-Tsingtao-Shanghai: from Tsingtao to Chefoo, and from Tsingtao to Shanghai.
Yap-Shanghai, Yap-Guam, and Yap-Menado (Celebes): from Yap Island to Shanghai, from Yap Island to Guam Island, and from Yap Island to Menado.

(2) That the Five Allied and Associated Powers shall jointly hold these cables together with any rights or privileges pertaining thereto for common agreement as to the best system of administration and control; and

(3) That the Five Allied and Associated Powers shall call as soon as possible an International Congress to consider and report on all international aspects of telegraph, cable and radio communication, with a view to providing the entire world with adequate communication facilities on a fair, equitable basis."

MR. LLOYD GEORGE thought it would be unwise to take any decision on this question in the absence of the Japanese Representatives.

PRESIDENT WILSON expressed the view that a preliminary discussion could be held in regard to the Atlantic cables.

(At this stage MM. Yamakawa and Saburi, and Vice-Admiral Takeshita[3] entered the Council Chamber.)

MR. BALFOUR said that since the last meeting he had been able to

[2] Now known as Constanta, a Rumanian port on the Black Sea.

[3] Tadao Yamakawa, Counselor in the Japanese Ministry of Marine; Sadao Saburi, Secretary in the Ministry of Foreign Affairs; and Vice Adm. Isamu Takeshita, Assistant Chief of the Naval General Staff.

make careful enquiries in regard to the actual position of the Atlantic cables. This aspect of the case, he thought, was very important as being relevant to the final decision, and it would throw light on what had actually happened. He felt bound to confess that he had only on that day been able to discover the actual position of affairs and, he thought, Mr. Lansing's previous information must have been equally imperfect, since he (Mr. Lansing) had told the Council at a previous meeting that Great Britain had control of too many cable lines. Now, the fact of the case was that Great Britain had control of no cable lines, with the exception of the one recently captured from Germany. This statement had greatly surprised him and it had led him to make further enquiries in order to obtain an explanation. It appeared that there existed 13 cable lines between the United Kingdom and America. Seven of these lines were actually owned by American companies, and the remaining 6 though owned by British companies were leased to American companies for a period which still had some 90 years to run. The explanation for this surprising state of affairs was, however, a very simple one. It showed how monopolies, to which the Heads of Government objected, worked. The fact was that a cable running, say between Land's End and New York, would be of no use unless the company owning the cable was able at New York to make satisfactory arrangements for the further transmission of messages along the internal telegraph lines. In Great Britain, the State owned all land telegraph lines: but in America these were apparently owned by two private companies, who so arranged their rates as to "freeze out" British owned cables. In consequence British companies had been driven to say to the American companies: "As we cannot work our cable lines under these conditions, we will lease them to you." The result was that all cables running between Great Britain and America were either owned or leased by American companies. The British did not grumble at the service, which was efficient and good, though the rates were somewhat high; but the fact remained that the whole control was American.

PRESIDENT WILSON thought the inference contained in the last part of Mr. Balfour's statement should be completed. In his opinion it was just as necessary to obtain land connections at the British end of the cable lines as it was at the American end.

MR. BALFOUR explained that the difference lay in the fact that in Great Britain the land telegraph lines were State owned and the policy of the British Government had been to encourage the laying down of cables, and with this object in view, very favourable terms had been given to the cable companies; so much so that the American Companies actually contemplated increasing the number of their cable lines. However that might be, the last thing he wished to do was to make a complaint about American companies. But he did wish to point out that one of the morals of the existing state of affairs was that it was no use to obtain the control of cable lines crossing the Ocean unless international agreements could, at the same time, be made in regard to the rates charged over land lines. Thus, if the Great Powers decided to take over, as suggested in President Wilson's resolution, the Trans-Atlantic cables, and if they quarrelled with the great American Companies owning the land lines, they would be just as helpless as the British cable companies had been and would be "frozen out." Consequently, the American Government would have to consider whether it would not have to modify its system, so as to obtain some control over its land lines. So much in regard to the question of the control of cables in time of peace. On the other hand, in time of war it would never be possible to take away the control which every nation naturally possessed over the landing places situated in her own country. No nation would agree to give up her sovereignty over such landing places. Thus, for instance, Great Britain would never agree to hand over Land's End. Consequently, in time of war, every nation would use its powers to prevent messages hurtful to its own national interests being transmitted from the landing stages. He fully admitted that his statement was based on the system which had existed in the past, and he agreed that other conditions might prevail in the future, owing to altered international relations. It would, however, be an illusion to suppose, firstly, that any international arrangement in regard to cables would necessarily yield satisfactory results unless the land telegraph lines were also controlled and, secondly, that effective control could only be exercised over cables which landed in a country which was at war.

Furthermore, he thought it would not be wise to try to limit the power of nations to lay cables between the different parts of their own Dominions, if they so wished. Thus, for instance, he thought the United States of America should have perfect liberty to lay cables, for instance, between America and the Philippines and America and Panama, and he held that a cable which began and ended on American soil should be wholly controlled by America. He doubted the propriety of preventing any such arrangement. On the other hand, it should be realised that as a result Great Britain would thereby be placed in a position to apply Empire preferential cable rates. He thought that this introduced a question which could not, however, be decided before the International Congress referred to in paragraph 3 of President Wilson's draft resolution, had been appointed.

MR. LLOYD GEORGE thought that the strongest argument against the kind of international control proposed by President Wilson in the event of war, was that it might become impossible any longer to cut enemy cables. Thus, for instance, had the Atlantic cable lines been controlled in 1914 by America, France, Great Britain and Germany, it would not have been possible to cut the cables, as had been done.

MR. BALFOUR agreed, but maintained that each nation could have stopped messages from passing through their territory. In his opinion this question chiefly affected the Great Sea Powers, for it was particularly advantageous to them to be able to cut cables in the event of war.

PRESIDENT WILSON enquired whether the Council was not arguing a question which was not yet in debate.[4] In his draft resolution he had merely attempted to make arrangements so that the cables in question could be placed under the best system of administration and control. As Baron Makino had stated at yesterday's meeting, the Allied and Associated Governments had taken certain liberties with international law in the Peace Treaty, and in his opinion a new decision in international law was being made in regard to taking possession of cable lengths which lay in No Man's Land, at the bottom of the sea, in order to connect the ends to form new cable systems. He agreed that no clear ruling on this point existed in international law; and such action could only be justified by analogies such as the seizure of private property. The point he wished to make, however, was this, namely, that it was not proposed to assign to one or two of a number of partners in the war, the indispensable means of international communication, though the other belligerents were also vitally interested. He thought, therefore, that all partners of the war should have a voice in the system of administration and control to be adopted in future. The five Allied and Associated Powers who would hold these cables as trustees in accordance with his draft resolution, were the very Powers upon whom the whole system of peace and international understanding would henceforth rest. Consequently power should be conferred upon this group of Great Powers to decide the whole question, and he felt confident they would be in a position to do so equitably. He fully agreed that it would be impossible to interfere with sovereign rights.

In regard to the question of rates and monopolies, he agreed that at the present moment the proposals contained in his draft resolutions would merely be applied to a small number of cables; but he thought means might eventually be devised to break down the existing high rates. It would be admitted that no international under-

[4] In this and the following paragraph, Wilson paraphrased and summarized W. S. Rogers to WW, May 2, 1919, TLS (WP, DLC).

standing could be effective unless international means of exercising pressure were at the same time accorded and, in this connection, it might be found useful for the Great Powers to lay additional cables in order to make new and better communications, and so obtain the means of controlling rates and of preventing the creation of monopolies. But these results could not be reached by conversations which would be held after the property in question had been definitely assigned to particular Powers.

MR. LLOYD GEORGE said that he could not altogether accept President Wilson's conclusion. At the present moment the Atlantic cables were almost wholly in the hands of American monopolies, which had been very skilfully engineered. These American companies preferred London for their operations, as it suited them better for practical reasons. The greater part of their business was in London, which was a great cable distributing centre; and, in addition, the British Post Office had been extremely liberal in its arrangements for the transmission of messages over British land lines. The fact remained, however, that the existing 13 cable lines were all controlled by Americans. During the war the British had captured a German cable and connected it with Canada, and the line now constituted the only Canadian State owned line. The Canadian Government had recently contemplated laying a second cable in order to bring pressure to bear with a view of reducing the rates charged by the monopolist companies. President Wilson, however, now proposed that the cable line in question should be placed under international control. If America desired to break down American monopolies, he thought the only way would be for additional cable lines to be laid. To lay a cable across the Atlantic cost between £700,000 and £800,000. Consequently, whoever wanted to break monopolies would have to pay that sum. On the other hand, he failed to see why Canada should be deprived of something which had been captured during the war just as legitimately as the capture of a ship; the latter representing communications over the seas, the former, communications under the seas.

To sum up, he failed to see the point of dispossessing Canada in order to set up a kind of international control over something which she regarded as essential to her business success, and which had cost her over £200,000 to organise.

PRESIDENT WILSON thought that Mr. Lloyd George had, in his statement, made various assumptions which were not necessarily justified. In the first place, it was not correct to say that America wanted to deprive Canada of the cable in question. Secondly, he did not propose to establish a permanent international control over the particular cable in question. His proposal had merely contemplated the setting up of some authority, which would possess the right to enquire as to how all existing systems could best be administered and controlled. In other words, should the cable in question be assigned to Canada by the Treaty of Peace, the United States of America would thereafter have no right to ask what it was intended to do with the cable, for the obvious reply would be that the cable belonged to Canada, and America could not interfere in its management. But since, at the present moment, the Allied and Associated Governments, were partners of war, he considered it to be part of his privilege to enquire what was to be done with the cable in question. He merely asked, therefore, that an initial enquiry should be made as to what was to be done with the cables mentioned in his draft resolution.

MR. LLOYD GEORGE said that he did not for a moment challenge President Wilson's right to examine what was to be done with any piece of property that had been seized from the enemy during the war. On the other hand, he thought it would be wiser to accept the proposal made by Admiral de Bon at yesterday's meeting, namely, that Germany should be informed that the cables which during the period of the war had been cut and utilised by the Allied and Associated Governments, would not be restored to her, and that they would remain the property of the Allied and Associated Governments. At the same time, an International body could be appointed to consider and report on the whole question of ocean cables.

PRESIDENT WILSON thought that the only difference between the two plans was that in accordance with his own proposals the cables would during the intermediate period be vested in trustees. With this exception, his proposal did not differ in principle from Admiral de Bon's.

MR. BALFOUR proposed the following amendments to President Wilson's draft resolution:

"(*a*) Para. 1.

The word 'jointly' to be omitted.

(*b*) Para. 2.

To be amended to read as follows: 'These cables shall continue to be worked as at present without prejudice to any decision as to their future status which may be reached by the five Allied and Associated Powers mentioned in the next paragraph.' "

PRESIDENT WILSON said he would accept the amendments proposed by Mr. Balfour.

MR. BALFOUR, continuing, said that Sir Robert Borden had suggested the following addition to the end of the new paragraph 2, namely: "And without prejudice to any vested right that may be claimed by reason of cutting, possession, expenditure and utilisation."

PRESIDENT WILSON thought that the latter addition would be

quite unnecessary. He suggested that the whole of the resolution should be re-drafted to embody Mr. Balfour's amendments and taken up the first thing at the meeting to be held on the following day.

VISCOUNT CHINDA wished to call attention to one important point in the draft resolution. He thought the submarine cable lines Chefoo-Tsingtao-Shanghai; Tsingtao-Chefoo; and Tsingtao-Shanghai should be omitted from the first paragraph of the resolution, since it had already been agreed by the Council of Four that these cables were to be renounced by Germany in favour of Japan.

(This was agreed to.)

Mr. Rogers[5] invited attention to the fact that Mr. Balfour's amended paragraph 2 merely related to cables at present being worked. He thought the wording should be amended so as to include cables and parts of cables not at present in use.

(This was agreed to.)

(It was agreed that the following draft resolution, as amended, should be considered at a Meeting to be held on Saturday, May 3rd, at 11 a.m.:

—1—

"Germany renounces, on her own behalf and on behalf of her nationals, in favour of the Principal Allied and Associated Powers, all rights, titles or privileges of whatever nature in the submarine cables set out below, or in any portions thereof:

Emden-Vigo: from the Straits of Dover to off Vigo.

Emden-Brest: from off Cherbourg to Brest.

Emden-Teneriffe: from off Dunkerque to off Teneriffe.

Emden-Azores (1): from the Straits of Dover to Fayal.

Emden-Azores (2): from the Straits of Dover to Fayal.

Azores-New York (1): from Fayal to New York.

Azores-New York (2): from Fayal to the longitude of Halifax.

Teneriffe-Monrovia: from off Teneriffe to off Monrovia.

Monrovia-Lomé:

from about { lat. 2 deg. 30′ N.
long. 7 deg. 40′ W. of Greenwich

to about { lat. 2 deg. 20′ N.
long. 5.30′ deg. W. of Greenwich

and from about { lat. 3 deg. 48′ N.
long. 0.00.

to Lomé.

Lomé-Duala: from Lomé to Duala.

Monrovia-Pernambuco: from off Monrovia to off Pernambuco.

Constantinople-Constanza: from Constantinople to Constanza.

[5] Walter Stowell Rogers.

Yap-Shanghai, Yap-Guam, and Yap-Menado (Celebes): from Yap Island to Shanghai, from Yap Island to Guam Island, and from Yap Island to Menado.

—2—

Such of the above-mentioned cables as are now in use, shall continue to be worked in the conditions at present existing; but such working shall not prejudice the right of the Principal Allied and Associated Powers to decide the future status of these cables in such way as they may think fit.

The Principle Allied and Associated Powers may make such arrangements as they may think fit for bringing into operation any of the said cables which are not at present in use.

—3—

The Principal Allied and Associated Powers shall as soon as possible arrange for the convoking of an International Congress to consider all international aspects of communication by land telegraphs, cables or wireless telegraphy, and to make recommendations to the Powers concerned with a view to providing the entire world with adequate facilities of this nature on a fair and equitable basis."

(The Meeting then adjourned.)

T MS (SDR, RG 256, 180.03101/67, DNA).

To Lord Robert Cecil

My dear Lord Robert: Paris, 2 May, 1919.

The enclosed message from Washington from our Acting Secretary of State raises an important question upon which I would be very much instructed by your opinion, if you would be kind enough to give it.[1]

In the hurry of the breaking up of the session the other day, I did not have an opportunity to congratulate you as you deserved to be congratulated, on the successful termination of the labors of the Commission on the League of Nations. I feel, as I am sure all the other members of the commission feel, that the laboring oar fell to you and that it is chiefly due to you that the Covenant has come out of the confusions of debate in its original integrity. May I not express my own personal admiration of the work you did and my own sense of obligation?

Cordially and sincerely yours, Woodrow Wilson

TLS (Cecil Family Papers, Hatfield House).

[1] About this matter, see R. Cecil to WW, May 4, 1919.

To Robert Lansing

My dear Lansing: Paris, 2 May, 1919.

I am very much disturbed about this Montenegrin situation. When I ask explanations of Mr. Vesnitch and others, they reply only with accusations against the King of Montenegro,[1] who is now in Paris and plays no direct part in Montenegrin affairs, and no indirect part either, for he is not permitted to communicate with his people. I cannot escape the impression that the Serbians have taken a very high-handed course and have done things that the opinion of the world would certainly condemn, if they were generally known, and I would very much like your advice as to how to handle the whole matter.

Would it be possible for you to see Mr. Plamenatz[2] and try in a personal interview to get a closer view of the whole situation than is possible through correspondence?

Cordially and faithfully yours, [Woodrow Wilson]

CCL (WP, DLC).

[1] That is, Nicholas I.

[2] That is, Jovan S. Plamenatz (Plamenac).

To William Shepherd Benson

My dear Admiral: Paris, 2 May, 1919.

I have your letter[1] about sending various vessels to assist the removal of the troops from Archangel when the ice breaks, and in reply would say that, so far as we are concerned, there are no plans whatever for active operations, and what is intended is merely to insure a safe withdrawal of our land forces.

Cordially and faithfully yours, [Woodrow Wilson]

CCL (WP, DLC).

[1] W. S. Benson to WW, May 1, 1919.

From William Shepherd Benson

My dear Mr. President, Paris, 2 May, 1919.

I beg to transmit herewith, for your information, the following despatch, which was sent by Admiral Andrews at 11:45 a.m. on April 30th:

"Additional troops have arrived at Sebenico. No demonstration any Adriatic port against Americans personally, except noisy demonstration YMCA." Very respectfully, W. S. Benson

TLS (WP, DLC).

A Translation of a Letter from Skevos Zervos and Paris Roussos[1]

Mr. President, Paris, May 2, 1919.

We have the honor to bring to the knowledge of Your Excellency the recent and grave happenings that have taken place in the Islands of the Dodecanese, the knowledge of which has just been transmitted to us by despatch. We permit ourselves at the same time to respectfully draw your attention to these facts.

All the inhabitants of the Dodecanese, having arisen as a single man, have proclaimed before God and before men that they no longer will be slaves and that they repel all tyranny.

Easter Day, after having been present at the mass, the Dodecanese proclaimed in churches and public squares the union of the Dodecanese to Greece.

Our prelates and priests, from the height of the pulpit, our notables and men of letters in the squares of the towns and villages, in the midst of enthusiastic acclamations of a crowd delirious with joy, declared before God resurrected and before the civilized world the union of our land, the Dodecanese, with our mother country, Greece.

At this news the local Italian Authorities and soldiers of the Army of Occupation, in an excess of rage, attacked our unarmed compatriots, killing our priests and our women, wounding the defenseless inhabitants, imprisoning bishops and notables, maltreating with an unheard of savagery our women and children, and behaved in general in a barbarous and odiously tyrannical manner.

For example, in the Island of Rhodes, while the people after having gone to the Easter Mass, proclaimed the union to Greece and were accompanying the Bishop[2] back to his home in the midst of enthusiastic acclamations and cries of joy, manifesting in a loud voice national sentiments and acclaiming Greece, troops of Italians threw themselves savagely on this defenseless crowd, and dispersed it by charging with bayonets.

The Military Governor[3] went to the seat of the Bishop, insulted the Bishop, forbade him any contact with his flock and made him personally responsible for the manifestations and threatened to bring him before a war council and to have him shot.

While these happenings were going on in the town of Rhodes, in the villages of Neochori and Misagros, Italian soldiers, despite all law, human and Divine, arrested and killed the priests for having proclaimed the union with Greece.

For the same reason in the village of Valanova they killed the Episcopal Bishop[4] in the very church where he was officiating. A great number of other villagers of both sexes were killed by these same soldiers. In the villages of Arkhanghelos, Coskinou, Calathos, Calathies, Lindos, Pylona, Lardos, Asclipios, Ghennadi, Trianta, Cremasti, Psinthos, Apollonas, Platani, and in general in all the villages of Rhodes, the Italians were guilty of acts of vandalism and unheard of atrocities.

In the island of Calymnos all the notables were arrested and thrown into prison and beaten without pity; they have been deprived of all food for several days.

Easter a young man was shot for having cried: "Long live the union! Long live Venizelos!" after having first been beaten with lances by the Italian soldiers and submitted to other cruel atrocities.

By these methods the Italians are endeavoring to terrorize the inhabitants of the Dodecanese. They are threatening them all with being shot or making them die of starvation.

Mr. President, in bringing these facts to your knowledge we protest energetically against these inhuman acts of the Italian Authorities and the odious proceedings which they are employing against the Dodecanese to the end of terrorizing the defenseless populations.

We protest to Your Excellency, we protest to the Congress of Peace and to the civilized world against the murder of so many innocent beings, we protest against the assassination of priests, of women and of defenseless citizens.

In the name of the rights of man, the most elementary liberty of humanity, also in the name of the rights of people, the principle of nationality and the Wilsonian Doctrine, and we beg you, Mr. President, we beg the Conference of Peace, to intervene by prompt and energetic action so as to put an end to the long and atrocious martyrdom of the Dodecanese.

We demand that our compatriots should no longer run the danger of being shot for the only reason that they are Greeks and because they have had the courage to affirm that they are Greeks for thirty centuries and that they will always remain Greeks.

We beg you, Mr. President, to accept the assurances of our profound respect.

Dr. Skevos Zervos
Paris Roussos

TCL (WP, DLC).

[1] Members of the delegation representing the inhabitants of the Dodecanese Islands before the Paris Peace Conference. The TLS is in WP, DLC.

[2] Apostolos, Greek Orthodox Bishop of Rhodes.

[3] Vittorio d'Elia, Italian Governor of Rhodes.

[4] Reports in the *New York Times*, May 2 and 6, 1919, indicate that a village priest (presumably Greek Orthodox) of Villanuova (the Italian spelling of what seems to have then been called Villa Nova), Rhodes, had been killed by Italian troops in late April when he sought to lead a demonstration.

Three Telegrams from Thomas Nelson Page to the American Mission

Rome, May 2, 1919.

285. IMPORTANT French Ambassador Barrère has, I hear, seen Baron Sonnino. The press this morning contains Poincaré's brief but warm statement to the journal FRANCE-ITALY.[1] It is reliably reported as coming from French Embassy that the French are much dissatisfied with the attitude we have taken in regard to Italian affairs and declare positively that France will not sign the Peace Treaty unless some arrangement is arrived at with Italy so that Italians will be able to sign also.

In well informed French circles there is a tendency to feel that France has lost the fruits of her victory owing to the stubbornness of President Wilson and the incompetency or what they term the old age of Clemenceau.

In French circles it is alleged that we are making peace with Germany at the expense of France and Italy for the advantage of Great Britain. They resent bitterly the Anglophile tendencies of our Peace delegates more especially the President.

It is alleged that the President had in his pocket a document regarding France and her territorial aspirations particularly that on the Sarre similar to the one which he issued regarding Fiume.

The Peace Treaty has been completed. It consists of 950 sections. It is not a preliminary document but is the final Peace Treaty and when signed negotiations will be over and there will be no further Peace Treaty of any kind. There is no doubt that Germany will be ready to sign. France, Great Britain and the United States have already signed but to make the document valid according to these sources the Italians' signature is necessary. Extraordinary attempts are being made to induce the Italians to return to Paris to sign the document.

Unaffected great concern exists here at present situation. I do not believe the Italian deputation will feel able to return Paris in view of present feeling Italy unless some olive branch be held out to them. The feeling in Italy is not in the least appreciated in Paris. I wish in the interest of future American Italian friendship some way might be opened for their return. Nelson Page

[1] See the minutes of the meeting of the Council of Four printed at May 1, 1919, 11 a.m., and n. 4 thereto.

Rome, May 2, 1919.

286. VERY CONFIDENTIAL AND URGENT.

I have reason to think from conversation with one I know to be well informed, that should an invitation come from Paris expressing desire to reopen negotiations touching Fiume there might be a chance doing so on the following conditions:

(1) Fiume proper to be absolutely free from all Slav sovereignty direct or indirect, that is through some kind of Commission.

(2) Susac from the river down the river to the sea to be absolutely free from Italian sovereignty and separate from Fiume, that is the river will be dividing line between Fiume and Susac.

(3) Fiume to be a free city and the port a free port.

(4) To be conceded from, as well as taken out of, the Pact of London the island of Pago and specially Dalmatian mainland coast except Zara and Sebenico with reasonable defensive ground behind them.

Unfortunately, I do not know whether these points for concession by Italy are new but if they present a chance for reopening discussion, the chance should not be thrown away. Cannot the President take the great step of proposing reopening the discussion and suggest confidentially the foregoing as a basis for new discussion and possible settlement? I know that in Paris some consider me too friendly to Italy but I say on my responsibility as the American Ambassador that the condition in Italy is not dreamed of in Paris and the friendship between the United States and Italy is profoundly imperiled. Nelson Page.

Rome, May 2, 1919.

288. ROUTINE Political conditions.

As reported last week, first effect publication President's Adriatic note was wave intense anger all over Italy against President and Americans which caused government to send troops to protect Embassy in fear of attack. Feeling ameliorated somewhat after a day or two though still strong enough and attempt made here to separate the President from American people, re-asserting friendship with latter but continuing violent attacks on President, this attitude being inspired by government. All consuls report same attitude. Although Italian resentment first directed only against Americans, tendency became apparent after a few days to fasten on France and England some share of responsibility under leadership of *Popolo Romano* and *Tempo* of Rome. Both reproduced remark which Clemenceau is supposed to have made to an Italian, namely that Italians requesting Fiume is like requesting moon. Some coinciding with belief that President is pulling chestnuts out of the fire for France and England. Great emphasis laid by Italian press on expression of sympathy from America exclusively from the Republican journals of America, representatives claiming this to be an indication of solidarity with Italy of general American public opinion. Lodge's speeches much cited.[1] Coincident with this were violent attacks on the President which have now somewhat calmed down probably because the Ambassador protested, bringing to the attention of government a realization that attacks on President might produce serious consequences. For last two days attitude of press with the exception of such ultra Nationalistic papers as IDEA NAZIONALE less inflammatory doubtless reflecting government's desire to show more conciliatory attitude without, however, making any renunciations. . . .

Events of the last week have heightened impression, rapproachment between France and Italy, all the more remarkable when one considers that only short time ago relations so strained that war was feared. Much emphasis laid on exchange of telegrams between former Premier Luzzatti and Clemenceau.[2] The latter, assures me that former French policy not that of scraps of paper. Much importance also attached to general sympathetic attitude of French press which appears in contradiction to position of Clemenceau regarding Fiume. French Embassy issued official statement denying that Clemenceau had inspired President's note. Situation continues very grave. Nelson Page

T telegrams (WP, DLC).

[1] Henry Cabot Lodge's major pronouncement on Italy and the Adriatic question at this time was not a speech but a telegram addressed to various Italian-American organizations in Boston. It reads as follows:

"In the discussion of the terms of peace I have always declared that the region known as Italia Irredenta and all adjoining regions where Italian culture and the Italian population are dominant, should be returned to Italy, and that Italy should have military and naval control of the Adriatic, not only for her own protection but as an essential barrier against any future attempt of Germany to attack the rest of the world as she did in the recent war. I have also said repeatedly that the Jugoslavs ought to have access to the Adriatic, which I regard as economically essential to their independence.

"To both these opinions I adhere, and I can see no reason why the matter could not have been arranged. From information given me by an Italian deputation whom I saw last Spring in Washington I was assured that Italy was entirely willing to give portions of the Dalmatian coast containing good ports to the Slav population of that region. If this be true, as I have no doubt it is, I cannot see why this arrangement should not have been made.

"The pact of London, according to the President's statement, provided for the return of Fiume to Croatia, but the dissolution of the Austrian Empire has vitally changed the situation contemplated by the secret treaty of London, and to that secret treaty the United States was not a party. I repeat that I think Italy should make arrangements to secure an access to the Adriatic to the Slavic populations which I hope will form a united independent barrier State.

"As to Fiume, if Italy is of the opinion that it is necessary to her safety and for her protection that she should hold Fiume, I am clearly of the opinion that it should be hers, especially as the people of Fiume, I understand, have voted to join with Italy. Italy regards

Fiume as the founders of our own republic regard[ed] the mouth of the Mississippi when it was said that any other nation holding the mouth of the Mississippi was of necessity an enemy of the United States.

"That which we desire to do for the Slavs is purely commercial and economic. Italy's demand for Fiume rests on the ground of national safety and protection. Italy has fought side by side with France, England, and the United States and has helped enormously in repelling the German onset. She has sacrificed a half million of her people. She has burdened herself with heavy debts. She has suffered grievously in her industries and in her food supply. She has taken possession of Fiume, which was part of the enemy territory, by her victory in the war. I do not see how the United States and the other nations with whom she was allied can properly refuse her request.

"I earnestly hope that Fiume may become an Italian possession so as to give her that security to which her armies and her sacrifice entitle her." H. C. Lodge to Rocco Brindisi *et al.*, April 29, 1919, *New York Times*, April 30, 1919.

[2] This exchange was discussed, and Clemenceau's telegram was quoted, in a brief article in the *New York Times*, April 27, 1919, which reads as follows:

"ROME, April 26. Engagements between France and Italy will be honored, according to a telegram received tonight by Prof. Luigi Luzzatti, former Premier and Minister of the Interior, from Premier Clemenceau of France, to whom Prof. Luzzatti sent an appeal this morning. The French Premier's telegram follows:

" 'You cannot doubt, my dear illustrious friend, that I am animated by the same sentiments toward Italy as are yours toward France, for I have esteemed it an honor to manifest them in darker days. At the hour of signing peace there can be no question of disregarding our reciprocal engagements. French policy is not 'a scrap of paper.'

" 'Your sincere and devoted friend, CLEMENCEAU.' "

From the Diary of Lord Robert Cecil

May 2 [1919].

Wiseman saw me in the afternoon, very denunciatory of the Prime Minister. He is particularly angry with him over Wilson's Italian statement, which he says—I think quite truly—was approved both by Ll. G. and Clemenceau, though of course they did not mean it to be published then. Now Ll. G. allows it to be said that he never saw the document and did not in any way approve of it. Wiseman also bitterly resented the continual abuse of the President from LL. G., which he says is in no way reciprocated; though I believe the President's secret opinions about our Prime Minister are certainly not more favourable than the P.M.'s opinions about him. Altogether he left me with a strengthened feeling of self-congratulation that I was no longer a member of the Government.[1]

T MS (R. Cecil Papers, Add. MSS 51071-51157, PRO).

[1] Although still a leading member of the British delegation in Paris, Cecil had resigned as Assistant Secretary of State, Foreign Office, in January.

To Charles Mills Galloway

My dear Mr. Galloway: Paris, 2 May, 1919.

I perfectly understood the embarrassment of the present situation for you personally,[1] and beg that you will let the whole question rest until I return to Washington and we can have a personal conference.

Please do not gather from this brief reply that I do not attach a great importance to your letter of April 14th. I am obliged to make all my letters as brief as possible nowa'days because of the constant pressure upon me, as I am sure you will understand.

Sincerely yours, [Woodrow Wilson]

CCL (WP, DLC).

[1] Wilson was replying to C. M. Galloway to WW, April 14, 1919, Vol. 57.

Three Telegrams from Joseph Patrick Tumulty

[The White House] May 2, 1919.

Number 89 stop Committee from American Federation of Labor called to see me last night in great distress and asked me to forward the following stop They say that if Sir Robert Borden's draft is accepted it will mean the united opposition of labor in this country to League of Nations quote Information cabled through State Department last Sunday was to the effect that text of clauses in part two of report of Commission on International Labor Legislation would be before Plenary Session on Monday April 28 at which time Mr. Barnes would move adoption of original text after which Sir Robert Borden would move an amended text stop There has been no information as to the outcome stop paragraph

The clauses referred to are the nine clauses which comma with their introductory paragraph comma form what is termed innerquote Labors Bill of Rights end innerquote paragraph

The redraft presented by Sir Robert Borden changes the whole bill of rights from one to which the signatories are pledged to one which is a mere statement of opinion comma abstract comma without force and in at least one of the most vital instances a repudiation of the original paragraph

The introductory paragraph in the original sets forth that innerquote The high contracting parties declare their acceptance of the following principles and engage to take all necessary steps to secure their realization end innerquote etc paragraph

The redraft in the last sentence of the introductory says that the innerquote methods and principles end innerquote outlined in the list of clauses innerquote seem to the high contracting parties to be of special and urgent importance end innerquote paragraph

The definite acceptance of the principles found in the original draft gives way to the weak sentiment that these things seem to be important which is merely an opinion that may be disagreed with or disavowed by any nation either before or after signing stop In that single sentence of the redraft the whole document loses its flavor, its character, its meaning and the high ideals expressed so frequently in the interest of advancement for labor are abandoned paragraph

Clause One in the numbered list of nine clauses declares in the original that innerquote In right and in fact the labor of a human being should not be treated as merchandise or an article of commerce stop end innerquote This is definite language with a positive meaning stop The redraft reads thus colon innerquote First the guiding principle above enunciated that labor should not be regarded merely as a commodity or article of commerce end innerquote paragraph

The insertion of the word innerquote merely innerquote reverses the meaning and thus sets up again the ancient barbaric doctrine that labor is a commodity and article of commerce stop This is a repudiation of the principle contained in the Clayton Act signed by President Wilson and impressively commented upon by him at that time and for which Mr. Gompers has given the best efforts of his life and which the American workers look upon as the definition of their true status in modern life and society stop The seriousness of this cannot be brought to the attention of Mr. Gompers at this time because of physicians' orders and were he to learn of it is likely that its effect would make his recovery a matter of serious doubt so keenly would he feel the gravity of the issue involved paragraph

The original in clause three says definitely that innerquote No child should be permitted to be employed in industry or commerce before the age of fourteen years end innerquote stop This is definite stop The redraft in its Clause Six makes innerquote The abolition of child labor end innerquote and such limitations as shall permit continuation of their education and innerquote assure their proper physical development end innerquote one of the matters that innerquote seem to be of special and urgent importance end innerquote but which may not be if signatories think otherwise after they have gone home stop This repudiation of the original draft will not only arouse the opposition of the workers but will be subjected to severe criticism by the entire educational world paragraph

Adequate wage equal pay for equal service by men and women, weekly rest and the vitally important right of association become in the redraft matters that innerquote seem to be innerquote important but which are in fact of the most extreme and vital importance to the wage earners, men as well as women stop The adoption of the redraft may also cause extreme opposition by the women of our country paragraph

Limitation of hours of work to a minimum [maximum][1] of eight hours a day and forty-eight hours a week is definitely provided in clause seven of the original but in the redraft is found in clause four merely innerquote as the standard to be aimed at end innerquote and subject to the general description of matters that innerquote seem to be important end innerquote stop In view of the universal acceptance of the principle of the eight-hour day this is a clear evasion of the declaration of the original draft paragraph

Almost complete change of phrasing in the redraft of the nine numbered clauses seriously weakens and impairs and makes indefinite each clause even without the devitalizing introductory which puts the whole program in the light of something that merely innerquote seems to be end innerquote important stop Added to this devitalizing process is the direct repudiation of the fine American principle that innerquote the labor of a human being is not a commodity or article of commerce end innerquote a principle that is part of American law expressing the ideal of America's forward looking people and that will be undermined and made the subject of world ridicule if inserted in the peace treaty by the adoption of the redraft presented by Sir Robert Borden paragraph

The rejection of the original draft and the acceptance of Sir Robert Borden's draft would be interpreted as a complete repudiation of the work of Mr. Gompers and the American labor movement and would give aid and comfort to that element in our country which is typified by what has come to be known as Bolshevism stop It would also be interpreted as a repudiation of the President's high ideals and the American people's conception of the modern status of labor as expressed in the Clayton Act and would make it most difficult and humiliating for the workers of America to support the whole scheme of the League of Nations upquote. Tumulty.

[1] "Minimum" also in the copy of this telegram in the J. P. Tumulty Papers, DLC.

[The White House, May 2, 1919]

No. 92 Sympathetic editorial in New York World with reference to Japanese settlement.[1] I have not given out statement as yet. It does not appear now as if any would be necessary. Tumulty.

[1] "JAPAN'S HONOR AND PRIDE," New York *World*, May 2, 1919. It read as follows:

"What the correspondents describe as a victory for Japan at the Peace Conference in the matter of the Shantung peninsula of China proves to be more sentimental than real. Japan's principal feat at arms during the war was the capture of Kiaochow from the Germans, who had gained that port by characteristic aggression and perfidy. Japan pledged itself then, as Baron Makino does now, to restore the province to China in due time, as to which Japan is to be the sole judge.

"In agreeing to this agreement, the Peace Conference dealt wisely with a question of great delicacy, which after all had more to do with the susceptibilities of Japan than with anything else. Japan is in possession of the peninsula. Its contention has been that to be ordered out of it would be incompatible with its dignity and a reflection upon its good faith. This may be punctilio, but when the United States, Great Britain and France yielded to it they did no more than proclaim their belief in the integrity of a nation which truly claims that it has never violated an engagement.

"Thus it is the honor and pride rather than the greed of Japan that the Associated Powers have recognized, and they have done it in a manner so gracious that their action must have good results. Not the least of these is the covenant of the League of Nations, under which, with Japan's assent, the problems of the Far East are to come at once under the jurisdiction of that body."

[The White House, May 2, 1919]

No. 94 It is urgent that you see Senator Harris about suffrage matters.[1] Tumulty.

T telegrams (WP, DLC).

[1] Senator William Julius Harris was at this time vacationing in Europe. Wilson saw him on May 8. See the extract from the diary of Dr. Grayson printed at that date and Christine A. Lunardini and Thomas J. Knock, "Woodrow Wilson and Woman Suffrage: A New Look," *Political Science Quarterly*, XCV (Winter, 1980-81), 669.

To Joseph Patrick Tumulty

Paris, 2 May, 1919.

Am perfectly willing to have you use your own discretion about the use you make of what I sent you about the Chinese-Japanese settlement. Sorry I cannot yet predict the date of my return though think it will be by June first. Am expecting to make tour of the country but even that is impossible to predict with certainty. Would be glad if you would give out the following as from me. QUOTE The labor programme which the Conference of Peace has adopted as part of the Treaty of Peace constitutes one of the most important achievements of the new day in which the interests of labor are to be systematically and intelligently safeguarded and promoted. Amidst the multitude of other interests this great step forward is apt to be overlooked and yet no other single thing that has been done will help more to stabilize conditions of labor throughout the world and ultimately relieve the unhappy conditions which in too many places have prevailed. Personally I regard this as one of the most gratifying achievements of the Conference. UNQUOTE Woodrow Wilson.

T telegram (WP, DLC).

From Albert Sidney Burleson

Washington May 2nd [1919]

I have given the following statement to the press. By direction of the President, the requisite orders have been issued restoring the various cable lines to the respective owners effective May 2, 1919. The Telegraph and Telephone lines will be returned to the various companies as soon as legislation can be secured from Congress safeguarding the interests of the owners thereof. For a number of years the postmaster general has advocated the Government ownership of the telegraph and telephone system and has urged that they should be blended with and become a part of the postal establishment as essential agencies of communication. He is firmly convinced if such a policy were entered upon that, where there are now three telegraph and telephone pole lines and sometimes four occupying the same highway, entailing immense waste, better and cheaper service could be given by one coordinate wire agency; that by the abolition of various supervisory forces of the wire systems which would then be unnecessary by complete unification of the systems, thereby eliminating the operating cost of the useless system by thoroughly coordinating the remaining telegraph and telephone services by the consolidation of offices and the utilization of post office buildings where practicable; by the use of stamps as a means of eliminating costly and complicated accountings and the utilization of the auditing and accounting forces of the post office department, thereby largely eliminating those of the wire systems, that such savings could be effected that would enable those in authority during normal times to materially reduce the cost of the wire service to the people. As to the wisdom of this course, the post-master general has not changed his views. At the time the government took over the control of the wires, extraordinary and abnormal conditions existed resulting in a constantly increasing and very high operating cost which has necessarily continued. The early coming of the armistice, the accentuated cost of operation and diminishing revenues, the uncertainty in the period of Government control presented such a situation that those in charge for the government were able to accomplish but little by way of unification or to go forward with their policies of economy and consequently were soon brought face to face with a very serious but quite simple problem, to wit, given increasing cost of operation plus diminishing revenues equals that there can be but one answer—increase of rates. This action was taken. It was quite unfortunate and was taken with deepest regret but it was imperative to an intelligent mind. This increase of rates constitutes no sound reason for a change of view on the original proposition that it is economically wise for the government to own the wire systems as a part of the postal establishment and in no sense tends to refute the soundness of the contention that through such ownership saving would be effected that would result in a reduction of rates. For example, street car companies and other public utilities—organizations throughout the country which are being operated under private control—are in many cases on the verge of bankruptcy and are petitioning for an increase in rates for their services and when same have been granted the increases sought often return with petitions for still further increase, basing their claims upon the higher wages and increased cost of material. The wire administration could not escape this condition which extended throughout the country in reaction in every form of service, public or private. There is quite a difference between government ownership and government control for a limited and very uncertain period. The present control affords no more a test of the virtues of government ownership than could be had through a temporary receivership in a court proceeding. That the contention of the postmaster general for a complete unification of the various wire systems is both wise from an economic standpoint and supported by sound business principles has been confirmed by the ablest experts on electrical transmission in America. That it should be brought about the postmaster general still believes perfectly through government ownership and operating as a part of the postal establishment, but if this is not done then through some means of unified control by private ownership over which the government should at all times exercise a wholesome regulatory supervision. About the desirability of this, the post-master general has had no reason to undergo a change of mind. However, for some time it has been apparent that the first of the alternatives does not meet with the approbation of the new Congress. Such being the case, there is but one course to pursue, and that is to return the various wire properties to their respective owners after urging proper legislation to safeguard the interest of all the properties in fairness to the investors and to insure proper service to the public. Having reached this conclusion the post-master general does not hesitate to [recommend] this line of action.

Burleson.

T telegram (WP, DLC).

From the Diary of Dr. Grayson

Saturday, May 3, 1919.

The President arose early and after breakfast went to his study where he disposed of matters requiring his attention. At 11:00 o'clock the Big Three met. Lloyd-George and Clemenceau talked a great deal concerning the matter of bringing about a reconciliation with Italy but offered no solution. They seemed to want to put the whole thing up to the President but presented no definite program for his guidance. It is common comment that they are trying to get Italy back into the Conference, and they are giving the impression on the outside that the President is to blame. However, when it comes to a show-down with him they offer no solution for the proposition. It is again very apparent how tricky and what politicians both of them are to the outside world. When it comes down to practical work on the inside they are quite meek and pretend to the President they are siding with him.

The President, Mrs. Wilson and I had lunch at one o'clock. Just before dinner the President conferred with Count Cellere,[1] the Italian Ambassador to the United States. He came and made a long plea for Italy, urging that she be allowed to come back into the Conference. The President assured him that no one would welcome her back more than he would but that he had to adhere to his stand concerning Fiume. The Italian Ambassador did most of the talking and offered no solution. The President told him that there was no use in debating any further; that they (Italy) knew the terms, and that when they would accept them, they would be welcomed back. He hoped with all his heart that they would come back but that he must be frank with them and tell them that he must adhere to his principles.

I have never seen the President more fatigued than he was at dinner time this evening. He could not have had a harder or more difficult and fatiguing day. Count Celere came with a statement which he could have made in about three minutes, but he remained for over an hour—all of which was most tiresome to the President. It was 7:45 when the President went to his usual seven o'clock dinner. He was 45 minutes late.

Ray Stannard Baker was here to get the news of the day. When I went in to see the President to announce Baker, he said: "Well, I am just so tired that I do not feel I could recall what has happened throughout the day. You know briefly about what occurred. Won't you go out and explain the situation to Baker? Tell him how I feel and express my apology for not seeing him."

After dinner I spent an hour with the President and Mrs. Wilson.

It was most refreshing to see how Mrs. Wilson entertained the President with light enjoyable conversation, detaching his mind from the heavy responsibilities to which he had been subjected during the day. Her attentions and affection for the President are truly touching and beautiful. No one but a member of the household could appreciate what a genuine and true helpmate she is to the President.

Before saying good-night to the President I begged him, owing to his fatigue, not to go to church tomorrow. This was not only because he greatly needed a Sunday morning's rest in bed, but it was very damp and I was afraid that the church might not be heated. Moreover, with many persons present with colds and coughing, the President in his run-down condition would be taking chances of catching cold. I said: "Really, too much is dependent on you now to take this chance." He looked up with a twinkle in his eye and said: "I am a Presbyterian, but I will have to agree with my physician."

[1] That is, Count Vincenzo Macchi di Cellere.

Hankey's Notes of a Meeting of the Council of Four[1]

President Wilson's House,
I.C.-180A Paris, May 3, 1919, 10 a.m.

1. M. KLOTZ was introduced by M. Clemenceau and read the letter which was to be sent to M. Crespi, in reply to the latter's letter referred to in the Minutes of the previous day.[2] This reply is identical with the draft approved on the previous day, except for an introduction in the following sense:

"I already had the pleasure to acknowledge the receipt of your letter etc."

(M. Klotz' letter was approved.)

(M. Klotz withdrew.)

2. MR. LLOYD GEORGE suggested that the Foreign Ministers should be introduced for the discussion on the subject of Italy.

M. CLEMENCEAU said he was willing.

PRESIDENT WILSON said it was not a matter of foreign affairs but rather for the Conference. There was no technical reason why the Foreign Ministers should be present.

MR. LLOYD GEORGE said that the decision to be taken was so important that he would like to have the presence of Mr. Balfour, who

[1] The complete text of these minutes is printed in *PPC*, V, 426-36.

[2] See the minutes of the Council of Four printed at May 2, 1919, 11 a.m., and Appendix I thereto.

had come over under the impression that the question of submarine cables was to be discussed at 10:00 o'clock.

(This was agreed to.)

(Mr. Balfour entered, and M. Pichon was telephoned for.)

PRESIDENT WILSON read a despatch from the United States' Ambassador in Rome, who, he said, was sympathetic to the Italians but thoroughly understood his own point of view.[3] The gist of it was that May Day had been quiet in Rome; that excitement had largely subsided; that the Italian Government had realized the dangerous position; that the troops as well as the gendarmes had been removed from the American Embassy; that there was a real desire for a settlement, but that the only possible settlement was a concession by the Allied and Associated Powers in regard to Fiume; if this could be agreed, everything else could be arranged; but that nothing would content Italy which left out Fiume.

He pointed out that the Italian Government had only themselves to blame for this result, as they had worked up public opinion.

MR. LLOYD GEORGE said that Mr. Erskine,[4] the British Chargé d' Affaires, had telegraphed that he had seen Baron Sonnino; that the latter had said he was doing his best to quiet excitement; but had ended by saying that the next move ought to be from Paris.

PRESIDENT WILSON said that these telegrams showed that the things that Baron Sonnino had contended were not popular items. What the public wanted were the items Signor Orlando had contended for, namely, those outside the Pact of London. Mr. Baker, who was in charge of the press arrangements for the United States Delegation, said that his Italian colleague had not latterly come to see him, but yesterday he had seen him and he had asked when the Italians were going to be invited back to Paris. His reply had been: "Who invited you to go?"

M. CLEMENCEAU was handed a despatch from M. Barrère, the French Ambassador in Rome, which had just arrived. M. Barrère said that he was telegraphing at midnight and had just received a letter from Baron Sonnino, commenting more particularly on the fact that the Delegates of Austria and Hungary had been asked to Paris without consultation with the Italians. This compelled him to give to some observations he had forwarded the character of formal protest.

(At this moment a message was received by Mr. Lloyd George from the Marquis Imperiali, who telephoned to the effect that he had received a cipher despatch from Rome and would postpone

[3] T. N. Page to Ammission, No. 282, May 1, 1919, T telegram (WP, DLC).

[4] William Augustus Forbes Erskine.

his visit to Mr. Lloyd George until it had been deciphered.)

PRESIDENT WILSON said that Baron Sonnino did not state the whole of the facts. The Italians had been informed of what was intended before they left for Rome.

MR. LLOYD GEORGE pointed out that the decision to invite the Austrians and Hungarians had been taken after the Italian Delegation had left. How, he asked, could the Italians have been consulted?

M. CLEMENCEAU said that they had been informed immediately the decision was taken.

PRESIDENT WILSON asked if the telegram drafted by Mr. Balfour, to which Mr. Lloyd George had alluded in conversation before the meeting, might be read.

MR. LLOYD GEORGE read the first draft, which had been prepared by Mr. Malkin,[5] a legal expert, and did not pretend to give more than a rough outline of the legal position in which Italy would be if she did not sign the Treaty of Peace with Germany (Appendix I). The gist of this was if Italy broke the Pact of London, the Allies were no longer bound by the Treaty of London.

MR. BALFOUR said that his own draft (Appendix II) was based on the idea that there would be great disaster to the world if Italy did not come back to meet the Germans. The breach between Italy and her Allies would become wider. There would be one Power outside the grouping of Great Powers and it might be impossible for that Power to come back. His idea was to give Italy a bridge, or at least the means of coming back.

MR. LLOYD GEORGE pointed out the difference between the effect the document would produce if signed simply by the British Government as a friendly warning and its dispatch as a formal warning from France, Great Britain and the United States of America. He then read Mr. Balfour's draft. (Appendix II.)

PRESIDENT WILSON said that the first document (Appendix I) was not adequate since it did not recite Italy's participation in all these transactions. For example (a) the Armistice; (b) the basis on which the Peace negotiations were undertaken and (c) Italy's share in drawing up the Peace Treaty itself, and (d) finally, Italy's withdrawal.

M. CLEMENCEAU then produced a document that he had prepared which, at his request, President Wilson read. (Appendix III.)

(During the reading of this document M. Pichon entered.)

PRESIDENT WILSON pointed out that each step of this kind tended to emphasize the isolation of the United States of America.

M. CLEMENCEAU said the document had been prepared by M. Tar-

[5] Herbert William Malkin.

dieu under his instructions entirely from the point of view of the signatories of the Treaty of London.

PRESIDENT WILSON pointed out that in effect this document (Appendix III) did indicate that if Italy came back on the basis of the Treaty of London, some agreement might be reached. The world knew, however, that the United States could not be a party to an agreement based on the Treaty of London and he would have to say so. This document amounted to a virtual promise to stand with Italy and the isolation of the United States would become more serious than ever. He wished to add that he was saying this in the most friendly spirit.

MR. LLOYD GEORGE said he had put precisely the same difficulty to his colleagues and had pointed out that we were in danger of a quarrel either with the United States or with Italy. The former would be far the more serious of the two. Putting the matter at its lowest, Germany would not sign the Peace in the former event so that this was a very serious possibility. This made him almost more afraid of the return of the Italian Delegates than if they stayed away.

MR. BALFOUR said that this was his view.

MR. LLOYD GEORGE said that Mr. Bonar Law, who had been in contact with elements in England that were perhaps less imbued with the principles on which the Peace was being based, was inclined to take a somewhat different view. He asked Mr. Balfour what the feeling was in England according to his information.

MR. BALFOUR said he had shown Sir Rendell Rodd[6] the memorandum handed by Mr. Lloyd George and M. Clemenceau to M. Orlando.[7] His view had been: "Are you really going to quarrel with Italy over a thing like that?" Sir Rendell Rodd had, however, rather changed his view after their conversation.

MR. LLOYD GEORGE said he did not wish to put M. Orlando in the position of being able to cast the responsibility on his Allies for their remaining away. Unless France and Great Britain said clearly: "We stand by the Treaty of London" M. Orlando could say: "You threw me over."

PRESIDENT WILSON thought that the same object could be secured in a different way although he was not prepared there and then to say exactly how. As he told M. Clemenceau and Mr. Lloyd George on the previous day, the whole trend of the Press was to show that France and Great Britain were not acting with the United States and that he had not the support of the Heads of these States. This was why he wanted the memorandum to Mr. Orlando to be

[6] Sir James Rennell Rodd, British Ambassador to Italy since 1908.

[7] That is, the document printed as Appendix I to the minutes of the Council of Four, April 24, 1919, 4 p.m.

published so as to show clearly that their views were similar to his own. This would show United States' opinion that he was not standing in isolation in this matter. It had been stated in Rome that President Wilson's declaration had been inspired by M. Clemenceau. He was informed that the French Embassy had issued an official denial to this. One Italian newspaper had said that M. Clemenceau had neither inspired or knew of his declaration.

M. CLEMENCEAU asked M. Pichon if this was correct.

M. PICHON said he had no information.

PRESIDENT WILSON said that it had only been in one newspaper. Whichever way, however, his statement was taken, it was news to him that his colleagues did not know, or that he had sent out his statement arbitrarily. He wanted to warn his colleagues that if they were not careful an impression would be given that there was a serious rift between France and Great Britain on the one hand and the United States on the other. The effect of this would be that United States' opinion would say: "We will get out of this."

MR. LLOYD GEORGE said it was necessary to speak very frankly in the intimacy of these conversations. It must not be forgotten that there was a growing feeling that Europe was being bullied by the United States of America. In London this feeling was very strong and that matter had to be handled with the greatest care. Any such rift would be the saddest possible ending to the present Conference. It would put an end to the League of Nations. He understood that the London Press had behaved extremely well and had not gone as far as British public opinion. The position was one of the real danger and wanted to be handled with the greatest care, otherwise we might have the worst catastrophe since 1914.

PRESIDENT WILSON said he did not speak with authority in regard to British public opinion. Nevertheless, he was sure of the fact that the so-called bullying was recognized by the common man as based on the principles which inspired the Peace. In his view, it was indispensable clearly to show Italy that in all essentials Great Britain, France and the United States were united, otherwise the Italians would continue to be troublesome.

MR. LLOYD GEORGE said that in fact they were not completely united. In regard to Fiume they were united. M. Clemenceau and he, however, were not in the same position as President Wilson, owing to the fact that they were bound by the Treaty of London.

PRESIDENT WILSON pointed out that Mr. Lloyd George and M. Clemenceau had both signed the memorandum to M. Orlando. This showed that they were united with him in judgment even though not in position.

MR. LLOYD GEORGE said that it was no use being united in judgment when a decision was wanted. France and Great Britain were bound by the Treaty of London. If Italy insisted he was bound to stand by the Treaty. He could not possibly help that. This was the bottom fact of the whole situation.

PRESIDENT WILSON thought that this was a position which could not be got out of. Moreover, it was an indefensible position. The treaty had been entered into when only a little group of nations was at war. Since then half the World had joined in. There could be no right in coercing other Parties to this Treaty which were just as much bound by conscience as Great Britain and France were by the Treaty. It was neither good morals nor good statesmanship.

MR. LLOYD GEORGE said that Great Britain had been brought into the war largely in protest against the breach of a Treaty. She could not contemplate herself breaking a Treaty at the end of the war when the other partner of the Treaty had lost half a million lives in giving effect to it. This had been worrying him for several days past.

PRESIDENT WILSON said this made it the more important to find some way out. The stage ought to be so set as not to encourage the Italians to come back. M. Clemenceau's document (Appendix III) was more than an invitation for them to return. It was a challenge. He would prefer the first document that had been read (Appendix I) with a recital of the facts added. A clear narration should be given of the facts and a very important statement in M. Orlando's letter to M. Clemenceau dated April 23rd in which he stated that:

"The terms of Peace with Germany may henceforth be considered a settlement in their essential elements" should be referred to. Then the case would be clear that if Italy were to break off the responsibility would be theirs.

MR. LLOYD GEORGE said that the Italians would then formulate a long reply, and a controversy would be commenced. He agreed to every word that President Wilson had said but he was really afraid that they might come back.

MR. BALFOUR said that as he understood the matter the policy that we wished to pursue was the same policy as the United States of America wished to pursue, and vice versa. Our difficulty arose from the fact that we were bound by a formal treaty, which, however, it was true, had been concluded in entirely different circumstances from those now applying. The difficulty was how to get a real agreement in conformity with our treaties. The only way seemed to be to get the Italians to admit that they had broken the treaty which they really had done.

PRESIDENT WILSON said that Italy had broken both treaties, because her demands were more than the Treaty of London gave her. He had never for a moment given the smallest indication that he agreed to the Treaty of London.

MR. LLOYD GEORGE said he could not altogether accept any suggestion that President Wilson's statement voiced the British view. He thought that Italy had a real case connected with her security in demanding the Islands in the Adriatic. President Wilson had agreed that the ethnic principle was not the only one that could be adopted by admitting that Italy should have a great part of the Tyrol. He himself would apply the same principle to the Islands, in default of which, Italy's east coast would be seriously menaced.

PRESIDENT WILSON agreed that against Austria-Hungary this was the case.

MR. LLOYD GEORGE said the same applied if Austria-Hungary had allies. If we were to say "you have broken the treaty," there would be an end of the matter. In M. Clemenceau's document (Appendix III) we said "you will have broken if you do not come back." If there must be a break, a break with Italy would be bad enough, but not a disaster; a break with the United States would be a disaster.

PRESIDENT WILSON asked why the Treaty of London should be mentioned in the Note. Mr. Lloyd George had been almost brutally frank with M. Orlando on this point. He wished that the memorandum to M. Orlando might be published. (M. Clemenceau interjected that this was his view.) All that was now necessary was to show that Italy was breaking the Pact. The first document read (Appendix I), however, did not prove the case sufficiently.

MR. BALFOUR explained that the first document was only a very hasty draft in which his legal adviser had jotted down his view on the legal point.

MR. LLOYD GEORGE adverted to a matter of drafting in M. Clemenceau's document (Appendix III). It called attention to the fact that the Treaty of London assigned Fiume to the Croats. In his view, it was imperative to point out that this meant Serbia—another Ally. He asked if the Serbs had known of this Treaty.

MR. BALFOUR thought not.

PRESIDENT WILSON said that that had been argued and set before the Italians sufficiently.

MR. LLOYD GEORGE said it was not quite sufficient to say that Fiume had been given to the Croats. There was no feeling for the Croats in the United Kingdom, but there was very strong feeling for the Serbs.

M. PICHON said that the Treaty of London had not been communicated to the Croats. At one of the conversations at the Quai d'Orsay, M. Vesnitch had said that he did not know the Treaty of London, and took no cognizance of it.

M. CLEMENCEAU said he would prefer to publish the memorandum signed by Mr. Lloyd George and himself first. If any other document were published first, the public would not understand the situation, which could not be made clear without the memorandum. There were certain objections, but by this means alone could the position be fully explained. He and Mr. Lloyd George had all along approved of the general lines of President Wilson's statement, and it must be made clear that they had not differed from it. On the eve of very serious events, it must be shown that Great Britain and France had always stood with the United States of America, otherwise if some other document were published first, it would be said that they had wavered. It was true that M. Orlando did not want the memorandum published, but this was a case of a choice between two evils and the least disadvantageous was to publish the memorandum.

MR. LLOYD GEORGE said he must make it clear that President Wilson had not put the view of the British Government in his statement, and that was why he had wanted a separate document to be sent to M. Orlando. Without it, M. Orlando would not know what the British attitude was.

PRESIDENT WILSON said that memorandum showed clearly what the British and French view was as matters stood. He said that he had to keep his private secretary in the United States reassured that there was no difference between him and Great Britain on this point.

MR. BALFOUR confirmed this by stating that he had received a telegram from Lord Reading who was about to make a speech in New York, and who had indicated that there was this idea of a separation between the American view and the British and French view. He had telegraphed back that there was not the smallest difference in policy between them.

PRESIDENT WILSON said that his private secretary, Mr. Tumulty, had an almost uncanny appreciation of public opinion in the United States. He himself had had to keep Mr. Tumulty reassured that there was no difference between himself and his British and French colleagues. If this opinion continued to gain ground American public opinion would be asking what he was going to do.

MR. LLOYD GEORGE asked what action was contemplated if Italy did not come back? What would be done if Italy remained in Fiume: Would she be left there? It would be no use sending her letters, in which we should merely have to say that the Austrian Peace had been settled on certain principles and that Fiume was to be a free port. Should we have to say to her, you must clear out?

M. CLEMENCEAU said not at present.

MR. LLOYD GEORGE said he was not shrinking from the results of our policy. The League of Nations, however, would be finished, if the first Power that defied it did so with impunity. Moreover, if Italy was left in Fiume, there would be fighting between her and the

Jugo-Slavs. Were we to allow the Italian armies to march to Belgrade? He only said these things to show that we were really determining a great policy at the present time.

PRESIDENT WILSON suggested that Mr. Lloyd George had been arguing that if the memorandum were published, it would prevent the Italians coming back.

MR. LLOYD GEORGE said he was, because the indications at the present time were that if the Italians came back, they would ask for impossible terms. He, himself, hoped that Italy might still be willing to accept the compromise that he had proposed, namely, that Fiume should remain an absolutely free port; that they should evacuate Dalmatia, perhaps with some provision for free cities; and that they would take the Islands.

M. CLEMENCEAU doubted if this was possible.

(The Meeting then adjourned to the room upstairs for the Meeting on Cables, reported in the other series of Minutes.)

I.C. 180-A

APPENDIX I.

The French and British Governments have been loyally endeavoring to carry out the provision of the Pact of London under which the signatories agreed not to conclude a separate peace. For several months discussions have been proceeding with the object of reaching an agreement as to the terms on which peace could be made in common. The action of the Italian representatives in withdrawing from these discussions, if persisted in, obviously makes it impossible for peace to be concluded in common; it renders the fulfilment of the promise in question by the French and British Governments impossible, and constitutes a breach by the Italian Government of the Pact of London.

I.C. 180-A.

APPENDIX II.

We are not sure that you fully realize the serious effects on the unity of the Allies and the settlement of Europe which must be produced by your absence from Versailles while peace with Germany is being arranged. It is true that we have no suggestion to make about Fiume, and the Adriatic, beyond those with which you are already acquainted. But these problems are not directly connected with the conclusion of peace with Germany, and their solution, if a solution is possible, will certainly not be hindered by the presence of Italian plenipotentiaries at Versailles. On the other hand, if Italy refuses her concurrence and cooperation she will not only be in our opinion violating the Pact of London, but she will be taking a step which will render future unity of action a matter of the extremist difficulty. To us such a result seems little short of disaster to civilization.

I.C. 180-A.

APPENDIX III.

1. The Governments of Great Britain and France had received no answer to the letter sent on the ______ April by Mr. Lloyd George and Clemenceau to Signor Orlando, in which the Prime Ministers of both countries urged their Italian Colleague to reconsider the situation. Since then the German Plenipotentiaries, in compliance with the invitation forwarded to them on the 17th April, notwithstanding Signor Orlando's reservations, by the Supreme Council of the Allied and Associated Governments, have arrived at Versailles. It is therefore necessary, in the common interest, that the situation thus created should be cleared up, and that it be known whether, as the Allies heartily trust, Italy will stand at their side to sign Peace with Germany at the same time as they will.

2. The letter of Signor Orlando to M. Clemenceau dated April 23rd stated that "*the terms of Peace with Germany may henceforth be considered as settled in their essential elements.*" The London agreement of April 26th, 1915, providing that "*none of the Allied Powers shall lay conditions of Peace without previous agreement with its Allies,*" has consequently been complied with, as regards Peace with Germany. The Governments of Great Britain and France therefore like to think that Italy will be ready to sign with them the Treaty which she has had an ample share in preparing, and with which, according to the above-mentioned letter, she has declared herself satisfied.

3. As regards the other agreement of April 26th, 1915, concerning the boundaries between Italy and Austria Hungary, the Governments of Great Britain and France, still prompted by the same spirit which had inspired their conduct in the negotiations of the last few months, recall the fact that the said Treaty, which they constantly declared themselves ready to carry out, assigns Fiume to the Croats. They consequently renew their regret that the claim laid to Fiume by the Italian Government—signatory of the Treaty which ascribes that town to the Croats—should make it impossible to execute an agreement by whose terms the said Governments are bound to abide, with respect to all parties concerned.

4. This being the case, the Governments of Great Britain and France, feeling they have faithfully fulfilled their obligations, on the one hand by preparing together with Italy the terms of peace with Germany, on the other hand by declaring their readiness to

stand by their engagements of the 26th April, 1915, as regards Italy as well as the Croats, are under the obligation to request the Italian Government to acquaint them with their final decision.

Were Signor Orlando, contrary to all their expectations, to come to a negative decision, the two Governments should have to hold the opinion that it would be owing to Italy that the two kinds of engagements taken in London on April 26th, 1915, would lapse.

In the latter case, Italy by withdrawing her consent to the conditions of peace with Germany, settled in agreement with the Italian Delegation, as well as to the arrangements regarding the Adriatic, would, in so doing, renounce being a party to the Treaty which is going to be considered at Versailles and benefiting by the provisions agreed upon in 1915 in the matter of the Adriatic.

5. The Governments of Great Britain and France still fervently hope that the Italian Government will be fully alive, as they are, to the danger of such a solution for that future of peace and justice for which Italy, in full solidarity with the Allied and Associated countries, has sacrificed so much of her blood. The present circumstances and the fact that the German Plenipotentiaries are now in Versailles make it a duty for Great Britain and France to ask Signor Orlando for an answer at the earliest possible moment.

They beg him to forward it to them and while heartily appealing to the high sense of the Italian interests and of the general weal entertained by the Government of Italy, they hereby bear witness to the unfailing affection of Great Britain and France for the Italian Nation.

T MS (SDR, RG 256, 180.03401/139, DNA).

Hankey's Notes of a Meeting of the Council of Four[1]

President Wilson's House,
I.C.-180B Paris, May 3, 1919, 11:30 a.m.

1. The following draft resolution was before the Meeting: [Here follows the text of the draft resolution at the end of Hankey's notes of the meeting of the Council of Ten printed at May 2, 1919, 5 p.m.]
(After some discussion it was decided to accept the first paragraph for inclusion in the Treaty of Peace, and to add to it a second paragraph in the following terms:

> "The value of the above mentioned cables or portions thereof, in so far as they are privately owned, calculated on the basis of the original cost, less a suitable allowance for depreciation, shall be credited to Germany in the reparation account."

It was further decided that paragraphs 2 and 3 of the draft should form the subject of a separate protocol between the principal Allied and Associated powers. The following modification to the second of these paragraphs was agreed upon. Instead of the expression "Powers concerned" the expression "principal Allied and Associated Powers" was substituted. The last clause of this paragraph therefore reads:

"and to make recommendations to the Principal Allied and Associated Powers with a view to providing the entire world with adequate facilities of this nature on a fair and equitable basis.")

T MS (SDR, RG 256, 180.03401/140, DNA).

[1] The complete text of these minutes is printed in *PPC*, V, 437-38.

From the Diary of Colonel House

May 3, 1919.

The burning question for the past two days has been that of the Italians. Clemenceau and George, particularly George, say if the Italians come back and demand the Treaty of London, they will have to live up to their obligations. The President told them that we would not sign a treaty which recognized the Treaty of London, and that France and England would have to choose between Italy and the United States. George and Clemenceau hoped that no such choice would have to be made, but if it came to that, they would have to recognize their obligation to the Treaty of London no matter what the consequences.

The President was disturbed and came immediately to the Crillon and had a conference with Bliss, White and myself, Lansing being absent. I tried to stir him from his inflexible position and made several suggestions regarding a settlement which might be satisfactory to both sides. The only one he seemed to favor was leaving the settlement to the League of Nations, but this he rejected because he said that the decision had to be unanimous and Italy will have a vote on the Council of Ten. I thought it might be arranged with the Italians to waive their right to vote.

I later talked with Congressman La Guardia,[1] who called soon after the President left. He is an Italian by birth and is now a Republican Congressman from New York. He has been in our Aviation Service and, during the war, did some flying in Italy. I mentioned the suggestion of the League of Nations, and he thought it might be acceptable to Italy. He will try it out on Crespi, who is still here, and will let me know in the morning.

The President, Lloyd George and Clemenceau are preparing a communication to send Orlando. They hope to put it in such form that Orlando will not come back to Paris. They all three hope that he will remain away and not sign the German Treaty because they are afraid he will demand the ratification of the Treaty of London and thereby bring about a difficult situation with the United States. The whole matter seems to me to have been stupidly managed. If the worst comes to the worst I shall try to persuade the President to sign the peace with the Germans and then let France and England settle with Italy the best way they can, we, however, refusing to join in the settlement and refusing to guarantee it in any way.

I have been busy again today with the organization of the League of Nations. I have also had up the matter of Syria which is not altogether in good shape.

Monsignor Francis Clement Kelly of Chicago[2] was an interesting caller. He is a clever man but inspires me with distrust. He wanted to know whether we desired to have certain bankers make a loan of two hundred and fifty millions of dollars to Carranza. The oil and other interests would back the loan if the Catholic Church would sanction it. He would sanction it, he said, if we desired him to do so. If we did not, he would have the loan refused, and in that event, he thought that by giving aid to de la Barra or Felix Diaz,[3] the Carranza Government might easily be overthrown.

He did not hesitate to suggest double-dealing on his part, but spoke unctiously several times of his interest in saving souls. He also wanted to know whether the President desired him, Kelly, to publicly give the President credit for what he termed "our clause" in Article 22 of the Covenant, which he said demands religious freedom. I was non-committal on everything. I listened to Kelly, asked a few questions and gave no opinions of my own further than if he called again in a week or ten days, I would give him the answers which he demanded, or would refuse to give them, as the case might be. I did this to get rid of him. I have no notion of mentioning the matter to the President, or of involving him or myself in any way whatsoever. If Kelly comes back, I shall tell him that he had better use his own judgment in both instances.

[1] That is, Fiorello Henry La Guardia, who had received the Italian War Cross for his service on the Italian-Austrian front. He had been an American consular agent in Fiume, 1904-1906.

[2] That is, the Most Rev. Francis Clement Kelley (not Kelly), about whom see the index references in Vol. 39 of this series.

[3] That is, Francisco Léon de la Barra and Felix Díaz, about whom see the index references in *ibid.*

From the Diary of David Hunter Miller

Saturday, May 3rd [1919]

I sent up to the President a memorandum,[1] with a copy of the four draft articles.[2]

I talked with M. Berthelot over the telephone, and asked him to come to the meeting which had been arranged last night; namely, that the Committee should meet at the President's house at 11:15 and that we should go in to the Council of Three at quarter of twelve.

I sent M. Berthelot a copy of the four articles.

The final French text of the Covenant is in a folder marked "Final French Text 3 May."

The report of the Committee is marked in pencil showing the changes made by the Council of Three. The Council of Three agreed in principle to the provisions of Article 3 and decided that those provisions should be inserted after further consideration of their language, in the separate Treaty with Poland. The exact action of the Council otherwise in adopting Articles 1, 2 and 4 is shown on the memorandum.

I asked the President whether Roumania was considered as a new State for the purposes of our Committee, and he said, "Yes"; also, he spoke to me about the difficulties which would arise if Italy did not come back and said that the expression, "Principal Allied and Associated Powers" had been adopted and would be defined in one clause of the Treaty as meaning either four Powers or five Powers, as the case might be. He said that the Council of Three had directed that the Covenant be changed accordingly, which I should think would mean simply in Article IV.

Mr. Balfour and Baron Makino were present at the meeting, and of course Hankey and the members of the Committee. There was no criticism of the language of items 1 and 2 of Article 3 but C and D of item 3 of that Article were criticised as being too broad. Lloyd George said that discrimination might be made against an inhabitant such as was made in the United States where only a native-born citizen could be President. The question of the rights of minorities was taken up and the sentiment was entirely against creating any communities such as the Jews want.

After the meeting I agreed with other members of the Committee to meet at the Quai d'Orsay on Monday at noon to discuss our subsequent procedure and principles.

In the afternoon I received from Harrison Treaty clauses regarding Czecho-Slovakia but I have no copies of these.

Mr. Marshall[3] came in and I told him that I did not feel at liberty to tell him what had happened, and I did not mention to him even about the appointment of the Committee. I did tell him that the ideas that they had about creating corporate entities would undoubtedly not be accepted.

I saw Colonel House in the afternoon and he thought that I should not discuss with the Jews any details of what had happened. I showed him the memorandum of the action taken by the Three.

Wiseman came in while we were talking and discussed the Italian situation, which Colonel House said was critical. I gathered that the effort to arrange it is still going on by some arrangement about Fiume. Colonel House said that the President would not accept the Pact of London and that a most difficult situation will arise if the Italians abandon their claim to Fiume and insist on the Pact of London. Wiseman thought that the Italians should be asked to sign the Treaty with Germany and that if they refused it should be signed anyhow. I pointed out that it would be necessary to guarantee Germany against an attack by Italy if she were left at war with that country and deprived of an army, and that this would be very difficult for the Allies of Italy to do.

While I was walking home Rappard[4] met me in the street and asked me if I would discuss with Huber[5] tomorrow the meaning of some of the clauses in the Covenant. I told him I did not think it would be proper for me to do so. He spoke of the Swiss Government writing to the Secretary General and I simply asked in reply what effect an answer of the Secretary General would have.

The final French text (subject to the amendment made at the Plenary session of April 28th) was printed.

I dined and spent the evening at home.

David Hunter Miller, *My Diary at the Conference of Paris, with Documents* (21 vols., New York, 1924), I, 286-88.

[1] It is printed as the following document.

[2] T MS (WP, DLC). These articles, with changes by Wilson as noted, are printed in Annexes A and B to the minutes of the Council of Four printed at May 3, 1919, 12:10 p.m.

[3] That is, Louis Marshall, president of the American Jewish Committee, who had recently arrived in Paris with Julian William Mack, president of the Comité des Délégations Juives in Paris.

[4] That is, William Emmanuel Rappard.

[5] Max Huber, Professor of Constitutional and International Law at the University of Zürich and a Swiss delegate to the Second Hague Peace Conference of 1907. A legal adviser to the Swiss Federal Council since 1918 and a strong advocate of the creation of an international peace organization, Huber was later elected to the Permanent Court of International Justice (1921-1930) and to the Permanent Court of Arbitration (1923-1940). He also became a member of the International Committee of the Red Cross in 1923 and served as its President and Acting President, respectively, from 1928 to 1947.

A Memorandum by David Hunter Miller

MEMORANDUM FOR THE PRESIDENT: 3 May, 1919.

The Committee appointed to consider Rights of Minorities, etc. in new States[1] hopes to present a report to the Council of Three this morning, subject to an agreement in detail with the French representative, M. Berthelot.

The substance of the report will be as follows:

1. The question of economic equality must be left for a subsequent treaty.

2. The subject of community rights of minorities must also be left for a subsequent treaty.

3. But provisions binding Poland to an agreement in these matters is essential in the Treaty of Peace. Such provisions will be presented as Annex A, which is Article 4 of the enclosed draft.[2]

4. Provisions as to citizenship and individual rights are deemed by me essential to be inserted in the Treaty of Peace. These are Article 3 of the enclosed draft. Mr. Headlam-Morley, of the British, agrees that such an Article is essential but thinks it can wait for a subsequent treaty, although if he could submit it to the British Legal Advisers he would be willing to have it go in now. This is the only point of difference between him and myself.

5. Articles 1 and 2 of the enclosed draft are preliminary to Article 3, but the British approve of them. David Hunter Miller

TS MS (WP, DLC).

[1] About this matter, see the minutes of the Council of Four printed at May 1, 1919, 11 a.m.

[2] See n. 2 to the extract from the Miller Diary just printed.

Hankey's and Mantoux's Notes of a Meeting of the Council of Four[1]

President Wilson's House,
I.C.-180C Paris, May 3, 1919, 12:10 p.m.

1. The Preliminary Report of the Committee on New States was presented for consideration (Appendix).

PRESIDENT WILSON proposed that for "the commerce of the Allied and Associated Powers" in the last line of Annex A, the words "the commerce of other nations" should be substituted.[2]

(This was agreed to, and it was decided that this clause should be inserted in the Treaty in substitution of the existing Article 7 of the Chapter relating to Poland.)

[1] The complete text of Hankey's minutes is printed in *PPC*, V, 439-44.

[2] Wilson made this change in the draft of the articles which Miller had enclosed with his memorandum printed as the previous document.

The Articles contained in Annex B were then considered. On the proposal of PRESIDENT WILSON, it was decided that Articles 1 and 2 should be sent to the Drafting Committee with instructions that they should be inserted in the Treaty with Germany, unless the points contained therein were already adequately covered by other articles.

With regard to Article 3, Mr. Headlam Morley explained that while accepting in principle the substance of the provisions contained in this Article, he had felt great apprehension as to the acceptance of the provisions as they stood, without a detailed consideration and without consultation with the legal authorities. It had been impossible in the very limited time at the disposal of the Committee either to consider proposals in detail or to consult the legal advisers.

MR. LLOYD GEORGE confirmed this view.

DR. MILLER pointed out that unless Article 3 or some provision of a similar character were inserted in the Treaty, there would be nothing in the Treaty binding Poland to accept provisions safeguarding the rights of individuals in the matter of citizenship.

To meet this objection President Wilson proposed that in the Article contained in Annex A, the inclusion of which in the Treaty had already been agreed to, the word "inhabitants" should be substituted for "communities" in Line 4.[3]

(This was accepted. The Article in Annex A was as amended then sent to the Drafting Committee.)

The Committee on New States was instructed to draft for embodiment in the separate Treaty with Poland clauses giving effect to the general principles of Article 3.

(It was decided that the decisions taken with regard to Poland should apply equally to Czecho-Slovakia, and that the necessary instructions should be sent to the Drafting Committee to this effect.)

MR. HEADLAM MORLEY then raised the question of the proposed Article regarding railway facilities. Some uncertainty appeared to have arisen as to whether this Article should be included or not.

(It was decided that the Article should be included.)

MR. HEADLAM MORLEY then proposed that Articles should be inserted in the Treaty containing provisions (a) to prevent the Germans building fortifications which might threaten the free navigation of the Vistula, (b) to prevent the Germans requisitioning in or otherwise injuring territory ceded by them to Poland during the interval which would elapse before the cession actually took place.

[3] *Idem.*

(This was approved and instructions were sent to the Drafting Committee accordingly.)

§ Mantoux's notes:

Messrs. Berthelot, Headlam-Morley, and David Hunter Miller are introduced.

Mr. D. H. Miller presents the text proposed for the recognition of Poland.

The discussion involves the question of knowing if the status of Poland will be included in the treaty with Germany or if it is preferable to place only a brief stipulation in the treaty, which would be followed by an agreement between the Allies and the Polish state.

It is decided that Annex A will be inserted into the treaty.

Headlam Morley. Since the question of the rights of minorities involves the very constitution of the state, it is preferable to have the time to examine it closely and to come to an agreement with the parties involved; it is better to make it the object of a special treaty.

Lloyd George. I read in your text that no distinction can be made among the "inhabitants" of Poland by reason of their race, their nationality, their language, or their religion. Is not the word "inhabitants" too vague and too broad?

Miller. We are obliged to use it, because the treaty says nothing about the right of citizenship in Poland. It is specified that the inhabitants of Prussian Poland will become Polish citizens. But nothing is indicated about the other inhabitants of Poland.

Lloyd George. It is better in fact to reserve this entire question for the treaty between ourselves and Poland. We do not have the time to do what is necessary in the very short period of time remaining to us.

Wilson. Antisemitism in Poland is very sharp; I remind you on this subject of the personal attitude of M. Dmowskí. On the other hand, the Jews form a considerable element of the population. Under these conditions, will we be able to negotiate by mutual agreement with the Poles about this question of religious equality? What does Mr. Miller think?

Miller. You will make Poland sign what you want, provided you ask her for it before the signing of the treaty which gives her her frontiers and her international status.

Lloyd George. So long as we will not have told them that we are resolved to hold out against the protests of the Germans concerning Danzig and Silesia, the Poles are in our hands.

In the text of Annex A, it is only a question of the liberty of the religious communities. Why not say "the inhabitants"?

Miller. That is better, because a strict interpretation of the word "community" would permit the exclusion not only of isolated individuals but of communities which could form later.

As for the word "inhabitants," I repeat that it was preferred to the word "citizens" because the latter would permit exclusion of the Jews.

Headlam Morley. What happened in Rumania must be avoided. The Rumanians have escaped their international obligations, which imposed upon them the equality of all the citizens of their state, by declaring that the Jews were not "citizens."[4]

Wilson. The best thing is to prepare a text of the treaty between ourselves and Poland.

Lloyd George. I repeat that we have a grip on the Poles as long as the treaty with Germany is not signed. §

M. 103 [Appendix]

The Committee on New States.
Report to the Council of Three.

In the unavoidable absence of M. Berthelot (French Representative), Dr. Miller (American Representative) and Mr. Headlam-Morley (British Representative) met on Friday, May 2nd and considered the instructions contained in Sir Maurice Hankey's letter of May 1st.

It was unanimously agreed that the matters raised by Sir Hubert Llewellyn Smith concerning the economic and other obligations which it might be necessary to impose on New States,[5] were of so extensive and complicated a nature that it was quite impossible to consider them in time to incorporate them in the Treaty of Peace with Germany.

It was therefore agreed that there must be separate Treaties negotiated between the Five Allied and Associated Powers on the one hand and the new States—for instance, Poland—on the other, in which these and other matters which might arise would be dealt with. A suitable form for those Treaties could be devised without much difficulty for though in most cases the new States have been recognised, in no case has the territory over which the Government has control been specified, and there are many matters consequential on recognition such as the establishment of consular relations, which will have to be dealt with.

Having agreed to this, the Committee then considered the question of the protection of Minorities. It was again agreed that the question, in particular so far as it affects the Jews in Poland, is so contentious and so difficult that it is impossible to come to precise conclusions about it in the short time available before the text of the Treaty with Germany is closed. It was agreed, therefore, that all the

[4] About this subject, see W. H. Taft to JPT, May 5, 1919, n. 1.

[5] See Appendix II to the minutes of the Council of Four printed at May 1, 1919, 11 a.m.

detailed clauses dealing with this matter should be placed in the separate Treaties referred to.

It was also agreed, however, that there must be inserted in the Treaty with Germany some general clause referring to the other Treaty, and that this should be made of a binding nature. The text of the clause proposed is annexed (Annex A).

It was agreed that it would be essential at some stage, either in the Treaty with Germany or in the separate Treaty to be negotiated with Poland, to insert clauses defining Polish citizenship and political and religious equality. This is necessary, as the experience of Roumania has shown, for the protection of the Jews and other minorities, and the importance of this has been very strongly pressed upon us by the Jewish representatives whom we have seen; it will be equally important for other minorities. Clauses have been drafted providing for this in such a form that they can be inserted in the Treaty with Germany (See Annex B).

It was agreed that it must be left to the decision of the Council of Three whether those clauses should be inserted in the Treaty with Germany or in the separate Treaty. While all were agreed that if there had been sufficient time it would have been preferable to insert them in the Treaty with Germany, the British Representative feels himself bound to point out that it has been impossible for him to consult the British Legal Advisers.

The American Representative is of the opinion that the insertion in the Treaty of Peace of some clause binding Poland in respect of the citizenship and rights of those millions of her population which are not German is essential.

The British Representative is inclined to think that the Article given in Annex A gives sufficient scope to enable the clauses in Annex B to be inserted in the separate Treaties.

Both are agreed that if there is time to get the consideration which is necessary from the French and British legal advisers, and if it is possible in the time to get these clauses through the Drafting Committee, they may well be inserted in the Treaty with Germany.

As to procedure, the most convenient arrangement would be that the special Treaty with Poland, at any rate, should be prepared as quickly as possible and should be ready for signature at the same time as the general Treaty with Germany. There are advantages in this that Poland would be bound, not as against Germany, but as against her Allies but at the same time the Germans would have cognisance of the separate Treaty which is, as will be seen, specifically referred to in the main Treaty.

In accordance with their instructions, the Committee started with their consideration of the Polish question. It is recognised that the same problems, though in a slightly different form, arise in the case of Czecho-Slovakia, and they are agreed that apart from any detailed modifications of form which may appear necessary, these clauses which have been drafted especially for the case of Poland, should be applied also to Czecho-Slovakia.

They have unfortunately, however, not been able to procure a single copy of the chapter of the Treaty dealing with Czecho-Slovakia in its final form, or to discuss the matter with those immediately responsible for dealing with Czecho-Slovakia, and are therefore not in a position to advise as to whether any alteration in the form or details may be required.

2.5.19

ANNEX A.

Recognition of Poland (and Czecho-Slovakia).

*Article*______

(Substitute for Article 7 of Chapter relating to Poland.)

Poland accepts and agrees to embody in a Treaty with the Five Allied and Associated Powers such provisions as may be deemed necessary by the Five Allied and Associated Powers to protect the interests of inhabitants in Poland who differ from the majority of the population in race, language or religion.

Poland further accepts and agrees to embody in a Treaty with the Five Allied and Associated Powers such provisions as may be deemed necessary by the Five Allied and Associated Powers to protect freedom of transit and equitable treatment of the commerce of other Nations.

Recognition of Poland (and Czecho-Slovakia).

ANNEX B.

Chapter______

Article 1.

Without prejudice to the effect of any previous recognition of Poland, Germany as well as the Allied and Associated Powers recognises Poland as a sovereign and independent State.

Article 2.

The boundaries of Poland not mentioned or determined by the provisions of this Treaty will be subsequently fixed by the Five Allied and Associated Powers.

Article 3.

Poland undertakes the following obligations to each of the other Allied and Associated Powers, and recognises them to be obligations of international concern of which the League of Nations has jurisdiction:

1. Without any requirement of qualifying or other proceedings, Poland admits and declares to be Polish citizens:

(a) all persons habitually resident in territories recognised to be Polish by this or any subsequent Treaty, except those who are citizens or subjects of one of the Allied or Associated Powers or of a Power which was neutral throughout the late war; and

(b) all persons hereafter born in Poland not nationals of another State.

The foregoing provisions shall not limit or affect any provision of Articles 4 and 5 of Chapter______

2. Poland agrees that all citizens of Poland shall enjoy equal civil and political rights without distinction as to birth, race, nationality, language or religion.

3. Poland assumes and will perform the following obligations:

(a) To protect the life and liberty of all inhabitants of Poland;

(b) To assure to all inhabitants of Poland the free exercise, whether public or private, of any creed, religion, or belief, whose practices are not inconsistent with public order or public morals;

(c) To allow all inhabitants of Poland the free use of any language, particularly in business transactions, in schools and other educational instruction, in the press, and at public meetings and assemblies; and,

(d) To make no discrimination against any inhabitant of Poland on account of birth, race, nationality, language, or religion.

4. Poland agrees that the foregoing obligations are hereby embodied in her fundamental law as a bill of rights, with which no law, regulation, or official action shall conflict or interfere, and as against which no law, regulation, or official action shall have validity or effect.

Article 4.

Poland accepts and agrees to embody in a treaty with the Five Allied and Associated Powers such provisions as may be deemed necessary by the Five Allied and Associated Powers to protect the interests of communities in Poland which differ from the majority of the population in race, language, or religion.

Poland further accepts and agrees to embody in a Treaty with the Five Allied and Associated Powers such provisions as may be deemed necessary by the Five Allied and Associated Powers to protect the freedom of transit and equitable treatment of the commerce of the Allied and Associated Powers.

4. Railway Facilities.

Germany and Poland undertake within one year of the conclusion of this Treaty to enter into a Convention of which the terms in case of difference shall be settled by the Council of the League of Nations, with the object of securing, on the one hand to Germany, full and adequate railroad facilities for communication between the rest of Germany and East Prussia over the intervening Polish territory, on the other hand to Poland, full and adequate railroad facilities for communication between Poland and the City of Danzig over any German territory that may, on the right bank of the Vistula, intervene between Poland and the City of Danzig.

T MS (SDR, RG 256, 180.03401/141, DNA); Mantoux, I, 474-75.

Hankey's and Mantoux's Notes of a Meeting of the Council of Four[1]

President Wilson's House,
I.C.-181A Paris, May 3, 1919, 4 p.m.

1. M. CLEMENCEAU raised the question of whether the invitation sent to the Austrian and Hungarian Governments to come to St. Germain should not be made public.

MR. LLOYD GEORGE said he was in favour of publication, but he thought it should be discussed as part of the whole question of the situation with Italy.

2. SIR MAURICE HANKEY reported that he had had a letter from Mr. Hurst, the British Member of the Drafting Committee, in regard to the Article approved on the previous afternoon on the subject of the denunciation of the Treaty of Brest-Litovsk (I.C.179.C, Minute 11).[2] In this letter Mr. Hurst pointed out that the clause approved on the previous day had been less far-reaching than the clauses already included in the Financial and Economic Sections of the Peace Treaty. In view of these circumstances and in order to avoid any obvious divergence between the Economic Article (Article 10 of the Economic Clauses), the Financial Article (Article 12, (vi) of the Financial Clauses) and the new political Article, certain changes had been made. (The new draft submitted by the Drafting Committee was approved.)[3]

(Sir Maurice Hankey was instructed to forward it immediately to the Secretary-General for communication to the Drafting Committee.)

3. SIR MAURICE HANKEY reported that he had received a letter from General Thwaites, the head of the British Military Section, enclosing a copy of the English draft of Clauses in regard to the Baltic

[1] The complete text of Hankey's minutes is printed in *PPC*, V, 451-62.
[2] Printed in *ibid.*, pp. 421, 424.
[3] See Appendix I, printed below.

States, to be inserted in the Treaty of Peace under Guarantees. The French translation as approved by Marshal Foch was also attached.

(These Articles were approved as a basis for an Article in the Treaty of Peace—Appendix II.)

(Sir Maurice Hankey was instructed to forward them to the Secretary-General for communication to the Drafting Committee with the least possible delay.)

4. MR. LLOYD GEORGE described an interview he had had with the Marquis Imperiali, who had communicated to him the gist of a telegram he had received from Rome. The Marquis had refused to communicate a copy and Mr. Lloyd George had to rely entirely on his memory. No-one else had been present at the conversation, which the Marquis Imperiali had said was a private one, although he had said that he must communicate his impression of it to Rome. The first part of the telegram, so far as Mr. Lloyd George could remember, was that M. Orlando had said that there was very little object in returning to Paris. There was no basis for an agreement in regard to Fiume. Moreover, he understood that Great Britain and France were not agreed with the United States. In the second part, M. Orlando had said, "You say you stand by the Treaty of London. How much better off are we? President Wilson will not accept it. What guarantees do our Allies propose to enforce the Treaty?" Mr. Lloyd George had then replied to the Marquis Imperiali, "What guarantees do you want? Do you expect us to declare war on the United States?" The Marquis Imperiali had replied "Oh, no." Mr. Lloyd George had asked him what he would suggest, and he could not suggest anything. The Marquis Imperiali had then made a suggestion which Mr. Lloyd George characterized as an impudent one, that the Allies were not keeping the Pact of London, because they were making a separate peace with Germany, without Italy. Mr. Lloyd George had told him that Italy was already on the point of breaking the Pact, that we would be within our legal rights, and that we were advised by our legal advisers that this was the case, in considering that Italy would break it by not being present to meet the Germans. If Italy was not present on Tuesday then the Allies would no longer be bound by the Pact. The Marquis had replied that this was a very serious situation. Mr. Lloyd George's rejoinder was that it was no more serious than he himself had in that very room warned the Marquis Imperiali that it would be. He had warned M. Orlando in exactly the same sense. He had also reminded him that M. Orlando had acted against the advice of M. Sonnino. The Marquis Imperiali had then said, "Won't you make us some offer?" Mr. Lloyd George had replied, "To whom shall we make it? Can you receive an offer?" The Marquis Imperiali replied that he could transmit one.

Mr. Lloyd George then said that it was impossible to deal with people who were hundreds of miles away, and had no responsible person with authority to act for them. If the Italian representatives did not come back, there was no official person with whom negotiations could take place. The Marquis Imperiali then said that the Italian representatives ought to know this. He was afraid that if they came back to Paris, and found that no agreement could be reached, the situation would be graver than ever. Mr. Lloyd George asked, "Why would it be more grave than it is now?" He had warned them a week ago. The Italians were in possession of Fiume contrary to the Treaty of London. He had asked what the position of the Italians would be, and what the general position would be if the Peace about to be secured with Austria gave Fiume to the Croats. The Marquis Imperiali had been somewhat perturbed at this and had said, "I suppose you could put the Germans off for a day or two if the Italian Delegation were returning?" Mr. Lloyd George then told him that the Italian Government would be under an entire delusion if they thought that they could get Fiume. The Allied and Associated Powers were absolutely united on that point. They were united quite apart from the question of principle, because the Treaty of London gave Fiume to the Croats. A compromise that had been suggested was that it might be arranged that Fiume should become a free port, instead of being given to the Croats, on condition that the Italians gave up to the Serbs-Croats the Dalmatian Coast. The Marquis Imperiali had asked Mr. Lloyd George if he would put this in writing, and Mr. Lloyd George had declined.

(In the course of the discussion below, it will be found that Mr. Lloyd George supplemented his statement from time to time, as the course of the discussion brought fresh points to his mind.)

M. CLEMENCEAU said he had had a conversation with the Italian Ambassador, Count Bonin, which had been almost identical with Mr. Lloyd George's but he had had one opportunity which Mr. Lloyd George did not have. Count Bonin had asked him what his point of view was. He had replied that he certainly would give it, and he had given him a piece of his mind. He had told him that Italy had entered the war with a bargain. This bargain had not been kept yet. Italy had postponed for more than a year going to war with Germany. The bargain had been that Italy was to get the Tyrol, Trieste, and Pola, and that Fiume would go to the Croats. Now Italy asked him to keep his word about their part of the Treaty, and to break it in regard to Fiume. This was a point the Italians did not seem to realise. He had told him that he could see what was the game they were playing, but they could not get a quarrel between the Allies and President Wilson about Fiume. Italy had broken the Treaty, and he had the written opinion of a jurisconsult to that effect, which could be produced if it were wished. Count Bonin had said "Why do you not make a proposal?" M. Clemenceau had replied, "We cannot, we have signed the Treaty." Instead of asking to talk, the Italians wanted their Allies to break the Treaty. Count Bonin had then said, "You are not in agreement with President Wilson." M. Clemenceau had replied, "I can discuss this with President Wilson and Mr. Lloyd George, but I will not discuss it with you." Then Count Bonin had dropped this topic. Finally, Count Bonin had said, "If we make a suggestion, would you help?" M. Clemenceau replied, "Certainly, if it is a feasible suggestion, but I cannot commit myself in advance." Then Count Bonin said that M. Orlando could not come back and conduct the negotiations, because he could not afford to fail. He added, "I suppose we must hurry up." M. Clemenceau replied, "Yes, you had better be as quick as you can." Then Count Bonin said, "Then you will help us." M. Clemenceau replied, "Certainly, if your proposal is a feasible one." Count Bonin then referred to Fiume, and M. Clemenceau had replied that he had better not refer to that in any proposal, and that was the end of the conversation, as far as he could remember it.

MR. LLOYD GEORGE recalled that the Marquis Imperiali had put forward a proposal that had appeared in the newspaper "Temps,"[4] but he had answered that he could not look at that.

[4] "Bulletin du Jour. La Question de Fiume," Paris *Le Temps*, April 29, 1919. The article began by stating that the entire discussion about the question of Fiume was turning in a vicious circle, since both sides in the controversy, Wilson as well as the Italian government, were employing Wilsonian principles to justify their respective positions. Wilson, in denying Fiume to the Italians, based his arguments on the second of his five principles for a just peace proclaimed in his speech in the Metropolitan Opera House on September 27, 1918. According to this second principle, no special interest of any single nation which was inconsistent with the common interest of all could be made the basis of any part of the settlement. The common interest dictated that the Yugoslavs should own a great port on the Adriatic, capable of serving the regions of Laibach and Agram (now Zagreb). A settlement that would fail to provide such an outlet would be detrimental to the commerce of all nations and would endanger world peace. Thus, in Wilson's view, Italy's claim to Fiume had to give precedence to the needs of the civilized world. On the other hand, Italy's demand for Fiume rested on the ninth of Wilson's Fourteen Points, which stated that Italy's frontiers should be readjusted "along clearly recognizable lines of nationality." Since nobody could deny that the great majority of the present population of Fiume was recognizably Italian, it was not surprising that even moderate Italian leaders categorically insisted on the award of Fiume to Italy.

However, the article continued, a solution to this stalemate had to be found, lest the present crisis result either in a new war with all its incalculable consequences or in the resounding defeat of one of the two great powers involved in the dispute. What did the Yugoslavs claim? A port. What did the Italians claim? A people. Hence, the article asked, if the Italians were to receive the population of Fiume and the Yugoslavs a port which would serve for them the same purpose as Fiume, would not the whole problem be solved?

The article then went on to describe the geographical peculiarities of the Dalmatian coast and the existing railway lines which connected it with the interior. One look at the map, the article maintained, would suffice to ascertain that the natural outlet for Croatia was not the Gulf of Quarnero with Fiume, but the Channel of Morlacca with such ports as Novi, Senj, and Lukovo. Fiume was chosen by Austria-Hungary as the site for a great

M. CLEMENCEAU expressed the view that in 24 hours suggestions would come from Italy.

PRESIDENT WILSON then said that Count Cellere, the Italian Ambassador in Washington, who had accompanied him to Europe, just as Lord Reading had done, and who was a man with whom he was personally friendly, had asked for an interview. He had not had time to grant it to him yet, but he had no doubt he would have to do so in the course of the day. He had no doubt that the interview would be on exactly the same lines as those of his colleagues, and he did not anticipate that it would add anything of value.

MR. LLOYD GEORGE recalled that he had impressed on the Marquis Imperiali that the Allied and Associated Powers had every intention of concluding a peace with Germany and Austria. The Marquis then asked whether they were going to do so without consultation with Italy, to which he replied that there was no-one to consult with in Paris. Italy, however, had been told the result of every decision immediately affecting her. Their intention was to press on with making these Treaties of Peace, and they could not delay simply because Italy would not settle on the subject of Fiume. He had impressed strongly on him that peace would be made.

PRESIDENT WILSON believed that the present line that was being

---

port for political and military reasons, and it had never been intended to serve as an outlet for Croatia. In fact, it would not at all be in Yugoslavia's interest to have its major port located at the extreme north of its coastline. If, on the other hand, one could build a great port in the region of Senj and connect it with the railway lines to Agram and Laibach, Yugoslavia would receive an outlet far more appropriate to its needs than Fiume. To be sure, it might take ten years to complete such a huge project, but the United States, France, and Great Britain would undoubtedly be glad to furnish the capital and provide the necessary material and expert advice. In the meantime, until the completion of the construction, the port of Fiume could be administered by the League of Nations in an arrangement similar to that adopted for the Saar Basin. Once the new port had been built and was ready for use, Fiume, in conformity with the wish of its inhabitants, could be returned entirely to Italy. By proceeding along these lines, the article concluded, one would not only solve the problem of Fiume but also simplify the entire Adriatic question; and the principle of nationality, having triumphed in Fiume, could be applied elsewhere. Since the Treaty of London would have been revised in regard to Fiume, which it had given to Croatia, it could also be modified in regard to Dalmatia, which had been attributed to Italy. In this way, the article was confident, one would return to the spirit of moderation cherished by the Latin people, the principle of logic appreciated by the French, and the Anglo-Saxon spirit of compromise.

Two days later, on May 1, 1919, *Le Temps* followed with a second, slightly revised proposal. In "Bulletin du Jour. Les Revendications de l'Italie," the paper repeated many of its previous arguments but, referring to a letter it had received from a French engineer, now suggested that the new Yugoslav port should be built at Buccari, in the vicinity of Fiume in the Gulf of Quarnero. Although, like Fiume, it had the disadvantage of being situated at the very north of the Yugoslav coastline, the Bay of Buccari was a great natural basin which could be turned into a major port without much effort in about two years. Moreover, Buccari was located only twelve miles from the railway line which connected Fiume and Agram, and a simple extension of that line would suffice to connect the new port with the interior. In any event, the article concluded, these details seemed rather uninteresting in comparison with the noble sentiments which the settlement of the Adriatic question would permit to be expounded, and it was important to show, by unimpeachable evidence, that the Allies had at hand an equitable and practical solution.

adopted was the best. No proposal should be made to Italy. The only question which had to be decided was as to what sort of notice should be given to Italy of our intentions. He suggested that the two conversations that had been described this afternoon might be sufficient. M. Clemenceau's conversation was more official perhaps than Mr. Lloyd George's, since it had been carried out between the President of the Conference and the Italian Ambassador in Paris. Count Bonin's visit had been an official one, whereas the Marquis Imperiali had described his as a private one. Surely M. Clemenceau's statement gave sufficient notice to the Italian Government.

MR. BALFOUR pointed out that even if the Marquis Imperiali's visit was a private one, Mr. Lloyd George had not said that his remarks were private.

MR. LLOYD GEORGE reverted to the fact that he had refused to give anything in writing, but the Marquis Imperiali had said he would report the conversation to his Government. On the whole he thought it could hardly be regarded as being so official as M. Clemenceau's conversation.

PRESIDENT WILSON pointed out that in any case, the two statements were practically identical.

MR. LLOYD GEORGE said they were identical except in the respect that the Marquis Imperiali had never said a word about President Wilson. He, himself, had had to say that he could not undertake that President Wilson was now prepared to agree to what he (Mr. Lloyd George) had thought he might be willing to agree to last week. The Marquis Imperiali had reminded him of the question of giving mandates to Italy for certain towns on the Dalmatian Coast and he had replied that this was the only point on which, perhaps, he had exceeded his authority from the Council.

PRESIDENT WILSON said the great point was as to whether the Italians had now received sufficient notice of the breach of the Pact of London.

MR. BALFOUR suggested that the Prime Minister would be entitled, if he thought fit, to write a letter to the Marquis Imperiali, somewhat in the following sense:

My dear Ambassador,

One point was raised at our conversation today which is of immediate importance, and on which there should be no misunderstanding. I write this line not to supersede or alter anything I said, but merely to state that the Allied and Associated Powers intend to meet the Germans next Tuesday, and we are advised that in all the circumstances, the absence of Italy will constitute a breach of the Pact of London.

PRESIDENT WILSON suggested that such a letter would come better from M. Clemenceau, as President of the Conference.

M. CLEMENCEAU thought it would be better to prepare a document explaining the whole case.

PRESIDENT WILSON asked if it would not be sufficient to confirm in writing what M. Clemenceau had already said at his interview with the Italian Ambassador.

MR. LLOYD GEORGE thought a document putting an end to the Alliance would be a very serious one, and could not be treated in too formal a manner. He was inclined to take M. Clemenceau's document read at the morning meeting. (Appendix III to I.C.180.B.)[5]

PRESIDENT WILSON said that this document had been too full of "ifs." It should contain no "ifs." The following phrase occurred to him as a suitable one: "Absence from signing the Treaty will constitute a breach."

M. CLEMENCEAU said the effect of this would be to bring the Italians back.

MR. LLOYD GEORGE said that he had made the Marquis Imperiali realise that the Allied and Associated Governments would not give way on the subject of Fiume.

PRESIDENT WILSON said that there was no need to mention Fiume. If you did, it would be an indication that there were other things on which you were prepared to discuss.

MR. LLOYD GEORGE said that the Italians would not trouble themselves much about anything except Fiume.

PRESIDENT WILSON said he did not believe a settlement could be reached without giving them Fiume.

MR. LLOYD GEORGE said that from many points of view he would rather they did not come back.

M. CLEMENCEAU recalled that Count Bonin had said that the only thing Italy could not accept was for Fiume to be Croat.

PRESIDENT WILSON pointed out that if the Italians insisted that Fiume should not be Croat, the British and French Governments would not be bound by the rest of the Pact. They could not free themselves from that part of the Treaty which gave Fiume to the Croats.

MR. LLOYD GEORGE said they could only do so as a compromise. He himself had told the Marquis Imperiali that he could only consent to Fiume not being Croat on the condition that the Italians would give up Dalmatia to the Jugo-Slavs.

PRESIDENT WILSON said that if one item of the Treaty was departed from, the whole Treaty was upset.

[5] Actually, Appendix III to I.C. 180A, i.e. the minutes of the Council of Four printed at May 3, 1919, 10 a.m.

MR. LLOYD GEORGE pointed out, however, that the Croats did not sign the Treaty of London.

PRESIDENT WILSON said that, nevertheless, the British and French Governments would not be morally bound if that part of the Treaty was not carried out.

MR. BALFOUR recalled that it was Russia who had made so strong a defence in the interests of the Slavs, when the Treaty of London had been concluded. This defence only broke down in the absence of Sir Edward (now Lord) Grey, when Mr. Asquith had been in charge of the Foreign Office, and had felt that in view of the general situation he must get Italy into the war and he had then forced the hands of the Czar.

MR. LLOYD GEORGE said that this was not the whole story. About that time the Allies had been trying to induce the Serbians to give up to Bulgaria a portion of Serbia which they believed ought to belong to Bulgaria, their object being to bring Bulgaria into the war. They had told the Serbians that they would get the whole of Jugo-Slavia in the end, and Fiume had been inserted in the Treaty in order that Serbia might eventually receive it, since this was part of the inducement to try and get them to make the concession to Bulgaria.

After some discussion on the subject of the attitude of the Germans (in the recent meetings on the subject of credentials) the Italian question was again resumed.

PRESIDENT WILSON asked if Mr. Balfour had expanded the note prepared by his legal adviser (Appendix I to I.C.180A).[6]

MR. LLOYD GEORGE said that he thought M. Clemenceau's document would be a better basis for a statement (Appendix III to I.C.180A).

PRESIDENT WILSON considered it too long and argumentative.

M. CLEMENCEAU said that he would like to make a suggestion. In his opinion the Drafting Committee would not be ready with the Treaty by Tuesday. He did not believe it could be ready to hand to the Germans before Thursday. He thought, therefore, that the best plan would be to leave the Italians alone for 24 hours, during which time they could consider the statements that he and Mr. Lloyd George had made to M. Bonin and the Marquis Imperiali.

MR. LLOYD GEORGE agreed. Their statements, he said, had been very blunt ones.

M. Clemenceau said that M. Klotz had handed the reply to M. Crespi[7] personally to M. Crespi, who had been very annoyed with the letter. He, himself, would try and reconsider the Memorandum

[6] *Ibid.*

[7] That is, the letter printed as Appendix I to the minutes of the Council of Four printed at May 2, 1919, 11 a.m.

he had submitted (Appendix III to I.C.180A). In his view, any statement sent to the Italians should contain one part which was from Mr. Lloyd George and himself, and one part from the Three. In the meanwhile he suggested that he should be allowed to let M. Bonin know that a decision would be taken on Monday.

PRESIDENT WILSON begged him not to do this. It would be a challenge to the Italians to return.

MR. LLOYD GEORGE doubted this in view of his statement that it was useless for the Italians to return unless they were ready to give up Fiume. MR. LLOYD GEORGE said that there was a good deal to be said for Mr. Balfour's plan of his writing a letter to the Marquis Imperiali confirming what he had said about the intention of the Allied and Associated Powers to meet the Germans next week. Two new factors had entered into the situation; one was that M. Orlando had said that it was no use coming back if the Allies would not enforce the Pact, and the second was his own statement that it was no use their coming unless they were prepared to give up Fiume.

PRESIDENT WILSON referred to the Marquis Imperiali's question about guarantees and warrantees. Supposing the Italians came back and said: "We will give up Fiume but we insist on the Treaty of London." The British and French Governments had said that they must give it them. Their guarantee was their word.

MR. LLOYD GEORGE recalled that he had also told the Marquis Imperiali that the Italian troops must leave Fiume before they would even discuss the question of Fiume.

PRESIDENT WILSON said that if they agreed to that and came back, they could say: "We have your promise about the Treaty of London"; this was a moral guarantee. In that case it would make it impossible for the United States to sign the Treaty.

MR. LLOYD GEORGE said that then we could not have peace with Austria.

PRESIDENT WILSON said that the Allies could sign the Peace. The Italians had their guarantee that Great Britain and France would fulfil their engagements regardless of what it involved. What better guarantee could they have? The Marquis Imperiali could have replied on the subject of guarantees: "We have your word."

MR. LLOYD GEORGE said that the Marquis had not answered on this point.

PRESIDENT WILSON said that a telegram from the United States Ambassador at Rome had been read to him on the telephone.[8] The gist of it was that, some person of the first authority, not named, had asked if a compromise could not be reached on the following lines:

[8] T. N. Page to Ammission, No. 286, May 2, 1919.

1. Fiume to be made independent.
2. Susak, while free from Italian sovereignty, not to be under Slavonian sovereignty. (At this point President Wilson produced a map of Fiume, showing how very difficult it was to distinguish the suburb of Susak from Fiume itself.)

It was agreed:

1. That no immediate statement should be sent to Italy warning them that their failure to sign the German Treaty would constitute a breach of the Pact of London.
2. That M. Clemenceau, Mr. Lloyd George, and Mr. Balfour should prepare fresh drafts of statements to be considered at the next meeting.

§ Mantoux's notes:

Clemenceau. I have some information about Brockdorff-Rantzau's state of mind. It seems that he is completely disappointed to discover that we are in agreement; he is disappointed not to have been able to enter into contact with the Americans and would like to have a "completely frank" conversation with a French statesman!

Wilson. The impression given by Brockdorff-Rantzau to those who saw him present his credentials is that of a man who is preparing himself for the supreme humiliation; if his legs did not tremble under him, he was near it. There is obviously a contrast between what the Germans hoped to find here and what they are finding in fact before them.

Lloyd George. According to Mr. Keynes, Mr. Melchior would be a bit more optimistic than he was earlier. That seems to indicate that he thinks that the German delegation will be able to sign, for that is what he himself wants. §

5. M. MANTOUX said that M. Clemenceau had asked him to arrange for the preparation of a reply regarding the decision of the previous day in regard to the Belgian request that the German colonies should be ceded, not to the Principal Powers, but to a named list of Powers, including Belgium and Portugal.[9] In view of the later discussion about mandatories, he wished to know the precise nature of the reply to be sent. Were the mandates to be granted by the Allied and Associated Powers, or by the League of Nations.

PRESIDENT WILSON pointed out that the exact position was that, if the allocation of mandates was postponed until the League of Nations was in operation, the decision would rest with the League. It had been agreed, however, that the mandates should be assigned by the Allied and Associated Powers in the meanwhile.

[9] For this part of the minutes of the meeting of the Council of Four on May 2, 1919, 4 p.m., see *PPC*, V, 419-20.

MR. LLOYD GEORGE said that to inform M. Hymans of this would be an incitement to him to obstruction. Lord Robert Cecil, with whom he had discussed the question in the morning, had begged him to get the question of the mandatories, and the nature of the mandates, settled.

PRESIDENT WILSON asked why, after deciding the mandatories, should the mandates also be immediately decided? The general lines of the mandates were provided for in the Covenant of the League of Nations, which contemplated various grades from virtual independence with advice, down to virtual dependence. It added certain provisions about liquor traffic, arms traffic, etc.

MR. LLOYD GEORGE said he was being strongly pressed to insert a new condition, somewhat similar to that that had been discussed in regard to Poland dealing with the question of religious equality. The Missionary Societies were afraid that otherwise certain churches would exclude other churches.

PRESIDENT WILSON said that he wanted to decide the question of mandatories, and that he was willing to decide the question of mandates.

MR. BALFOUR said his view was that the mandates should be worked out first.

MR. LLOYD GEORGE pointed out that this was the opposite view of his own view.

PRESIDENT WILSON pointed out that the mandatories was the only controversial part of the question.

SIR MAURICE HANKEY said that he believed that mandates had been discussed a good deal between the experts of the various countries.

MR. LLOYD GEORGE said that the real difficulties would arise in giving mandates to possessions in Turkey.

PRESIDENT WILSON agreed, and thought Palestine would be especially difficult, owing to the Zionist question, on which the British and the United States, and he thought also the French, Governments were to some extent committed. There was, however, he pointed out, plenty of time, since the League of Nations would not be in operation until the Peace Treaty with Germany had been ratified, and that would take a long time.

6. M. CLEMENCEAU said that he had received very serious complaints of the action of the British in Syria. He undertook, at Mr. Lloyd George's request, to send him a paper on the subject.

§ Mantoux's notes:

Clemenceau. We have to respond to the letter from M. Hymans, who asks for assurances about the fate of territories conquered by the Belgians in German East Africa.

Wilson. We have settled the question concerning all the German colonies; they will be administered by mandate of the League of Nations, and the assignment of mandates, for the first time, will be made by the great powers.

Lloyd George. I reckon that it is necessary to settle the system of mandates as soon as possible. Lord Robert Cecil fears difficulties if we delay making this settlement. It is a matter of clearly determining the conditions of the mandates and perhaps of adding new clauses to them, notably one which would prevent religious missions from persecuting one another.

Wilson. Is not the most urgent matter the naming of the mandatories?

Lloyd George. I do not know why Lord Robert Cecil is in such a hurry to define the form of mandates. That is not without difficulties, notably for Asia Minor, where there will obviously be different kinds of mandates. I think, moreover, that we will be able to agree without difficulty and that the choice of mandatories is, as you think, what must concern us first.

Wilson. We have the time; the League of Nations will not begin its functions before the ratifications of the treaty will have been exchanged. In my opinion, the place where the problem arises in the most difficult way is Palestine. Our governments, at least the British and American governments, have undertaken a commitment toward the Jews to establish something which resembles an Israelite state in Palestine, to which the Arabs are very much opposed.

Balfour. I recall that this terrible Treaty of London is still mixed into the question, because of our agreements with Italy about Asia Minor.

Wilson. The mandate in Palestine will have to require a system of guarantees for the different populations toward the Jews, and vice versa. §

7. SIR MAURICE HANKEY said that Mr. Balfour had received a request which he had passed on to him (Sir Maurice Hankey) from the Chinese Delegation, for a copy of the Clauses to be introduced in the Treaty of Peace in regard to China,[10] as well as for the proceedings of this Council in regard to them. He presumed that the proceedings, being of a very intimate, personal, and confidential character, would not be communicated. There was no precedent for communicating these proceedings to persons who had not been present. He asked for instructions, however, as to the Articles.

M. CLEMENCEAU said that he saw no objection to their receiving the Clauses.

[10] See Appendix IV to the minutes of the Council of Four printed at April 30, 1919, 11 a.m.

PRESIDENT WILSON said that if they received the Clauses they should certainly receive a copy of the statement which the Japanese intended to make.

8. SIR MAURICE HANKEY read extracts from a letter he had received from the Chinese Delegation, enclosing a letter which had been addressed to the Chairman of the Financial Commission, drawing attention to the omission from the Clauses proposed by that Commission of a Chinese proposal to the following effect:

> "In cases where one of the High Contracting Parties has a silver standard of currency, payments of debts shall be made in the currency stipulated in the contract, and at the rate of exchange on the date of settlement."

SIR MAURICE HANKEY, after reading further extracts from the letter, stated that Mr. Keynes, who was acting for Mr. Montagu (who had resigned from the post of Chairman of the Financial Commission) had replied in the sense that the exception could not be made in the case of one country.

PRESIDENT WILSON said he would be very glad if something could be done to meet China in this respect, as China was not coming very well out of the Peace Treaty.

MR. LLOYD GEORGE suggested that China was not really so badly treated.

9. PRESIDENT WILSON showed Mr. Lloyd George a draft of an agreement in regard to the disposal of German ships captured in American ports.[11]

In reply to Sir Maurice Hankey he said that this did not affect the Treaty of Peace.

MR. LLOYD GEORGE said that he would be prepared to assent, if President Wilson would make an alteration in the Treaty so as to remove a reference to Congress.[12] His objection to this Clause was that the British Parliament might protest against mention being made of the United States Congress and not of the British Imperial Parliament.

[11] Undated CC MS, enclosed in H. M. Robinson to WW, May 4, 1919, TLS (WP, DLC). About this matter, see the minutes of the Council of Four printed at April 23, 1919, 4 p.m.

[12] The article in question read as follows: "As the ships and boats so to be retained will, in the case of Brazil, China, Cuba, Siam and the United States, exceed the total amount of tonnage which would be allocated to those countries where the total enemy tonnage captured, seized, detained or still in existence shared in proportion to losses of ships and boats during the War, in each such case a reasonable value on the excess of ships and boats over the amount which would result from such a division will be determined. The amount of the value so fixed will be paid over by each such Government to the Reparation Commission for the credit of Germany towards the sums due from her for Reparation in respect of submarine losses of merchant ships, unless as regards the United States, the Congress shall otherwise determine." From the CC MS cited in n. 11 above.

PRESIDENT WILSON said he would get over the difficulty by annexing a note to the Clauses on the subject.[13]

(The meeting then adjourned.)

APPENDIX I TO I.C.181.A.

Germany acknowledges and agrees to respect as permanent and inalienable the independence of all the territories which were part of the former Russian Empire.

In accordance with the provisions of Article ______ of Part IX and Article ______ of Part X Germany accepts definitely the abrogation of the Brest-Litovsk Treaty, and of all treaties, conventions and agreements entered into by her with the Maximilist[14] Government in Russia.

The Allied and Associated Powers formally reserve the right of Russia to obtain from Germany restitution and reparation based on the principles of the present Treaty.

APPENDIX II TO I.C.181.A.

Alternative 'C.'

DRAFT CLAUSE.

As a guarantee for the execution of the Article by which the German Government undertakes to annul the provisions of the Brest-Litovsk Treaty, and in order to ensure the restoration of peace and good government in the Baltic Provinces and Lithuania, all German troops at present in the said territories shall return to within the frontiers of Germany as soon as the Allies shall think the moment suitable, having regard to the internal situation of these territories. These troops shall abstain from all requisitions and seizures and from any other coercive measures, with a view to obtaining supplies intended for Germany, and shall in no way interfere with such measures for national defence as may be adopted by the Provisional Governments of Esthonia, Latvia and Lithuania.

No other German troops shall, pending the evacuation or after the evacuation is complete, be admitted to the said territories.

T MS (SDR, RG 256, 180.03401/143, DNA); Mantoux, I, 480, 482-83.

[13] See H. M. Robinson to WW, May 4, 1919, and the two memoranda of agreement printed at May 8, 1919.

[14] Again, Bolshevik.

To Robert Lansing

My dear Lansing: Paris, 3 May, 1919.

I am pretty clear in my view that the case of Finland stands by itself.[1] It never was in any true sense an integral part of Russia. It has been a most uneasy and unwilling partner, and I think that action in regard to the recognition of the Finnish Government would not commit us or embarrass us with regard to the recognition of any other part of the former Russian Empire that might be separately set up. I am very keen for the recognition of Finland, as you know.[2]

Cordially and faithfully yours, [Woodrow Wilson]

CCL (WP, DLC).

[1] Wilson was replying to RL to WW, May 1, 1919 (third letter of that date).

[2] As instructed by the Council of Four on April 30, 1919, 11 a.m., the Council of Foreign Ministers took up the question of the recognition of Finland on May 3, 1919, 4 p.m. Since France had already recognized the independence of Finland as early as January 6, 1918, the discussion involved mainly the positions of the United States, Great Britain, and Japan. The council agreed that the United States and Great Britain would "forthwith severally recognise the independence of Finland and the *de facto* Government"; that the Finnish government should be urged to accept the decisions of the peace conference about the frontiers of Finland; and that the Japanese government, after being informed of the council's decision, would be requested to follow suit. See *PPC*, IV, 662-65.

The United States recognized the independence of Finland and the *de facto* government on May 7, 1919, and, on May 24, appointed its consul at Helsingfors, Thornwell Haynes, as Commissioner of the United States to Finland with the rank of Minister Plenipotentiary. For a detailed discussion, see Juhani Paasivirta, *The Victors in World War I and Finland: Finland's Relations with the British, French and United States Governments in 1918-1919*, trans. Paul Sjöblom (Helsinki, 1965), pp. 78-114.

From Robert Lansing

My dear Mr. President: Paris, May 3, 1919.

I enclose herewith a memorandum[1] relative to the time of release to the press in the United States of the sections of the Peace Treaty and will be very glad if you will indicate to me your wishes in the matter. Faithfully yours, Robert Lansing.

TLS (WP, DLC).

[1] It is missing in WP, DLC.

To Robert Lansing

My dear Mr. Secretary: [Paris] 3 May, 1919.

I am sorry to learn that Mr. Patchin[1] has been permitted to send the official text of the Treaty, piece by piece, to the other side of the water, because every part of the treaty is subject to revision until the last moment, and I hope that the Department will be warned by you, yourself, to observe the utmost care to keep the treaty to itself.

I am clear in my judgment that no sentence of the official text ought to be given to the press until the treaty is signed. A careful summary of the treaty is being prepared for presentation to the Plenary Conference itself (since it is not practicable to communicate the official text), and I hope that the Department will be instructed not to release anything except under explicit instructions as to what is to be released. This is a hasty reply to your letter of yesterday [*sic*].

Cordially and faithfully yours, [Woodrow Wilson]

CCL (WP, DLC).

[1] That is, Philip Halsey Patchin, Executive Secretary of the A.C.N.P.

From Robert Lansing, with Enclosure

My dear Mr. President: Paris, May 3rd, 1919.

In accordance with the request expressed in your letter of May 1st, 1919,[1] regarding participation on the part of the United States in connection with granting certain assistance to Roumania, I have spoken to General Bliss on the matter and am transmitting to you herewith a copy of the memorandum which he has submitted on this subject. Faithfully yours, Robert Lansing

TLS (WP, DLC).

[1] WW to RL, May 1, 1919 (second letter of that date).

E N C L O S U R E

MEMORANDUM

1. At 6:15 p.m., March 27, in an interview with the President at his residence, he stated, substantially, as follows:

That, during the conference of the Council of Four that afternoon several telegrams were considered relating to the serious situation at ODESSA;[1] that it appeared that that place would have to be evacuated unless it could receive immediately reinforcements and considerable supplies; that after some discussion in the Council of Four they sent for Marshal Foch and presented the case to him; that Marshal Foch stated that he did not believe that it was worth while to continue the occupation of Odessa, and that it would be better to withdraw its garrison and send it to Roumania; that the Allies should immediately provide assistance for the Roumanian Army, etc. etc.

2. The President said that in the discussion which followed Mr. Lloyd George agreed that some assistance, in the way of supplies, would be given by England to the Roumanian Army; that the

French also agreed to do something; that he was then asked what he would do in the way of sending surplus supplies from the American Army here in France; that he replied that he did not know what he could do under the laws of the United States but that he would take advice on the matter.

3. In the interview mentioned in the first paragraph above the President asked what he could do under the law. He was informed, first, that enquiry would have to be made to ascertain whether there were any surplus stores of the American Army in France; second, that enquiry would have to be made of the financial agents of the United States Treasury Department here in Paris as to what financial arrangements would be necessary. He was informed that enquiries would be made on these subjects and the facts communicated to him at the earliest possible moment.

4. On the following day he was informed that, if he decided it to be legal so to do, he could direct the Secretary of the Treasury in Washington to open a credit with Roumania, on application therefor by that Government, for an amount equal to the value of the supplies to be furnished to Roumania; that the supplies, if any surplus existed in France, could then be furnished to Roumania on the furnishing by the latter of whatever security the law required. He was informed that it would be most desirable for him to consult the financial experts of the government before taking further steps in the matter.

5. Since that date nothing is known as to the President's action in this matter.

6. The French General Staff were fully informed as to the foregoing and said that the case was fully understood by them. Nevertheless, although the United States cannot deal with France in the matter but only with the government of Roumania, the French have repeatedly asked for the delivery to them of supplies, presumably to be transported to Roumania. This cannot be done until the preliminary financial arrangements are made between the United States government and the government of Roumania, in which case, presumably, the stores will be delivered to an accredited agent of the Roumanian government.

7. It is not known whether the Roumanian government has taken any step to comply with the American law on this subject.

8. Subsequent to all of the foregoing, the United States Liquidation Commission informed the French General Staff that it was prepared to sell to the Roumanian government, after compliance by the latter with the requirements of the law, certain surplus stores of the United States army in France.

9. The me[m]orandum herewith from the French Ministry of For-

eign Affairs to the American Ambassador in Paris[2] refers to "a decision of the Council of Four." The statement of the President at the above mentioned interview of March 27 was to the effect that there was no decision of the Council of Four insofar as it concerned the United States. The French Minister of Foreign Affairs requests the appointment of representatives having authority to fix the rules for the distribution of the financial expenses. Nothing is known about an agreement as to the distribution of financial expense by the Council of Four and it would be necessary to have an official extract from the minutes of the session of the Council of Four in order to determine what was agreed upon. So far as is known, the only question discussed at the Council of Four was as to the contribution that could be made by each of the Allied and Associated Governments from their surplus military stores for the support of the Roumanian army.

So far as is known, the only questions to be determined are the following, and these cannot be determined in a conference with the French authorities, but only by the authorities of the United States:

a) What are the surplus supplies of the United States Army in France that Roumania desires?
b) Does Roumania desire to ask a credit of the United States to cover the value of these supplies? and if so, is it legal for the United States to grant her this credit?
c) Does Roumania desire to purchase these supplies, for cash or for approved securities, from the Liquidation Commission?

10. So far as is known, whatever transaction is had on this subject must be between the Roumanian government and the government of the United States and not through the intermediary of the French Government or of any other government whatsoever.

T MS (WP, DLC).

[1] For this discussion, see the minutes of the Council of Four printed at March 27, 1919, 3:30 p.m., Vol. 56.

[2] It is printed as an Enclosure with RL to WW, April 25, 1919.

From Jovan S. Plamenatz

Mr. President, Neuilly-sur-Seine, 3rd May, 1919.

In the official report of the Peace Conference of the 28th April it is said that the delegates of all the allied countries have taken part in the plenary sitting, held on that day with the object of creating the pact of the League of Nations.

The name of Montenegro, as an ally, does not appear therein.

I protest emphatically against this new violation of the sovereign rights of Montenegro, war ally of the Great Powers.

Could the justice and morality of the allies have permitted that in the organisation of this Society of Nations should take part the States which have not shed a single drop of blood for the common cause. On the other hand, allied Montenegro, which has sacrificed so much in men and material, was not invited to participate in the same.

These unjust proceedings can never be excused before History. Moreover, they will carry the germ of new bloody conflicts, fatal to the development of Humanity.

Such proceedings should not be allowed in this holy alliance of the nations. They would make it resemble too much that of Vienna in 1814, which was founded upon injustice and as such soon recognised as fallacious.

I have the honor to be, Mr. President,

Your most obedient, humble servant, J. S. Plamenatz

TLS (WP, DLC).

From William Shepherd Benson, with Enclosures

My dear Mr. President: Paris, May 3, 1919.

With reference to our conversation of yesterday afternoon, I beg to transmit herewith, copies of orders which have been issued in compliance with your instructions. Certain detail orders, which have also been necessary, have been omitted as not being essential.

I shall keep you fully and promptly informed of all information which may be received from Naval sources regarding the question which makes these movements necessary.

Sincerely yours, W. S. Benson.

TLS (WP, DLC).

ENCLOSURE I

[Paris] 2 May 1919

For Rear Admiral Andrews.

President very anxious to get exact and reliable information as to what is going on in and about Fiume. Unless you know excellent reasons exist to make it undesirable proceed in the Olympia to Fiume, arrange to get despatches through to Paris and keep me informed as to what troops of various powers are in or near Fiume, any movements of these troops of whatever character. Acknowledge.

Benson

T telegram (WP, DLC).

ENCLOSURE II

[Paris] 2 May 1919.

Proceed immediately to Smyrna in NAHMA or NOMA whichever most suitable, taking two destroyers with you if available; otherwise two will be directed report to you there. Keep me informed constantly of other forces naval and military, in that vicinity. Ascertain diplomatically all information possible as to conditions, actions of other powers, particularly Italy. Be most circumspect. ARIZONA ordered to report to you Smyrna. State when you will reach Smyrna and with what force. Acknowledge. Benson[1]

Note—Rear Admiral Bristol left Constantinople May first in U.S.S. Nahma (Yacht) for Smyrna. Should have reached there following day. W. S. Benson

T telegram (WP, DLC); hw W. S. Benson.

[1] This telegram is W. S. Benson to M. L. Bristol.

ENCLOSURE III

[Paris] 2 May 1919.

For Commanding Officer, USS ARIZONA.[1]

Proceed Smyrna Syria immediately and report Rear Admiral Bristol. Inform me probable date passing Gibraltar and Malta; also probable date arrival Smyrna. Keep close watch for radio. When will you sail. Acknowledge. Benson

[1] John Havens Dayton, Captain, U.S.N.

ENCLOSURE IV

[Paris] 2 May, 1919.

Mission Number 453 for Opnav.[1]

Send MISSISSIPPI if available to Brest immediately—if MISSISSIPPI not available send next best dreadnaught for President—ARIZONA diverted to other duty. Both orders by direction President. Acknowledge. Benson

[1] William Sowden Sims.

ENCLOSURE V

[Paris] 2 May 1919

PRIORITY My 1134. Modify as follows: Direct three destroyers now at Gibraltar or vicinity to join USS ARIZONA when that vessel passes Gibraltar and proceed with her to destination. Paragraph.

Issue necessary instructions to destroyers concerned and USS ARIZONA. Acknowledge. Benson

T telegrams (WP, DLC).

From Henry White

Dear Mr President, Saturday Eveg. [May 3, 1919] 7.30

I hasten to send you the enclosed clipping from today (Saturday)'s London Times, which has been brought to me by W. Buckler who returned with it from London.[1] Certain marked passages in the telegrams from here & from Washn. will be of interest, I think, to you as they certainly are to me. I hope our French & British friends will be content to "sit tight" for a day or two longer on the Italian question which is evidently (I mean the position in which they have got themselves) causing an increasing amount of mischief each day in that country. Yours in haste, Henry White

I am leaving this on my way to dinner. The Times of today will not be seen generally in Paris until tomorrow morning.

ALS (WP, DLC).

[1] "American Views on Fiume," and "At Versailles," London *Times*, May 3, 1919, clipping (WP, DLC). The first article, written by a correspondent who had just toured the entire Pacific Coast region, observed that the "underlying sentiment" of the people in this strongly Republican part of the country was "enthusiastic for the League of Nations." The idea of the League transcended the personal popularity of Senators Poindexter and Borah, and even the Republican leaders in the western states had dissociated themselves from the views of their Washington representatives and had cautioned them not to take their opposition to the League too far. "The general feeling in the Far West," the article declared, "is that Mr. Lodge's Republican leadership has been proved to be unwise, because he is endeavouring to lead the party into a position of opposition to such a popular issue as the League. Mr. Lodge's attitude on the Italian question, it is feared, may prove similarly embarrassing with the Republican Party, which is put in the position of harassing the President and then being forced to acquiesce in his point of view." In fact, the article continued, Wilson's "somewhat diminishing prestige" had received an impetus by his announcement on Fiume, since bold and open diplomacy was admired as direct and unhypocritical in this section of the United States. Moreover, much of the wartime feeling of nonpartisanship in questions of foreign policy had survived, and it was thus not unusual to "find the whole West rising in support of the President." The article emphasized that even Wilson's bitterest critics, such as the editorial writers of the Portland *Oregonian* and Senator Johnson of California, had openly endorsed his stand on Fiume, and it concluded: "The unquestionable wave of enthusiasm for Mr. Wilson's stand in the Italian controversy came as much from the knowledge that Great Britain and France supported his claim as from the convincing nature of his statement. Few pronouncements from Mr. Wilson have carried as much conviction. . . . The clear fact is that the Far West believes that the annexation of Fiume might disturb the peace of Europe, if not the world, again, and that it believes that Italy must recede or accept a compromise."

The second article, after discussing such topics as the arrangements for the stay of the German delegation at Versailles, the exchange of credentials with the German delegates, and Belgian claims for reparation, also commented on the Italian situation. It stated that "Italian official and semi-official diplomacy" was very active, both in Rome and in Paris, in trying to persuade the Allied governments to take some step which could be interpreted as an invitation to the Italian delegates to return to the peace conference. However, in spite of "sundry suggestions" by the Italian Ambassador in Paris and by the Italian government, there was no sign so far that Italy's point of view of the situation was entirely shared by the British or the French governments. "The Italians chose to absent themselves from the Conference," the article continued, "and they are free to return whenever they think fit. They were not sent away, and consequently there is no obvious ground for asking them to come back." In fact, there was reliable information that at least one of the Italian delegates "considered the spectacular withdrawal from the Conference and the appeal to the Italian Parliament a serious tactical mistake," and that this view was "widely shared" in Italian political circles. "By far the soundest course for the Italian Delegation," the article concluded, "would be to return to Paris without fuss, before the other leading Delegations get into the habit of working without it."

To Norman Hezekiah Davis, with Enclosure

My dear Mr. Davis: Paris, 3 May, 1919.

In view of the enclosed letter from Mr. Hoover, I hesitate to send the order you suggested to the Secretary of the Treasury,[1] terminating the credit to Belgium, and beg that you will bring the matter again to the consideration of the Secretary with the expression of my judgment that it would be wise in the circumstances to continue advances to the Belgian Government for food purchases until the balance of the forty millions credit is exhausted. I hope that your own judgment will coincide with this.

Cordially and sincerely yours, [Woodrow Wilson]

[1] See N. H. Davis to WW, May 1, 1919.

E N C L O S U R E

From Herbert Clark Hoover

My dear Mr. President: Paris, 2 May 1919.

The letter addressed to you by Mr. Davis at the request of the Secretary of the Treasury has been called to my attention. The proposal of the Treasury is apparently to stop all advances to Belgium for foodstuffs, and they are asking for your approval for the withdrawal of a credit authorized by you to Belgium, of which there is an unexhausted balance of $22,250,000.

I, of course, do not know all of the Treasury's reasons, but the statement made that it is because of the completion of the operations of the Relief Commission does not meet the point. In an endeavor to secure the gradual development of the various relieved countries from the nursery stage of relief, I had insisted that the Belgians should take over their entire relief measures and thrust the responsibility up to them as from the first of May, with the full anticipation that they would continue to draw from the United States Treasury such sums as were needed for their foodstuffs. Under the proposal of the Treasury, the Belgians will be out of foodstuffs within sixty days, and I do not think we have any more right to withdraw credits from Belgium for food, than we would from England, France, Italy, or any of these countries, without proper and ample notice. More especially is this the case in the rather delicate situation in Belgium and in connection with the peace negotiations at the present time.

With the retirement of the Relief Commission we had arranged for the reduction of the Belgian food programme from approximately $20,000,000 a month to $15,000,000 a month. Since that time, I have been able to sell some accumulated Belgian stocks to the Germans, with the intention of re-investing the realized sums in foodstuffs, and if the Treasury could see their way to grant to Belgium the balance of the authorized credit, that is $22,250,000, I think we could establish a situation by which their food supply would be taken care of until the end of August. I do earnestly recommend that the Treasury should take this course, and if you approve I enclose a draft letter[1] which I would suggest should be addressed to Mr. Davis. I simply do not see how Belgium is to be fed otherwise. Faithfully yours, [Herbert Hoover]

CCL (WP, DLC).

[1] T MS (WP, DLC); not printed.

Ray Stannard Baker to Cary Travers Grayson

Dear Admiral: [Paris, c. May 3, 1919]

Here is our Summary of the Treaty.[1] It presents in short space a pretty good idea of the dose we are administering to the Germans.

I think the President may desire to look it over. If he does I'd like to have it back again soon with any suggestions or corrections. I suppose now our time on it is brief.

Sincerely Ray Stannard Baker

ALS (WP, DLC).

[1] T MS (WP, DLC).

Two Telegrams from Thomas Nelson Page to the American Mission

Rome, May 3, 1919

287. The Rome press is still filled with harsh attacks on President Wilson but its tone towards United States is less angry. The decisions [declarations] of Senator Lodge and Senator Curtis,[1] which are continually reprinted in Italian newspapers, and the attitude of the Republicans, is given to lead the Italians to believe there is wide divergence between the American people and their Chief executive. All sorts of devices are employed to promulgate this view, including suppositious declarations by myself of divergence of our views.

In the editorials of the two leading morning newspapers are rather suggestive references to the Italian attitude toward the Peace Conference. "IL TEMPO" in a leader which has been mutilated by censor suggests hypothesis that Barrere, the French Ambassador, has returned to Rome bringing certain proposals which may make for settlement. It praises government and men who have maintained dignity of Italy and borne great responsibility last few days but it adds "This phase of our history is now closed" and to meet the new needs new men should arise. IL TEMPO is naldis paper.[2] The editorial is interpreted not only as attack on cabinet but also as demand for appointment of new delegation to Peace Conference.

MESSAGGERO discusses various interpretations given by "experts" in international law to Pact of London and concludes that Pact of London needs no special interpretation. It says that in three days which remain the Allies can formulate a proposal in accord with rights and sentiments of Italy and one which does not exclude the spirit of conciliation.

Baron Sonnino has stated that he would get out if he stands in the way of settlement.

These suggestions, the veiled suggestion that a new delegation be appointed, and the hint that formula of conciliation may be found, are significant, especially as made by representative newspapers. The hint that government may carry out policy of conciliation is also borne out, leading article heavily censored in POPOLO ROMANO fiercely criticising government for adopting such attitude.

I believe the government really most anxious to find some solution of present situation whose difficulty here I do not believe at all realized in Paris. However wicked the means adopted to excite the people they are now absolutely solidly for extreme assertions of Italy's claims. Even the extreme socialists, who have stood out throughout the war against Italy's claims to Dalmatia, do not now venture to oppose demand for annexation. The situation is in fact very grave.

It is said on Italian authority that President Wilson has issued a new statement in answer to Orlando's and that it has been held up by Italian censor. Sonnino states he has no knowledge of such new statement.

A forecast of action of Italian troops in occupying Konia is given in letter from Smyrna correspondent of the TEMPO which is published today. It states that the Greeks have been slowly taking possession of Smyrna and secretly building up a formidable civic organization. Side by side with this Greek movement a strong and steady British penetration has been going on. The British have taken possession of railway leading from Smyrna to Konia and there have been British troops at Konia for some time. Correspondent intimates that Italy must take action to save her interests. "CORRIERE D'ITALIA" says that Italians probably acted upon request of General Allenby. It is plain that all three powers interested are acting without waiting decision at Paris.

EPOCA published yesterday evening, republishes this morning, letter of George Herron in support of Italian claims and alleges that opposition to them centered in and owing to international financial circles which desire concessions.[3] This statement regarded as important by Italians for they believe Herron to be close to President, but they do not by any means take this statement as expressing President's thought.

Gabriele Dannunzio, who was prevented from coming Rome last Tuesday is expected today and announcement has been made of large conference to be held by him this afternoon at Campidoglio which will be made occasion for demonstration. Whatever he says will undoubtedly be with the approval of the Government.

He will speak tomorrow at Augusteo Auditorium, not at Capitol. It is certain that the Government will try to have his speech milder and more tranquilizing tone than is expected. My interpretation of Government's permission for him to speak is that it has not strength to oppose him. Nelson Page.

[1] That is, Charles Curtis.

[2] "Naldis" is a garbled decode. In any event, the Editors have been unable to identify the owner of *Il Tempo*. However, according to one authority, *Il Tempo* was "generally regarded as expressing the Giolittian point of view, . . . berating the government for its laxity in pushing the Italian demands, while playing up at the same time the social unrest of which the Socialists were the chief promoters." Albrecht-Carrié, *Italy at the Paris Peace Conference*, p. 125.

[3] About this allegation and Wilson's reaction, see n. 2 to the House Diary printed at May 12, 1919.

Rome, May 3, 1919.

289. IMPORTANT.

Learn from my French colleague that Italian Government received yesterday evening communication through Italian Embassy, Paris, made by Peace Conference that the Austro-Hungarians have been invited to send peace delegations to Versailles about May 14th. To this communication Italian Government sent French Ambassador reply and protest at midnight which French Ambassador considered sufficiently urgent to report without a moment's delay to his government. He has seen both Orlando and Sonnino today and found them greatly moved and incensed at what they consider attempt to coerce them against all rights of Italy. French Ambassador states that he has presented strongly his views on such increasing difficulty in situation already very difficult. I agree with him in this view of case unless it be proved that intention immediately to invite Italy to return to Peace Conference. Without such a step, and it should be made immediately, not only Italian Government but the entire Italian people will be unquestionably greatly inflamed. I understand that the publication of the information received will be withheld from press for the present.

Referring my telegram last night[1] I urge that immediate invitation in above sense be sent coupling it with and as a part of communication made to Italian Government through Italian Embassy, Paris. Unless this course followed result can hardly be other than to throw Italy into a state of upheaval which may be a catastrophe.

Nelson Page

T telegrams (WP, DLC).

[1] TNP to Ammission, May 2, 1919 (second telegram of that date).

Sir Robert Borden to Sir Thomas White, with Enclosure

SECRET

Dear Sir Thomas White, Paris, May 3rd, 1919.

I now beg to enclose General Memorandum No. 19, which is descriptive of events that have occurred since the evening of Saturday, 26th April. Yours faithfully, R. L. Borden

TLS (R. L. Borden Papers, CaOOA).

E N C L O S U R E

SECRET

Paris, May 3rd, 1919

GENERAL MEMORANDUM NO. 19

. . . 3. Sir Robert Borden presided at a meeting of the British delegations on Monday last and was in conference with Mr. Lloyd George both before and after the meeting. The first conference related to a paragraph in the Labour Convention which is designed to debar the British Dominions from election to the Governing Body, to which further reference will be made in this memorandum. The second conference related to the strong feeling expressed by the representatives of the Dominion at the proposal of the Council of Four to override the report of the Commission on Responsibilities of the War,[1] and to substitute therefor a proposal drafted by President Wilson.[2] As neither the Report of the Commission nor President Wilson's proposal has been brought before the British Delegations for discussion, and as there was a strong division of opinion on the subject, Sir Robert Borden was asked to communicate with Mr. Lloyd George and to represent to him the extreme undesirability of having the subject discussed at the Plenary Conference that afternoon, although it had been placed upon the agenda. Mr. Lloyd George entirely agreed with this view and stated that the item had been placed on the agenda without his knowledge. At his request, Sir Robert Borden met President Wilson and Mr. Clemenceau to whom he had made the same representations. They concurred in the view expressed by Mr. Lloyd George. . . .

5. On Sunday the 27th, Sir Robert Borden finally succeeded in securing agreement between the representatives of the various nations as to the form of the nine Articles respecting labour which are to be inserted in the Peace Treaty.[3] After the League of Nations Covenant had been adopted, Mr. Barnes proposed the original draft and Sir Robert Borden moved the new draft in amendment. He was supported by Mr. Vandervelde and the sitting closed with the usual formula by Mr. Clemenceau "Adopté. La séance est levé[e]." The question as to discussion of the proposed Articles respecting punishment of the Kaiser, etc., had solved itself with the kind assistance of M. Bourgeois and of the gentlemen from Honduras and Panama. There was no time for further debate.

6. In pursuance of a request from President Wilson, conveyed through Mr. Lloyd George, Sir Robert Borden had an interview on Tuesday 29th April, with Mr. Robinson, who is the Chief American Expert on labour conditions. The discussion related to the elimination from the Labour Convention (ARTICLE VII) of the following words:

"No Member, together with its Dominions and Colonies, whether self-governing or not, shall be entitled to nominate more than one member."

The interview was unsatisfactory as Mr. Robinson seemed to be greatly oppressed by the condition of public opinion in the United States with regard to the influence of the British Empire in the League of Nations and in the International Labour organizations. The result of the interview and the position taken by the Canadian Ministers thereon is sufficiently set forth in a letter from Sir Robert Borden to Mr. Lloyd George, dated 29th April, copy of which is attached.[4]

7. In connection with this question and with respect to the construction of the League of Nations Covenant, Sir Robert Borden had an interview with President Wilson on Thursday afternoon[5] while in attendance at a meeting of the Council of Four at the Quai d'Orsay. Lord Robert Cecil, General Smuts and Mr. Hurst, all agree that under the Covenant as it has been adopted, the representatives of the Dominions are eligible under Article IV for election by the Assembly to the Council of the League.[6] Mr. Sifton and Mr. Doherty[7] are inclined to entertain the opposite view. The question is doubtless arguable but it should not be settled upon a purely technical or narrow construction. At the interview in question, President Wilson entirely agreed with the view that representatives are so eligible. Sir Robert Borden has asked Mr. Lloyd George to have this understanding brought up and confirmed by President Wilson and the First Delegates of the other Powers, either in the course of the conversations in the Council of Four, or otherwise. . . .

9. With respect to the Labour Convention, the following extract from a letter addressed to Mr. Lloyd George by Sir Robert Borden on the 2nd instant sufficiently explains the present situation:

"This difficulty I also discussed yesterday at the Quai d'Orsay with President Wilson and I found him quite sympathetic. So far as Canada is concerned he would have no difficulty whatever; but he explained that there was considerable difficulty with respect to some other Dominions and especially India. In reply I told him that we could not ask to be placed in a different position from them. As our position has been conceded (in the view above indicated) with respect to the League of Nations, there is a far weightier reason why it should apply also to the Labour Convention having regard to three principal considerations: (a) the essential and striking differences in labour conditions, (b) our great industrial development, and (c) the larger representation of the governing body under the Labour Convention (twenty-four) as compared with that on the League of Nations Council (nine).

Unless the offending paragraph in the Labour Convention is suppressed I shall be obliged to make a public reservation when the Peace Treaty is presented to the Plenary Conference. The motion which I proposed and which was unanimously accepted at the second last Plenary Conference[8] affords ample ground, in my judgment, for its suppression. A direction from the Council of Four to the Drafting Committee would effect its suppression." . . .

T MS (R. L. Borden Papers, CaOOA).

[1] See n. 4 to the minutes of the Council of Four printed at April 2, 1919, 4 p.m., Vol. 56.

[2] See the minutes of the Council of Four printed at April 9, 1919, 11 a.m., Vol. 57.

[3] See the Enclosure printed with H. M. Robinson to WW, April 27, 1919.

[4] It is missing.

[5] That is, May 1, 1919.

[6] After the Commission on the League of Nations had finished its work on April 11, 1919, and the final English version of the Covenant had been printed on April 21, 1919, the British Dominions and India had continued to insist on another important alteration. Their criticism had been directed at Article 4 of the Covenant, which concerned the composition of the Council of the League of Nations and read in part as follows: "The Council shall consist of Representatives of the United States of America, of the British Empire, of France, of Italy, and of Japan, together with Representatives of four other States which are members of the League of Nations." The article then went on to use the words "State" or "States" several times more in defining the membership of the council. The Dominions had objected that this particular wording would make them ineligible to serve on the council, since, although members of the League, they were not strictly speaking "states." Hence, on April 21, they had asked that, throughout the Covenant, all references to "state" or "states" should be deleted and substituted by "member of the League" and "members of the League," respectively. Two days later, Cecil, House, and Wilson had agreed to the proposed changes, and they had been incorporated in the draft presented to and adopted by the Plenary Session on April 28, 1919. See the diaries of Lord Robert Cecil, April 21, 1919, and of Colonel House, April 22 and 23, 1919, both not printed; and Miller, *My Diary at the Conference of Paris*, I, 264-70, *passim*. For a detailed discussion of this question, see David Hunter Miller, *The Drafting of the Covenant* (2 vols., New York and London, 1928), I, 477-82. The draft of the Covenant of April 21, 1919, is printed in *ibid.*, II, 683-94. The Covenant as adopted is printed in this volume at April 28, 1919.

[7] That is, Arthur Lewis Sifton and Charles Joseph Doherty, Ministers of Customs and Justice, respectively, and plenipotentiary delegates of Canada at the peace conference.

[8] In his efforts to secure for the Dominions the right to become members of the Governing Body of the International Labour Office, Borden, during the Plenary Session of April 11, 1919, which had adopted the Labour Convention, had introduced an amendment which had instructed the Drafting Committee to make such alterations "as may be necessary to have the Convention conform to the Covenant of the League of Nations in the character of its membership and in the method of adherence." The minutes of this session, together with the draft of the Labour Convention, are printed in *PPC*, III, 280-84. For a summary, see n. 5 to the extract from the Grayson Diary printed at April 11, 1919, Vol. 57. See also Miller, *My Diary at the Conference of Paris*, IX, 415-16, and James T. Shotwell, ed., *The Origins of the International Labor Organization* (2 vols., New York, 1934), I, 210-11.

From the Diary of Ray Stannard Baker

Saturday the 3rd [May 1919].

The President has had a hard day. The *Three* put nearly the finishing touches on the treaty to-day so that it can now go to the printer: but the troublesome Belgian & Italian problems remain unsettled. They are trying to force Wilson's hands on the Italian question: & after the Three adjourned the Italian Ambassador to America, Celleri, appeared & nearly wore the President out with talk—delaying his dinner for half an hour. I have never seen the President look so worn & tired. A terrible strain, with everyone against him. He was so beaten out that he could not remember without an effort what the council had done in the forenoon. I told Grayson afterwards that he ought to keep the President absolutely quiet over Sunday, else I did not see how he could stand it. Grayson agreed wholly with me. . . .

The Chinese statement which I was able to delay came out, at last, to-day.[1] It is sharp & strong—and true. Looking at it from the point of abstract justice it is unanswerable: & yet the President is *right*. . . .

The Treaty, which I have been reading the last few days, is a terrible document: a document of retribution to the verge of revenge, a fearful indictment, such a dispensation of hard justice as I never read before. Too hard? I think the Germans at Versailles will fall in a swoon when they see it. Will they sign it? I am doubtful. If they do, it will be with crossed fingers! They will be slaves under it for half a century. I can see no real peace in it.

Even the President said the other day, talking of some of the provisions: "If I were a German I think I should never sign it."

They have tempered justice with no mercy.

President too much a gentleman: trusts himself in the Conferences without any secretary, & only once with a stenographer (when the Italians were there) Minutes kept by Sir Maurice Hankey when the Japanese were there the other day. Mantoux there with Clemenceau. What guarantees do the Japanese give for the faithful performance of their agreements with China?

The President always advising me not to mind if the others broke over on their agreements regarding publicity "We've got to keep to our arrangement." Loneliness of the President: rarely anyone to luncheon or dinner. Other commissioners in a round of dinners & teas & receptions.

—Weariness at night.

[1] This statement, which was actually released on May 2, 1919, declared that the Chinese delegation, having been informed orally about the outlines of the proposed Shantung settlement, could not but "view it with disappointment and dissatisfaction." The German rights in Shantung, the statement pointed out, had "originated in an act of wanton aggression," which, by the transfer of these rights to Japan, was now being confirmed. While such a virtual substitution of Japan for Germany in Shantung was serious enough in itself, it assumed grave dimensions if considered in connection with Japan's position in Manchuria and Eastern Mongolia, since it would make the Chinese capital of Peking nothing "but an enclave in the midst of Japanese influence." Moreover, the statement continued, by China's declaration of war against the Central Powers and by the abrogation of all treaties between them and China, the German rights had automatically reverted to China. Thus, the Chinese delegation maintained: "It appears clear, then, that the Council has been bestowing on Japan the rights, not of Germany, but of China; not of an enemy but of an ally. The more powerful ally has reaped a benefit at the expense,

not of the common enemy, but of the weaker ally." If it was the intention of the council to restore Shantung to China, it was difficult to see what consideration of principle or of expediency could justify its transfer, in the first instance, to an alien power, which would then "voluntarily" return it to its rightful owner.

As for the basis of Japan's claim to the German rights, the Chinese delegation argued that it had been Japan's aggressive policy which had forced China to sign the treaties of May 1915 and September 1918. The Chinese delegation realized that the decision of the council was prompted by the fact that, in February and March 1917, Great Britain and France had promised to support Japan's claims to the German rights. However, China had not been a party to any of these secret agreements, nor had she been informed of their contents when invited to enter the war on the Allied side. Thus, the fortunes of China seemed "to have been made objects of negotiation and compensation" after she had already joined the Allies, and it was at least open to question how far the secret agreements were still applicable in these circumstances. Apart from all these considerations, the statement continued, the claims of Japan were hardly compatible with the Fourteen Points, and it concluded:

"If the Council has granted the claims of Japan in full for the purpose of saving the League of Nations, as is intimated to be the case, China has less to complain of, believing, as she does, that it is a duty to make sacrifices for such a noble cause as the League of Nations. She cannot, however, refrain from wishing that the Council had seen fit, as would be far more consonant with the spirit of the League now on the eve of formation, to call upon strong Japan to forego her claims animated by a desire for aggrandizement, instead of upon weak China to surrender what is hers by right.

"China came to the conference with a strong faith in the lofty principles adopted by the allied and associated powers as the basis of a just and permanent world peace. Great, therefore, will be the disappointment and disillusion of the Chinese people over the proposed settlement.

"If there is a reason for the Council to stand firm on the question of Fiume, there would seem to be all the more reason to uphold the claim of China relating to Shantung, which includes the future welfare of 36,000,000 souls and the highest interest of peace in the Far East." *New York Times*, May 4, 1919.

To Joseph Patrick Tumulty

Paris, 3 May, 1919.

Please tell Mr. Gompers that the redraft of the clauses to which his cable refers are the best that could be got out of a maze of contending interests in the conference.[1] Woodrow Wilson.

T telegram (WP, DLC).

[1] Wilson was replying to JPT to WW, May 2, 1919 (first telegram of that date).

To Walker Downer Hines

Paris, 3 May, 1919.

For Director General Hines. I have followed the controversy between the Railway Administration and the Industrial Board as well as I could from this distance and take the liberty of suggesting that perhaps it would not be wise to continue it longer. I have advised Mr. Redfield[1] that perhaps it would be best to discontinue the Industrial Board particularly in view of the fact that the Attorney General, I am told, regards its action as questionably consistent with the law.

Woodrow Wilson.

T telegram (WP, DLC).

[1] See WW to WCR, April 21, 1919 (first telegram of that date), Vol. 57. However, see also JPT to WW, April 22, 1919, *ibid.*

From Joseph Patrick Tumulty

The White House, 3 May 1919.

#95 Think call for special session should issue immediately so that members may arrange to be here. Tumulty.

T telegram (WP, DLC).

To Joseph Patrick Tumulty

Paris, 3 May, 1919.

Please tell Secretary of the Treasury confidentially that I expect to summon Congress for the 15th of May.

Woodrow Wilson.

T telegram (WP, DLC).

From the Diary of Edith Benham

May 4, 1919

Nothing much to record yesterday. The place, of course, is seething over the Chinese question. Mrs. W. said the P. has not been able to sleep from worry over it and that the question is not precisely the same as Fiume, since the Japanese had taken it, and he also felt they would administer it better. Then he knew the Italians, Japanese, Russians and Germans would make an alliance and where would we be. He felt he would rather sacrifice himself than have that happen, and let people criticize him. Of course I think this is poor business in one way, for it is not insistence upon the 14 points, and I think the Chinese have us in their reply. In other words, this peace instead of being made on the high moral principles and the note it sounded of care for the weaker nations is made on some of the old lines. On the whole it has been better, but not altogether now. I must say those crafty little devils, the Japanese, had him coming and going as they had the Allies before. . . .

The P. had a conference with Count Cellere in the afternoon and I was amused in looking out of the window into the court below to see an international tableau. The French guard was standing indifferently in a corner, the Italian soldier who had come with Count

Cellere was looking sullenly at the big American guard who was striding up and down with an expression of withering contempt on his face.

From the Diary of Dr. Grayson

Sunday, May 4, 1919.

The President remained in bed until ten o'clock; he had breakfast at 10:30. At 11:00 o'clock I went down to see him, and after a brief conversation he asked if I would not join him and Mrs. Wilson; that he had some things he wanted to read aloud. He read a diary by the son of [Albert] Gallatin.[1] We were all very much struck by the similarity of occurrences of the Peace Conference of Ghent 100 years ago as compared with what the President is going through today.

We had lunch at one o'clock, and immediately afterwards went for a motor ride in an open car on the road to Fontainebleau. When we got within a few miles of that place we turned to the right and went to the village of Barbizon. This is the home of artists. Many famous paintings have been inspired here. We drove all through the village and around it. During the afternoon we were compelled to stop twice on account of tire trouble. Each time, although the President was wearing a golf-cap, he was recognized by the passersby, especially by pedestrians. At one place where a tire was being adjusted an old French woman came up to the car. She was plainly dressed, showed evidence of having worked hard all her life; her hands were rough; her face was worn, but it was a face with a kindly expression. She took a long look at the President seemingly trying to ascertain whether it was really the President or not. Finally, she calmly walked off to the edge of the field, pulled some wild flowers, and walked back to the car, handing them to the President, at the same time bowing most profoundly, and expressing, in French, the gratitude that the poor people of France had for the justice that the President was trying to do for them. To my mind it was one of the most simple yet touching tributes I have ever seen paid the President. He was very much moved by the incident.

A great many pedestrians were to be seen along the road. At one place two American soldier boys were walking along with their arms around two French girls. The President called attention to them, saying: "There is an instance of international entente."

We returned home at about 6:30. The President spent a quiet evening with Mrs. Wilson, and retired early, making it a complete day of rest.

[1] James Gallatin, *A Great Peacemaker: The Diary of James Gallatin, Secretary to Albert Gallatin, 1813-1827* (New York, 1914).

From Lord Robert Cecil

Dear Mr President Paris. 4 May 1919.

I have to thank you very cordially for your exceedingly kind letter.[1] It has been a great honour for me to have had the opportunity of working with you in so great a cause & if you think that my efforts have really been of assistance that is much more than sufficient reward for any exertions that I have made. The acceptance of the Covenant which owes so much to you is the first step. But in itself the Covenant is no more than a bare skeleton. We have next to clothe it with flesh and muscle. Even so it will be but a dead body unless a spirit can be infused into it. For that we must look under God to the peoples of the World & especially to those of America & England. May they be rightly inspired!

On the point raised by Mr Polk the Covenant will come into force when the Treaty does so. I understand that a clause is to be inserted in the Treaty providing that it will become effective as soon as certain of the Powers have ratified it. So that no special provision in the Covenant seems necessary.

Again thanking you from my heart

Yours very sincerely Robert Cecil

ALS (WP, DLC).

[1] WW to R. Cecil, May 2, 1919.

From Henry Mauris Robinson

Dear Mr. President: [Paris] 4 May 1919

Feeling that the suggested method for the execution of the Ship Agreement might give rise to serious trouble, I presumed to discuss the matter with Messrs. McCormick, Lamont, Dulles and Bradley Palmer. All agreed that the agreement must contain any reservation in relation to the application of funds in one of three ways, viz:

Preferably in the body of the agreement.

A statement setting out the specific reservation, immediately preceding your signature, or

A statement before your signature that the United States had a reservation set forth in a separate memorandum.

All agreed that the first method would be altogether the best.

I then discussed the question with the British Shipping Representative,[1] who is quite in accord with us that to embody any reservation desired, in the body of the agreement is so much the best way as to really preclude the other suggestions. He also agreed that to make a special reservation for the United States would be a mistake.

A copy of the redraft is enclosed[2] and you will find after the word "determined" in the third line on page 2, the formula agreed to by the British representative and ourselves.[3] In other respects the agreement is the same except for a few minor drafting changes agreed to by the British.

This text has been passed by Mr. Dulles and Mr. Palmer. The British representative has told Lord Cunliffe that in his opinion this is the only thing to do. My understanding is that Lord Cunliffe's reply resembled a grunt, but that in all probability there will be no difficulty in getting the Prime Minister to accept the Agreement in this form.

While no definite conclusion has been arrived at with the French, it may be during the day and possibly before this is sent you. I am sending this to you so that the matter may not be finally overlooked.

When signed by Great Britain, France and the United States, the situation will be reasonably safe, though the full list of signatories will include about thirteen. The interest of the three states named is, on the basis of losses, approximately ninety per cent of the whole. I am also returning the draft[4] with the lead pencil emendations for possible use if discussion arises.

Very respectfully yours, Henry M. Robinson
Sunday, 5 p.m.

P.S. Owing to a meeting of the French Cabinet Ministry, I have been unable up to this time to get a meeting with M. Clementel to determine finally the French attitude.

TLS (WP, DLC).

[1] Charles Hipwood, Assistant Secretary of the Board of Trade and an adviser on economic questions in the British delegation at the peace conference.

[2] It is printed, as amended by Wilson, as the first of the two memoranda of agreement on May 8, 1919.

[3] It read as follows: "The amount of the value so fixed will be paid over by each such State to the Reparation Commission for the credit of Germany towards the sums due from her for Reparation, in respect to war losses of merchant ships, unless the competent legislative authority of any such State shall affirmatively determine otherwise."

[4] That is, the document cited in n. 11 to the minutes of the Council of Four printed at May 3, 1919, 4 p.m.

From Henry White

My dear Mr. President: Paris, May 4, 1919.

This is merely a line of warning in respect to the question of Bavaria, which is likely to be brought tomorrow to the attention of the Council of Three; not by the Committee on Credentials, which decided this morning that the credentials of the German Delegates are in order, but probably by M. Clemenceau at the instance of M. Cambon. The latter, after the decision of the Committee but before it adjourned, said that he ought to call its attention to the fact that there is a political side to the case of Bavaria, to which, in his opinion, the attention of your Council should be called, and he suggested that the Committee on Credentials send a message to the Council of Three, stating that the credentials of the German Delegates had been found in order, but before notifying them thereof, it felt that "The Three" be asked whether some guarantee should not be required of the German Delegates as to their power to bind Bavaria to the terms of any Treaty which they might sign.

I objected to this proposal on the ground (1) that the Committee on Credentials was fully empowered to decide upon the validity of the powers of the various delegates; (2) that it had arrived at a decision in respect to those of the German Plenipotentiaries; (3) that it would be going beyond its province to make any further suggestions to the Council of Three, besides giving the latter an unnecessary piece of work, and that (4) while M. Cambon was naturally at liberty to make any observations that might seem to him appropriate to his own Government, they should be made on his own responsibility and not in behalf of the Committee on Credentials.

My position in the matter was supported by the Japanese and British Plenipotentiaries;[1] and it was decided to notify the Germans that their powers are in order. My object in this note is, therefore, to suggest that, should this question be brought up at your meeting tomorrow, it will save you trouble merely to say that the Committee on Credentials having pronounced those of the Germans to be valid, you see no reason why any further question should arise as to Bavaria's not being bound by the Treaty signed by them.

Yours very sincerely, Henry White

P.S. The accompanying brief statement will explain some of the Credentials Committee's reasons for its action.[2]

TLS (WP, DLC).

[1] Keishiro Matsui and Andrew Bonar Law.

[2] T MS (WP, DLC). It pointed out that the present German government was a "revolutionary government" which had taken over all the powers of the former Emperor, including the power to declare war and to conclude peace in the name of the former empire. Furthermore, the Treaty of Brest-Litovsk had been concluded "without any assent having been asked or given thereto on the part of Bavaria." In addition, a law passed by the National Assembly at Weimar on February 10, 1919, provided as follows: "The National President represents the nation under international law; he may make treaties with foreign Powers in the name of the nation. War is declared and peace is made by national law."

From William Shepherd Benson

My dear Mr. President, Paris, 4 May 1919.

In accordance with your desire to be kept informed of conditions in the Adriatic, I have the honor to quote below for your information the following despatches, received this day from Rear Admiral Phillip Andrews, Commanding U. S. Naval Forces in the Eastern Mediterranean:

> "I will go to Fiume on Maury. Can get complete data in one or two days. Know now that British have 6100 soldiers and French about the same. Situation American zone now excellent but withdrawal of Olympia and both senior officers likely to allow trouble to begin. Think necessary Olympia remain here at present. Military situation at and near Fiume probably cannot be fixed."

"Flag temporarily in Maury proceeding Fiume."

Very respectfully, W. S. Benson

TLS (WP, DLC).

Thomas Nelson Page to the American Mission

Rome. May 4th, 1919.

290. Press this morning rather more moderate but continues to make much of Herron's published letter and of D'Annunzio expected speech. This speech was delivered this morning in great Augusteo Auditorium. It was very inflammatory and closed with order of the day as follows: "The Romans convoked in general assembly take notice of the free and declared will of Fiume to be annexed to Italy. It defies the Allied Governments to present to the German delegates in the absence of Italy the preliminaries of peace which act would be understood as a formal violation of the Declaration of London. It invokes the immediate annexation of the territories included in the Pact of London, recalling to the government the duty to set free also the other Italian cities not yet redeemed and especially Spalato and Trau and that the government take immediate steps to restore all its limitations which it holds adapted to prevent any possible foreign reprisal."[1]

Publication in press of speech much censored. Prime Minister Orlando requested me to call on him this afternoon, and, greeting me with much friendliness, stated that he was profoundly pained by the speech and requested that I telegraph his sincere regrets to my Government. He stated that he had an hour's talk with D'Annunzio yesterday for the purpose of impressing on him the importance of moderation and of not speaking in a way to excite the people and the latter promised that he would not do so, but the Premier said he had not kept his promise. The Premier expressed sentiments of personal friendliness and appreciation of our people and of the President; he showed me the protocol with the exchange of expressions of good will between him and the President at their last meeting in Paris.[2] He added that D'Annunzio speech was not more a defiance to the Allied Governments than it was to himself and to the Italian Government. I rather think that he feels that the people may get so out of hand now that nothing he can say will quiet them. The mistake was made in permitting D'Annunzio, who is an officer in the army, to come to Rome and speak. He was promoted yesterday from major to lieutenant colonel.

The Premier said further that the censor had not in the early publication of D'Annunzio's (#) censured enough but the later editions were more fully censored.

Meantime I hear that Italy has taken possession of Fiume and is fortifying it.

I think on the whole there is a greater feeling of hopefulness on the part of government people of some settlement being arrived at. Also of being invited to return to Paris. If invited I think they will be able to make more concessions than if they should go without being invited. I do not believe that without being invited they would dare to return to Paris and make any concessions. The French Ambassador who had seen both Sonnino and Orlando yesterday came to see me this afternoon and I think holds the same view.

Nelson Page.

T telegram (WP, DLC).

[1] For additional extracts from D'Annunzio's speech, see Mayer, *Politics and Diplomacy of Peacemaking*, pp. 707-708.

[2] See the minutes of the Council of Four printed at April 24, 1919, 4 p.m.

From the Diary of Ray Stannard Baker

Sunday May 4th [1919]

A lazy day at last. No meetings of the Three. The President drove down to Fontainbleau & to Barbizon & looked at the fields in which Millet painted the Angelus. I took up to him this evening the precious confidential summary of the Treaty, which we have been so energetically at work upon. I do hope they let it go as we have prepared it: but I fear they will want still to muffle it & take care lest the people see & know. The Chinese got out their second statement today—very sharp.[1] I took it up to the President. It is a hard situation.

—Of General Bliss—letter on Chinese question:[2] letter on selling of armament to small nations:[3] simple, robust, honest.

[1] This statement, issued by the Chinese Press Bureau in Paris, declared that new light on the settlement of the Shantung question had made the Chinese delegation "indignant." Although the delegation had as yet received no details of the settlement and was "still waiting in suspense," it had learned that the proposed clauses went even further than had been expected. The statement then briefly summarized the major provisions of the Shantung agreement and argued that Japan was "given everything Germany obtained from China by aggression, and more." Although China had the "best title" to the German rights, not a word was said in the draft clauses about what China might expect to recover for herself. It was entirely left to Japan to say what she would be pleased to return to China and what she would retain "for her own enjoyment." The statement concluded: "Reading the draft clauses together with the outlines the council has proposed in settlement, it is clear that the council makes China lose both ways. It has given Japan not only more than Germany had in Shantung, but also more than Japan claims from China in the treaty of 1915 and the notes of 1918. . . . The more the Chinese delegates study the proposed settlement, the less they understand its meaning and purpose, and the more they feel aggrieved. It will be difficult to explain to the Chinese people what the Peace Conference really means by justice." *New York Times*, May 5, 1919.

[2] THB to WW, April 29, 1919.

[3] THB to RL, April 19, 1919, printed as an Enclosure with RL to WW, April 19, 1919, Vol. 57.

From Jessie Woodrow Wilson Sayre

Dearest, dearest Father, [Cambridge, Mass.] May 4th [1919].

Have you time in the immense pressure of events over there to read just a wee note of love and adoring reverence from your little daughter over here? Oh I can't tell you how my heart beats with exulting pride and joy at every word you say and at everything you do. And I know you will win out. I don't see how anyone can stand out against the right course when it is so simply and clearly put. It must be an intense strain but I know that you don't allow yourself to think of that or even to feel it. You are sustained, I know, by thousands and hundreds of thousands of loving confident yearning prayers both here and over there.

Our little family is flourishing here. Woodrow is not as fat as he should be. When you caught cold he followed suit and is only beginning to gain now. But he is good as gold and no trouble at all.

The children are adorable with him and so careful of him and helpful, eager to run errands and to help in other ways with him.

We leave here in about a month now for Martha's Vineyard, a whole afternoon nearer mainland than S'conset is, because Frank has to teach here all summer. We are very near Margaret and Lewis Perry[1] and right on the water's edge with beautiful bathing right there at our steps. It looks most promising and we are eager to begin.

Perhaps we shall see the Mayflower at the Vineyard Haven dock some fine day this summer. Wouldn't that be jolly. And we might arrange for the Christening there, but all that's unimportant and premature just now.

Frank joins me in dearest love to Edith and your darling darling self, my dear dear Father.

Ever your own little girl Jessie.

ALS (WP, DLC).

[1] Lewis Perry, B.A. Williams 1898; M.A. Princeton, 1899; former Professor of English and Literature at Williams College and, since 1914, Principal of the Phillips Exeter Academy; and Margaret Lawrie Hubbell Perry. They were old friends of the Wilsons.

From the Diary of Dr. Grayson

Monday, May 5, 1919.

The President arose early and had breakfast at 8:15. After breakfast he went to his study, and at 11:00 o'clock he attended a meeting of the Big Three here at the temporary White House. They discussed the question of the Italians returning to the Peace Conference. The Italians had made a request that they would return if invited. Lloyd-George and Clemenceau again were disposed to put the whole thing before the President. They suggested that the President invite the Italians to return to Paris. The President held to his former views. The morning's meeting was another instance of Clemenceau killing time, and Lloyd-George doing one of his mental somersaults.

The President again brought up the question of allowing the newspapermen to be present at the presentation of the terms to the German delegates at Versailles. Clemenceau and Lloyd-George both reiterated their statements of several days ago that it would be undignified to have the newspapermen present, and, furthermore, that there was no room for them. The President sharply disagreed with them on both points and made the proposition that they go there and see for themselves just what accommodations were available for a final conference. He proposed that they go individually and meet there at 2:30—to give no previous notice of their going, so that they could be there alone, without any onlookers, and then on the spot determine the question under consideration.

The President had lunch at one o'clock. Immediately after lunch the President read a note to me saying that Orlando and Sonnino would return to Paris Wednesday morning in the hope of joining the Peace Conference at Versailles. He told me to notify Ray Stannard Baker to tell the newspapermen that they (the Italians) were coming on their own initiative and not by invitation from any one.

The President left the house for Versailles at about two o'clock, unattended and unaccompanied by any one. Mrs. Wilson and I asked whether we could go along, and he said: "No; according to the bargain made with Lloyd-George and Clemenceau each was to go alone, unattended and unannounced." In a joking spirit, he added: "I regret to tell you that you both are not invited."

It developed, the President told me afterward, that the three had agreed to permit newspapermen to the number of forty-five to be present at the meeting—to be divided equally among the Five Great

Powers, and representatives of certain of the smaller powers. It was evident that there was ample room for the accommodation of 45 men, and the subject of lack of dignity by having newspapermen present was not further discussed. The President alone won this victory for the newspapermen and for the publicity of the proceedings. He claimed that the world was entitled to have a first-hand description of the scene and of the proceedings of the settlement of peace for practically the entire world.

Immediately after lunch the President called up Secretary Lansing and requested that the members of the American Peace Commission assemble in his (Lansing's) suite at the Crillon Hotel at 3:30 for a conference. The President met with the Commission at that hour and they discussed the questions of the procedure for Wednesday's session.

Upon the President's return he immediately went to the residences of Lloyd-George and Clemenceau for individual conferences. When he returned at about 6:30 he saw Ray Stannard Baker and gave him an outline for the newspapers of matters that had been discussed during the day.

He then had dinner, Mr. Charles H. Grasty, Chief Editorial Writer of the New York Times, being a guest. Mr. Grasty is under my treatment and is now recovering from a severe illness of ptomaine poisoning. At the invitation of the President and Mrs. Wilson he came here to occupy a spare-room, where he thought he could be near me and receive more home-like attention. Mr. Grasty had been living in an apartment alone.

After dinner Mr. Grasty, Mrs. Wilson and I accompanied the President down to his sitting-room, where we spent a half hour in conversation. Grasty recalled that he wrote an editorial for the President proposing Mr. Wilson for President of the United States. The editorial was written for the Baltimore Sun either in 1894 or 1904, he could not recall the date.[1] Grasty said: "I am trying to distinguish myself by being the first man to mention you in an editorial for President of the United States." During the conversation a note was received from one of the experts of the American Commission calling attention to the fact that Premier Clemenceau had made a radical change in the League of Nations covenant before it was adopted at the Fifth Plenary Session. These changes were made by Clemenceau without consulting any one, so far as the President could ascertain this evening. The President at once got in communication with Premier Clemenceau and demanded that this be immediately deleted. The reason for this demand was because the document is being put in printed form tonight, and it was necessary for the President to take decisive action. Clemenceau at first demurred and said he would bring up the question at the Plenary Session and have it adopted, but the President would not stand for this. The President thereupon issued directions to the expert to remove the clause that had been inserted without proper permission. The President was very much disturbed over this, not only on account of the important point in question, but it opened his eyes as to the possibility of a change or changes being made in the treaty which is about to be presented to the German delegates. It is practically impossible for him to read it all over, as the document covers 85,000 words; it is a good-sized book. He feels that to a certain extent he must depend upon his experts. It was necessary, as may well be understood, to leave the phrasing of the peace document to the experts.

The President told me that Clemenceau said to him today that he (Clemenceau) regretted very much the attitude that the French papers had taken on the Italian question advocating Italy's claims to Fiume. He said: "The French papers have been bought by Italian money to further Italy's cause." The President said to me: "Italy's money borrowed from the United States."

This morning after breakfast I had a conversation with the President and I told him that I would remain out until after midnight for the purpose of getting some views from the various newspaper people as to their attitude concerning the Japanese-Chinese situation. I had a long conversation with Senator Peter Gerry of Rhode Island, who had just arrived from the United States and who brought the latest information concerning public affairs at home. I repeated all this to the President. He was much interested in the news from Senator Gerry.

At 11:45 tonight Sir Maurice Hankey came here and asked to see the President. He brought several pages of the treaty showing still another change that had been made by Clemenceau without permission of the Peace Delegates—a change which he (Clemenceau) had made personally. Sir Maurice wanted to call the President's attention to this. I went down and woke up the President, Sir Maurice accompanying me into his bed-room. The President noted the change and immediately got Mr. Clemenceau on the telephone. He insisted on the deletion of the words inserted by Clemenceau, and Clemenceau, of course, had to acquiesce. He made a feeble explanation. The President directed that the words be deleted and Lloyd-George concurred in the President's action.

[1] The Editors have been unable to find any such editorial. Indeed, it seems unlikely that Grasty wrote an editorial of this kind in either of the years referred to by Grayson, certainly not in 1894, when Wilson was still a Princeton professor. Moreover, from 1892 to 1908, Grasty was editor and proprietor of the *Baltimore Evening News* and was not associated in any way with the *Baltimore Sun* until 1910.

A Translation of a Telegram from Baron Sidney Sonnino to Stéphen Jean Marie Pichon

[Rome, May 5, 1919]

"Having received the amplest confirmation of the confidence which the Parliament and the nation have placed in the Government of the King, aiming to attain the fulfilment of the greatest national aspirations of liberation and security; desiring not to complicate, in this moment already very grave, the political and moral situation of Europe by any positive or negative act which might be interpreted by whomever it be as a pretext to put off the peace which the entire world desires; relying on the assurances of the Allied Governments and on their good dispositions, aiming to facilitate an agreement capable of solving to the common satisfaction and in the general interest, the questions affecting the interests of Italy in the Adriatic, the President of the Council and I have decided to leave Monday evening for Paris, where we shall arrive Wednesday morning in the hope of being able to participate in the first meeting with the German Delegates."

T MS (WP, DLC).

Hankey's Notes of a Meeting of the Council of Four[1]

President Wilson's House,
I.C.-181B Paris, May 5, 1919, 11 a.m.

1. SIR MAURICE HANKEY read the following communication, which had been received from the Drafting Committee:

"On account of the important part which the Covenant of the League of Nations plays in the draft Treaty of Peace, the Drafting Committee forward the annexed proof indicating the changes which have been made in the text since Friday, May 3rd. The alteration in Article 22 was made under instructions given personally to M. Fromageot by M. Clemenceau, the President of the Conference.

"See Article 4, p. 11—Italy is omitted.
" " 22, p. 17.
" Annex I, p. 19.—Italy being *omitted.*
" " p. 20.—where Italy is *included.*"

M. CLEMENCEAU said that it was very important to France that some words should be put in to enable her to utilise native troops for the defence of French territory just as she had done in this war. He was not responsible for the actual wording employed.

[1] The complete text of these minutes is printed in *PPC*, V, 463-73.

PRESIDENT WILSON drew attention to the previous discussion which had taken place on this subject at the Council of Ten on January 30th, (I.C.128, Minute 1),[2] when it had been agreed that precisely similar wording in the resolutions on the subject of mandates, namely, "for other than police purposes for the defence of territory," would cover France's needs. He asked Sir Maurice Hankey to bring the matter to Lord Robert Cecil's attention and ask him what alteration, if any, there should be in the League of Nations Covenant.

2. (At this point Colonel Henri was introduced.)[3]

COLONEL HENRI, who is the officer in charge of the arrangements for the security of and communication with the Germans at Versailles, said that on the previous evening the Germans had sent him a message to the effect that they had been kept waiting so long that they proposed to return to Berlin. This morning, a subordinate official had reported to him that 14 persons would be leaving this evening. Colonel Henri had asked for their names, but the subordinate said he did not know them. Colonel Henri had insisted that he could not make the arrangements for motor cars, etc., unless he knew who the persons were, and a reply had been promised by mid-day. He was to see Baron Lassneer[4] in the afternoon.

M. CLEMENCEAU suggested that Colonel Henri should be authorised to inform the Germans of the date on which the Treaty would be handed over. This raised the question of the date. He was informed by M. Dutasta that the American Representative on the Drafting Committee thought a meeting was possible on Wednesday afternoon, but the British and French Representatives considered Thursday was the earliest possible date.*

M. CLEMENCEAU, continuing, said that he had just received news that M. Orlando was coming back and this would involve altering the first two pages of the Treaty.

MR. LLOYD GEORGE said it would be better not to alter the Treaty in print, but to alter it in writing if they came back, which would show the Germans that we had intended to go on without the Italians.

PRESIDENT WILSON proposed that the Germans should be informed that the Treaty would be handed to them on Wednesday morning.

*(*Note by the Secretary*. Mr. Hurst informs me that he pressed very strongly that the Treaty could be ready by Wednesday afternoon.)

[2] See the minutes of the Council of Ten printed at Jan. 30, 1919, 3:30 p.m., Vol. 54.

[3] Lt. Col. Marie Joseph Henry of the French General Staff, head of the liaison group with enemy peace delegations.

[4] Actually, Baron Kurt von Lersner, former representative of the Foreign Office at the German General Headquarters at Spa and a German representative at the Armistice Commission in Spa; at this time, a representative of the German Foreign Office in the German peace delegation.

MR. LLOYD GEORGE preferred Wednesday afternoon.

M. CLEMENCEAU gave Colonel Henri instructions to inform the Germans as follows:

1. The delay in printing the Peace Treaty was due to the time taken in examining the full powers.
2. The Treaty was now being printed.
3. The Meeting with the Germans would be at 3 p.m. on Wednesday next, May 7th.

(Colonel Henri withdrew.)

(It was decided that no alteration should be made in the first two pages of the Treaty of Peace owing to the fact that the Italians had announced their intention of returning.)

3. (It was decided to hold a Plenary Meeting on the following day, Tuesday, May 6th, at 3 p.m.)
4. (M. Pichon then entered.)

M. PICHON said he had had a verbal note from M. Bonin, conveying a message from Baron Sonnino. The gist of this was that, having received a vote of complete confidence from the Italian Parliament, and not desiring to complicate the situation at this very serious moment by any positive or negative act which might be interpreted as putting back the peace, and confident in the assurance by their Allies and their desire to obtain a peace satisfactory to all and in the general interest, the President of the Council and Baron Sonnino had decided to leave for Paris, arriving on Wednesday morning, with the hope of being present when the Treaty of Peace was handed to the Germans.

SIR MAURICE HANKEY again asked definitely whether the Drafting Committee were to alter the printing of the first two pages of the return of the Italians.

MR. LLOYD GEORGE replied that they should not do so. Any alteration should be made in writing at the last moment.

PRESIDENT WILSON agreed.

(MR. LLOYD GEORGE retired to interview the Marquis Imperiali, but returned very shortly after to say that the Marquis merely had the same message for him as M. Pichon had already received from M. Bonin.)

PRESIDENT WILSON drew attention to the following information, which related to the Italian question:

1. Additional Italian troops had been sent to Sebenico.[5]
2. There had been serious oppression by the Italians in the Dodecanese and in a village in Rhodes (?) named Alanova (?) [Villa Nova] a bishop had actually been killed in the church

[5] See W. S. Benson to WW, May 2, 1919.

where he was officiating, while a woman had also been killed by the Italians.

This information had been conveyed to him by a Greek named Russes (?).[6]

MR. LLOYD GEORGE said he had received the same information.

(At this point, General Sir Henry Wilson entered with maps.)

MR. LLOYD GEORGE said he had invited General Wilson to come here because he felt that the Italian movements in the East were, when considered in the aggregate, highly suspicious, and he thought his colleagues ought to be made acquainted with them.

GENERAL WILSON explained on a map the general military position in the East as regards the Italians. At the present time, there were about 30,000 Italians in Bulgaria. General Franchet d'Esperey was responsible for making those dispositions. There were two French divisions in this region, but they were troops who had come from Odessa, very tired and not the best French troops. In Hungary there were four Roumanian divisions, two weak French divisions, and, on the other side, opposing the Roumanians, two Hungarian divisions.

MR. LLOYD GEORGE said that in Asia Minor the Italians had occupied the harbour of Marmaris, nominally as a coaling station. They had a battalion at Konia, which had been sent there by agreement. They had landed troops at Adalia without consulting the Allied and Associated Powers and other movements were reported.

GENERAL WILSON said there were unconfirmed reports of landings at various places on the coast of Asia Minor, including Alaya.

MR. LLOYD GEORGE re-called that the Italian expedition to Tripoli[7] had been uncommonly well concealed. He was suspicious of a similar expedition now to Asia Minor. According to his information, the Italians were arming the Bulgarians and stirring them up to attack both the Greeks and the Serbians, but especially the latter. They were the only nation not demobilising.

M. CLEMENCEAU said this was a fact.

M. LLOYD GEORGE thought that the situation in the East was not being very well handled by the Allies. The Bulgarians were a most formidable people and were not being disarmed.

M. CLEMENCEAU disputed this. He said he had despatches in regard to the breach blocks of the Bulgarian guns which proved this.

[6] See S. Zervos and P. Roussos to WW, May 2, 1919.

[7] At the beginning of the Turco-Italian war of 1911-1912, as a result of which Turkey, in exchange for an indemnity, handed over to Italy sovereignty over Tripolitania and Cyrenaica (which now comprise Libya). For detailed studies, see Francesco Malgeri, *La Guerra Libica (1911-1912)* (Rome, 1970), and William C. Askew, *Europe and Italy's Acquisition of Libya, 1911-1912* (Durham, N. C., 1942).

MR. LLOYD GEORGE said that the breach blocks were being taken to Sofia, where there were no Allied troops except Italians.

M. CLEMENCEAU said he had ordered them back.

MR. LLOYD GEORGE said that the Italians were the only considerable force in this region. He wished General Henrys[8] was in charge, as he thought that for this particular work he was more suited than General Franchet d'Esperey.

M. CLEMENCEAU asked where General Henrys was.

GENERAL WILSON said he was on his way back from Warsaw.

MR. LLOYD GEORGE said that the British had a division and a half in the Caucasus. He would like to have examined the effect of bringing them back from the Caucasus.

PRESIDENT WILSON recalled the report of the Military Representatives on the distribution of forces in Turkey.[9]

MR. LLOYD GEORGE thought the question ought to be re-considered. Any day it might be found that the Italians had captured Anatolia and it would be difficult to get them out of there once they had occupied it. The mandates for Turkey could not be settled now, owing to the decision to send out a Commission. He thought, therefore, that we should fall back on his original proposal of a re-distribution of the forces of the occupation. The United States troops ought to go to Constantinople and to provide troops for Armenia. The British would come out of the Caucasus and the French might put a garrison in Syria, while the Greeks should be allowed to occupy Smyrna, since their compatriots were actually being massacred at the present time and there was no one to help them.

M. CLEMENCEAU said the Italians had seven battleships at Smyrna.

MR. LLOYD GEORGE said he would like to settle the forces of occupation in Turkey before the Italians returned to Paris: this afternoon, if possible.

PRESIDENT WILSON said he could not do it so hastily.

MR. LLOYD GEORGE said if they discussed it with the Italians, they would anticipate them.

PRESIDENT WILSON said he did not know where he was to find the American troops. Marshal Foch would be nervous if he withdrew United States' troops from the occupied zone in Germany.

GENERAL WILSON said that one United States division would be required for Constantinople and the Straits to replace one British division and the few French battalions that were there. He could not

[8] That is, Gen. Paul Prosper Henrys.

[9] See the memorandum by T. H. Bliss printed at Feb. 8, 1919; the minutes of the Supreme War Council printed at Feb. 10, 1919, both in Vol. 55; and the minutes of the Council of Four printed at March 20, 1919, 3 p.m., Vol. 56.

estimate the number required for Armenia, as this would depend on how far into the country they had to penetrate. At the present moment, the British were under an agreement to let the Italians go to the Caucasus.

MR. LLOYD GEORGE said that all he had said was that he would like the British to come out of the Caucasus and the Italians had said they would like to go in, as there was oil there.

PRESIDENT WILSON said he did not approve of the Italians going to the Caucasus.

M. CLEMENCEAU said he had made no agreement on the subject.

MR. LLOYD GEORGE recalled the report of the Military Representatives, which, however, he was reminded by Sir Maurice Hankey, had never been formally approved. He understood that, in any event, the British were coming out.

PRESIDENT WILSON asked why any troops should replace the British.

GENERAL WILSON said that unless some civilised Power was in occupation, there would be the most terrible massacres.

MR. LLOYD GEORGE agreed and pointed out that we could not persuade Denikin from entering Georgia.

GENERAL WILSON said he was most anxious to get the British troops out.

PRESIDENT WILSON said that the British troops were the only ones accustomed to this kind of business, although the French had some experience. United States officers would be quite unaccustomed to it.

MR. LLOYD GEORGE said that the United States troops would be wanted in Armenia and would not meet with difficulties, although it was not the same in the Caucasus. In reply to President Wilson, he said he feared the effect of the Italians going to the Caucasus would be very serious. He was convinced that the forces of the occupation should be settled at once and then the Commission could go out.

PRESIDENT WILSON said this was too important a matter to be settled in a hurry. He must confer with his military advisers first.

GENERAL WILSON said that the British problem was very simple, as it merely involved taking the troops out of the Caucasus.

MR. LLOYD GEORGE said it had been proposed to put these troops in the region of Constantinople for the present, in order to have them ready to counter any move by the Italians.

M. CLEMENCEAU said that he, himself, intended to take action today as regards Bulgaria.

PRESIDENT WILSON said he was not at all sure as to what military troops he could dispose of.

MR. LLOYD GEORGE said that there was a general idea that the British were imperialistic in their desires, but as a matter of fact they were not willing to take any more responsibility.

PRESIDENT WILSON said it did not seem a question of assuming more responsibility but a question of their withdrawing their existing responsibility.

MR. LLOYD GEORGE pointed out that the Caucasus was very rich, but it would be a big job to look after it and the British Empire could not assume those additional responsibilities.

PRESIDENT WILSON feared that to let the Italians into the Caucasus would prove to be very serious and threaten the peace of the world.

MR. LLOYD GEORGE said that to take the 1½ British divisions from the Caucasus and put them in Constantinople would safeguard the position against the Italians. Otherwise, the Allied and Associated Powers might find their hands forced. The situation ought to be tackled at once to avert this possibility.

(It was agreed:

1. That General Wilson should at once see General Bliss (to whom President Wilson sent a message by telephone) and should post General Bliss with the whole situation, in order that General Bliss may confer with President Wilson in the afternoon.
2. That the Naval Authorities should be invited to co-operate, when the naval elements entered into the problem.)

(General Wilson withdrew.)

5. In reply to a telephone message from M. Pichon, it was agreed that the fact that the Italian Delegation was returning to Paris should be published.

6. MR. LLOYD GEORGE said that a few days ago an old friend of his, formerly a Welsh member of Parliament, had called on him in Paris, and said he was just leaving for Rome. He had told Mr. Lloyd George that he was convinced that the Italians were anxious for an excuse to come back, and had asked if there was anything he could do. Mr. Lloyd George had explained the general situation to him, without, of course, giving him any authority to act. Last night he had received a telegram from his friend in Rome, the gist of which was that he had seen M. Orlando, who had said he was willing to stand by the Pact of London but had intimated that when Italy had got Dalmatia and the Islands, she would go to Croatia and make a bargain for the exchange of Fiume.

PRESIDENT WILSON pointed out that all this fitted in with the naval and military movements that the Italians were making.

MR. LLOYD GEORGE said that the Italians had already broken the Treaty by occupying Fiume.

M. CLEMENCEAU pointed out, however, that the Italians had not occupied it alone: Allied troops were also in Fiume.

PRESIDENT WILSON recalled that the Armistice had given the right to the Allies to advance troops for the maintenance of order, and the Italians had used this excuse to push forward troops to Fiume, in which they had been joined by their Allies. This prevented us from saying that the Italians were outside their rights.

MR. LLOYD GEORGE said that he would like to tell the Italians they must withdraw. If they should plead the Armistice as an excuse for staying, we must say: "Then let the Serbians go in; they are Allies."

PRESIDENT WILSON pointed out that the Italians were sending troops to Sebenico. They were not entitled to do that under the Armistice.

MR. LLOYD GEORGE said we ought to insist on adherence to the Armistice. They were playing the Pact of London against Great Britain and France, and it was Great Britain and France that must meet them. Our line should be to say: "You must clear out of Fiume and leave it to the Croatians, in accordance with the Pact." They could not afford to do that.

PRESIDENT WILSON said he had just received a message from Mr. Lansing to the same effect as M. Pichon's and the Marquis Imperiali's messages, namely, that the Italians would be back on Wednesday morning. The message also stated that they were coming in the hope that they could take part in the meeting with the Germans. This meant that they were in the hope that the Allied and Associated Governments would make this possible for them.

MR. LLOYD GEORGE said this could not be done on Wednesday morning.

7. M. CLEMENCEAU said that the Germans had assumed that the Allied and Associated Powers were going to make a communication of the terms published and had asked that as theirs could not be ready they might be allowed to use the one issued by the Allied and Associated Powers. M. Cambon had given him this information.

MR. LLOYD GEORGE said he had received a message from General Smuts, who considered that the Germans would obtain a considerable diplomatic advantage if the treaty were published. In such a gigantic document there would have to be a good many alterations, and the Germans would claim these to be a diplomatic victory for them. He pointed out that in many parts of the Treaty he himself had had to trust to experts who were not really looking at the Treaty as a whole. He anticipated, when he read the Treaty as a whole, that he might find a good many unexpected clauses, some inconsistent with others, just as had happened to him sometimes in introducing a complicated Bill into Parliament.

M. CLEMENCEAU did not think it possible to keep publication back, but he would only publish a summary.

PRESIDENT WILSON agreed that the text ought not to be published.

MR. LLOYD GEORGE pointed out that M. Tardieu's summary was so long that it would occupy three whole sheets of the "Times."

PRESIDENT WILSON said that Mr. Baker, who was in general charge of the United States Press arrangements, had prepared a summary.

MR. LLOYD GEORGE said that Mr. Baker's summary had been prepared in co-operation with Mr. Mair,[10] who had done a large part of it, but even Mr. Mair's summary would occupy two sheets of the "Times."

(It was agreed that M. Tardieu, Mr. Baker and Mr. Mair should be invited the following morning to meet the Council of Three.)

8. M. CLEMENCEAU asked how the question of Responsibilities stood.

PRESIDENT WILSON said he understood that it had been held up at a recent Plenary, owing to some objection by the British Dominions.

MR. LLOYD GEORGE said it was too late now to bring it before the Plenary. He understood that General Botha thought that the names of the Germans whom it was proposed to try should be given. He had pointed out that the British had made the same demand in South Africa. General Botha had agreed to all their other demands, but would not give way on that, and had insisted that he should be given the names. General Botha had then asked Lord Kitchener whether, in his place, he would give up men to be tried without knowing their names, and Lord Kitchener had replied that as a soldier, he would not. Consequently, the negotiations had been broken off, and the war had gone on for 17 months. In the end, only three names had been given for trial.

PRESIDENT WILSON said he had always felt that this was the weak spot in the Treaty of Peace.

MR. LLOYD GEORGE pointed out that this depended on the mentality of the Germans.

9. (A memorandum by the Secretary-General was considered with the result that it was agreed to proceed to Versailles that afternoon, and meet the Secretary-General there.)

10. MR. LLOYD GEORGE pointed out that the cost of the Army of Occupation was to have precedence over indemnities and reparation. The present Armies of Occupation were costing £300,000,000 a year. At present no limit was placed on the size of the total army to

[10] George Herbert Mair, director of the press section of the British delegation at the peace conference.

be maintained. Unless some limitation were arranged, there would be nothing left for indemnity.

M. CLEMENCEAU said that this did not affect the Treaty of Peace, but was a matter that should be arranged between the Allied and Associated Governments.

PRESIDENT WILSON said that in a previous conversation it had been arranged that the British and United States forces would be very small—only sufficient to show the flag.

(It was agreed that a Committee composed of General Bliss, for the United States of America, General Sir Henry Wilson for the British Empire, and a French Officer to be designated by M. Clemenceau, should meet to consider the size of the Army of Occupation of the Rhine Provinces, after conclusion of the Treaty of Peace.)

11. MR. LLOYD GEORGE pointed out a difficulty which had arisen about the organisation of the League of Nations. The United States of America could not devote any money to the League until the Treaty was ratified. It was absolutely necessary, however, to get the organisation of the League ready, as certain duties would fall on it very soon after the signature of the Treaty of Peace. It was not considered desirable to proceed at once to Geneva, where sufficient buildings were not available. He asked authority, therefore, on behalf of Sir Eric Drumond, Secretary-General, to establish himself temporarily in London, where he would build up the organisation of the League.

PRESIDENT WILSON said he had no objection.

M. CLEMENCEAU said he had no objection.

(It was agreed that the Secretary-General of the League of Nations should be authorised to establish the temporary and provisional organisation of the League of Nations in London.)

12. The Council had before it a memorandum from the Secretary-General, entitled "Free Circulation for the German Delegation." (Appendix.)[11]

M. CLEMENCEAU considered that the couriers allowed to the German Delegation were quite sufficient.

PRESIDENT WILSON thought that the Allied and Associated Powers should be as liberal in these matters as possible.

MR. LLOYD GEORGE pointed out that there was nothing for the Germans to spy on at the present time.

M. CLEMENCEAU agreed to adopt a liberal attitude.

(It was agreed that the German Delegates at Versailles should be permitted to send to Germany and vice versa, in addition to the or-

[11] It is printed in *PPC*, V, 473.

dinary couriers bearing the official mail, other persons, including journalists, in such proportion as they may deem necessary.)

13. M. CLEMENCEAU said he had received a protest from the Marquis Saionji against decisions having been taken in regard to affairs in China and Siam without consultation with the Japanese. No complaint was made against the substance of the Articles in the Treaty of Peace that had been agreed on, but as Japan had special interests in the Far East, he considered that the Japanese Plenipotentiaries should have been present at the discussion.

PRESIDENT WILSON pointed out that as he had no objection to the substance, the matter was not very material. No-one present could recall any decision in regard to Siam, and the clauses in regard to China had been prepared by experts, but had not been discussed at any meeting.

14. MR. LLOYD GEORGE said he was very anxious to settle the question of the mandates before the Treaty of Peace.

PRESIDENT WILSON said that it could hardly be settled in 48 hours. In regard to Turkey in particular, it was impossible for him to give a decision at present as to whether the United States could take a mandate.

MR. LLOYD GEORGE said that as far as Great Britain was concerned he would make no objection to a settlement of the Turkish mandates, though he realised President Wilson's difficulty. What he was pressing for at present was the German Colonies.

M. CLEMENCEAU said he was ready at any time to discuss the matter.

PRESIDENT WILSON said that to all intents and purposes it had been agreed that the mandate for German South-West Africa should be given to South Africa, for New Guinea and the adjacent islands to Australia, for Samoa to New Zealand.

MR. LLOYD GEORGE said that there was still the remaining African Colonies.

M. CLEMENCEAU said there was perfect agreement on these too.

MR. LLOYD GEORGE urged early consideration of this question, as he was most anxious to be able to announce the mandates to the Press at the time when the Peace Treaty was issued.

PRESIDENT WILSON said he was very anxious to avoid the appearance of a division of the spoils being simultaneous with the Peace.

T MS (SDR, RG 256, 180.03401/144, DNA).

From the Diary of Colonel House

May 5, 1919.

The President called at the Crillon during the afternoon and much to my alarm and surprise he said that he, Lloyd George and Clemenceau had decided to have Italy's name not only eliminated from the Peace Treaty but also from the Covenant of the League of Nations. He did not seem to realize that the three of them have no right to touch the Covenant of the League. He also astonished me by saying that Clemenceau, without authority from anyone, had asked the Treaty Drafting Committee to add in Article 22 of the Covenant the words, "or of the mother country." The sense of this change is that when one country becomes the mandatory for another country, they would have the right to make the country over which they exercise the mandatory, to raise and send troops for the defence of the so-called mother country.

This would be a perversion of the entire mandatory system. For instance, if Great Britain is a mandatory over Arabia and France a mandatory over Syria, and should Great Britain go to war with France, Great Britain would be asking one part of Arabia to fight for her while France would be asking what is practically another part of Arabia to fight for her.

After fussing with these matters nearly all day, bringing in both Miller and Cecil, Miller went to the Quai d'Orsay in the evening where the Drafting Committee were at work, and in the name of both Great Britain and the United States protested against any changes being made in the Covenant. Therefore Italy's name will appear and the words which Clemenceau instructed to go in will be left out.

The conception which the Council of Three have as to their powers is amazing. The Covenant was adopted at the Plenary Conference last Monday, and no one excepting another Plenary Conference has the right to change a dot or a comma. I can foresee trouble in the early days of the League's life, for both Cecil and I are determined that it shall be what it is intended to be, a league of the world and not a league that can be dominated by any particular power or powers. I have tried to impress this upon Drummond and I think he understand[s] that he is no longer in the service of the British Government, but in that of the Governments of the subscribing powers to the League.

The President said he had signed and sent the letter I wrote for him to send Paderewski.[1] I am glad of this because there is a fight being made upon Paderewski in Poland and this letter may save the situation.

The President seemed to have no idea of the affront which the leaving of Italy's name out of the Treaty and the Covenant would be. He seemed to think, as also did Lloyd George and Clemenceau, that it was quite the right thing to do. They thought Italy's name could be written in afterward in the event the Italian Delegation participated in the Treaty. Of course, the thing to do is to have the name of Italy printed in and if they refuse to sign, obliterate it. However, for the moment, that trouble is averted.

[1] WW to I. J. Paderewski, April 26, 1919.

From the Diary of Lord Robert Cecil

May 5 [1919].

In the afternoon, a very brief and business-like meeting of the League Organisation Committee. They accepted everything we wanted. After the meeting, the President came up to the room to tell me that Clemenceau was demanding an alteration which would enable the natives in Mandatory States to be used for the defence of the Mandatory State itself. We were agreed that this would be practically to destroy the prohibition against arming natives, and the President then sent down Miller, the American lawyer, with Baker,[1] to the Quai d'Orsay to protest against any alteration being made. Later I saw Hankey on the same point. He was apparently inclined to make the concession to Clemenceau, but I told him my views and he then assured me that when the clause had been under consideration at the beginning of the Conference, not by the League of Nations Commission—which never had anything to do with it—but by the Prime Ministers and Foreign Secretaries, Clemenceau had evidently been assured both by Ll. G. directly and by the President less directly, that this use of natives would be allowed, and was indeed permitted under the phrase actually used. However, I was immovable and went back to the Hotel to dine with the Bakers[2] and go to the play. Owing to a ridiculous mistake I spent the next three quarters of an hour trying to find the Bakers' house, when all the time they were waiting for me at the Majestic.

While I was away, House rang me up. I got on to him when I returned and he then told me that the President intended to stick to his view, in which I encouraged him.

[1] Philip John Baker (later Noel-Baker), at this time Vice-Principal of Ruskin College, Oxford, and a member of the League of Nations section of the British delegation at the peace conference.

[2] Philip John Baker and Irene Noel Baker.

From the Diary of David Hunter Miller

Monday, May 5th [1919]

After the meeting was over and there was nobody there but Colonel House, Cecil, Baker,[1] Frazier, Capt. Montgomery,[2] and myself, the President came in and said that he was very much disturbed about an addition which had been made in the Covenant to Article XXII. He said that he had been told of it by Hankey and that it had been made by direction of Clemenceau, and that he (the President) had told Clemenceau that nobody could give such a direction, not even the Three. The President then suggested that I should go over and examine the treaty text to see whether there were any other changes. I told him that if he approved I would examine both the English and the French texts and report to him. He did approve, and I took Baker of the British and went over to the Quai d'Orsay and got the French and English texts from Hurst. These are (in my files). We came back and read them very carefully. I read the French text with Warrin, and Baker read the English with Hudson.[3] There were some typographical errors in the French text which are shown in pencil,[4] and the differences in English text are shown. I made a memorandum of these for the President,[5] and told Colonel House about the matter before I sent this up to the President. Colonel House was very much disturbed by the change in place of the name of Italy.

I got back to the Hotel Meurice about 8:30 and the President called me up on the telephone. He said he had my memorandum and that he strenuously objected to the words added in Article XXII going in. I spoke to him about the change in the Annex in the name of Italy and told him the Italians would object very much too, and explained to him just what the change was. He then said he would like that changed, but he was insistent that the other words should not go in and told me to take it up with Doctor Scott. I called up Dr. Scott, who was out, getting Mrs. Scott[6] on the telephone; and after getting a little something to eat I went over to the Quai d'Orsay and saw Dr. Scott and told him what the President objected to. He said it would be changed. I also told him about the change in the position of the name of Italy, and he said that would be changed.

I then went back and reported to Colonel House, who was very much delighted and said it was the best hour's work that had been done here, and while I was there he telephoned the President and told him about it and told me that the President had said that he was very much relieved.

Miller, *My Diary at the Conference of Paris*, I, 290-92.

[1] That is, Philip John Baker.

[2] Capt. Stuart Montgomery, a secretary for territorial questions in the Secretariat of the A.C.N.P., secretary of the Polish Commission, and chief of the Secretariat's Russian Division.
[3] That is, Manley Ottmer Hudson.
[4] For a list of these errors, see Miller, *My Diary at the Conference of Paris*, IX, 274.
[5] It is printed as the following document. The differences not specifically mentioned in this memorandum are listed in *ibid.*, I, 291.
[6] Adele C. Reed Scott.

From David Hunter Miller

MEMORANDUM FOR THE PRESIDENT: 5 May, 1919.

The English and French texts of the Covenant in the Treaty (fifth proof) have been carefully compared with the texts as reported by the Commission.

The amendment to Article V adopted by the Conference has been made.

There is a change in language in Article IV, of which you are aware; namely, the substitution of "Principal Allied and Associated Powers" for the names of the Five Great Powers.

The name of Italy has been taken from the list of signatories in the Annex and placed in the list of invited States.

The change which you mentioned in Article XXII, fifth paragraph, by the addition of the words, "and of the territory of the mother country" appears in the Treaty text.

Otherwise, there are no differences except a few of a trifling nature, such as punctuation and corrections.

David Hunter Miller

TS MS (WP, DLC).

To David Lloyd George[1]

My dear Mr. Prime Minister: [Paris] 5 May, 1919.

I have carefully considered your recent communication enclosing a scheme suggested for the re-establishment of more normal and economic financial conditions in Europe.[2] I am fully alive to the confused conditions that now exist and to the very great importance of trying to clear and improve them, especially in respect of the situation of the new and weaker nations that are to be set up under the Treaty of Peace.

I am sorry to say, however, that Mr. Keyne[s]'s plan does not seem feasible from the American point of view. Our Treasury, and our financial delegates here in Paris are convinced that the plan as presented lacks many elements of economic and financial soundness. I have asked our Treasury representatives here, Mr. Davis and Mr. Lamont, to explain in detail to your financial advisors the serious objections to the plan as they present themselves to us. Personally, I am convinced of the soundness of these objections. I am convinced, moreover, that it would not be possible for me to secure from the Congress of the United States authority to place a financial guarantee upon bonds of European origin. Whatever aid the Congress may see fit to authorize should, in my judgment be rendered along independent lines. By that I do not mean in ways that would not involve close and cordial cooperation with European Governments, for such harmony and cooperation I consider indispensable. I mean merely that such cooperation should not, so far as America is concerned, take the form of a guarantee upon bonds. Our Treasury also holds the view (and in this again I concur) that to the very limit of what is practicable, such credits as it may be wise to grant should be extended through the medium of the usual private channels rather than through the several governments. Your Treasury, I understand, and certainly ours, believes it wise to retire at the earliest possible moment from "the banking business."

In order, however, that practical progress may be made, I have asked our local advisors here to present to me their views as soon as possible. Meantime, may I not call to your attention the following facts and considerations with regard to Germany's present and prospective financial situation:

(a) Germany requires working capital. Without that, she will be unable to start her industrial life again, and therefore unable to make any substantial progress in the way of reparation, but

(b) The provisions of the reparation clauses of the proposed treaty demand that Germany shall deliver over at once all her working capital, that is, practically the whole of her liquid assets;

(c) Simultaneously the suggestion is in effect made that America should in large measure make good this deficiency, providing in one form or another credit, and thus working capital, to Germany.

Throughout all the reparation discussions the American delegation has steadily pointed out to the other delegations that the plan proposed would surely deprive Germany of the means of making any appreciable reparation payments. I, myself, as you know, have frequently made the same observation. But whenever any of us was urgent on this point, he was accused of being pro-German. Our delegation finally gave assent to the reparation clauses as drawn, only because the reparation problem was one that chiefly concerned France, Great Britain, Belgium, and the other European countries, and not America.

I venture to point this situation out to you, in order that I may make the following point clear. America has, in my judgment, always been ready and will always stand ready to do her full share, financially, to assist the general situation. But America has grave difficulties of her own. She has been obliged within two years to raise by means of war loans and taxes the sum of forty billion dollars. This has been a very heavy burden, even for our well-to-do commonwealth, especially in view of the fact of the short period during which such sums of money had to be raised, and our Treasury informs me that our investing public have reached, and perhaps passed, the point of complete saturation in respect of investment. Such is our situation.

You have suggested that we all address ourselves to the problem of helping to put Germany on her feet, but how can your experts or ours be expected to work out a *new* plan to furnish working capital to Germany, when we deliberately start out by taking away *all Germany's present* capital? How can anyone expect America to turn over to Germany in any considerable measure new working capital to take the place of that which the European nations have determined to take from her? Such questions would appear to answer themselves, but I cannot refrain from stating them because they so essentially belong to a candid consideration of the whole difficult problem to which we are addressing ourselves, and to which our American advisors will address themselves with as sincere a desire as that of their colleagues, to reach a serviceable conclusion.

Cordially and sincerely yours, Woodrow Wilson.

TCL (RSB Coll., DLC).

[1] The following letter was drafted by Lamont and Davis, extensively amended by Wilson, and then retyped. The draft, with WWhw and WWsh changes, is in WP, DLC.

[2] D. Lloyd George to WW, with Enclosure, April 23, 1919.

Two Letters from Thomas Nelson Page

Personal

My dear Mr. President: Rome May 5. 1919.

I wrote you in January, recalling to you that I have always wished to return home on the restoration of Peace,[1] and renewed then my request to be relieved when this consummation, so devoutly to be wished, should be attained.

Although I have not had a reply to the letter, I have, of course, known that you have had the matter in mind and I have gone ahead making the necessary arrangements for my return home, where my presence is needed on many accounts, very imperatively.

I have not written you since further on this matter because I have been unwilling to add in the slightest degree to your burdens. But feeling confident that Peace would be signed in due time I completed arrangements to give up the apartment occupied by me in the Palazzo del Drago as the Embassy, and to sail from England on the 28th of June.

I still believe that the Peace will be concluded duly and as the time is drawing near I feel that I should write you again so that should it appear easier for you to fill my place immediately I might resign immediately that is, after the present crisis passes, instead of waiting until after arriving in America. In any event, I desire to time my resignation so as to have it in accord with what you may think most convenient and for the best interests of our Country.

I cannot add more than I have already said of my appreciation of the high privilege it has been to me to serve under and with you in this great crisis of the progress of Humanity, or of my profound recognition of your part in saving the Liberty of Mankind.

I beg you to believe that I shall be always at your service in the work which must still be done and that I am, with the highest sense of your kindness to me, as always,

Your most sincere friend, Thos. Nelson Page

ALS (WP, DLC).

[1] The Editors have been unable to find this letter; however, see WW to RL, Jan. 25, 1919, Vol. 54.

Confidential.

My dear Mr. President: Rome, May 5, 1919.

I am just sending off a telegram[1] containing translation of a memorandum of a basis of compromise which I received to-day from the French Ambassador, who requested the British Ambassador[2] and me to meet him at noon in order that he might deliver to us the result of his conferences with Signor Orlando and Baron Sonnino.

You will have seen the telegram, so I need not go into any detail about that. I will only say that the memorandum appeared to meet fully the views of both the French and British Ambassadors, who expressed themselves as believing that it contained the final concession which the Italian Government would make—or indeed could make—in the present state of public feeling here in Italy.

I can scarcely define just what this feeling is, or what the change in its manifestation signifies. I think, however, it is not only very widely diffused now, but, for the present, at least, is very deep. I understand that the organization under Dr. White,[3] which has been working here for months in the anti-tuberculosis campaign, has been notified that American nurses can not be longer utilized, and a conference which had been arranged a week or so ago for Miss

Holt,[4] relating to the teaching of the blind, has been called off, perhaps indefinitely, but at least for several days in consequence of d'Annunzio's speech yesterday. D'Annunzio was, as you know, the trumpet that called Italy into the war. He is billed all over town to speak this evening at the Campidoglio. I telegraphed yesterday of Orlando's having sent for me yesterday evening and expressed his profound regret that d'Annunzio had made such a speech, and not only professed himself profoundly pained by it, declaring that d'Annunzio had promised him faithfully not to indulge in anything inflammatory, but requested me to telegraph to my Government the expression of his profound regret and displeasure. Orlando further indicated, I thought, that d'Annunzio had become too strong for him to curb. I also heard this morning from the French Ambassador that Sonnino had said he considered d'Annunzio's coming to Rome a disaster.

I confess myself somewhat mystified by the present situation here. The tremendous reverberation of the first explosion has almost passed away and I would say that the people show certain signs of being bored by all that has gone on. They have, however, never been permitted to learn anything of the other side of what happened in Paris, and I see no chance at present of their hearing this as the press is unanimous in keeping up its campaign, only in a somewhat less violent form.

I wish very much that some settlement could be made of this Adriatic question, for I feel that it contains a real peril against the friendly relations of our two countries and Peoples. The danger is that the people who have been misled and excited beyond measure will not be controlled or guided longer even by the men in the Government, and I think this is appreciated by the latter.

The plan proposed in the memorandum, a copy of which I enclose in the original,[5] contains, I think, about that proposed in the Paris *Temps* of some days ago[6] (which, as I telegraphed the Commission,[7] was extensively re-produced in the Rome papers) with certain modifications, such as the concession about the Island of Pago, and of the Dalmatian mainland, except the cities of Zara and Sebenico, which I obtained information regarding and telegraphed about on Friday night.[8] I do not know what, if anything, lies behind this French suggestion. I feel very sure that both the French and British Ambassadors believe sincerely that the present situation is one which requires immediate solution, and that this can only be arrived at under present conditions by a compromise, something like that set forth in this memorandum. I, accordingly, have united in the recommendation that the negotiations be re-opened with a view to arriving at this or some similar compromise which will enable the peace proceedings to go on without further let or hindrance on the part of the Allies. Universal regret is expressed at the violence of the attacks by those with whom I am brought into contact, and I believe that when the whole truth is known there will be a very general feeling of shame that they were made on you.

I pointed out to Orlando Cavour's opinion of the perilous folly of attacking the head of other States in the public press. Cavour said that while violent attacks in the press of a country against individuals or even the sovereign only involved those making them and applied to those against whom they were directed, who had their redress under the law, attacks against the heads of other States involved the whole people and, if continued, inevitably resulted in creating hostility between the two peoples. He assured me of his great desire to prevent the continuance of such attacks.

I have no doubt that you are giving to this whole question your profound attention and thought, nor have I any doubt that you will be able to solve it in a way to meet the substantial justice and the verities of the situation. It is because of this that I feel it my duty to give you all the facts at my command, and to express with entire frankness my opinion, based on these facts, and informed by devotion to our Country and to the principles which you have set forth as the sole guide of your action.

I cannot but feel that when three Ambassadors unite in the same view as to a situation, it must be considered as having a serious foundation.

Believe me, always, my dear Mr. President,

Yours most sincerely, Thos. Nelson Page

TLS (WP, DLC).

[1] It is printed as the following document.

[2] That is, Sir James Rennell Rodd.

[3] William Charles White, M.D., medical director of the Tuberculosis League of Pittsburgh, and director of the American Medical Red Cross division for relief and prevention of tuberculosis in France (1917-1918) and Italy (1918-1919).

[4] That is, Winifred Holt, about whom see EBW to Sallie W. Bolling and others, Dec. 24, 1918, n. 2, Vol. 53. She had recently opened, or was about to open, a "Lighthouse" for the blind in Rome.

[5] T MS (WP, DLC), in the French language.

[6] About which, see n. 4 to the minutes of the Council of Four printed at May 3, 1919, 4 p.m.

[7] See TNP to Ammission, No. 288, May 2, 1919, T telegram (WP, DLC).

[8] See TNP to Ammission, No. 286, May 2, 1919.

Thomas Nelson Page to the American Commissioners

Rome. May 5, 1919.

291. URGENT, CONFIDENTIAL.

Yesterday evening the French Ambassador informed me that he would probably have by noon today something definite to go on from the Italians in the form of a proposition of compromise regarding Adriatic claims. Last night he wrote me asking me to meet the British Ambassador and himself at noon today. This I did and found that he has had from both Sonnino and Orlando the following as a basis of compromise which he states has been formally accepted by the Italian Government. Following is translation of the French text:

"The basis of an accord to be carried out by the three Allies and the Associated Power would be the following: One, Fiume to belong to the Italians after the realization of the conditions contained in Article No. 2; two, construction in determinate number of years, to be fixed after having consulted engineers and in any case not beyond the 30th of June 1923, and by an international association (consortium), of a port for Jugo-Slavs either at Signa or at Buccari and of a uniting thereof by railroad line with the Agram line; three, until the realization of conditions contained in Article number 2, Administration of Fiume in the name of Society of Nations; four, after the verification of the claims within the time and condition agreed on and in any case not later than the 30th of June 1923, of the works provided for in Article 2, Fiume shall belong to the Italians; five, Dalmatia to belong to the Jugo-Slavs except Zara and Sebenico which shall be given to Italy; six, Islands (except Pago) and the remainder to be as in the convention of April 26th, 1915; seven, a reciprocal concession of special guarantees to be determined; for example in educational and religious matters to be given in favor of element of Italian race comprised within Jugo-Slavs territory and element of Jugo-Slavs race comprised within Italian territory; eight, the right to select their nationality on the part of the Italians of Trau, Spalato, Ragusa and for the Jugo-Slavs of Fiume, Zara and Sebenico."

This, both of the other Ambassadors will urge their respective governments to accept and extend an invitation to the Italian delegates to return to Paris. I do the same. The difference between this and what I telegraphed Friday night is that while in latter it was said that Fiume would probably be agreed to as a free city, now in this proposal it is to be Italian after June 30th, 1923, and on the condition mentioned regarding creating another port at Segna or Buccari and a connecting railway. I think it just possible that Sebenico might eventually be accepted as a free city. On the other hand the advantage of this present proposal is that according to the French Ambassador the Italian Government has formally agreed to accept it.

Nelson Page.

T telegram (WP, DLC).

From Robert Lansing, with Enclosure

My dear Mr. President: Paris, 5th May, 1919.

I am transmitting herewith for your information, a copy of a report which has been prepared by Mr. E. L. Drasel [Dresel], a member of the American Commission who has recently returned from an official mission to Berlin.

Faithfully yours, Robert Lansing.

ENCLOSURE

Ellis Loring Dresel to the American Commissioners

Sirs: Paris, May 5, 1919.

On my return to Paris it may be well to summarize as briefly as possible the attitude in Germany towards peace. Comment is rendered difficult by the fact that conditions are only surmised through newspaper reports, which doubtless are in ma[n]y cases misleading.

In all interviews which I had, almost without exception a claim was made to the effect that French feeling showed such deep-seated enmity and chauvinism towards Germany as to make impossible any conditions which would not involve the ruin of Germany. On the other hand, constant emphasis was laid on the sincere desire of Germany to conclude a peace strictly on the basis of the President's Fourteen Points. In addition I note:

1. *Attitude of Government circles.* On my arrival in Germany, I found that a very evident effort at propaganda against signing peace was being carried on by the Government through the papers and by interviews. The reasons for this Government attitude may be stated as follows:

(a) The desire of the Government, in answer to criticisms of its weak and vacillating policy, to take an energetic stand and acquire support of the nationalist groups.

(b) The prevalent idea that a split among the Allies might still be possible to accomplish.

(c) The belief that neither a military occupation, which would lead to mutinies of Allied forces, nor a further blockade, which public opinion among the proletariat of all nations would render impracticable, could be carried out.

(d) The argument that a severe peace would mean the revival of militarism endangering the republic.

(e) The possibility that close political and commercial relations with Russia might yet save the situation.

To what extent this Government attitude will be maintained is, of course, exceedingly difficult to say. It is evident, however, that it must be partially discounted.

2. *Attitude of the nationalist and reactionary elements.* This is undoubtedly strongly against a severe peace, but at present these circles can carry but little weight except insofar as they help to support the Government.

3. *Attitude of Independent Socialists.* These are strongly in favor of accepting almost any conditions of peace. One possible limitation will be indicated below.

4. *Attitude of bourgeoisie, well-to-do people, bankers, captains of industry, etc.* These are in favor of accepting peace, as by this means only will they be able to keep what they have acquired. With this class the questions of indemnity and shipment of raw materials are more important than territorial questions.

As far as special questions are concerned, though opinions differed widely as to acceptability of the different conditions, an almost universal opinion was noticed that the control of Danzig by the Poles is the point to which most objection will be made. Even by the Independent Socialists this is looked on as a dismemberment of Germany and a violation of the Fourteen Points of the President.

Next to this, the control of the Sarre Basin by France is felt directly to lead the way to an annexation of the district. The Germans freely offer to deliver to France the whole output of the Basin for a period of years, but insist that it shall remain under German control.

In the next place, the annexation of the upper Silesian coal fields by Poland is looked on as utterly destructive to the possible rebuilding of Germany.

Further, the surrender of the colonies is looked on as utterly unjust and as contrary to the President's announced principles.

Questions of indemnity were not discussed in great detail by most of the people with whom I talked, as it seems to be assumed that full opportunity will be afforded Germany to make representations as to this. In a prolonged conversation which I had with Dernburg,[1] Minister of Finance, he explained at great length the almost hopeless financial and industrial situation of Germany. Sixty great industrial enterprises taken at random, of which he holds statistics, showed a monthly loss in operation of 108 million marks. A million workmen were out of work for want of raw materials, 800,000 prisoners would shortly be returned, and there were 3 million war invalids. This meant a class of 4,800,000 persons to whom an average wage of ten marks a day would have to be furnished. The issue of unsecured currency now amounted to 69 billion marks. The budget for the coming year was 25 billion marks and so far provision had only been made for raising 7 billions of this by taxation.

I hesitate very much to formulate a judgment in regard to this extremely intricate situation, but on the whole my opinion is that the German delegates will sign if assurances are given them that their present bankrupt state will be taken into account in fixing the indemnity terms, that raw materials necessary for the revival of their industries will be given them on easy terms, and that some slight concessions will be made on territorial questions, which will enable them to claim that they achieved some results by negotiation and that they did not merely accept a peace of violence. To my mind, too much stress can hardly be laid on what may seem a minor matter, viz: the attitude towards the German delegates. The German frame of mind is one of extreme depression, nervousness and excitability, coupled with fear that they will be treated as outlaws. Whatever minor concessions of an unimportant nature can be made to them, whatever opportunity can be given for informal personal discussions, and whatever willingness is shown to meet any reasonable requests that they may make, can hardly fail to have a favorable influence on the signing of peace.

The above statement is merely preliminary and will be followed by a detailed report on my journey.[2]

I have the honor to be, Sirs,

Your obedient servant, Ellis Loring Dresel

TLS (WP, DLC).

[1] That is, Bernhard Jakob Ludwig Dernburg.

[2] It is printed in *PPC*, XII, 103-17.

From Robert Lansing

My dear Mr. President: Paris, 5 May, 1919

I saw Mr. Paderewski this morning[1] and he assures me that none of Haller's Army will be used against the Ukranians. I also explained to him that the Conference would view the attempt to employ force, even though done to obtain a just right, with concern and might even dispose them to reject what otherwise they would grant.

Faithfully yours, Robert Lansing

TLS (WP, DLC).

[1] Lansing was replying to WW to RL, May 1, 1919 (first letter of that date).

From William Shepherd Benson

My dear Mr. President: Paris, 5 May, 1919.

Since the last conference[1] on the question of final disposition of enemy war vessels I have been collecting all possible data and opinions in regard to the subject from our various naval colleagues. Thinking it may be interesting for you to have the result of these efforts I will submit them.

The naval representatives of the five Great Powers[2] are unanimous in personal and professional opinion that all of these vessels should be sunk. This includes the French and Italian representatives as well as the British, American and Japanese. The Italian representative consented to breaking up on account of public opinion and the pressure of his Ministry of Marine. The French representative has opposed sinking for the same reason. Admiral De Bon informs me that he has tried very hard to persuade his Minister of Marine; but was unsuccessful, and his attitude in regard to distribution was in compliance with the directions of the civilian officials of his Government. I mention this to show you what is the naval professional opinion in regard to the increase of naval armament.

The Japanese representative has given me a memorandum in which he very frankly states that if the other powers agree to sinking or breaking up he will also agree, but if any powers receive any of these vessels that he will insist that his Government receive its share.

In order that you may get an idea of the view taken by the representatives of the other Governments in regard to how these vessels would be distributed, I am enclosing herewith a copy of a memorandum that I have been able to obtain from the French and British representatives.[3] Attention is invited to what goes to Great Britain and what goes to the United States.

In this connection, Mr. President, I beg to, I might almost say, solemnly invite your attention to the fact that, in view of what has passed during the various conferences in Paris and the attitude assumed by the other powers, there will at all times be an European and an American interest which will always differ. It must be quite evident to you that in practically all questions that have come up Great Britain has been able to maintain her position and carry through her claims largely through the dominant influence exerted in consequence of her tremendous naval superiority. It is quite evident to my mind that if this condition of inequality of naval strength is to continue the League of Nations, instead of being what we are striving for and most earnestly hope for, will be a stronger British Empire.

For the six months that I have been constantly in conference with the representatives of the various powers I have tried in every possible way to interpret your views and to anticipate your ideals and objects of the League of Nations, and in these conferences have been prompted by these motives, and I have, from the very beginning, had forced upon me the fact above stated; that American interests, the American viewpoint, American aims and ideals were entirely foreign to those of the other powers and that in practically all important cases the representatives of the other powers have agreed with the representatives of Great Britain. The alliance between France, and Japan and Great Britain, together with their interests, is so intimately connected that any addition to the naval strength of the former two powers will simply be so much more practically added to the strength of Great Britain. The conclusion therefore is most evident to my mind that everything should be done to decrease or at least to prevent an increase in the naval strength of Great Britain, France and Japan, as I am most thoroughly convinced that in order to stabalize [stabilize] the League of Nations and to have it develop into what we intended it to be the United States must increase her naval strength to such a force as will be able to prevent Great Britain at least from dominating and dictating to the other powers within the League.

It is with great hesitancy that I express myself as forcibly as I have in this letter, but I really feel that I would be neglecting my duty to you as well as to my country if I failed to do so.

An extended discussion on this subject will be found in papers Nos. 1,[4] 24,[5] and 65,[6] submitted to you from time to time, on naval questions. Sincerely yours, W. S. Benson.

TLS (WP, DLC).

[1] Presumably of the Inter-Allied Military and Naval Committee. See the minutes of the meeting of the Council of Four printed at April 25, 1919, 5:30 p.m.

[2] That is, Benson, Rear Adm. Hope for Great Britain, Vice-Adm. de Bon for France, Rear Adm. M. Grassi for Italy, and Vice-Adm. Takeshita for Japan.

[3] CCI MS, dated May 5, 1919 (WP, DLC). The British proposal listed by classes of ships all the losses sustained by the five great powers during the war, the number of German and Austrian ships available, and the suggested proportional distribution of these ships based upon the losses of each of the five powers. According to this plan, Great Britain, for example, would receive thirteen dreadnoughts, four battle cruisers, fourteen light cruisers, eighty-one destroyers, forty-six torpedo boats, and ten monitors. France would receive four dreadnoughts, three light cruisers, fourteen destroyers, and thirty-two torpedo boats, while the United States would receive only one light cruiser and three destroyers. The French proposal, which, according to Benson, had been arrived at by "going through a system of mental gymnastics based on untenable premises," distributed the total available tonnage of 740,000 tons as follows: 288,000 tons to Great Britain; 260,000 tons to France; 166,000 tons to Italy; 19,000 tons to the United States; and 7,000 tons to Japan. Translated into terms of ships, the French thus claimed five dreadnoughts, three battle cruisers, eight light cruisers, and forty destroyers.

[4] W. S. Benson, "CONFIDENTIAL. U. S. NAVAL ADVISORY STAFF. SUBJECT: QUESTION I *and* RECOMMENDATIONS," Dec. 17, 1918, TS MS (WP, DLC). This memorandum on the final disposition of the German and Austrian warships recommended that all enemy war-

ships, including submarines, which were either interned by the Allies and the United States at the time of the Armistice or which, according to the terms of the Armistice, were to be surrendered to them, "should be destroyed by sinking without any previous temporary distribution for any purpose whatever." "No German vessel delivered into the hands of the Allies," the memorandum continued, "should ever be used to increase the naval armaments of any Power whatever." The remaining enemy warships, whether already built or still under construction, which had been neither interned nor surrendered, should be left at the disposal of the German government without any restriction or, in the case of Austria-Hungary, should be retained by such part or parts of the former Hapsburg Empire as decided upon by the peace conference. However, all submarines still in German possession, whether completed or still under construction, should also be destroyed.

In a brief Appendix, the Naval Advisory Staff outlined the "underlying motives" of its recommendations. The destruction of the German ships interned at Scapa Flow, the advisers argued, would discourage Germany from resuming her military and naval aspirations and reduce the "tendency towards heavy armament burdens." The distribution of these ships among the Allied and Associated Powers, even for "experimental or other temporary purposes," the memorandum continued, was dangerous, since it might lead to a permanent distribution. As the advisers warned: "The only certain way to prevent such a distribution is destruction in the first instance." As to the destruction of all submarines, Benson and his colleagues pointed out that this suggestion was preliminary to a future recommendation prohibiting the possession of any submarines by the Central Powers for a number of years. Moreover, it was entirely possible that all powers would agree voluntarily to abandon submarine warfare. Finally, the memorandum stated that the removal of any restrictions on the employment of Germany's remaining warships would promote peace and "prevent the fostering of bitter feeling." Germany's financial situation would, in any case, prevent her from resuming a large-scale naval building program and induce her to maintain a navy of minimum size.

[5] Printed as an Enclosure with W. S. Benson to WW, March 14, 1919 (first letter of that date), Vol. 55.

[6] W. S. Benson, "PLANNING SECTION MEMORANDUM No. 65. SUBJECT: *United States Naval Interests in the Armistic terms*," Nov. 4, 1918, TS MS (WP, DLC). The observations of this memorandum on the probable strength of the fleets of the principal naval powers after the war were based on four premises: that all of the great powers which were now considering armistice terms and peace terms with the Central Powers were endeavoring "astutely and consistently" to achieve a settlement which would strengthen to the utmost their respective positions in the world; that there was an agreement between "Great Britain, France, and Italy by which Great Britain and France dictated the German armistice terms" and Great Britain and Italy dictated those with Austria; that a secret understanding existed between France, Italy, and Great Britain as to the distribution of the German and Austrian warships; and that there was strong evidence of an agreement between Great Britain and Japan about the transfer of at least five British dreadnoughts to Japan after the signing of the peace.

In four detailed tables, the memorandum went on to show, respectively, the present number of dreadnoughts, battle cruisers, destroyers, and submarines of the major naval powers; the assumed distribution of the German and Austrian warships among the Allied and Associated Powers; the probable postwar strength of the six greatest naval powers; and a comparison of the relative strength in terms of capital ships of the principal naval powers before and after the distribution of the enemy warships. In commenting on these figures, the naval advisers drew the following conclusions: "Assuming the distribution made as indicated, the United States with seventeen modern capital ships would be faced at once with an alliance between Great Britain and Japan controlling a total of sixty-seven capital ships. Even with Japan left out Great Britain would face us with *three* times the number of capital ships that we have. This in itself is an intolerable situation, but if we join to the mere recital of figures, political considerations which we know have governed in the past, we shall see more clearly that our national interests demand that this distribution of vessels shall not take place." Thus, the memorandum warned, the United States, the latest in a succession of powers "to compete with Great Britain for commercial supremacy on the seas," had to be vigilant, lest it share the fate of its predecessors and be defeated by Great Britain.

The memorandum then continued with an analysis of the effect that the destruction of the surrendered or interned German and Austrian war vessels would have on the overall naval situation. In that case, the advisers argued, other European nations would require no increase in their fleets, since French and Italian interests would not conflict and neither nation could compete with Great Britain at sea. The relative naval strength of Great Britain, France, Italy, and Japan would remain unchanged, but, due to the absence of the balancing influence of Germany on the activities of the British fleet, the position of the United States would be greatly weakened. While Japan would require no augmentation of her fleet, unless her intentions were hostile to the interests of the United States, the alliance between Great Britain and Japan would "still be strong in relation to the United States in the proportion of fifty-six capital ships to seventeen." Thus, the memorandum pointed out, if Great Britain should insist upon a distribution of the enemy warships, she would do so solely in view of her future relations with the United States. Unless the United States succeeded in leaving in Europe "some restraining influence on British naval power," Great Britain would be able to exert throughout the world an influence unknown to her in peacetime in the recent past. Although it might be "right and proper," the memorandum continued, that Great Britain should have a greater navy than any other European power, it was not "in the interest of humanity" that she should occupy so commanding a naval position that she would regulate the high seas throughout the world "in accordance with her will." To counter these British designs, the naval advisers made the following recommendations:

"1. All German and Austrian submarines should be destroyed.

"2. No German or Austrian Naval vessel should be used to increase the Naval armament of any power whatever.

"3. The German Navy should remain after this war sufficiently strong to exercise a distinctly conservative influence on the application of British sea power.

"4. The United States should never permit the transfer of British capital ships to Japan, as the move would be distinctly hostile to American interests."

From the Diary of Ray Stannard Baker

Monday May 5 [1919]

We are still in the struggle to get a representation of journalists—establish the principle—at the initial meeting with the Germans: So far without success. I have had it up twice to the President, who told me he discussed it with the three—to no avail. I do not believe he himself really favors it. He likes publicity in the abstract, but shrinks from the specific application. They "pass the buck" from one to another: and it now looks as though they would try to keep all the correspondents behind the hedge in the grounds of the Trianon Palace Hotel.

Two Telegrams from Joseph Patrick Tumulty

[The White House, May 5, 1919]

No. 97 Scott Ferris has telegraphed me protesting against the new schedule of rates increasing telephone charges in Oklahoma from 50 to 100 per cent. In this telegram to me he says, "Three years of drouth, two years of war, and the intense loyalty of our state to the Government makes this action impossible of explanation by the friends of the Government. Is there no one who can appeal to you to prevent this additional burden and this injustice upon people who already have more than they can carry?" This is typical of other telegrams of protest which have reached here. A similar situation prevails in Rhode Island, Massachusetts, New Jersey and Illinois and throughout the West. I have discussed the matter with the Postmaster General and have told him that in view of the return of the telephones within a month or two, these increases are most unwise. Evidently I made no impression. My own feeling is that some of the gentlemen whom the Postmaster General has consulted from among the directors of the telegraph and telephone companies are putting through these increases with the idea that they will be made permanent, and our administration will have to bear the blame. On all personal telephone bills that are being sent throughout the country there is a notice attached that increases are made necessary by reason of the action of the Postmaster General. Could you not suggest to the Postmaster General that in view of the impending return of the telegraph and telephone systems, these increases might well be held in abeyance? Tumulty.

[The White House, May 5, 1919]

Number 98 A large delegation of labor men called here today comma recommending that you encourage comma in American shipyards comma the building of foreign ships comma urging that if there is to be no interruption of the shipping business comma foreign orders must be had in the immediate future stop They claim that we are today comma without restraint comma shipping steel and other material to certain foreign nations comma which are rapidly expanding their own ship building facilities and that foreign shipyards are being built up at the expense of American ship yards stop This affects over three hundred thousand men directly employed in the ship yards and seven hundred thousand more employed in manufacturing auxiliaries for these ships stop The coal [Coast][1] newspapers are clamoring for the raising of this embargo. Tumulty

T telegrams (WP, DLC).

[1] Correction from the "telegram sent" in the J. P. Tumulty Papers, DLC.

William Howard Taft to Joseph Patrick Tumulty

My dear Mr. Tumulty: Washington, D. C. May 5, 1919.

I am very much troubled that this conference at Paris was unable to adopt a provision in favor of religious freedom throughout the world. There is no necessity for such a resolution in respect to the allied countries, because there is now religious freedom there. The acute necessity for it is with respect to Poland, Rumania, and those other new States carved out of Russia, Austria and Germany. I would like, therefore, to have you transmit to the President, as coming from me, a cable message of the following purport:

"The Jews of the United States are greatly disturbed over reliable reports coming to them of continued abuses of their co-religionists in Poland, Rumania and in the new Slav States created under the auspices of the conference. Is it not possible to impose on these States, as a condition of their recognition and membership in the League, the maintenance of religious freedom under their respective governments? What was done in the Berlin Conference of 1879[1] ought to be possible in the more favorable atmosphere of this conference, with the additional securities of performance that the League will give."[2]

I understand that unless something of this sort is done, there will be a strong movement among the Jews to attack the League, and I do not need to tell you that there are men in the Senate who will seize every opportunity of this kind as an instrument to defeat its ratification. Sincerely yours, Wm H Taft

TLS (WP, DLC).

[1] Taft meant the Congress of Berlin which convened on June 13, 1878. A conference of the major European powers, the congress met to solve the international crisis caused by the Russo-Turkish war of 1877-1878 and the Treaty of San Stefano (March 3, 1878), which had greatly extended Russia's influence in the Balkans, had established the independence of Montenegro, Serbia, Rumania, and a greatly reduced Bulgaria, and had all but eliminated the Ottoman Empire from Europe. The Treaty of Berlin of July 13, 1878, which revised the previous settlement, stripped Russia of most of its gains, reinstated Turkish rule in Macedonia and Eastern Rumelia, and permitted Austria to occupy Bosnia-Herzegovina. The treaty also affirmed the independence of Montenegro, Serbia, Rumania, and a greatly reduced Bulgaria. Moreover, as a result of protracted and vigorous efforts by Jewish groups throughout Europe, the treaty obliged each of the new states as well as the Turkish Empire to refrain from discrimination of any kind against religious minorities, to grant full civic and political rights to all inhabitants, regardless of faith or creed, and to guarantee the freedom of religious association and practice. As it turned out, these stipulations, which were primarily intended to protect the 250,000 to 300,000 Jews living in Rumania, were completely disregarded by future Rumanian governments and, notwithstanding repeated protests by the major European powers, anti-Semitism remained rampant in the country. The minutes of the congress, as well as the text of the Treaty of Berlin, are printed in French and German in Imanuel Geiss, ed., *Der Berliner Kongress 1878. Protokolle und Materialien* (Boppard am Rhein, 1978). For a general discussion, see also W. N. Medlicott, *The Congress of Berlin and After. A Diplomatic History of the Near Eastern Settlement, 1878-1880* (2d edn., London, 1963), and William L. Langer, *European Alliances and Alignments, 1871-1890* (New York, 1931), pp. 121-69. About the Jewish question, see N. M. Gelber, "The Intervention of German Jews at the Berlin Congress 1878," in Leo Baeck Institute, *Year Book*, V (1960), 221-48; and Fritz Stern, *Gold and Iron: Bismarck, Bleichröder, and the Building of the German Empire* (New York, 1977), pp. 351-93.

[2] Tumulty sent this message as JPT to WW, No. 100, May 6, 1919, T telegram (WP, DLC).

From the Diary of Dr. Grayson

Tuesday, May 6, 1919.

The President arose early and had breakfast at 8:00 o'clock. He remained in his study until 11:00 when the Big Three met. They decided to have a meeting at the Quai d'Orsay in the afternoon. The

President, Mrs. Wilson and I had lunch, and during the lunch the President said: "A pun was made this morning which Mr. Clemenceau entirely missed, as he does not understand English very quickly. Lloyd-George said to me: 'Will the *Pres-dent* meet us at the Quai d'Orsay this afternoon at our session?' Clemenceau only heard the word "press." He said: 'Oh, no, we will not allow the press there this afternoon.' I said: 'But you will if you add the *dent*.' Lloyd-George laughed very heartily but Clemenceau did not know what was going on."

The President said the Italians had telegraphed asking that the delivery of the Peace terms to the Germans be postponed for 24 hours, as Orlando and Sonnino were on their way from Rome to Paris, and their train was due to arrive at 12:00 o'clock noon, Wednesday; and as they (Orlando and Sonnino) understood that the Peace terms were to be delivered to the Germans at three, they feared their train might be late and they would be prevented from participating at the meeting. Their request was not granted. The Big Three agreed that the Italians had plenty of time to make arrangements for their return in time for the ceremony.

The President told me: "Since I have been studying the European countries I have made up my mind that they would immediately repudiate any altruistic views they might entertain and grab for their own selfish interest anything they might want. America is the only altruistic country."

In the afternoon a secret Plenary Session was held at which the context of the Peace Treaty was communicated to the smaller nations and a general debate took place which was marked by sharp exchanges.[1] There was quite a tilt between Foch and Clemenceau over military questions. There is a clique between Poincaré, the President of the French Republic, and Marshal Foch against Premier Clemenceau.[2] While Foch was on the floor Clemenceau came over and said to the President: "You must save me from these two fools." The President asked Foch some very pointed questions and Foch was unable to answer them; the only way he answered them was by shrugging his shoulders and saying that he was unable to reply. This was concerning the creation of a buffer state in the Rhine and in connection with military reenforcements there. He (Foch) wanted to put there what seemed to be an excessively large number of troops. The President said to me: "Foch may be a great soldier but he appeared to be very simple and seemed to have no ideas for planning. He either did not know how to answer questions or did not seem to know what he was talking about. I was very much disappointed in him."

The President told me that the Big Three received word this

morning from the Germans that they were here and that if the Treaty was not ready they would go home. Word was sent back to them that they had better reflect over the consequences should they take such action. So they "piped down."

The President had dinner at seven o'clock, Mr. Charles H. Grasty being the guest. The President and Mrs. Wilson were very solicitous and particularly kind to him, making every effort to make his stay here at the house as comfortable as possible.

After dinner Grasty and I joined the President and Mrs. Wilson in the President's sitting-room for a half-hour. Grasty spoke of many things of interest concerning the war. He was in France during the entire period of the war. The conversation was in a light vein. The President retired early.

[1] At this Plenary Session, Foch doggedly argued once again that the Allied nations should occupy the territory of Germany up to the Rhine River "as long as you wish to retain guarantees," that is, at least as long as Germany was required to make reparation payments. During the same session, the former Premier and chief delegate of Portugal, Afonso Augusto da Costa, made a strong plea that his nation receive a fair, if modest, share of German reparations, and Lu Cheng-hsiang made a brief but strong protest against the Shantung settlement. Silvio Benigno Crespi, on behalf of the still absent Italian delegates, entered a reservation to any clauses of the treaty which might have been modified during their absence. The full text of the minutes of the Plenary Session is printed in *PPC*, III, 333-90. The remarks summarized above are in *ibid.*, 379-88. The exchanges between Foch and Clemenceau and between Foch and Wilson mentioned by Dr. Grayson below do not appear in the official record.

[2] For the background of the Poincaré-Foch "clique" against Clemenceau on the subject of Rhineland policy, see Jere Clemens King, *Foch versus Clemenceau: France and German Dismemberment, 1918-1919* (Cambridge, Mass., 1960), pp. 60-70.

From the Diary of Lord Robert Cecil

May 6 [1919].

Early this morning I received a message from House's secretary and son-in-law, Auchincloss, that the President had sent a peremptory communication to the printers that they were to print the Covenant exactly as it was passed by the Plenary Conference. Later I heard that Clemenceau had abandoned his proposed amendment as the Italians were coming back, after all the outcry about the President's message (which indeed I thought a great mistake). He will be more than ever confident that he can do anything he likes in Europe. As on the whole I agree with his policy, I do not mind.

Hankey's and Mantoux's Notes of a Meeting of the Council of Four[1]

President Wilson's House,
I.C.-181C Paris, May 6, 1919, 11 a.m.

SIR MAURICE HANKEY said he had received a communication from the Secretary-General, stating that for the indispensable material arrangements, such as protocol drafting, placing of the Delegations, assignment of cards and seats, arrangements with representatives of the Press, etc. one Secretary per Great Power and two Secretaries for the Secretary-General would be insufficient. M. Dutasta had therefore asked that the numbers might be raised to two Secretaries each for the United States of America, United Kingdom, France, Italy, and Japan, with one Secretary for each of the other Delegations, and three members of the Secretary-General's Secretariat.

(The above proposal was agreed to.)

2. M. CLEMENCEAU pressed very strongly that the guarantee by the British Empire and the United States of America, which it had been agreed should be given to France, should be furnished immediately, as it was important to him to be able to make an announcement on the subject.

M. TARDIEU said that after discussion with Mr. Frazier, he suggested that the undertaking should be announced simultaneously with the signing of the Treaty of Peace to the Press, but should not form part of the Treaty. He then read the attached form (Appendix I).

PRESIDENT WILSON said he did not like this form, which confused the question. It was provided in the Treaty that Germany should not maintain permanent facilities for mobilization west of the Rhine. If that was put in, as M. Tardieu contemplated, it would look as though, if Germany should do so, the United States would have at once to send troops. This was not what was intended. Troops were only to be sent in the event of an act of aggression. He then read Mr. Balfour's draft, which had been handed to him by Mr. Lloyd George (Appendix II), and which stated the matter perfectly clearly. In Mr. Balfour's draft, however, he detected an error in paragraph 2, where the word "any" should be substituted for "either." He himself would be quite prepared to sign a similar document, the paragraph in regard to Dominions of course being omitted.

M. CLEMENCEAU said he would be satisfied with this.

MR. LLOYD GEORGE said he would be prepared to sign. He said that he had already informed the Imperial War Cabinet of the decision.

[1] The complete text of Hankey's minutes is printed in *PPC*, V, 474-90.

M. TARDIEU said he could alter his draft to meet President Wilson's criticisms.

PRESIDENT WILSON said he considered Mr. Balfour's draft sufficient. M. Tardieu's draft gave the impression of a triple agreement, which the United States, of course, would object to. The agreement was triple in effect, but not in form.[2]

M. CLEMENCEAU then raised the question of the form which the announcement should take.

M. TARDIEU proposed a draft in some such words as the following: "So far as the question of the French frontier on the Rhine is concerned, the United States Government and the British Government are in agreement to submit to their respective legislatures the text of the Treaty according to the terms of which the Republic of the United States of America and Great Britain will immediately bring their assistance in case of an unprovoked German aggression."

PRESIDENT WILSON pointed out that the mention of the approval of the League of Nations had been omitted.

M. TARDIEU proposed to introduce the words "with the approval of the League of Nations" after the words "respective legislatures."

MR. LLOYD GEORGE said that the mention of the League of Nations would assist him in getting it through Parliament.

PRESIDENT WILSON then proposed the following alternative draft: "In addition to the securities afforded in the Treaty of Peace, the President of the United States of America has pledged himself to propose to the Senate of the United States, and the Prime Minister of Great Britain has pledged himself to propose to the Parliament of Great Britain an engagement subject to the approval of the Council of the League of Nations to come immediately to the assistance of France in case of unprovoked attack by Germany."

(It was agreed

(1) That the announcement should be made in the words proposed by President Wilson.

(2) That President Wilson on behalf of the United States of America and Mr. Lloyd George and Mr. Balfour on behalf of Great Britain, should respectively send letters to M. Clemenceau, based on Mr. Balfour's draft (Appendix 2).)

(At this point the Drafting Committee was introduced.)

3. MR. HURST said that the Drafting Committee had found itself in a difficulty. On Friday, May 2nd, the text of an article had been approved by the Supreme Council in regard to the renunciation by

[2] Mantoux, I, 493: "Wilson. I will make another observation. We must not give our commitments the appearance of a pact among three powers: the American Senate would object. I propose to indicate clearly that there are two separate commitments made toward France by Great Britain and by the United States."

Germany of the Brest-Litovsk Treaty, and other matters relating to Russia. This had been forwarded to the Drafting Committee (I.C.171.C Minute 11).[3] The Drafting Committee, however, had found that this article was less far-reaching than articles already included in the Financial and Economic Sections of the Peace Treaty, and had accordingly submitted a revised draft which was approved by the Supreme Council and duly transmitted to the Drafting Committee to supercede the original draft (I.C.181.A. Minute 2).[4] Today, however, the Drafting Committee had been told that the original clause was to be reinserted.

In reply to Mr. Lloyd George he said he thought the new instructions had been given to M. Fromageot by M. Pichon.

M. CLEMENCEAU said that if the revised draft had been approved by the Supreme Council it ought to stand.

(It was agreed that the revised draft approved on May 3rd should stand and the Drafting Committee was given verbal instructions to carry this out.)

4. MR. HURST said that on May 2nd, the Supreme Council had approved the following Article for incorporation in the Treaty of Peace, which had been duly notified to the Drafting Committee:

"Germany acknowledges and will fully respect the independence of Austria within the frontiers established by the present Treaty as inalienable except by consent of the League of Nations." (I.C.179.C. Minute 12.)[5]

The difficulty in which the Drafting Committee found themselves was that the frontiers of Austria had not been fixed. It was true that the frontiers between Germany and that part of the Old Austrian Empire which was now comprised in the new Czecho-Slovak State had been fixed, but nothing had been said either about the frontiers between Germany and the new Austria, or about the other frontiers of Austria.

MR. LLOYD GEORGE proposed that the 1914 frontier between Austria and Germany should be adhered to.

PRESIDENT WILSON pointed out that this only provided for the boundary between Germany and Austria, whereas the Article quoted above referred to "the frontiers established by the present Treaty," and contemplated the whole of the boundaries of Austria.

MR. HURST said that the Drafting Committee had proposed an amendment to the effect that Germany should recognise Austria within frontiers which might be approved by the Allied and Associated Powers.

[3] Actually, I.C.-179C., i.e., the minutes of the Council of Four, May 2, 1919, 4 p.m.; the complete text is printed in *PPC*, V, 418-25.

[4] See the minutes of the Council of Four printed at May 3, 1919, 4 p.m.

[5] See the minutes of the Council of Four printed at May 2, 1919, 4 p.m.

(The Drafting Committee's proposal was agreed to, and the Drafting Committee was given verbal instructions to amend the Treaty accordingly.)

§ Mantoux's notes:

The members of the Drafting Committee are introduced.

Mr. James Brown Scott reads the text concerning Russia. One modification was made to the original text, in order to avoid a contradiction with other articles of the treaty. This modification had been approved by the Council of Four. The Drafting Committee today received a note asking it to return to the old text, and it wishes instructions on this subject. Its impression is that there is a misunderstanding.

After a short exchange of observations, the modified text is maintained.

Scott. The question of the frontier between German and Austria is not mentioned in the treaty. At the very least it must be indicated that it will be resolved, as well as the questions concerning the other frontiers of Austria in another treaty.

Lloyd George. Must it not be said that the frontier between Germany and Austria must remain what it was in 1914?

This proposal is adopted. §

5. MR. LLOYD GEORGE said he had an appeal to make in regard to Canada. Sir Robert Borden had pointed out that Canada was, by the existing wording, ruled out of the League of Nations Council.[6]

PRESIDENT WILSON pointed out that it was not the League of Nations Council but the Labour Convention to which he understood Sir Robert Borden referred.

MR. LLOYD GEORGE said that Sir Robert Borden's point was not so much that he wanted Canada at present to be represented on the Council, but that he wanted the regulation so altered that Canada could be included in the Council. He had pointed out that South American Republics such as Nicaragua, Honduras, etc. could be represented, and he maintained that the United States influence in those countries was greater than the influence of the United Kingdom in Canada.

PRESIDENT WILSON demurred to this, but said he did not want that point to be made in order to convince him of the justice of Sir Robert Borden's contention. This Convention, however, had been drawn up by a Commission which had now dispersed, and passed by the Plenary Conference, and it was difficult to change it.

MR. LLOYD GEORGE said that Sir Robert Borden had actually moved and passed a resolution through the Plenary Conference,

[6] See the Enclosure printed with R. Borden to T. White, May 3, 1919.

which he believed to be adequate, but the Drafting Committee did not consider it adequate. Sir Robert Borden had said that if the Drafting Committee's view was upheld, he would have to raise the question at the Plenary Session in the afternoon, and Mr. Lloyd George wanted to avoid this if possible.

PRESIDENT WILSON asked if anyone had the exact terms of the resolution moved at the Plenary.

MR. HURST said the substance of it had been that the Drafting Committee was instructed to bring the Labour Covenant into line with the League of Nations Covenant.

MR. LLOYD GEORGE asked if M. Clemenceau would agree to put Canada in the same position in regard to the Labour Convention as it was in regard to the League of Nations Covenant.

M. CLEMENCEAU agreed.

PRESIDENT WILSON said that that was his understanding of the situation. He was so anxious not to hold up the printing of the Peace Treaty that he thought alterations of this kind might be put into an errata.

MR. HURST asked that the form in which the correction should be made might be left to the Drafting Committee.

(It was agreed [1] that the necessary alterations should be inserted in the Labour Convention, to place the Dominions in the same position as regards representation on the governing body of the Labour Convention as they were already in as regards representation on the Council of the League of Nations.

2. That the form in which this should be incorporated in the Treaty of Peace should be left to the Drafting Committee.) The Drafting Committee were given verbal instructions to carry out this decision.*

NOTE: At the end of the meeting, Sir Maurice Hankey received a note from Mr. Hurst to say that the decision would be carried out by suppressing the following sentence in Article 393 (Labour Convention): "No member, together with its dominions and colonies, whether self-governing or not, shall be entitled to nominate more than one member."

§ Mantoux's notes:

Lloyd George. Sir Robert Borden, in the name of the Canadian government, asks for Canada the right to be represented in the labor section of the League of Nations. I recall the important role that Sir Robert Borden has played in the commission for labor legislation, and Canada would not understand if no place was reserved for her

* *Note by the Secretary*. At the Plenary Meeting in the afternoon the attached statement (Appendix VI) was signed by M. Clemenceau, President Wilson, and Mr. Lloyd George, the original being retained by the Prime Minister of Canada.

in the League of Nations, given her importance in comparison with other American states which, not being attached to a great empire like ours, regard themselves as independent states. In fact, the influence of the United States on these states is much greater than ours is on Canada, and I do not need to recall the significant role which Canada played during the war.

Wilson. I have no objection to make; but your ideas about the relation between the small American powers and the United States are not altogether exact.

The proposal is adopted. §

(M. Loucheur was introduced at this point together with Lord Cunliffe.)

NOTE: The following passages were extremely difficult to follow, as all present were standing up, and the conversation was very general.

6. M. LOUCHEUR handed in the attached document proposing a drafting alteration in the text of Article 232 of the Treaty of Peace (Appendix III).

(The object of this alteration, as explained by M. Loucheur, was understood to be to prevent the Germans from giving too narrow an interpretation of this Article. Annex 1 to the Reparation Clauses[7] includes among the categories of damage for which compensation may be claimed pensions to naval and military victims of the war, whereas the actual text of this Article, although referring to Annex 1, indicates that it is only damage done to the civilian population that shall be compensated. This was the reason for inserting the words "and generally for all damage in accordance with the definition contained in Annex 1.")

M. CLEMENCEAU insisted very strongly on this alteration, which was merely a drafting one, was essential to him, as his colleagues pressed very strongly for it.

MR. LLOYD GEORGE said the question was really a legal one, and he greatly regretted the absence of Lord Sumner. After consulting Lord Cunliffe and Mr. Hurst, he said that so far as he was concerned, he would accept the change.

PRESIDENT WILSON, after consulting Mr. Brown-Scott, also accepted it.

(It was agreed that the alteration proposed by M. Loucheur should be approved, and the Drafting Committee was given verbal instructions to amend the Treaty of Peace accordingly.)

§ Mantoux's notes:

Clemenceau. I have to ask for the modification of the article

[7] That is, the so-called Categories of Damages, for which see the minutes of the Council of Four printed at April 7, 1919, 4 p.m., Vol. 57.

which contains the general stipulations on reparations. After having mentioned the reparations due to the civilian population, the article ends thus. "* * * as they are defined in Appendix I."

It has been called to my attention that Appendix I mentions clearly the pensions which must be given to disabled soldiers or to the families of soldiers killed by the enemy, but that, according to a narrow interpretation, the Germans could claim that it is a question uniquely of direct damages to the civilian population, such as are defined in that appendix. In order to avoid any discussion on this point, I propose to insert: "and generally all damages defined by Appendix I."

Wilson. I do not see the point of this modification. We ourselves have declared in the memorandum published at the time of the Armistice that by "reparation" we meant reparation of damages suffered by the civilian population, and, on the other hand, we all agreed to recognize that pensions had to be included in the list, which we indicated in the clearest fashion in Appendix I. What more do you want?

Clemenceau. I want to prevent any interpretation which could give rise to arguments. I want to prevent certain recriminations which arose among my own colleagues. I am asking you urgently to consent to the modification which I present to you.

The proposed amendment is adopted.§

7. M. LOCHEUR raised a question, which he said had up to now been overlooked in regard to Reparation. It was provided by the terms of the Armistice of November 11th, 1918, and the Conventions renewing it, for certain restitutions, including the surrender of ships, to take place regularly during the Armistice. Unless some provision was made for a continuation of these restitutions, they would come to a stop on the signature of Peace, and would not be renewed until the Treaty was ratified. He said that Mr. Lamont and Mr. MacCormick were in agreement with him on the subject. He urged, therefore, that some clause should be inserted to provide for this defect.

(This was agreed to.)

8. MR. LLOYD GEORGE said that on the previous evening M. Paderewski had pointed out to him that, under the Reparation Clauses, the old Government buildings and forests of Poland, which had during the war been seized by Germany, and had now reverted to Poland, would have to be paid for by the Poles.

MR. HURST, in reply to a question by Mr. Lloyd George, said that under the Reparation Clauses, all State property would have to be valued and accounted for to the Reparation pool by Poland.

President Wilson said that the Reparation Committee had powers to remit in such cases as these.

MR. HURST said it would involve a diminution in Poland's share in the pool.

(On President Wilson's suggestion, it was agreed that the Reparation experts should prepare a clause to provide for this difficulty, which should be forwarded to the Drafting Committee for insertion in the Treaty of Peace.)

9. M. LOUCHEUR said that M. Crespi had communicated with him to say that the decision as regards the participation of Italy in reparation was contrary to Article 11 of the Treaty of London, namely, "Italy will receive a part corresponding to her efforts and her sacrifices in the eventual war indemnity." M. Crespi had asked that this provision might be withheld.

MR. LLOYD GEORGE said it was too late.

PRESIDENT WILSON agreed. He said it would involve a most elaborate alteration.

MR. LLOYD GEORGE said it created an awkward situation, but he pointed out that Italy had not declared war against Germany for more than 12 months after she signed the Treaty of London.

PRESIDENT WILSON pointed out that reparation was provided for, but no war indemnity.

MR. LLOYD GEORGE thought that this narrow interpretation of indemnity would hardly be fair to Italy. Italy's real weak point was that she had not declared war against Germany until nearly two years after the beginning of the war. Her efforts against Germany had been by no means great.

PRESIDENT WILSON pointed out that the formula on April 30th (I.C.178.C. Minute 1)[8] related to the attacks on Italy by Germany, and not Italy's operations against Germany.

MR. BROWN SCOTT suggested that the matter might be settled in the Treaty with Austria.

PRESIDENT WILSON said that this meant that Italy would receive nothing. It was a very complicated business to make a change now.

M. LOUCHEUR read a draft Article which he proposed should be substituted for the present Article.

(The Secretary was unable to obtain this.)

MR. LLOYD GEORGE said that the effect of M. Loucheur's proposal would be a protest on behalf of Serbia and Roumania.

[8] It read as follows: "War damages resulting from hostilities on any one of the fronts shall be compensated by Germany and her allies *pro rata* with the military and naval force supplied by each of them on that front. The proportions will be determined by the Reparations Commission." See the minutes of the Council of Four, April 30, 1919, 5:30 p.m., printed in *PPC*, V, 387-88.

M. LOUCHEUR then suggested that the original text should be restored.

(This was agreed to.)

(At this point, the Drafting Committee and M. Loucheur withdrew, M. Tardieu having withdrawn during the discussion.)

M. Dutasta, Secretary-General of the Conference, was introduced.

10. PRESIDENT WILSON asked M. Dutasta which Governments had been invited to attend the Plenary in the afternoon.

M. DUTASTA said the whole of the Plenary Conference had been invited.

In reply to a further question from President Wilson, he said that in addition to the great powers, the following States would be represented to meet the Germans:

Belgium, Brazil, Greece, Poland, Portugal, Roumania, Serbia, and Czecho-Slovakia.

PRESIDENT WILSON pointed out that many other States, including some of the Central and South American States had declared war on Germany and would have to sign the Treaty.

MR. LLOYD GEORGE said this was because of the League of Nations. Some neutrals, however, were to join the League of Nations, and these would not be present to meet the Germans.

PRESIDENT WILSON said he hoped at any rate the Chinese would be included.

MR. LLOYD GEORGE and M. CLEMENCEAU agreed.

SIR MAURICE HANKEY said he was informed that Siam had sent aviators to the theater of war.

MR. LLOYD GEORGE said in these circumstances it would be difficult to leave Siam out.

(It was agreed that China and Siam should be added to the list of States represented when the Treaty of Peace was handed to the Germans.)

§ Mantoux's notes:

M. Dutasta, Secretary General of the Conference, is introduced.

Wilson. A certain number of states have not been invited to the session tomorrow, where the text of the plan for the treaty will be transmitted to the Germans; I refer to the states which declared war on Germany without actually going to war.

Lloyd George. In fact, it was decided to admit only the belligerents.

Wilson. You do not admit China, at the very least?

Clemenceau. I think sympathy must be shown toward her, and it is difficult to exclude a state which represents 400 million inhabitants.

Lloyd George. Besides, 200,000 Chinese worked behind our lines, and some even fought at Amiens.

Dutasta. There is also a claim from Siam.

Clemenceau. Siam sent us some aviators.

The admission of China and Siam is decided. §

11. M. DUTASTA handed in a Memorandum in regard to the neutral zone of Savoy, of the Free zones of Savoy, and of the Gex district (Appendix IV),[9] as well as an Article proposed by the French Government for incorporation in the Treaty of Peace (Appendix 5).[10] He said that the text of this Article had been agreed between the French and Swiss Governments.

PRESIDENT WILSON said he knew nothing about the matter.

MR. LLOYD GEORGE said that he knew nothing of it either. He proposed that the Foreign Ministers should be invited to meet at once, with full powers to decide the question.

(It was agreed that the Council of Foreign Ministers should be summoned at once by the Secretary-General, and should meet with full powers to decide the questions raised in the documents presented by the Secretary-General.)

12. SIR MAURICE HANKEY was instructed to notify M. ORLANDO that a meeting of the Supreme Council would be held on the following day at President Wilson's house in the Place des Etats-Unis, at 11 a.m.

13. MR. LLOYD GEORGE drew attention to an article in the "Matin," which was generally well informed about Italian affairs. This indicated that Italy would now claim the sovereignty of Fiume under the League of Nations.[11]

PRESIDENT WILSON asked how long it would take the Italians to realise that they could not get Fiume under any circumstances. The only advantage in letting the Italians have Fiume would be that it would break the Treaty of London, which he was disturbed to find allotted the Dodecanese to Italy.

M. CLEMENCEAU said he had bad news of Italian military movements.

MR. LLOYD GEORGE asked what the result of President Wilson's enquiries in regard to the proposed Military re-disposition of forces in Turkey had been.

PRESIDENT WILSON said he regretted to have to say that his legal advisers informed him that he had no authority to send troops to Turkey. One result of the United States policy of isolation had been that laws had been placed on the Statute Book restricting the move-

[9] Printed in *ibid.*, pp. 487-89.

[10] Printed in *ibid.*, p. 489.

[11] About this latest Italian proposal, see T. N. Page to Ammission, May 5, 1918.

ments of troops outside of the United States. Under existing laws it would not even be possible for him to agree to send troops to Turkey, nor could he send them unless at war with Turkey. He had tried his best to find some way out but could not. The most he could do at present, and though that was not much it might do to steady the Italians, was to express his willingness to propose to Congress legislation on the subject when he submitted the Treaty of Peace. Such legislation would practically form part of the scheme of mandates.

MR. LLOYD GEORGE pointed out that in the meanwhile Italy might establish herself in Anatolia.

PRESIDENT WILSON said that in that case Italy would be compelled to get out again. The United States was the only country where Italy could get credits for essential purposes.

MR. LLOYD GEORGE said that no discussion had taken place in regard to the mandates for Anatolia.

PRESIDENT WILSON said that a certain authoritative Turk had expressed the view that the whole of Turkey ought to be under a single mandate. He himself thought that this was more than he could induce the United States to undertake. The Turks were hated in the United States, and the only ground on which a mandate would be accepted over Turkey would be to protect subject races against the Turks. He was assured that to put in a disturbing authority in Anatolia would inevitably cause trouble with the Greeks on one side and the Italians on the other. There would be constant friction between them. Moreover, when the Italian people saw what additions were involved to their budgets they would not like the arrangements. He could not understand the position of the Italian Government in this matter. He compared it to the popular clamour against the destruction of warships, the fact not being understood how heavy was the cost of their upkeep.

§ Mantoux's notes:

Lloyd George. M. Orlando and M. Sonnino will be here tomorrow morning. What are we going to do with them if they show up at our meeting? Tomorrow morning, I think we will have enough to do before meeting the Germans without recommencing the discussion of the Italian questions. If our Italian colleagues tell us that they want to enter into the question of Fiume immediately, I propose to answer them that we cannot do it, that we do not have the time.

Hankey. Should I inform them of the time of the meeting, as I have always done?

Lloyd George. Undoubtedly. *Le Matin*, which I read to inform myself about what the Italians want, indicates that they will ask for sovereignty over Fiume, under a regime to be established by the League of Nations.

Wilson. How long will it take them to learn that they cannot have Fiume—under any condition? The only reason which would lead me to give them Fiume is that, by so doing, we would destroy the Treaty of London. I have noticed that this treaty also gives them the Dodecanese.

Clemenceau. That is true, and it is a shame.

Wilson. The United States cannot sanction such a treaty. In the Dodecanese islands, the Italians, as we saw the other day, are oppressing the population because it declares itself to be Greek, and are killing the priests in their churches. In every way they are conducting themselves in the fashion of tyrants.

Concerning the present movements of the Italians in Asia Minor and your desire to see American troops participate in the occupation of different Asiatic regions, I am sorry to tell you that this participation will not be possible, because I am bound by the Constitution of the United States: I do not have the right to send American troops into a country with which the United States is not in a state of war. All that I can do is to ask Congress, as I will do anyway, to approve a law which will permit the execution of the peace treaty and in particular the functioning of the system of mandates under the authority of the League of Nations. But the decision of Congress cannot be taken immediately.

Lloyd George. In the meantime, if we allow them to do so, the Italians will have occupied all of Anatolia. We have not even discussed yet among ourselves the question of mandates for that part of Asia.

Wilson. I am told that the Turks wish that the regions inhabited by their race not be divided, and also that there is a movement among them in favor of an American administration.

Lloyd George. That would not surprise me; of all Westerners, the Americans are those against whom they have the fewest grievances.

Wilson. I have no hope that American opinion will consent to it. Hatred of the Turk is unbelievable in America. What American opinion will approve is the protection of the Armenians or of some population which stands against the Turks. It will also approve the occupation of Constantinople, if it is conferred on us, because in that way Constantinople will be taken away from the Turks. But I confess that, to put as turbulent a power as Italy in Anatolia, seems dangerous to me, as much because of the Turks and their possible reactions as when I think of the relations which will be established between the Italians and the neighboring mandatories. As for the Italians, I do not know if they will be very satisfied to have great mandates in Asia when they see the costs that that will impose upon their budget.

Lloyd George. It is a bit like the dreadnoughts which one proposes to keep instead of destroying them: those who will keep them will see what it will cost them, to say nothing of keeping them up.

Wilson. It is like the official yacht of the President of the United States, the *Mayflower*: I do not use it four times during the year, and its maintenance, along with the pay for the crew, costs something like one hundred thousand dollars per year. §

14. SIR MAURICE HANKEY stated that he had received a letter from M. Berthelot stating that the Committee set up on May 1st (I.C.178B, Minute 8)[12] had established that the problem applied equally to certain countries such as Roumania and Greece which would receive territorial increases very much in the same conditions as new States like Poland, Czecho-Slovakia and the kingdom of the Serbo-Croats and Slovenes. The question was especially important by reason of guarantees to be formulated for the Jews of Roumania and the Mussulmans of Thrace and Albania. The Committee therefore asked for an extension of its terms of reference to include Roumania and Greece.

The above proposal was approved and Sir Maurice Hankey was instructed to notify M. Berthelot accordingly.

15. PRESIDENT WILSON drew attention to the position the Italians had assumed in Albania.

MR. LLOYD GEORGE said that a Protectorate had been announced without informing any of their Allies.

PRESIDENT WILSON said that Albania ought to be independent.

MR. LLOYD GEORGE doubted if sufficient unity could be ensured.

16. MR. LLOYD GEORGE said he thought some attempt ought to be made to proceed further in regard to Turkey. Otherwise the Italians would establish themselves there. M. Clemenceau on the previous day had told them that Italy had seven battleships at Smyrna. This meant that they intended to land troops. It was said that Italy was making trouble between the Greeks and Turks, and having done so they would land troops with the ostensible object of keeping the peace.

PRESIDENT WILSON remarked that they would have to be informed that if they did not evacuate they would get no money.

MR. LLOYD GEORGE said that America had had a good deal of experience of bankrupt countries in Central America, and Europe had had a good deal of experience of the same kind in the Balkans and Turkey. The one thing these countries could always do was to make war.

PRESIDENT WILSON suggested that they did it by living on the country.

[12] Actually, I.C.-178D, i.e., the minutes of the Council of Four printed at May 1, 1919, 11 a.m.

17. MR. LLOYD GEORGE said he thought it ought to be decided that M. Venizelos should be allowed to land two or three Divisions at Smyrna to protect his fellow-countrymen in Turkey.

PRESIDENT WILSON pointed out that the report of the Greek Commission was now unanimously in favour of giving this area to Greece.

M. CLEMENCEAU said he was ready to allow M. Venizelos to send troops.

PRESIDENT WILSON said that undoubtedly he was ready.

M. CLEMENCEAU recalled the agreement of St. Jean de Maurienne.[13]

MR. LLOYD GEORGE said that the agreement of St. Jean de Maurienne had been conditional on Italy playing an adequate part in the war against Turkey, and had also been subject to the agreement of Russia. He asked for a decision that M. Venizelos might be authorized to send troops on board ship to Smyrna to be kept there ready for landing in case of necessity.

PRESIDENT WILSON asked why they should not be landed at once? The men did not keep in good condition on board ship.

MR. LLOYD GEORGE said he had no objection.

§ Mantoux's notes:

[Wilson.] I too have received news from Albania:[14] the inhabitants are protesting against the idea of being subjected to an Italian protectorate in a permanent way.

Lloyd George. The history of the Italian protectorate over Albania is rather curious. The Italians acted surreptitiously and unexpectedly. Afterward, they denied having established a protectorate over Albania.

Wilson. The Albanians are horrified at the idea of being subjected to Italy. I think they must be allowed their independence.

Lloyd George. I really don't know what they will do with it, if not cut each other's throats. Their independence will resemble that of the highlands of Scotland during the fifteenth century.

Wilson. Do not speak ill of the mountains of Scotland; it is my family's country of origin.

Lloyd George. It also seems to me good to acknowledge the old Celtic blood sometimes.

I insist again that in Asia we do not allow Italy to present us with a *fait accompli.* We must allow the Greeks to land troops at Smyrna.

[13] Concluded in April 1917 between Great Britain, France, and Italy, and subject to the assent of Russia, it stipulated that, in the event of the dismemberment of the Ottoman Empire at the end of the war, France would obtain the Adana (Seyhan) region, while Italy would receive the remainder of southwestern Anatolia, including Smyrna.

[14] The Delegates of the Albanian Colony of Turkey, the Albanian Political Party of America, the Albanian Colony of Rumania, and the National Albanian League of America to WW, May 5, 1919, TLS (WP, DLC).

Wilson. The best means to stop the Italian ventures is the financial means. The moment might come when we will tell them that, if they do not evacuate such and such a territory, they must not expect us to furnish them with the money necessary to maintain them.

Lloyd George. Have we ever prevented the Turks and the Balkan powers from making war, even though they have always suffered from lack of money? My opinion is that M. Vénisélos must be told to send troops to Smyrna. We will give our admirals instructions to allow the Greeks to land everywhere where there is a threat of troubles or massacres.

Wilson. Why not tell them to land now? Do you have an objection?

Lloyd George. None.

Clemenceau. I do not have any either. But must the Italians be warned?

Lloyd George. I don't think so. §

18. SIR MAURICE HANKEY read a letter he had received from Mr. Hughes, Prime Minister of Australia, in his capacity of Chairman of the Third Sub-Commission[15] of the Commission on Reparation enclosing a report presented by the Third Sub-Commission. The last paragraph of this report read as follows:

> "Under all the circumstances the Sub-Commission thinks that no useful purpose can be served by proceeding to make recommendations unless the Supreme War Council expresses a wish that it should do so."

Sir Maurice Hankey was authorized in replying to this letter to thank Mr. Hughes for his letter and report, and to state that as this aspect of reparation had been dealt with as part of the general discussions of the Supreme Council, it would not be necessary for the Sub-Commission to make further recommendations at present.

19. At the conclusion of the meeting a message was received from the Marquis Imperiali stating that the Italian Delegation could not arrive from Rome on the following day before 12 o'clock even if the train was punctual; as the Italian Delegation would wish to establish contact with the Allied and Associated Governments before meeting the Germans, he asked for a postponement of this meeting for twenty-four hours.

MR. LLOYD GEORGE pointed out that the Italian credentials had not yet been presented. He suggested that M. Pichon ought to ask M. Bonin whether he wished the Italian credentials to be presented.

PRESIDENT WILSON said it would be impossible to change the date

[15] That is, the Commission on Measures of Control and Guarantees.

of the meeting. The Italians were entirely responsible themselves for the delay in their return, and must take the consequences. He agreed with Mr. Lloyd George that M. Bonin should be asked if he wished the Italian credentials to be presented. Italy had left the Conference without any justification and no postponement was possible.

M. CLEMENCEAU agreed, and pointed out that the Italians could have returned earlier.

MR. LLOYD GEORGE agreed.

(It was agreed that M. Pichon should be asked to consult M. Bonin as to whether he wished the Italian credentials to be presented to the Germans.)

Just as the Meeting was dispersing the question was raised in the ante-room by Mr. Baker and Mr. Mair who were waiting there, as to the date on which the summary of the Treaty of Peace should be made public.

Sir Maurice Hankey consulted M. Clemenceau who was already in his Motor car, and President Wilson and Mr. Lloyd George who were in the ante-room, with the result that it was agreed that the summary of the Treaty of Peace should be published in the morning newspapers of Thursday, May 8th; that arrangements should be made to secure publicity simultaneously in all the countries concerned; and that no publicity should take place before that date.

(The question of publicity by wireless telegraphy was left to be decided when the Council of Three met in the afternoon at the Plenary Conference.)

APPENDIX I TO I.C.181.C.

(Translation)[16]

COMMUNIQUÉ

The President of the United States has addressed to M. Clemenceau the following letter:

(text of letter)[17]

The Prime Minister of Great Britain has addressed to M. Clemenceau the following letter:

(text of letter)[18]

The engagement foreseen in these two letters, for which legislative approval will be requested by the Governments, will be founded upon the following bases:

(1) Any violation by Germany of the engagements undertaken by her concerning the left Bank of the Rhine and 50-kilometre zone on

[16] From *PPC*, V, 485-86.
[17] Printed as Appendix II to the minutes of the Council of Four, May 6, 1919, 5:30 p.m.
[18] Printed as Appendix II below.

the right Bank (Articles 42 and 43 of the Treaty of Peace) will be considered by the signatories as an act of hostility against them and as calculated to disturb the peace of the world.

(2) The signatory (the United States in one case, the British Empire in the other) will immediately give its assistance to France, if any move of unprovoked aggression is directed against France by Germany.

(3) This agreement will be submitted for the approval of the Council of the League of Nations by majority vote.

(4) The agreement remains in force until the signatories consider that the League of Nations itself constitutes a sufficient guarantee.

APPENDIX II TO I.C. 181.C.

To MONSIEUR CLEMENCEAU, 6th May, 1919.

Président du Conseil de la République Française.

The stipulations relating to the Left Bank of the Rhine contained in the Draft Treaty of Peace with Germany are as follows:

(1) Germany is forbidden to maintain or construct any fortifications either on the left bank of the Rhine or on the right bank to the west of a line drawn fifty kilometres to the east of the Rhine.

(2) In the area defined above the maintenance and the assembly of armed forces, either permanently or temporarily, and military manoeuvres of either kind, as well as the upkeep of all permanent works for mobilisation are in the same way forbidden.

(3) So long as the present treaty is in force Germany undertakes to co-operate in any enquiry which the Council of the League of Nations, acting if need be by a majority, may deem necessary.

As these conditions may not at first provide adequate security and protection to your country, H.M.G. agree to ask Parliament to authorise a treaty with France by which Great Britain shall be bound to come immediately to her assistance in the event of any unprovoked movement of aggression against her being made by Germany.

The Treaty will be in similar terms to that entered into by the United States and will come into force when the latter is ratified.

The Treaty must be recognised by the Council of the League of Nations as being consistent with the Covenant of the League, and will continue in force until on the application of one of the parties to it, the Council of the League agrees that the League itself affords sufficient protection.

The obligation imposed under this Treaty shall not be binding on the Dominions of the British Empire until the Treaty is ratified by the Parliament of the Dominion concerned.

(Signed) D. LLOYD GEORGE.
ARTHUR JAMES BALFOUR.

APPENDIX III.

REPARATION.

Article 2.

ACTUAL TEXT.

The Allied and Associated Governments recognise that the resources of Germany are not adequate, after taking into account permanent diminutions of such resources which will result from other provisions of the present Treaty, to make complete reparation for all such loss and damage.

The Allied and Associated Governments, however, require, and Germany undertakes, that she will make compensation for all damage in accordance *with the definition contained in Annex I* hereto done to the civilian population of the Allied and Associated Powers and to their property during the period of the belligerency of each as an Allied and Associated Power against Germany by such aggression by land, by sea and from the air.

(*Article* 232 of the Treaty)

TEXT AS PROPOSED BY THE FRENCH DELEGATION.

(Approved by M. Clemenceau, President Wilson, and Mr. Lloyd George, 6th. May 1919.)

The Allied and Associated Governments recognise that the resources of Germany are not adequate after taking into account permanent diminutions of such resources which will result from other provisions of the present Treaty, to make complete reparation for all such loss and damage.

The Allied and Associated Governments, however, require, and Germany undertakes, that she will make compensation for all damage from the air *and generally for all damage* in accordance with the definition contained in Annex I hereto.

APPENDIX VI TO I.C.181.C.

Notes of a meeting held
at President Wilson's
house May 6, 1919.

The question having been raised as to the meaning of Article IV of the League of Nations Covenant, we have been requested by Sir Robert Borden to state whether we concur in his view, that upon the true construction of the first and second paragraphs of that Article, representatives of the self-governing Dominions of the British Empire may be selected or named as members of the Council. We have no hesitation in expressing our entire concurrence in this view. If there were any doubt it would be entirely removed by the fact that the Articles of the Covenant are not subject to a narrow or technical construction.

Dated at the Quai d'Orsay, Paris, the sixth day of May, 1919.

(Sgd) G. CLEMENCEAU.
WOODROW WILSON.
D. LLOYD GEORGE.

T MS (SDR, RG 256, 180.03401/145, DNA); Mantoux, I, 493-94, 494-95, 496, 497-98, 498-99.

From the Diary of Colonel House

May 6, 1919.

The main business of today was the meeting at the Quai d'Orsay and the reading of an abstract of the Treaty. As usual with these large meetings it was stupid beyond endurance, and I left with Wallace after an hour of it. A few minutes after it started, I sent a note to the President suggesting that the English translation be dispensed with. He got up, took my note to Lloyd George and Balfour who both agreed, and then Balfour went around the table to all the other English speaking delegates and obtained their consent to it. The President then announced the result to Clemenceau, who in turn instructed Tardieu who was reading the abstract in his monotonous way, to discontinue.

The President returned my note with the lines indicated drawn upon it which he intended to represent the setting of Tardieu's reading to music. While the meeting was in progress, the President whispered that he hoped I would see that Tardieu was not put on the Council of the League of Nations. He said he distrusted him and had caught him in two musstatements [misstatements] today. As a matter of fact, someone is prejudicing the President against Tardiue [Tardieu]. I have been trying to find out who it is. I suspect Jusserand and I also suspect Baruch, though I am not certain of either.

The President is the most prejudiced man I ever knew and likes but few people. I notice in the matter of appointments he seldom suggests friends of his own. In recalling appointments during his two administrations I can remember enthusiasm in regard to two only. One was Professor Fry[1] of Princeton for Ambassador to Germany, and again when he appointed his friend Thomas Jones on the Federal Reserve Board, the Senate refusing to confirm it.[2]

The President, Lloyd George and Clemenceau have worked assiduously since the President's return, and in the last few weeks they have worked intelligently. I wish to do them this justice. The only objection that could be raised, as far as I can see, to their present method is that it smacks too much of secrecy and autocracy. Nevertheless, one can never get things done just right, and if they had leaned in the direction I have indicated as desirable, they would probably have been less effective.

The President is still lacking in any kind of organization around him. I believe I can do more work in a day than he can do in a week for the reason that I have the very highest type of advisers and secretaries about me. If he had someone in his immediate entourage that measurably compared with the force I have, a tremendous burden would be lifted from his shoulders. The people with me, directly or indirectly, can do most of the things that come up better than I can do them myself or than the President could do them. He has never learned this lesson and, I take it, never will.

After I left the Plenary Session yesterday, Foch and the Portuguese Delegate and one or two others raised a disturbance.[3] I shall not go into detail for I take it the *Proces Verbal* will have covered their remarks. With Foch it is the trouble that has been brewing for a long while and of which I have spoken before.

[1] He meant Henry Burchard Fine, Dean of the Faculty of Princeton University.

[2] That is, Thomas Davies Jones. About this controversy, see the index references under his name in Vol. 30 of this series.

[3] He meant the Plenary Session of May 6, about which see n. 1 to the extract from the Grayson Diary printed at this date.

Hankey's Notes of a Meeting of the Council of Four[1]

I.C.-181D Quai d'Orsay, May 6, 1919, 5:30 p.m.

1. It was agreed that all belligerent Allied and Associated States should be present when the Treaty of Peace was handed to the Germans.

2. MR. HURST on behalf of the Drafting Committee reported that an important article had by mistake been left out of the final Draft of the Treaty. On the previous evening he recalled that the Drafting Committee had received a document purporting to come from M. Clemencau in substitution for the articles that they had drafted on this subject. He had taken this fresh draft to Sir Maurice Hankey, who had also been approached on the subject by M. Tardieu, and Sir Maurice Hankey had obtained a consent to it of Mr. Lloyd George and President Wilson at a very late hour. A new text had then been incorporated in the final Draft of the Treaty, but on examination it was found that the following important article had been omitted:

> "In case Germany violates in any way whatever the provisions of Articles 42 and 43, she shall be regarded as committing an hostile act against the Powers signatory to the present Treaty and as intended to disturb the peace of the world."

[1] The complete text of these minutes is printed in *PPC*, V, 491-95.

PRESIDENT WILSON pointed out that this draft differed slightly from the original draft which he had prepared. He handed the original draft to Mr. Hurst.

(It was agreed that Mr. Hurst should inform the Drafting Committee that this article was to be reinstated with the wording changed so as to correspond more closely to the original draft.)

3. With reference to the decision taken in the morning that the summary of the Peace Treaty should be published on Thursday morning in the Press of all countries, it was further decided that no radio telegraphic summary should be sent out before mid-night on Wednesday, May 7th.

(M. Tardieu undertook to communicate this decision to the Secretary General.)

4. MR. LLOYD GEORGE said the only difficulty arose about Togoland and the Cameroons in regard to which he was not personally well informed.

M. Clemenceau, with the consent of his colleagues, sent for M. Simon,[2] the French Minister of the Colonies.

MR. LLOYD GEORGE said in regard to Togoland, he understood the British had captured one half, and the French the other half. The French wanted the capital named Lomé. In regard to the Cameroons, the British and French had each helped to capture it. He did not know what arrangement had been reached but he understood that Lord Milner had made some arrangement.

In regard to the Pacific, he said he understood that the Mandates would be allotted as follows:

Australia should receive a Mandate of New Guinea, and the islands in the Bismarck Archipelago to the east of New Guinea.

New Zealand should receive the Mandate for Samoa.

The Japanese could receive a Mandate for certain islands north of the Equator.

PRESIDENT WILSON agreed in all the above.

MR. LLOYD GEORGE said having regard to the island of Nauru, some difficulty had arisen as the Governments of the United Kingdom, Australia and New Zealand all had certain interests. He suggested the best plan would be to give the Mandate to the British Empire which would arrange exactly how it would be dealt with.

PRESIDENT WILSON said that if a Mandate was once assigned it could not be handed over to one of the Dominions.

MR. LLOYD GEORGE said that the island was very valuable owing to phosphate deposits, and the United Kingdom, Australia and New Zealand were all interested in these.

PRESIDENT WILSON said that the policy of the open door would

[2] That is, Henry Simon, French Minister for Colonies.

have to be applied. He drew attention to Article 22 of the Covenant of the League of Nations, which provided for "equal opportunities for the trade and commerce of other members of the League."

MR. LLOYD GEORGE suggested that it was essential that the Mandatory should have the right to apply a tariff as this was the only method by which they could raise revenue.

PRESIDENT WILSON pointed out that the United States possessed islands in the Samoan group.

In assigning the German Islands to New Zealand, difficulties would arise if a tariff were applied.

(At this point, M. Simon entered.)

M. CLEMENCEAU asked M. Simon to state what arrangements had been made as regards Togoland.

M. SIMON said none had been written. The position was that the British occupied one part and the French another. He himself had been authorised by the French Government to discuss the matter with Lord Milner, and they had searched for a basis of agreement. It would probably suit both parties if the French part were joined on to Dahomey and the British part to Ashanti. The only railway was occupied by the British. He had asked Lord Milner to make a division which would be suitable to both countries and in regard to the Tribes. Lord Milner had then left for England, and the negotiations had been broken off at a time when, in his opinion, an understanding had nearly been reached.

In regard to the Cameroons there was complete agreement. The Cameroons he stated were divided by a mountain range, and he explained on a map how one part could be conveniently joined to Nigeria and the other part to French territory. He had agreed this with Lord Milner, and they had arranged their scheme to suit the Tribes.

MR. LLOYD GEORGE made the following proposal that France should become the mandatory for the Cameroons, subject to an arrangement between France and Great Britain for a readjustment between the Cameroons and Nigeria, this agreement being submitted to the approval of the League of Nations.

In regard to Togoland he understood that mandates were difficult. The country was cut into small bits, and it would be found that half of a tribe was under a mandate, and the other was not. He suggested that the principle of mandates should not apply in this case.

PRESIDENT WILSON thought it was difficult to avoid mandates under the Treaty Clauses.

MR. LLOYD GEORGE stated that the Treaty Clauses would merely hand over Togoland with the other former colonies to the Allied and Associated Powers, which would have a free hand to arrange for their disposal.

PRESIDENT WILSON agreed that the arrangement must be accommodated to the circumstances.

MR. LLOYD GEORGE proposed that M. Simon should before 11 a.m. on the following day prepare a scheme on the following lines:

Great Britain and France to make a joint recommendation to the League of Nations in regard to the division of Togoland. France to have a mandate for the Cameroons, subject to a joint recommendation which the British and French Governments would make to the League of Nations for rearrangement of the boundary between Nigeria and the Cameroons.

(The above was agreed to.)

(M. Simon withdrew, but shortly afterwards returned and asked that the portion of the Cameroons which the Germans had forced France to give up in 1819 [1911] should not be subject to a mandate.)

PRESIDENT WILSON suggested that this should be included in the joint recommendation.

(This was agreed to.)

5. PRESIDENT WILSON asked if any answer had been received to the invitation to Austria and Hungary to send representatives to Paris.

M. CLEMENCEAU said the Hungarian Government had fallen,[3] and no answer had been received. A message had been sent by the French Representatives in Vienna stating that an answer had been sent, but it had not yet been received.

6. At the end of the Plenary Meeting, which preceded this meeting, Mr. Lloyd George on behalf of Great Britain and President Wilson on behalf of the United States of America handed to M. Clemenceau an undertaking to come to the assistance of France in the event of aggression by Germany. (Appendix.)

APPENDIX I TO I.C.181.D.

To MONSIEUR CLEMENCEAU, 6th May, 1919.

Président du Conseil de la République Française.

The stipulations relating to the Left Bank of the Rhine contained in the Draft Treaty of Peace with Germany are as follows:

(1) Germany is forbidden to maintain or construct any fortifications either on the left bank of the Rhine or on the right bank to the west of a line drawn fifty kilometres to the east of the Rhine.

[3] In the wake of the advance of Rumanian armed forces to the east bank of the Tisza River less than eighty miles from Budapest, similar incursions into Hungary by Czech armies, and mounting internal economic and political problems, rumors of the imminent demise of the Hungarian Soviet Republic were common at this time. Actually, however, Béla Kun and the new People's Commissar for Defense, Vilmos Böhm, were just undertaking a *levée en masse* in order to rejuvenate the Hungarian Red Army, which would soon begin a successful offensive against the Czech invaders. See Mayer, *Politics and Diplomacy of Peacemaking*, pp. 734-49.

(2) In the area defined above the maintenance and the assembly of armed forces, either permanently or temporarily, and military manoeuvres of either kind, as well as the upkeep of all permanent works for mobilisation are in the same way forbidden.

(3) So long as the present treaty is in force Germany undertakes to co-operate in any enquiry which the Council of the League of Nations, acting if need be by a majority, may deem necessary.

As these conditions may not at first provide adequate security and protection to your country, H.M.G. agree to ask Parliament to authorize a treaty with France by which Great Britain shall be bound to come immediately to her assistance in the event of any unprovoked movement of aggression against her being made by Germany.

The Treaty will be in similar terms to that entered into by the United States and will come into force when the latter is ratified.

The Treaty must be recognised by the Council of the League of Nations as being consistent with the Covenant of the League, and will continue in force until on the application of one of the parties to it, the Council of the League agrees that the League itself affords sufficient protection.

The obligation imposed under this Treaty shall not be binding on the Dominions of the British Empire until the Treaty is ratified by the Parliament of the Dominion concerned.

(Signed) D. LLOYD GEORGE.
ARTHUR JAMES BALFOUR.

APPENDIX II TO I.C.181.D.

To MONSIEUR CLEMENCEAU 6th May, 1919.
Président du Conseil de la République Française.

The stipulations relating to the Left Bank of the Rhine contained in the Draft Treaty of Peace with Germany are as follows:

(1) Germany is forbidden to maintain or construct any fortifications either on the left bank of the Rhine or on the right bank to the west of a line drawn fifty kilometres to the east of the Rhine.

(2) In the area defined above the maintenance and the assembly of armed forces, either permanently or temporarily, and military manoeuvres of either kind, as well as the upkeep of all permanent works for mobilisation are in the same way forbidden.

(3) So long as the present treaty is in force Germany undertakes to co-operate in any enquiry which the Council of the League of Nations, acting if need be by a majority, may deem necessary.

As these conditions may not at first provide adequate security and protection to your country, I agree to submit to the Senate for its advice and consent, a treaty with France by which the United States of America shall be bound to come immediately to her assistance in the event of any unprovoked movement of aggression against her being made by Germany.

The Treaty will be in similar terms to that entered into by Great Britain and will come into force when the latter is ratified.

The Treaty must be recognised by the Council of the League of Nations as being consistent with the Covenant of the League, and will continue in force until on the application of one of the parties to it, the Council of the League agrees that the League itself affords sufficient protection. (Sgnd) WOODROW WILSON.

ROBERT LANSING.[4]

T MS (SDR, RG 256, 180.03401/146, DNA).

[4] There is a WWT outline with WWsh, a TC, and a CC of this letter in WP, DLC, and a TC in the D. H. Miller Papers, DLC.

From the Diary of David Hunter Miller

Tuesday, May 6th [1919]

After the meeting the President, who had gone to the other side of the room, beckoned to me and handed me a paper. I think the paper at that time did not have any writing on it. He told me that this was the note which had been signed by the British and that he would sign a similar note on behalf of the United States and asked me if I would have it gotten up, pointing out that it would have to be changed in some places, such as "H.M.G. agree, etc." I told him I would have it done immediately and I went to the office and prepared a similar note. Copies of this are in the files, although they are not carbon copies, only two of which were made. I took the note up to the President and saw him in his study. I explained to him just where the note had been changed. He agreed, although he wondered whether he would not have to do more than simply agree to submit the matter to the Senate. I told him that that was a similar engagement to that undertaken by the British and it bound him to do everything except exchange ratifications, in doing which the honor of the Government would be involved. He agreed with this and signed the note. He told me that Lloyd George had slipped in a paragraph into the British note about ratification by the United States and that he (the President) did not think Clemenceau had noticed it. He also said that he considered this practically an advance determination by the Council in place of the determination which they might make if there was such an aggression. I told him I agreed with this idea.

The President told me to get the note signed by Mr. Lansing and to deliver it to M. Clemenceau. In addition to this he spoke about the publicity and gave me a paper, which he said he had written out and had read to Clemenceau who had approved it.

It happened that as I left the Quai d'Orsay previously I had spoken to Philip Kerr, Lloyd George's secretary, and also to Ray Stannard Baker, and I had understood that the text of the note was going to be given to the press. The President said that he would prefer this statement to be given out only, and I told him I would try to arrange it.

Coming back, I stopped at the Majestic and saw Philip Kerr at the door. I showed him the original American note signed by the President. He said he did not want back the copy of the French note and he wrote in the names of Lloyd George and Balfour at the end of it.

Kerr said that he had agreed with Tardieu that simply this statement should be given out, and he agreed with me that that would be what the British and Americans would give out.

I left with the President a copy of the British note which had been made out at my office. I also left with him one of the carbon copies of the American note.

After stopping at the office to get some copies of the press statement made I went in to see Mr. Lansing and he countersigned the American note, and I left with him the other carbon copy of it.

I then went over to the Quai d'Orsay and as I was driving in met Dutasta driving out. I told him I wanted to see Clemenceau and he asked me to go around with him to the Ministry of War, which I did in his car, my own following. He took me up to Clemenceau's office and Clemenceau pulled the original British note out of his pocket and handed it to me, and asked me to read it to him aloud while he read the American note. There was only one other person present besides Dutasta. I do not know who he was and was not introduced to him.

I then went back to the office and wrote a memorandum for the President,[1] which I sent up to him.

Ray Stannard Baker came in and I gave him copies of the statement to be released when the Summary of the Treaty is released at six o'clock tomorrow, Paris time. This is what Kerr told me that he had agreed to with Tardieu and what I agreed to with him.

Miller, *My Diary at the Conference of Paris*, I, 293-95.

[1] It is printed as the second document below.

A Statement

[May 6, 1919]

In addition to the securities afforded in the Treaty of Peace, the President of the United States has pledged himself to propose to the

Senate of the United States and the Prime Minister of Great Britain has pledged himself to propose to the Parliament of Great Britain an engagement, subject to the approval of the Council of the League of Nations, to come immediately to the assistance of France in case of unprovoked attack by Germany. Woodrow Wilson

WWhw MS (F. D. Roosevelt Papers, NHpR).

A Memorandum by David Hunter Miller

6 May, 1919.

MEMORANDUM FOR THE PRESIDENT

After counter signature by Secretary Lansing the note was delivered by me to M. Clemenceau. At his request I read to him aloud the original British note while he read the American note. He asked me to thank you very much.

The statement prepared by you[1] is being released to the French, British, and American press at the same time as the release of the Summary of the Treaty. M. Tardieu agreed to this with Mr. Carr [Kerr], the Private Secretary of Mr. Lloyd George, and Mr. Carr agreed to it with me. A copy of the statement is transmitted herewith. David Hunter Miller

TS MS (WP, DLC).

[1] That is, the statement just printed.

To William Allen White

My dear Mr. White: Paris, 6 May, 1919.

I have delayed replying to your deeply appreciated letter of April 29th until I could report some progress in my effort to get the representatives of the press admitted to the meeting with the Germans. I have had a partial success at least, as you probably have learned, and do not feel that I can complain because I believe that forty-five (the number of newspaper men provided for) is really all that can be gotten into the room with dignity.

I want you to know how delightful it is to me to have won your approval and confidence. Somebody told me the other night of having heard a lecture by you in which you had made what he regarded as a most extraordinarily successful exposition of what I had been trying to do and of the movements of public opinion in connection with it, and I feel that I ought to thank you personally for what you have of course intended as a public service but it is necessarily also a great personal service to me by way of fortifying and forwarding the work I am trying to do amidst these mazes of difficulties over here. Cordially and gratefully yours, [Woodrow Wilson]

CCL (WP, DLC).

To Charles Prestwich Scott

My dear Mr. Scott: Paris, 6 May, 1919.

I cannot deny myself the pleasure of just a line to say how much good your letter of April 30th did me. I need such letters very much these days, and deeply appreciate the friendship which prompted yours, besides being immensely cheered by your favorable judgment. Cordially and sincerely yours, [Woodrow Wilson]

CCL (WP, DLC).

To James Cardinal Gibbons

My dear Cardinal Gibbons: Paris, 6 May, 1919.

I have received with the greatest interest your letter of April fifteenth[1] with regard to the Holy Places in the Holy Land, and will of course take pleasure in keeping the whole matter in mind in attempting to deal with the perplexing matters which concern Palestine. The information you give me about the Holy Places is novel to me, and I shall try to make myself acquainted with the problem in the most sympathetic way.

Cordially and sincerely yours, Woodrow Wilson

TLS (Baltimore Cathedral Archives).

[1] J. Card. Gibbons to WW, April 15, 1919, TLS (SDR, RG 256, 185.5137/112, DNA), requesting Wilson to use his influence at the peace conference to prevent the Greek Orthodox Church from encroaching upon the historic rights of the Roman Catholic Church in Palestine, particularly concerning Holy Shrines.

To Norman Hezekiah Davis

My dear Mr. Davis: Paris, 6 May, 1919.

Before I withdraw my approval from the Roumanian credit which you mention in this letter,[1] which I am temporarily returning, I wish you would read the enclosed papers which give a true account of an important matter. I feel bound to give aid to Roumania so far as I can in the methods outlined by General Bliss.[2]

Cordially and sincerely yours, [Woodrow Wilson]

CCL (WP, DLC).

[1] N. H. Davis to WW, May 2, 1919, TLS (WP, DLC). Davis stated that Carter Glass had asked him to request that Wilson withdraw his approval of the establishment of credits for $5,000,000 each to Rumania, Czechoslovakia, and Serbia.

[2] See the memorandum printed as an Enclosure with RL to WW, May 3, 1919.

To William Shepherd Benson

My dear Admiral Benson: Paris, 6 May, 1919.

No apology was needed for your letter of yesterday. I recognize the high sense of duty from which you are acting, and take very much the view of the matter that you do. While it was impossible to get the words that you and I desired into the Treaty, I do not yet at all despair of bringing about the same result, chiefly because I do not believe that the taxpayers of these countries will consent to bear the burden of a larger naval establishment.

Cordially and sincerely yours, [Woodrow Wilson]

CCL (WP, DLC).

From Henry Mauris Robinson

Dear Mr. President: [Paris] 11:45 a.m., May 6, 1919

I feel that I should report that up to this hour I have not seen M. Clementel or the new Minister of the Merchant Marine.[1] I have endeavored all morning to get an appointment, and they have tentatively named five o'clock this afternoon.

Inasmuch as you may want to discuss this with the Prime Minister before I can report the result of the meeting with M. Clementel, I would say that the percentages of the total net war losses of Allied and Associated Powers respectively are: Great Britain, 77.65; France, 6.75; Italy, 6.70; and the United States 3. And, if all enemy tonnage is pooled and shared on the basis of losses, France would receive 361,632 gross tons, while if each Allied or Associated Power keeps all tonnage now in her possession and on the basis set out in the agreement you have signed,[2] France would receive 328,598 gross tons, the actual difference being only thirty-three thousand gross tons as between the two methods. As is obvious, the loss to France by reason of Brazil's retention of ships is but 13,500 gross tons.

As I read the statement submitted by M. Clementel, it indicates a desire to open up the whole discussion again. And, inasmuch as we are in agreement with Great Britain whose interest is over 75 per cent of the whole and over ten times that of France, it would seem as though it was not becoming for France to raise any question in regard to this.

Very respectfully yours, Henry M. Robinson

TLS (WP, DLC).

[1] He meant the Commissioner for Maritime Transport and the Merchant Marine, who served under Clémentel, the Minister of Commerce and Industry. The holder of this office was Ferdinand Émile Honoré Bouisson. Bouisson had announced his resignation on May 4 in protest against the government's handling of the rioting in Paris on May 1. However, he soon resumed his office. *New York Times*, May 5, 1919.

[2] See the first of two memoranda of agreement printed at May 8, 1919.

Henry Churchill King to Edward Mandell House

[Paris] 6 May 1919.

From: Mr. King.
To: Colonel House.
Subject: The appointment of French members of the Commission on Mandates in Turkey.

My dear Colonel House:

It is six weeks tomorrow since I was asked to serve as one of the American members of the International Commission on Mandates in Turkey and, so far as I have been able to discover, the French members are still not appointed. It seems reasonable to ask that that delay should not continue. Weather conditions are fast getting unfavorable for the Syrian visit, and valuable time is being lost. The French might well consider, also, that this continued delay almost inevitably prejudices their case, and tends to drive the American Commissioners into the arms of the British.

In the interests of a just and wise settlement of the whole problem of the Commission, I sincerely hope that the French appointments may be promptly made.

Very sincerely yours, Henry Churchill King.

TLS (WP, DLC).

Sir Robert Borden to Sir Thomas White

Paris, May 6th, 1919.

X300. Secret.

At secret session of Plenary Conference to-day terms of Peace Treaty were made known. Enormous length of Treaty made any real discussion impossible within limited time available. Much to astonishment of all present Marshal Foch made strong attack upon dispositions of Treaty from military point of view. He declared that there was an entire absence of military safeguards and that France could only be secured by military occupation of Germany up to Rhine. His speech produced great sensation and at its close Clemenceau declared session adjourned. Subsequently Clemenceau engaged Foch in exceedingly animated conversation in Conference Hall. It was announced by French Government during secret session that President Wilson and Lloyd George had undertaken to recommend to their respective legislatures a Treaty guaranteeing France against unprovoked aggression by Germany. This announcement was made practically in terms cabled to you last evening. No further request has been made to us for adherence to any such Treaty and possibly it will not be made. After long fight we succeeded in eliminating from Labour Convention obnoxious clauses which prevented selection of Dominion representatives for place on governing body. President Wilson has acted extremely well in this respect as he overrode advice of his Labour experts. I also secured signed statement from Clemenceau, Wilson and Lloyd George removing any possible doubt as to qualification of Dominion representatives to be selected or named as members of Council under article four of League of Nations Covenant. Borden

T telegram (R. L. Borden Papers, CaOOA).

Frank Lyon Polk to the American Commissioners

Washington, May 6th, 1919.

1877. In response to inquiry for his views as to recognition of Omsk Government, Ambassador Morris replies as follows:

"May 3rd, 12 a.m. If Great Britain and France decide to recognize the Kolchak Government, I think we should do likewise and urge similar action by Japan. Unity of action in Siberia is more important than the character of the action taken. Frankly, I would prefer to see recognition postponed until the Kolchak Government shows more willingness to define its purpose and policy, and less subserviency to reactionary influence. If, however, the Associated governments decide that the general situation in Russia as a whole calls for recognition of Siberian Government, important that a statement will be first obtained from Kolchak and his colleagues defining their own position and the fundamental issues of the revolution, the land problem, the state of self-government, freedom of speech and uncensored communications and the calling as soon as practicable of a constituent assembly."

In this connection Stevens[1] at Harbin reports as follows:

"April 30th, 4 p.m. Reports from technical board. Anti-Siberian

Government has threatened (?) plan to stop transportation, weaken government railway men. I believe now is the psychological moment to extend some measure recognition Siberian Government, strengthen hands. Whatever it is there is nothing other than it in sight that gives promise of maintenance of order, failing which, unrestrained anarchy. Such action would greatly assist in restoration of American prestige, which is badly damaged."

The following telegram from Consul Caldwell[2] bears further on the necessity for a united policy on the part of the governments represented in Siberia: "278, May 5th, 7 p.m. Referring to my telegram No. 262, April 24th, 5 p.m.[3] and to General Graves' 281, May 4th,[4] contention of Omsk Government that if we are not actively assisting them we are hindering and I am convinced that American troops in Siberia acting under present policy are not only accomplishing no useful purpose, but are doing actual harm in tending to prolong the disturbed conditions. The time has come for us to either withdraw our troops or to actively support the Omsk Government, preferably the latter. If troops are withdrawn all foreign troops should go together, but it would be better to leave the field to the Japanese military, prejudicial as this would be both for Siberia and other foreign interests, than to continue as we are now. Support to Omsk Government should be given by all the Allies acting in unison and should not involve any use of military force beyond that which is already provided for in the railway agreement,[5] but in so doing it should be understood that we are supporting (following subject to correction) the Omsk Government which in its turn should be made to issue a definite statement as to calling a constituent assembly and certain other reforms. At the same time we should see that the various trouble making military leaders claiming to support Omsk Government in this district receive orders from that government prescribing proper conduct for forces and we should see that these orders are obeyed. This would checkmate support to these various factions, being given with the knowledge and consent of all the Allies and through the Omsk Government.

This of course necessitates a new declaration from all the foreign nations having troops in Russia which can be brought into line. This declaration should show that Allies support the Omsk Government in its endeavors to build up a real government through the methods set forth in the declaration of that government regarding constituent assembly referred to above.

This telegram has been written after consultation with, and has the full approval of, General Graves, as well as Captain Watts."[6]

To my mind these telegrams bear out opinion that all the governments concerned in the railway plan should recognize the Omsk

Government as a de facto government in Siberia and in such other parts of Russia as may now or hereafter be under its actual control.

Upon taking the oath of office Admiral Kolchak solemnly declared that the power conferred on him would be relinquished to the all Russian Government which would be created by a properly constituted constituent assembly.

Referring to your 1880 [1890], May 4th, 6 p.m.,[7] I am confident that if the Omsk Government were aware that recognition was at hand they would willingly issue a satisfactory statement providing for the convening of a constituent assembly or more constitutional means for ascertaining the will of the people at the earliest date when such a meeting would be practicable and also make adequate recommendations regarding the freedom of the press, of speech, and of meeting, and the safeguarding of private life and property and the observance of foreign obligations and undertakings. The recognition would of course be provisional upon such a declaration being made. Polk, Acting.

T telegram (SDR, RG 256, 861.00/605, DNA).

[1] That is, John Frank Stevens, head of the Inter-Allied Technical Board, which had supervised the Trans-Siberian Railway since 1918.

[2] That is, John Kenneth Caldwell.

[3] J. K. Caldwell to FLP, April 29 [not 24], 1919, *FR 1919, Russia*, p. 490. The significant portion of this telegram read as follows: "There is imminent possibility of American troops being forced into armed conflict with Russians, troops of Ivanoff-Rinoff or peasant Bolshevik bands or even both. Situation cannot be permanently improved without adoption of uniform policy by all Allied Governments. Support of Ivanoff-Rinoff, Semenoff, and Kalmikoff with arms, military supplies and money by . . . any one country without knowledge definite assent of other associated countries must be stopped and this cannot be effected here." The three Russian officers mentioned were Pavel Pavlovich Ivanov-Rinov, Grigorii Mikhailovich Semenov, and Ivan Pavlovich Kalmykov.

[4] Printed as an Enclosure with THB to WW, May 9, 1919.

[5] About which, see n. 4 to FLP to RL, Dec. 30, 1918, Vol. 53.

[6] Capt. William Carleton Watts, U.S.N., commanding the cruiser *U.S.S. Albany*.

[7] A.C.N.P. to FLP, May 4, 1919, *FR 1919, Russia*, p. 339. It read as follows: "There is a feeling here among some that it would be unworthy (*unwise*) to recognize the Omsk Government even provisionally because it seems to be a military dictatorship. If Koltchak were to take steps at once to summon a Constituent Assembly it might lessen opposition to some form of recognition. What are your views as to the possibility of inducing such action by Koltchak?"

Two Telegrams to Joseph Patrick Tumulty

Paris, 6 May, 1919.

Please ask Glass to advise me immediately the latest date he thinks it safe to name for the meeting of Congress.

Please assure the representatives of the steel and shipbuilding industries that I am giving a great deal of thought to what they say and shall hope to cooperate. Also please give same message to labor men concerned.[1]

Please say to the Committee of the Federation of Labor which cabled me about Sir Robert Borden's amended form of the labor clauses[2] that I really think they will find upon reflection that the view set forth by Mr. Robinson in his telegram to Mr. Hurley and Mr. Gompers is a true interpretation of what was done.[3] I would deeply regret any serious disappointment on their part in a matter to which I, like them, attach the highest importance.

Senator Harris just returning to Paris. Have arranged to see him. You can assure the Treasury people that none of us had any idea of consenting to a guarantee by the United States of the German bonds.[4] Woodrow Wilson.

[1] Wilson was here replying to JPT to WW, May 5, 1919 (second telegram of that date).

[2] Wilson was here replying to JPT to WW, May 2, 1919 (first telegram of that date).

[3] H. M. Robinson to E. N. Hurley and S. Gompers, T telegram enclosed in H. M. Robinson to GFC, May 5, 1919, TLS (WP, DLC), which reads as follows:

"[Paris] 3 May 1919

"Replying to cable from Oyster on behalf of Gompers dated May 1.

"While I would have preferred to have had the statement of the principles in text passed by the Commission retained there were certain of the principles that could not be assented to by certain of the Nations without the modifications contained in the Borden Preamble and concluding clause. We had a very considerable difficulty getting the outlines of the nine points set up.

"On your statement that 'Clause 1 as redrafted repudiates the American principle enunciated in the Clayton Act' I feel that I must entirely disagree and take the position:

"1. That there is no possible adverse effect on the Clayton Act and that as it appears in Borden's text it becomes the underlying principle upon which all the other principles enunciated as well as those that may be enunciated in the future rest. In my opinion the preamble and first clause combined constitute a complete declaration of the principles of the Clayton Act as a minimum to which the most unwilling of the Nations must subscribe.

"It is clear to me then that:

"1. No part of American labor legislation has been affected.

"2. The principle underlying American labor legislation has been accepted with the result that

"3. The American labor legislation as of today is accepted as the pattern for all the Nations to be arrived at from time to time by such individual nations as by reason of the limitations recognized in the original text proposed by the Commission, Paragraph 7, are not now in position to immediately enforce the Clayton law principle which however they do now accept as the goal of their striving."

[4] Wilson was here responding to JPT to WW, No. 90, May 2, 1919, T telegram (WP, DLC). Tumulty stated that he concurred in the views of Russell C. Leffingwell on "the possibilities of obtaining favorable action at the hands of Congress, in the matter of international guarantee of German bonds." R. C. Leffingwell to JPT, May 1, 1919, TLS (WP, DLC), reveals that Leffingwell believed that favorable action by Congress on any such proposal was a "political impossibility," and that he had so informed Norman H. Davis in a telegram sent about May 1. That telegram is missing in WP, DLC.

Paris, 6 May, 1919.

Please send following message to State Chairman Wolfe[1] of Texas.[2] QUOTE I am deeply interested, as every lover of the country must be, in the vote to be taken by the people of Texas on the twenty-fourth on the Constitutional amendment giving the women of Texas the right to vote, and take the liberty of expressing my confident hope that this exceedingly important amendment will be adopted. UNQUOTE. Woodrow Wilson.

T telegrams (WP, DLC).

[1] Manson Horatio Wolfe, cotton exporter of Dallas and chairman of the State Democratic Executive Committee of Texas.

[2] Wilson was replying to M. H. Wolfe to WW, May 2, 1919, T telegram (WP, DLC). Wolfe gave Wilson the details on the constitutional amendment repeated in Wilson's reply. "The friends of suffrage," Wolfe said, "would be gratified to have an expression from you as leader of the Democratic party favoring suffrage amendment."

From Joseph Patrick Tumulty

[The White House, May 6, 1919]

Glass away. Talked with him yesterday, when he said it was urgent that session be called for fifteenth. Tumulty.

T telegram (WP, DLC).

To Henry Mauris Robinson, with Enclosure

My dear Mr. Robinson: Paris, 6 May, 1919.

Will you not be kind enough, when you next communicate with Hurley, to say that my own judgment goes with the recommendation made in this cable?

Cordially and sincerely yours, Woodrow Wilson

TLS (WP, DLC).

E N C L O S U R E

Washington [May 2, 1919]

1831. URGENT. IMPORTANT.

For the President only. From Hurley.

"If the situation induced [indeed] is such that in your opinion it would be advisable to authorize our shipyards to build for France or Italy or other foreign account it would relieve the situation here. If you would grant the Shipping Board that authority, such building would of course in each instance be subject to the approval of the Shipping Board as regards the type of vessel, price, possible interference with American work, flag under which operated and liability to requisition in time of war. Should you approve this request no deliveries could be made for nearly a year and then but few deliveries. At some of the yards now building small ships there is considerable material, the nature of which could be used in construction for

France or Italy or South American countries. This would facilitate our disposal of these particular contracts which at the present moment are not a desirable asset to us because we have more ships of this type than their need. The Association of Shipbuilders which cabled you recently is unnecessarily alarmed about cancellations. No steps in this direction will be taken without your approval. Signed, Hurley." Polk, Acting.

T telegram (WP, DLC).

From the Diary of Dr. Grayson

Wednesday, May 7, 1919.

The President had an early breakfast and attended to a number of matters before the 11:00 o'clock meeting. He sent a cablegram to Secretary Tumulty directing him to give out a message from him (the President) to the effect that Congress will be called for an extra session on Monday, May 19th.

At 11:00 o'clock the Big Three met. They had no intimation that Orlando would be present, but while the meeting was in progress the Italian Premier made his appearance. They were all tremendously surprised,—so much so that every one seemed a bit embarrassed. This embarrassment was especially pronounced as they were discussing a matter of Italy and Greece at the time Mr. Orlando entered the room. It was a subject they did not care to discuss in his presence, so for a few minutes they all indulged in general conversation and talked over a number of matters at random about the Peace Treaty; and then decided to adjourn. Later on the three met at Lloyd-George's apartment, across the street, and concluded their discussion of the Italian-Grecian situation without the presence of Orlando.

It is interesting to note that when Orlando entered the room he walked in and took a seat in the chair which he had occupied before his departure for Rome. He sat down and joined in the meeting as naturally as if nothing had happened. The President told me this story apropos to Orlando's return:

A young boy imagining that he was dissatisfied with his home-life decided to run away from home. After he had been away from home for a while he discovered that he had no definite place to go, whereupon he returned to his home. Upon entering the house he found the family sitting around the fireside. He took his accustomed seat without saying a word. No one appeared to notice that he had even been away or that he had come back. Finally, the boy upon noticing the old black cat in the corner, said: "Well, the old black cat is still here." And so today Mr. Orlando found his vacant chair still here.

The President, Mrs. Wilson, Mr. Grasty and I had lunch at one o'clock. Grasty was speaking of the causes that won the war. He named two things for which the President was responsible and which took a lot of courage to put into effect. At the time the President gave the order to do these two things he was severely criticised. The first was for the barrage of the North Sea—the laying of the mines and nets. The second was the order for sending disorganized units to France instead of waiting to train an army in the United States and organize it into regiments, brigades and divisions. Grasty said these two decisions won the war. The first was called the big sea decision, and the second the big land decision. He said that he was in London when Admiral Sims received the order about the sea decision. The Admiral bitterly opposed it by saying: "The President is butting into naval matters that he doesn't know anything about." Grasty said: "Sims soon found out that he was mistaken." The President replied: "Sims is a good executive but he is poor in planning."[1]

Grasty told the President that it was really remarkable the way in which the American raw recruits who were sent over here developed what he (Grasty) termed "squirrel" sense. He said these men seemed to be able naturally to protect themselves both in the trenches and in the wooded sections where the fighting took place. The allusion to "squirrel sense" brought forth from the President the following story:

In Maine before they had prohibition there was a great enterprise in manufacturing a brand of whiskey which made one intoxicated immediately. The best known brand that accomplished this was the one known as "squirrel whiskey." A fellow in a local town after taking a drink or two of this squirrel whiskey developed a desire to travel. While this desire was uppermost a train pulled into the station, which he boarded. One of his friends missed him and discovered that he had boarded the train. They immediately wired the conductor, describing him as a man who had just boarded the train, who was drunk, and who did not know where he was going. They asked the conductor to put him off and arrange to have him sent back on the next train. The conductor wired back: "Impossible; there are several men on this train so drunk that they can't tell their names or their destination."

The President thought the general prospects for peace with the Germans were good. He said that the Germans would doubtless complain of the severity of the terms, but, considering everything, he thought they (the terms) were just. He said to me today that he

[1] For another view of the reasons for Sims' opposition, see Elting E. Morison, *Admiral Sims and the Modern American Navy* (Boston, 1942), pp. 413-17.

disliked very much seeing the Germans because the fellows who had been sent here as representatives of the German government are a job lot, and that it was difficult for him to take any interest in them one way or another. He then went on to say that von Bethmann Hollweg had invented the phrase "scrap of paper" (referring to the Belgian Treaty). This, the President said, greatly illuminated the innermost thoughts and fancies of the German statesman. Grasty interrupted by saying that he (Bethmann Hollweg) was a big scoundrel. The President replied: "Yes, but he was something more than that: he was a representative of the Junker type of the Prussian."

In speaking of Foch Grasty remarked that there is considerable comment around Paris to the effect that Foch is getting a swelled head. He used to be a popular, democratic, genial man, full of animation. He had seen him at the French military headquarters in the Ministry of War get down under a table in order to show you a war maneuver. Now, since people had begun to bestow praise upon him for winning the war, and telling him that he did it all, the praise has gone to the Marshal's head and caused it to swell up. Grasty said that he had seen a great deal of him from the very beginning of the outbreak of the war, and that he did not consider him a big man.

General Pershing called at 2:15 for a five-minute engagement with the President. Grasty asked Pershing what his opinion was of Foch, about whom we had just been speaking. The General replied that he was a good Generalissimo but that he did not have any plans during the war except to wait for the Americans.

After coming in contact with Lloyd George, Clemenceau, General Pershing, Marshal Foch and Mr. Balfour my impression is that the President is the best informed and the most skilled diplomatist in the European countries today. He knows the details of all countries and the philosophy of their governments as a whole. He allows himself to be angered by many of the things that come up at these conferences, but it is amazing how he can control his temper, especially after unearthing proof of deception and trickery of the men with whom he has been dealing here.

At 2:30 the President went to Versailles to attend the ceremony of turning over the Peace terms to the German delegates. He went unaccompanied by either Mrs. Wilson or myself. There had been so much discussion as to the accommodations at Versailles and as to who should be allowed and not allowed to go that he (the President) decided to take no one with him.

The proceedings at Versailles were extremely simple but they conclusively demonstrated the bitterness of the German feeling and they also showed that the President was entirely right when he described the German delegates as a mediocre lot. There was the usual crowd about the Trianon Palace Hotel, in the big dining-room of which the terms were handed over. French soldiers kept the people who did not have credentials entitling them to enter the building at a good distance from the structure. The President arrived at the Hotel about 15 minutes before three o'clock. Clemenceau and the British delegations had preceded him, and they stood in the main reception hall chatting together while the delegates who were entitled to be present came in. It was 2:50 o'clock when the President and Clemenceau headed the procession into the big oblong dining-room in which the delegates assembled. The room had been arranged practically as a duplicate of the Clock Room in the Quai d'Orsay, the tables having been placed to form a parallelogram along the sides of the room. Clemenceau, wearing his usual yellow gloves, took his seat at the head of the table with the President on his right and Lloyd-George on his left. As soon as all of the delegates had been seated Paderewski, the Polish President, living up to his dramatic training in the United States, attempted a spectacular entry. He stalked through the door at the end of the room, throwing his gray head far back, and essaying a dignified and diplomatic walk. The performance fell flat. Not two people in the room saw him, because just as he came through the door the German newspaper correspondents were escorted through the back entrance, and they proved more of an attraction than did the former pianist. Paderewski endeavored to save the situation by making an elaborate bow towards the front of the room, but even this did not carry inasmuch as at that very particular moment Clemenceau was telling a story to the President and Lloyd-George that apparently amused them inasmuch as they smiled broadly. Meanwhile, Paderewski settled down in his seat with a look of utter chagrin covering his features.

At 3:02 the chief usher of the French Foreign Office, in black livery, with silk stockings, and knee breeches, and wearing a heavy silver chain around his neck entered the room, followed immediately by the German plenipotentiaries. He announced them as "The Delegates Allemand." And they filed to their seats while the Allied and Associated Peace Conference Delegates arose to receive them. As soon as they were seated Clemenceau arose and delivered an address, after which he handed over to the Secretary-General of the Conference a printed copy of the terms and the latter transmitted them to the chairman of the German delegation. . . .[2]

It was a matter of sharp comment that the German spokesman (Brockdorff-Rantzau) failed to stand while he was delivering his ad-

[2] Here follows a transcript of the seventh Plenary Session of May 7, 1919; it is printed in *PPC*, III, 413-20.

dress. The British were inclined to assume that this was a studied insult. Men who watched the Count closely, however, were convinced that the reason that he did not stand up was that he could not. He was trembling violently when he entered the room and his hand fumbled with his chair before he finally took his seat. It was also noted that while he gripped the table with his elbows firmly to prevent his hands shaking, his knees were trembling during the entire time that he was repeating his speech.

On returning to the house the President told me of the afternoon's developments, and he (the President) mentioned these points: He said that it was very apparent that the chairman of the German delegation did not accept the situation as it existed. Rather he had snarled and failed to show the slightest sporting disposition. He plainly admitted that he knew that Germany had been whipped but it was also evident that he was desirous of placing responsibility somewhere else than upon the armies that had succeeded in accomplishing the task. The President also told me that the Count had snarled through his mention of the President's fourteen points, making a frantic endeavor to take advantage of those points from the German viewpoint. The President further called attention to the fact that the Count had devoted a good part of his speech to a discussion of the question of the Kaiser's responsibility and also of the disposition that was to be made of the German prisoners of War—two topics that were completely disposed of in the treaty terms, which had just been communicated to the Germans and which were not at that time known to them. It was just a case of having jumped at conclusions.

The President, Mrs. Wilson, Mr. Grasty and I had dinner at seven o'clock. After dinner the conversation drifted to the Italians. The President said that Mr. Clemenceau had shown him a poster in which the Italians claimed that they had won the war, making exaggerated and false statements. He also said that they had distributed posters designed to indicate that he (the President) was pro-German and picturing him in a Prussian helmet. The President laughed at it all and told an incident which took place at a meeting of the Allied War Council. The English were admonishing the Italians for not sending their fleet out, and the Italian Admiral replied that the Italian fleet had been very successful; that in comparison with the English fleet the English fleet had gone out and had lost a great many ships; the Italian fleet had remained in port and had not lost one ship. At this point General Bliss got up and left the Council, since questions were being discussed that he had nothing to do with. He excused himself and went out into the hall for a smoke. Someone remarked to him in the hall: "I understand that the Council is at sea over their discussion." "No, the trouble is," the General replied, "the Italians are a bunch of cowards and you cannot get them to go to sea."

Poincaré is very unpopular with the people of France. They regard him as a coward. During the early days of the war when Paris was in some danger of being seized by the Germans, Poincaré and Madame Poincaré sneaked out of town by a secret railroad station and did not let any one know of their departure. Ever since that the French people have had the feeling that he was a quitter.

Grasty suggested to the President that it was very important that he (the President) write a history of his administration, and especially of the war. Grasty said: "I would like to make you an offer to write one editorial a week for the Baltimore SUN, for which they would gladly pay you $25,000 a year. It would be a great thing for the paper and it would mean much to the country and the world to have expressions from you on current topics." The President said to him: "I am much obliged but I would not do it for $100,000 a year. When I leave public life I don't want to be under contract, as I have been all my life. I want to be free. I feel very much like the Irishman, who was asked what he would do if he had a million dollars: 'I would hire me a room in the best hotel in the town; I would leave a call every morning to be awakened at six o'clock and to be told to get up and go to work; then when the knock came on the door and I was told to go to work I would tell the man who called me to go to hell, I don't have to go.' " It was evident that Grasty was putting in a lick for his paper, and while his offer was nipped in the bud he could not help but laugh at the President's reply.

Hankey's and Mantoux's Notes of a Meeting of the Council of Four[1]

President Wilson's House,
I.C.-181E Paris, May 7, 1919, 11 a.m.

1. M. DUTASTA was introduced, and was given authority to issue one copy of the Treaty of Peace to each Delegation with a notice that it was strictly confidential.

2. M. DUTASTA was instructed with reference to paragraphs that had appeared in the Press, that no photographs were to be taken of the meeting with the Germans. Sketches, however, would be allowed.

§ Mantoux's notes:

[1] The complete text of Hankey's minutes is printed in *PPC*, V, 496-500.

M. Dutasta, Secretary General of the Conference is introduced.

Clemenceau. We still have to settle some details about this afternoon's session. A copy of the treaty will be given to each delegation.

Lloyd George. That almost amounts to the same thing as publishing the treaty.

Clemenceau. We will send each delegation a letter indicating that this communication is being made confidentially.

Lloyd George. So be it.

I read in the French newspapers that the French press would be accompanied by a photographer; we agreed among ourselves that photographers would be excluded.

Clemenceau. M. Dutasta asks if this exclusion extends to sketches.

Lloyd George. The objection is not the same, and besides, I do not see how we can prevent a journalist or any other person from sketching.

Clemenceau. Then no photographers.

M. Dutasta withdraws.

Lloyd George. I want to explain my position regarding the Irish from America,[2] who are asking to be heard by the conference. They came to see me at the time of their arrival in Europe, and I advised them to go to Ireland—not forgetting Ulster—and to see the situation for themselves. They soon jumped into the arms of the Sinn Feiners, took part in a great number of separatist and republican demonstrations, and worked with agitators of sedition to such a point that Field Marshal French[3] wanted to arrest them. At present, to my very great regret, it is impossible for me to receive them. §

3. SIR MAURICE HANKEY brought to notice a letter from General Botha, the Chairman of the Polish-Ukrainian Armistice Commission, asking for authority for the Secretary General to despatch the following telegram under the auspices of the Commission:

"Secretary of State, Stanislau-Tarnopol:[4]

Since the Ukraino-Polish negotiations have been commenced under auspices of the Peace Conference at Paris, warn High Command of our army to beware of every provocation of the enemy in-

[2] That is, Francis Patrick Walsh, Edward Fitzsimons Dunne, and Michael J. Ryan.

[3] That is, Field Marshal John Denton Pinkstone French, Viscount French of Ypres and of High Lake, at this time Lord-Lieutenant of Ireland.

[4] Tarnopol, or Ternopol, and Stanislau, Stanisławow, or Stanislav, both located near Lvov in the Galician section of the Ukraine, had been the successive seats of government of the so-called Western Ukrainian National Republic, later called the Western Province of the Ukrainian National Republic. It is not possible to identify the specific person to whom this telegram was addressed since all ministers in the Western Ukrainian government were called Secretaries of State. See Volodymyr Kubijovyč, ed., *Ukraine: A Concise Encyclopaedia* (2 vols., Toronto, 1963-71), I, 770-75.

structing the whole army to retain composure and dignity at any price during the negotiations.

Secretary of State
Dr. Paneyko."[5]

and in addition asking that general authority should be given to the Polish-Ukrainian Armistice Commission to authorise the despatch by the Secretariat-General of such telegrams as the Commission should from time to time consider necessary in connection with its duties.

PRESIDENT WILSON was in favour of the necessary authority being given.

M. CLEMENCEAU did not altogether like having telegrams sent before he had seen them, but said that he would agree with the President of the United States of America.

(At this point M. Orlando and Count Aldrovandi entered.)

(It was agreed

(1) That the Secretary-General should have authority to send the above telegram on behalf of the Polish-Ukrainian Armistice Commission.

(2) That the Polish-Ukrainian Armistice Commission should be given general authority to authorise the despatch by the Secretariat-General of such telegrams as the Commission should from time to time consider necessary in connection with its duties.)

Sir Maurice Hankey was instructed to notify the Secretary-General accordingly.

4. MR. LLOYD GEORGE said the situation in Russia was developing in a very remarkable manner, and would have to be dealt with soon. There had been a curious collapse of the Bolsheviks, and the British Cabinet were pressing for a decision. It seemed that Koltchak had made such progress that he might soon be in a position to join hands with the forces based on Archangel. On the other hand, it was possible that he might march direct on Moscow. This was M. Paderewski's view. Hence, in short time, the Allied and Associated Powers might be faced with a Koltchak Government in Moscow. According to information furnished by M. Tschaikowski[6] and M. Paderewski, Koltchak was simply a soldier and nothing more. Denikin was said to be pro-German or at any rate in the hands of a pro-German Chief of Staff. All this pointed to the desirability of imposing some conditions on Koltchak and Denikin before further supplies were fur-

[5] Vasil Paneyko, or Basil Paneiko, as it is sometimes spelled, Secretary of State for Foreign Affairs in the Western Ukrainian (Galician) government, headed the diplomatic delegation of that entity in Paris and was also a member of the delegation of the Ukrainian National Republic.

[6] That is, Nikolai Vasil'evich Chaikovskii.

nished. Koltchak's political programme was vague and indefinite, containing such items as "there must be land reform."

M. Paderewski was afraid of a very powerful military Russia developing under Koltchak.

M. CLEMENCEAU pointed out that M. Paderewski, like all Poles, was anti-Russian.

PRESIDENT WILSON suggested that we should demand a programme of reforms and insist that our continued support depended on its being adopted.

MR. LLOYD GEORGE said that he and General Wilson had both formed a very high opinion of M. Tschaikowski. He thought that his colleagues ought to see him. He was sent to Siberia by the Czarist Government owing to his liberal views, and was urging that the Allies should prevent Russia from becoming Imperial again. He himself feared that more than he did Bolshevism.

M. CLEMENCEAU was afraid of both.

PRESIDENT WILSON said Bolshevism must collapse, whereas an Imperial Russia might remain. There was nothing in the Treaty with Germany to prevent the Germans from forming a powerful industrial and commercial union with Russia. He asked what the assistance given to Russia consisted in.

MR. LLOYD GEORGE said arms and supplies.

PRESIDENT WILSON asked if they had been able to build up stocks.

MR. LLOYD GEORGE thought not. Koltchak's success was probably due to the fact that the Bolshevists had no coal or oil.

(M. Simon, the French Minister of the Colonies, entered.)

5. M. SIMON said that the document he had been asked to prepare required a very careful text, and was not yet ready.

MR. LLOYD GEORGE said he had telephoned to Lord Milner about the Colonies, and hoped to receive an answer that afternoon. In the meanwhile, he would ask M. Simon to consult with an official of the Colonial Office for whom he had sent in regard to an agreement which he handed to him. (Appendix.)

6. PRESIDENT WILSON said he had received a letter[7] from a gentleman who signed himself President of the Council and Minister of Foreign Affairs for Montenegro, claiming a place at the Conference in the afternoon on the ground that Montenegro had been an effective belligerent. He did not raise the question of his being present this afternoon, but he thought a decision ought to be taken in regard to Montenegro before the Austrian settlement was concluded.

(This was agreed to.)

§ Mantoux's notes:

[7] J. S. Plamenatz to WW, May 6, 1919, TLS (WP, DLC).

Wilson. I have a letter from the Montenegrins, signed by Mr. Plamenatz, who calls himself "President of the Council"; they ask for a seat at the Conference, as an allied and belligerent power.

Lloyd George. It is true that they fought on our side; but they certainly betrayed the Serbs.

Wilson. In any case, the question of the presence of the Montenegrins does not arise for today's session; it will arise when it is a matter of negotiating with the Austrians.

Lloyd George. We have never taken a decision about the position of Montenegro; I think we declared that she had the right to be represented at the conference, but we added that we did not know by whom she could be represented at the present time.

Wilson. My impression is that the Montenegrins have for some time been treated rather brutally by the Serbs. I commented about this to Mr. Vesnić; he answered me with accusations against the King of Montenegro, which might be perfectly justified, but which are beside the point in question. What must be known is what decision we will take about the subject of the participation of the Montenegrins in the negotiation of the Austrian treaty. §

7. PRESIDENT WILSON said that he understood that the Persians were much depressed at not being consulted in regard to the Peace Settlement. They said that their interests were not being considered.

MR. LLOYD GEORGE pointed out that the Austrian problem had not yet been discussed in any detail. When it was discussed, he wished the Council to hear what the representatives of India had to say, particularly in regard to Constantinople and the future of Islam. He thought that Persia ought then to be heard.

8. M. CLEMENCEAU reported that the Austrian Government had accepted the invitation to send a delegation. He then read a despatch from the French representative in Vienna,[8] somewhat in the following terms:

> "The Press Bulletin of Berne has announced that the Austrian Delegation will be called to Paris only in the second half of the month. The Minister of Foreign Affairs asks if this is correct. I replied that the Austrian Delegation must be ready to leave on Saturday evening. Will you let me know whether the date of arrival on the 12th is maintained. A difficulty has arisen as regards the selection of delegates. The Christian Socialists were a powerful political party and insist that the views of the Allied and Associated Powers should be met and that the Head of the Delegation should not be Dr. Klein, who is an out and out supporter of union

[8] Henry Allizé, a career diplomat who headed the French mission in Vienna.

with Germany. Hence, the exact composition of the Delegation cannot yet be indicated, although it will not exceed the numbers already indicated."

He then read another telegram from the Head of the French Mission in Vienna, according to which the Head of the British Mission[9] had asked to see him to ask if the arrival of the Austrian Delegates at Paris could not be postponed, and he had replied that his own instructions came from the President of the Conference, and he had no authority to discuss the matter.

MR. LLOYD GEORGE said he knew nothing of this, and gave instructions for enquiries to be made.

9. MR. LLOYD GEORGE said he did not see why the Austrians should be mixed up in the settlement with the Jugo-Slavs and other parts of the old Austrian Empire. He suggested that Austria should be told that the general settlement was our affair, and that as far as she was concerned, it was only proposed to draw her frontiers. No difficulty would arise about the frontiers between Austria and Italy. All the difficulties concerned Croatia and Italy.

PRESIDENT WILSON said he would like time to think this proposal over.

M. ORLANDO, in reply to Mr. Lloyd George, said that peace with Austria-Hungary could not be made, because there was now no Austro-Hungarian State in the sense that there had been before the war. Austria-Hungary having disappeared, could not become a High Contracting Party. What would take place, he said, was a general settlement of the boundaries of the new States and Austria was one of these states. Hence, it was necessary to determine the frontiers with other states at the same time.

MR. LLOYD GEORGE agreed, but could not see that Austria had anything to do with the boundaries of other States than those contiguous to her.

PRESIDENT WILSON said that as M. Orlando had indicated, the boundaries of all the states of Austria-Hungary must be made simultaneously, and a general settlement reached. The Czechs had fought for the Allied and Associated Powers, and the Jugo-Slavs had remained at war with them practically to the end. He thought the boundaries of the whole of the states must be settled together.

MR. LLOYD GEORGE suggested that a beginning had to be made somewhere. Why, he asked, should Austria starve because peace had not been made with Croatia. Bolshevism and difficulties of that kind would increase in Austria the longer the delay. There was no difficulty, he understood, between the boundary of Hungary and Croatia.

[9] Lt. Col. Sir Thomas Andrew Alexander Montgomery-Cuninghame.

PRESIDENT WILSON said the Peace Settlement could not be made so easily, namely, by merely cutting up the countries into bits.

M. ORLANDO suggested that the various negotiations should be carried out simultaneously.

PRESIDENT WILSON agreed, and suggested that every step should be taken as completely as possible in order that it might not transpire afterwards that there were no guarantees of the execution of the Treaty.

(The Meeting was then adjourned to the Offices of the Supreme War Council, after the Meeting with the Germans.)

APPENDIX I TO I.C. 181.E.

It is agreed that in the case of:

TOGOLAND. France and Great Britain shall make a joint recommendation to the League of Nations as to its future.

CAMEROONS. The mandate shall be held by France subject to a rectification of the Western boundary in favour of Nigeria—a recommendation as to the nature of the rectification to be made to the League of Nations by France and Great Britain.

GERMAN EAST AFRICA. The mandate shall be held by Great Britain.

GERMAN SOUTH-WEST AFRICA. The mandate shall be held by the Union of South Africa.

THE GERMAN SAMOAN ISLANDS. The mandate shall be held by New Zealand.

THE OTHER GERMAN PACIFIC POSSESSIONS SOUTH OF THE EQUATOR, excluding the German Samoan Islands and Nauru, the mandate shall be held by Australia.

NAURU. The mandate shall be given to the British Empire.

GERMAN ISLANDS NORTH OF THE EQUATOR. The mandate shall be held by Japan.

T MS (SDR, RG 256, 180.03401/147, DNA); Mantoux, I, 504-505, 506-507.

Hankey's Notes of a Meeting of the Council of Four[1]

I.C.-181F

Mr. Lloyd George's Residence,
Paris, May 7, 1919, at noon.

1. The Conference had before it the conclusions of a conference held in the Hotel Astoria, Paris, on May 6th, 1919. (*Appendix.*)

M. VENIZELOS said that a Greek Division could very well be sent from Macedonia; General Franchet d'Esperey had announced that the Greek Division was not required there.

MR. LLOYD GEORGE asked what troops Greece had immediately available to send to Smyrna.

[1] The complete text of these minutes is printed in *PPC*, V, 501-505.

M. VENIZELOS said the total was two divisions without weakening the position in Macedonia, but troops could not be spared from Thrace until Greek troops had been brought from Russia.

MR. LLOYD GEORGE asked how soon two divisions could be transported to Smyrna.

ADMIRAL HOPE[2] said that a transport had been ordered to carry one division as soon as possible from Salonika and Kavalla to Smyrna. At the present time, however, the ships were very much scattered and, at the moment, he could not say what ships could be made available in the Eastern Mediterranean, or how soon. Once the ships were assembled it would only take about a day to transport them from Salonika to Smyrna. In reply to President Wilson, he said he had no means of guessing how long it would take to assemble the ships. In reply to Mr. Lloyd George, he said that he was going back to London tomorrow and in a day or two would be able to let him know the exact position.

PRESIDENT WILSON suggested that in the meantime the divisions should be got ready.

M. VENIZELOS said that one division was ready now, and it was proposed that they should be embarked at the port of Leftera.

ADMIRAL HOPE said he understood that there was no heavy artillery attached to this division, only mountain artillery; in that case it could be embarked in the Bay of Kavalla, but heavy artillery could only be embarked from Salonika.

GENERAL WILSON, in reply to Mr. Lloyd George, said that, between Salonika and the Dardanelles, the Turks only had about three divisions. During the war the strength of the Turkish division had been reckoned at about 6,000 men but towards the end of the war they had died down to almost nothing. Of course, however, a division could be filled up.

M. VENIZELOS said that a Greek division comprised 9,000 rifles, and 16,000 of all ranks. He understood that many of the Turkish divisions were reduced to the size of a regiment.

GENERAL WILSON thought that probably there was no very formidable Turkish force in this region.

MR. LLOYD GEORGE suggested that the British ships at Smyrna might supply some information.

ADMIRAL HOPE doubted if they had any facilities for obtaining information as to the military forces.

GENERAL WILSON said that his news all came from Constantinople.

PRESIDENT WILSON said he supposed that the Armistice gave the Allies the right to send troops.

[2] That is, Rear Adm. George Price Webley Hope.

M. VENIZELOS said that more than 30,000 Greek citizens in the town of Smyrna were in danger from the Turks.

PRESIDENT WILSON said that this provided a very strong reason for protecting them.

GENERAL WILSON said that it was true the Allies had power to land troops, but the Italians also had the right.

M. VENIZELOS pointed out that the Italians had landed in Adalia without consulting the Allies.

PRESIDENT WILSON said that if Greek troops were sent, the Italians could hardly land troops unless they intended to break with the Allies.

GENERAL WILSON raised the question of the command of the troops. He understood that the Greek divisions were to come away from the command of General Franchet d'Esperey without being placed under the command of General Milne[3] or any other Allied commander. They would constitute an allied force under Greek command.

M. CLEMENCEAU, PRESIDENT WILSON, and MR. LLOYD GEORGE agreed in this.

PRESIDENT WILSON raised the question as to whether the Turkish Government ought to be warned of the intention to land troops.

M. VENIZELOS thought that they ought, but only just before the landing took place. He, himself, knew the Turks well and he thought that if they received no warning, except just before the event, no resistance would be offered. Of course, however, there were some risks. All the facilities for landing were available.

MR. LLOYD GEORGE asked whether there was not a danger that the Commander of the Fort would fire on the Greek ships when the landing began.

M. VENIZELOS said that the danger would be of their firing from the forts when the ships were entering the Gulf of Smyrna.

PRESIDENT WILSON thought that they would not fire on the transports.

M. VENIZELOS agreed that they probably would not fire, if the transports were convoyed.

M. CLEMENCEAU suggested it would be safer to warn the Turks.

PRESIDENT WILSON agreed that this would undoubtedly be the correct procedure. But if the Turks were warned too far in advance they would make preparations. He suggested that no communication should be made to the Turks until the troops were on board.

MR. LLOYD GEORGE asked if M. Venizelos had warned the Greeks to keep the matter quiet.

M. VENIZELOS said he had taken all possible measures with this

[3] That is, Lt. Gen. Sir George Francis Milne.

object. All available Greek ships were being collected but they were mostly very small. It would be necessary to crowd the ships very closely but Greek soldiers would not object to this. The ships should be dispatched as soon as possible.

MR. LLOYD GEORGE, summing up the conclusions of the meeting, said that:

1. Admiral Hope was to proceed to England to ascertain all details about the number of ships available for transport and the time required; to give orders for the concentration of these ships at Salonika; and to inform him as soon as possible of the results of his mission.
2. M. Venizelos was to collect as many Greek transports as possible at Kavalla, and to arrange for the troops to be ready to embark.

M. VENIZELOS said that one division was sufficient to start with.

M. CLEMENCEAU, in reply to Mr. Lloyd George, said that General Franchet d'Esperey already knew of the expedition. He asked if anything was to be said to the Italians.

MR. LLOYD GEORGE was reminded by Sir Maurice Hankey that Admiral Calthorpe,[4] who was at the same time the British Naval Commander-in-Chief in the Mediterranean and Diplomatic Representative at Constantinople, had repeatedly insisted on the importance of his being informed whenever any redisposition of troops was made in the Eastern Mediterranean. He had, for example, complained of not being informed when the Italian battalion was sent to Konia. The reason for this was that he wished to be able to make such dispositions as might be necessary to safeguard against the reaction of these movements in other parts of Turkey.

MR. LLOYD GEORGE said that the fewer people who were informed, the better.

ADMIRAL HOPE said that Admiral Calthorpe must be told, as he was Commander-in-Chief of the Mediterranean Fleet. He suggested that this should be done by the Secretary of State for Foreign Affairs.

PRESIDENT WILSON suggested that Admiral Calthorpe should be cautioned as to the great importance of secrecy.

M. VENIZELOS said that it would be extremely difficult to keep the matter secret as the concentration of ships would soon become known.

(The Meeting then adjourned.)

SECRET. APPENDIX.

CONCLUSIONS of a Conference held in Hotel Astoria, Paris, at 4:30 p.m., 6th May, 1919.

[4] Adm. Sir Somerset Arthur Gough-Calthorpe.

PRESENT.

M. Veniselos, Admiral Hope, General Belin,
General Bliss, General Sir H. Wilson.

1. The Supreme Council having agreed to the immediate despatch of Greek troops to SMYRNA and the occupation of that town by purely Greek forces, we decided:

(a) To notify General Franchet d'Esperey.
(b) To order one Greek division to prepare to embark at SALONIKA.
(c) To order a second Greek Division to get ready.
(d) To collect transport for the move of one Division as rapidly as possible.
(e) To examine what steps may be necessary to safeguard the journey.
(f) To take steps to keep up the necessary communication between GREECE and SMYRNA.

2. We are of opinion that these troops are under Greek Command and in no sense under International Command except possibly during the sea-transit.

3. We are of opinion that if the Turks or the Italians or both oppose a landing we shall find ourselves in face of a difficult problem and we draw attention to this possibility.

4. We presume the Italian and Turkish Governments will be informed as we are not sure whether such action is covered by the Armistice Terms.

T MS (SDR, RG 256, 180.03401/148, DNA).

Remarks at a Plenary Session by Count Ulrich von Brockdorff-Rantzau

Gentlemen, [May 7, 1919]

We are deeply impressed with the lofty character of the task which has brought us together with you, namely, to give the world a speedy and enduring peace. We cherish no illusions as to the extent of our defeat—the degree of our impotence. We know that the might of German arms is broken. We know the force of the hatred which confronts us here, and we have heard the passionate demand that the victors should both make us pay as vanquished and punish us as guilty.

We are required to admit that we alone are war-guilty; such an admission on my lips would be a lie. We are far from seeking to exonerate Germany from all responsibility for the fact that this world war broke out and was waged as it was. The attitude of the former German Government at the Hague Peace Conferences, their actions and omissions in the tragic twelve days of July, may have contributed to the calamity, but we emphatically combat the idea that Germany, whose people were convinced that they were waging a defensive war, should alone be laden with the guilt.

None of us will wish to assert that the calamity dates only from the fateful moment when the Heir to the throne of Austria-Hungary fell a victim to the assassin's hand. During the last fifty years the imperialism of all European States has chronically poisoned the international situation. The policy of retaliation and that of expansion, as well as disregard of the right of peoples to self-determination, contributed to the disease of Europe, which reached its crisis in the world war. The Russian mobilisation deprived statesmen of the possibility of effecting a cure and placed the decision in the hands of the military authorities.

Public opinion in all the countries of our adversaries is echoing with the crimes which Germany is alleged to have committed during the war. Here, again, we are ready to acknowledge wrong which has been done. We have not come here to belittle the responsibility of the men who conducted the war politically and economically, and to disown breaches of international law which have been actually committed. We repeat the declaration which was made in the German Reichstag at the beginning of the war: wrong has been done to Belgium and we wish to redress it.

Moreover, as regards the method of conducting the war, Germany was not alone at fault. Every European nation knows of deeds and persons on whose memory their best citizens are reluctant to dwell. I do not wish to answer reproaches with reproaches, but if it is from us that penance is demanded, then the Armistice must not be forgotten. Six weeks passed before we obtained it, and six months before we learnt your conditions of Peace. Crimes in war may not be excusable, but they are committed in the struggle for victory, in anxiety to preserve national existence, in a heat of passion which blunts the conscience of nations. The hundreds of thousands of non-combatants who have perished since the 11th November through the blockade were killed with cold deliberation, after victory had been won and assured to our adversaries. Think of that, when you speak of guilt and atonement.

The measure of the guilt of all participants can only be determined by an impartial enquiry by a neutral Commission, before which all the principal actors in the tragedy should have their say, and to which all records should be disclosed. We have demanded such an enquiry and we repeat the demand.

Though we stand alone at this Conference, without allies, and confronted by our numerous adversaries, yet we are not defenceless. You yourselves have brought us an ally: Justice, which was guaranteed to us by the agreement relating to the bases of Peace.

Between the 5th October and 5th November, 1918, the Allied and Associated Governments abandoned the idea of a peace of violence and inscribed the words "Peace of Justice" on their banner. On the 5th October, 1918, the German Government put forward the principles of the President of the United States of America as a basis of Peace, and was informed on the 5th November by Mr. Lansing, Secretary of State, that the Allied and Associated Powers had accepted this basis with two specific reservations. President Wilson's principles therefore became binding upon both belligerent parties—upon you as well as upon us, and also upon our former allies.

These principles taken individually demand of us grievous national and economic sacrifices; but the sacred and fundamental rights of all nations are protected by this agreement. The conscience of the world is behind it; no nation will be permitted to violate it with impunity.

On this basis you will find us prepared to examine the Peace Preliminaries which you lay before us, with the fixed purpose of sharing with you the common task of rebuilding that which has been destroyed, of righting the wrongs that have been done, first and foremost the wrong done to Belgium, and of pointing mankind to new goals of political and social progress. In view of the bewildering number of the problems which beset the fulfilment of our common purpose, we ought to refer the principal questions individually at the earliest possible moment to special Commissions of experts, for discussion on the basis of the draft presented by you. In this connection it will be our chief task to build up anew the shattered human energy of the nations concerned, by international protection of the life, health, and liberty of the working classes.

I consider our next aim to be the restoration of the territory of Belgium and Northern France, which were occupied by us and devastated by the war. We solemnly accepted the obligation to do this, and are determined to carry it out to such extent as may be agreed upon between us. To do this we are thrown back on the co-operation of our former adversaries. We cannot complete the task without the technical and financial participation of the victors; you can only carry it through with our aid. It must be the desire of impoverished Europe that reconstruction should be carried out as successfully and economically as possible. This desire, however, can only be fulfilled by means of a clear and businesslike understanding in regard to the best methods. The worst method would be to continue to have the work done by German prisoners of war. Such labour is certainly cheap. It would, however, cost the world dear, if hate and despair were aroused in the German people at the thought of their captive sons, brothers, and fathers continuing to languish in their former bondage after the Peace Preliminaries. We can attain to no enduring Peace without the immediate settlement of this question, which has dragged on far too long already.

Our experts on both sides will have to study how the German people can best meet its obligation of financial reparation without breaking down under the heavy load. Such a collapse would deprive those entitled to compensation of the advantages to which they have a claim, and would entail irreparable confusion in European economic existence as a whole. Both victors and vanquished must be on their guard against this threatening danger and its incalculable consequences. There is only one way of warding it off: unreserved recognition of the economic and social solidarity of peoples, of a free and comprehensive League of Nations.

Gentlemen, the lofty conception that the most terrible calamity in the history of the world should bring about the greatest advance in human progress has been formulated and will be realised. If the goal is to be attained, if the slain in this war are not to have died in vain, then the portals of the League of Nations must be thrown open to all peoples of good will.

The German nation is earnestly prepared to accommodate itself to its hard lot, provided the foundations agreed upon for peace remain unshaken. A Peace which cannot be defended in the name of justice before the whole world would continually call forth fresh resistance. No one could sign it with a clear conscience, for it would be impossible of fulfilment. No one could undertake the guarantee of fulfilment which its signature would imply.

We will examine the document submitted to us with all good will, and in the hope that the final result of our meeting can be subscribed by us all.

Printed in *Peace Congress (Versailles) Protocol No. 1* . . . (SDR, RG 256, 180.0201/9, DNA), pp. 5-7.

Sir Robert Borden to Sir Thomas White

Paris, May 7th, 1919

X.304. The trees practically in full leaf and the glorious weather of an early summer day gave a fine setting to the arrival of the Allied Plenipotentiaries at Versailles this afternoon. No places were vacant as Signor Orlando and Baron Sonnino, looking cheerful and smiling, took their seats with the other Allied Plenipotentiaries. The Prime Minister of France held an informal reception before the session opened, and many of the Delegates surrounded Marshal Foch, active and alert as ever, notwithstanding the tremendous burdens which he has carried for nearly five years. Promptly at three o'clock the Allied Plenipotentiaries took their places. Sir Robert Borden sat next to the Delegation from the United Kingdom and with him was Mr. Sifton. At five minutes past three the German Delegates entered, preceded by a French Officer, who announced them. They were, Brockdorff-Rantzau, Lansberg, Giesberts, Leinert, Schücking and Melchior. They were accompanied by three principal Secretaries or experts, Von Stockhammern,[1] Dr. Simons and Dr. Von Haniel. The Allied Plenipotentiaries arose as a matter of courtesy when the Germans entered and then all were seated. Without delay, M. Clemenceau addressed them. On his right was President Wilson and on his left was Mr. Lloyd George. He spoke very briefly, declaring that it was not a time to use superfluous words. Germany had cruelly and wantonly brought this war upon the Allied Powers and upon the world. The German Government desired Peace. Here were the Plenipotenitaries of the Allied Nations prepared to make peace with them. The conditions of peace were set forth in a volume which would be delivered to the German Delegates and for consideration of its terms a reasonable time would be allowed to them. Within a maximum period of fifteen days or as much earlier as they desired the Germans must present in French and English, their written observations on the whole of the Treaty, the headings of which are as follows: League of Nations, Geographical frontiers of Germany, Political clauses for Europe: Belgium, Luxemburg, Sarre, Alsace-Lorraine, Austria, Czecho-Slovachia, Poland and Eastern Prussia, Denmark, Helgoland, clauses concerning Russia and the Russian States, recognition of new European States. Political clauses for countries outside Europe: General clause of renunciation colonies Siam, Liberia, Morocco, Egypt, Turkey and Bulgaria, Shantung. Military, naval and aerial clauses, War prisoners, Responsibilities and penalties, Reparations and restitutions, Financial clauses, Economical clauses, Ports, Waterways, rivers and railways, Aerial navigation, Organisation of Labour, Guarantees and occupation of territories. Final clauses, Execution of the armistice, end of the war, state of Peace. The Germans would be entitled to send their reply on particular headings of the Treaty or to ask questions in regard to them. After having examined any observations presented by the German Plenipotentiaries, the Supreme Council of the Allied Nations would send their answers in writing to the German Delegates and determine the period within which a final definite answer must be given by them. If the Germans desired information on any particular point or question it would be afforded without unnecessary delay. Finally the Germans would be treated with the courtesy which was the privilege of civilized nations. The speech of M. Clemenceau was translated first into English and then into German. Count Brockdorff-Rantzau then read a carefully prepared speech which is said to be substantially the same as one which he delivered not long since in the German Parliament at Weimar. The fact that he remained seated during its delivery occasioned surprise and not a little irritation among the Allied Plenipotentiaries, some of whom desired M. Clemenceau to direct that the speaker should rise. This however was not done and possibly the apparent discourtesy of Count Brockdorff-Rantzau was due to his highly nervous condition which has greatly impressed those who have met him in making the arrangements for today's conference. He is a tall spare thin lipped man of the Prussian junker type with a harsh metallic voice. His speech was delivered in German and translated first into French and then into English. Two interpreters were brought for this purpose with the German Delegation. The English translation was not very good but the French somewhat better. It is believed that the speech of Count Brockdorff-Rantzau was designed for effect in Germany, Neutral Countries and the United States. Summarized its principal points were as follows. He admitted that the policy of the late German Government had contributed to the war but he urged that there were other causes among which he named the imperialistic policy as he termed it, of all the European States during recent years. Further he admitted that the Germans had sinned in their methods of conducting the war but he contended that there was default in this respect among the Allied Nations as well and that the maintenance of the blockade since the armistice had resulted in death and suffering in Germany. He declared the willingness of Germany to make reparation for the wrong done to Belgium and for the devastation wrought by the German forces in France. The Germans could only make reparation with the assistance and co-operation of the Allied Nations. It was cruel to detain German prisoners and to compel them to work like slaves since the armistice. Germany had consented to make peace upon the terms proposed by President Wilson and she will accept terms of peace so far as they conform to the principles thus laid down as modified by the proposals of the Allies in agreeing to an armistice. He enlarged on the advantages of a League of Nations and made references to Germany's intense desire to improve the conditions of workingmen throughout the world. One of the Allied Plenipotentiaries observed that the speech might also be construed as suggesting that the improvement of conditions of the labouring classes throughout the war was the chief motive with which Germany had undertaken the war. The speech throughout was full of high sounding phrases and its frequent abruptness in tone was somewhat heightened by the imperfect English translation. On the whole the speech made a distinctly unfavourable impression upon those who heard it. Its effect strengthens the impression that as the Germans were at the commencement of the war, so are they still, if the spirit of a Prussian junker fairly represents that of the German people. As to this there is of course grave doubt. The clumsy attempts throughout the latter part of the speech to appeal to President Wilson were not regarded as either well designed or effective.

In short the chief German Plenipotentiary exhibited the characteristic German inability to comprehend the mind or spirit of other nations. Even bearing this in mind the speech was regarded as foolishly irritating and provocative. At its close M. Clemenceau inquired whether any of the German Plenipotentiaries desired to be heard and upon receiving a reply in the negative declared the session closed. And so the curtain rang down upon the first scene of the last Act of the terrible drama which has occupied the world's stage for nearly five years. Borden.

T telegram (R. L. Borden Papers, CaOOA).

[1] Franz Edler von Stockhammern, Director of the Economic Division of the German Foreign Office.

From the Diary of Colonel House

May 7, 1919.

I started for Versailles shortly after two o'clock. I drove very rapidly and made what is usually a forty to forty-five minute trip in a half hour. Clemenceau and a few others were already there. Balfour soon followed with the other members of the British Delegation. Orlando and Sonnino came in shortly after and I suggested to Balfour that we walk down the hall to meet them. This seemed to please the Italians very much.

Everyone was seated in the room where the Treaty was to be presented promptly by three o'clock except Paderewski, who, as usual, came in late. He evidently cannot get it out of his head that he is not giving one of his great concerts in which the audience is always supposed to be seated before he enters.

After we were seated, the Germans were notified and were brought in by Col. Henry. We all arose when they entered, an action I was glad to see. Clemenceau made a speech of a few minutes. He did it in his usual composed though energetic fashion. The translation however into English and Germans [German] was badly done. Mantoux was evidently nervous and his English was poor. The French officer who undertook to put it into German also did badly. Much to our surprise, Brockdorff-Rantzau began to read a long reply. Clemenceau stood when he delivered his address, but Rantzau remained seated. White and I wondered whether it was not because he was too nervous to stand steadily upon his feet. When White went last Thursday to see their credentials, he said he never saw a greater exhibition of nervousness in a diplomat; that his knees literally knocked together, and White thought that he might at any moment faint.

The speech he made in reply to Clemenceau's was an able one but it seemed to me out of place. If I had been in his position I should have said: "Mr. President, and gentlemen of the Congress: War is a great gamble; we have lost and are willing to submit to any reasonable terms."

After Brockdorff-Rantzau had delivered his speech, Clemenceau asked if there was anything else to say; Rantzau replied in the negative, and Clemenceau then declared the Congress adjourned. The Germans went out in advance, and the balance broke up into groups to discuss the occasion together. I congratulated both Lloyd George and Clemenceau, particularly Clemenceau, and told him that it was a great hour not only for France but for him. He showed some emotion and, as usual, patted me on the shoulder and said to the President who was standing by, "This is our great friend. You will not mind my saying so."

I took out two of my secretaries, Arthur Hugh Frazier[,] and Major Stephen Bonsal. Soldiers were stationed at different intervals all the way from St Cloud to Versailles, some of them holding red flags to stop automobiles that were not expected at the Congress. While all the Delegates had tickets of admission and laissez-passer, no one stopped our car. I have been here so long and so many times I suppose I was easily recognized.

To Raymond Poincaré

My dear Mr. President: Paris, 7 May 1919.

M. Clemenceau was kind enough to hand me your letter of April 28th concerning the occupation of the Rhine territory, and I have retained it for a few days in order to give it full consideration. I have already heard several times a very impressive argument from the same point of view from Marshal Foch,[1] and along with my colleagues had again and again considered the highly important matter upon which you dwell, but it was of course my duty at your request to consider it once more, as I have faithfully done. As in every other matter of such gravity there are, I realize, two sides to this question and it is exceedingly difficult to be sure that one has properly weighed them against one another, but after repeated consideration of this matter I am convinced that it would not be wise to go further than we have gone in the Treaty in respect to the occupation of the Rhine territory.

Thanking you for setting the matter so fully and carefully forth,

Sincerely yours, [Woodrow Wilson]

CCL (WP, DLC).

[1] See the memorandum of January 10, 1919, by F. Foch, printed as an Enclosure with F. Foch to WW, March 14, 1919, Vol. 55; Foch's memorandum printed at March 31, 1919; and the minutes of the Council of Four printed at March 31, 1919, 3 p.m., Vol. 56.

From Robert Lansing

Dear Mr. President: Paris, May 7, 1919.

I am sending you enclosed herein copies of two telegrams received today from Peking showing that a rather serious situation has been created in China by the report of the decision made with regard to Japanese claims in Shantung Province.[1]

Faithfully yours, Robert Lansing

TLS (WP, DLC).

[1] There were actually three telegrams from Paul S. Reinsch, dated May 1, 2, and 3, 1919. That of May 1 was embodied in FLP to A.C.N.P., May 5, 1919, No. 1861; those of May 2 and 3 were included in FLP to A.C.N.P., May 5, 1919, No. 1862; T telegrams (WP, DLC). Reinsch's telegram of May 1 stated that the Peking government had received a dispatch from Paris outlining the decision of the peace conference upon the Shantung problem but that he considered it to be fraudulent since he believed it "impossible to conceive" that the five Allied and Associated Powers could have imposed such an unjust settlement upon China. In his telegram of May 2, Reinsch conceded that the dispatch from Paris was authentic. He commented as follows: "People and officials are deeply depressed and feel utterly helpless in the presence of this negation of their fundamental rights and the approval of the most iniquitous, ruthless and corrupt acts of aggression. The acting Minister of Foreign Affairs [Ch'en Lu] states that the Government does not see how it can accede to a treaty sanctioning such spoliation. They are about to instruct the delegation not to sign, although they fear reprisals, as they are now at the mercy of the Japanese military gang. They fear a great national uprising, in universal popular indignation and despair." Reinsch warned that the proposed Shantung settlement might create "a violent anti-foreign movement" in China. If Japan's aggressive policy toward China received the sanction of the western powers, Japan would obtain "such dominant prestige in Asia" that, within a few years, she "would become a serious menace to even the greatest power." Reinsch's telegram of May 3 reported as follows: "There is great excitement among the people particularly at Peking, Shantung and Shanghai. Large meetings of protest are planned for today and tomorrow. The substance of all appeals may be summarized as follows: We call upon the Government immediately to instruct Chinese delegates in Paris not to sign the Peace Treaty."

From Bernard Mannes Baruch

My dear Mr. President: Paris, May 7, 1919.

German militarism has been destroyed and the peoples of the world set free from political domination not of their own choosing. The rights of self-determination and political freedom are coming to the whole world which finds itself exhausted from the struggle to attain these ends—exhausted mentally, physically and financially. It is staggering under huge debts. The consequent grave industrial problems will require the strongest and most sympathetic treatment. But unless great care is taken, military domination will be succeeded by financial domination.

All of the countries owe large debts, for the most part to the United States, England and France. Exchange has depreciated and commercial and economic life is prostrate.

In order that a government like Italy and new governments such as the Baltic Provinces, Poland, Czecho-Slovakia and Jugo-Slavia, and the Balkan States such as Roumania and Bulgaria may establish themselves financial assistance must be given. Otherwise these people will find themselves financially shackled for years to come by a domination more severe and more difficult to throw off than was the military domination.

Permit me to say that I think it is the duty of the United States, which has done so much to free these people and to establish high purpose and ideals in the world, to complete its work of freeing these people by giving them an equal opportunity in the world.

I recommend that aid be given to stricken Europe by the United States, in cooperation with England, France and any other country that desires to join; that the aid be not given jointly but independently; that the United States, England and France should each, by consultation, know what the others are doing in order that there may be no duplication of effort.

A prime condition of our granting aid should be the establishment of equality of trade conditions and removal of economic barriers. Any credits we give should be contingent upon the cancellation of preferential treaties and trade agreements now existing, and upon an understanding that the monies advanced by any of the governments should not be held as a special charge against the customs or duties or public utilities of any country. All advances should be made with the understanding that the nationals of all countries should receive equal opportunity to do business in the country to which the money has been advanced, and that no preference or special concession should be given to the country making the advance, except that where commercial credits are granted the material should be bought in the country making the advance.

The restoration of economic life in Europe, particularly in the new states which are being constituted by the terms of the Peace Treaty, require the following:

One: The secretary of the Treasury should be empowered, with the approval of the President, where necessary, to adjust and change the terms of payment of principle and interest of the loans made to other governmen(t)s. Exchange in all countries has depreciated and it will be difficult, until economic conditions improve, to pay in dollars in some cases even the interest on these loans. If the Secretary of the Treasury funded the loans over long periods and deferred the interest payments (taking notes for the interest for periods of from three to five years) these countries would be freed from the immediate necessity of finding money for this purpose. This would relieve the exchange situation tremendously, have a tonic effect upon financial conditions in Europe, and give these countries an opportunity to rehabilitate and readjust their systems of taxation and finance.

Two: The secretary of the Treasury should be empowered, with the approval of the President, to establish special commercial credit advances to the various nations which it may be desirable to assist, such credits or advances to be used in payment for raw materials, railroad aupplies [supplies], machinery, etc., required from America. Modification of War Finance Corporation provisions may accomplish this. The necessity of all such purchases, and the method of purchase, should be supervised. Such loans should not be available for military purposes or for any form of public improvement or investment in fixed property, but should be used solely to assist the commerce of the country.

These loans should be made through the interested governments with the guaranty of the borrowing government, the guaranty of its banks, and on the individual note or credit of the borrowing merchant or grouped industry. This method is recommended not alone that we may have a combined credit, but that we may have the combined judgment and responsibility of the government, the banker and the merchant in passing upon the necessity for the loan. This will prevent wild and unnecessary expenditures. An agent or agency acting in cooperation (not joint agency) should be established in each country to pass upon the necessity of the commercial loans requested. It, in conjunction with the government and the banks of the borrowing country, should investigate the needs and see that the money is expended for the purpose for which it is advanced.

Each Allied, Associated or neutral government would have an opportunity to take its share in any or all advances; but a country would make a loan only for purchases from its nationals. There are already banks in most of these countries, and others could be readily established by the peoples of the countries in question. The banks in the borrowing countries should not be permitted to charge more than one percent. in addition to what the lending government would receive. It would not be necessary to extend these credits for more than three years. In most instances the money would be paid back before this time.

It might appear on the surface that this is a complicated and difficult plan, but it is not. The expenses could be paid by a charge of something less than one-quarter of one percent. The organization could be quickly formed, made to function and bring to the peoples whom we desire to help the fre[e]dom and liberty of action that would go further to bring about normal and peaceful conditions than many times the money spent to restore order by force of arms.

There will be great competition among the financial and commercial interests of the various countries to make these loans. In many cases the exporting or selling house would assume part of the advance. Before long the government's place would be taken by private concerns. Once the plan is started, the final result will be that the treasuries of the various countries will be obliged to advance less money than is now thought necessary.

Three. To the newer countries some advances will have to be made in order to carry on their governments until the revenues come in from their restored industrial and economic life. But none of these monies should be used for military works or public improvements, except for such things as railroad facilities. The Secretary of the Treasury should be, with the approval of the President, empowered to do this.

Whatever the amount may be, it is an obligation that we cannot escape. It is a part of the obligation that the rich nations of the world, and America in particular, must carry out. America entered the war with a high purpose. It has written that purpose into the terms of the Peace. It must now carry through that purpose, in order that peace may be maintained by the restoration of normal conditions and by the granting of an equal opportunity to all.

Economic inequality and barriers were among the causes of the war. They have not been removed; in many cases they have been increased. No greater use can be made of our resources and I know of no more fitting climax to the part that America has played in the war, and to your own great work, than the accomplishment of this project. Very sincerely yours, Bernard M Baruch

TLS (WP, DLC).

From Bernard Mannes Baruch and Others,[1] with Enclosure

Memo. for the President. [c. May 7, 1919]

Loucheur of the French Ministry greatly fears that we are making it impossible for the Germans to sign the Treaty, by reason of the fact that they see no possible hope for their economic life in the clauses as drawn. He believes that the only way in which it is possible to show the Germans that the Treaty can be worked out, without their becoming hopeless slaves, is for a few—a *very* few of our experts (business men) to sit down with similar members of the German Delegation & point out to them *how* their metallurgical & industrial life is *not* to be destroyed. Loucheur fears that unless we give the Germans some ray of hope that we shall listen to reasonable points that they may raise, they may take a position that will be impossible of solution for both them and us.

We believe there is a very important point in this and we suggest that the Council may see fit to meet it immediately by allowing to become known some statement like the attached. Loucheur thinks that M. Clemenceau & Mr. L George will adopt promptly *any* suggestion you make on this matter. But Loucheur's name should *not* be brought in. Respectfully submitted: B.M.B.

N.H.D.

TWL.

HwI MS (WP, DLC).

[1] Norman H. Davis and Thomas W. Lamont.

E N C L O S U R E

For the Press

In case the German Delegation, in its communication upon the Treaty which is to be made on Thursday, raises any points which, in the judgment of the Council of Four, justify oral explanations in order to clarify possibly obscure points in the Treaty, the Council will permit its experts to meet members of the German Delegation in person at Versailles, for the purposes indicated.

Hw MS (WP, DLC).

From Henry Mauris Robinson

Dear Mr. President: [Paris] 7 May 1919

After several discussions M. Clementel and M. Clavielle[1] will not concede the retention by Brazil, Cuba, China and Siam of the vessels taken over by them during the war, but are entirely willing to recommend to M. Clemenceau that the French Government should enter into an agreement for the retention by the United States of her seized ships. Enclosed is a draft which M. Clementel and I prepared and which I have been assured will be given you by M. Clemenceau immediately.[2]

This leaves the question of the French interest in the ships taken over by Brazil, Cuba, etc., open for negotiations between France and those States.

As I read the Treaty Provisions, distribution of merchant ships and other commodities, services, and even money, is to be made among the Allies under such agreements as they may make in advance of the distribution. This apparently leaves everybody free to negotiate as they see fit.

We have endeavored in every way to protect Brazil's interest, but now it appears to be Brazil's duty to protect her own interest in the negotiations which will be taken up with her by the French immediately.

The British Representative is taking the matter up with Japan.

Jointly we took it up with Italy this morning. Italy presents a new question which does not affect us—the Italian representative stated that they were entirely willing to concede the United States title but want to write into the Agreement some method of determining a new problem. The new problem is this: If Italy, under the Treaty of Peace, is to have Trieste, taking over as she does all of the property of Trieste, does she take over such ships as were registered in Trieste? This is of importance to France and Great Britain as Italy would propose not to apply such ships on her part in the pooled ships and, pro tanto, it would reduce the dividend to the other Allies who receive ships out of the pool. This last is for your information, and you will be informed as the negotiations progress.

As a part of the arrangement with France, acting under your authority I have indicated that we will endeavor to sell her some steel cargo ships not to exceed seventy thousand tons in all, while probably the amount we could presently deliver would be thirty-five thousand. They ask for the five-thousand deadweight ton ship but acknowledge that they will take part in other tons. I have cabled the Shipping Board asking them to fix the number of ships, type, and prices.

In conclusion, I think we are entirely right from every standpoint in taking the memorandum from France, the copy of which is enclosed.

I expect to go to London for a day or two, leaving Friday morning, and if you desire me to give further information I shall be very glad to do it any time tomorrow.

Very respectfully yours, Henry M. Robinson

TLS (WP, DLC).

[1] Albert Claveille, not Clavielle, French Minister of Public Works and of Transport and a technical adviser on communications questions in the French delegation to the peace conference.

[2] T MS (WP, DLC). Under this draft agreement, the French and American governments agreed that, insofar as any interest of the French government was concerned, the United States should retain all ships captured, seized, or detained by her during the war prior to November 3, 1918. Since the tonnage thus retained would exceed that which the United States would get were the total enemy tonnage allocated in proportion to the losses suffered by all Allied and Associated nations during the war, a "reasonable value" was to be placed on the excess retained above this proportional amount, and the United States would pay the resulting sum to the Reparation Commission for the credit of Germany toward the sums due her.

From William Shepherd Benson

My dear Mr. President: Paris, May 7, 1919.

I beg to quote the following despatches which have just been received from Rear Admiral Andrews in the Adriatic:

> "18,000 troops under Italian Generals Fiume District about 40,000 more spread out along bound[a]ry line to North about 50,000 more about Trieste field guns mountain batteries and all preparations. Trenches dug barbed wire entanglements put up all ready in case of attack by Jugo-Slav army. Italian troops here about restlessly moved about."
>
> "Slavs at Fiume claim only 20 percent population want annexation Italy. Italian Commanding General[1] claims all here want it. Only an impartial count could tell truth. Commanding General evidently fearing not to be given to Italy said conciliation is possible if officer Peace Commissioners would come here. Gave as his personal suggestion that the wedge of Fiume starting between mountain spurs could be made republic or autonomous state."
>
> "Attitude of Italy's Commanding General most friendly and apparently reasonable. He says has noted movements of Serb troops in violation of Armistice line. Finds it his duty to make military disposition to guard against accidental collision. Says Serb sentries generally polite and careful. Italian troops specially warned to avoid trouble." Sincerely yours, W. S. Benson.

TLS (WP, DLC)

[1] Lt. Gen. Francesco Saverio Grazioli.

Thomas Nelson Page to the American Commissioners

Rome. May 7th, 4 PM 1919.

294. URGENT.

The Press is manifestly more hopeful of some solution that will settle the present critical situation, that is to say, that will give Fiume to Italy. This has been the crucial question overshadowing all others. I hear that some government officials are less hopeful, fearing America may not yield. A man fully informed as to Italian sentiments stated to me this morning: "If Orlando and Sonnino return from Paris with Fiume all will be well and within a week the old relations between America and Italy will be as before the trouble arose. If they return without Fiume, they will be chased out of Italy. It will be a catastrophe. There will be a revolution and government and throne both may go. President Wilson has absolutely in his hands to-day, the destiny of 40,000,000 Italians, either by saying yes or no." This undoubtedly represents the feeling of a great part of those in Rome. They say Bolshevism will be the result. I feel that if a settlement is not arrived at and Orlando and Sonnino return without one, the situation here will be irremediable. I am ready to go to Paris if my presence there will contribute in any way towards solution. But the present situation here ought to be recognized frankly and met without delay. Nelson Page.

T telegram (WP, DLC).

From the Diary of Ray Stannard Baker

Wednesday the 7th [May 1919]

I had a talk with the President at 6:30. He is much relieved at having the German treaty off his hands. I asked him what he thought of the Rantzau speech. "Not frank & peculiarly Prussian!" He told me he had called a special session of Congress for May 19.

We also gave out the news of the exact terms of the American-British guarantee to France.

It was a wonderfully fine spring day with the lilacs & chestnuts just beginning to bloom.

He [Wilson] also spoke of the speech as "stupid," which with him is severe condemnation: a kind of crime. It did not so impress me. It had everything in it: explanation, appeal, defiance—and it was emotional—but it left in my mind a still more pronounced feeling that the inclination of the Germans was to sign the treaty. The British criticise Brockdorf[f]-Rantzau for remaining seated while speaking: they call it an insult. To me he looked ill—very pale & worn: but he might have explained! Clemenceau was crisp, out right & vigorous as a presiding officer. The Allies all rose when the German delegates came in—led by Clemenceau. The Germans were evidently nervous & ill at ease—especially the interpreters. The interpreting into English & French of Rantzau's German was abominable. The French never show their nervousness: they have savoir faire.

—Only one woman was present—a Miss Alison, British stenographer.

—There was much heartburning in our delegation over inability to get to the great sitting: not even Admiral Benson, or Admiral Grayson: nor Lamont, Baruch, Davis, Miller & other experts were there. The spectators were cut down to the bone.

—Nothing could be lovelier than the view of the park through the great glass windows—the new leaves of spring, the chestnuts & lilacs just coming into bloom. But the French kept all the windows & doors hermetically sealed.

From the Diary of Edith Benham

May 7, 1919

Great excitement downstairs this morning when the Italians returned. The P. told us that he, L. George and Clemenceau were sitting peacefully in his room downstairs where the small conferences are, and as he said, they are always like old cats, each one going to his own corner, and the places by the windows occupied by the various secretaries, who need the light. Into the midst of this peaceful picture of home life enters Orlando. We all asked impatiently what he did and what they all did. "Why nothing. I think we were all too stunned to say anything, and we acted as though he had never been away and went along peaceably about our business." Mrs. W. and I met Orlando as we were coming home from our morning walk and he looks very badly. . . .

At luncheon the P. said how he hates to meet any of these Germans. He wouldn't mind the old crew so much, but not these nondescripts. Grasty asked him what he thought about the peace, if he felt it was all right, and he said "Yes, as far as it was possible and the Germans would be the only ones to object," but he didn't feel it was unduly severe for them.

He paid his compliments to Admiral Sims of whom he doesn't think highly because he became so utterly dominated by English influence. Grasty spoke of the splendid feat of laying the mine barrage and the P. said it was done contrary to Sims's advice and the British. He cabled Sims asking him about the idea. Sims cabled back "British Admiralty advises strongly against it." The P. said he wrote the message and signed it with his own name, "If entirely independent of British and acting on your own responsibility would you advise barrage." Sims cabled back again, "British Admiralty advises against barrage." I don't know that I have quoted every word, but that is the sense. The P. said, "I took his message and finished with him then." In regard to Leonard Wood he says he is a mischief maker and disloyal. He turned against Gen. Scott, who had recommended his retention as Chief of Staff. Pershing said he didn't want him here for that reason. Grasty said when Wood came over he invited him to luncheon for he admired him and he found out very soon what he was and everyone in Paris found out the same thing.

To Joseph Patrick Tumulty

Paris, 7 May, 1919.

Please issue call in my name for Congress to meet on Monday the 19th of May. I will cable message to Congress later. Please convey the following to the Postmaster General. QUOTE Is it not feasible to postpone the telephone and telegraph increases of rates until the companies are returned to their private owners? I receive many messages about it[1] and they all incline me to believe that this would be the wise and prudent course but I wish your judgment in the matter. UNQUOTE.

Woodrow Wilson.

T telegram (WP, DLC).

[1] Wilson was replying to JPT to WW, May 5, 1919 (first telegram of that date).

Two Telegrams from Joseph Patrick Tumulty

[The White House, May 7, 1919]

No. 103 Republican Congress will attempt to pass resolution suggesting opening of all shipyards to contracts for foreign ships. The criticism directed against us by our failure to do this most acute. If we consent after asking opening of Congress, our Republican friends will get credit. ______ [Labor] greatly interested. Now is the time [Is it not the time] to suggest that Hurley consent to this.

Tumulty.

[The White House, May 7, 1919]

No. 104 Stories here carrying peace terms,[1] announce that "Italy gets Fiume in 1923 as a basis of resuming participation in peace negotiations." The story follows: "Premier Orlando accepts the proposal that Italy administer Fiume as a mandatory of the League of Nations until 1923, when Fiume will revert to Italian sovereignty." This story, with another from the Associated Press that "United States reported in pact to defend France" will cause a great deal of unfavorable comment and difficult to explain. Tumulty.

T telegrams (WP, DLC).

[1] Evening papers, such as the New York *Evening Post*, printed on May 7 an official summary of the peace treaty with Germany made public by the Committee on Public Information on that date. Morning newspapers in New York and elsewhere printed the summary on the following day. The official summary included the following supplementary statement: "In addition to the securities afforded in the Treaty of Peace, the President of the United States has pledged himself to propose to the Senate of the United States, and the Prime Minister of Great Britain has pledged himself to propose to the Parliament of Great Britain an engagement, subject to the approval of the Council of the League of Nations, to come immediately to the assistance of France in case of unprovoked attack by Germany." New York *Evening Post*, May 7, 1919. The story about Italy becoming the mandatory for Fiume appeared in a separate dispatch from the Associated Press datelined Paris, May 7 and was printed in *ibid.* on May 7 and in other newspapers on May 8. Some papers, e.g., the New York *World*, May 8, 1919, also carried another Associated Press dispatch about the proposed French security treaty.

From Albert Sidney Burleson

[Washington] May 7 [1919]

No. 102 From the Postmaster General:

In my opinion before the wires are returned to their owners laws should be passed providing for some measure of governmental regulation, also adequate rates fair alike to the companies and the public, and that the machinery for establishing these rates should not be subject to interference by any other agency. Also that wasteful attempts at competition should be ended and unification into one thoroughly coordinated wire system brought about. It is believed that efficient service to the public cannot be maintained if the complex, contradictory and overlapping control of states and municipalities over rates and operating conditions is to continue. As requested, the form for recommendation to Congress is submitted:

"When the war was at a critical stage and the resources of the nation were being most actively mobilized for its prosecution, it was deemed a wise and necessary precaution for the Government to take control and management of the telegraph and telephone systems of the country. The emergency which justified and required that action is passed. The problems involved in their early return to the owners should have the prompt and thoughtful consideration of the Congress. Without further legislation these properties will go back to their owners automatically upon the proclamation by the President of the fact of ratification of the treaty of peace. In the interest of the public and the owners they ought not to be returned without further legislation by the Congress. Fundamentally the problem is closely akin to that involved in the railroad situation dealt with in my address to the Congress on December 2, 1918. The same alternative courses which I pointed out then would seem to be open with respect to these wire systems now. We cannot simply release the wires and go back to the old conditions of private management, wasteful attempts at competition and multiform regulation by state and federal authorities; or we can establish complete government control, accompanied if necessary by actual government ownership; or we can adopt an intermediate course of modified private control under a more unified and affirmative public regulation and under such alterations of the law as will prevent wasteful competition and effect desirable unification in the operation of the various systems. To return to the old conditions is manifestly not advisable.

"The telegraph and telephone facilities of communication have ceased to be local. It is generally true and should be universally the case that every telephone user should be able to reach any other telephone user at any place in the country. The development of the art makes this practicable. Communication of intelligence is a matter of national governmental concern, no less so when carried on electrically by telephone and telegraph than through the mails. Ownership and operation by the United States is not a necessary corollary to this proposition, but the necessity for some measure of regulation and control by the National Government does logically follow.

"Aside from these general underlying considerations, the immediate situation confronting the wire companies as a result of the high costs of labor and material which culminated during the war and the uncertainty of future changes in the present level of prices introduces another and very important consideration calling for the immediate action of Congress. These properties cannot in fairness to their owners or to the general public be returned under the burden of these increased costs of operation without assurance of rates adequate to cover such increases and at the same time afford a fair return on the investment; for otherwise deterioration of the properties and the service will inevitably result and the public as well as the owners be disastrously affected. Manifestly the former rates are inadequate to produce the necessary revenue to meet existing requirements. To maintain and operate these properties new material must be purchased at market prices and skilled labor employed at prevailing wages. Because of these extra-ordinary changes in the operating conditions of these properties a serious responsibility rests on the Government to adopt every means possible consistent with some policy to protect the owners so as to enable them to operate their properties free from the dangers of receiverships or the serious impairment of their value or the deterioration of this important service of the public." Tumulty.

T telegram (WP, DLC).

From the Diary of Edith Benham

May 8, 1919

The P. said the Germans made a most unfortunate impression on everyone. In the first place, as I may have written, he, L.G. and Clemenceau went out to see about the arrangement of the rooms and if the table could be placed so that they would not have the appearance of prisoners at the dock, but they could not arrange it differently. Then they had arranged that they should stand when the Germans came into the room. Of course, as you have seen by the papers, Von Brockdorff Rantzau (I hope I have spelled it straight) sat when he made his speech. Mr. White had told us that when he went up to meet them when they came that B.R. looked like a ghost and his knees shook so he could hardly stand, so he may not have been able to stand, but he certainly, as the P. said, should have given some explanation. He said that the sight of them, for they were arrogant still, aroused all the old animosities and hatreds which had been dormant in part in the desire to bring Germany to a realization of the part she would have to play to be admitted into the society of decent nations.

As I wrote you this afternoon we all went junketing to the races. I can't say they were very much in the way of gaiety, for there were not many people there. The Princess Murat[1] expressed it well for she said it was sad to look around and see so many young faces missing—so many who had been killed. Lady Paget[2] came over to talk to Mrs. W. and the P. She must have been a beautiful woman years ago and now is certainly fearfully and wonderfully made up. She was an American but I am a little uncertain who she was. I don't think the P. is as popular here as he was for he had very little applause when he was leaving. He is always irritated when he speaks about the way the French forget how they implored our aid and he says the censors (Foreign) never allowed the fact to go through how desperate the need was and how our men literally turned the day. In conference the other day the French and British were saying what their men had done and how wonderful this and that had been. This kept up for some time with no reference to the Americans and he said, "Gentlemen, have you forgotten there was an American Army?" Foch, of course, is the leader in all this anti-American agitation.

[1] Cécile, Princess Murat, wife of Joachim Napoléon, 5th Prince Murat, Prince of Ponte-Corvo.
[2] That is, Lady Mary Fiske Stevens Paget, wife of Gen. Sir Arthur Henry Fitzroy Paget.

From the Diary of Dr. Grayson

Thursday, May 8, 1919.

The President had breakfast at 8:30. He has a habit of going to the window every morning after dressing, and, with the window wide open, practice deep-breathing exercises. He always looks out of the window and waves "good-morning" to the members of the guard on duty in the garden. This has become a regular routine and the soldiers look for the wave of his hand every morning.

The Big Four met at 11:00 o'clock. The Austrian situation was discussed. They decided not to have a meeting in the afternoon.

The President in the afternoon, feeling greatly in need of recreation and fresh air, motored out to the Longchamps Race Course at my suggestion, which was pleasing to Mrs. Wilson. The President enjoyed the afternoon. Lord Derby, the British Ambassador to France, Prince Murat, Mr. B. M. Baruch and the racing officials came up to the box and talked with the President and Mrs. Wilson. It was the first time the President had seen races on the turf. He was intensely interested in watching the crowd as well as the races. It was a most refreshing afternoon for him. Incidentally, it was the first time since the term of General U.S. Grant that a President of the United States had been present at running races.

Upon his return home he conferred with Senator William Harris of Georgia. Senator Harris told the President that he had finally decided that he would vote for the adoption of the Woman's Suffrage Amendment when it came before the Senate at the extra session. This insured the adoption of suffrage inasmuch as one vote was needed in the Senate to total the two-thirds majority required to amend the Constitution and give the women the right to vote.

At seven o'clock the President had dinner with Mrs. Wilson, Dr. Stockton Axson and myself. After dinner we talked on various subjects, including the Germans and the peace treaty, the attitude of the French and the English toward the Germans and America. The President then talked to me about prospective political conditions in America, and discussed with me the pros and cons of the candidates—Democrats and Republicans—for the next Presidential campaign. He also dwelt upon himself telling me what he could do and what he could not do.

A telephone message came from Mr. Bernard M. Baruch saying that he had discovered that the French had changed the wording of an important clause which was serious.[1] The President remarked: "The French seem to be always up to some skullduggery; the word 'honorable' doesn't seem to mean anything to them." The evidence before the Big Four was conclusive that M. André Tardieu was the one who made this change.

The relaxation and enjoyment of the races and the evening at home free from business clearly showed the elasticity of his physical and mental make-up, and although much run down from the heavy strain to which he has recently been subjected, he shows that he is able to come back if given a proper chance. From the benefits received by the President during the short afternoon at the races, I was more than ever convinced that sunshine, fresh air, and good horses with the colors up is a tonic that is second to none in benefitting a mind wearied man, whether he is a President or just a common layman.

[1] See B. M. Baruch to WW, May 8, 1919.

Hankey's and Mantoux's Notes of a Meeting of the Council of Four[1]

President Wilson's House,
C.F.-1 Paris, May 8, 1919, 11 a.m.

1. There was some discussion on the subject of the meeting with the Germans on the previous day, in the course of which M. Clemenceau said that he had heard on good authority that Count Brockdorff-Rantzau said he would not sign the terms of peace.

M. CLEMENCEAU raised the question as to whether Brockdorff-Rantzau's proposal for joint Commissions to examine the proposals on technical matters in the Treaty of Peace[2] should be adopted.

PRESIDENT WILSON said he thought that Brockdorff-Rantzau's proposal had related to the responsibilities of the war rather than to technical matters.

M. CLEMENCEAU said that the Commission he had proposed on this matter was a neutral one: he had really made two proposals. He then read the draft of a reply which was to the following effect:

(1) The proposed neutral Commission on responsibilities for the war would be contradictory to the articles in the Treaty of Peace on this subject.

(2) In regard to the proposal for technical commissions he must inform Brockdorff-Rantzau that verbal communications are

[1] The complete text of Hankey's notes is printed in *PPC*, V, 510-18.
[2] That is, in his remarks at a Plenary Session printed at May 7, 1919.

and remain excluded. The German delegation must have its own Commissions and send replies to the Secretary-General.

Before finally approving this draft it was agreed: that the text of Brockdorff-Rantzau's statement on the subject should be consulted.

Later in the meeting Brockdorff-Rantzau's statement was available from which the following extract was read: "Having regard to the disconcerting multiplicity of the problems which are raised by this aim pursued in common we must as rapidly as possible have the principal matters discussed by special expert commissions on the basis of the draft which you are submitting." (Translated from the French Summary.)

MR. LLOYD GEORGE suggested that this did not constitute a definite proposal which need be replied to.

M. CLEMENCEAU agreed that it would be better to take no notice.

PRESIDENT WILSON agreed and suggested that one possible interpretation of the phrase was that if the Germans signed the Treaty they would want the assistance of the Allied and Associated Powers in carrying it out.

It was agreed:

That no reply should be made to this statement in Brockdorff-Rantzau's speech.

2. PRESIDENT WILSON read a summary prepared by the American Delegation of the present position in regard to the settlement of the territorial boundaries of former Austro-Hungarian territory, as well as Bulgarian territory.[3] The summary pointed out that the United States, British and French experts had agreed in regard to Bulgaria, the Greek frontiers, the Czecho-Slovak frontiers, the Roumanian frontiers, and the Jugo-Slav frontiers. The question of the frontiers between Belgium and Holland had not been dealt with. In regard to the Polish frontiers, agreement had not been reached, except with regard to Germany and the frontier between Poland and Czecho-Slovakia. The frontiers of Albania and of Russia were also unsettled.

MR. LLOYD GEORGE suggested that the best plan would be the one he had suggested on the previous day, namely, deal first with the frontiers of Austria and of Hungary, and to determine their boundaries and their conditions. Once these were out of the way, the more contentious questions which arose between the Allies could be dealt with.

PRESIDENT WILSON pointed out that once peace was made with Austria and with Hungary, and once these countries had been made separate, and the Treaties of Peace with them had been completed,

[3] S. E. Mezes to WW, May 5, 1919, T MS (WP, DLC).

the present Conference would have no further authority. To leave it to the component parts to arrange matters between themselves would cause very serious trouble. He urged the importance of retaining the peace-making power in the present Conference.

MR. LLOYD GEORGE said that the difficulty could be surmounted by inserting an Article in the Treaty of Peace, binding Austria and Hungary, respectively, to recognise the States contiguous to them, within the boundaries arranged by the Allied and Associated Powers as a whole.

PRESIDENT WILSON pointed out that this clause would not bind the new States to respect the decision of the principal Powers. If they did not, this would mean launching out in a new sea of negotiation.

MR. LLOYD GEORGE said that if his Italian colleagues would pardon him, and he did not ask them to agree or to disagree in what he was about to say, the present atmosphere was not a favourable one for settling the more controversial questions. There was great public excitement, which was partly artificial and partly genuine. The best plan would be to give time for that to subside. It was not essential for peace between the Allied and Associated Powers and Austria and Hungary, that these controversial questions should be settled.

PRESIDENT WILSON said that he was anxious to arrange that the boundaries between various States should not be left to separate agreement. He proposed, therefore, that it should be provided in the Treaty of Peace that Austria and Hungary respectively should recognize the States contiguous to them, within boundaries which should be stated, where possible, but where they could not be stated, were determined by some definite authority, for example, the League of Nations.

MR. LLOYD GEORGE suggested that the League of Nations ought not to be burdened at the outset with these tremendously difficult problems. They should be settled by the Allied and Associated Governments.

PRESIDENT WILSON suggested the best plan would be to have them settled by the *principal* Allied and Associated Governments. The important thing was that the latter should not divest themselves of their authority.

MR. LLOYD GEORGE agreed that the matter could be dealt with on these lines. Austria and Hungary were both starving and Peace Treaties with them ought to be concluded as soon as possible. The only part of Brockdorff-Rantzau's speech on the previous day which had made him feel uncomfortable was the passage where he had alluded to the starvation which had occurred since the Armistice had been signed.

M. CLEMENCEAU said that his statement had to be proved.

MR. LLOYD GEORGE said that, at any rate, there was no doubt that Austria and Hungary were starving.

PRESIDENT WILSON told M. Clemenceau that we ought not to blink facts because we were annoyed with Brockdorff-Rantzau. There was no doubt that people had been starved because through no-one's fault it had not been possible to get the Treaty of Peace ready earlier.

MR. LLOYD GEORGE drew attention to an Article by Mr. Hervé[4] in the 'Victoire,' in which he said that, after reading the summary of the Treaty of Peace, he withdrew all his attacks on the slowness in preparing the Treaty of Peace.

M. CLEMENCEAU told President Wilson that he could give him an order to visit women from fourteen years of age to sixty, who had been violated by the Germans.

MR. LLOYD GEORGE said that Sir Ernest Pollock[5] had told him that documents before the Commission on breaches of the laws of war had been so bad that only parts of them were read. The Commission had become perfectly sick with reading them.

M. CLEMENCEAU said that they had an awful case against the Germans.

PRESIDENT WILSON summed up the decision as regards the boundaries as follows: Wherever they can be fixed, this shall be done, but where they cannot be fixed, the High Contracting Parties shall be bound to accept what the principal Allied and Associated Powers decide.

(There was no dissent from this.)

MR. LLOYD GEORGE raised the case of the Ukraine. Could the principal Allied and Associated Powers settle that?

PRESIDENT WILSON said they could settle the boundary between the Ukraine and Poland. One difficulty was that the Ukraine declared herself independent of Russia.

MR. LLOYD GEORGE said that this was part of the general Russian question, and he hoped that a special day would shortly be set apart for discussing this.

PRESIDENT WILSON suggested that the Council of Foreign Ministers should be asked to make a comprehensive enquiry and to make recommendations as to all the frontiers of former Austro-Hungarian territory, except those specially concerning Italy.

BARON SONNINO recalled that there was one portion of the frontier between Jugo-Slavia and Austria which was closely connected with the Italian problem. He thought the best plan would be for the For-

[4] Gustave Hervé, proprietor of *La Victoire*, a right-wing French newspaper.

[5] Sir Ernest Murray Pollock, Solicitor General of Great Britain and a technical adviser on legal questions in the British delegation to the peace conference.

eign Ministers to examine what the experts had proposed and to make recommendations.

(It was agreed:

1. That the Council of Foreign Ministers should be asked to consider at once, and to make recommendations in regard to the territorial boundaries of Austria and Hungary, and of the new States created out of former Austro-Hungarian territory, and States contiguous thereto, as dealt with in the reports of the various Commissions set up by the Preliminary Peace Conference.
2. That the Council of Foreign Ministers should be asked to hold their first meeting on this subject on the afternoon of to-day, May 8th.)

   (Although no formal resolution was adopted, it was also substantially agreed that the Treaties of Peace with Austria and with Hungary should contain an Article binding the High Contracting Parties to recognise the frontiers of the various States formed out of the former Austro-Hungarian territory, within boundaries which should be fixed, wherever possible, but in cases where it was not possible to fix them, in time for the Treaties, within such boundaries as might be decided by the principal Allied and Associated Powers.)

3. MR. LLOYD GEORGE suggested that this question [reparation clauses in the Austrian and Hungarian treaties] should be referred to the same group of financial experts which had dealt with Reparation under the instruction of the Supreme Council, in connection with the German Treaty of Peace.

M. ORLANDO said he understood that the reparation experts were meeting to consider this subject on that very day, more particularly in connection with the scheme that he himself had proposed for a debit and credit account in regard to the countries formerly constituting part of the Austrian Empire.

PRESIDENT WILSON said that nevertheless there would be no harm in approving Mr. Lloyd George's proposal.

(The following resolution was agreed to:

That the group of financial experts which, under the immediate direction of the Supreme Council, completed the Articles for insertion in the Treaty of Peace with Germany on the subject of reparation, shall re-assemble to prepare for the consideration of the Supreme Council draft Articles for insertion in the Treaty of Peace with Austria and in the Treaty of Peace with Hungary.)

4. (On the proposal of Mr. Lloyd George, the following resolution was agreed to:

That the group of experts which, under the supreme direction of the Supreme Council, completed the Financial Clauses for insertion in the Treaty of Peace with Germany, shall re-assemble to prepare for the consideration of the Supreme Council draft Articles for insertion in the Treaty of Peace with Austria, and in the Treaty of Peace with Hungary.)

5. MR. LLOYD GEORGE suggested that the Drafting Committee should be asked to start work on the Austrian Treaty and on the Hungarian Treaty.

PRESIDENT WILSON said that the Drafting Committee were entitled to a rest after their very heavy labours in preparing the German Treaty.

(This was agreed to.)

6. After a short discussion, a resolution on the following lines was agreed to:

That the Military Representatives of the Supreme War Council at Versailles, with whom shall be associated representatives of the Naval and Air Services of the United States of America, Great Britain, France and Italy, should prepare for the consideration of the Supreme Council of the principal Allied and Associated Powers draft military, naval and air articles for insertion in the Treaty of Peace with Austria and in the Treaty of Peace with Hungary.

(It was also agreed that the exact text of this resolution should be left to M. Clemenceau, who would then forward it as an instruction to the Military Representatives.)

7. After a short discussion, a resolution on the following lines was agreed to:

That the Military Representatives of the Supreme War Council at Versailles should prepare for the consideration of the Supreme Council of the Principal Allied and Associated Powers a draft Convention in regard to the military occupation of the territories West of the Rhine, as provided for in Article 432 of the Treaty of Peace presented to the German Plenipotentiaries.

It was also agreed that the military representatives should invite the co-operation of a Belgian representative. The exact terms of the reference to the Military Representatives was left to M. Clemenceau, who undertook to give the necessary instructions.

8. After a short discussion, a resolution on the following lines was agreed to:

That the Military Representatives of the Supreme War Council at Versailles should prepare for the consideration of the Supreme Council of the principal Allied and Associated Powers a scheme for the size of the Army of Occupation of the German territory West of the Rhine, as provided for in Articles 428 and 429 of the Treaty of Peace presented to the German Plenipotentiaries.

It was also agreed that the Military Representatives should invite the co-operation of a Belgian Representative.

The exact terms of the reference to the Military Representatives was left to M. Clemenceau, who undertook to give the necessary instructions.

§ Mantoux's notes:

Lloyd George. Since the questions of frontiers are on the whole settled for both countries we wish to attend to first, Austria and Hungary, the most pressing question is to request from our technical advisers:

(1) a report on the disarmament of Austria, which can be modeled on the text relating to Germany;

(2) a report on the indemnities and the reparations owed by Austria;

(3) a draft of financial clauses relative to Austria.

The same work could be done for Hungary.

Orlando. The Reparation Commission has already taken up, following a discussion among ourselves, the question of reparations owed by Austria and Hungary.

Lloyd George. I am going to inform myself about that. In that case, it would only be necessary to continue the work begun. Who will summon the military experts to study the plan for Austria's disarmament?

Clemenceau. I will do it.

Lloyd George. The resolution which I have before me proposes to us to entrust that study to Marshal Foch and his experts. But Marshal Foch has, on disarmament, ideas which are not ours, and he holds them very strongly. I believe that it is preferable to entrust this study to our military representatives in Versailles.

This proposal is adopted.

Lloyd George. I suppose that we are now going to discuss among ourselves the bases of the peace with Austria such as it is now constituted—the former Duchy of Austria, if you prefer. This will simply consist of fixing the frontiers of this state and determining its status.

Wilson. I fear that if we treat separately the question of Austria and that of the other states born of the dissolution of the Austro-Hungarian monarchy, we will subsequently find ourselves in a difficult situation in which to impose the execution of our terms. Let me explain myself.

If you wish to impose your will upon all these states, it is necessary to preserve the power which enables you either to grant or to refuse them peace. If, for example, you determine today the frontier between Austria and the Yugoslavs, and Austria accepts it, that does not suffice. The Yugoslavs must also accept it, and they will not do so until they too have signed the peace.

Lloyd George. What I wish is not to delay the resolution of problems which are ripe for solution because others need more time. The frontiers of Yugoslavia can be fixed only when the question of the Adriatic will have been settled. Given the current agitation on that issue, I believe it is preferable to wait and to settle the Austrian questions in the meantime.

Wilson. The way to get around this difficulty could be the following: we would ask Austria to recognize in advance all the frontiers of her neighbors. We will include in the treaty that the Austrian state agrees to recognize the frontiers of all the states of the former Austro-Hungarian monarchy such as they will be approved by the League of Nations. The same stipulation will subsequently be inserted in the other treaties.

Lloyd George. I do not think it is necessary to mention here the name of the League of Nations; we must say: "the Allied and Associated Powers."

Wilson. I agree. The important thing is to preserve our authority; without that, we shall never be able to settle the still more delicate question of the frontiers of Russia. Let us remember that we will have to determine, for example, the frontier between Poland and the Ukraine.

Lloyd George. Concerning the Ukraine, everything I have learned shows me that the country is a veritable creation of Germany. Mr. Bark,[6] the former Finance Minister of the Russian Empire, whom I met yesterday, told me that he himself was born in the Ukraine and that no one had ever seriously thought of this country other than as a part of Russia.

Wilson. I do not completely agree with you. I believe that a true desire for autonomy exists in the Ukraine.

Lloyd George. For autonomy, agreed; but regarding a complete separation from Russia, I think this movement is temporary.

Wilson. Concerning the states of the former Austro-Hungarian monarchy, can we not ask the Council of Foreign Ministers to present us with recommendations on the frontiers already settled by the experts?

Sonnino. Do you mean the frontiers between the small states?

Lloyd George. And that part of the Italian frontier upon which accord has been established.

Sonnino. I will point out that the frontier between Austria and the

[6] That is, Petr L'vovich Bark, at this time living in England.

Yugoslavs is not definitely fixed, and that this question concerns Italy, because there is involved a railway which connects Trieste to Vienna. It is a matter of knowing whether it should not pass from Italian territory to Austrian territory without crossing any part of Yugoslavia: that can be done easily.

The question of frontiers is referred to the Council of Foreign Ministers.

Wilson. And the question of responsibilities? Do you intend to pose the question in Austria as in Germany?

Lloyd George. It does not arise concerning the Emperor Charles: he was not there when war was declared, and his responsibility is nil.

Wilson. Do we wish to extend to Austria the system of prosecution for individual crimes against international law?

Orlando. we can produce a great number of cases which render these prosecutions necessary.

Sonnino. What was done by Austrian submarines must also be mentioned.

Wilson. The difficulty is to determine what are the crimes which have been committed by German submarines and what are those which must be imputed to Austrian submarines.

Lloyd George. In any case, some orders had to be given by Austrian authorities to the submarines, and the authors of these orders must be punished for organizing piracy.

Hankey. I will remind you that the Commission on Railways and Navigable Waterways had to draw up a special draft of its conclusions in order to insert them in the treaty with Germany. An analogous draft for the treaty with Austria will be necessary.

The Commission on Ports, Railways, and Navigable Waterways will receive instructions to this effect.

Lloyd George. We have already spoken of the effectives of the army of occupation on the left bank of the Rhine. It is a question, above all else, of avoiding an excessive financial charge which would weigh heavily on the total sum of reparations. I propose to have this question examined by a commission.

Wilson. I do not know whether this commission should be named immediately, because we could not avoid placing Marshal Foch on it, who is not exactly in the state of mind which is necessary to envisage a reduction in the occupation forces.

Lloyd George. I accept the adjournment proposed by President Wilson: surgeons say it is better to operate on patients without fever. That applies perhaps also to the case of Fiume.

Orlando. Perhaps.

Wilson. Colonel Hankey tells me that a plan already exists, prepared by Generals Wilson, Weygand, and Bliss, on a question relative to the army of occupation; but it deals with relations with the German population in the occupied zone.

Clemenceau. The best thing is to refer this question and that of the effectives of the army of occupation to the Supreme War Council in Versailles.

This proposal is adopted.

Lloyd George. I return to what M. Clemenceau said earlier about Brockdorff-Rantzau's statements: I am not sure that he specifically demanded the institution of mixed commissions.

Wilson. The sentence he used can be interpreted both ways.

Clemenceau. In that case, it is best to say nothing to him and to let him do whatever he wants. §

9. SIR MAURICE HANKEY reported that the Supreme Economic Council had forwarded various resolutions for the consideration of the Supreme Council of the principal Allied and Associated Powers, dealing with such matters as: Supply of Raw Materials to Czecho-Slovakia and Poland: Blockade of Germany and Hungary: and other matters.

He suggested that the most convenient procedure for dealing with these questions would be for the Supreme Council to meet the principal representative of the Supreme Economic Council.

MR. LLOYD GEORGE pointed out that all these questions were bound up with the elaboration of some scheme for providing credits for European countries, in regard to which he had already submitted a scheme.

PRESIDENT WILSON agreed, but said it would be necessary to find some alternative proposal, as the scheme submitted by Mr. Lloyd George did not command itself to the United States experts.

MR. LLOYD GEORGE pointed out that the British Government was in the position not only of owing large amounts to the United States, but of being guarantors of what other countries owed to the United States. Great Britain was both a creditor and a debtor nation, but if she could collect all that was due to her from other nations, the balance would be on the right side. Hence, he felt in a good position to make this proposal. He pointed out that the United States of America had made large profits out of the belligerents during the early part of the war, when she had not herself been a belligerent. He did not say this in any spirit of criticism whatever, as she was merely in the position that Great Britain had been in in 1870.

PRESIDENT WILSON pointed out that the wealth which the United States had drawn from these sources had not gone to the Government, but to particular financiers and to particular classes of the nation. Congress would take the view that the Government ought not to accept on behalf of the nation any obligation because certain interests in the nation had made profits.

MR. LLOYD GEORGE said that unless the United States of America and Great Britain agreed on some scheme for re-starting Europe, a very serious state of affairs would arise.

(It was agreed that the leading representatives of the principal Allied and Associated Powers on the Supreme Economic Council should be invited to attend at 10.30 on the following day to raise the various questions referred to the Supreme Economic Council.)

§ Mantoux's notes:

Hankey. The Supreme Economic Council requests that a decision be taken on the question of raw materials. As long as that question remains unresolved—says the communication of the council—there will be no real hope of peace for Europe.

Lloyd George. This question particularly concerns the United States and Great Britain, who are together holding the greatest part of the indispensable raw materials; furthermore, it is linked to the question of credits in America. We are charged with the burden of a rather considerable debt vis-à-vis the United States. It is necessary that the question of credits be settled, regardless of the difficulties raised by the treasuries; for, if Europe does not obtain these raw materials, she will find herself in a position worse, in certain respects, than that of wartime.

Wilson. The difficulty for the American Treasury lies in furnishing the guarantee that one demands of it for the German bonds.

Lloyd George. Without stressing this argument too much, I could tell you that the United States, by being neutral during the first two years of the war, realized enormous profits—and this is not a reproach, for the same thing would have happened to us if we had remained neutral. But it seems to me possible and indispensable that the United States guarantee these bonds.

Wilson. The difficulty is that we will only be able to do so through the means of taxation, which would fall in great part on persons who derived no benefits from the war trade.

Lloyd George. If we could renounce all debts owed us by our allies, on the condition that you would forgive ours, I assure you that we would accept, even though the balance would be unfavorable to us. It is absolutely necessary for us to deal with this question without delay.

The members of the Supreme Economic Council are convoked for tomorrow, Friday, May 9, at 10:30.§

10. MR. LLOYD GEORGE read a telegram he had received from the

Allied Naval Armistice Commission in London, to the effect that the Germans were continuing to delay the surrender of German merchant-ships in Spain by raising questions affecting cargoes, and neglecting to instruct their Captains to hand over the ships to the representatives of France.

On April 21st a warning had been sent to the German Government that if the matter was not expedited a reference would be made to the Supreme War Council. A consultation had since taken place at Rotterdam, but as no action had resulted the matter was now brought before the Supreme War Council with a recommendation that pressure should be put on the Governments concerned to proceed with the delivery to France of these ships.

PRESIDENT WILSON suggested that the pressure of the present treaty should be enough. In two weeks the Germans would be compelled to sign the whole treaty. He had only wanted to give them time to read and digest it, and get used to the idea that it would have to be accepted. He had never contemplated any additional matter being added.

(After some discussion it was agreed that Admiral Wemyss, on behalf of the Supreme Council of the principal Allied and Associated Powers should be instructed, through the Armistice Commission, to draw attention to the failure to carry out this undertaking, and, in the event of no satisfactory reply being received, to make recommendations as to the action to be taken.)

11. PRESIDENT WILSON asked if it was necessary to go into the question of breaches of the laws of war in connection with the Austrian and the Hungarian Treaties.

M. SONNINO said that there were a certain number of personal cases, although the question was less serious than in the case of Germany.

MR. LLOYD GEORGE pointed out that it had been agreed that the Austrian Emperor was not in any way responsible for the war.

M. ORLANDO said that there was a terrible record of crimes against some Austrians.

M. SONNINO pointed out that there were some bad cases in connection with submarines.

PRESIDENT WILSON asked if it was possible to distinguish German from Austrian submarines.

M. SONNINO said that in most cases it was not possible, but there was evidence in some cases.

MR. LLOYD GEORGE pointed out that someone in Austria-Hungary must have taken the decision and given the necessary authority, so that there ought to be clauses in the Treaties on this subject.

(This was agreed to.)

12. It was agreed that the Commission on Ports, Waterways and Railways should be instructed to prepare articles for inclusion in the Treaties with Austria and with Hungary.

§ Mantoux's notes:

Mr. Lloyd George reads aloud a document establishing that the Germans are not carrying out, as required by the conditions of the Armistice, the delivery of their ships which are in Spanish ports.

Wilson. Why concern ourselves with that affair when we approach the signing of the treaty which will deliver all these ships to us?

Clemenceau. I consider it essential to require the execution of the Armistice agreement and to pursue it right up to the signing of the treaty, all the more so since we greatly need the ships which the Germans delay giving up.

Wilson. What I wish is not to multiply the points of friction and irritation if one can avoid it.

After an exchange of observations, it is decided that Admiral Wemyss will be charged with admonishing the German government about the nonexecution of the clauses of the Armistice relative to the delivery of enemy ships in neutral ports. If these admonitions are not followed by results, the Admiral should immediately report to the Supreme Council of the heads of government.

T MS (SDR, RG 256, 180.03401/1, DNA); Mantoux, II, 6-10.

From Bernard Mannes Baruch, with Enclosure

My dear Mr. President: [Paris] May 8, 1919.

Here is a memorandum showing the chief points which, in going over the final draft on Reparation in the text of the Treaty, we feel should have your earnest attention.

The two most important features (paragraphs 9 and 16), as stated to you over the telephone, are the one[s] relating to the dropping out of the clause permitting withdrawal from the Reparation Commission, and the one which apparently commits America as well as the other Governments to military action in case of any default by Germany in reparation payments, whether such default is willful or not. You will recall that you and Mr. Lloyd George both approved the omission of sweeping and drastic sanctions, and thought it preferable, in the Treaty itself, to set forth that, in case of willful default, certain financial and economic pressure might be resorted to.

Paragraphs 1 and 2 are also worthy of serious consideration.

McCormick, Davis, and Lamont have been studying this phase and make the point that the arrangement to be made by the Chiefs of State with the Belgians has not yet been definitely executed. This is ready for presentation at any time.

I am told that there will be a Committee on Errata, and that various corrections in the draft of the Treaty will be suggested by the different Governments. If this be so, the correction of the clauses referred to will not be difficult.

Believe me, my dear Mr. President,

Faithfully yours, Bernard M Baruch

TLS (WP, DLC).

E N C L O S U R E

May 8, 1919.

MEMO TO: Messrs. Baruch, Davis, Lamount [Lamont] and McCormick,

FROM: Mr. John Foster Dulles.

In comparing the text of reparation clauses, as handed to the Germans yesterday, with the text of these clauses as last known to me, the following points of substance, as distinct from mere drafting changes, are to be observed: (References are to attached revise of May 1st).[1]

(1) In paragraph 2 after the words "their property" are introduced the words "during the period of the belligerency of each as an Allied and Associated Power against Germany."

This change, I assume, is intended to give effect to what I understood was the decision of the Council of Three that Governments such as Poland and Czecho-Slovakia could not recover for damage which occurred prior to their *recognition* as Governments. The actual words employed, however, refer not to the date of the recognition of such States but to the period of belligerency. This would exclude, e.g., damage to the United States while neutral and damage to Italy prior to her declaration of war against Germany, which was considerably after her declaration of war against Austria. This is probably a matter of indifference to the United States, as it is understood that we propose to take care of our claims which arose when we were neutral through recourse to A.P.C.[2] property as authorized by the Economic Clauses.

(2) In paragraph 2 in lieu of the words "in accordance with the definition contained in Annex 1" are inserted the words "and in general all damage as defined in Annex 1 hereto."

I have already commented on this change as proposed to me by the French, and which I refused to accept in the language submitted on the ground that it made it appear in the face of the Treaty that we were adding something to the declaration of the Allies of November 4, 1918. I understand that the present language was accepted by the Council of Three on May 5th.[3]

(3) As a new paragraph to Article 2 is set out the provisions relative to a special bond issue to cover borrowings by Belgium. The language employed is that submitted by me to the Central Drafting Committee, except that the words "as a consequence of the violation of the Treaty of 1839" precede instead of follow the words "to make reimbursement of all sums which Belgium has borrowed from the Allied and Associated Powers up to November 11, 1918."

The effect of this change is that the violation of the Treaty of 1839 becomes a reason for Germany's assuming this special obligation, but, on the other hand, there is no qualification of Belgium's borrowings, so that all sums which she has borrowed up to November 11, 1918, are reimbursable by Germany irrespective of whether or not such borrowings were necessitated by the violation of the Treaty of 1839.

(4) In Article 8 the word "documents" is omitted. I had advised the Central Drafting Committee that this word should be inserted as part of our arrangement with Belgium. Possibly it was felt that the introduction of this word would be unnecessary on the theory that "objects of every nature" would be construed by the Commission to include "documents."

(5) There is added to Article 8 a provision to the effect that pending the establishment by the Reparation Commission of a new procedure for restitution, restitution shall continue in accordance with the Armistice of November 11, its renewals and protocols.

(6) Article 10 still requires Germany to give information relative to military operations which may be necessary for the assessment of Germany's liability for reparation as defined in Annex 1.

This requirement was introduced at the time when Germany's liability was to depend upon her military effort. In eliminating the text of "military effort," the Drafting Committee failed to make the corresponding change in Article 10, which while now unnecessary, probably is harmless.

Palmer says matter OK as now stands B.B.

(7) Article 12 remains as originally proposed by Mr. Palmer. I had filed with the Central Drafting Committee, on May 4th, notification to the effect that the British, French and American members of the Economic delegations desired Article 12 changed so as to leave open the possibility of securing redress under the Reparation Clauses for damage to property of the character dealt with by the Economic Clauses.

(8) There is an additional Article to the effect that German cables

are dealt with in Annex 7, which is a new Annex not drafted by the Reparation Committee.

(9) In Annex 2, paragraph 2, the provision for withdrawal from the Reparation Commission has been stricken out and does not appear in the Treaty. N.B.

(10) In annex 3, paragraph 8, there is an additional sentence to the effect that the handing over of the German mercantile marine shall continue pursuant to the Armistice conditions.

(11) I had filed with the Central Drafting Committee, on May 4th, a new Article, agreed to by the British and United States shipping experts, to the effect that Germany took over from her subjects and agreed to cancel claims on account of seizure or requisition of German ships. This new Article is not included.

(12) In Annex 4, Article 3, the date for filing the lists of articles to be taken from Germany is changed from 60 days "after the date of the signature of this treaty" to "60 days after the coming into force of the present treaty."

It had been intended to maintain the earlier date as the preparation by France and Belgium of lists of what they desire had no relation to the coming into force of the Treaty, and what was desired was to insure a filing of lists as early as possible.

(13) There is an additional sentence at the end of Annex 4 to the effect that deliveries of agricultural machinery shall continue under Article 3 of the armistice renewal of January 16, 1919.

(14) There is an additional provision in paragraph 10 of Annex 5 to the effect that the provisions of Article 6 of the Armistice of November 11 remain in force until new demands for coal are made pursuant to this Annex.

(15) The provisions for the restoration to Louvain of documents, etc., and the restoration of certain works of art are contained as "special clauses" and do not form a part of Annex 4 as was indicated to the Central Drafting Committee when the clauses in question were filed with it.

The effect of this is that there is no requirement that Germany be credited with the value of the articles so restored unless, pursuant to the general clause in Article 13 of the Principal Reparation Clauses, the Reparation Commission decides that in its judgment Germany should be given a credit on account of these transfers.

(16) In the part of the Treaty dealing with military occupation there is the following provision:

> "In case either during the occupation or after the expiration of the fifteen years referred to above the Reparation Commission finds that Germany has failed to observe the whole or part of her obligations under the present Treaty, the whole or part of the

areas specified in Article 429 will be reoccupied immediately by the Allied and Associated forces."

If this Article had been prepared in conformity with the spirit of the provision of Annex 2, paragraph 18, dealing with guarantees, it would have referred to "voluntary failure" and would have used the word "may" instead of "will" with reference to military reoccupation. It is arguable that the effect of the clause as drafted is to require the Allied and Associated Governments (including the United States) to occupy German territory up to the Rhine, including the bridgeheads, if Germany, despite her best efforts, fails to meet her full reparation obligations.

(17) In the European political clauses there is a provision relative to Russia, to the effect that the Allied and Associated Powers formally reserve all rights for Russia to obtain from Germany the restitutions and satisfactions based on the principles of the present Treaty. J.F.D.

TI MS (WP, DLC).

[1] REPARATION. *May 1st. 5th Revise*, copy in WP, DLC.

[2] Alien Property Custodian.

[3] Actually on May 6, 1919. See the minutes of the Council of Four of that date, 11 a.m.

From Edward Mandell House

Dear Governor: Paris, May 8, 1919.

Sonnino came to see me this afternoon to ask that I say to you that he and Orlando were exceedingly sorry because of the intemperate things that had been said in Italy both in public speeches and in the press. He said they did their best to curb it and that they would like you to know that they in no way sympathized with it. He spoke in a very conciliatory tone and hoped that a way out would be found. He had nothing to suggest.

Affectionately yours, E. M. House

TLS (WP, DLC).

From Robert Lansing, with Enclosure

Dear Mr. President: Paris, May 8, 1919.

I am sending you two more telegrams relating to the serious situation in China.[1]

The Department suggests that a statement be made either by yourself, by the Conference or by me which will reach the people of China, allay their fears and suspicions and subdue their anger.

Mr. Polk adds that it ought to include approval of the actions both of Dr. Koo and Mr. C. T. Wang, who represent the two factions now endeavoring to effect a reconciliation in Shanghai.

I believe a statement by yourself would be most likely to meet with a favorable reception. Will you kindly let me know your feeling in regard to the suggestion.

Faithfully yours, Robert Lansing.

TLS (SDR, RG 256, 185.1158/115, DNA).

[1] The most important of these two is printed as an Enclosure. The second, FLP to Ammission, No. 1883, May 7, 1919, T telegram (SDR, RG 256, 185.1158/115, DNA), reads as follows: "Legation Peking reports disorders in Peking resulting from decision of Paris Conference and states communication with Peking by telegraph to be broken off except to Siberia. Report fully and promptly any information you may have, or can obtain."

E N C L O S U R E

Washington. May 4th, 1919.

1870. IMPORTANT

For the Secretary of State.

Advices from Peking indicate there is a good deal of resentment and manifestations of public indignation over the award of German rights in (Sha[n]tung?) to Japan. Besides the cables which we have forwarded to you[1] we are today advised that the Chinese Minister to Japan[2] has been assaulted by a mob of students and that the house of Tsao Ju-lin[3] has been burned and that he himself has taken refuge in the Legation quarters. The demonstrations are expression of anger and resentment and are possibly superinduced by the fact that they do not fully understand situation. It is just possible that their temper may lead them to some action which will cause trouble and which might be avoided if they understood all of the facts. The situation is such that it may be capitalized by the leaders of the south in an effort to overthrow the present government and it is not without the bounds of possibility that if that should happen and a civil war should again break out that the Japanese might feel justified in intervening which would lead to further complications and might be the occasion for still further demands on their part.

Of the latter I have to suggest that if possible and consistent, some communication be made which will reach the people of China and will allay their present fears and suspicions and will in some measure subdue their anger, and should proceed from you or from the President or from the Peace Conference. If it is possible that this be done and there could be included in it expressions of approval of the actions of the Chinese delegates to the Conference, especially Doctor Koo and C. T. Wang, whose affiliations are respectively with the north and the south, it might help to solidify the national sentiment and prevent any further factional manifestations.

Polk, Acting

T telegram (SDR, RG 256, 185.1158/102, DNA).

[1] See the telegrams summarized in n. 1 to R. Lansing to WW, May 7, 1919.

[2] Chang Tsung-hsiang.

[3] Ts'ao Ju-lin, Minister of Communications in the Peking government. Chang was staying at Ts'ao's house at the time of these incidents on May 4. The mob action marked the beginning of the so-called May Fourth Movement, a major force in modern Chinese history. See Chou Tse-tsung, *The May Fourth Movement: Intellectual Revolution in Modern China* (Cambridge, Mass., 1960), pp. 84-116.

From Robert Lansing

Dear Mr. President: Paris, 8 May 1919.

I enclose for your information three telegrams,[1] dated yesterday, received by the Commission from Ambassador Page in Rome, indicating his feeling that he might aid you by going to Paris for a couple of days in order to present the situation personally: and that he is now actually enroute. Your colleagues on the Commission feel that Mr. Page's decision was an unfortunate one and that his departure from Rome at this moment may cause embarrassment and be misinterpreted in Italy.

I am, dear Mr. President,

Very sincerely yours, Robert Lansing

TLS (WP, DLC).

[1] See T. N. Page to the American Commissioners, May 7, 1919. Page's other two telegrams of this date are Nos. 295 and 296, T telegrams (WP, DLC). In the first, sent at 5 p.m., he said that, if the situation in regard to Fiume did not "clear up tomorrow," he thought that he "might aid by coming Paris for couple of days, see President and other American plenipotentiaries, and present situation personally." He noted also that the French Ambassador was going to Paris on the following day. In the second telegram, sent at 8 p.m., Page wrote as follows: "After conference with French Ambassador, have decided to leave for Paris tomorrow, Thursday [May 8] morning; due Paris afternoon Friday. Please arrange appointments for me."

From William Shepherd Benson

My dear Mr. President: [Paris] 8 May, 1919

The following despatches have just been received from Rear Admiral Andrews, with regard to the situation in the vicinity of Fiume. These despatches were all sent by Admiral Andrews on the morning of the 6th instant:

"Actual number of Serbian soldiers this vicinity about 1000 as sentries along Armistice Line as everywhere on this coast. Where Serbs have a picket of 2 men, Italians confront this with 30 men. Italians state movement of Slav troops seen but do not state any large number seen. If many Slav soldiers were known to be around they would proclaim it. Their silence is proof of few."

"Activity of Italy mainly through fear of Serb attack. They have said it would happen. Now they believe it. Incidentally Italians have large number of troops in their hope of holding Fiume. Here they do not seem positive of what the decision may be."

"Small chance of hostile collision in this vicinity. Possible sentry collision through ignorance. Italys every act is as if at war. Serbs wish to avoid trouble with Italy stands well with Allies. Finally the situation is not now critical though necessarily a little uncertain."

Very sincerely yours, W. S. Benson.

TLS (WP, DLC).

From Felix Frankfurter

My dear Mr. President, Paris May 8th. 1919.

Conscious of the duty of every American not to take from your time and energy, I am nevertheless compelled to bring to your attention the conditions that now confront Jewry, above all Eastern Jewry.

You are familiar with the problems and have stated their solution. The controlling Jewish hope has been—and is—your approval of the Balfour Declaration and your sponsorship of the establishment of Palestine as the Jewish National Home. The appointment of the Interallied Syrian Commission and the assumed postponement for months, but particularly beyond the time of your stay here, of the disposition of Near Eastern questions, have brought the deepest disquietude to the representatives of the Jewry of the world. As a passionate American I am, of course, most eager that the Jews should be a reconstructive and not a disruptive force in the new world order. I have reassured their leaders with the conviction born of knowledge of your purposes. They have faith; I venture to think no people in Paris have more faith—the faith of 2000 years. But they also have the knowledge of the suffering of millions of Jews, and the hopes of Jews the world over, which nothing will assuage except the rededication, at last, of Palestine as a Jewish Homeland.

Moreover it is not merely a Jewish question. An extended delay in the Near Eastern settlement is bound to intensify the existing unrest by giving dangerous opportunities to Young Turk intrigue[1] and to the stimulation of religious animosities.

The English authorities are eager to have Dr. Weizmann and me go to Palestine to assure moderation in the Jewish population. We are doing all that can be done and I am confident the Jewish population will maintain restraint. But I dare not leave here while the Turkish issues are undetermined and while you are still in Paris to decide them.

You will forgive me for writing, but circumstances have made me the trustee of a situation that affects the hopes and the very life of a whole people. Therefore I cannot forbear to say that not a little of the peace of the world depends upon the disposal, before you return to America, of the destiny of the peoples released from Turkish rule.

Faithfully yours, Felix Frankfurter.

TLS (WP, DLC).

[1] The Young Turk movement was the loose coalition of reform groups which arose in various parts of the Ottoman Empire and among Turkish exiles abroad in the 1870s and 1880s. One of these groups, the Committee of Union and Progress, became a dominating political force in the empire: it played a leading role in the restoration of the Ottoman Constitution and the revival of Parliament in 1908 and in the deposition of Sultan Abdul Hamid II in 1909. The CUP, as the committee was usually known, effectively took control of the Ottoman government in 1913. A triumvirate of CUP leaders, Talat Paşa, Cemal Paşa, and Enver Paşa, formed a virtual dictatorship, and it was they who were chiefly responsible for bringing the empire into the war on the side of the Central Powers and for conducting the Turkish war effort to the bitter end. The CUP regime collapsed with the Turkish surrender in October 1918, and Talat, Cemal, and Enver fled into exile on a German freighter on November 2. Frankfurter's remark about "Young Turk intrigue" certainly refers to the real or alleged activities of the discredited CUP, and perhaps more specifically to the triumvirate. For a discussion of the Young Turk movement and the CUP, see Stanford J. Shaw and Ezel Kural Shaw, *History of the Ottoman Empire and Modern Turkey* (2 vols., Cambridge, 1976-77), II, 255-59, 263-67, 273-339.

From Ignace Jan Paderewski

Mr. President, Paris, 8th May 1919.

The letter which you so kindly addressed to me on the 27th of April[1] was a letter of farewell, graciously written under the impression that I was about to leave at the time.

I beg to thank you for this fresh proof of your generous interest in the cause of my country as well as for the words of lenient appreciation with which you have thought fit to honour me.

These terms of appreciation coming from you, who have been the first to utter the noble and lofty principles of justice, according to which Poland is to become united and free, I cannot accept as a legitimate reward of my personal merits. I came here exclusively as my country's servant, as the faithful interpreter of Poland's wish formulated by our most representative and democratic Diet. I have been true to the Mission with which my country has entrusted me. Therefore the views and, I dare say, the just claims, so respectfully submitted to you and your illustrious colleagues, were not only personal views of my own, but are the expression of my country's will and right. On account of this your favourable and highly appreciated opinion about the broad views taken by me on all the subjects connected with the solution of the complex problem of Poland is solely due to the spirit of liberalism and toleration which always have guided and will always guide the Polish nation.

Your beautiful letter has once more proved to me that in all matters of justice your judgment is unerring. Fully confident that this is the case and that I have understood the meaning of your words, I feel sure that the Polish cause will receive entire satisfaction at your magnanimous hands.

With the expression of deepest gratitude and the assurance of my most profound respect, I beg to remain, Mr. President,

Your most obedient and humble servant I J Paderewski

TLS (WP, DLC).

[1] See WW to I. J. Paderewski, April 26, not 27, 1919.

Three Memoranda of Agreement

[May 8, 1919]

The Allied and Associated Governments whose signatures are hereto affixed, severally agree as regards merchant shipping as follows:

1. The Reparation Commission will as soon as possible compile a list giving fullest particulars available on all enemy ships still in existence, captured, seized or detained by any Allied or Associated Governments during the war, and also all other enemy ships or boats which the enemy Powers are required to cede under the Treaty of Peace.

2. The Reparation Commission will take such steps as will secure that each of the Allied and Associated Governments will retain as its own the complete title to and use of all ships captured, seized or detained during the war as a war measure and prior to November 11, 1918, and will own the same free from any claim of any of the other Allied or Associated Governments.

In all cases where the ships and boats so to be retained by any Allied or Associated Governments are in excess of the claims of such Governments respectively for war losses in merchant ships, such Governments shall not make any claim for a share in other ships and boats ceded under the Treaty of Peace.

3. In all cases where the ships and boats so to be retained by any such Governments are insufficient to satisfy in full the claims of such Governments respectively for war losses in merchant ships, the enemy ships which remain and which are to be ceded under the Treaty of Peace will be divided into three classes, viz. liners, other merchant ships, and fishing boats, and will be distributed to such

Governments on the basis of ton-for-ton and class-for-class of the ships and boats lost and not replaced by the ships and boats retained, but in proportion to the balances due on the claims of such Governments respectively.

4. As the ships and boats so to be retained will, in the case of Brazil, China, Cuba, Siam and the United States, exceed the total amount of tonnage which would be allocated to those countries were the total enemy tonnage captured, seized, detained or still in existence shared in proportion to losses of ships and boats during the War, in each such case a reasonable value on the excess of ships and boats over the amount which would result from such a division will be determined. The amount of the value so fixed will be paid over by each such State to the Reparation Commission for the credit of Germany towards the sums due from her for Reparation, in respect to war losses of merchant ships.

5. As soon as the Reparation Commission has collected the necessary information, and is in a position so to do, they will give public notice that after an interval of two months they will proceed to divide the vessels except those captured, seized or detained by the Allied and Associated Governments which are to be retained by them respectively as hereinbefore provided. If within one month of the publication of the notice any Allied, Associated or Neutral Government, person or corporation a national of such Government and acting through such Government, notifies the Commission that they have an equitable claim against any vessel which has not been, or is not being satisfied by the enemy Governments, that claim will be considered on its merits by the Commission which may adopt any procedure it thinks fit, provided it is expeditious and is calculated to do substantial justice as between the Allied and Associated Governments on the one hand and the claimant on the other.

The Commission will have power to determine claims so presented, and such determination will be conclusive and the Commission will also have power to enforce its findings.

DATED May [blank], 1919.

Woodrow Wilson
subject to the explanation
contained in the attached
memorandum.[1]
D Lloyd George

TS MS (E. M. House Papers, CtY).

[1] WWhw.

MEMORANDUM.[1]

I deem it my duty to state, in signing this document, that, while I feel confident that the Congress of the United States will make the disposal of the funds mentioned in clause four which is there agreed upon, I have no authority to bind it to that action, but must depend upon its taking the same view of the matter that is taken by the joint signatories of this agreement.

WWT MS (E. M. House Papers, CtY).

[1] After attempting to sign the preceding document, Wilson seems to have given up trying to write with his right hand.

8 mai 1919

Pending the outcome of the negociations, which we hope will enable us to accept and sign the general agreement heretofore signed by President WILSON and Mr. LLOYD GEORGE relating to distribution of enemy ships, the French Government agrees with the United States Government:

That in any case the United States, in so far as any interest of the French Government is concerned, shall retain all ships captured, seized or detained by them during the war as a war measure and prior to November 3rd 1918, the same to be free of any claim of the French Government for reparation;

And that the Reparation Commission will take such steps as will secure that the United States retain as their own the complete title to and the use of all said ships in so far as the interest of the French Government in these particular ships is concerned.

As the tonnage of the ships and boats so to be retained by the United States will exceed the total amount of tonnage which would be allocated to them, were the total enemy tonnage,—captured, seized, detained or still in existence to be ceded under the Treaty of Peace—shared in proportion to the losses of ships and boats during the war, a reasonable value on such excess of ships and boats over the amount which would result from such a division will be determined.

The amount of the value so fixed will be paid over by the United States to the Reparation Commission for the credit of Germany towards the sums due from her for reparation in respect to war losses of merchant ships; subject however to the power of the Congress of the United States to make disposal of such funds under the resolution approved May 12, 1917. Clemenceau

TS MS (E. M. House Papers, CtY).

To Joseph Patrick Tumulty

Paris, 8 May, 1919.

Please say to Mr. Taft[1] that the necessity of protecting the Jews is fully appreciated here and that we are endeavoring to take substantially the action that he suggests. Woodrow Wilson.

T telegram (WP, DLC).

[1] Wilson was replying to W. H. Taft to JPT, May 5, 1919.

Four Telegrams from Joseph Patrick Tumulty

[The White House, May 8, 1919]

No. 105 In your cable you spoke of forwarding message to Congress.[1] Have you made up your mind as to what you will discuss? Would like to suggest certain things I believe vital.

Tumulty.

[1] See WW to JPT, May 7, 1919.

[The White House, May 8, 1919]

No. 106 Secretary Glass suggests the following message to him. The loan has been ______ [sagging], but great impetus given to it by publication of terms of peace this morning. Following message if received today will put it over. Please send it as quickly as possible.

"Through you I appeal to my fellow-citizens on the eve of the consummation of a victorious peace to sustain the honor and credit of our country and to pay tribute to the valor and sacrifices of our fighting men, by making this last Liberty Loan not only a financial success, for that it must be, but a great popular thank offering in which every American will share according to his ability."

Tumulty.

[The White House, May 8, 1919]

No. 107 The recommendation of the Postmaster General in relation to the telephone and telegraph lines[1] seems to me to be fraught with grave peril and embarrassment to the administration. The Government's control of these systems has produced nothing but criticism and discontent. The sooner we can get rid of them, the better. To adopt the Postmaster General's suggestion would put us in the same hole with respect to the telephone and telegraph lines as we now are in in relation to the railroads, as having said that they must not be returned without adequate legislation and being unable to get the legislation. I suggest that you announce at once your intention of returning the telegraph and telephone lines on the first of July, unless Congress should meanwhile by joint resolution indicate its desire to the contrary; that you intend to ask of Congress the prompt appropriation of such fund, if any, as may be necessary to recompense the telegraph and telephone lines for any losses suffered under federal control; that you should lay before Congress, not as a condition to the return of the lines but as a measure for their general consideration, the question of the propriety of legislation leading to improvement of service, etc., but without specific demand for such legislation. No legislation embodying the Postmaster General's recommendation in his cables to you would receive the sanction of either House and therefore it would result in prolonging the control, a thing which is harassing us at every turn. Mr. Mackay, of the Postal,[2] is begging for the return of his systems, claiming that no legislation is necessary to protect his property. You can have no idea of the intensity of the people in these matters. Only last night the Attorney General told me that thirty-seven states were represented by their attorneys-general at the hearing before the Supreme Court yesterday, protesting against the rate increases of the Postmaster General. Tumulty.

[1] See ASB to WW, May 7, 1919.
[2] That is, Clarence Hungerford Mackay, president of the Postal Telegraph-Cable Co.

[The White House, May 8, 1919]

No. 108 Publication of peace treaty here great triumph for you; opposition stunned. There will be no serious opposition to it. Affectionate regards. Tumulty.

T telegrams (WP, DLC).

From the Diary of Dr. Grayson

Friday, May 9, 1919.

The President arose early and after breakfast he went to his study. At 11:00 o'clock in the morning and at 4:00 in the afternoon the Big Four discussed the procedure to be followed in framing the Austrian-Hungarian treaties. Although Orlando was present no reference was made to the Adriatic. As a matter of fact, it has been tacitly agreed to that the Adriatic problems will be allowed to take care of themselves for the time being, and that the other matters which deal directly with Austria and Hungary will be hastened as much as possible.

In the evening the President attended Sir Thomas Barclay's[1] dinner. It was a small affair, with twenty guests present. The gathering was a representative one—people in different walks of life—some in very humble circumstances—were present. Very laudatory speeches were made in behalf of the President for what he had done for the peace and justice of the world. Speeches were made by Sir Thomas Barclay and by ex-Prime Minister of France Painlevé and others. The Prince of Monaco made a fine address in English. The President in his address referred to the laudatory remarks which had been made and which, he stated, made him feel uncomfortable because they could see him at such close range at a small gathering like this. He said it reminded him of the story of an old woman who went to the circus for the first time. She was very much disturbed by seeing a magician read a newspaper through a two-inch board. Getting up suddenly she said: "This is no place for me to be with a thin calico dress on." The President afterwards asked that this story be not given to the press as a part of his speech.

Some of the "better" class in France rather frowned on the idea of the President going to a dinner where there was such a mixed gathering. But the President is a real democrat and he loves to get in elbow touch with all classes of people. He thoroughly enjoyed the evening.

[1] Sir Thomas Barclay was an English barrister, prolific author on international law; vice-president of the International Law Association; and active in the Institute of International Law. He was an old acquaintance of Wilson. See Thomas Barclay, *Une conversation avec le Président Wilson en 1903* (Paris, 1917). See also his *Le Président Wilson et l'évolution de la politique étrangère des États Unis* (Paris, 1918). No reporter was present at this private dinner, hence the newspapers, e.g., the *New York Times*, May 11, 1919, and the London *Times*, May 12, 1919, printed only the transcript prepared by Charles L. Swem.

Close wrote a brief account of the affair to his wife on May 10. He said that, the night before, he had attended a dinner given to the President by Sir Thomas Barclay and, Close added, "the guests were mostly high-brows, intellectually or otherwise. Among them two Princes, Prince Bonaparte and the Prince of Monaco." G. F. Close to Marva Close, May 10, 1919, TCL (G. F. Close Coll., NjP). Prince Bonaparte was Roland-Napoléon Bonaparte, grandnephew of Napoléon I; the Prince of Monaco was Albert Honoré Charles, Prince of Monaco. However, according to Sir Thomas, in his introduction of Wilson (T MS, WP, DLC), most of the guests were members and officers of the Institute of International Law.

Grayson apparently was not present at the dinner. If workingmen had been present, Close would surely have noted the fact. Moreover, Swem's transcript gives no evidence of any excision of Wilson's old story about the woman at the circus with the thin things on. We were not able to find Swem's shorthand notes of this speech in his shorthand notebooks in the C. L. Swem Coll., NjP. However, looking at the typed transcripts in the Wilson Papers and the Swem Collection, it would appear that Swem typed up his transcript hurriedly, making a few corrections, in order to hand copies to reporters on the night of May 10.

We are therefore forced to conclude that Grayson fabricated his account after reading Close's transcript, which is printed below, in order to cast Wilson's odd remarks in a reasonable context.

Hankey's Notes of a Meeting of the Council of Four[1]

President Wilson's House,
C.F.-3 Paris, May 9, 1919, 10:30 a.m.

1. LORD ROBERT CECIL, speaking on behalf of the Supreme Economic Council, and on the invitation of President Wilson, stated the general economic problem confronting the Associated Governments. He said that the most important part of the problem was to get Europe to work again. A great proportion of the population were out of work in most countries in Europe. It was useless merely to provide food; in fact the danger to social order was likely to become worse and not better if people were merely fed. It was essential that raw materials should be made available. Poland might be taken as a typical case. Her great textile industry, on which Lodz for instance was absolutely dependent, was entirely stopped for want of cotton and wool, although her factories and their machinery were practically intact. The trouble was simply that she had no money to buy raw materials and no exports (a large part of which formerly went to Russia) to send in exchange for them. Even agriculture was affected by the absence of raw materials, as the want of proper boots and clothing for agricultural labourers reduced their capacity to work. The problem then was how to provide credit. Personally he would not advise giving unlimited funds or even limited funds uncontrolled to the Polish Government who might spend them on military undertakings.

The problem, therefore, was twofold (a) to devise means of providing money, and (b) to devise means for seeing that it was used to set industry going. As far as he could see the position was getting worse and not better. What he had said of Poland, which he had taken merely as an instance, was generally true of Germany and other countries in Europe and the problem must be treated as a whole. Personally he regretted that there had not been a further relaxation of the Blockade some time ago. The problem was largely psychological and the continuance of the Blockade with a consequent feeling of distrust all over Europe was a large part of the difficulty. In the case of Belgium, for instance, it was clear that the provision of credit in itself was not sufficient as credits had there been offered without effecting a solution.

MR. LLOYD GEORGE asked whether prices did not constitute a large part of the difficulty, i.e., the anticipation that prices would fall had the effect of holding back orders.

LORD ROBERT CECIL agreed that this was a part of the difficulty but he said it was clear that it was necessary for a serious attempt to be

[1] The complete text of Hankey's minutes is printed in *PPC*, V, 521-25.

made at once to see that raw materials were obtained by the countries to which he referred. This was mainly a financial problem.

2. In addition, however, LORD ROBERT CECIL desired to make two following specific proposals with regard to the Blockade:

(a) That semi-public communications should be at once entered into with the border neutrals with a view to securing from them such undertakings as would, if necessary, enable the Blockade to be re-imposed even more effectively than before.

(b) That a public statement should at once be issued making clear what modifications in the Blockade have already been made and concluding with a statement that all the rest of the Blockade against Germany would be removed the moment Peace was signed.

(It was agreed that the above action (a) and (b) should be taken, it being understood that the removal of the Blockade would not apply to Bolshevist Russia.)

3. Lord Robert Cecil, continuing, said that, personally, he had no specific financial proposal to make and considered the problem was one to which the experts should devote themselves at once. He wished, however, to refer to a special and important difficulty in the case of Germany. We had provided Germany with the full amount of food she had paid for. In addition we had large quantities afloat for which payment had not been arranged. The Germans had always warned us that they could not find sufficient money to pay for their rations up to the harvest, and the attempts to help the situation by allowing exports had broken down. A paper had been prepared by the Finance and Food Sections of the Supreme Economic Council for delivery to the President of the German Financial Commission. This paper after describing the exact present position concluded with the statement that shipments would at once be stopped unless the German Government took certain immediate measures to provide further gold. This memorandum included the following statement as to the present position:

(i)	Food delivered to May 10	£19,050,000
(ii)	Foodstuffs afloat on May 10 or landed for delivery	£14,850,000
(iii)	Loading for May delivery	£5,100,000
(iv)	Balance collected for May delivery	£13,750,000
(v)	Foodstuffs collected for June delivery by German tonnage	£10,670,000
(vi)	Further United Kingdom supplies available for June	£5,000,000
	TOTAL:	£68,420,0000

The payment situation is as follows:

		Millions.
(i)	Original payments in gold and neutral currencies	6
(ii)	First deposit in Brussels	11
(iii)	Second Brussels deposit	7½
(iv)	Further deposit promised	10
	TOTAL:	34½

showing a deficit of over £30 million even when the further deposit promised was paid.

In answer to a question by Mr. Lloyd George, MR. HOOVER stated that he thought that if the Germans could find £75,000,000 sterling in all (i.e. about £7,000,000 more than the amounts required for the supplies referred to above) they could with the addition of their foreign credits manage to carry through to the harvest.

LORD ROBERT CECIL continuing, stated that one difficulty resulted from the smuggling of German private securities abroad. Some of these were said to be taken by aeroplane; others to have got across into the occupied territory and so to neutrals.

MR. NORMAN DAVIS said the German Government were in fact continuing to requisition securities.

MR. LLOYD GEORGE asked whether a large part of the Brazilian debt was not in fact in German hands.

MR. KEYNES stated that the part so held did not amount to very much. The German Government had obtained about £1,000,000 from this source.

(It was resolved that the Memorandum prepared for communication to the German Financial Commission should not be presented in view of the possible effect at this moment of a formal document of that character on the Peace negotiations. It was agreed, however, that the representatives of the Associated Governments should discuss the question verbally with the German representatives along the lines of the statement.)

4. PRESIDENT WILSON considered that the general financial problem could not be discussed to a conclusion at the present meeting but that further expert advice must first be obtained. On his motion it was resolved that:

"a Committee composed of two economic advisers from each of the Principal Allied and Associated Powers be requested to submit a systematic suggestion with regard to the means of assisting the nations which are in immediate need of both food, raw material and credit."

5. LORD ROBERT CECIL subsequently raised the question of the control of the Danube. He stated that the river was at present partly

under French and partly under British control, that there was general agreement that it was desirable to co-ordinate the control under a Commission of Four representing the four principal Associated Governments, but that a decision was required as to who should act as Chairman of this Commission. He himself hoped that Admiral Troubridge[2] would be chosen.

MR. HOOVER explained the practical obstruction to barge navigation resulting from the present complicated permit system, and he agreed with the proposal.

M. CLEMENCEAU stated that he considered it necessary that the whole should be under the supervision of the military Authorities but that subject to that he thought it would be suitable that Admiral Troubridge should be Chairman of the Commission, and he agreed to write to General Franchet d'Esperey suggesting that he should propose the appointment of Admiral Troubridge to this position.

6. MR. HOOVER raised the question of the restriction on export of food from the Banat to Austro-Hungary. He pointed out that the need for food in the latter country was desperate and that the Associated Governments were in fact with much difficulty importing food from great distances. At the same time there was actually a surplus of food in the adjacent Banat for which there were sufficient commodities in Austro-Hungary to provide payment. The Serbs, however, were refusing to allow the export of this food.

(It was agreed that M. Clemenceau should communicate with the Serbian Government intimating that the Associated Governments regarded it as of great importance that facilities for the export of foodstuffs from the Banat to German-Austria and, if a stable Government were established, to Hungary, should at once be given.)

T MS (SDR, RG 256, 180.03401/3, DNA).

[2] Adm. Sir Ernest Charles Thomas Troubridge, former head of the British naval mission to Serbia and admiral commanding on the Danube.

Hankey's Notes of a Meeting of the Council of Four[1]

President Wilson's House,
C.F.-2 Paris, May 9, 1919, 11:25 a.m.

(Mr. Hurst was introduced.)

PRESIDENT WILSON pointed out that the text of Article 430 of the Treaty of Peace differs from the instructions on the subject which were given to the Drafting Committee. The instructions to the Drafting Committee were as follows:

"In case either during or after this 15 years' delay, the Inter-Allied

> Commission of Reparations recognise that Germany refuse to execute the whole or part of the conditions agreed upon by her according to the present Treaty, the international re-occupation of part or the whole of the areas defined by Article 2 will take place immediately."

Article 430 of the Treaty reads as follows:

> "In case either during the occupation or after the expiration of the 15 years referred to above, the Reparation Commission finds that Germany has failed to observe the whole or part of her obligations under the present Treaty, the whole or part of the areas specified in Article 429 will be re-occupied immediately by the Allied and Associated forces."

The essential difference between the two texts, President Wilson pointed out, is that in the Article in the Peace Treaty the words "Germany has failed to observe" have been substituted for the original words "Germany refuse to execute."

MR. HURST pointed out that the change was a very small one. It was an Article in regard to which no action would take place for at least five years, and then it would only affect a relatively small area of territory.

MR. LLOYD GEORGE pointed out that there was considerable difference between refusal and failure to execute the Treaty.

PRESIDENT WILSON pointed out a further difference, namely, that the original draft, though loosely worded, was only intended to apply to Reparation, whereas Article 430 applied to the whole Treaty. The Reparation Commission had nothing to do with anything but Reparation. He agreed, however, that the original text was partly misleading.

MR. HURST said that this would entail the modification of Article 430, and no doubt an opportunity would arise during the negotiations with the Germans. The alteration would be to Germany's advantage, so that Germany was not likely to object. He undertook to arrange for a Meeting of the Drafting Committee in the afternoon, and to present a fresh draft by the following morning.

PRESIDENT WILSON asked whether the word "may" should not be substituted for "will" in the last line.

M. CLEMENCEAU asked what the original text was.

MR. HURST said it was "will."

M. CLEMENCEAU said he would prefer to adhere to the original text, owing to the effect of a change on the French people.

MR. HURST said the difficulty could be surmounted by using the future tense in the French text.

(It was agreed that the Drafting Committee should prepare a

fresh draft of Article 430 to be presented to the Supreme Council of the Principal Allied and Associated Powers on the following morning.)

(Mr. Hurst withdrew.)

(It was agreed in the afternoon to discuss the action to be taken in the event of a failure on the part of the Germans to sign the Treaty of Peace.)

(Sir Maurice Hankey was instructed to circulate a memorandum by Marshal Foch.

He circulated at the Meeting the memorandum by the Allied Admirals on the Naval action to be taken.)

T MS (SDR, RG 256, 180.03401/2, DNA).

[1] The complete text of these minutes is printed in *PPC*, V, 519-20.

From Tasker Howard Bliss, with Enclosure

My dear Mr. President: Paris, May 9th, 1919.

Just as I am leaving my hotel for a conference with Marshal Foch at his office, I received the enclosed telegram which I send you at once.

Mr. Baker's statement in the last paragraph offers one or the other of two alternatives without recommendation as to which should be taken nor as to which one public sentiment at home favors.

If Congress and the people want war to be made upon Bolshevism by force of arms, we should, in my opinion, undertake that war with such a force as would enable us to be independent of any Japanese, Chinese or Russian allies. If General Graves is ordered to make war on Bolsheviks and to support Kolchak's government, it will be impossible for him to do this without being under the command of the Japanese commander-in-chief. I do not think that this under any circumstances should be permitted.

On the other hand, if we send a large force, it should be kept in mind that in all certainty the Japanese will send a still larger one in order that they may keep the upper hand.

Sincerely yours, Tasker H. Bliss.

TLS (WP, DLC).

E N C L O S U R E

[Washington] 7th May [1919]

NDB 13 RUSH FOR THE PRESIDENT.

The following message has just been received from General Graves at Vladivostok:

"MAY 4TH SECRET

Paragraph 1 Slaughter[1] telegraphs that Soukin,[2] foreign minister, has just told him in substance as follows: That reports as to conduct of army transportation places the government in a very delicate position on account of the railroad guards in which American soldiers are coming toward Irkutsk; that contact and cooperation with American soldiers is impossible because America is not yet convinced of the right and justice of our cause and so fails to sympathize with us; that American troops who do not sympathize with the Russian government coming so close to the seat of government would weaken this government without in any way assisting it; that it migh[t] promote a feeling that America in her position of spectator is passively against the government and so encourage resistance to our authority which is now making itself felt in this region; that small incidents so close to them would be more easily seized by Japanese propagandists to still further antagonize Russian people and create a feeling between Russia and America; that we are sincere in this statement and unless the American troops can come as the open and avowed enemies of Bolshevism we believe that their coming constitutes a real danger for the government and for the traditional friendship of Russia and America. In pursuance of these beliefs General Romanoffsky[3] has been instructed to protest to the Railroad Committee as to the distribution of foreign troops as guards. The British and French have been instructed to sustain his objection and believe that American troops should not come to Irkutsk. End of statement.

Paragraph 2 Colonel Morrow[4] has just telegraphed from Verkhneudinsk that the Russian general, citing authority of Kolchalk, states Russian guards in Baikal sector assigned to Americans must not be changed and the Russians are increasing their guard, and will not vacate railroad and guard barracks in our sector(s)

Paragraph 3 This action of Kolchalk shown by these two telegrams might indicate that object mentioned in my cable 238[5] has been accomplished. I am inclined to think, however, that the Kolchalk adherents believe they are able to handle the situation without our military, and by our policy of non-interference we are a source of weakness to Kolchalk. This is probably true as a great percentage of Russians consider the American Government as the ideal government for themselves. The fact that we are the only foreign power here not supporting Kolchalk causes Russians who believe in American form of government to mistrust and oppose him. This creates a situation demanding immediate consideration. The Cossacks are just as opposed to us as they are to peasants and others who will not support them. The Japanese control these armed Cossacks in Eastern Siberia and will embroil us with them when it suits their purpose to do so. Ivanoff's[6] troops are now interfering with the operation of Eastern section of railroad under American guard, and General Michaloff[7] is doing the same thing in Baikal section. We cannot submit to interference, if we do we fail in our duty to keep trains moving. Russian military claims it is a military necessity. Any troubles with Cossack troops will be used by Japanese for propaganda purposes against the United States.

Paragraph 4 The conduct of American soldiers has been very good, although many false and malicious reports are made against them, such as American soldier committed some specified offense but never in such detail that falseness of charge can be established. I will not move from Lake Baikal to any other part of the railroad and such a proposition is an insult to the United States.

Paragraph 5 The British and French military here have no troops and are not guarding any part of the railroad but are determined if possible to force the use of American troops to act against all armed forces not supporting Kolchalk. My belief is the people in Eastern Siberia have no confidence in Kolchalk representatives here consequently they lack confidence in his promises. Ivanoff Rinoff has sent punitive expeditions to various parts of this province and the Japanese have sent such expeditions to various parts of Amur province. I have absolute proof that Ivanoff's troops have tortured killed and robbed the people. I also have similar reports with reference to actions of Japanese troops but have no means of establishing the truth of these reports. This has created a situation which I believe will have to be fought out by the Russian factions in Eastern Siberia. If we continue our policy here we will almost surely have armed conflicts with Russian troops as they are determined we cannot remain in Siberia and continue the policy of non-interference and they claim such policy is impossible under existing conditions. The Bolsheviks call attention to our failure to help Kolchalk and this has great influence with the peasants.

Paragraph 6 We are now squarely up against the proposition of using force or getting out as the Russian military are coming our sector and evidently are not going to ignore us but practically attempt to take over our duties in guarding railroad. Graves."

Paragraph Either General Graves should be directed to cooperate with the Kolchalk government or he ought to be withdrawn.

Baker.

T telegram (WP, DLC).

[1] That is, Maj. Homer Havron Slaughter.

[2] That is, Jean Sookine.

[3] That is, B. S. Romanovskii.

[4] Col. Charles H. Morrow, commander of American troops in the Lake Baikal region.

[5] Not found.

[6] That is, Gen. Pavel Pavlovich Ivanov-Rinov.

[7] Grigorii Mikhailovich Semenov.

Hankey's and Mantoux's Notes of a Meeting of the Council of Four[1]

President Wilson's House,
Paris, May 9, 1919, 4 p.m.

C.F.-4

1. SIR MAURICE HANKEY handed M. Clemenceau the draft of a letter prepared at M. Clemenceau's request, and agreed to by Mr. Hoover and the British Experts, inviting M. Pasitch to permit the export of food-stuffs from the Banat to Hungary.

M. CLEMENCEAU approved that the terms of the letter carried out the decisions reached in the morning, and undertook to despatch it.

2. The Council had before them the following documents:

1. A Note from Marshal Foch (Appendix I) as to the military action to be taken in the emergency contemplated.
2. A Note from the Naval Representatives of the Allied and Associated Powers on the Naval steps to be taken in the same contingency (Appendix II).

MR. LLOYD GEORGE pointed out that no very drastic proposal was contained in either of these documents.

PRESIDENT WILSON said that what was most disturbing him was that a certain period of time was allowed for the execution of the naval and military clauses, the maximum amount allowed being three months for the destruction of certain fortifications. For this period after the ratification of the Treaty of Peace, a much larger force would have to be maintained on the Rhine than thereafter. As far as he could recollect, his military advisers estimated it at 30 divisions. The United States' share of this would be such that they would have to stop sending troops home. By June 1st they would have reached the minimum contingent to be supplied by the United States—some 6 or 8 divisions. This was rather a serious problem, and serious not

[1] The complete text of Hankey's minutes is printed in *PPC*, V, 526-36.

only to the United States of America. It would mean a number of transports lying idle for some three months. Once ships were fitted as transports they were unsuited for commercial purposes. It would probably not be worthwhile to convert them for commercial purposes and then reconvert them for transport purposes.

MR. LLOYD GEORGE said that General Wilson had told him he was anxious and rather alarmed at the rapid withdrawal of the United States forces. He had asked him to speak to General Bliss on the matter before it was raised at the Supreme Council.

PRESIDENT WILSON said that at present the United States were shipping 300,000 men a month homewards.

MR. LLOYD GEORGE speculated as to the number of troops required for the occupation of Berlin. These were possibilities that ought not to be excluded from purview, and this was the reason for General Wilson's anxiety.

M. CLEMENCEAU thought 6 divisions would be enough.

MR. LLOYD GEORGE thought to this it would be necessary to add the occupation of the Lines of Communication. He asked the distance, however, from Berlin to the Rhine, and to the sea.

SIR MAURICE HANKEY estimated the distance from Frankfurt to Berlin at about 250 to 300 miles, and the distance from Berlin to Stettin about 90 miles.

NOTE. The discussion was adjourned at this point and resumed later. It will be more convenient to continue the record at this point.

MR. LLOYD GEORGE said he would like the Military representatives at Versailles specifically to consider what forces would be required for the occupation of Berlin. It was unnecessary for the Council to commit itself to a decision because it asked for this information. In his view, there was a good deal to be said for the occupation of Berlin if Germany refused to sign the Treaty. It would be the outward and visible sign of smashing the Junkers. They would never be convinced otherwise. He felt sure of this after hearing Brockdorff-Rantzau's speech.

PRESIDENT WILSON said the hope rested on the remainder of Germany ridding themselves of the Junkers. Apart from Brockdorff-Rantzau, the other German delegates had looked reasonable men.

MR. LLOYD GEORGE pointed out that none the less they had allowed the Junkers to take the lead. They could not free themselves from the sense of servitude to the Junkers.

PRESIDENT WILSON thought that Mr. Lloyd George's theory was correct that the insolent parts of Brockdorff-Rantzau's speech had been his own and the reasonable parts supplied by the other delegates.

MR. LLOYD GEORGE pointed out that there was no cohesion or unity of thought in the document.

M. CLEMENCEAU suggested that Marshal Foch should be invited to the Council to give his views as to the amount of force required for the occupation of Berlin.

MR. LLOYD GEORGE suggested that Marshal Foch should also be asked to consider whether the Poles ought to make any advance on Berlin.

(It was agreed that Marshal Foch should be heard at 11 o'clock on the following day.)

3. PRESIDENT WILSON presented a military problem to his colleagues. The United States, he said, as agreed between the Allied and Associated Powers some time back, had been trying to send supplies to the Civilian population of Siberia from Vladivostock. By agreement between the Allies and a Mr. Stevens,[2] who, long ago in the days of the old regime had been in Siberia, had become the head of a somewhat inconvenient Commission to run the railroads of Siberia, the United States had agreed to police the railroads as far west as Irkutsk. The position was that the United States Government did not believe in Koltchak. The British and French military representatives in Siberia, however, were supporting him. Koltchak had become irritated by the presence on the railway of United States soldiers, whom he regarded as neutrals. Moreover, the impression had got abroad among the peasants of Siberia that the United States was the standard of a free Government which they ought to imitate. When they saw the attitude of neutrality taken up by the United States soldiers, they thought there must be something wrong with the Government of Koltchak. Further, the Cossacks were out of sympathy with the United States soldiers and he suspected that the Japanese would be glad to have a collision between the Cossacks and American soldiers. As a consequence of this state of affairs the United States Government found itself faced with the two following alternatives:

1. To take sides with Koltchak and send much stronger forces to Siberia.
2. To withdraw.

If the former alternative were adopted and the United States increased their forces it was certain that the Japanese would increase theirs still more. The original agreement had been that the Japanese and the United States should send roughly equivalent forces.[3]

[2] That is, John Frank Stevens.

[3] As on several previous occasions, Wilson said what he had become convinced was a fact. Actually, the Japanese government had said that it intended to send 12,000 men to Siberia. However, it very explicitly reserved the right to send additional troops if, in its

When the United States sent 9,000 men the Japanese sent 12,000 men. He had not objected to this slight discrepancy, but the numbers of Japanese had subsequently gone up to 70,000, which had afterwards been reduced to a nominal 30,000. This, however, left a great disproportion. If the United States troops continued merely to guard the railway and to maintain, as it were, a neutral position, he was advised that collisions were bound to occur. If United States soldiers were attacked, it could not be expected that they would do nothing. If they were withdrawn, the field would be left to the Japanese and Koltchak, who was supported by the Allies.

He then read a series of telegrams from General Graves[4] commanding the United States forces in Siberia, bearing out the above summary of the position, and pointing out that if the present policy were continued, there would almost certainly be a collision between the United States troops and Russian troops.

MR. LLOYD GEORGE said that this strengthened his view as to the need of arriving at a policy in regard to Russia. Koltchak was advancing Eastward at a very remarkable rate. He was in a position either to move Northwards and join hands with the forces based on Archangel, or to march on Moscow.

PRESIDENT WILSON said he had always been of opinion that the proper policy of the Allied and Associated Powers was to clear out of Russia and leave it to the Russians to fight it out among themselves.

MR. LLOYD GEORGE asked that before a decision should be taken, the Council should hear M. Tchaikowsky.[5]

PRESIDENT WILSON agreed.

MR. LLOYD GEORGE suggested that President Wilson should send a reply to General Graves asking him to take no action for the moment, as the whole problem was being considered by the Allied and Associated Powers.

PRESIDENT WILSON said the risk of this was that there might be a collision between the United States and Russian troops. He suggested that the Allied and Associated Powers should simultaneously ask Koltchak what his programme was.

MR. LLOYD GEORGE suggested he might be asked two definite questions:

(1) Will you allow the peasants to retain the land or do you propose to restore the old seigneurial rights?

(2) Are you prepared to revive the Constituent Assembly?

judgment, it proved necessary to do so. See the index entry, "Russia—Siberia, intervention in," Vol. 49.

[4] For example, W. S. Graves to FLP, March 5, 1919, embodied in FLP to RL and V. C. McCormick, March 13, 1919, Vol. 55; and, particularly, the Enclosure just printed with THB to WW, May 9, 1919.

[5] That is, Nikolai Vasil'evich Chaikovskii.

PRESIDENT WILSON, in regard to the first point, said that a few days ago he had asked a very Russophile friend[6] whether the peasants had really got the land out of all the chaos in Russia. His friend had replied that they had only got it in a very inequitable way, each man having seized the land nearest to him. The difficulty would not only be to distribute the land to the peasants, but to systematise the existing distribution involving in some cases dispossession of individuals and groups.

(After some further discussion during which Mr. Lloyd George produced a map showing the great advance that Koltchak's troops had made, it was agreed that M. Tchaikowsky should be heard on the following day at noon.)

Mr. Lloyd George undertook that Mr. Philip Kerr, who knew his address, should summon him.

§ Mantoux's notes:

Wilson. I have to talk to you about a rather embarrassing problem for the American government, that of Siberia. When we first attempted to send food to the Russian populations, the Allies had agreed to send an American, Mr. Stevens, to the first revolutionary government of Russia, who was placed at the head of a commission entrusted above all with assuring the operation of the Trans-Siberian Railway. Since then, American troops have guarded the railroad between the Pacific and Irkutsk.

Our government does not have confidence in Admiral Kolchak, who is supported by France and England. Kolchak's partisans are irritated by the presence of the American soldiers, whom they view as neutrals, because of their attitude. This attitude, moreover, makes an impression upon the peasants who regard the United States as the democracy *par excellence* and conclude from America's refusal to declare itself in favor of Kolchak that the latter does not deserve to be supported.

The Cossacks are clearly hostile toward us, and the Japanese could not ask for anything better than to see a collision between the Americans and the Cossacks take place. In these conditions, we should either support Kolchak and reinforce our army of occupation or withdraw completely. But if we increase our effectives, Japan will do the same. When we went to Siberia, we had reached an agreement with Japan to send equal forces there. In fact, we sent 9,000 men and Japan 12,000. But little by little, she increased her effectives and brought them up to 70,000 men.

Lloyd George. She has promised to reduce them to 30,000.

Wilson. Even if 30,000 Japanese remain in Siberia, the number is

[6] Probably Charles R. Crane, who was still in Paris.

all out of proportion to our own. If we confine ourselves to guarding the line as we have done so far, exposing American soldiers to difficulties with Kolchak's partisans, I fear incidents. If, on the other hand, we reinforce the troops who guard the railroad, I fear a coalition between the Cossacks and the Japanese against us.

I am obliged to take an immediate decision. We have received a note on this subject from Admiral Kolchak's Minister of Foreign Affairs, which complains about the attitude of the Americans.[7]

President Wilson reads this note aloud and adds: In short, we must either act with Kolchak or else withdraw.

Lloyd George. This question is connected to another, vaster one: it is becoming necessary for us to agree upon a common policy in Russia. According to our information, Admiral Kolchak is rapidly advancing west of the Urals, and that seems to demonstrate that either the Bolsheviks no longer have the force to resist, or they are completely lacking in transportation. What is the latest news?

Hankey. The latest telegrams show that Admiral Kolchak is sending forces at the same time in the direction of Archangel and toward the Southwest.

Wilson. For myself, I have always been of the opinion that we should withdraw from Russia and let the Russians settle their own affairs themselves.

Lloyd George. I suggest we hear M. Tchaikovsky, the head of the government in Archangel. He is, as I have already said to you, a liberal of truly advanced ideas, and he believes that, by intervening in time, we can impose conditions of government on Kolchak.

Wilson. We will be able to obtain promises from him: but then how to force him to keep them?

Lloyd George. The fact that Bolshevism will have finally failed because it encountered the opposition of the world will be a lesson for Kolchak. Besides, he will be much more in our hands than the Bolsheviks could ever have been, because the Bolsheviks fed off the country like a worm on a leaf, but now only the membranes remain. The Russian government, whatever it is, will not be able to acquire locomotives without us, will not be able to acquire rolling stock; and without locomotives, it could never govern Russia.

M. Bark, the former Finance Minister of the Russian Empire, with whom I very recently had a conversation, says that Kolchak is a fairly reliable soldier, for whom there are no grounds for distrust. He also contests that Denikin is, as it has been said, a Germanophile, although he had as chief of staff an obviously czarist and militaristic schemer.[8] Kolchak is not only a man whom we can trust,

[7] Again, see the Enclosure printed with THB to WW, May 9, 1919. The Acting Minister of Foreign Affairs in the Kolchak government was Jean (John, Ivan) Sookine.

[8] Gen. B. S. Romanovskii.

but he is surrounded by young men who, before the revolution and in its beginnings, had taken an advanced position. I think we can impose conditions upon Kolchak if we do it now. I make a complete distinction between Kolchak and a man like Iudenich,[9] who is in Finland and is threatening Petrograd: the latter belongs to the old Russia.

Wilson. What conclusion should I draw with respect to keeping American troops in Siberia?

Lloyd George. I think it is better to postpone your decision until we have determined our policy in Russia. You might inform your representatives that we are first examining the overall question.

Wilson. What they fear is precisely the danger of the status quo.

Lloyd George. It is not a question of prolonging it; we will take a decision as soon as possible.

Wilson. We certainly have the right to ask Kolchak what his intentions are.

Lloyd George. His program is rather vague.

Wilson. He will have to be asked for precise details.

Lloyd George. First upon the agrarian question: he must be asked whether he is really determined not to take back land from the peasants.

Wilson. According to the information I have received from a man who knows Russia and her present situation very well, the peasants seized land randomly and haphazardly. The present distribution is the result of violence and has created new inequalities. It would obviously be necessary, in all justice, to regularize the operation and, in many cases, to redistribute lands; but it must be acknowledged that this would not be easy.

Lloyd George. It is necessary to resign oneself to some irregularities in this kind of revolution: the same occurred at the time of the French Revolution. After the agrarian question, the second question which should be raised would be that of the Constituent Assembly. We must force Kolchak to convene a truly representative Constituent Assembly.

Clemenceau. I am entirely of that opinion.

Wilson. When shall we hear M. Tchaikovsky?

Lloyd George. The sooner the better.

Wilson. I do not wish to run the risk of a collision between the American troops and the Cossacks of Siberia.

Lloyd George. We will have to take another decision: should our troops in Archangel go to meet Kolchak?

Wilson. The American troops in Archangel are not really secure.

[9] Gen. Nikolai Nikolaevich Iudenich, former czarist general, at this time living in Finland.

Lloyd George. If Admiral Kolchak can join us, it is the end of Bolshevism: that will prove its irremediable weakness, and, as we advance to the south, a very large number of Russians will rally to us. If Kolchak is on the point of succeeding, now is the time to impose our conditions and to negotiate with him.

Wilson. It is always dangerous to interfere in foreign revolutions.

Lloyd George. Here, it is the Russians who are taking the initiative; we will only support them.

Wilson. You have more experience than we do in far-flung expeditions. You have an officer corps which has a long tradition in this respect. As for ourselves, except in the Philippines, we have never had the same reason to act at a great distance, and the American officer remains first and foremost a citizen.

In accordance with your request, I am postponing my decision on the subject of Siberia. §

4. SIR MAURICE HANKEY reported that he had communicated to the Secretary-General the decision of the Supreme Council that the Commission on Responsibility for Breaches of the Laws of War should be asked to prepare draft articles for insertion in the Treaty of Peace with Austria. In reply, he had merely received articles contained in Annex IV to the report of the Commission,[10] with a letter stating that these were intended to apply equally to the cases of Germany, Austria, Hungary, Bulgaria and Turkey.

Sir Maurice Hankey pointed out, however, that these draft articles had been superseded by other articles prepared by the Supreme Council.

(After a short discussion it was agreed:

(1) That Articles 228, 229 and 230 of the Conditions of Peace handed to the German Delegates should be taken by the Drafting Committee as the basis for the preparation of corresponding articles in the Treaties of Peace with Austria and with Hungary.

(2) That the Treaties of Peace with Austria and with Hungary should contain no article corresponding to Article 227 of the Conditions of Peace, handed to the German representatives, since it was not desired to arraign the Emperor of Austria.)

Sir Maurice Hankey was instructed to communicate this decision

[10] REPORT PRESENTED TO THE PRELIMINARY PEACE CONFERENCE BY THE COMMISSION ON THE RESPONSIBILITY OF THE AUTHORS OF THE WAR AND ON ENFORCEMENT OF PENALTIES, March 29, 1919, printed report (WP, DLC). "Annex IV, Provisions for Insertion in Treaties with Enemy Governments" appears on p. 65. The six articles required each "Enemy Government" to recognize the right of the Allied and Associated Governments to set up a tribunal to try war criminals; to recognize the decisions of the tribunal and allow the execution of penalties imposed by it; to make all efforts to deliver up for trial any person alleged to have committed war crimes; and to furnish, upon demand, the names of persons who might be liable for trial, as well as all documents needed for such trials.

to the Secretary-General for the information of the Drafting Committee.

5. SIR MAURICE HANKEY produced a report signed by Admiral Benson, Admiral Hope, Admiral de Bon, Admiral Grassi and Admiral Isamu Takeshita on the subject of the disposal of submarines. With the exception of Admiral de Bon, it was unanimously recommended that all the submarines, submarine salvage vessels and docks surrendered by Germany should be broken up. Admiral de Bon did not, however, agree in this view and considered that the destruction of submarines and the future of submarine warfare could not be separated.

(The subject was postponed for future consideration.)

6. SIR MAURICE HANKEY read the following letter from Lord Cunliffe:

"Dear Sir Maurice—It has been suggested that before the Committee which is to report on what Austria could and should pay can make any real progress the "Big Four" must decide whether the new States, Poland, etc., are to bear any portion of the costs of the war. Could you get this point settled? Yours very truly, Cunliffe."

(The subject was postponed for further consideration.)

7. MR. LLOYD GEORGE said he had had a letter from Sir George Riddell[11] drawing attention to the risk that when the German delegates made communications to the Allies, German journalists would telegraph them to Germany where efforts would be made to influence public opinion throughout the world in favour of the German point of view.

M. CLEMENCEAU said he did not much care if they did.

(It was agreed to take no action.)

8. SIR MAURICE HANKEY produced the formula which he had drafted in an attempt to give effect to a decision which, broadly speaking, he thought had been arrived at on the previous day.

There was a short discussion in the course of which M. Orlando said he would like to consider the draft carefully before taking a decision.

Sir Maurice Hankey's draft is attached in Appendix 3. The alterations suggested in the course of the discussion are underlined.

APPENDIX I TO C.F.4.

No. 32/Me. MINISTRY OF WAR. PARIS. April 11th, 1919.

The President of the Council, Minister of War, to Mr. Lloyd George, Prime Minister.

[11] Sir George (Allardice) Riddell, proprietor of several newspapers and magazines, at this time liaison between the British press and the British delegation at the peace conference.

I have the honour to transmit to you the accompanying copy of a Note from Marshal Foch.

This Note records the opinions expressed by Marshal Foch, General Bliss, General Sir Henry Wilson and General Diaz in the course of a meeting which they held on April 8th in pursuance of a decision of the Supreme Council of the Allied and Associated Governments.

For the Minister and by order. [G. Clemenceau]

General Division

Head Military Cabinet.

Commander-in-Chief of the Allied Armies.

April 9th. 1919. No. 19

NOTE.

In pursuance of the decision of the Supreme Council of the Allied and Associated Governments dated April 8th,[12] Marshal Foch and Generals Bliss, Sir Henry Wilson and Diaz met on April 8th. at 5 p.m.

They expressed the following opinion:

We still possess to-day sufficient forces to undertake operations which might be necessary to overcome all difficulties likely to arise from the signature of Peace, for we shall not be confronted by armies properly organised or of equal value to our own. It is, however, clear that this advantageous situation is changing daily to our prejudice as time goes on and that it may be reversed whenever we have only reduced forces under arms.

1. *Question put*: "In the case of the Enemy Powers (Germany, Austria, Hungary, Bulgaria and Turkey) refusing to sign the Treaty of Peace."

In that case it would be a question of resuming the war in the form of operations directed against the centres of resistance of the Enemy Powers and, since the resistance would presumably come from Governments, directed in principle against the capitals or seats of those Governments.*

2. *Question put*: "In the case where such disorder prevailed in one or other of the Enemy countries, that there was no Government to sign a Treaty of Peace."

In that case operations would be resumed in an attempt to achieve thereby the ends which the absence of any Government would leave in suspense; for instance, the payment of indemnities. For this purpose operations would be directed in such manner as to take possession of the centres of enemy wealth such as, so far as Germany is

* The United States could not participate in any action against Bulgaria or Turkey, since they are not at war with those Powers.

[12] See the minutes of the Council of Four printed at April 8, 1919, 11 a.m., Vol. 57.

concerned, the Mines of the Ruhr Basin, with a view to securing by the occupation and exploitation of those centres the fulfillment of the Clause set forth in the Treaty.

With regard to Austria, however, where the employment of such means might prove deficient, it appears especially urgent to check the development of Bolshevism by a prompt occupation of political centres and railways having their termini therein, in order to secure the communications of the troops of occupation.

3. *Question put*: "In the case in which the German Government would be able to sign the Treaty of Peace on behalf of the whole of Germany, with the exception of Bavaria, on account of its jurisdiction neither being recognised nor existing in point of fact in that country."

In that case it would be necessary, after having treated with Germany, to reduce Bavaria by military action taken in concert with Italy, an operation which at the present time offers no difficulties.

In any one of the cases contemplated it would no doubt be necessary to revert to a certain extent to the enforcement of the Blockade; this question is not dealt with here, as it is in the province of the Admirals who are being likewise consulted.

(Signed) FOCH.

APPENDIX II TO C.F.4.

SECRET.

M. 79.

NAVAL ACTION IN THE EVENT OF NON-SIGNATURE BY ENEMY POWERS OF THE TREATIES OF PEACE.

In conformity with the request of the President of the Supreme Council of 8 April, addressed to Admiral Wemyss, the Admirals representing in Paris the Navies of the United States of America, the British Empire, France and Italy met on 10 April to consider the steps to be taken in each of the contingencies mentioned in the President's memorandum. They submit the attached report for the consideration of the Council.

2. If any of the enemy Powers refuse to sign the Treaty of Peace, hostilities against such Power no doubt would be resumed, but in the second contingency, where the non-signature of the Treaty resulted from there being no responsible Government, military occupation only might be necessary.

3. The operations to which the Allied navies could contribute would be:

(a) The establishment of a formal blockade.

(b) Military operations against defended ports in conjunction with the Allied armies.

(c) Occupation of surrendered ports.

The two latter would necessitate joint study and mutual understanding by the Military and Naval Staffs.

4. As the navies are not concerned in the case of Bavaria, the attached report refers only to contingencies Nos. (1) and (2) of the President's memorandum.

		For
(Signed)	W. S. BENSON, Admiral	The United States of America.
(")	GEORGE P. W. HOPE Rear-Admiral (on behalf of Admiral Wemyss who concurs in the report.)	The British Empire.
(")	de BON	France.
(")	M. GRASSI,	Italy.

PARIS,
10 April, 1919.

NAVAL ACTION POSSIBLE IN CERTAIN CONTINGENCIES.

I. GERMANY.

So far as Germany's sea forces are concerned her submarines have all been surrendered or rendered useless, and the Allied Naval Armistice Commission reports that the surface ships-of-war left in Germany are in such a condition that their value as a fighting force may be regarded as negligible. It would, therefore, appear impossible for Germany to raise an efficient naval fighting force in a reasonable time under the existing conditions of material and discipline; and, even if such a force were raised, the Allies could muster sufficient ships in the North Sea and Baltic to deal with the situation.

2. With regard to the principal German ports, it must be borne in mind that so far as is known the forts defending them are still effective, and strong opposition must be anticipated to any attempt to occupy them. Further, the maintenance of a *naval force alone* in a German port would be both difficult and hazardous, and its presence would bring no more pressure to bear on the German people as a whole than the ordinary measures of an effective blockade.

3. The following are considered the only *purely* naval measures which could be taken:

(a) The officers and men of the ships interned at Scapa made prisoners-of-war.

(b) The interned ships at Scapa seized.

(c) All fishing by German vessels prohibited.

(d) All German vessels found at sea, either with or without permits, seized.

(e) The blockade re-established by declaring a formal blockade of the whole of the enemy coast.

4. The Blockade has been gradually relaxed and in its present form is becoming increasingly difficult to maintain.

In order to enforce a formal blockade in the Baltic, the Allied force in that sea would require strengthening and bases would have to be established at Libau or elsewhere. It would probably be necessary to occupy such bases by a military force, transported by sea.

In the case of the North Sea the minefields in the Bight would prevent a close blockade.

5. In the event of Germany refusing to sign the peace terms, some action of an immediate and striking nature would be desirable.

Naval bombardments or demonstrations without the co-operation of the military on land would be both objectionable and ineffective.

Blockade can only act slowly, whilst the remaining measures mentioned in paragraph 3 would not produce the desired effect.

6. The Admirals therefore conclude that no naval measures *by themselves* are likely to be effective, and that any naval operations, such as the occupation of selected ports, must necessarily be carried out in conjunction with, or in continuation of, the operations of the land forces of the Allies.

II. AUSTRIA AND HUNGARY.

All vessels-of-war are already interned or in Allied hands on the Danube.

The principal ports are in the occupation of the Allies.

2. With regard to economic pressure, the present system of inspection of all ships could be adjusted to reduce imports as considered desirable, and the establishment of a formal blockade of the Adriatic appears unnecessary.

3. With regard to the Danube, all the monitors and other armed craft are now under the control of the Allies. They have recently retired below Baja, and if an advance up the river is contemplated it could only take place in conjunction with military measures.

III. BULGARIA.

Although the blockade has been raised there should be little difficulty in re-establishing it.

The Danube, so far as Bulgaria is concerned, is already under control.

IV. TURKEY.

The blockade, which has been raised, could be re-established.

2. All forts and other defences commanding the passage between

the Mediterranean and the Black Sea are now in the hands of the Allies. They should be completely destroyed as soon as possible.

APPENDIX III TO C.F.4.

It is agreed:

That the Treaties of Peace with Austria and with Hungary shall each contain Articles binding *Austria and Hungary as well as the other* High Contracting Parties to recognise the frontiers of the various States formed out of the former Austro-Hungarian Empire and of all contiguous States. Wherever possible the complete boundaries of all these States are to be fixed in the said Treaties of Peace with Austria and with Hungary. In cases, however, where it is not found practicable to fix the whole of these boundaries before the signature of these Treaties *Austria and Hungary as well as the other* High Contracting Parties shall *agree to* recognise these States within such boundaries as may be subsequently determined by the Principal Allied and Associated Powers. This will, of course, not apply to Austrian-Hungarian territory, the boundaries of which will be fixed by the respective Treaties of Peace.

9th May 1919.

T MS (SDR, RG 256, 180.03401/4, DNA); Mantoux, II, 16-19.

To Georges Clemenceau

My dear Mr. President: Paris, 9 May, 1919.

You were kind enough to hand me and recommend to my attention the important letter from the President of the Republic[1] concerning the occupation of the Rhine territory, and I have retained it for a few days in order to give it full consideration. I had already heard several times a very impressive argument from the same point of view from Marshal Foch, and, along with my colleagues, had again and again considered the highly important matter upon which the letter dwells, but it was of course my duty, at your request, to consider it once more, as I have faithfully done.

As in every other matter of such gravity, there are, I realize, two sides to this question and it is exceedingly difficult to be sure that one has properly weighed them against one another; but after repeated consideration I am convinced that it would not be wise to go further than we have gone in the Treaty in respect to the occupation of the Rhine territory.

Thanking you for letting me see a letter which so fully and carefully sets the matter forth,

Sincerely yours, [Woodrow Wilson]

CCL (WP, DLC).

[1] See R. Poincaré to G. Clemenceau, April 28, 1919, and WW to R. Poincaré, May 7, 1919.

From Edward Mandell House, with Enclosure

Dear Governor: Paris, May 9, 1919.

I herewith enclose you a copy of a letter which has just come from Lloyd George and which he says he is giving to the press. Shall I make any reply? If so, what would you suggest?

George begins his letter with a misstatement. I never asked him to see Messrs Dunne, Walsh and Ryan. They called here they said at your request and asked if it would be possible to get the consent of the British to permit the delegates of the so called Irish Republic to come to Paris in order to lay their case before the Peace Conference.

I took up the matter through Wiseman who upon investigation thought that the Foreign Office would be willing to give them passports but before giving a definite answer, they preferred getting the consent of the Prime Minister. Later, I was told, the Prime Minister would like to discuss the subject directly with me. He did so and told me that he would like to see Messrs Ryan, Walsh and Dunne himself.

He held them here for more than ten days without setting a day. They made it clear to me that they never asked or desired to see the Prime Minister, but they merely wished an answer to their request concerning the Irish delegates. George then insisted that they wait for another week for him to see them. They consented to do this provided, in the meantime, they might be given passports to go to Ireland. This was granted.

These are the facts.

Affectionately yours, E. M. House

TLS (WP, DLC).

E N C L O S U R E

David Lloyd George to Edward Mandell House

Dear Colonel House, Paris. 9th May 1919.

You will remember that about a fortnight ago you asked me whether I would consent to see three American citizens who had come over to Paris in connection with the Irish problem and listen to what they had to say. As you informed me that they were responsible men who had rendered excellent service to the Allied cause during the war, I readily consented. I did so because I thought that it would not only be a good thing for me to hear at first hand the views of the representatives of some millions of American citizens of Irish descent, but that it might also be useful if they could learn direct from me the difficulties which even those British statesmen who were most sympathetic to Irish self-government had had to encounter when attempting to settle the Irish problem. I think that my record justifies my claim to consistent sympathy with Ireland's cause. Since I have been in Parliament I have voted for every Home Rule Bill which has been introduced including Mr. Gladstone's, and I have supported every proposal for conceding to Ireland the largest measure of self-government which was consistent with the maintenance of the Union of the United Kingdom. This is the only form of Home Rule which has ever been asked for by Parnell, Davitt, Dillon and Redmond.[1]

As at the time I was too busy with the Peace Treaty to meet the Irish American representatives, I received a message asking if I had any objection to their going to Ireland in order to study conditions on the spot. I replied that I had none, but I suggested that if they went to Ireland they should make a special point of getting into touch with Ulster opinion, in order that they might be able to judge fairly of the problem as a whole. There, as you are aware, you have a solid block of population alien in race, religion and traditions to the rest of Ireland and in the name of self-determination resisting subordination to an Irish Parliament. To my amazement I now find that these gentlemen, so far from investigating the Irish problem in a spirit of impartiality, announced on arrival in Dublin that they had come there to forward the disruption of the United Kingdom and the establishment of Ireland as an independent Republic. Thus the "Freeman's Journal" quotes Mr. Walsh as stating:

> "We do not appear in Paris or in Ireland in any position except as that of advocates of the recognition of the present Irish republic and we have no duty to perform except to assist the representatives of Ireland in any steps which they may find suitable to carry on without interference the governmental functions necessary to the well-being and development of their own land in their own way."[2]

In addition they have not hesitated to take part in great public demonstrations with men who, during the war, at the very moment when hundred of thousands of Americans, including American Irishmen were rushing across the Atlantic to stem and throw back the last desperate thrust of the Prussian autocracy, were actually conspiring with Germany to add to their perils and to thwart their aims. Not satisified with this, one of their number, who is, I believe a Judge in the United States[3] has been delivering speeches which are a distinct incentive to rebellion against the Constitution of the United Kingdom, from which I may quote the following:

> "We have come from a country in which men died and made tremendous sacrifices that they might be able to assert the right of self-determination—the establishment of a republic. We and those before us have lived in the great republic for some one hundred and forty years and we appreciate the beneficent results of a constitution selected with the consent of the Government under a republican form of government. Therefore we are here simply to express our symp[a]thy with you and for the other people of the world who are struggling for self-determination and a republican form of Government."

I am extremely anxious not to add to anyone's embarrassment at this time, but you will see that it is impossible for the British Government to permit inflammatory speeches of this kind to be delivered. I am also sure that you will agree with me that it is now quite impossible for me to see men who have so strangely abused an opportunity for helping to bring about that real reconciliation in Ireland which I so long to see and which I know that you also have so much at heart. There is nothing that I more desire than real friendship between all sections in Ireland and thereby a lasting settlement of the Anglo-Irish problem. But I cannot believe that this kind of action can lead to anything but further bitterness and deeper divisions. The conduct of these gentlemen is exactly as if responsible Englishmen had gone to the United States during the controversy between the North and the South and delivered speeches inciting the Confederacy in the name of self-determination to destroy the Union. I think I know what action President Lincoln would have taken in such a case and no Englishman would have complained.

As these gentlemen have quoted my name very freely in Ireland I feel sure that you will have no objection to my sending this letter to the Press. Yours sincerely, D Lloyd George

TLS (E. M. House Papers, CtY).

[1] That is, Charles Stewart Parnell, Michael Davitt, John Dillon, and John Edward Redmond.

[2] *The* (Dublin) *Freeman's Journal and National Press*, May 5, 1919.

[3] Lloyd George was mistaken. He must have been thinking of Daniel Florence Cohalan, a justice of the Supreme Court of New York. The quotation below is from a speech by Edward Fitzsimons Dunne in Dublin on May 5, printed in *ibid.*, May 6, 1919. Dunne had been Democratic governor of Illinois, 1913-1917.

Edward Mandell House to David Lloyd George

Dear Prime Minister: Paris. May 9, 1919.

In reply to your letter of today which has just come I would like to make it clear that Messrs Walsh, Dunne and Ryan did not ask to see you. They wished me to ascertain whether the British Government would be willing to give the delegates of the so called Irish Republic safe conduct to Paris. This request was passed to you and you expressed a desire to talk the matter over with them.

Because of your great preoccupation you found it impossible to make an engagement for a week or ten days. They became impatient at the delay and requested that in the meantime they be given passports to visit Ireland. However, they did not couple this request with the statement that they desired "to study conditions on the spot."

I am, my dear Prime Minister,

Yours very sincerely, [E. M. House]

CCL (E. M. House Papers, CtY).

From Douglas Wilson Johnson, with Enclosure

My dear Mr. President: Paris, May 9, 1919.

I beg to inform you that I have drafted a formula for the settlement of the Adriatic question which has the unanimous approval of the American territorial specialists concerned with the Fiume and Dalmatian problems, with the exception of the Chief of the Austro-Hungarian division[1] who is absent. I discussed this formula to-day with M. Trumbic and he told me that with certain slight reservations it would be acceptable to the Yugo-Slavs.

Colonel House has recommended me to ask you to receive me as he believes it preferable that the details of this formula should be communicated to you direct and not at second hand. Under these circumstances I shall be grateful if you will be good enough to let me know when you can receive me.

Respectfully yours, Douglas Johnson.

TLS (WP, DLC).

[1] That is, Charles Seymour.

E N C L O S U R E

SUGGESTED FORMULA FOR ADRIATIC SETTLEMENT

1. Italy to receive the Sexten Valley[1] (shaded green on accompanying map), a strategic gateway into northern Italy (not included in Treaty of London).

2. Italy to receive the Tarvis[2] district (shaded green on map), a railway junction of much strategic and commercial importance (not included in Treaty of London).

3. Italy to receive the natural geographic frontier in Julian Venetia[3] shown by heavy black line on the accompanying map.

4. Italian troops to be immediately withdrawn from areas east of this line. A plebiscite to be held within a period to be fixed by the League of Nations, and under appropriate safeguards, to determine whether the area shaded blue on the accompanying map shall belong to Italy or Jugo-Slavia.

5. Italian troops to be immediately withdrawn from the vicinity and city of Fiume, which shall be administered, within the Jugo-Slav customs regime, by the League of Nations until its future status is determined. The city and district of Fiume, together with its moles, docks, basins and other port instrumentalities, to be ceded to Italy when and if the following conditions are fulfilled:

(a) By a plebiscite held within a period to be fixed by the League of Nations, and under appropriate safeguards, the city and district of Fiume by a majority of all votes cast manifests its desire to be annexed to Italy under condition that and as soon as the provisions in (b) have been satisfied.

(b) Within six months after the plebiscite provided in (a) has been held, and in case this plebiscite results favorably to the annexation of Fiume to Italy under the conditions specified, Italy shall proceed to the construction in and about the bay of Buccari[4] of all the port works, including moles, docks, basins, warehouses, office-buildings, railway tracks and all other port instrumentalities, necessary to provide for Jugo-Slavia and neighboring states a port whose facilities and possibilities of future development shall not be inferior to those of the present port of Fiume; and shall construct rail connections between the new port and the Fiume-Agram and Fiume-Laibach[5] railways not inferior to the existing rail connections between Fiume and the interior. Construction shall proceed under the supervision of an international commission of experts appointed by majority vote of the Council of the League of Nations, which shall certify that the port works, when completed, are not inferior to the present port of Fiume in facilities, possibilities of future development, and rail connections with the interior. The works to be completed within a period to be determined by majority vote of the Council of the League of Nations, and to be transferred without encumbrance to Jugo-Slavia under such conditions as to free port provisions as the Council of the League of Nations may by majority vote determine.

(c) Italy shall assure in perpetuity, to all nations concerned, the free and unhampered transit across the city and district of Fiume of persons and goods en route between points outside the territory of said city and district. (None of the territory to be ceded to Italy in accordance with the provisions of Section 5 was promised to Italy by the Treaty of London.)

In case any of the above conditions remain unfulfilled at the end of a period to be fixed by majority vote of the Council of the League of Nations, Fiume shall be transferred to Jugo-Slav Sovereignty with such restrictions as to free port provisions as the Council of the League of Nations may by majority vote determine.

6. Italy to receive the islands of Lussin[o], Unie, Sansego, Asinella, Lissa and its adjacent islets including Busi and San Andrea,[6] and the Pelagosa[7] group (Pelagosa Grande, Pelagosa Piccola, Cajola, and immediately adjacent islets), (enclosed in green circles on accompanying map).

7. The town of Zara[8] to be made a free city.

8. Italian troops to be immediately withdrawn from all parts of the Istrian and Dalmatian islands and Dalmatian mainland not mentioned in paragraphs 6 and 7. A plebiscite to be held within a period of one year from date of this Treaty, under appropriate safeguards, prescribed by a majority of the Council of the League of Nations, to determine whether the area shaded red on the accompanying map shall, as a whole, belong to Italy or to Jugo-Slavia.

9. Italy to receive Valona and a sufficient hinterland for its defense.

10. The entire east Adriatic coast, from the former Austro-Italian frontier to the northern frontier of Albania, to be neutralized under the League of Nations. No fortresses to be allowed on any part of the coast, and no war vessels of any kind to be permitted in the waters bordering this coast. This provision to be accompanied by guarantees for the free passage of Jugo-Slav merchant vessels through the southern Adriatic and Straits of Otranto, even in time of war.

CC MS (WP, DLC).

[1] A narrow valley located near the Plöcken, or Monte Croce, Pass over the Carnic Alps between Austria and Italy.

[2] Now known by its Italian name, Tarvisio.

[3] Now known as Venezia Giulia.

[4] Now known by its Yugoslavian name, Bakar.

[5] Now Rijeka-Zagreb and Rijeka-Ljubljana.

[6] Now known as Losinj, Unije, Sušak, Ilovik, Vis, Bisevo, and Sveti Andrija, respectively.
[7] Now known as the Pelagruz, or Palagruza, Islands.
[8] Now Zadar.

From Norman Hezekiah Davis, with Enclosure

My dear Mr. President: Paris, May 9, 1919.

With further reference to credits for Roumania, I desire to state that the United States Liquidation Commission, created by law for the purpose of disposing of Army stocks, is authorized, with the approval of the Treasury, to sell such stocks on credit, the credit so extended having no connection with credits already established by the Treasury Department for relief purposes in Europe. The withdrawal of your approval for the establishment of the credit of $5,000,000 for Roumania would not, therefore, interfere with the sale of Army supplies on credit to this Government, as contemplated in General Bliss' memorandum.[1] The Roumanian credit which you had previously authorized was for the purchase of food for relief, but Roumania has obtained a credit for a like amount from the Canadian Government, and as Mr. Hoover informed me that the Roumanian relief programme could probably be completed without this credit from the United States, I transmitted the Secretary of the Treasury's request for the withdrawal of your approval.

I am enclosing a memorandum on this general subject should you care to look into it further, and am also returning the letters which you sent to me, in case you desire to withdraw your approval of the proposed credit of $5,000,000 for Roumania.

I am, my dear Mr. President,

Faithfully yours, Norman H. Davis

TLS (WP, DLC).
[1] See THB to WW, March 26, 1919, Vol. 56.

ENCLOSURE

Memorandum for The President: Paris, 7th May, 1919.

The Roumanian Prime Minister[1] told me in March, before the subject was presented to the Council of Four, that the British and French Governments had agreed to furnish the credits necessary for the support of the Roumanian Army, but that he desired to obtain from the American Treasury credits for food, raw materials, and certain supplies from the American Army, principally for the civilian population. In a very recent conversation with the Prime Minister, he told me that he had not been able to obtain from England and France, expecially the latter, the contemplated credits. According to the list of supplies for the Roumanian Army, which was presented to me, it appears that the British and American Armies can supply about 90% of the requirements of the Roumanian Army and that the French can only supply approximately 10%.

Credit for Army supplies sold to Roumania should be given by the Army instead of the Treasury because the appropriation for credits to be established by the Secretary of the Treasury is almost exhausted. Roumania should be able after the harvest to obtain credit through private channels for her other requirements.

I have withheld my formal approval of sales of these supplies on credit pending more definite information as to Roumania's requirements, and as to your desire that they should be met, and also the completion of an agreement with Roumania regarding the credits given by the Army and by the Treasury. I had been informed that financial assistance to Roumania was being withheld by France and England subject to an agreement by Roumania to grant certain monopolistic concessions. The Roumanian Prime Minister admitted to me that he had received proposals to that effect (not mentioning any particular parties, however) but that he had not accepted them. I told him that, under the circumstances, we would desire to have, in connection with our credits, an undertaking on the part of the Roumanian Government that it would not grant concessions to any Governments or its nationals which would discriminate against the American Government or its nationals. I explained to him that we did not ask for any concessions or advantages, but that it would be difficult for the American Government to justify giving financial support to the Roumanian Government if advances from other Governments were given preference as to guarantee or otherwise. He told me that he had been able to remain free, but that if we did not continue to assist his Government financially he might be compelled to give concessions to other countries in order to get financial assistance. I then told him that it would probably be a protection to Roumania as well as to our Government if he would merely undertake not to grant any such concessions as long as his Government owes money to the United States. He told me he would think this over and expected to give a favorable reply, but that he feared that certain Governments (he did not mention which) might demand, as a condition of supporting Roumania's aspirations as to boundaries, certain concessions relative to the control and exploitation of the oil industries. N.H.D.

P.S. Roumania undoubtedly needs funds for the purchase of certain raw materials, but the Secretary of the Treasury is of the opinion that it would be in violation, at least of the spirit, of the law authorizing credits to foreign governments to make advances now for such purpose. If such were not the case, it would be, in my opinion, advisable to defer withdrawing your approval for the credit of $5,000,000 to Roumania.

T MS (WP, DLC).

[1] That is, Ionel (or Ion I. C.) Brătianu.

Two Letters from Josephus Daniels

My dear Mr. President: U.S.S. CORSAIR, 9 May, 1919.

When I was in Brussels I had a delightful visit to our Minister, Hon. Brand Whitlock, and in talking with him and others found that there was a deep seated feeling that a brief visit from you to Belgium before your return to America would do more than anything else to hearten and cheer that country.

I thought at the time of my visit there that I might again be in Paris and see you before returning home and to speak to you about this in the earnest hope that you could spare a day to visit Belgium. I found the King clear headed man with broad views and I know he and his people would feel honored if you could run over there even though only for a short time and I trust you may be able to do so.

Faithfully yours, Josephus Daniels

My dear Mr. President: U.S.S. CORSAIR, 9 May, 1919.

I am leaving in a few minutes from Brest for New York, and I am writing after a visit to Camp Pontanezen to express the earnest hope that when you leave France you will give yourself time enough at Brest to visit this Camp.

There are now 85,000 there and through it have passed hundreds of thousands since the armistice. Secretary Baker was there for a short time, and as you know, this camp came in for much criticism, and the officers have understood you had in mind a visit to the camp upon your return to America.

I believe it would do very much good not only to the men who are there but to the whole Army and to our country. It is only a mile or two from Brest and they will have automobiles to take you out. It will delay you only a short while and I think it is well worth it. Gen. Smedley Butler[1] was put in charge of the Camp after the armistice and has done wonderful work here which has been greatly appreciated by Secretary Baker and Gen. Pershing.

I know the great strain you have been under and are anxious to get home as soon as possible but I do not wish to add greatly to your burdens yet this will be heartening and cheering to the men who have done so much.

I had a very pleasant visit in England and our Ambassador[2] was good enough to say it did much good. My wife sends her love to Mrs. Wilson. Faithfully yours, Josephus Daniels

TLS (WP, DLC).

[1] Brig. Gen. Smedley Darlington Butler, U.S.M.C.

[2] That is, John William Davis.

From Herbert Clark Hoover

My dear Mr. President: Paris, 9 May 1919.

I feel the time has come when it is necessary to take some more definite action with regard to the situation in the three Baltic States of Esthonia, Latvia and Lithuania. I enclose herewith a sketch map showing approximately the ethnological boundaries and at the same time the present military status.

The food conditions in these states are simply terrible. From a shipping, finance and food point of view, we could overcome them if some kind of order could be established. We are gradually extending our distribution along the coastal fringe of the non-Bolshevik area, but even in such areas the hinterland is in a state of chaos due to Bolshevik invasions, with the resultant arson and slaughter. About one-half of the coast area is held by the Bolshevik, or is in such a state of anarchy as to make it impossible to send in ships. At Riga, for instance, the Red Army withdrew some days ago, leaving the town in the hands of a starving mob, as a result of which some twenty thousand bourgeois women and children have been driven onto an island in the bay, and the results are beyond all description.

From a relief point of view, the situation is hopeless for all except a few coastal towns, unless we can have some sort of order and protection. The Germans, of course, occupy Lithuania, and some instructions must be given them to cease interfering with the development of the government there, for some order must be established to succeed the German occupation.

The population in none of these states is Bolshevik. In many places they are putting up a good fight to try and establish their independence of the Moscow tyranny. They insist if they were given military supplies they require no other help to establish their boundaries and to maintain order, and our people concur in this opinion.

The problem seems to me as follows:

(a) To place enough naval strength (not large) in each of the ports to protect the relief of all the coastal towns;

(b) To furnish military supplies to the established governments so as to enable them to maintain order in the interior and to defend their borders.

Sheerly as a matter of preserving life, it does appear to me worth while to give them this support. All this requires collective action by the Allies, and a definition of policies.

The situation is one that is so appealing from every human point of view, that I am wondering whether or not it would be possible for yourself and the Premiers to set aside a short period, when the British and American naval authorities, who are familiar with this situation, could appear, together with myself on the food side, in the hope that some definite political and relief policy could be arrived at.

Faithfully yours, Herbert Hoover

Advise Mr. H. to consult British naval authorities.[1]

TLS (WP, DLC).

[1] Transcript of WWsh.

From Norman Hezekiah Davis, with Enclosure

My dear Mr. President: Paris. 9th May, 1919.

For your information I am enclosing copy of cable received from Mr. Leffingwell, Assistant Secretary of the Treasury, on the general subject of financial assistance in Europe, about which we have been in cable communication. I am sending you this cable because I think it will be of interest to you.

Faithfully yours, Norman H. Davis

TLS (WP, DLC).

ENCLOSURE

Washington, May 7, 1919.

1894. For Davis from Leffingwell.

Referring to your D-259 and 266,[1] there was never any doubt here that your position was as outlined in D-266, but we thought it might help with Lloyd-George for you to have our views vigorously stated.[2] It is perhaps unfortunate, but nevertheless true, that public sentiment in this country is in no mood to tolerate the assumption by government of further financial burdens in aid of Europe. One of the gravest difficulties in the way of the success of the Victory Liberty Loan has been the inability of our people to understand why we go on lending such huge sums to the Allies. Since the Armistice have been in the neighborhood of a billion and three quarters dollars.

Such loans in the month of April alone exceeded $400,000,000. We are looking forward to making further loans up to the statutory limit of $10,000,000,000. This means that we shall have loaned to Europe in the neighborhood of $3,000,000,000 since the cessation of hostilities, our total loans to the time of the armistice having been in the neighborhood of $7,000,000,000. You can imagine that, having successfully carried on the fight for permission to continue our foreign loans to the Allies after the armistice, and having failed originally to obtain general extension of authority for government loans to the Allies, and believing that the very fact that we are making these loans is a great obstacle to the success of the Victory Liberty Loan, I am strongly apprehensive of the popular and political effect of any suggestion of government loans or guarantees in aid of former enemies. The American people have lived an existence of provincial isolation for one hundred years; foreign trade has never been an important factor in our commercial or industrial life; we think of ourselves as having performed heroic deeds and borne great sacrifices to save France and Italy and hence England from annihilation by the Hun; and now we are inclined to feel that there is a disposition on Europe's part to exploit our generosity and to take advantage of us in financial matters. Unfortunate though it be, these are partly views of the average American. On the other hand War Finance Corporate was recently authorized by Congress to extend aid to American exporters up to a maximum of $1,000,000,000. To this extent the Treasury has been successful in obtaining authority to meet the situation to which your D-259 refers and in which you say the President is interested, namely devising some practicable plan for affording assistance to Europe with especial reference to the Governments which have been newly constituted.

The committees and members of both houses of Congress, though unanimously opposed without distinction of party to further government loans, were induced by the Treasury to accept amendments to the War Finance Corporation Act for this purpose. These amendments were incorporated in Victory Liberty Loan bill signed by the President March 3rd, last. The passing of this bill during the closing days of Congress, in the midst of a bitter partisan fight to force a special session, was thought here to be an important achievement of the Treasury. It would be very disappointing not to say humiliating to the Treasury to have the means thus devised for meeting the situation to which the President calls attention ignored, and no serious effort made to take advantage of them. You have already been fully advised as to the nature of this War Finance Corporation legislation; it in effect provides adequate machinery for reasonably long time credit for the movement of goods out of America. The problem is, therefore, to get American exporters and the business men in the territories which the President has in mind in contact with each other for the purpose of doing business. I think you can be helpful in suggesting to the governments concerned that America is ready to supply the goods and to finance their movement in the way indicated and that thing to do is to bring their intelligent and substantial business men in contact with American exporters for the purpose of developing some real business. You can, I think, be helpful in bringing the matter to the attention of such men now in Europe as Alexander Legge, whom you know very well, and whom we here regard very highly. If the Harvester Company, the Steel Company, and Ryan[3] Copper interests would start something on these lines I believe we should have taken a very important step towards the solution of the problem during the period of war. Government aid has furnished an easy and prompt cure for everybody's troubles. It is hard for business men, even in this country, to realize that the time has come for reliance upon individual initiative. I realize how hard it must be, therefore, for business men in the countries which have been devastated by war to begin again. That is, however, what must be done if sound and permanent relief is to be given. We are doing all in our power to bring the importance of this situation to the attention of American business men and to make them realize that the War Finance Corporation is prepared to finance their operations for a substantial period. The question is not, therefore, whether America will help, but whether Europe has adaptability enough and vigor enough to work out some business transactions and interest American business men in their financial and economic restoration. There are signs of increasing interest among our people such as Farrell[4] for steel, Ryan for copper, and among the cotton people. I hope the War Finance Corporation will immediately send two or three men to Europe with a view to looking over the field and possibly making some helpful suggestion for the purpose of expediting these operations. Polk, Acting.

T telegram (WP, DLC).

[1] N. H. Davis to Albert Rathbone, Assistant Secretary of the Treasury, and R. C. Leffingwell, D-259, transmitted as Ammission to State Department, No. 1856, April 29, 1919, T telegram (SDR, RG 256, 102.1/325, DNA); and N. H. Davis and T. W. Lamont to A. Rathbone, R. C. Leffingwell, and A. Strauss, D-266, transmitted as Ammission to State Department, No. 1911, May 1, 1919, T telegram (SDR, RG 256, 102.1/341d, DNA).

[2] After the American Mission, on April 25, 1919, had informed the Treasury Department of the so-called Keynes plan for the financial rehabilitation of Europe (about which, see D. Lloyd George to WW, April 23, 1919, and its Enclosure), Leffingwell, Rathbone, and Strauss had all argued against the implementation of the scheme, which they believed to be "financially indefensible" and "politically impossible." See Ammission to Department of State, No. 1774, April 25, 1919, T telegram (SDR, RG 256, 102.1/322a, DNA); R. C. Leffingwell and A. Rathbone to N. H. Davis, transmitted as FLP to Ammission, No. 1757, April 26, 1919, T telegram (SDR, RG 256, 102.1/325, DNA); A. Strauss to N. H. Davis and T. W. Lamont, transmitted as FLP to Ammission, No. 1768, April 28,

1919, T telegram (SDR, RG 256, 102.1/330, DNA); R. C. Leffingwell to N. H. Davis, transmitted as FLP to Ammission, No. 1769, April 28, 1919, T telegram (SDR, RG 256, 102.1/331, DNA); and A. Rathbone to N. H. Davis, transmitted as FLP to Ammission, No. 1770, April 28, 1919, T telegram (SDR, RG 256, 102.1/332, DNA).

In their replies, cited in n. 1, Davis and Lamont had agreed with the view of the Treasury Department that the proposal was impractical and unacceptable and had stated that Keynes' plan had been submitted for information only.

[3] That is, John Dennis Ryan.

[4] That is, James Augustine Farrell.

After-Dinner Remarks[1]

Paris, May 9, 1919

Sir Thomas and gentlemen: I esteem it a very great pleasure to find myself in this distinguished company and in this companionship of letters. Sir Thomas has been peculiarly generous, as have the gentlemen at the other end of the table, in what they have said of me, but they have given me too high a role to play up to. It is particularly difficult to believe one's self to be what has been described in so small a company as this. When a great body of people is present, one can assume a pose which is impossible when there is so small a number of critical eyes looking directly at you.

And yet there was one part of Sir Thomas's generous interpretation that was true. He was kind enough to say that in what I had said I was revealing rather my country than myself, and I think that is literally true, gentlemen. What I have tried to do and what I have said in speaking for America was to speak the mind of America, to speak the impulse and the principles of America. And the only proof I have of my success is that the spirit of America responded, responded without stint or limit, and proved that it was ready to do the thing which I was privileged to call upon it to do.

And we have illustrated in the spirit of America something which perhaps may serve as a partial guide for the future. May I say that one of the things that has disturbed me in recent months is the unqualified hope that men have entertained everywhere of immediate emancipation from the things that have hampered them and oppressed them. You cannot in human experience rush into the light. You have to go through the twilight into the broadening day before the noon comes and the full sun is upon the landscape; and we must see to it that those who hope are not disappointed by showing them the processes by which hope must be realized, processes of law, processes of slow disentanglement from the many things that have bound us in the past. You cannot throw off the habits of society immediately any more than you can throw off the habits of the individual immediately. They must be slowly got rid of, or, rather, they must be slowly altered. They must be slowly adapted. They must be slowly shaped to the new ends for which we would use them. That is the process of law if law is intelligently conceived.

I thought it a privilege to come here tonight, because your studies were devoted to one of the things which will be of most consequence to men in the future, the intelligent development of international law. In one sense this great unprecedented war was fought to give validity to international law, to prove that it had a reality which no nation could afford to disregard; that, while it did not have the ordinary sanctions, while there was no international authority as yet to enforce it, it nevertheless had something behind it which was greater than that—the moral rectitude of mankind. If we can now give to international law the kind of vitality which it can have only if it is a real expression of our moral judgments, we shall have completed in some sense the work which this war was intended to emphasize. International law has perhaps sometimes been a little too much thought out in the closet. International law has—may I say it without offense?—been handled too exclusively by lawyers. Lawyers like definite lines. They like systematic arrangements. They are uneasy if they depart from what was done yesterday. They dread experiments. They like charted seas, and if they have no chart, hardly venture to undertake the voyage. Now we must venture upon uncharted seas to some extent in the future. In the new League of Nations, we are starting out upon uncharted seas, and therefore, we must have, I will not say the audacity, but the steadiness of purpose which is necessary in such novel circumstances. And we must not be afraid of new things, at the same time that we must not be intolerant of old things. We must weave out of the old material the new garments which it is necessary that men should wear.

It is a great privilege if we can do that kind of thinking for mankind, human thinking, thinking that is shot through with sympathy, thinking that is made up of comprehension of the needs of mankind. And when I think of mankind, I must say I do not always think of well-dressed persons. Most persons are not well-dressed. The heart of the world is under very plain jackets. The heart of the world is at very simple firesides. The heart of the world is in very humble circumstances. And, unless you know the pressure of life on the humbler classes, you know nothing of life whatever. Unless you know where the pinch comes, you do not know what the pulse has to stand; you do not know what strain the muscle has to bear; you do not know what trial the nerve has to go through to hold on, hold on. To hold on when there is no glee in life is the hard thing. Those of us who can sit sometimes at leisure and read pleasant books and think of the past, the long past, that we had no part in, and project the long future—we are not specimens of mankind. The specimens of mankind have not time to do that, and we must use our leisure when we have it to feel with them and think for them, so that we can translate their desires into fact, as far as that is possible, and see that that most complicated and elusive of all things that we call justice is accomplished. An easy word to say, and a noble word upon the tongue, but one of the most difficult enterprises of the human spirit! It is hard to be just even to your nearest friend, and if it is hard to be just to those with whom you are intimate, how much harder it is to conceive the problems of those with whom you are not intimate and be just to them. To live and let live, to work for people and with people, is at the bottom of the kind of experience which must underlie justice.

The sympathy that has the slightest touch of condescension in it has no touch of helpfulness about it. If you are aware of stooping to help a man, you cannot help him. You must realize that he stands on the same earth with yourself and has a heart like your own, and that you are helping him standing on that common level and using that common impulse of humanity. In a sense the old enterprise of national law is played out. I mean that the future of mankind depends more upon the relations of nations to one another, more upon the realization of the common brotherhood of mankind, than upon the separate and selfish development of national systems of law; so that the men who can, if I may express it so, think without language, think the common thoughts of humanity, are the men who will be most serviceable in the immediate future. God grant that there may be many of them, that many men may see this hope and wish to advance it, and that the plain man everywhere may know that there is no language of society in which he has not brothers and colaborers, in order to reach the great ends of equity and of high justice.

T MS (WP, DLC).

[1] As we said in n. 1 to the extract from the Grayson Diary printed at May 9, 1919, Close's brief account of this dinner is the only one extant, other than Grayson's, and Sir Thomas Barclay and Close are the only persons who describe the guests.

In his introduction, Sir Thomas said that the Institute of International Law took special interest in Wilson's work, and particularly in the League of Nations. We leave it to the reader to assess the appropriateness of Wilson's remarks. He did begin by discussing the League of Nations. However, the last two paragraphs bore no relationship to the subject at hand and consisted of a combination of sentences drawn from campaign speeches. Also, Wilson's remarks were directly insulting to the diners, all of whom, we may be sure, wore evening clothing. It seems to us likely that Wilson became disoriented, forgot where he was, and fell back upon his memory bank of well-worn sentences and ideas for the last half of his remarks.

From Robert Lansing

My dear Mr. President: Paris, May 9, 1919.

As I said to you over the telephone the other day my health requires me to take a few days rest, otherwise I am afraid that I will break down. I plan therefore to leave Sunday for London and to remain four or five days as the guest of Ambassador Davis. Mrs. Lansing will of course accompany me.

I have arranged my work here so that it will progress as well I think as if I was here, and I will be in daily touch with it. In the event, however, that anything demands my presence or if you desire me to return at any time I shall be glad to come back on receiving telegraphic notice.

Trusting that you will understand that I would not leave Paris at this time except that it seems necessary to keep myself in condition to proceed with the work in hand, I am

Faithfully yours, Robert Lansing.

TLS (WP, DLC).

From the Diary of Ray Stannard Baker

Friday [May 9, 1919]

The President seems much relieved & far more cheerful than for many days. He told me they were working on Austria-Hungary & I found Ambassador Page of Rome at the House when I went up but the President refused to see him. Page is bubbling over with excitement over the Italian situation & is critical of our attitude. The President, I think, detests him.

I invited Senator Harris to my office for a talk with the correspondents. He told the President last night that he had decided to vote for the Woman Suffrage amendment. His one vote gives the necessary 2/3 to carry it.

Two Telegrams to Joseph Patrick Tumulty

Paris, 9 May, 1919.

The story you quote about Fiume in your one hundred and four[1] is absolute fiction and has no foundation whatever so far as I am concerned. Woodrow Wilson.

T telegram (WP, DLC).

[1] Wilson was replying to JPT to WW, May 7, 1919 (second telegram of that date).

Paris [May 9, 1919]

Happily there is no mystery or privacy about what I have promised the Government here.[1] I have promised to propose to the Senate a supplement in which we shall agree, subject to the approval of the Council of the League of Nations, to come immediately to the assistance of France in case of unprovoked attack by Germany, thus merely hastening the action to which we should be bound by the Covenant of the League of Nations.

I would very much appreciate advice as to what my message to Congress should contain. Of course I shall address the Congress immediately after I reach home on the whole subject matter of what has been accomplished here. Woodrow Wilson.[2]

T telegram (J. P. Tumulty Papers, DLC).

[1] Wilson here was replying to the final sentence of JPT to WW, May 7, 1919 (second telegram of that date), and to JPT to WW, May 8, 1919 (first telegram of that date).

[2] There is a WWT of this telegram in WP, DLC.

Four Telegrams from Joseph Patrick Tumulty

[The White House, May 9, 1919]

No. 109 It is certain that as soon as Congress convenes the Republicans will pass resolutions to restore telegraph and telephone lines. In an appeal by Mr. Mackay of the Postal Telegraph Company, published in all the papers this morning, he promises to reduce telegraph rates on Postal lines within the United States within twenty-four hours by twenty per cent after they are restored by the Government. In his appeal to the Postmaster General he says he can save American people a million dollars a month if the Postal Telegraph lines are returned to him. If we wait to take action in this matter until after Congress convenes, we will lose a great advantage.

Rabbi Wise has been making helpful speeches all over the country. He has been your strongest advocate. Writing me he says, "The most serious difficulty has been created for the President by those who have skilfully played up the dependent province of Great Britain. The whole question lies with Great Britain. If only Great Britain would be wise enough to do the thing that is just and fitting with respect to Ireland, otherwise I fear there will be great difficulties for the President." I know how difficult your situation is in this matter and wish you could help. Tumulty.

[The White House, May 9, 1919]

No. 110 Former Secretary McAdoo asks me to send the following message:

"I would suggest that you defer any reference to railroads and wires in your forthcoming message to Congress until you return. I think [the situation] should be carefully weighed, in the light of existing conditions. W. G. McAdoo." Tumulty.

[The White House, May 9, 1919]

NUMBER 111. I sincerely hope you will consider advisability of raising the embargo on beer. The most violent reaction has taken place since the enactment of this law, especially in the larger cities. It is not the reason of Brewery Propaganda. It comes from many of the humbler sort who resent this kind of federal interference with their rights. Our party is being blamed for all this restrictive legislation because you insist upon closing down all breweries and thus making prohibition effective July first. Even the Prohibitionists, themselves, fearing reaction, are hoping that something will be done to realize lifting this embargo on beer.

Congressman Mondell[1] this morning, in a talk with me, told me that the Prohibitionists were anxious to have the embargo raised and this attitude is verified by stories emanating from Prohibition Headquarters appearing in the newspapers. My own feeling is that even the Prohibitionists themselves would feel grateful to you for this and that in doing this you would be serving the cause of real temperance for them. The country would be more ready to accept prohibition brought about by constitutional amendment instead of having it made effective by Presidential ukase.

The psychological effect of raising this embargo would be of incalculable benefit to America in every way at this time. The Act approved November 21, 1918, provides that "After June 30, 1919, and until the conclusion of the present War, and thereafter until the termination of demobilization, that date which shall be determined and proclaimed by the President of the United States, for the purpose of conserving the manpower of the nation * * * it shall be unlawful to sell for beverage purposes any distilled spirits * * * " If then on June 30, 1919, demobilization has been carried to the point where the number of men remaining in the service is no larger than the number discharged from the Army, which I understand is five hundred thousand, cannot you declare by proclamation the demobilization complete for the purpose of this act. The probability [is] that the treaty of peace will be made by the first of July and that war will thus be ended both in theory and practice and it would be illogical thereafter to continue an extraordinary war measure. There is another reason, we are entering upon a critical period of economic reconstruction and unrest in which it is desirable that there shall be no strikes and disturbances and it would be disastrous to have a nationwide strike over an entirely extraneous issue. To avert such a possibility, there is good reason for immediately abolishing the provision for nationwide prohibition on July first and postponing until January first, next, when nationwide prohibition becomes effective by constitutional amendment, at which time the processes for reorganization will be sufficiently advanced to enable us to endure such disturbances. As the Springfield Republican says: "The establishment of national prohibition by federal statute, through the mere action of Congress, does not appeal to one as so desirable as the establishment of national prohibition by the direct action of three fourths of the States."

Remember the prohibition law, according to the text of that act, was enacted "for the purpose of conserving the manpower of the nation and to increase efficiency in the production of arms, munitions, ships and food for Army and Navy."

As the New York World says in an editorial: "This wartime prohibition act is breeding social, industrial and economic discontent every day. What makes it still more infamous is that under its provisions the rich man, because he has money can accumulate for his personal consumption whatever stocks of wines and liquors he pleases, but the working man, because he cannot afford to lay in a supply of anything, is deprived even of a glass of beer with his evening meal. There has never been another such measure of outrageous class and social discrimination on the statute books of the United States. It should never have been enacted by Congress. It should never have been signed by the President. If it is not repealed it is bound to cause more trouble than any other piece of federal legislation since the fugitive slave law."

By taking vigorous action in this matter you would do more for the cause of real temperance and incidentally help our party in all parts of the country and hearten those people who feel the sting of the wave of intolerance which is now spreading over the country, than anything you could think of. I wish I could meet you face to face and try to impress upon you the utter necessity for this action. You will have to take action soon if thousands of men are not to be thrown out of employment within the next week or two. Tumulty.

[1] Frank Wheeler Mondell, Republican of Wyoming.

The White House, 9 May, 1919.

Number 112. Consensus of opinion is that it would be a mistake, in opening session of Congress, to avoid the question of foreign and domestic problems. The country looks to you for a definite word. Beg to make the following suggestions. 1. It would be desirable to deal *generally* with reconstruction problems, accentuating their importance and picturing the field that is open to American enterprise, pleading for the proper American spirit in undertaking these tasks. 2. With reference to foreign commerce. Emphasize America's opportunity for legitimate enterprises. American business ought to have encouragement, making clear America's friendly attitude toward other countries, their sovereignty; so that program should be formulated, which would be helpful to an understanding between shipping interests and financial interests. 3. As to Labor. Industrial democratization must be considered and workmen's right to participation in all decisions affecting wages, hours and working conditions. The English plan, known as the Whitley plan,[1] might be suggested as a basis for industrial democratization, which provides for workmen's and employers' committees in industrial establishments, which provide a clearing house for the best industrial thought of the nation. Suggestion of a labor conference committee to coordinate and direct the conciliation parties already created, might be considered. 4. The question of a revision of the revenue laws ought to be considered. The removal of unnecessarily burdensome taxes, like the luxury tax (which Congress will repeal immediately). 5. Tariff. It might be possible for Taussig to suggest certain definite things in the way of legislation on the tarriff, to block any wholesale revision by Republicans, especially taking care of such essential industries as have been developed during the war, like chemicals, dyes, etc. 6. I assume that there ought to be a recommendation favoring the passage of the Federal Woman's Suffrage. 7. I assume that the passage of the bills suggested by Secretary Lane with reference to land for soldiers, etc., should be urged. 8. I am not sure but that it would be well to advocate further Child Labor legislation. I understand that the last law, which is intended to meet the constitutional objections to the first law, has also been declared unconstitutional.[2] While this is not a decision of the Supreme Court (I refer to the last decision) it might be well for Congress to consider the framing of legislation which would avoid all constitutional questions. 9. It will be necessary to deal with the railroad situation. Personally, I think that the sooner the railroads can be turned back, the better it will be for the Democratic Party. I think our position generally should be that they were taken over as a war measure, that the exigency no longer exists, that the people have not passed upon the general subject of national ownership and that is only fair to restore the antebellum situation. Of course, there will have to be proper safeguards, proper government control and other measures to protect the public and serious consideration will have to be given also by Congress or by some commission to the question of governmental assistance in a financial way to the railroads. 10. The telephones and telegraphs fall in the same category as do the railroads. 11. Budget. Sentiment in favor of government budget continues to grow. 12. Merchant Marine. This subject should be covered in a big, broad way. The Republicans think only of the subsidy plan.

Tumulty.

T telegrams (WP, DLC).

[1] About which, see R. Meeker to WW, Feb. 11, 1919, n. 1, Vol. 55.

[2] For the decision of the United States Supreme Court on June 3, 1918, which held that the Keating-Owen Child Labor Act of 1916, the "first law" referred to by Tumulty, was unconstitutional, see S. Gompers to WW, July 19, 1918, n. 1, Vol. 49. The advocates of the abolition of child labor immediately sought another means to achieve that end. The scheme ultimately settled upon was an amendment, originally proposed by Senator Atlee Pomerene on November 15, 1918, to the revenue bill of 1918 which, as finally enacted on February 24, 1919, provided that the net profits of mines and manufacturing establishments making use of child labor were to be subject to an excise tax of 10 per cent. 40 *Statues at Large* 1138. The executive committee of the Southern Cotton Manufacturers quickly brought a case to test the constitutionality of the new law. James Edmund Boyd, judge of the United States District Court for the Western District of North Carolina and the same judge who had originally declared the Keating-Owen Act unconstitutional, declared on May 2, 1919, that the child-labor tax was also unconstitutional. Although he did not even bother to write a formal opinion, his remarks from the bench indicated that he found the tax invalid on the grounds that Congress could not tax out of existence the practice of child labor which it had been forbidden by the Supreme Court to prohibit directly, and that the law invaded the regulatory authority of the states. The case was appealed to the Supreme Court and was argued before it on December 10, 1919, but the court was then unable to render a decision. However, a reconstituted and more conservative court invalidated the child-labor provision of the Revenue Act of 1918 in 1922 on the ground that it violated the Tenth Amendment by invading the right of the states to regulate conditions of labor. The decision was rendered in Bailey *v.* Drexel Furniture Co. (259 U.S.20).

Joseph Patrick Tumulty to Cary Travers Grayson

[The White House, May 9, 1919]

It is highly important that Senator Harris give out public statement in Paris saying that President has asked him to vote for suffrage and that he has consented to do so. Tumulty

T telegram (WP, DLC).

APPENDIX

WILSON'S NEUROLOGIC ILLNESS AT PARIS

EDITORS' INTRODUCTION

It became obvious to us, while going through the documents from late April to about mid-May 1919, that Wilson was undergoing some kind of a crisis in his health.

The first evidence of this malaise came in the dramatic deterioration in what little handwriting Wilson did during these weeks. Whatever happened to Wilson seems to have occurred when he was signing letters in the morning of April 28. The first illustration below is Wilson's signature to a letter to Paderewski, which approximates Wilson's normal signature at this time. The signature to the letter to House, which follows, reveals that Wilson was already beginning to write with difficulty. The signature to the next letter, to Henry M. Robinson, shows that Wilson was by now writing only with extreme exertion.

As the following illustrations make clear, Wilson's handwriting continued to deteriorate even further. It grew increasingly awkward, became more heavily slanted to the right, was more and more heavily inked, and became almost grotesque until about May 13. As Wilson's signature to the letter to House of that date indicates, Wilson's right-handed writing was beginning to improve, but not markedly. Indeed, from this time, and during the next two months, he wrote very little with his right hand and occasionally used his left hand for writing—when he wrote at all by hand. In the light of the earlier pattern of Wilson's neurologic illness, we began to wonder if he might possibly have suffered a "slight" stroke, or lacunar infarction, on about April 28, and additional bleeding in the brain during the next two weeks or so.

There were enough other evidences of uncharacteristic Wilsonian behavior between late April and mid-May to prompt us to seek the advice of specialists who had done significant work on Wilson's history of neurologic illness. We asked Bert E. Park, M.D., a practicing neurosurgeon, trained historian, and author of *The Impact of Illness on World Leaders* (Philadelphia, 1986), which contains a long chapter and appendix about Wilson's neurologic illness, to write an essay on the impact of illness on Wilson in Paris. He generously accepted our invitation, carefully read all the volumes, published and unpublished, for the period of the Paris Peace Conference, spent an extended period in the *Papers* office going through the documents themselves, and wrote the article which we print below. Once we had Dr. Park's manuscript in hand, we submitted it for review and critique to Edwin A. Weinstein, M.D., Professor Emeritus of Neurology at the Mount Sinai Medical School and author of *Woodrow Wilson: A Medical and Psychological Biography* (Princeton, N. J., 1981), and to James F. Toole, M.D., Teagle Professor of Neurology in the Bowman Gray School of Medicine of Wake Forest University and former President of the American Neurological Association (1984-1985), who, since the early 1960s, has been one of our principal consultants on Wilson's medical history. Both replied that they thought that Dr. Park's article was excellent and a notable contribution to Wilsonian biography. We print their comments below.

We are extremely grateful to these three busy physician-scholars, and particularly to Dr. Park, for their contribution to our understanding of Woodrow Wilson during one of the critical periods of his life. It goes without saying that their political liberty and advancement of mankind.

I am, my dear Mr. Paderewski,

Sincerely yours,

Woodrow Wilson

Hon. Ján Paderewski,
President of Poland,
Paris.

To Paderewski, April 26

but I do not know anything about Mr. Joseph P. Chamberlain suggested by Mr. Shotwell and would defer to Mr. Robinson's judgment in that matter.

Affectionately yours,

Woodrow Wilson

Colonel E. M. House,
Hotel Crillon, Paris.

To House, April 28

Gompers did not regard as a real substitute.

Cordially and sincerely yours,

Woodrow Wilson

Hon. Henry M. Robinson,
Hotel Crillon, Paris.

To Robinson, April 28

Mr. L. G. says that these little American republics welcome the League as protection against us.

Note to House, April 28

course you indicate.

Cordially and sincerely yours,

Woodrow Wilson

Admiral Wm. S. Benson, U. S. Navy,
Hotel Crillon, Paris.

To Admiral Benson, May 3

Cordially and sincerely yours,

Woodrow Wilson

His Eminence,
James Cardinal Gibbons,
408 North Charles Street, Baltimore.

To Cardinal Gibbons, May 6

Paris, 7 May, 1919.

My dear Mr. President:

~~M. Clemenceau was kind enough to hand me your letter of April 20th~~ concerning the occupation of the Rhine territory, and I have retained it for a few days in order to give it full consideration. I ~~have~~ had already heard several times a very impressive argument from the same

Example of left-handed script, to Clemenceau, May 7

May , 1919.

Woodrow Wilson

Subject to the explanation contained in the attached memorandum.

D Lloyd George

Signature and Note, to Anglo-American Agreement, May 8

In haste,

Affectionately yours,

Woodrow Wilson

Colonel E. M. House,

Hotel Crillon.

To House, May 13

opinions and conclusions are their own. We print their comments here as an appendix.

It is not surprising that these diagnoses differ. Even today, when a patient is under direct observation, physicians are not always in agreement. As Dr. Toole concludes, "How can we be definitive when the trail is cold and the records are scant and often secondary?" And Dr. Park is quite aware of "the risk of falling prey to retrospective medical reductionism."

But as the Editors are on record as stating: "We are interested only in discovering as much of the truth about Woodrow Wilson as we can. . . . We have no personal investment in any theories whatsoever about Wilson's pathology or psychological make-up." *Journal of American History*, LXX (March 1984), 955. The question of Wilson's health from April to the autumn of 1919 is of ever-increasing relevance, and, despite the difficulties of assessing its bearing upon his behavior, we think that it is incumbent upon us as Editors to exploit to the full whatever light modern medical opinion can cast on the records available. In coming to our own conclusions, we fully recognize that there is ample ground for disagreement, and also, we hope, ground for better understanding.

The subject is so important that, in the face of its intrinsic uncertainties, exhaustive efforts at analysis are warranted. Our position continues to be: "Let investigation of Wilson's physical and mental health abound!"

THE IMPACT OF WILSON'S NEUROLOGIC DISEASE DURING THE PARIS PEACE CONFERENCE

BY

Bert E. Park, M.D., M.A.

Few scholars disagree that Woodrow Wilson was an increasingly restricted, if not drastically changed, individual following his major strokes in Pueblo, Colorado, on September 25-26 and in the White House a few days later, on October 2, 1919. Virtually all also acknowledge that the President's intransigence and isolation during his seven-month convalescence from this cerebrovascular accident had a direct impact on Wilson's behavior during the conflict over ratification of the Versailles Treaty. Nevertheless, controversy remains regarding whether or not illness directly affected the President's conduct at the Paris Peace Conference earlier that year. Even among those medical scholars who believe that illness played some role there, disagreement exists as to its underlying pathogenesis.

The first physician to examine Wilson's health in a comprehensive fashion was Dr. Edwin A. Weinstein, who deserves credit for drawing attention to the deleterious effects of neurologic illness on the President's capacity to lead.[1] A detailed review of the extant primary sources, however, suggests that some revisions are required in Weinstein's synthesis. First, it is by no means certain (and probably unlikely) that Wilson suffered cerebrovascular insults or transient ischemic (insufficiency of blood, in this case in the brain) attacks on the bases of *large-vessel atherosclerosis or embolism* prior to his devastating stroke that *did* occur on this basis in late September 1919. Certainly there is little evidence to support ophthalmic artery embolism as the cause of Wilson's partial left eye blindness in 1906 (as others have pointed out).[2] Nor can it easily be de-

[1] Edwin A. Weinstein, *Woodrow Wilson: A Medical and Psychological Biography* (Princeton: Princeton University Press, 1981).

[2] Michael Marmor, "The Eyes of Woodrow Wilson," *Ophthalmology*, 92 (1985):454-65.

fended that he had experienced bilateral brain injury on the basis of large-vessel atherosclerosis as early as 1913. Moreover, most medical experts who have examined the recently available records of the Paris Peace Conference no longer accept the conclusion that Wilson suffered from viral encephalitis on April 3, 1919 (as Weinstein proposed in a revision of his own earlier hypothesis), leading, perhaps, to some imprudent compromises being incorporated into the preliminary peace treaty.

In an effort to discredit Weinstein's analysis, a few investigators have zealously denied that illness had any role at all to play in Wilson's conduct in Paris, his later major strokes in 1919 notwithstanding.[3] The literary skirmishes in this academic conflict have been blessed by an increasing degree of sophistication; yet the strong stands taken have largely obscured the middle road that leads the impartial examiner to a different, and more defensible, assimilation of the data heretofore ignored by all.

The opposing sides do agree that Wilson was afflicted with hypertension at a relatively early age, which offers the medically trained historian a single, unifying disease that can account, not only for virtually all aspects of Wilson's poor health, but also for most of his later behavioral and cognitive changes. Not only are most of the neurologic events Weinstein previously ascribed to large-vessel atherosclerosis more compatible with tiny strokes occurring on the basis of hypertension, but poorly controlled blood pressure probably accounted for the retinal hemorrhage of the left eye that Wilson experienced in 1906. Then, too, hypertension is a frequent cause of congestive heart failure, and the record is clear that Wilson was victimized by this condition in 1919. Of singular importance to the conduct of Wilson's presidential affairs, and basic to the new thesis, chronic elevations of blood pressure arguably accounted in part for much of his intransigence and character transformation that occurred from 1918 onward. On the basis of hypertension's effect on small penetrating blood vessels deep within both sides of the brain, Wilson most likely suffered significant ischemic injury over the years, enough to induce a perceptible degree of dementia as defined by specific medical criteria. This process[4] accelerated significantly following his severe large-vessel, atherosclerotically induced strokes in 1919, but was arguably manifest even before he ventured to Paris in January of that year.

Criteria for establishing a diagnosis of dementia include the following:

1. Cognitive loss interfering with occupational or social obligations.
2. Memory impairment.
3. *One* of the following: impaired abstract thinking; impaired judgment; personality change.
4. No impairment of consciousness.
5. A suggested underlying etiology.[5]

With regard to cognitive loss sufficient enough to interfere with occupational obligations, some of Wilson's associates suggested that the year 1918 was a watershed in his conduct of his office. Louis D. Brandeis later recalled that, after August 1918, Wilson's judgment was no longer infallible and that he was prone

[3] Juliette L. George, Michael F. Marmor, and Alexander L. George, "Issues in Wilson Scholarship: References to Early 'Strokes' in the *Papers of Woodrow Wilson*," *Journal of American History*, 70 (1984):845-53.

[4] In medical terminology, this condition is termed a "lacunar state," which results from multiple small clinical or subclinical strokes ("lacunes"), and is a leading cause of multi-infarct dementia.

[5] Charles E. Wells, "Organic Syndromes: Dementia," in *Comprehensive Textbook of Psychiatry*, 4th ed., edited by H. Kaplan and B. Sadock, 1:854 (Baltimore: Williams and Wilkins, 1985).

to do things which were "unnatural" for him. Before that period he had been a bold and imaginative leader.[6] Wilson's responses to certain perceived Allied affronts at this time were judged by many to be occasionally inappropriate.[7] Others described the President as having a one-track mind from that point onward.[8]

Wilson himself seemed to have been aware of increasing difficulty with his memory, the second criterion required to support a diagnosis of dementia. He revealed to Newton D. Baker as early as August 1917 that he was becoming absent-minded.[9] A year later Wilson referred to his mind becoming "leaky" after being unable to recall the specifics of a meeting with his Minister to China. Thereafter he required written memoranda to be submitted by individuals with whom he had spoken, but still forgot some critical decisions that he had made.[10]

Although Wilson's powers of abstraction may not have been grossly impaired prior to going to Paris, there is little doubt that some changes in personality and impairment of his judgment were already manifest as early as 1918. Weinstein cites many examples of his increasingly secretive, suspicious, and defensive manner—among them his refusal to allow the Fourteen Points address to be known in advance, his ill-natured criticism of Taft and other moderate Republicans among the League to Enforce Peace, which Wilson had supported heretofore, and his appointment of men to the American Commission to the peace conference whom he felt would support his positions without question.[11] From the start, he also sought to eliminate the Senate from any participation in affairs concerning the impending peace conference and became less discreet in his personal criticisms, strong supporters such as Senator Gilbert M. Hitchcock included.[12] Moreover, Wilson's judgment of political events was impaired, at least on occasion. Not only did he dismiss without consideration unwelcome advice regarding the disadvantages of his attending the peace conference despite his self-perceived repudiation in the November elections, but Wilson also similarly ignored the vindictive election and parliamentary mandates which Lloyd George and Clemenceau had received in kind. Indeed, many described the wording of Wilson's call for a referendum on his policies in November 1918 as both a political and diplomatic blunder. Then, too, his poor organizational efforts, relative disdain for detail, and limited preparation prior to going to Paris reflected a significant divergence for one who prided himself on being so precise and methodical.

If significant loss of abstractive capacity would arguably not become obvious until after Wilson's return from Paris, a few examples nevertheless suggest some restriction of this faculty as early as 1918. Wilson viewed the forthcoming conference in black and white: negotiations would hinge on abstract morality pitted against the wicked forces of self-interest, which he was certain he would find there. Yet he failed to recognize that his whole perception of the League threatened to undercut its potential strength: either the League as Wilson per-

[6] Memorandum of Louis D. Brandeis, March 23, 1929, the Papers of Ray Stannard Baker, Library of Congress.

[7] House Diary, March 28, 1918, CtY; W. B. Fowler, *British-American Relations, 1917-1918: The Role of Sir William Wiseman* (Princeton: Princeton University Press, 1969), pp. 213-16.

[8] Fowler, p. 207.

[9] Wilson to N. D. Baker, August 17, 1917, Woodrow Wilson Papers, Library of Congress.

[10] House Diary, August 19, 1918.

[11] Weinstein, *Medical and Psychological Biography*, pp. 322-25, *passim.*

[12] *Ibid.*

ceived it would be too supranational for the United States Senate to accept, or else it would be rendered impotent by the high idealism underpinning it.[13]

The final criterion necessary for establishing a diagnosis of dementia is a plausible definition of its cause, which the hypertensive lacunar-state thesis provides. As has been implied, this condition differs significantly from the other cause of multi-infarct dementia originally proposed by Dr. Weinstein. Briefly stated, I believe that Wilson's clinical history fits the hypertensive form of the disease more precisely, as I have argued in detail in a recent publication.[14] Hypertensive multi-infarct dementia follows a patchy, stepwise deteriorating course. It is not rapidly progressive, nor are the neurologic insults that occur usually as dramatic as those seen in large-vessel, atherosclerotic-induced disease. Indeed, overt neurologic deficits and symptoms, such as weakness of an extremity, do not have to appear at all.

As one expert has described hypertensive multi-infarct dementia: "It is much less characteristic of multiple strokes clinically than is the first large-vessel, atherosclerotic type. . . . The onset is more insidious and the course slowly progressive, without episodes of acute exacerbation and remission. Focal neurologic symptoms and signs are considerably more rare than in the first type of multi-infarct dementia. . . . Hypertension may be the only clinical clue to the vascular origin of the dementia."[15] Given the presence of untreated hypertension in Wilson's clinical history as early as 1906, at which time significant involvement of the retinal vessels of the eye was already manifest (considered an *end-stage* of the accelerated phase of the disease), it is not surprising that thirteen further years of the untreated condition predisposed Wilson to the development of incipient hypertensive multi-infarct dementia long *before* his viral illness in early April 1919 and his devastating large-vessel atherosclerotic strokes in September and October of the same year.

Physicians are aware that, in the earliest stages of dementia, certain behavioral changes may only be recognized in retrospect as nascent manifestations of the disease that later becomes obvious in time. The extant sources suggest that, once having arrived in Paris, Wilson continued to manifest several features suggestive of early dementia.

In its formative stages, the afflicted individual shows a loss of enthusiasm for usually satisfying activities (during the latter half of the conference Wilson abstained from golf and had to be pushed by his physician to take walks or to take car rides—all three activities from which Wilson had derived such pleasure before). He experienced a lowered frustration tolerance (this was particularly noticeable during the last week of March and came to a head during Wilson's illness in early April). The individual becomes more self-absorbed (a noticeable characteristic of Wilson that all associates underscored). He manifests lack of sensitivity and consideration for others (certainly Clemenceau and the German delegates were victimized by this, not to mention Lansing during the entire conference and House during its latter half). Those afflicted demonstrate an unaccustomed suspiciousness and compulsiveness. Not only was Wilson as suspicious of alleged French spies as he later became of advice from his most trusted subordinate; his compulsion to complete the work on the conference

[13] This is but one example of patients with dementia or brain damage failing to employ the abstract attitude. See Kurt Goldstein, "Functional Disorders in Brain Damage," in *American Handbook of Psychiatry*, 2nd edn., edited by Sylvano Arieti (New York: Basic Books, 1975), 4:182-207.

[14] Bert E. Park, *The Impact of Illness on World Leaders* (Philadelphia: University of Pennsylvania Press, 1986).

[15] Wells, "Dementia," 1:859.

within a ten-day time limit was highlighted, for example, by his insistence on having all participants hurriedly sign the memorandum on the Kaiser's guilt shortly after reversing himself on the same issue.

Afflicted persons also demonstrate a notable lack of attention to detail (Ray Stannard Baker, among others, pointed out that one of Wilson's shortcomings was his refusal to deal with specifics: the League itself, based on the Fourteen Points, would suffice to overcome all obstacles, in Wilson's way of thinking; nor did other details such as economic matters hold much interest for him). Unexpected facetiousness or jocularity is manifest (Wilson's occasional quips that often startled his associates as being somewhat inappropriate, if not out of place; e.g., his reference to the Queen of Rumania as "traveling in high gear," his allusion to the "late Lloyd George," or to himself as suffering from "Klotz on the brain").

Finally, although memory for recent events is usually compromised, the afflicted individual may turn to more familiar themes to disguise this lack of facility. In early May, Wilson admitted to being so fatigued that he could not remember the events that had transpired in the Council of Four that morning.[16] A noted authority on dementia and its manifestations has stated the case succinctly, and his observations may have singular importance for Woodrow Wilson's conduct: "A diagnosis of dementia is *seldom made* during its early phase, and the changes that characterize this period usually must be assembled in retrospect [italics mine]."[17] Given the later changes that occurred in Wilson's behavior after the conference, it is not surprising in retrospect that he appears to have fulfilled virtually every criteria of *early* dementia while still in Paris.

The presence of a modest organic brain syndrome in an individual of Wilson's acknowledged intellect, however, might not necessarily translate into compromised leadership or negotiating skills. Changes in cognition, memory, and abstraction must be assessed *relative to* his formidable premorbid (i.e., before illness) intellectual quotient. Such a gifted person may well function adequately enough in the early stages of dementia to match wits with intellects of lesser caliber. This may account for the failure of many of Wilson's associates (and some later scholars) to recognize the subtle changes that nevertheless were evolving. With regard to the Paris Peace Conference itself, the primary sources suggest that Wilson may have been affected by illness on three separate occasions while there. In judging the President's effectiveness both as a leader and a negotiator during these interludes of early April, early May, and mid-June, the three periods in question warrant examination within the context of what transpired.

What, then of the impact of his first illness on April 3, 1919, in relation to Wilson's underlying neurologic condition? To begin with, the argument that Wilson may have suffered from central nervous system involvement on the basis of encephalitis lethargica is untenable.[18] On the other hand, despite the difficulty inherent in retrospectively identifying the specific causal agent for Wilson's severe systematic illness, a strong case can still be made for the influenza virus as being responsible, as his physician, Dr. Cary T. Grayson, originally suspected. It is of no consequence that Grayson did not use the term influenza until April 5. Nor is it important that the phrase "influenza" was a catch-all term used by

[16] *Ibid.*; Grayson Diary, May 3, 1919, *Wilson Papers*, 58:367.

[17] Wells, "Dementia," 1:859.

[18] The virus of encephalitis lethargica predominantly affects the central nervous system, with 75 percent of those afflicted demonstrating neurologic deficits, usually disorders of eye movements resulting in diplopia. See A. B. Baker, "Viral Encephalitis," in *Clinical Neurology* (Hagerstown, Md.: Harper and Row, 1975), 17:47.

all physicians during this period to describe any viral illness. What is important is that the descriptive term "influenza" may have precisely defined the virus responsible for Wilson's illness. To argue the point, one should consider the term's meaning both in relation to what it implied for physicans of Grayson's day, as well as its precise definition today.

On what basis would Grayson have made his diagnosis of influenza? The 1907 edition of Osler's *Modern Medicine* (being a standard text of its day with which any practicing physician would have been familiar) identified the salient features of influenza. An antecedent prodrome (a premonitory symptom) is usually lacking. The patient is suddenly afflicted with fever, chills, headache, and generalized pains. The degree of malaise and prostration is striking and often out of proportion to the fever. Catarrhal respiratory symptoms are striking.[19] Although the respiratory symptoms were described as being virtually always present, gastrointestinal and neurologic symptoms may supervene. The former, though somewhat unusual with influenza, may manifest itself as diarrhea in persons with antecedent gastrointestinal disease (which Wilson had). With regard to neurologic symptoms, the clinical picture of influenza was described as being incomplete without "minor nervous phenomena," such as "headaches and neuralgic pains."[20]

Virtually every aspect of Wilson's presenting symptoms parallel this early description of influenza. By Osler's description alone, one can infer that Wilson's systemic infection was serious (as Grayson admitted): "In more severe attacks, pulmonary secretions are abundant. . . . There may be delirium[21] and great weakness. With invasion of deeper parts of the lungs, cough may be very distressing."[22] Not only was a racking cough Wilson's most troublesome symptom early on, but by the third day of his illness, Grayson was referring to accumulations of mucous in Wilson's bronchial tree.[23] Acknowledging that the most severe cases go on to bronchopneumonia or chronic influenza (persistent cough) thereafter, Grayson's concern that Wilson might have been predisposed to develop this complication was, then, not unfounded.

Subsequent medical descriptions of influenza not only remain consistent with Osler's earlier account of the disease but define the case by inference even more distinctly on Wilson's behalf. As the 1928 edition of Cecil's *Textbook of Medicine* described influenza: "The principal manifestations are sudden onset with . . . marked prostration" (Wilson was unable to sit up in bed for four days),

[19] William Osler, *Modern Medicine: Its Theory and Practice* (Philadelphia and New York: Lea Brothers & Co., 1907), 2:474.

[20] *Ibid.* The editorial comment in the *Papers of Woodrow Wilson* (56:558, fn. 2) is in error in asserting that Wilson did not suffer from headaches. As Wilson himself described his symptoms (in Grayson's words): ". . . owing to intense pains in my back and stomach and *head*" (56:557). Emphasis added.

Editors' note: Actually, there is only one reference during this illness to a headache—during an *afternoon* meeting of the Big Four on April 3. There are no further references to headaches during this illness. See the extract from the Grayson Diary, April 3, 1919. However, in the note just cited, we were trying to make the point that it was most unlikely that Wilson suffered from an attack of Spanish influenza. As the authority on the pandemic of 1918 points out, patients with Spanish influenza complained, in addition to a generalized headache, of "special aching, at the back of the eyes, or inside the head in front, the patient generally putting his hand low down across the forehead to indicate the site." A. A. Hoehling, *The Great Epidemic* (Boston, 1961), p. 122. Wilson's symptoms did not include this type of headache. Indeed, it is most likely that, if Wilson had had Spanish influenza, it would have gone into pneumonia and killed him, as it did most other victims.

[21] This important feature will be discussed in detail below.

[22] "The cough is at first dry and the sputum scanty. If the finer bronchi are invaded, the cough is more distressing and may be paroxysmal." Osler, *Modern Medicine*, 2:475.

[23] Grayson Diary, April 5, 1919, *Wilson Papers*, 57:3.

"severe aching pains in the back and extremities" (precisely Grayson's description of the initial attack), "and a rapidly progressive inflammation of the respiratory mucous membrane." Shortly after onset, a dry, irritative cough begins (which bothered Wilson so during the first two days of his illness). Gastrointestinal symptoms are usually insignificant except in those with previous disease of the alimentary tract. Overt encephalitis is unusual with influenza. Nevertheless, and this point is important, stupor and delirium often occur as secondary manifestations of the systematic illness, particularly at fever levels of 102-105 degrees.[24]

Although Grayson may have been using the term as but a descriptive phase for any viral illness of that period, his diagnosis was nevertheless quite consistent with the disease as recognized by reputable contemporary sources. Moreover, the argument for influenza being the *precise* etiology may be strengthened by modern knowledge of the specific viruses influenza A and B (influenza C, or Asian flu, was not described until the 1940s). Consider this summation of influenza taken from a modern-day text: influenza A usually occurs in the early months of the year in northern temperate zones. Known as the "three day fever," its symptoms are remarkably constant in uncomplicated cases. The headache, myalgia (muscle aches) and asthenia (weakness and prostration) are severe and out of proportion to the symptoms originating from involvement of the respiratory tract. Patients with influenza almost invariably cough, although usually this is not productive of sputum. The disease is abrupt in onset and lasts two to five days in the absence of complications.[25]

The evidence is strong, then (though certainly not conclusive), that on the basis of textbook descriptions of both Grayson's time as well as today, the influenza virus was responsible for Wilson's systemic infection from April 3 through April 7. At least two infectious disease experts have already suggested that possibility.[26] This is of singular importance both in a negative and a positive sense for the now-refuted diagnosis of encephalitis, since most authorities agree that, with either influenza A or B, overt encephalitis is distinctly unusual. That is, the negative corollary supports the assumption that the disease itself would not have impacted on Wilson's conduct or the decisions made during the critical period of April 3 through April 15.

Yet there is a positive corollary which suggests that, whatever the virus involved, the illness may indeed have had some effect on Wilson's thinking and behavior. High fever in and of itself is a frequent cause of metabolic encepha-

[24] Russell L. Cecil, *A Textbook of Medicine* (Philadelphia and London: W. B. Saunders Co., 1929), pp. 7, 11. Although diarrhea is uncommon with influenza, Wilson suffered from an ill-defined disease of his alimentary tract at a younger age (Weinstein, *Medical and Psychological Biography*, pp. 53, 55, 60-63, *passim*), perhaps predisposing to the appearance of diarrhea, as Cecil's description implies. A few other viruses such as parainfluenza and myzoviruses closely resemble influenza. Adenovirus is the most difficult to distinguish from influenza, but prostration is less, the onset less sudden, and sore throat or laryngitis is more common with this entity. That Grayson was treating Wilson's nose and throat prior to April 3 at least suggests that the adenovirus in particular cannot be ruled out as the cause of his viral infection, as sore throat and rhinitis are more common with adenovirus than with influenza. See Cecil, *Textbook of Medicine*, edited by Paul B. Beeson and Walsh McDermott (Philadelphia and London: W. D. Saunders Co., 1967), p. 24.

[25] *Ibid.*

[26] See editorial comment, *Wilson Papers*, 56:557-58. Although the diagnosis of encephalitis per se is dubious, I nevertheless support Weinstein's assertion that "Wilson's brain involvement . . . was *the effect* of . . . the influenza virus." Weinstein, *Medical and Psychological Biography*, p. 338. Emphasis added, suggesting a *secondary* rather than direct effect.

lopathy (clouding of mental processes) in the elderly, particularly those with underlying cerebrovascular disease or organic brain syndromes.[27] A lowered threshold for delirium is known to exist in such patients, leading to transient sensorial changes during the height of the fever, often with some delay (if not failure altogether) in returning to cognitive levels or behavioral patterns antedating the illness. As a noted authority on delirium has observed: "Severe hyperthermia may itself be a cause of delirium. . . . Preexisting brain damage . . . and certain underlying medical disorders bring the patient close to this threshold . . . so that relatively small metabolic changes such as fever may then push the patient beyond the threshold into delirium."[28]

Equally important, dementia need not be a requisite antecedent; stress and certain features of the premorbid personality may alone predispose to a lowering of delirium thresholds. As Dr. Lawrence Kolb suggests: "The intensity of the symptoms is dependent less upon the height of the fever than upon the integration of the personality and the importance of psychogenic factors."[29] Even if one were to discount the argument for dementia, it cannot be ignored that certain aspects of Wilson's personality (alluded to by Alexander and Juliette George as "temperamental defects"),[30] coupled with the trying circumstances of the period itself, may have had more to do with the President's literally feverish state of mind at this interval than has been recognized to date.

Some might argue that Wilson showed no obvious signs of delirium during the illness in early April. Nevertheless, Grayson discreetly referred to Wilson experiencing two very "restless nights" (April 3 and 4) despite ostensibly displaying unremarkable behavior during the day. Physicians are aware that manifestations of delirium are characteristically worse at night, when the ordinary background of sensory input is reduced.[31] Most investigators attribute this circumstance to alterations in the sleep-wakefulness cycle in which dreams become superimposed on reality. Indeed, the most common form of delirium encountered in a patient with an organic brain syndrome from whatever cause is the so-called "nocturnal confusion." Not surprisingly, the casual observer during the day may miss the diagnosis, since delirium's manifestations may be limited to nighttime.[32] The absence, then, of overt disorders of perception, hallucinations, or inappropriate behavior, which the layman commonly equates with delirium, does not assure its absence in Wilson's case during this interlude. As such, Gilbert F. Close's observations as late in the illness as April 7, that he had never known the President to be "in such a difficult frame of mind as he is now," and that "even while lying in bed he manifests peculiarities,"[33] may have more significance than many scholars have chosen to admit.

The identification of a delusional state, like dementia, rests on subtle yet spe-

[27] Wells, "Dementia," pp. 847, 854.

[28] *Ibid.*, p. 843.

[29] Lawrence E. Kolb, "Multi-infarct Dementia and Delirium States," in *Modern Clinical Psychiatry*, p. 141.

[30] Alexander L. George and Juliette L. George, *Woodrow Wilson and Colonel House: A Personality Study* (New York: The John Day Company, 1956), p. 196.

[31] Kolb, *Modern Clinical Psychiatry*, p. 141.

[32] Z. Lipowski, *Delirium: Acute Brain Failure in Man* (Springfield, Ill.: Charles C. Thomas, 1980), p. 541. As Lipowski warns the physician: "Such confusion is quite characteristic and should be inquired about *since patients often do not report it spontaneously*," p. 200, italics mine.

[33] Arthur Walworth, *Woodrow Wilson*, 2nd rev. ed. (Boston: Houghton Mifflin Co., 1965), Vol. 2, p. 297; Gilbert F. Close to his wife, April 7, 1919, Close Coll., Firestone Library, Princeton University; Irwin Hood Hoover, *Forty-Two Years in the White House* (Boston and New York: Houghton Mifflin, 1934), p. 98.

cific criteria.[34] Dr. Zbigniew Lipowski points them out in listing common sources of error in making the diagnosis: (1) A patient suffering from mild symptoms of delirium is likely to look normal and behave appropriately. It is only, perhaps, in conversation that the wary observer may notice the patient voicing suggestive complaints or displaying cognitive or attentional defects. (2) It is erroneous to believe that delirium always, or even usually, features excited, loud, and restless behavior, frightening hallucinations, and persecutory delusions. (3) And, most important, the degree of psychological disturbance (delusions and hallucinations) does not correlate with the degree of deficiency of attention and information processing.[35]

With regard to Wilson's viral illness in general, a few observations by distinguished investigators bear emphasis, at least by inference. For example, viral infections may give rise to delirium without invading the nervous system, whether the patient is febrile or not.[36] Then, too, impairment of concentration and reduction of speed of mental activity are among the earliest symptoms of many viral infections, even though delirium as such may not yet be appreciably manifest.[37]

The relation of delirium to the influenza virus in particular is even more intriguing in the historical circumstance under discussion. Decrements in concentration and abstraction may be regarded as early, prodromal symptoms of impending influenzal-induced delirium. Indeed, the influenza virus is the most frequently cited predisposing agent to delirium among the systematic viral illnesses.[38] As Lipowski relates: "Loss of interest in reading, difficulty in marshalling one's thoughts, mild depression, and a tendency to withdraw . . . are additional features of an early phase of viral infection, such as influenza."[39] These early manifestations of delirium may eventually emerge full-blown if the illness becomes severe and/or the patient has pronounced susceptibility to the syndrome.

In retrospect, then, the four-to-five-day period of turbulence *prior* to Wilson's physical collapse on April 3, during which time Wilson was being treated by Grayson for "a cold," may deserve more careful scrutiny than has heretofore been undertaken, assuming that this represented the prodrome of the more serious stage of his illness. It has already been suggested that Wilson possessed a requisite "susceptibility" toward delirium on the basis of diffuse cerebrovascular disease superimposed on a rather rigid personality profile, enough to have accelerated the process. More intriguing still, Lipowski points out that it is often

[34] Specifically:
(1) Clouding of consciousness with reduced capacity to attend to environmental stimuli.
(2) Two of the following: perceptual disturbances such as hallucinations or incoherent speech; disturbance of the sleep-wake cycle; or altered psychomotor activity such as restlessness.
(3) Disorientation or memory impairment.
(4) Acute or subacute progression, with variability in clinical symptoms.
(5) The identification of a specific cause. (Taken from the *Diagnostic and Statistical Manual of Mental Disorders* and cited in Wells, "Organic Syndromes: Delirium," in *Comprehensive Textbook of Psychiatry*, 1:842). During the April 3-7 illness, Wilson fulfilled the criteria substantiating the presence of a transient delirium. See text.

[35] Lipowski, *Delirium*, p. 202.

[36] J. Gould, "Virus, Disease and Psychiatric Ill Health," *Brit. J. Clin. Pract.*, 11 (1975): 1-5.

[37] E. A. Alluise, W. R. Beisel *et al.*, "Behavioral Effects of Tularemea and Sandfly Fever in Man," *J. Infect. Dis.*, 128 (1973):710-17.

[38] Lipowski, *Delirium*, pp. 410, 414, 416.

[39] *Ibid.*, p. 416.

impossible to judge if delirium is a "manifestation of encephalitis due to the virus or it if represents an encephalopathy lacking focal neurologic signs." Patients with influenza may develop either of these complications and manifest delirium.[40]

In summary, these investigators are emphasizing that, with systemic viral infections in general (and influenza in particular), cognitive and behavioral changes may occur *prior* to the overt onset of serious illness—such as occurred in Wilson's case on April 3. With that point in mind, it would be instructive to point out what some observers might perceive as disturbing conduct on Wilson's part immediately preceding that date. On March 27, House expressed surprise when Wilson confided to him that he would accept Clemenceau's demand for a separate security treaty between France and the United States. As House described it, "in a moment of enthusiasm he committed himself to Clemenceau."[41] This pattern of decision making, ostensibly in isolation, might arguably have been recapitulated on April 1 and 2, when Wilson dismayed his commissioners by agreeing to the Anglo-French scheme for reparations, including pensions and disability. Equally disturbing to some was his wording in informing his advisers that he "did not feel bound by considerations of logic," nor did he feel that the matter need be settled, according to John Foster Dulles, "in accord with strict legal principles"—both very uncharacteristic Wilsonian declarations. Perhaps there was more than met the nonmedical eye in one associate's description that Wilson seemed "fresh" and "a trifle impatient of prolonged discussion" at the time.[42]

It had been on March 28, in fact, that virtually all diary accounts, from those of the discreet Grayson to those of the fawning Benham, recorded how fatigued and tired the President appeared.[43] Nor was Wilson at all hesitant to display invective against virtually all of his negotiating partners. On that day, Grayson confided in his diary that Wilson "could not resist the opportunity" to tell Tardieu just what he thought of him.[44] Not surprisingly, this was the day of the famed row between Clemenceau and Wilson in which House recorded that the two "came near calling one another names."[45] Following this confrontation, both House and Lansing agreed that it had been a mistake for Wilson to have come to Paris. Depression engulfed the President. Edith Benham observed this to have been one of the few times she had seen the President "thoroughly down and out."[46]

Interestingly enough, Wilson was being treated by Grayson for a cold by March 29. Within two days, the President had officially agreed to French ownership of the Saar coal mines and was exposed to Smuts' influential memorandum concerning reparations payments. A day later, more than one observer noted how irritated, vituperative, and rigid Wilson had suddenly become. His angry outburst over Henry Wickham Steed's letter on April 1 concerning the Saar amazed and perplexed the man who delivered it, as he later recounted.[47] Wilson's irascibility extended to his discussion of disability allowances and pensions on the same day (see above). A stormy conference on the morning of April 2 concerning such less pressing matters as the Polish army transport problem and French restrictions on German couriers so "completely disturbed the Pres-

[40] *Ibid.*; Grayson Diary, *Wilson Papers*, 56:428, 525.
[41] House Diary, *Wilson Papers*, 56:336.
[42] *Wilson Papers*, 56:499-502.
[43] Grayson Diary, *ibid.*, 56:348; McCormick Diary, 56:353; Benham Diary, 56:355.
[44] Grayson Diary, 56:348.
[45] House Diary, 56:349.
[46] Benham Diary, 56:355.
[47] *Wilson Papers*, 56:517, n. 1.

ident" that he was "not prepared to go further into . . . any of the matters that directly affected the French."[48] Edith Benham had "never seen him so irritated, so thoroughly in a rage."[49] For the first time Wilson began to consider risking breaking up the conference for the sake of saving his principles, a position he had refused to consider before.[50]

It would be the height of folly and a flagrant surrender to medical reductionism to ascribe the decisions made solely to an early delirium antedating a serious viral illness. Nevertheless, a review of this period with reference to certain medical opinion not heretofore emphasized suggests the need for further investigation of this very critical period of the Paris Peace Conference.

More readily defended is the assertion that the impact of the illness in itself had serious implications for Wilson's underlying hypertensive cerebrovascular condition. Therein lies the true significance of the viral infection (the previous observations regarding its possible direct impact on affairs in Paris notwithstanding). It has been suggested that a transient delirium, fever-induced and medically defined, affected Wilson for a brief span, perhaps as early as late March and extending into the height of the illness in early April. This has relevance both for Wilson's behavior at the time and the progression of his underlying multi-infarct dementia, as the observations of several medical experts have implied. Dr. Lawrence Kolb has outlined those implications clearly enough: "Patients with multi-infarct dementia are peculiarly apt, on the occasion of a mild infection, to suffer from episodes characterized by confusion, disorientation, . . . anxiety, fear reaction, suspiciousness, and delusional trends."[51] In short, Kolb is describing a delirium, some aspects of which Wilson demonstrated during his illness.

In distinguishing delirium from dementia, it is important to emphasize features peculiar to delirium such as its diurnal variation (lucid periods during the course of the day alternating with confusion at night), rapid shifts in psychomotor activity, and disturbances of the sleep-wakefulness cycle, all of which distinguish it from the more permanent cognitive impairment of dementia.[52] Nevertheless, Lipowski emphasizes that the two processes feed upon each other—allowing for delirium to intervene during brief systematic illnesses among the demented, while accelerating the process of dementia itself by the former's transient occurrence: "Psychopathological manifestations . . . shade over into each other and overlap. They may be viewed as a continuum of pathological states related to diffuse cerebral pathology, which may be completely, partly, or not at all reversible. Delirium may be the first manifestation of multi-infarct dementia. . . . Furthermore, delirium may be superimposed upon dementia, as is often the case in degenerative cerebral diseases."[53] In one study of 534 patients, for example, 70 per cent of those experiencing an acute delirium had a chronic brain syndrome. This suggests that dementia predisposes a person to the development of delirium and that the two syndromes often coexist.[54] Moreover, transient delirium may augment an underlying chronic brain disorder by inducing increased demands on cerebral metabolic rate. In brain cells

[48] Grayson Diary, 56:524.
[49] Benham Diary, 56:541.
[50] Baker Diary, 56:542.
[51] Kolb, "Multi-infarct Dementia and Delirium States," p. 252. Certainly Wilson's behavior during the height of his illness fits Lipowski's succinct description of a patient afflicted with delirium, who "tends to be either lethargic, or agitated and restless." See Lipowski, *Delirium*, p. 543.
[52] *Ibid.*, p. 214.
[53] *Ibid.*, p. 215.
[54] *Ibid.*, p. 539.

already rendered relatively anoxic (oxygen deprived or deficient) by hypertensive cerebrovascular changes, this may lead to stable cognitive and emotional impairment thereafter.[55]

These observations in themselves may represent the true significance of Wilson's illness in April, somewhat removed from its plausible if unproved direct impact on what transpired at the time. This is not to say (as has already been implied) that Wilson's frame of mind may not have indirectly prompted some notable compromises in his heretofore rigid positions. Yet, paradoxically, insofar as the brief illness may have augmented his underlying multi-infarct organic brain syndrome, a perceptible hardening of his attitudes (rather than compromise) and other behavioral disturbances became manifest once the effects of his transient setback subsided. It is not therefore surprising that Irwin H. Hoover remarked that "something queer was happening in [Wilson's] mind" and that "he was never the same after this little spell of sickness"; or that Herbert Hoover would observe that, before his illness, Wilson was sharp and attentive, but after it, "he sometimes groped for ideas."[56]

Critics of the above argument might point out not only that such secondary effects of delirium are delayed, but also that the facts surrounding the illness of April 3 suggest that the sensorial changes, if they occurred at all, were strikingly brief. Moreover, they would argue that the data from the Wilson Papers covering this period indicate that, apart from Wilson's reversal on the issue of bringing the Kaiser to trial (and possibly with regard to some aspects of French occupation of the Rhineland), none of the other critical decisions made during the April 3-April 14 period represented reversals of Wilson's prior positions—much less do they bear the imprint of a serious yet brief illness from which the President ostensibly recovered completely.[57]

Perhaps. Yet what *is* discernible, and bears emphasis not heretofore established, was a decided shift in Wilson's conduct toward a sense of temporal urgency, with a penchant for more rigid thinking and less compromise thereafter.[58] Only with later events judged retrospectively does the medically trained historian begin to appreciate that such changes were consistent with the earliest stage of a heretofore mild organic brain syndrome on the basis of hypertension-related small-vessel cerebrovascular disease.

That such of Wilson's behavior and decision making after the Paris Peace Conference reflected this insidious condition can be defensibly argued. Yet the question remains: what role might this disease have played in the events as

[55] *Ibid.*, pp. 539-41; E. M. Nemoto, "Pathogenesis of Cerebral Ischemia-anoxia," *Crit. Care Med.*, 6 (1978):203-14.

[56] I. H. Hoover, *Forty-Two Years in the White House*, pp. 98-99; Herbert Hoover, *The Memoirs of Herbert Hoover* (New York, 1951-1957), 1:468.

[57] Wilson did make a few impulsive decisions toward the end of his illness, many of which were frivolous (e.g., in a fit of pique, declaring that he would not negotiate anymore with the French government; *Wilson Papers* 57:50). One such impulse, however, bore fruit. On April 6, Wilson ordered the *George Washington* to Brest, vowing to go home if the deadlock was not broken; *ibid.*, 57:61ff.

[58] Many characteristics which Wilson later carried back with him to the League fight became magnified toward the end of this brief illness: suspicious (e.g., his attitudes toward House's assessment of Clemenceau and the perceived need of his once-trusted subordinate to make untimely concessions); aloof, predetermined, and hard-driving (e.g., R. S. Baker's description of Wilson as John Knox and Calvin rolled into one "on too large a scale"); self-perceived as a martyr (e.g., "I will have to stand alone"); rigid and unyielding (e.g., "peace must be made on the principles of the 14 Points," while vowing to fight for his principles even if he were to lose peace and lose his own prestige). Virtually all of these characteristics endured following the April 3 illness. Though not necessarily having affected the issues directly, this physiologic setback appears to have galvanized certain features of Wilson's premorbid personality.

they transpired from April 3 through April 14? The answer is equally defensible: not as much as at first thought, and then, perhaps, only indirectly. In a recent publication,[59] I originally accepted the premise that some of the decisions Wilson made after April 3 may have been a direct reflection of his compromised health. A review of heretofore unavailable sources has forced some revisions in my thinking, but not so much as to abandon the premise altogether.

On balance, the record simply does not sustain the suggestion that Wilson's compromised health necessarily translated into compromised decisions by the President during and immediately after the April illness. To argue the point, it is necessary to examine the key issues in some detail, and with an eye to chronology. Three of the most controversial disputes and Wilson's role in their resolution immediately come to mind: the reparations question; the twin issues of the Saar coal mines and the occupation of the Rhineland; and the Kaiser's guilt, insofar as he could be tried for war crimes, whether on moral or legal grounds. Other issues, of course, deserved and received equal billing (such as the Polish question, the naval conflict with Great Britain, Italy's demand for the port of Fiume, and the Shantung dispute). Yet few scholars have argued that Wilson's position (perhaps the naval accord ultimately agreed to excepted) perceptibly changed from beginning to end on these questions. No such unanimity of opinion exists, however, with regard to the issues of reparations, the Rhineland, the Saar, and the Kaiser's guilt.

With regard to the first, Wilson had agreed to the inclusion of disablement pensions and separation allowances in the articles on reparations, a decision that ran counter to the opinion of the broad majority of his advisers. Rather than a reversal as some have argued, however, Wilson's position was arguably more an extension of the understanding arrived at during the pre-Armistice negotiations of November 1918 (i.e., "compensation will be made . . . for all damages done to the civilian population of the Allies"), as forcefully proposed in the Smuts memorandum written on March 31. True, just two days before, during the meeting of the Council of Four on March 29, Wilson had expressed doubts as to whether an article including pensions and allowances could be incorporated into the text of the treaty. Still, at this late date Wilson was not adamantly opposed, and he moved for adjournment to consider the options with his experts who, two days later, were nevertheless "dismayed" by his decision. Moreover, it has been surmised that Wilson had agreed to ask the Germans to hand over a "blank check" on the amount of reparations (with pensions calculated on the French basis of payments), whereas he had argued forcefully on at least three earlier occasions to present the Germans with a precise figure. Smuts himself was "surprised" by the influence that he carried on this issue, and John M. Keynes worded his verdict in a fashion that caught the eye of Wilson's critics: This represented "the most decisive moment in the disintegration of the President's moral position and the clouding of his mind."[60]

These caveats notwithstanding, it should not be ignored that, whatever compromises Wilson accepted on the reparations issue, his intent was still consistent, as the Smuts memorandum cogently argued. Equally important, Wilson learned on April 1 that the Germans would accept reparation responsibility for civilian damages.[61] These factors in themselves greatly influenced the President's shift toward a more conciliatory role vis-à-vis his negotiating partners.

[59] Park, *Impact of Illness on World Leaders.*

[60] John Maynard Keynes, *The Economic Consequences of the Peace* (New York, 1920), pp. 52-53.

[61] *Wilson Papers*, 56:496.

Above all, Wilson formulated his position *before* the onset of his illness on April 3 and not after, as other investigators have mistakenly maintained.

With regard to the Saar and the Rhineland, Wilson's position remained firm (with perhaps one exception) both before and after the illness in early April. Although both House and Charles H. Haskins suggested that sovereignty, as well as the mines themselves, should be awarded to France, Wilson never went any further than to surrender ownership of the mines alone, without transferring the sovereignty of the region. In the face of House's intimation on April 1 that the President was becoming "stubborn and angry," if not "unreasonable," over this issue,[62] Wilson never turned away from his position throughout the remainder of the conference. Indeed, the French soon surrendered to Wilson's position in favor of a later plebiscite.

Similarly, Wilson stood firm in his resolve not to surrender sovereignty of the Rhineland to France or to create an independent Rhenish state. Concerning further French demands with regard to the Rhineland, he again and again in early April refused to compromise, except insofar as to agree to a nominal suspension of German sovereignty there. Yet he never surrendered it. Perhaps to placate Clemenceau, he nevertheless accepted the French scheme on April 14 concerning occupation forces. This decision was made in the spirit of compromise (which Clemenceau acknowledged with thinly disguised elation), given the concessions that the French Premier had made on the issue of sovereignty.[63]

The question concerning the Kaiser's guilt deserves careful scrutiny, since this was the one issue in which Wilson clearly reversed himself during the period immediately following his illness. Perplexing to some was his willingness to follow Lansing's advice on the issue, when he had held his adviser at arm's length on many other occasions. Indeed, Wilson was originally of the opinion that there was no legal precedent for trying the Kaiser, and that his punishment should consist of the "moral opprobrium of mankind." As he stated for the record on April 2: "It is not just to make an act of this type an individual crime after it was committed." As late as April 6, the President still stood against the concept of total German war guilt, enough to delete the phrase "and the enemy accepts" from the reparation agreement.[64] Yet in the Council of Four meeting on April 8, we find Wilson uncharacteristically being swayed by the arguments of Lloyd George and Clemenceau. Still, it was on the basis of the moral rather than the criminal argument that the Allies won the day, as the President was willing to recognize the sanctity of treaties which the Kaiser had willfully violated—a position that arguably coincided with his moral perception of international law.

Perhaps Wilson was aware how far public opinion had pushed the Allied negotiators themselves to yield to domestic political considerations. On that basis, there is some merit in the Georges' assertion that having to acknowledge the pressures of his own public opinion regarding the inclusion of the Monroe Doctrine into the Covenant sensitized Wilson to the need for conciliation.[65] On the other hand, Weinstein implies that the euphoria during the recovery phase of

[62] House Diary, *ibid.*, 56:517-18.

[63] As House described both Wilson's surrender and Clemenceau's response: "I obtained [Wilson's] consent to everything that Clemenceau desired me to put through for him . . . I also got him to tentatively consent to the putting of Fiume . . . under the League of Nations." Clemenceau later "embraced me, saying . . . he would never forget how much I had done for France" (*ibid.*, 57:353). Such an implied blanket surrender by Wilson, including his accepting a compromise on Fiume that he had "dismissed as not being feasible" (57:352) the day before, was admittedly uncharacteristic of the President.

[64] *Wilson Papers*, 56:532-34; House Diary, April 30, 1919, n. 1.

[65] George and George, *Wilson and House*, p. 264.

his illness was responsible. My views are more in accord with the Editors' comment suggesting that Wilson had other grounds for euphoria rather than the effect of illness per se, and that Wilson accepted the compromise only insofar as the Kaiser's act represented a violation of international law and morality but was not a criminal offense.[66] As such, this was not necessarily a rejection of his principles. Nevertheless, it should be acknowledged (which the same editorial comment does not) that his agreement to bring the Kaiser *to trial* was a reversal of his prior position, regardless of the justification for doing so.* House himself felt that Wilson surrendered more than he expected on the issue, and it cannot be denied that Wilson's conciliatory attitude on this point was out of keeping with his intransigence on other issues, the French scheme for occupation of the Rhineland excepted.

Perhaps the strongest argument against the pervasive impact of illness on these three issues is, I think, the variable response Wilson applied to each within a roughly equivalent time-frame: refusing to yield at certain points, conferring with his advisers on others, and even placating his negotiating partners on occasion. It might be argued, on the other hand, that Wilson's illness at least imbued him in part with a sense of urgency to complete the process of peacemaking, to the point of ordering the *George Washington* to Brest at precisely the time he was stricken by his serious illness. Cynics of the medical argument should not ignore the fact that delirium may be accompanied by either a reduced or enhanced susceptibility to environmental stimuli. Indeed, fever has been demonstrated to speed up the subjective estimate of time in those so afflicted.[67] The record suggests time and again thereafter that Wilson was intent on drawing all matters to a close on an accelerated time schedule. Moreover, his impatience with what he perceived as obstructionist tactics became even more apparent during the final weeks of the conference and its aftermath. If such qualities as intransigence, impatience (and even paranoia) are consistent with elderly individuals victimized by a delirium superimposed on the early stages of dementia, this observation should not ignore that, on several occasions during the month of March, Wilson had been advised (and appeared to accept the need) to set a timetable within which the negotiations must be concluded.[68] Contrary to previous accounts (including my own), the evidence does not then conclusively support the hypothesis that illness played a major role in any of the alleged concessions Wilson made to the Allies during this period—although it may have arguably prompted a potential crisis earlier than anticipated.

If Wilson's viral illness cannot conclusively be tied to specific compromises that he made on critical issues during the first two weeks of April, another neurologic illness may have surfaced later that month which warrants discussion. An editorial comment in Volume 56 of *The Papers* suggests that a previously undisclosed affliction on or about April 28 was "so serious that, at times, it rendered him incompetent."[69] This involves an alleged difficulty the President had with his right hand, manifested by a noticeable deterioration in Wilson's handwriting. Some examples included his signature; others entailed hastily

[66] Editorial comment, *Wilson Papers*, 57:147-48.

* That Wilson's compromise formula for the trial of the former Emperor was tactical—a move to break the log jam in the Council of Four—is again demonstrated by what Wilson said to Grayson on July 6, 1919, on the trip home aboard the *U.S.S. George Washington*. See the entry from the Grayson Diary printed at that date. Editors' note.

[67] Lipowski, *Delirium*, pp. 203, 413.

[68] See, for example, *Wilson Papers*, 56:61 and 56:408.

[69] Editorial comment, *ibid.*, 56:558.

scrawled notes during conference sessions.[70] The reliability of these items in question as indicators of neurologic disease is out of the scope of my expertise and falls under the purview of a skilled handwriting analyst. Nevertheless, there *is* circumstantial evidence in the primary sources to suggest that Wilson once again was having difficulty wrestling with his pen—the very same circumstance that recurred repeatedly from 1896 onward, and upon which Weinstein originally based his case for multiple strokes having afflicted Wilson at an early age. Far removed from the direct impact this possible neurologic event may have had in relation to the deliberations in Paris in late April, the issue is important insofar as it may have signified an ongoing illness with which Wilson had struggled for over twenty years. It also reopens the controversy as to whether there were other medical conditions that may have accounted for this recurring disability, and as such, deserves our consideration.

On April 26, Wilson apologized to Margot Asquith for dictating his letter to her.[71] This was not all that unusual, as he frequently resorted to dictating his letters. Yet in conjunction with a noticeable deterioration in his handwriting, the question arises as to whether he was again having difficulty with his right hand. Indeed, on April 30, he typed on his own typewriter (his "pen") a letter to Arthur Balfour and felt compelled to apologize for doing so.[72] Nevertheless, there was no mention in Grayson's diary entries during this period of any alleged disability of the President's right arm.[73] Although an element of rigidity and intransigence in Wilson's positions on Fiume and Shantung emerged during this period, the available evidence does not suggest a direct cause-and-effect relationship between the President's apparent difficulty with his right hand and the agreements reached over the issues he was negotiating. The latter point is not surprising, and certainly does not negate the possibility of yet another lacunar stroke having occurred on the basis of Wilson's hypertension, since it is chararcteristic of these strokes that deficits in attention, cognition, abstraction, and judgment are not observed at the time they occur.[74]

If, on the other hand, one views Wilson's underlying illness in the proper perspective of a continuum, an appreciable increase in references to certain aspects of the President's state of mind are found in the record at this juncture. As early as April 25, Wilson admitted that he was unable to appreciate the similarities between the Italian and Japanese demands, implying himself that there might be something important he was missing: "He told me [Ray Stannard Baker] he could not see clearly just where his principles applied & remarked . . . that he had been reading over the 14 points to refresh his memory!"[75] On April 29, Baker observed how tired and worn the President appeared.[76] Grayson, referring a day later to the Japanese dilemma, admitted that these were "terrible days for the President *physically* and otherwise" [ital-

[70] See the sample of Wilson's handwriting reproduced above.

[71] *Wilson Papers*, 58:155.

[72] *Ibid.*, 56:660.

[73] Grayson's assessment of Wilson and his role in the conference must be viewed cautiously, since he virtually always portrayed Wilson in the best light. For example, in describing certain aspects of the Shantung settlement, Grayson's conclusions would be questioned both by his contemporaries and by later scholars. Other diary sources suffer from their own peculiar biases: the anti-French bias of Baker; the self-serving slant of House's entries; the reverential references of Benham, and, of course, the frequently obsequious tenor of Grayson's comments.

[74] H. J. Barnett, B. M. Stein, J. P. Mohr, and N. Y. Yatsu, *Stroke: Pathophysiology, Diagnosis, and Management* (New York and London: Churchill, Livingstone, 1986), 2:483-84.

[75] Baker Diary, *Wilson Papers*, 58:142.

[76] *Ibid.*, 58:229.

ics mine].[77] Was the discreet physician making an oblique reference to a new turn in Wilson's health?

If there were no overt discrepancies in Wilson's negotiations concerning the Fiume and Shantung issues during this period (the President's failure to see the similarities in the circumstances obvious to others perhaps excepted), he clearly erred on May 1 in allowing the striking from the draft concerning the Kaiser's guilt the words implying that the Emperor had *not* committed any offenses against criminal law.[78] This error clearly negated the hard-fought victory he had won on April 9. Although the Editor's comment that Wilson may have been "in a daze and did not know what was going on"[79] is a rather harsh and subjective assessment, it does appear that on this occasion at least, Wilson failed to appreciate how much he had violated his own principles.

Moreover, the President's memory seems to have taken a turn for the worse at this time. On May 3, Wilson was unable to give Baker an accounting of the day's events and implored Grayson to brief Baker on his behalf, claiming that he was too tired to recall what had transpired.[80] If, as has been argued, Wilson occasionally (and unaccountably) surrendered positions he had embraced in the past, he nevertheless remained inflexible on issues with which he was currently dealing that required less recall. The Italian question was a case in point. House was disturbed by Wilson's inflexible state of mind and wrote that the President was running the risk of making his allies choose between Italy and the United States over an issue that had been "stupidly managed" from the start.[81] Briefly stated, the evidence suggests that Wilson was unable to shift reflectively from one issue to the next, particularly if some were rather far removed. A deficient memory only complicated the problem. Both deficits are defined as qualities compatible with an evolving organic brain syndrome.

That all was not well is further suggested in a speech Wilson made to a gathering of esteemed international lawyers on May 9. This was one of his poorest speaking performances on record. In mid-stream, Wilson appears to have lost the train of his thought and fell back upon an oft-repeated discourse on the virtues of the common man that had little relevance to the original subject at hand—much less to the audience he was addressing.[82] Those afflicted with memory impairment frequently attempt to rescue themselves from an embarrassing situation by redeploying hackneyed themes or resurrecting vignettes and stories they have recounted in the past. This is but one of the many defensive (if reflexive) measures often employed by those unable temporarily to shift reflectively.

Nevertheless, a review of the primary sources during the period April 28 through May 10 argues for some reservations regarding the thesis that Wilson's health adversely affected what transpired. For example, the inadvertent deletion of the clause concerning the Kaiser's guilt on May 1 may have occurred on the basis of Wilson's fatigue, and nothing more. Two nights before the morning conference during which the error was made, Wilson admitted that he had been unable to sleep as he ruminated until the early hours of the morning over the complexities of the Shantung issue.[83] Moreover, a review of his conduct in

[77] Grayson to J. P. Tumulty, April 30, 1919, 58:248.

[78] Council of Four, 58:277-78. The Drafting Committee later reverted to Wilson's formula.

[79] Editorial comment, 58:278.

[80] Grayson Diary, 58:367.

[81] House Diary, 58:379-80.

[82] *Wilson Papers*, 58:598-600.

[83] Grayson Diary, 58:244.

the Council of Four on that day and thereafter reveals no noteworthy changes in conduct or thought processes, and on three separate occasions within the week that followed he signed documents bearing the indelible Wilson signature, implying that whatever disturbance of right hand function that had occurred had cleared rapidly and without noticeable residual. Then too, if one compares the theme of Wilson's speech of May 9 with those of two later speeches in June concerned with the needs and aspirations of the common man (to be discussed below), the critical scholar perceives a continuity in the President's thought processes that argues against overt disorders of perception having occurred at this interval.

Wilson's intransigence (yet another facet of the same underlying disease) was admittedly never mollified thereafter. Intimating that the important work of the conference had already been completed,[84] his rigidity thereafter presaged the methodology he would carry back to the United States in his impending battle with the Senate. Wilson's rigid mindset was underscored on May 5 both by his refusal to ask the Italians to return to the conference, and by his demand to allow correspondent coverage of the presentation of terms to the German delegates at Versailles.[85]

This is not to imply that Wilson's cognitive compromise was a pervasive condition from that point onward. Permanency of deficits on a day-to-day basis is neither consistent with dementia in general in its earliest stages, nor did Wilson's condition in particular reflect that. For example, in a letter to Lloyd George on May 5, Wilson recognized the weaknesses inherent in the reparation clauses he had agreed to in early April.[86] Not that he was willing to renegotiate the entire issue; still, his powers of abstraction and judgment were not so compromised as to preclude his recognition that some errors may have been made.*

Events of the preceding days compelled House to point out one of the grave defects in Wilson's character: his "prejudice and self-will." As House described the President's conduct: "He is always running the risk of getting into an inextricable situation," and House cited the President's antagonism of the Republicans in the Congress as an example. For all the self-serving tenor of House's comments, he nevertheless was prescient in predicting that this characteristic of Wilson would only complicate matters in the future.[87] House further conceded on May 12 that, either on the basis of fatigue or intransigence, Wilson was now closing his eyes to bad news. House had offered to show Wilson an Associated Press article critical of Wilson and the Fourteen Points. Wilson refused to read it, and his self-serving, if irascible, posture was revealing: he assured himself that "the American people were satisfied with the peace, and he did not care whether Germany was or not."[88]

Individuals victimized by even modest degrees of dementia frequently magnify certain aspects of their character as the disease progresses. In a word, they become caricatures of themselves. Wilson had always been highly principled and strong-willed. It can now be argued that, by May 1919, such traits shaded

[84] See, for example, the transcript of his discussion of the treaty with the American delegation on June 3, 1919, to be printed in *Wilson Papers*, Vol. 60.

[85] Grayson Diary, 58:429.

[86] *Wilson Papers*, 58:446-48.

* This is all quite true; however, Wilson's letter to Lloyd George was an emended form of a draft letter prepared by Norman H. Davis and Thomas W. Lamont. See WW to D. Lloyd George, May 5, 1919, n. 1, Vol. 58. Editors' note.

[87] House Diary, May 10, 1919, *Wilson Papers*, 59: (forthcoming).

[88] *Ibid.*, May 12, 1919, 59: (forthcoming).

into prejudice on the one hand, and intransigence on the other, as his cognitive compromise accelerated. Taking the evolution of the condition one step further, those afflicted first ignore views contrary to their own, ultimately to the point of withdrawing altogether from input they perceive as distasteful. It is precisely this quality that marks the premature aging individual as temperamental. What is frequently ignored is that moodiness may reflect physiologic changes of dementia, as good days characteristically alternate with bad in the early stages of the disease. Perhaps it is not surprising, then, that Charles Seymour underscored Wilson's unstable temperament as well as his tendency to follow his own lead when the advice he received ran counter to his views. Seymour also alluded to Wilson's "one-track mind," highlighting in bold relief the assertion that, by mid-May, at least on occasion, Wilson was unable to shift reflectively.[89]

If a more labored script or if a too frequent oratorical "flight beyond the azure main"[90] were ever any indication of a recurrence of Wilson's neurologic condition, a few such alleged aberrations from the indelible Wilsonian style a month later at least deserve passing comment in completing this review. Those scholars most familiar with Wilson's penmanship have surmised that the President was inexplicably writing with his left hand on June 20. One handwritten note on this date in particular to King Albert of Belgium bore certain characteristics reminiscent of Wilson's left-handed script of an earlier period.[91] Then, too, two successive speeches on June 19 and 20 have been judged by some to be similar to his perplexing speech on May 9 to the society of international lawyers previously discussed. Does this admittedly sketchy evidence suggest that Wilson once again was plagued by a recurrence of neurologic illness?

To prove the hypothesis, significant changes both in Wilson's style and conduct must be demonstrated—and here the proposition falls short of the necessary criteria to argue the case with conviction. Comparative analyses of Wilson's script on June 20, for example, with extant examples of his penmanship on May 10 reveal similarities both in the slant of the script and the individual letters in question, at least insofar as I am capable of judging. Perhaps the skills of a handwriting analyst would shed greater light on this matter. Until such an analysis is undertaken, this intriguing hypothesis simply cannot be authoritatively argued.

Moreover, if one compares the themes and metaphors of the three speeches in question, a striking similarity (rather than contrast) in style and content is manifest. For example, Wilson's June 19 address to the Belgian Parliament alluded to the same references concerning the common man that appeared in the President's after-dinner remarks of May 9. Wilson's allusions to the needs of the common lot gathered around simple dinner tables on June 19 recapitulated his earlier references to plain jackets and simple firesides in his speech the month before. In like manner, the familiar Wilsonian metaphor advising against "rushing into the light" without first going "through the twilight," expressed on May 9, was repeated in his speech on June 20 at the University of Louvain, when Wilson beseeched his audience not to "operate in the dark, but . . . where the light is full."[92]

One suspects that, through these speeches, rather than representing flights of fancy or inappropriate remarks, Wilson was intent toward the close of the

[89] *Ibid.*, May 14, 1919, 59: (forthcoming).

[90] Lloyd George, as quoted in George and George, *Wilson and House*, p. 230.

[91] Not only was the script more upright and less distinct, as was typical of Wilson's previous left-handed style, but certain individual letters were also suggested to have differed strikingly from their right-handed counterparts.

[92] *Wilson Papers*, 58:598-600; June 19 and 20, to be printed in Vol. 61.

conference on portraying himself as the standard-bearer in the struggle against aristocratic forces on behalf of the common man—much as he had fought his negotiating partners from the vantage point of New-Order versus Old-Order politics. If Wilson's oratory was arguably inappropriate for his audience on occasion, as some have argued, it cannot be ignored that the themes he developed (and the metaphors that he used) were consistent from beginning to end. Moreover, a review of his conduct during meetings of the Council of Four in mid-June reveal no obvious inconsistencies in position or compromise of behavior that one would expect if Wilson had been victimized by an acute exacerbation of illness at this juncture. Nor do the diary entries of June 19, 20, and 21 (most notably Grayson's) make any reference to illness or altered behavior on Wilson's behalf. The data simply are not compelling enough at present to make much of this period in mid-June relative to Wilson's underlying neurologic condition. This does not negate the dementia thesis; but to argue that the incipient manifestations of his still pervasive condition adversely affected what transpired at Paris in mid-June runs the risk of falling prey to retrospective medical reductionism.

In summary, the primary sources in Volumes 51-59 of *The Wilson Papers* suggest that a perceptible deterioration in the President's mind-set was occurring during the years 1918-1919 on the basis of hypertensive cerebrovascular disease, to the effect that, by mid-May 1919, a recognizable syndrome compatible with multi-infarct dementia had emerged. Of singular importance to the debate which has evolved over the presence or absence of significant neurologic disease during this period is that specific identifiable strokes are not necessarily required to establish the diagnosis of dementia on a hypertensive basis. Therefore, whether or not alleged deficiencies in Wilson's right hand were due to neurologic disease is arguably immaterial to the thesis presented (although, retrospectively, the deficits described from 1896 onward are more compatible with lacunar strokes than writer's cramp, median nerve entrapment at the wrist, or cervical disc disease, as has previously been suggested).[93] What is required to establish the diagnosis are recognizable features of dementia and an identifiable cause for its occurrence. By May 1919, both criteria appear to have been fulfilled. Nevertheless, a review of the extant sources now casts doubt on the supposition that this disease process impacted negatively on what was agreed to at Paris. The same cannot be said, however, for the period following the peace conference, a position that will be argued in a subsequent volume of *The Wilson Papers*.

WOODROW WILSON'S NEUROPSYCHOLOGICAL IMPAIRMENT AND THE PARIS PEACE CONFERENCE

BY

Edwin A. Weinstein, M.D.

Woodrow Wilson had a history of hypertension and small-stroke disease prior to his incapacitating strokes of September and October 1919. The cognitive and emotional changes which resulted from his cerebral vascular disease, interacting with Wilson's personality and motivations, affected his preparation for the Paris Peace Conference, his conduct of the negotiations, and his efforts to gain the Senate's consent to ratification of the treaty.

[93] Park, *Impact of Illness on World Leaders*, p. 339, nn. 11, 12.

Following a retinal hemorrhage associated with hypertension and resulting in partial permanent blindness in his left eye in 1906, Wilson was examined regularly by the ophthalmologist, Dr. George de Schweinitz of Philadelphia. Dr. de Schweinitz's records have not survived, but Dr. Edward S. Gifford who was familiar with them has written:

> When Dr. de Schweinitz died in 1938, his records passed to Dr. Alexander G. Fewell, who had assisted Dr. de Schweinitz every morning from 8 until 10 for many years. Dr. Fewell's records and practice came to me.
>
> But sometime in the fifties, Dr. Fewell destroyed Dr. de Schweinitz's records, which pained me considerably because I knew those records contained historical material about many prominent people. Before destroying those records, however, Dr. Fewell read that of Woodrow Wilson and talked to me about it.

According to Dr. Fewell, Woodrow Wilson suffered from a very high blood pressure and his fundi [retinas] showed hypertensive vascular changes with advanced angiosclerosis, angiospasticity, and exudates (white spots on the retina resulting from vessel damage and/or lipid deposits). These observations were made while Wilson was President.[1]

I have cited Dr. Gifford's report in detail because it is one of the few statements of Wilson's pathology by a physician. The retina, along with the brain, heart, and kidneys, is a target organ for hypertension, and the state of the retinal vasculature is an index of the condition of blood vessels in the brain.

Pathology often precedes clinical manifestations, and Wilson was in reasonably good health until 1918, when he complained a good deal of fatigue and frequently spent much of the working day in his private quarters. The first recorded instance of a change in the President's habitual emotional behavior came in December 1917. Edmund Starling, a Secret Service agent assigned to the White House, described how Wilson reprimanded a watchman who had scolded his driver for going through a stop sign.[2] The incident in itself is trivial, but it impressed Starling because it showed the President so out of character. Wilson was invariably polite to subordinates. He was especially fond of motoring and had insisted that all White House staff members, including his own chauffeur, observe traffic regulations strictly. On a similar occasion, he had gone to pains to point out that not even a President was immune from the law.[3]

Throughout 1918, Wilson grew increasingly egocentric, suspicious, and secretive, and less discreet in his public references to people. He became extremely proprietary about the proposed League of Nations: he refused to discuss it with anyone but Colonel House, rejected the ideas of a committee to coordinate plans with the British, and spoke scathingly of "butters-in."[4] When House and Wilson attended a service at the Washington Cathedral, it seemed to Wilson that the minister had intended to preach about deficiencies in the War Department, but changed the subject when he saw the President in the congregation.[5] Wilson used intemperate language in turning down the suggestion that William Howard Taft and Elihu Root—both strong League supporters—be appointed Peace Commissioners. Aboard the *George Washington*, Wilson, ap-

[1] Edward S. Gifford to the author, Sept. 27, 1968, quoted in Edwin A. Weinstein, *Woodrow Wilson: A Medical and Psychological Biography* (Princeton, 1981), pp. 296-97. De Schweinitz examined Wilson in Philadelphia, among other times, on August 20, 1915.

[2] Thomas W. Sugrue and Edmund W. Starling, *Starling of the White House* (New York, 1946), pp. 97-98.

[3] Cary T. Grayson, *Woodrow Wilson: An Intimate Memoir* (New York, 1960), p. 48.

[4] WW to E. M. House, March 20, 1918, E. M. House Papers, CtY.

[5] House Diary, Feb. 24, 1918, *ibid.*

parently still smarting from his defeat in the congressional elections, charged that David Lloyd George and Georges Clemenceau did not truly represent their peoples. In Paris, in January, after Lloyd George had brought Wilson the news of the death of Theodore Roosevelt, he was horrified by the "outburst of acrid detestation" in which Wilson denounced the former President.[6]

There are scattered reports of memory impairment in 1918. In August 1917, Wilson noted to Newton D. Baker that he was getting absent-minded.[7] A year later, after telling Colonel House that his mind was becoming, "leaky," he adopted the practice of having memoranda written by people to whom he had spoken.[8] Wilson appointed two men whom he disliked intensely to the secretariat of the Peace Commission and later forgot about it.[9] Wilson's fatigue has been attributed to stress and overwork, but it is more likely that his state of health made him more susceptible to stress and fatigue.

Wilson's attack of viral illness in early April had both transient and enduring effects on his behavior. It affected not only the respiratory and gastrointestinal systems but other organs, including the heart, brain, and prostate, and there is evidence that in Wilson's case all of these were involved. The most common cerebral manifestation is so-called postgrippal asthenia (loss of strength, debility), now thought to represent an autoimmune reaction, but Wilson's mental symptoms were too severe to be explained on this basis. Whatever the etiology, the effects of Wilson's viral infection were more marked because of his underlying cerebral vascular disease.

While still in bed, the President sent for his secretaries in order to dictate, and when he learned that they, along with the White House Head Usher, "Ike" Hoover, had driven out to Versailles, issued an order forbidding the staff to use cars for other than official business. Wilson had apparently forgotten that the secretaries, Gilbert F. Close and Charles L. Swem, had gone out only after first ascertaining that their services would not be needed that day. The action struck Hoover as peculiar because, prior to his illness, Wilson had been extremely solicitous in urging the staff to take as much recreation as possible. When Wilson spoke with Close the following day, the incident was not mentioned.[10]

After Wilson was able to get out of bed, he developed the delusion that all of the French servants—cooks, maids, waiters, and porters—were spies who spoke perfect English, overheard everything he said, and reported his words back to the French government. Hoover and the Secret Service agents investigated but found only one servant who could speak more than a few words of English. Despite this negative report, the President was not convinced and ordered an agent to remain in his room to guard his papers while he was out. Espionage, of course, was not unknown, but it is highly unlikely that the French had organized such an elaborate system and that all the French servants spoke "perfect English."

The *content* of Wilson's behavioral alterations was closely related to personality and motivational factors. Along with his passion for motoring, Wilson had an intense emotional investment in "perfect English." It was a major source of

[6] David Lloyd George, *The Truth About the Peace Treaties*, 2 vols. (London, 1938), 1:232.

[7] WW to Newton D. Baker, August 17, 1917, Wilson Papers, DLC.

[8] House Diary, Aug. 19, 1918.

[9] Lawrence E. Gelfand, *The Inquiry: American Preparations for Peace, 1917-1919* (New Haven and London, 1963), pp. 177-78.

[10] I. H. Hoover, "The Facts about President Wilson's Illness," MS in the Papers of I. H. Hoover, DLC; G. F. Close to Arthur Walworth, May 7, 1951, letter in Walworth's possession.

identity and self-esteem and had been a strong bond in his relationship with his father, and it may have been a way of symbolically representing his problems with the French. The *occurrence* of the delusion was a sign of disordered thinking based on Wilson's underlying brain damage.

The most astonishing change in Wilson's political behavior following his acute illness was the momentary reversal of his attitude toward the Germans. Wilson had been reluctant to ask Congress for a declaration of war and justified his decision by a vision of a league of nations, of which a viable, democratic Germany would be a member. His reluctance was enhanced by his knowledge of some of the secret treaties—the clandestine arrangements among the Allies to acquire territories of the Central Powers—gross violations of Wilson's principle of self-determination. The first of the Fourteen Points called for open diplomacy and forbade private international understandings of any kind. Wilson believed that the causes of the war lay in the imperialist rivalries of the Great Powers and the influence of the German General Staff over the Kaiser. Wilson opposed French expansion beyond Alsace and Lorraine and Britain's desire to cripple Germany as a commercial rival. Whereas the French wanted to humiliate the German delegates, Wilson insisted that they be accorded diplomatic privileges.

On April 2, the day before Wilson was stricken, Lloyd George and Clemenceau introduced a resolution to try the former German Emperor. Wilson replied that a dangerous precedent would be established if the victors in a war were also the judges and gave a number of legal arguments against a criminal trial. When Lloyd George suggested that the Americans were fearful of a procedure which might be used against a President, just as the Japanese did not want a precedent which might affect their Emperor, Wilson noted that, while Congress declared war, he bore the real if not the legal responsibility. On the day after Wilson's return to the Council of Four, he opened the meeting with a resolution to bring the ex-Kaiser to judgment not for "an offense against criminal law but as a supreme offense against international morality and the sanctity of treaties." He rejected suggestions that the signing be delayed until the Japanese could be present, and he personally passed the document around the table for the others to sign. That evening he triumphantly announced to Dr. Grayson that progress had been made "not through the match of wits, but simply through my hammering and forcing them to decisions."[11]

Wilson also exhibited a personal animosity toward and contempt for the German delegates—referring to them as "a job lot." He told Edith Benham that the sight of the arrogant Germans aroused in him all the hatreds and animosities which had lain dormant in the past.[12] (Nevertheless over the years of American neutrality, Wilson had striven to deal with Britain and Germany in evenhanded fashion.) When the chief German delegate, Count Ulrich von Brockdorff-Rantzau, denied sole guilt for the war and stated Wilson's own expressed views of the origin of the conflict, Wilson remarked that Brockdorff had not shown the "slightest sporting disposition."[13]

Wilson's change of attitude toward the Germans has both psychological and neurological aspects. It is related to both an alteration of brain function and motivational factors. It was a way of denying Wilson's own feelings of guilt and responsibility for American participation, and such denial is greatly enhanced by the presence of brain damage. Such patients deny or minimize their incapaci-

[11] Council of Four, *Papers of Woodrow Wilson*, 56:530-34; Grayson Diary, April 9, 1919, MS in the possession of James Gordon Grayson and Cary T. Grayson, Jr.

[12] Edith Benham Helm, *The Captains and the Kings* (New York, 1954), p. 107.

[13] Grayson Diary, May 7, 1919.

ties and concerns, or project them on to others.[14] The denial may not be complete, and patients show their feelings and concerns in less conscious fashion, in humor, slips of the tongue, or various figures of speech. In going over a draft of the resolution, Wilson failed to notice the striking of words which indicated that the ex-Kaiser was not guilty. This may possibly have been the result of carelessness or fatigue, but in my opinion, it was a highly meaningful omission, related to Wilson's emotional status and state of brain function.*

Wilson's hard-line policy toward the Germans took place in a setting of increasing memory loss and cognitive difficulties. Following a session of the Council of Four on May 3, he told Grayson and Baker that he was so fatigued that he could not remember what had happened in the meeting.[15] When Wilson told Grayson that Clemenceau's memory seemed to be affected and that the Frenchman was avoiding decisions, he was displacing his own problems. Wilson's insistence that the Fourteen Points had been fulfilled, and his refusal to attend to reports of opposition at home, are further examples of the denial of reality resulting from his brain damage.

A number of lay observers noted the change in Wilson. Herbert Hoover wrote that prior to his illness in April, Wilson had been incisive, quick to grasp essentials, unhesitating in his conclusions, and willing to listen to advice. Afterwards, he groped for ideas and his mind constantly strove for precedents.[16] Ray Stannard Baker recalled his leave-taking of Wilson on their arrival in America. "Although I had seen him daily for months—not one word did he say about it either commendatory or otherwise or intimate that he cared ever to see me again. He said goodbye as he would have to a visitor of an hour."[17] This lack of empathy and impairment of his ability to relate to others was one of the most striking features of Wilson's condition.

Wilson's speech at the dinner given in his honor by Sir Thomas Barclay on May 9 was perhaps the worst of his presidency. It was devoid of relevant content; it did not state the purposes and problems of the League in referential language, or address the legal aspects. Rather, Wilson carried on with his favorite metaphors of darkness and light, sailing on uncharted seas, and making new garments out of old material. Shifting abruptly from the figurative to the literal, he talked of the plain clothing of poor people, their unhappiness and the strains on their pulses, nerves, and muscles—possibly in reference to his own condition. Seemingly indulging his old prejudice against lawyers, he told his audience that they were too limited in their thinking to have so much to do with international law. He closed by stating that the future of mankind depended on replacing the selfish and separate systems of national law with the common thought of humanity which had no language.[18]

Dr. Grayson, on the return voyage to America, noted that Wilson had difficulties in organizing his thoughts for his presentation of the Versailles Treaty to the Senate. The President, in what had now become a characteristic way of

[14] Edwin A. Weinstein and R. L. Kahn, *Denial of Illness: Symbolic and Physiological Aspects* (Springfield, Ill., 1955).

* However, following his recovery in mid-May, Wilson became increasingly responsive to German protests against certain provisions of the treaty, particularly on the matter of reparations, the terms of the Allied occupation of the Rhineland, Germany's early admission to the League of Nations, etc. [Editors' note.]

[15] Grayson Diary, May 3, 1919; Baker Diary, May 3, 1919, R. S. Baker Papers, DLC.

[16] Herbert Hoover, *The Memoirs of Herbert Hoover*, 2 vols. (New York, 1951-57), 1:468.

[17] Baker Diary, July 9, 1919.

[18] Address at Sir Thomas Barclay's dinner, Paris, May 9, 1919, Wilson Papers, DLC.

denying his problems and projecting them on to others, explained that he had made a false start because he had so little respect for the audience which would receive his message.[19] The speech was a failure as Wilson, in effect, denied the problems and difficulties he had encountered and portrayed the accomplishments of the conference in glowing terms.

Wilson's memory impairment, his emotional preoccupation with his moral responsibility for American entry into the war, and the compromises he had been forced to make in Paris set the background for his remarkable testimony before the Senate Foreign Relations Committee on August 19. Under questioning from Senators William E. Borah and Hiram W. Johnson, Wilson denied that he had known of the secret treaties prior to going to Paris. When Johnson asked if the Fourteen Points had not been laid down to counter the Allied war aims embodied in the secret treaties, Wilson stated that this was not the case. The amnesia was highly selective. At the same meeting, the President readily answered questions on the Shantung settlement also based on secret arrangements but actually unknown to him before the peace conference. Wilson may have been consciously lying, but, as Link has suggested, he had nothing to gain politically by not saying he knew about the treaties, and he might even have gained credit had he admitted his prior knowledge and pointed out how the treaties had added to his difficulties in Paris.[20] On his subsequent western tour to gain support for the treaty, Wilson repeatedly referred to the secret treaties and the difficulties they had caused him.

In summary, there is a great deal of evidence that Wilson suffered from progressive cerebral vascular disease which affected his behavior even before his incapacitating strokes of 1919. In the absence of modern procedures which examine the structure and metabolism of the brain directly, and the results of neurological examination and mental testing, the exact nature and location of the brain pathology cannot be stated. The combination, however, of memory loss and other cognitive impairment, emotional disturbances, and a denial syndrome, along with Wilson's hypertension and retinal pathology, lead to a clinical diagnosis of multi-infarct dementia.

SOME OBSERVATIONS ON WILSON'S NEUROLOGIC ILLNESS

BY

James F. Toole, M.D.

Mark Twain once remarked, "There is something fascinating about science; one gets such wholesome returns of conjecture out of such a trifling investment of fact."[1] The same could be said of the controversy which has developed regarding the degree to which failing health might have affected the ability of President Woodrow Wilson to negotiate an equitable treaty at Versailles. The medical records have been destroyed; the remaining documents describing his behavior and allusions to his medical condition are at times colored by the political persuasion of the writer; and, when he died, there was no postmortem examination. Because of the acrimony which this subject has engendered, it is wise to put the evidence into perspective so that some of the more speculative theories and extrapolations might be properly balanced.

[19] Grayson Diary, July 1, 1919.

[20] Arthur S. Link, *Woodrow Wilson: Revolution, War, and Peace* (Arlington Heights, Ill., 1979), p. 78.

[1] Mark Twain, *Life on the Mississippi*.

First, even though the syndrome was unknown at the time, the evidence contained in the records[2] convinces me, as it did Geschwind,[3] that Wilson was ambidextrous, dyslexic, and suffered from dyscalculia.

Second, in 1906, during his tenure as president of Princeton University, Wilson had a sudden loss of vision in his left eye. George de Schweinitz, M.D., a preeminent ophthalmologist, examined him with an ophthalmoscope and saw hemorrhage in his retina. The cause most probably was retinal vein occlusion, which is usually the result of hypertension with or without concomitant atherosclerosis.[4]

Third, Wilson's physicians undoubtedly suspected hypertension, but its effects on the brain were unknown at the time, and there was no method for its measurement until the Riva-Rocci sphygmomanometer[5] was introduced in the United States by Dr. Harvey Cushing in 1901, after which it required many years for its general adoption into medical practice.

Fourth, Wilson had recurrent focal neurologic deficits which some attribute to psychosomatic,[6] others cervical root irritation,[7] and still others recurrent strokes.[8] One insightful medical observation hitherto not considered is the description by Dr. Thewlis recounted by Dr. Walter Alvarez.

Dr. Malford Wilcox Thewlis, a neuropsychiatrist, trained by Babinski and Gilbert in Paris, visited President Wilson in Paris on the very day when he had awakened with a very different personality and a markedly lessened ability. To quote Dr. Alvarez: "Dr. Thewlis said President Wilson told him that that morning when he got up, his hand was so shaky he could not shave himself. At the time, the doctors were reporting that he had a cold, but recently I received a letter from Gene Smith who wrote a splendid life of Wilson[9] in which he told me that Dr. Grayson said he knew that the President had had several little strokes—some of them before he left for Paris. Incidentally, Gene Smith's book should be read by every physician who would like to understand what little and big strokes can do to a man."[10]

In Paris, Irwin Hood Hoover, the White House Head Usher, immediately saw that, after the bad morning, his Chief was a very different man. As Hoover wrote later, the President, who before had always been kind and thoughtful of the comfort of those around him, suddenly became crabbed, difficult, unreasonable, and fussy. Wilson also thought that his residence in Paris was filled with spies.[11]

[2] A. S. Link, personal communications.

[3] Norman Geschwind, M.D., to August Heckscher, May 12, 1983, photocopy (WC, NjP).

[4] M. F. Marmor, "The Eyes of Woodrow Wilson," *Ophthalmology*, 92 (1985):454-65; Sohan Singh Hayreh, M.D., personal communications, 1987.

[5] S. Riva-Rocci, "Un nuovo sfigmomanometro." *Gazz. Med. Turin*, 47 (1896):981.

[6] S. Freud and W. C. Bullitt, *Thomas Woodrow Wilson: A Psychological Study* (Houghton Mifflin, 1967); M. F. Marmor, "Wilson, Strokes and Zebras," *N. Engl. J. Med.* 307 (1982):528.

[7] J. L. George, M. F. Marmor, and A. L. George, "Issues in Wilson Scholarship: References to Early 'Strokes' in the Papers of Woodrow Wilson," *J. of Amer. Hist.* 70 (1984):845-53.

[8] W. J. Friedlander, "Woodrow Wilson's Cerebral Arteriosclerosis and the Failure of the League of Nations," *Stroke*, 1 (1966):11-14. E. A. Weinstein, *Woodrow Wilson: A Medical and Psychological Biography* (Princeton University Press, 1981); J. F. Toole, "Woodrow Wilson's Strokes—A Continuing Controversy," American Academy of Neurology, 36th Annual Session, April 10, 1984; and B. E. Park, *The Impact of Illness on World Leaders* (University of Pennsylvania Press, 1986).

[9] Gene Smith, *When the Cheering Stopped: The Last Years of Woodrow Wilson* (New York, 1964).

[10] W. C. Alvarez, *Little Strokes* (J. B. Lippincott Co., 1966), p. 34.

[11] Weinstein, pp. 340-41.

From my review of these publications, I believe that chronic hypertension and its complications are the likely explanation for Wilson's recurring weakness, first of one and then the other arm. These events probably represented lacunar infarctions, an expected complication of untreated hypertension.[12] Furthermore, the recurrent bouts of behavioral change suggested by some to have been depression or psychoneurotic can also be ascribed to this etiology.[13]

One of the reasons why some have considered Wilson's periodic incapacity psychiatric in nature is his capacity to substitute one for the other hand, each with its characteristic script. Because of his mixed dominance, when he had his first episode of right brachial paresis (paralysis of the right arm) in 1896, he was able to use his left hand.

Regarding changes in Wilson's behavior over time, diseases of the body or of the brain or both can affect brain function expressed as shortened attention span, impaired judgment, diminishing capacity for conceptualization, and lack of motivation and drive. Furthermore, chronic stress can result in depression, fatigue, diminished alertness, aberrant behavior, and impaired judgment.[14] Overworked, overtired, and overstressed as Wilson undoubtedly was at Paris, it is easy to see that he might occasionally have lost his thread of thought or become upset by minutiae. Attempts to determine which of these etiologic possibilities best explain President Wilson's actions are speculative at best, but again, a leading possibility is his documented chronic hypertension which might well have caused multiple lacunar infarctions. If in fact this was the case, it is particularly ironic that President Wilson was living in Paris where the concept of *état lacunaire*—small cerebral infarcts situated deep within the substance of the brain—had just been introduced by Parisian neurologists.[15] At the time, the importance of hypertension as its usual cause had not been considered.[16] Wilson's neurologic disorders and their cause exceeded medical knowledge of the time. This is even better illustrated by the fact that the first nine editions of William Osler's authoritative textbook, published 1897-1910, do not cite hypertension (synonym hyperpiesis), in the index or describe it in the text. The 1912 edition considers for the first time, "Hypertension, arteriosclerosis due to. . . ."[17]

We now know that lacunar infarctions occur most often in the distribution of arteries arising from branches of the middle cerebral artery. Their course is often stepwise, progressing over hours or days, and they may affect movement or sensation only in one limb or one half of the body. Episodes may vary from side to side and, in up to 30 per cent of cases, attacks last less than twenty-four hours.[18] In others, they remain static for days or even permanently.

The precise delineation of the great variety of syndromes produced by lacunar infarctions has been delineated only since 1975 with the advent of computerized cranial tomography. In the succeeding ten years, transitory loss of use of one arm and then the other, akin to Wilson's affliction, have been described.

[12] J. F. Toole, "Hypertension, Lacunar Infarctions and Hypertensive Encephalopathy," in *Cerebrovascular Disorders* (Raven Press, 1984), pp. 280-88.

[13] J. F. Toole, "Behavioral Abnormalities and Intellectual Decline Caused by Cerebrovascular Disorders," *ibid.*, pp. 271-80.

[14] A. Trafford, "It May Not Be Lonely at the Top but It's Stressful," *Washington Post*, National Weekly Edition, March 2, 1987.

[15] P. Marie, "Des foyers lacunaires de désintégration et de différents autres états cavitaires du cerveau," *Rev. Med.*, 21 (1901):281-98.

[16] J. C. Gautier, personal communication, 1987.

[17] W. Osler, *The Principles and Practice of Medicine* (D. Appleton Co., 1912).

[18] G. A. Donnan and P. F. Bladin, "Capsular Warning Syndrome: Repetitive Hemiplegia preceding Capsular Stroke," 12th International Joint Conference on Stroke and Cerebral Circulation, Tampa, Florida, February 1987.

Furthermore, transitory or permanent speech disturbances, inability to write, dementia, confusion, and disorientation have all been documented.[19]

On the other hand, isolated lacunes may exist without causing recognizable symptoms and most specifically without any changes in intellect or behavior. However, the summation of many lacunes can cause devastating changes in personality and even dementia.[20] Typically, a person suffering from multi-infarct dementia due to lacunar state loses interest, enthusiasm, and spontaneity, is easily distracted, and displays a lack of clarity in his communications by using a limited vocabulary. Furthermore, he is subject to radical mood shifts and displays impaired judgment in regard to appropriate courses of action. It is important to remember that dementia is the result of disease and not a consequence of normal, healthy aging. However, Wilson, before the autumn of 1919, escaped the end stages of lacunar state, in which a characteristic combination of permanent gait abnormality, speech dysfunction, inappropriate laughter and crying, various degrees of intellectual impairment, and incontinence of urine and feces ensue.

It is my belief that the sequence of recurrent neurologic deficits beginning in 1896, accompanied by left retinal hemorrhage in 1906, elevated blood pressure documented by Dr. Francis Darby Boyd in Edinburgh in 1906, the prescription of a bland and presumably low-salt diet by Dr. Grayson in 1913, and the observations of Dr. Thewlis in 1919, culminating in July, September, and October 1919 with incontrovertible stroke, add up to strong circumstantial evidence that he had chronic hypertension causing recurrent cerebrovascular events.

Whether disease of the brain affected concentration, insight, judgment, and behavior and whether acute or chronic systemic illness caused malaise which affected stamina is a lively controversy, debated even today when TV records events and observations in a far more sophisticated and candid way than they were in Wilson's era. How can one be definitive when the trail is cold and the records are scant and often secondary?

EDITORS' COMMENTARY

In our opinion, Dr. Park, in his article printed above, places the incident or incidents of late April to mid-May 1919 squarely in the context of Wilson's medical history. The main theme of that history, which Dr. Park explains in detail in his *The Impact of Illness on World Leaders*, is that Wilson, from at least 1896, suffered from untreated hypertension, which in turn caused "small" strokes in 1896, 1906, and perhaps at later dates until about the middle of his presidency. The etiology of these strokes, according to Dr. Park, was not the occlusion of major arteries or veins in the brain but rather what are now called lacunar infarctions, which result in bleeding in the brain from the lacunes, or small vessels, that run from the base to the top of the brain.

In earlier volumes, we said that Wilson, in 1896 and 1906, suffered from strokes due in the first instance to the occlusion of his right carotid artery. We made our diagnoses of these two incidents in a letter to the Editor, printed in *The Journal of American History*, LXX (March 1984), 945-55. In this communication, we also emphasized that the strokes of 1896 and 1906 were merely

[19] See n. 12.

[20] See n. 13; H. L'Etang, *Fit to Lead?* (William Heinemann Medical Books, London, 1980), p. 45; E. A. Weinstein, "Denial of Presidential Disability: A Case Study of Woodrow Wilson," *Psychiatry*, 30 (1967):376-91.

manifestations of a larger syndrome of untreated hypertension, arteriosclerosis, and other aspects of cerebrovascular disease. Along with Dr. Weinstein, the chief proponent of the etiology in which the right carotid artery was the chief culprit, we are now convinced that Wilson's strokes of 1896 and 1906 were more likely caused by lacunar infarctions rather than by hemorrhages of major veins and arteries of the brain. But whatever the etiology was, the important fact is that Wilson was long the victim of a dangerous cerebrovascular disease, and that this disease had an important impact on his behavior during critical periods of Wilson's life. We also agree with Dr. Park's conclusion, stated so well in his article printed above, that Wilson's illness from late April to mid-May 1919 was transitory and had no significant impact upon Wilson's positions and policies at the peace conference. However, the illness was portentous in that it signaled a renewal of Wilson's cerebrovascular disease. It would reoccur soon—on July 19, 1919—in a much more virulent form and with momentous consequences for the nation and the world.

We have two minor differences with Dr. Park. The first is his conclusion that, beginning in the early morning of April 3, 1919, Wilson most likely suffered an attack of Influenza A or B, instead of a gastrointestinal viral infection. The specialists in infectious diseases quoted in note 2 to the extract from the Grayson Diary printed at April 3, 1919, Vol. 56, all agree that it was possible that Wilson had either Influenza A or B. However, both these strains of the influenza virus usually attack in epidemics, and there was, to our knowledge, no influenza epidemic in Paris or, for that matter, in any part of western Europe or the United States in March or April 1919. Moreover—and we think that this is also a significant fact—such gastrointestinal disturbances as affected Wilson are very rare in cases of Influenza A and B. Dr. Park admits this fact but says that Wilson's stomach disturbance and diarrhea might have accompanied his influenza because he had "antecedent gastrointestinal disease." But insofar as the Editors know, Wilson had not suffered from this disease since the spring of 1913.

In all fairness, we must admit that we are coming close to the point of nitpicking. The important point, which Park makes very well, is that Wilson had a viral infection that had a profound neurologic impact, all the more profound because Wilson was at this time near the point of physical and nervous exhaustion.

Our second criticism is that Dr. Park failed to mention one of the most important pieces of evidence that suggests that Wilson might have had a stroke on April 28. It is the story related by Dr. Alvarez, which Dr. Toole has adverted to. In *Little Strokes*, p. 34, Dr. Alvarez writes as follows:

> My old and very interesting friend, Dr. Thewlis, once told me of a day when he was in Paris, and had dropped in to visit President Wilson. It turned out to be the sad day when the President had wakened with a little stroke so destructive that it had made of him a changeling with a very different personality, and a markedly lessened ability. Dr. Thewlis said Dr. Wilson told him that morning when he got up, his hand was so shaky he could not shave himself.

Dr. Thewlis probably saw Wilson on April 29 rather than April 28, but that is a matter of no consequence. Both Alvarez and Thewlis were distinguished physicians of great probity, and there is no reason to doubt Dr. Alvarez's report of what Dr. Thewlis told him, anecdotal though it is. Obviously, Dr. Grayson had asked Thewlis to examine Wilson earlier, probably when Wilson had his viral infection. In part, on a basis of this evidence, Dr. Toole said to the Editor: "It is not a question of whether Wilson had a stroke in Paris, but only of what kind of stroke it was."

These criticisms seem captious in light of Dr. Park's achievement, both in his book and in his article just printed. We believe that he has provided a solid and convincing basis for a general agreement upon the etiology, nature, and consequences of Wilson's longtime hypertension and cerebrovascular disease.

We remind our readers that, in "A Special Note" in the Introduction to Volume 54, we said the following:

> The Woodrow Wilson Foundation, the Editors of *The Papers of Woodrow Wilson*, and Princeton University Press edit and publish this series in order to broaden public understanding of the career of a great statesman and of a complex personality.

It is with this objective in mind that we have printed this Editorial Note.

INDEX

NOTE ON THE INDEX

THE alphabetically arranged analytical table of contents at the front of the volume eliminates duplication, in both contents and index, of references to certain documents, such as letters. Letters are listed in the contents alphabetically by name, and chronologically within each name by page. The subject matter of all letters is, of course, indexed. The Editorial Notes and Wilson's writings are listed in the contents chronologically by page. In addition, the subject matter of both categories is indexed. The index covers all references to books and articles mentioned in text or notes. Footnotes are indexed. Page references to footnotes which place a comma between the page number and "n" cite both text and footnote, thus: "418,n1." On the other hand, absence of the comma indicates reference to the footnote only, thus: "59n1"—the page number denoting where the footnote appears.

The index supplies the fullest known form of names and, for the Wilson and Axson families, relationships as far down as cousins. Persons referred to by nicknames or shortened forms of names can be identified by reference to entries for these forms of the names.

All entries consisting of page numbers only and which refer to concepts, issues and opinions (such as democracy, the tariff, and money trust, leadership, and labor problems), are references to Wilson's speeches and writings. Page references that follow the symbol Δ in such entries refer to the opinions and comments of others who are identified.

Four cumulative contents-index volumes are now in print: Volume 13, which covers Volumes 1-12, Volume 26, which covers Volumes 14-25, Volume 39, which covers Volumes 27-38, and Volume 52, which covers Volumes 40-49 and 51.

INDEX

WOODROW WILSON

APPEARANCE AND IMPRESSION OF

APPOINTMENT SUGGESTIONS, APPOINTMENTS AND RESIGNATIONS

FAMILY AND PERSONAL LIFE

HEALTH